THE POEMS OF ALEXANDER POPE
VOLUME IX
TRANSLATIONS OF HOMER

The Twickenham Edition of the
Poems of Alexander Pope

GENERAL EDITOR: JOHN BUTT

VOLUME I

PASTORAL POETRY and AN ESSAY ON CRITICISM. E. Audra, formerly Professor of English, Lille University, and Aubrey Williams, Professor of English, University of Florida.

VOLUME II

THE RAPE OF THE LOCK and other poems. Geoffrey Tillotson, Professor of English, Birkbeck College, University of London.

VOLUME III i

AN ESSAY ON MAN. Maynard Mack, Sterling Professor of English and Fellow of Davenport College, Yale University.

VOLUME III ii

EPISTLES TO SEVERAL PERSONS (MORAL ESSAYS). F. W. Bateson, Fellow of Corpus Christi College, Oxford.

VOLUME IV

IMITATIONS OF HORACE and AN EPISTLE TO DR ARBUTHNOT and THE EPILOGUE TO THE SATIRES. John Butt, late Regius Professor of Rhetoric and English Literature, University of Edinburgh.

VOLUME V

THE DUNCIAD. James Sutherland, Lord Northcliffe Professor of English, University College, University of London.

VOLUME VI

MINOR POEMS. Norman Ault and John Butt.

VOLUMES VII–X

HOMER'S ILIAD AND ODYSSEY. Editor: Maynard Mack. Associate Editors: Norman Callan, Professor of English, Queen Mary College, University of London; Robert Fagles, Associate Professor of English and Comparative Literature, Princeton University; William Frost, Professor of English, University of California, Santa Barbara; Douglas M. Knight, President, Duke University, Durham, North Carolina.

Pope at thirty-four, when the *Odyssey* project was launched

ALEXANDER POPE

THE
ODYSSEY OF HOMER

Books I–XII

Homerus

★

Edited by
MAYNARD MACK

Associate Editors
NORMAN CALLAN
ROBERT FAGLES
WILLIAM FROST
DOUGLAS M. KNIGHT

LONDON: METHUEN & CO LTD
NEW HAVEN: YALE UNIVERSITY PRESS

First published 1967
Editorial matter © 1967
MAYNARD MACK
Norman Callan, Robert Fagles,
William Frost, Douglas M. Knight
Printed in Great Britain by The Broadwater Press Ltd
Welwyn Garden City, Hertfordshire

In Memoriam

JOHN BUTT

1906 – 1965

CONTENTS

Volume VII

THE ILIAD, BOOKS I–IX

Volume VIII

THE ILIAD, BOOKS X–XXIV

Volume IX

THE ODYSSEY, BOOKS I–XII

[*Pope does not give titles to all the books. Those added by the editor are set within square brackets*]

Volume X

THE ODYSSEY, BOOKS XIII–XXIV

LIST OF PLATES
Volume VII
THE ILIAD, BOOKS I–IX

Volume X

THE ODYSSEY, BOOKS XIII–XXIV

Notes on the plates in this volume

Plate 1. Frontispiece. Pope at thirty-four. Oil on canvas. $28\frac{1}{2}$ by 24 in. By Sir Godfrey Kneller, signed and dated 1722 ("G. Kneller / 1722"). The Viscount Harcourt, Stanton Harcourt, Oxfordshire. Wimsatt, 7.1.

By this date Pope's fame as the British Homer was consolidated and he was already involved with Broome and Fenton in translating the *Odyssey*. The book under his arm is again visibly Homer, but this time (it may be safe to guess) it is one of the quarto volumes of his own translation of the *Iliad*.

Plate 2. This is the first page of manuscript of the *Odyssey* translation and perhaps for that reason shows slightly more correction by Pope than is normal in Fenton's pages. Some of Pope's comments in the *Correspondence* tend to support Sherburn's belief that the manuscripts preserved represent a second working by Fenton after Pope's revisal of his first, but the evidence is far from certain. Except for further slight changes in lines 18 and 21, and larger changes in lines 13–14, the corrected text on this leaf is the text as published.

Plate 3. The first page of Fenton's translation of *Odyssey* IV bespeaks the efficiency with which Pope revised his collaborators' work, clarifying a situation here (line 6), excising an orotundity there (line 4), indicating the need for an alteration elsewhere (lines 1–2), etc.

Plates 4–5. William Kent's head and tail pieces for *Odyssey* v. These, with Plates 8–11 below, indicate the care that by 1725–6, feeling no doubt the eminence and affluence of his position, Pope lavished on the ornamentation of his *Odyssey* as compared with the *Iliad*, the plates of which he had left to Lintot. The *Odyssey*, as Pope proudly advertised, had "Ornaments on Copper, . . . fifty in number, designed by Mr. Kent." These consisted of Kent's design for the title-page of Volume 1 (see below, Plate 11 in this volume), a headpiece for the prefatory "General View of the Epic Poem, . . . Extracted from Bossu", and head and tail pieces for each of the twenty-four books. The head and tail pieces shown here are those of Book v, the book in which Hermes is sent to warn Calypso to let Odysseus go (he is seen descending to Calypso's grotto behind the central medallion), and in which Odysseus, after the wreck of his raft, is saved by the scarf of the sea nymph Leucothea, who is presumably the subject of the fantastic tailpiece.

Plates 6–7. Frontispieces of the *Iliad* and the *Odyssey*. Pope's will bequeaths to his friend Murray, later the famed Lord Mansfield, a "*Marble Head of* Homer *by* Bernini" that I am not able to identify (*The Life of Alexander Pope, Esq. With a True Copy of His Last Will and Testament* (Charles Corbett, 1744), p. 59). That it was actually by Bernini is highly improbable. The inventory of his goods taken after his death (*Notes and Queries*, 6th series, volume v (13 May 1882), pp. 363–5) shows that Pope had a drawing of Homer in one of his upstairs bedrooms, another drawing of him "In the Great Parlor", and a marble bust of him "In the Libʳ" along with other marble busts of Sir Isaac Newton, Spenser, Shakespeare, Milton, and Dryden. This bust is probably the same as the supposititious "*Head . . . by* Bernini".

Whatever Pope had in this kind, we may be confident it was based on the conception of Homer implied in these plates, which show the frontispieces of his *Iliad* and *Odyssey*. This is the Homer of Horace's tribute (*Epistles* I ii 3–4), who teaches better than philosophy, the blind seer on whom in part Milton models his own persona in *Paradise Lost*, the great conscious artist whose essential character, in Winckelmann's enormously influential phrase, is "a noble simplicity and calm grandeur" ("*eine edle Einfalt und eine stille Grösse*"). For the *Iliad*, Pope used the best-known ancient bust of Homer, then in the Farnese collections, now in the Museo Archeologico, Naples. For the *Odyssey*, he used a bust brought from Constantinople for the Earl of Arundel in the early seventeenth century, which in 1721 had been purchased by Pope's friend, Dr Richard Mead. It is now in the British Museum and is no longer thought to be Homer, but "a Poet".

Plates 8–9. These plates show the head and tail pieces of *Odyssey* IX. Plate 9 is "pictorially" illustrative in what in general was an older manner—that represented in the anonymous designer's headpieces for the *Iliad*. It is the only tailpiece of this kind in the entire *Odyssey*. Plate 8, like 4 and 5 above, is "ornamentally" illustrative. We are still shown the subject of the book, the one-eyed Polyphemus with mouth apparently twisted in pain as if he had already lost his sight, and the sheep, cauldrons, and pipes that are emblems of his way of life. But we have moved from history-painting to design, the species of many-motived classicizing design that Kent was to impress on domestic interiors for a generation.

Plates 10–11. The title-page of Pope's quarto *Iliad* is self-explanatory. The design by Kent for that of the *Odyssey* shows the tomb of Achilles, on which is inscribed the final phrase of *Odyssey*, III 109: "ἔνθα δ' Ἀχιλλεύς". This phrase makes part of Nestor's poignant lament for friends and kinsmen dead at Troy, when Telemachus visits Pylos seeking news of his father: "There all our best were slain. There lies warlike Ajax, there Achilles, there Patroclus . . ." The figure approaching the tomb is Homer; the figure resting on it is Achilles, from behind whose head a sunburst of rays strikes wonder or terror into the gazing poet. The allusion is to an ancient story reported by Leo Allatius (*De Patria Homeri*, 1640, pp. 145–7) to the effect that "*Homer*, keeping some sheep near *Achilles's* Tomb, obtained, by his Offerings and Supplications, a Sight of the Hero, who appeared to him surrounded with so much Glory, that *Homer* could not bear the Splendor of it; and that he was not only dazzled but blinded by the Sight." Pope knew Allatius (*Correspondence*, I 225), but may have found the story in Bayle's *Dictionary*, from whose version of it (Engl. tr., 1710, I 65: art. *Achillea*, note D) I quote. See also Volume VII, p. 31.

LIST OF ABBREVIATIONS

(Authors whose names identify the work intended, e.g. Herodotus, Strabo, Lucretius, etc., are not included. For commentators and poets cited by Pope in his Notes, see also the index in Volume x, which for main entries is analysed by work.)

BARNES = Ὁμήρου Ἰλιὰς καὶ Ὀδύσσεια. *Opera, Studio, et Impensis*, Josuae Barnes (2 vols., Cambridge, 1711).

BOCHART = Samuel Bochart's *Geographia Sacra, in Opera Omnia* (3 vols., Leyden, 1712), Volume I.

BOIVIN = Jean Boivin de Villeneuve, *Apologie d'Homère, et Bouclier d'Achille* (Paris, 1715).

BOSSU = René Le Bossu's *Traité du Poëme Epique* (Paris, 1675).

CHAPMAN = George Chapman's translations of the *Iliad* (1611) and *Odyssey* (1615?). The work intended is indicated by the context.

CORRESPONDENCE = *The Correspondence of Alexander Pope*, ed. George Sherburn (5 vols., Oxford, 1956).

DACIER = Anne Lefevre Dacier, whose name when unaccompanied by any further citation refers to her translation of the *Iliad* (3 vols., Paris, 1711) in Pope's *Iliad* notes, and to her translation of the *Odyssey* (3 vols., Paris, 1716) in the notes to his *Odyssey*.

DACIER (when used in conjunction with a reference to Aristotle's *Poetics*) = André Dacier, *La Poëtique d'Aristote avec des Remarques* (Paris, 1692).

DINDORF = *Scholia Graeca in Homeri Odysseam* (2 vols., Oxford, 1855) and *Scholia Graeca in Homeri Iliadem* (6 vols., Oxford, 1875–88), ed. K. W. Dindorf. The intended collection is indicated by the context in which the reference occurs.

DRYDEN = Dryden's translation of the *Aeneid* (unless otherwise indicated).

EC = *The Works of Alexander Pope*, ed. Whitwell Elwin and J. C. Courthorpe (10 vols., London, 1871–89).

GRIFFITH = R. H. Griffith, *Alexander Pope: A Bibliography* (2 parts, University of Texas Press, 1922–6).

HOBBES = Thomas Hobbes's translations of the *Iliad* (1676) and *Odyssey* (1677). The work intended is indicated by the context.

JOHNSON = Samuel Johnson, *Lives of the English Poets*, ed. G. B. Hill (3 vols., Oxford, 1905).

KNIGHT = D. M. Knight, *Pope and the Heroic Tradition: A Critical Study of the Iliad* (Yale University Press, 1951).

LA MOTTE = Houdart de La Motte, *Oeuvres* (4 vols., Paris, 1754). (The specific works usually cited from this collection are his *Discours sur Homère* (1714) and his *Réflexions sur la Critique* (rev. and enl. edn, Paris, 1716).

NAUCK = *Tragicorum Graecorum Fragmenta*, ed. J. A. Nauck (Leipzig, ed. 1889).

OGILBY = John Ogilby's translations of the *Iliad* (1660) and *Odyssey* (1665). The work intended is indicated by the context.

PERRAULT = Charles Perrault's *Parallèle des Anciens et des Modernes* (4 vols., Paris, 1688–96).

PROUDFOOT = L. Proudfoot, *Dryden's Aeneid and Its Seventeenth-Century Predecessors* (Manchester University Press, 1960).

PTOLEMY = Claudius Ptolemaeus' *Geography*.

QUINTILIAN = *Institutio Oratoria*.

RAPIN = René Rapin, *Oeuvres* (2 vols., The Hague, 1725). (The individual work usually cited is his *Comparaison d'Homère et de Virgile*.)

SANDYS = Sir J. E. Sandys, *A History of Classical Scholarship* (3 vols., Cambridge, 1903–8).

SCALIGER = J. C. Scaliger, *Poetices Libri Septem* (Geneva, 1561).

SHERBURN = George Sherburn, *The Early Career of Alexander Pope* (Oxford, 1934).

SPENCE = Joseph Spence, *Anecdotes, Observations, and Characters of Books and Men*, ed. S. W. Singer (London, 1820). References are made to page numbers in this edition and to anecdote numbers in the forthcoming edition by J. M. Osborn.

SPINGARN = J. E. Spingarn, *Critical Essays of the Seventeenth Century* 3 vols., Oxford, 1908).

SPONDANUS = *Homeri Opera*, ed. Jean de Sponde (Geneva, 1606).

SÜHNEL = Rudolf Sühnel, *Homer und die englische Humanität: Chapman und Popes Übersetzungkunst im Rahmen der Humanistischen Tradition* (Tübingen, 1958).

TERRASSON = Jean Terrasson's *Dissertation Critique sur l'Iliade d'Homère* (2 vols., Paris, 1715).

TE = The Twickenham Edition of Pope's *Poetical Works* (Vols.
I–VI: the original poems, London, 1938–61; vols. VII–X: the
Homer translations, London, 1967).

WARREN = Austen Warren, *Alexander Pope as Critic and Humanist*
(Princeton University Press, 1929).

THE
ODYSSEY
OF
HOMER.

A GENERAL VIEW of the

EPIC POEM

And of the

ILIAD and *ODYSSEY*.

Extracted from *BOSSU*.

SECT. I.[1]

Of the Nature of Epic Poetry.

THE Fables of Poets were originally employ'd in representing the *Divine Nature*, according to the notion then conceiv'd of it. This sublime Subject occasion'd the first Poets to be call'd Divines, and Poetry *the Language of the Gods*. They divided the divine Attributes into so many Persons; because the infirmity of a human Mind cannot sufficiently conceive, or explain, so much Power and Action in a Simplicity so great and indivisible as that of God. And perhaps they were also jealous of the advantages they reap'd from such excellent and exalted learning, and of which they thought the vulgar part of mankind was not worthy.

They could not describe the Operations of this Almighty Cause, without speaking at the same time of its Effects: so that to Divinity they added *Physiology*, and treated of both, without quitting the umbrages of their Allegorical Expressions.

But *Man* being the chief and the most noble of all that God produc'd, and nothing being so proper, or more useful to Poets than this Subject; they added it to the former, and treated of the doctrine of *Morality* after the same manner as they did that of Divinity and Philosophy: And from Morality thus treated, is form'd that kind of Poem and Fable which we call *Epic*.

The Poets did the same in Morality, that the Divines had done

---

1. Numerals between pointed brackets indicate the book and chapter in Bossu's *Traité du Poëme Epique* (Paris, 1675) from which the parts of this "View" are extracted. The English follows rather closely the translation by "W.J." (London, 1695).

in Divinity. But that infinite variety of the actions and operations of the Divine Nature, (to which our understanding bears so small a proportion) did as it were force them upon dividing the single Idea of the Only One God into several Persons, under the different names of *Jupiter*, *Juno*, *Neptune*, and the rest.

And on the other hand, the nature of Moral Philosophy being such, as never to treat of things in particular, but in general; the Epic Poets were oblig'd to unite in one single Idea, in one and the same Person, and in an Action which appear'd singular, all that look'd like it in different persons, and in various actions; which might be thus contain'd as so many *Species* under their *Genus*.

The Presence of the Deity, and the Care such an august Cause is to be suppos'd to take about any action, obliges the Poet to represent this action as great, important, and manag'd by *Kings and Princes. It obliges him likewise to think and speak in an elevated way above the vulgar, and in a style that may in some sort keep up the character of the Divine Persons he introduces.† To this end serve the poetical and figurative Expression, and the Majesty of the Heroic Verse.

But all this, being divine and surprising, may quite ruin all Probability: Therefore the Poet should take a peculiar care as to that point, since his aim is to instruct, and without Probability any action is less likely to persuade.

Lastly, since Precepts ought to be ‡concise, to be the more easily conceiv'd, and less oppress the memory; and since nothing can be more effectual to this end than proposing one single Idea, and collecting all things so well together, as to be present to our minds all at once; therefore the Poets have reduc'd all to one §single action, under one and the same design, and in a body whose members and parts should be homogeneous. ⟨1 ii⟩

What we have observ'd of the nature of the Epic Poem, gives us a just Idea of it, and we may define it thus:

"The Epic Poem is a discourse invented by art, to form the

---

* *Res gestæ regumque ducumque.* Hor. Art. Poet. ⟨73⟩.

† *Cui mens divinior atque os magna sonaturum, des nominis hujus honorem.* Horat. ⟨Sat. 1 iv 43⟩.

‡ *Quicquid præcipies esto brevis, ut cito dicta percipiant animi dociles, teneantque fideles.* Hor. ⟨Ars⟩ Poet. ⟨335⟩.

§ *Denique sit quodvis simplex duntaxat, & unum.* ibid. ⟨23⟩.

Manners, by such instructions as are disguis'd under the allegories of some One important Action, which is related in verse, after a probable, diverting, and surprizing manner." ⟨I iii⟩

SECT. II.

The Fable of the Iliad.

IN every design which a man deliberately undertakes, the end he proposes is the first thing in his mind, and that by which he governs the whole work, and all its parts: Thus since the End of the Epic Poem is to regulate the Manners, 'tis with this first view the Poet ought to begin.

But there is a great difference between the Philosophical and the Poetical doctrine of Manners. The Schoolmen content themselves with treating of Virtues and Vices in general: the instructions they give are proper for all States, People, and for all Ages. But the Poet has a nearer regard to his own Country, and the necessities of his own nation. With this design he makes choice of some piece of morality, the most proper and just he can imagine: And in order to press this home, he makes less use of the force of Reasoning, than of the power of Insinuation; accommodating himself to the particular customs and inclinations of those, who are to be the subject, or the readers, of his work.

Let us now see how *Homer* has acquitted himself in all these respects.

He saw the *Grecians*, for whom he design'd his Poem, were divided into as many States as they had capital Cities. Each was a Body Politick apart, and had its form of government independent from all the rest. And yet these distinct States were very often oblig'd to unite together in one body against their common Enemies. These were two very different sorts of Government, such as could not be comprehended in one maxim of morality, and in one single Poem.

The Poet therefore has made two distinct Fables of them. The one is for *Greece* in general, united into one body, but compos'd of parts independent on each other; and the other for each particular state, consider'd as they were in time of peace, without the former circumstances and the necessity of being united.

As for the first sort of government, in the Union or rather in the Confederacy of many independent States; experience has always made it appear, "That nothing so much causes success as a due subordination, and a right understanding among the chief commanders. And on the other hand, the inevitable ruin of such confederacies proceeds from the heats, jealousies and ambition of the different leaders, and the discontents of submitting to a single General." All sorts of States, and in particular the *Grecians*, had dearly experienc'd this truth. So that the most useful and necessary instruction that could be given them, was, to lay before their eyes the loss which both the People and the Princes must of necessity suffer, by the ambition, discord, and obstinacy of the latter.

Homer then has taken for the foundation of his Fable this great Truth; That a Misunderstanding between Princes is the Ruin of their own States. "I sing (says he) the Anger of *Achilles*, so pernicious to the *Grecians*, and the cause of so many Heroes' deaths, occasion'd by the Discord and Separation of *Agamemnon* and that Prince."

But that this truth may be compleatly and fully known, there is need of a second to support it. 'Tis necessary in such a design, not only to represent the Confederate States at first disagreeing among themselves, and from thence unfortunate; but to show the same States afterwards reconciled and united, and of consequence victorious.

Let us now see how he has joyn'd all these in one general action.

"Several Princes independent on one another were united against a common enemy. The person whom they had elected their General, offers an affront to the most valiant of all the Confederates. This offended Prince is so far provoked, as to relinquish the Union, and obstinately refuse to fight for the common cause. This Mis-understanding gives the enemy such an advantage, that the Allies are very near quitting their design with dishonour. He himself who made the separation is not exempt from sharing the misfortune which he brought upon his party. For having permitted his intimate friend to succour them in a great necessity, this friend is kill'd by the enemy's General. Thus the contending Princes being both made wiser at their own cost, are reconcil'd, and unite again: Then this valiant Prince not only obtains the victory in the publick cause, but revenges his private wrongs by killing with his own hands the author of the death of his friend."

This is the first Platform of the Poem, and the Fiction, which reduces into one important and universal Action all the particulars upon which it turns.

In the next place it must be render'd Probable by the circumstances of times, places and persons; Some persons must be found out, already known by History or otherwise, whom we may with Probability make the actors and personages of this Fable. *Homer* has made choice of the siege of *Troy*, and feign'd that this action happen'd there. To a Phantome of his brain, whom he would paint valiant and cholerick, he has given the name of *Achilles*; that of *Agamemnon* to his General; that of *Hector* to the Enemies Commander, and so to the rest.

Besides, he was oblig'd to accommodate himself to the manners, customs, and genius of the *Greeks* his Auditors, the better to make them attend to the instruction of his Poem; and to gain their approbation by praising them: So that they might the better forgive him the representation of their own faults in some of his chief Personages. He admirably discharges all these duties, by making these brave Princes and those victorious people all *Grecians*, and the fathers of those he had a mind to commend.

But not being content, in a work of such a length, to propose only the principal point of the Moral, and to fill up the rest with useless ornaments and foreign incidents, he extends this Moral by all its necessary consequences. As for instance in the subject before us, 'tis not enough to know, that a good understanding ought always to be maintain'd among Confederates: 'Tis likewise of equal importance, that if there happens any division, care must be taken to keep it secret from the enemy, that their ignorance of this advantage may prevent their making use of it. And in the second place, when their concord is but counterfeit and only in appearance, one should never press the enemy too closely; for this would discover the weakness which we ought to conceal from them.

The Episode of *Patroclus* most admirably furnishes us with these two instructions. For when he appear'd in the arms of *Achilles*, the *Trojans*, who took him for that Prince now reconciled and united to the Confederates, immediately gave ground, and quitted the advantages they had before over the *Greeks*. But *Patroclus*, who should have been contented with this success, presses upon *Hector* too boldly, and by obliging him to fight, soon discovers that it was not the true *Achilles* who was clad in his armour, but a Heroe of much inferior prowess. So that *Hector* kills him, and regains those advantages which the *Trojans* had lost, on the opinion that *Achilles* was reconciled. ⟨i viii⟩

SECT. III.

The Fable of the Odyssey.

THE *Odyssey* was not design'd, like the *Iliads*, for the instruction of all the States of *Greece* join'd in one body, but for each State in particular. As a State is compos'd of two parts; the Head which commands, and the Members which obey; there are instructions requisite for both, to teach the one to govern, and the others to submit to Government.

There are two Virtues necessary to one in authority, Prudence to order, and Care to see his orders put in execution. The Prudence of a Politician is not acquir'd but by a long experience in all sorts of business, and by an acquaintance with all the different forms of Governments and States. The Care of the Administration suffers not him that has the Government to rely upon others, but requires his own presence: And Kings who are absent from their States, are in danger of losing them, and give occasion to great disorders and confusion.

These two points may be easily united in one and the same man. "A King forsakes his Kingdom to visit the courts of several Princes, where he learns the manners and customs of different nations. From hence there naturally arises a vast number of incidents, of dangers, and of adventures, very useful for a Political Institution. On the other side, this Absence gives way to the disorders which happen in his own kingdom, and which end not till his return, whose presence only can re-establish all things." Thus the Absence of a King has the same effects in this Fable, as the Division of the Princes had in the former.

The Subjects have scarce any need but of one general maxim, which is, To suffer themselves to be govern'd, and to obey faithfully; whatever reason they may imagine against the orders they receiv'd. It is easy to join this instruction with the other, by bestowing on this wise and industrious Prince such Subjects, as in his absence would rather follow their own judgment than his commands: and by demonstrating the misfortunes which this disobedience draws upon them, the evil consequences which almost infallibly attend these particular notions, which are entirely different from the general Idæa of him who ought to govern.

But as it was necessary that the Princes in the *Iliads* shou'd be cholerick and quarrelsome, so it is necessary in the Fable of the *Odyssey* that the chief person should be sage and prudent. This raises a difficulty in the Fiction; because this person ought to be absent for the two reasons aforemention'd, which are essential to the Fable, and which constitute the principal aim of it: But he cannot absent himself, without offending against another maxim of equal importance; *viz.* That a King should upon no account leave his Country.

It is true, there are sometimes such necessities as sufficiently excuse the Prudence of a Politician in this point. But such a necessity is a thing important enough of it self to supply matter for another Poem, and this multiplication of the action would be vicious. To prevent which in the first place, this Necessity and the departure of the Hero must be disjoin'd from the Poem; and in the second place, the Hero having been oblig'd to absent himself, for a reason antecedent to the action and plac'd distinct from the Fable, he ought not so far to embrace this opportunity of instructing himself, as to absent himself voluntarily from his own Government. For at this rate, his Absence would be meerly Voluntary, and one might with reason lay to his charge all the disorders which might arrive.

Thus in the constitution of the Fable, he ought not to take for his action, and for the foundation of his Poem, the Departure of a Prince from his own country, nor his voluntary stay in any other place; but his Return, and this return retarded against his will. This is the first Idea *Homer* gives us of it. *His Hero appears at first in a desolate Island, sitting upon the side of the Sea, which with tears in his eyes he looks upon as the obstacle that had so long oppos'd his Return, and detain'd him from revisiting his own dear Country.

And lastly, since this forc'd delay might more naturally and usually happen to such as make voyages by sea; *Homer* has judiciously made choice of a Prince whose Kingdom was in an Island.

Let us see then how he has feign'd all this Action, making his Hero a person in years, because Years are requisite to instruct a man in Prudence and Policy.

"A Prince has been oblig'd to forsake his native Country, and to

* *Odyss. 5.*

B*

head an Army of his Subjects in a foreign expedition. Having gloriously perform'd this enterprise, he was marching home again, and conducting his Subjects to his own State. But spite of all the attempts, with which his eagerness to return had inspir'd him, he was stopp'd by the way by tempests for several years, and cast upon several countries differing from each other in Manners and Government. In these dangers his Companions, not always following his orders, perish'd through their own fault. The Grandees of his country strangely abuse his absence, and raise no small disorders at home. They consume his estate, conspire to destroy his son, would constrain his Queen to accept of one of them for her Husband; and indulge themselves in all violence, so much the more, because they were persuaded he would never return. But at last he returns, and discovering himself only to his son and some others, who had continu'd firm to him, he is an eye-witness of the insolence of his enemies, punishes them according to their deserts, and restores to his Island that tranquility and repose to which they had been strangers during his absence."

As the Truth, which serves for foundation to this fiction is, that the Absence of a person from his own home, or his neglect of his own affairs, is the cause of great disorders: So the Principal point of the Action, and the most Essential one, is the Absence of the Heroe. This fills almost all the Poem: For not only this real absence lasted several years, but even when the Heroe return'd, he does not discover himself; and this prudent disguise, from whence he reap'd so much advantage, has the same effect upon the Authors of the disorders, and all others who knew him not, as his real absence had before, so that he is absent as to them, 'till the very moment of their punishment.

After the Poet had thus compos'd his Fable, and join'd the Fiction to the Truth, he then makes choice of *Ulysses*, the King of the Isle of *Ithaca*, to maintain the character of his chief Personage, and bestow'd the rest upon *Telemachus*, *Penelope*, *Antinous*, and others, whom he calls by what names he pleases.

I shall not here insist upon the many excellent advices, which are so many parts, and natural consequences of the fundamental Truth; and which the Poet very dextrously lays down in those fictions, which are the Episodes and Members of the entire Action. Such for instance are these advices: Not to intrude one's self into the Mysteries of Government, which the Prince keeps secret: This is represented to us by the winds shut up in a bullhide, which the miserable Companions of *Ulysses* would needs be so foolish as to pry into. Not to suffer ones self to be led away by the seeming Charms of an idle and inactive life, to which the [*] *Sirens' Songs* invited. Not to suffer ones self to be sensualiz'd by pleasures, like those who were chang'd into brutes by *Circe:* And a great many other points of Morality necessary for all sorts of people.

This Poem is more useful to the People than the *Iliad,* where the Subjects suffer rather by the ill conduct of their Princes, than through their own miscarriages. But in the *Odyssey,* 'tis not the fault of *Ulysses* that is the ruin of his Subjects. This wise Prince leaves untry'd no method to make them partakers of the benefit of his return. Thus the Poet in the *Iliads* says, "He sings the anger of *Achilles,* which had caused the death of so many *Grecians;*" and on the contrary, in the † *Odyssey* he tells his Readers, "That the Subjects perished through their own fault." ⟨1 x⟩

SECT. IV.

Of the Unity of the Fable.

ARISTOTLE bestows great Encomiums on *Homer* for the Simplicity of his design, because he has included in one single part all that happen'd at the siege of *Troy.* And to this he opposes the ignorance of some Poets who imagin'd that the Unity of the Fable or Action was sufficiently preserved by the Unity of the Heroe: and who compos'd their *Theseids, Heracleids,* and the like, wherein they only heap'd up in one Poem every thing that happen'd to one Personage. ⟨1 xvi⟩

He finds fault with those Poets who were for reducing the Unity of the *Fable* into the Unity of the *Heroe,* because one man may have performed several adventures, which 'tis impossible to reduce under any one and simple head. This reducing of all things to Unity and Simplicity is what *Horace* likewise makes his first Rule. *Denique sit quodvis simplex duntaxat, & unum.*

According to these Rules, it will be allowable to make use of

---

[*] *Improba Siren desidia.* Horat. ⟨Sat. II iii 14–15⟩

† Αὐτῶν γὰρ σφετέρῃσιν ἀτασθαλίῃσιν ὄλοντο. Odyss. I ⟨7⟩.

several Fables; or (to speak more correctly) of several Incidents which may be divided into several Fables; provided they are so ordered, that the Unity of the Fable be not spoil'd. This liberty is still greater in the Epic Poem, because 'tis of a larger extent, and ought to be entire and compleat.

I will explain my self more distinctly by the Practice of *Homer*.

No doubt but one might make four distinct Fables out of these four following Instructions.

1. *Division between those of the same Party exposes them entirely to their enemies.*

2. *Conceal your Weakness, and you will be dreaded as much, as if you had none of those imperfections, of which they are ignorant.*

3. *When your strength is only feign'd, and founded only in the Opinion of others; never venture so far as if your strength was real.*

4. *The more you agree together, the less hurt can your Enemies do you.*

'Tis plain, I say, that each of these particular Maxims might serve for the Ground-work of a Fiction, and one might make four distinct Fables out of them. May one not then put all these into one single *Epopea?* Not unless one single Fable can be made out of all. The Poet indeed may have so much skill as to unite all into one Body, as Members and Parts, each of which taken asunder would be imperfect; and if he joins them so, as that this Conjunction shall be no hindrance at all to the Unity and the regular Simplicity of the Fable. This is what *Homer* has done with such success in the composition of the *Iliads*.

1. *The Division between* Achilles *and his Allies tended to the ruin of their Designs.* 2. Patroclus *comes to their relief in the Armour of this Heroe, and* Hector *retreats.* 3. *But this young Man pushing the advantage, which his disguize gave him, too far, ventures to engage with* Hector *himself; but not being master of* Achilles*'s strength (whom he only represented in outward appearance) he is killed, and by this means leaves the* Grecian *Affairs in the same disorder, from which in that disguise he came to free them.* 4. Achilles *provok'd at the death of his Friend, is reconciled, and revenges his loss by the death of* Hector. These various incidents being thus united, do not make different Actions and Fables, but are only the uncompleat and unfinish'd parts of one and the same Action and Fable, which alone can be said to be compleat and entire: And all these Maxims of the Moral, are easily reduc'd into these two parts, which in my opinion cannot be separated without enervating the force of

both. The two parts are these, *That a right Understanding is the preservation, and Discord the destruction of States.

Tho' then the Poet has made use of two parts in his Poems, each of which might have serv'd for a Fable, as we have observ'd: Yet this Multiplication cannot be call'd a vicious and irregular *Polymythia*, contrary to the necessary Unity and Simplicity of the Fable; but it gives the Fable another qualification, altogether necessary and regular, namely its Perfection and finishing stroke. ⟨I xv ii⟩

SECT. V.

Of the Action *of the Epic Poem.*

THE Action of a Poem is the Subject which the Poet undertakes, proposes, and builds upon. So that the Moral and the Instructions which are the End of the Epic Poem are not the Matter of it. Those the Poets leave in their Allegorical and figurative obscurity. They only give notice at the *Exordium*, that they sing some *Action*. The *Revenge of* Achilles, the *Return of* Ulysses, *&c.*

Since then the Action is the Matter of a Fable, it is evident that whatever incidents are essential to the Fable, or constitute a part of it, are necessary also to the Action, and are parts of the Epic Matter, none of which ought to be omitted. Such for instance, are the contention of *Agamemnon* and *Achilles*, the slaughter *Hector* makes in the *Grecian* Army, the Re-union of the *Greek* Princes; and lastly, the Re-settlement and Victory which was the consequence of that Re-union. ⟨II i⟩

There are four qualifications in the Epic Action: the first is its *Unity*, the second its *Integrity*, the third its *Importance*, the fourth its *Duration*.

The Unity of the Epic Action, as well as the Unity of the Fable, does not consist either in the Unity of the Heroe, or in the Unity of Time: Three things I suppose are necessary to it. The first is, to make use of no Episode but what arises from the very platform and foundation of the Action, and is as it were a natural member of the body. The second is, exactly to Unite these Episodes and these Members with one another. And the third is, never to finish any Episode so as it may seem to be an entire Action; but to let each

---

* *Concordia res parvæ crescunt : discordia magnæ dilabuntur.* Salust. de bello Jug. ⟨x vi⟩

Episode still appear in its own particular nature, as the member of a body, and as a part of itself not compleat. ⟨vii⟩

Of the Beginning, Middle, and End of the Action.

   Aristotle ⟨*Poetics*, xxiii 1⟩ not only says that the Epic Action should be One, but adds, that it should be entire, perfect, and compleat, and for this purpose ought to have a *Beginning*, a *Middle*, and an *End*. These three parts of a whole are too generally and universally denoted by the words, Beginning, Middle, and End; we may interpret them more precisely, and say, That the Causes and Designs of an Action are the Beginning: That the Effects of these Causes, and the Difficulties that are met with in the execution of these designs, are the Middle; and that the Unravelling and Resolution of these difficulties are the End. ⟨ii ix⟩

The Action of the Iliad.

   Homer's design in the *Iliads* is to relate the Anger and Revenge of *Achilles*. The Beginning of this Action is the Change of *Achilles* from a calm to a passionate temper. The Middle is the Effects of his Passion, and all the illustrious Deaths it is the Cause of. The End of this same Action is the Return of *Achilles* to his Calmness of temper again. All was quiet in the *Grecian* Camp, when *Agamemnon* their General provokes *Apollo* against them, whom he was willing to appease afterwards at the cost and prejudice of *Achilles*, who had no part in his fault. This then is an exact Beginning: It supposes nothing before, and requires after it the Effects of this Anger. *Achilles* revenges himself, and that is an exact Middle; it supposes before it the Anger of *Achilles*, this Revenge is the Effect of it. Then this Middle requires after it the Effects of this Revenge, which is the Satisfaction of *Achilles*: for the Revenge had not been compleat, unless *Achilles* had been satisfied. By this means the Poet makes his Heroe, after he was glutted by the Mischief he had done to *Agamemnon*, by the death of *Hector*, and the Honour he did his Friend, by insulting o'er his Murderer; he makes him, I say, to be moved by the Tears and Misfortunes of King *Priam*. We see him as calm at the End of the Poem, during the Funeral of *Hector*, as he was at the Beginning of the Poem, whilst the Plague raged among the *Grecians*. This End is just, since the Calmness of temper *Achilles* re-enjoy'd, is only an Effect of the Revenge which ought to have preceded: And after this no Body expects any more of his Anger. Thus has *Homer* been very exact in the Beginning, Middle and End of the Action he made choice of for the Subject of his *Iliads*.

The Action of the Odyssey.

His Design in the *Odyssey* was to describe the Return of *Ulysses* from the Siege of *Troy*, and his Arrival at *Ithaca*. He opens this Poem with the complaints of *Minerva* against *Neptune*, who opposed the Return of this Heroe, and against *Calypso* who detain'd him in an Island from *Ithaca*. Is this a Beginning? No; doubtless, the Reader would know why *Neptune* is displeas'd with *Ulysses*, and how this Prince came to be with *Calypso*? He would know how he came from *Troy* thither? The Poet answers his Demands out of the Mouth of *Ulysses* himself, who relates these things, and begins the Action, by the Recital of his Travels from the City of *Troy*. It signifies little whether the Beginning of the Action be the Beginning of the Poem. The Beginning of this Action is that which happens to *Ulysses*, when upon his leaving *Troy* he bends his Course for *Ithaca*. The Middle comprehends all the Misfortunes he endured, and all the Disorders of his own Government. The End is the re-instating of this Hero in the peaceable possession of his Kingdom, where he was acknowledg'd by his Son, his Wife, his Father, and several others. The Poet was sensible he should have ended ill had he gone no farther than the death of these Princes, who were the Rivals and Enemies of *Ulysses*, because the Reader might have look'd for some Revenge which the Subjects of these Princes might have taken, on him who had kill'd their Sovereigns: But this Danger over, and the People vanquished and quieted, there was nothing more to be expected. The Poem and the Action have all their Parts, and no more.

But the Order of the *Odyssey* differs from that of the *Iliads*, in that the *Poem* does not begin with the Beginning of the *Action*. ⟨II xi⟩

Of the Causes and Beginning of the Action.

The *Causes of the Action* are also what the Poet is oblig'd to give an Account of. There are three sorts of Causes, the Humours, the Interests, and the Designs of Men; and these different Causes of an Action are likewise often the Causes of one another, every Man taking up those Interests in which his Humour ingages him, and forming those Designs to which his Humour and Interest incline him. Of all these the Poet ought to inform his Readers, and render them conspicuous in his principal Personages.

Homer has ingeniously begun his *Odyssey* with the Transactions at *Ithaca,* during the absence of *Ulysses.* If he had begun with the Travels of his Heroe, he would scarce have spoken of any one else, and a Man might have read a great deal of the Poem, without conceiving the least Idea of *Telemachus, Penelope,* or her Suitors, who had so great a share in the Action; but in the beginning he has pitch'd upon, besides these Personages, whom he discovers, he represents *Ulysses* in his full Length, and from the very first opening one sees the Interest which the Gods take in the Action.

The Skill and Care of the same Poet may be seen likewise in inducing his Personages in the first Book of his *Iliads,* where he discovers the Humours, the Interests, and the Designs of *Agamemnon, Achilles, Hector, Ulysses,* and several others, and even of the Deities. And in his Second he makes a Review of the *Grecian* and *Trojan* Armies; which is full Evidence, that all we have here said is very necessary. ⟨ıı xii⟩

Of the Middle or Intrigue of the Action.

As these *Causes* are the *Beginning* of the Action, the opposite Designs against that of the Hero are the *Middle* of it, and form that Difficulty or *Intrigue,* which makes up the greatest part of the Poem; the Solution or *Unravelling* commences when the Reader begins to see that difficulty remov'd, and the doubts clear'd up. *Homer* has divided each of his Poems into two Parts, and has put a particular Intrigue, and the Solution of it, into each Part.

The first Part of the *Iliads* is the Anger of *Achilles,* who is for revenging himself upon *Agamemnon* by the means of *Hector* and the *Trojans.* The *Intrigue* comprehends the three days Fight, which happen'd in the Absence of *Achilles*: and it consists on one side in the resistance of *Agamemnon* and the *Grecians*; and on the other in the revengeful and inexorable Humour of *Achilles,* which would not suffer him to be reconcil'd. The Loss of the *Grecians* and the Despair of *Agamemnon,* prepare for a solution by the satisfaction which the incens'd Heroe receiv'd from it. The death of *Patroclus* join'd to the Offers of *Agamemnon,* which of it self had prov'd ineffectual, remove this Difficulty, and make the unravelling of the first part.

This death is likewise the Beginning of the second Part; since it puts *Achilles* upon the design of revenging himself on *Hector*. But the design of *Hector* is opposite to that of *Achilles*; This *Trojan* is valiant, and resolv'd to stand on his own defence. This Valour and Resolution of *Hector*, are on his part the cause of the Intrigue. All the Endeavours *Achilles* us'd, to meet with *Hector* and be the death of him; and the contrary Endeavours of the *Trojan* to keep out of his Reach, and defend himself; are the intrigue; which comprehends the battle of the last day. The unravelling begins at the death of *Hector*; and besides that, it contains the insulting of *Achilles* over his Body, the Honours he paid to *Patroclus*, and the Intreaties of King *Priam*. The regrets of this King and the other *Trojans*, in the sorrowful Obsequies they paid to *Hector*'s body, end the unravelling; they justifie the satisfaction of *Achilles*, and demonstrate his Tranquillity.

The first part of the *Odyssey* is the return of *Ulysses* into *Ithaca*. *Neptune* opposes it by raising tempests, and this makes the Intrigue. The unravelling is the arrival of *Ulysses* upon his own Island, where *Neptune* could offer him no farther injury. The second Part is the re-instating this Heroe in his own Government. The Princes that are his Rivals, oppose him, and this is a fresh Intrigue: The Solution of it begins at their deaths, and is compleated as soon as the *Ithacans* were appeas'd.

These two Parts in the *Odyssey* have not one common Intrigue. The Anger of *Achilles* forms both the Intrigues in the *Iliads*; and it is so far the Matter of this *Epopéa*, that the very Beginning and End of this Poem depend on the Beginning and End of this Anger. But let the Desire *Achilles* had to revenge himself, and the Desire *Ulysses* had to return to his own Country, be never so near ally'd, yet we cannot place them under one and the same Notion: For that Desire of *Ulysses* is not a Passion that Begins and Ends in the Poem with the Action; 'tis a natural Habit; nor does the Poet propose it for his Subject as he does the Anger of *Achilles*. ⟨ii xiii⟩

We have already observ'd what is meant by the *Intrigue*, and the *Unravelling* thereof; let us now say something of the Manner of forming both. These two should arise naturally out of the very Essence and Subject of the Poem, and are to be deduced from thence. Their Conduct is so exact and natural, that it seems as if their Action had presented them with whatever they inserted, without putting themselves to the Trouble of a farther Inquiry.

What is more usual and natural to Warriors, than Anger, Heat, Passion, and Impatience of bearing the least Affront or Disrespect?

This is what forms the Intrigue of the *Iliads*; and every thing we read there is nothing else but the Effect of this Humour and these Passions.

What more natural and usual Obstacle to those who take Voyages, than the Sea, the Winds, and the Storms? *Homer* makes this the Intrigue of the first Part of the *Odyssey*: And for the second, he makes use of almost the infallible effect of the long Absence of a Master, whose return is quite despair'd of, *viz.* the Insolence of his Servants and Neighbours, the Danger of his Son and Wife, and the Sequestration of his Estate. Besides an Absence of almost twenty Years, and the insupportable Fatigues joyn'd to the Age of which *Ulysses* then was, might induce him to believe that he should not be own'd by those who thought him dead, and whose Interest it was to have him really so. Therefore if he had presently declar'd who he was, and had call'd himself *Ulysses*, they would easily have destroy'd him as an Impostor, before he had an Opportunity to make himself known.

There could be nothing more natural nor more necessary than this ingenious Disguise, to which the advantages his Enemies had taken of his Absence had reduc'd him, and to which his long Misfortunes had enur'd him. This allow'd him an opportunity, without hazarding any thing, of taking the best measures he could, against those persons who could not so much as mistrust any harm from him. This way was afforded him by the very Nature of his Action, to execute his Designs, and overcome the Obstacles it cast before him. And 'tis this contest between the Prudence and the Dissimulation of a single Man on one hand, and the ungovernable Insolence of so many Rivals on the other, which constitutes the Intrigue of the second Part of the *Odyssey*. ⟨II xiv⟩

Of the End or Unravelling of the Action.

If the *Plot* or *Intrigue* must be natural, and such as springs from the very Subject, as has been already urg'd : Then the *Winding up* of the Plot, by a more sure claim, must have this Qualification, and be a probable consequence of all that went before. As this is what the Readers regard more than the rest, so should the Poet be more exact in it. This is the End of the Poem, and the last Impression that is to be stamp'd upon them.

We shall find this in the *Odyssey*. *Ulysses* by a Tempest is cast upon the Island of the *Phæacians*, to whom he discovers himself, and desires they would favor his Return to his own Country which was not very far distant. One cannot see any reason why the King of this Island should refuse such a reasonable Request, to a Heroe whom he seem'd to have in great esteem. The *Phæacians* indeed had heard him tell the Story of his Adventures; and in this fabulous recital consisted all the advantage they could derive from his Presence; for the Art of War which they admir'd in him, his Undauntedness under Dangers, his indefatigable Patience, and other Virtues, were such as these Islanders were not used to. All their Talent lay in singing and dancing, and whatsoever was charming in a quiet life. And here we see how dextrously *Homer* prepares the Incidents he makes use of. These People could do no less, for the Account with which *Ulysses* had so much entertain'd them, than afford him a Ship and a safe Convoy, which was of little expence or trouble to them.

When he arriv'd, his long Absence, and the Travels which had disfigur'd him, made him altogether unknown; and the Danger he would have incurr'd had he discover'd himself too soon, forced him to a Disguise: Lastly, this Disguise gave him an Opportunity of surprizing those young Suitors, who for several years together had been accustomed to nothing but to sleep well, and fare daintily.

It was from these Examples that *Aristotle* drew this Rule, "that Whatever concludes the Poem should so spring from the very constitution of the Fable, as if it were a *necessary*, or at least a *probable* consequence". ⟨II xv⟩

SECT. VI.

The Time of the Action.

THE *Time* of the Epic Action is not fix'd, like that of the Dramatic Poem: It is much longer, for an uninterrupted Duration is much more necessary in an Action which one sees and is present at, than in one which we only read or hear repeated. Besides, Tragedy is fuller of Passion, and consequently of such a Violence as cannot admit of so long a Duration.

The *Iliads* containing an Action of *Anger* and *Violence*, the Poet allows it but a short time, about *forty days*. The Design of the *Odyssey* required another Conduct; the Character of the Hero is *Prudence* and *Long-suffering*; therefore the Time of its Duration is much longer, above *eight Years*. ⟨II xviii⟩

The Passions of the Epic Poem.

The *Passions* of Tragedy are different from those of the Epic Poem. In the former, *Terror* and *Pity* have the chief place; the Passion that seems most peculiar to Epic Poetry, is *Admiration*.

Besides this *Admiration*, which in general distinguishes the Epic Poem from the Dramatic; each Epic Poem has likewise some *peculiar Passion*, which distinguishes it in particular from other Epic Poems, and constitutes a kind of singular and individual difference between these Poems of the same Species. These singular Passions correspond to the *Character* of the *Hero*. *Anger* and *Terror* reign throughout the *Iliad*, because *Achilles* is angry, and the most Terrible of all Men. The *Æneid* has all *soft* and *tender Passions*, because that is the Character of *Æneas*. The Prudence, Wisdom, and Constancy of *Ulysses* do not allow him either of these Extremes, therefore the Poet does not permit one of them to be predominant in the *Odyssey*. He confines himself to *Admiration* only, which he carries to an higher pitch than in the *Iliads*: And 'tis upon this account that he introduces a great many more Machines in the *Odyssey* into the Body of the Action, than are to be seen in the Actions of the other two Poems. ⟨iii ix⟩

The Manners.

The *Manners* of the Epic Poem ought to be *poetically good*, but it is not necessary they be always *morally* so. They are poetically good, when one may discover the Virtue or Vice, the good or ill Inclinations, of every one who speaks or acts: They are poetically bad, when Persons are made to speak or act out of Character, or inconsistently, or unequally. The Manners of *Æneas* and of *Mezentius* are equally good, consider'd poetically, because they equally demonstrate the Piety of the one, and the Impiety of the other. ⟨iv iv⟩

Character of the Heroe.

'Tis requisite to make the same distinction between a Heroe in Morality and a Heroe in Poetry, as between moral and poetical Goodness. *Achilles* had as much right to the latter as *Æneas*. *Aristotle* says, that the Heroe of a Poem should be neither good nor bad; neither advanc'd above the rest of mankind by his Virtues, or sunk beneath 'em by his Vices; that he may be the properer and fuller Example to others, both what to imitate and what to decline. ⟨iv v⟩

The other Qualifications of the *Manners*, are, that they be *suitable* to the Causes which either raise or discover them in the Persons; that they have an exact *Resemblance* to what History or Fable have delivered of those persons to whom they are ascrib'd; and that there be an *Equality* in them, so that no man is made to act or speak out of his character. ⟨IV vii⟩

Unity of the Character.

But this Equality is not sufficient for the *Unity of the Character*: 'tis further necessary that the same Spirit appear in all sort of Encounters. Thus *Æneas* acting with great *Piety* and *Mildness* in the first part of the *Æneid*, which requires no other Character; and afterwards appearing illustrious in Heroic valour in the wars of the second part, but there without any appearance either of a hard or a soft disposition, would doubtless be far from offending against the *Equality* of the Manners: But yet there would be no *Simplicity* or *Unity* in the Character. So that besides the Qualities that claim their particular place upon different occasions, there must be One appearing throughout, which commands over all the rest: And without this we may affirm 'tis no Character.

One may indeed make a Heroe as valiant as *Achilles*, as pious as *Æneas*, and as prudent as *Ulysses*. But 'tis a meer Chimæra to imagine a Heroe that has the Valour of *Achilles*, the Piety of *Æneas*, and the Prudence of *Ulysses*, at one and the same time. This Vision might happen to an Author, who would suit the character of a Heroe to whatever each part of the Action might naturally require, without regarding the Essence of the Fable, or the Unity of the Character in the same person upon all sorts of occasions: This Heroe would be the mildest, best-natur'd Prince in the world, and also the most cholerick, hard-hearted, and implacable creature imaginable; he would be extreamly tender like *Æneas*, extreamly violent like *Achilles*, and yet have the indifference of *Ulysses*, that is incapable of the two extremes. Would it not be in vain for the Poet to call this Person by the same name throughout?

Let us reflect on the effects it would produce in several Poems, whose Authors were of opinion, that the chief character of a Heroe is that of an accomplish'd Man. They would be all alike, all valiant in Battle, prudent in Council, pious in the acts of Religion, courteous, civil, magnificent; and lastly endued with all the prodigious Virtues any Poet could invent. All this would be independent from the Action and the Subject of the Poem; and upon seeing each Heroe separated from the rest of the work, we should not easily guess, to what Action and to what Poem the Heroe belong'd? So that we should see that none of those would have a Character, since the Character is that which makes a person discernable, and which distinguishes him from all others. ⟨IV xii⟩

This commanding Quality in *Achilles* is his Anger, in *Ulysses* the art of Dissimulation, in *Æneas* Meekness. Each of these may be stil'd, by way of eminence, the Character in these Heroes.

But these Characters cannot be alone. 'Tis absolutely necessary that some other should give them a lustre, and embellish them as far as they are capable: Either by hiding the defects that are in each, by some noble and shining Qualities; as the Poet has done the Anger of *Achilles*, by shading it with an extraordinary Valour: Or by making them entirely of the nature of a true and solid Virtue, as is to be observ'd in the two others. The Dissimulation of *Ulysses* is a part of his Prudence; and the Meekness of *Æneas* is wholly employ'd in submitting his Will to the Gods. For the making up this Union, our Poets have joyn'd together such Qualities as are by nature the most compatible; *Valour* with *Anger*, *Meekness* with *Piety*, and *Prudence* with *Dissimulation*. This last Union was necessary for the Goodness of *Ulysses*; for without that, his Dissimulation might have degenerated into Wickedness and Double-dealing. ⟨IV xi⟩

SECT. VII.

Of the Machinery.

WE come now to the *Machines* of the Epic Poem. The chief Passion which it aims to excite being *Admiration*, nothing is so conducive to that as the *Marvellous*; and the importance and dignity of the Action is by nothing so greatly elevated as by the *Care and Interposition of Heaven*.

These Machines are of three sorts. Some are *Theological*, and were invented to explain the nature of God. Others are *Physical*, and represent things of Nature. The last are *Moral*, and are the Images of Virtues and Vices. ⟨v i⟩

Homer and the Ancients have given to their Deities the Manners, Passions and Vices of Men. Their Poems are wholly Allegorical; and in this view it is easier to defend *Homer* than to blame him. We cannot accuse him for making mention of many Gods, for his bestowing Passions upon them, or even introducing them fighting against men. The Scripture uses the like figures and expressions.

If it be allowable to speak thus of the Gods in *Theology*, much more in the Fictions of *Natural Philosophy*, where if a Poet describes the Deities, he must give them such Manners, Speeches, and Actions as are conformable to the nature of the things they represent under those Divinities. The case is the same in *Moral* Deities: *Minerva* is wise, because she represents Prudence; *Venus* is both good or bad, because the Passion of Love is capable of these contrary qualities. ⟨v ii⟩

Since among the Gods of a Poem some are good, some bad, and some indifferently either; and since of our Passions we make so many allegorical Deities; one may attribute to the *Gods* all that is done in the Poem, whether good or evil. But these Deities do not act constantly in one and the same manner.

Sometimes they act invisibly, and by meer Inspiration; which has nothing in it extraordinary or miraculous: being no more than what we say every day, "That some God has assisted us, or some Dæmon has instigated us."

At other times they appear visibly, and manifest themselves to men, in a manner altogether miraculous and præternatural.

The third way has something of both the others: It is in truth a miracle, but is not commonly so accounted: This includes Dreams, Oracles, &c.

All these ways must be *Probable*; for so necessary as the Marvellous is to the Epic Action, as nothing is so conducive to Admiration; yet we can on the other hand admire nothing that we think impossible. Tho' the Probability of these Machines be of a very large extent, (since 'tis founded upon Divine Power) it is not without limitations. There are numerous Instances of allowable and probable Machines in the Epic Poems, where the Gods are no less Actors than the Men. But the less credible sort, such as *Metamorphoses*, &c. are far more rare.

This suggests a Reflection on the Method of rendring those Machines probable, which in their own nature are hardly so. Those which require only *Divine Probability*, should be so disengag'd from the Action, that one might subtract them from it without destroying the Action. But those which are essential and necessary, should be grounded upon *Human Probability*, and not on the sole Power of God. Thus the Episodes of *Circe*, the *Sirens*, *Poly-*

phemus, &c. are necessary to the Action of the *Odyssey*, and yet not humanly probable: Yet *Homer* has artificially reduc'd them to human Probability, by the Simplicity and Ignorance of the *Phæacians*, before whom he causes those recitals to be made. ⟨v iii⟩

The next Question is, Where, and on what occasions Machines may be used? It is certain *Homer* and *Virgil* make use of them every where, and scarce suffer any Action to be perform'd without them. *Petronius* ⟨*Satyricon* 118⟩ makes this a Precept: *Per ambages, deorumque ministeria* &c. The Gods are mention'd in the very *Proposition* of their Works, the *Invocation* is addressed to them, and the whole *Narration* is full of them. The Gods are the *Causes* of the Action, they form the *Intrigue*, and bring about the *Solution*. The precept of *Aristotle* ⟨*Poetics*, xv 10⟩ and *Horace* ⟨*Ars Poet.* 191–2⟩, that the unravelling of the Plot should not proceed from a Miracle or the appearance of a God, has place only in Dramatic Poetry, not in the Epic. For it is plain that both in the Solution of the *Iliads* and *Odyssey* the Gods are concern'd: In the former, the Deities meet to appease the Anger of *Achilles*: *Iris* and *Mercury* are sent to that purpose, and *Minerva* eminently assists *Achilles* in the decisive combate with *Hector*. In the *Odyssey*, the same Goddess fights close by *Ulysses* against the Suitors, and concludes that Peace betwixt him and the *Ithacensians*, which compleats the Poem. ⟨v iv⟩

We may therefore determine, that a Machine is not an Invention to extricate the Poet out of any difficulty which embarrasses him: But that the Presence of a Divinity, and some Action surprizing and extraordinary, are inserted into almost all the parts of his work, in order to render it more Majestic and more Admirable. But this mixture ought to be so made, that the Machines might be retrench'd without taking any thing from the Action. At the same time it gives the Readers a lesson of Piety and Virtue ⟨v v⟩; and teaches them, that the most brave and the most wise can do nothing, and attain nothing great and glorious, without the assistance of Heaven. Thus the Machinery crowns the whole work, and renders it at once, *Marvellous*, *Probable*, and *Moral*.

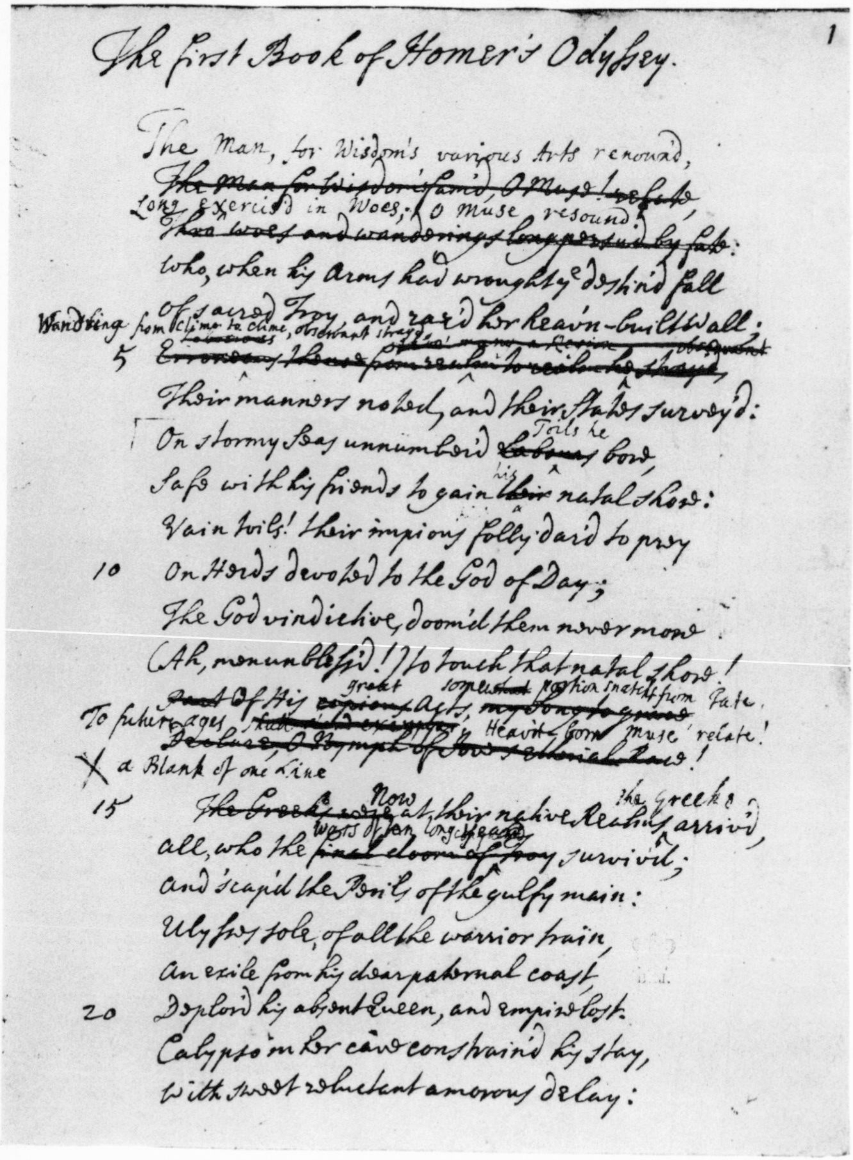

The first Book of Homer's Odyssey.

The Man, for Wisdom's various Arts renown'd,
~~The Man for Wisdom fam'd, O Muse rehearse,~~
Long exercis'd in Woes, O Muse resound;
~~Whose woes and wand'rings long pursued by fate:~~
Who, when his Arms had wrought Troy's destin'd fall

Wand'ring from Of sacred Troy, and raz'd her Heav'n-built Wall;
clime to clime,

5   ~~Erroneous, &c.~~

Their manners noted, and their states survey'd:
⌐ On stormy Seas unnumber'd ~~Labours~~ Toils he bore,
Safe with his friends to gain his natal shore:
Vain toils! their impious folly dar'd to prey
10   On Herds devoted to the God of Day;
The God vindictive, doom'd them never more
(Ah, men unbless'd!) to touch that natal shore!

To future ages
great
&c.   Heav'n from muse relate!

✗ a Blank of one Line

Now   the Greeks
15   ~~The Greeks~~ at their native Realms arriv'd,
were ~~of ten long years~~
all, who the ~~dire doom of Troy~~ surviv'd;
and 'scap'd the Perils of the gulfy main:
Ulysses sole, of all the warrior train,
An exile from his dear paternal coast,
20   Deplord his absent Queen, and empire lost:
Calypso in her cave constrain'd his stay,
with sweet reluctant amorous delay:

Plate 2   First leaf of Fenton's translation of *Odyssey* I,
with Pope's corrections

THE
FIRST BOOK
OF THE
ODYSSEY.

The ARGUMENT.
Minerva's Defcent to *Ithaca.*

The Poem opens within forty eight days of the arrival of Ulysses *in his dominions. He had now remain'd seven years in the island of* Calypso, *when the Gods assembled in council proposed the method of his departure from thence, and his return to his native country. For this purpose it is concluded to send* Mercury *to* Calypso, *and* Pallas *immediately descends to* Ithaca. *She holds a conference with* Telemachus, *in the shape of* Mentes *King of the* Taphians; *in which she advises him to take a journey in quest of his Father* Ulysses, *to* Pylos *and* Sparta, *where* Nestor *and* Menelaus *yet reign'd: then after having visibly display'd her divinity, disappears. The suitors of* Penelope *make great entertainments, and riot in her palace till night.* Phemius *sings to them the return of the* Grecians, *till* Penelope *puts a stop to the song. Some words arise between the suitors and* Telemachus, *who summons the council to meet the day following.*

THE Man, for Wisdom's various arts renown'd,
Long exercis'd in woes, oh Muse! resound.
Who, when his arms had wrought the destin'd fall

We shall proceed in the same method thro' the course of these Annotations upon the *Odyssey*, as in those upon the *Iliad*; considering *Homer* chiefly as a Poet, endeavouring to make his beauties *understood*, and not to praise without a reason given. It is equally an extreme, on the one hand to think *Homer* has no human defects; and on the other to dwell so much upon those defects, as to depreciate his beauties. The greater part of Criticks form a general character, from the observation of particular errors, taken in their own oblique or imperfect views; which is as unjust, as to make a judgment of the beauty of a man's body from the shadow it happens to cast, in such or such a position. To convince the Reader of this intended impartiality, we readily allow the *Odyssey* to be inferior to the *Iliad* in many respects. It has not that sublimity of spirit, or that enthusiasm of poetry; but then it must be allow'd, if it be less noble, it is more instructive: The other abounds with more Heroism, this with more Morality. The *Iliad* gives us a draught of Gods and Heroes, of discord, of contentions, and scenes of slaughter; the *Odyssey* sets before us a scene more amiable, the landschapes of nature, the pleasures of private life, the duties of every station, the hospitality of ancient times; a less busy, but more agreeable portrait. The *Iliad* concludes with the ruin, the *Odyssey* with the happiness of a nation. *Horace* was of the same opinion, as is evident from the epistle to *Lollius* ⟨1 ii 15–18⟩.

> *Seditione, dolis, scelere atque libidine, & ira,*
> Iliacos *intra muros peccatur & extra.*
> *Rursus, quid virtus & quid sapientia possit,*
> *Utile proposuit nobis exemplar* Ulyssem.

 1. *The Man, for Wisdom,* &c.] *Homer* opens his Poem with the utmost simplicity and modesty; he continually grows upon the reader,

> *Non fumum ex fulgore, sed ex fumo dare lucem*
> *Cogitat, ut speciosa dehinc miracula promat.*

⟨Horace, Ars Poet. 143–4⟩.

Cicero lays this down as a rule for the Orator, *principia verecunda, non elatis intensa verbis* ⟨*Orator* xxxvi 124–5⟩; and *Horace* for the Poet, *Nec sic incipies, &c.* ⟨*Ars Poet.* 136⟩. He proposes the beginning of the *Odyssey* as a pattern for all future poems, and has translated them in his Art of poetry ⟨141–2⟩.

> *Dic mihi, Musa, virum, captæ post tempora Trojæ,*
> *Qui mores hominum multorum vidit, & urbes.*

May I be forgiven the arrogance, if I should offer a criticism upon this translation? The *sufferings* of *Ulysses* are the subject of the whole *Odyssey*, and yet *Horace* has omitted the mention of those sufferings: ὃς μάλα πολλὰ πλάγχθη. There is another word also which seems essential, that is, πολύτροπον, this is likewise omitted. For the sufferings of *Ulysses*, and the wisdom by which he extricated himself from them, enter into the very design of the Poem. But indeed in another place he has plainly had regard to all these circumstances,

> *Qui* domitor Trojæ, *multorum* providus *urbes*
> *Et mores hominum inspexit, latumque per æquor*
> *Dum sibi, dum sociis, reditum parat,* aspera multa
> Pertulit— *Epist. ad Loll.* ⟨*Epist.* 1 ii 19–22⟩.

I must also refute a criticism of *Rapin*, who will have it that the word πολύτροπος includes a character of craft and low cunning, unworthy of a brave spirit ⟨Comparaison xv, 1 157⟩: But *Eustathius* admirably vindicates the Poet in this respect, he shews us that τρόπος nowhere in *Homer* signifies (ἤθη) or Morals; and that it implies a man who could accommodate himself to every condition of life; one who in the worst estate had still a reserve to free himself from it; it therefore, says he, signifies a man that thro' experience has learn'd wisdom. I have likewise the authority of *Horace* for this sense, in the above-cited passage,

> *Qui domitor Trojæ multorum* providus *urbes.*

I take *providus* in this place to signify not only a man who noted the manners of various nations with care, but also one who in calamity could foresee methods to extricate himself from it. And surely nothing can be more unjust than what *Rapin* objects against *Ulysses*, in employing his wisdom only in his own preservation, while all his companions were lost: *Homer* himself sufficiently refutes this objection, and directly tells us, that he employed his wisdom in the care of their safety, but that they thro' their folly defeated his wisdom. The words of *Homer*, says *Eustathius*, shew that a wise man neglects not his friends in adversity. But, says *Rapin*, what could oblige *Homer* to begin with so dishonourable an action, and place the greatest weakness of his Heroe in the very frontispiece of his Poem? and invoke his Muse to sing the man who with difficulty saved himself, and suffer'd his companions to be destroy'd? There had been some weight in this objection, if *Ulysses* had saved his own, with the loss of their lives; but I cannot see any dishonour, in his preserving himself by wisdom, when they destroy'd themselves by folly: It was chiefly by storms that they perish'd; it can be no imputation to his character, not to be able to restrain the effects of a tempest: he did all that a wise man cou'd do, he gave them such admonitions upon every emergency, that if they had pursued them, they had been preserved as well as *Ulysses*.

For Wisdom's various arts renown'd.] *Bossu's* observation in relation to this Epithet πολύτροπος, given to *Ulysses*, is worth transcribing ⟨IV ix⟩. The Fable of the *Odyssey* (says he) is wholly for the conduct and policy of a State: Therefore the quality it requires is *Wisdom*, but this virtue is of too large an extent for the simplicity which a just and precise *character* requires; it is therefore requisite it should be limited. The great art of Kings is the mystery of *Dissimulation*. 'Tis well known, that *Lewis* the eleventh, for the instruction of his Son, reduc'd all the *Latin language* to these words only, *viz. Qui nescit dissimulare nescit regnare.* 'Twas likewise by this practice that *Saul* began his reign, when he was first elected and as yet full of the spirit of God. The first thing we read of him in holy Writ is, that he made as if he did not hear the words which seditious people spoke against him [*Ille vero dissimulabat se audire.* Reg. lib. I ⟨i.e. I Sam., 10 : 27⟩].

This then is the *character* which the *Greek* Poet gives his *Ulysses* in the Proposition of his Poem, he calls him ἄνδρα πολύτροπον; to denote this prudent dissimulation, which disguised him so many ways, and put him upon taking so many shapes.

Without mentioning any thing of *Circe*, who detain'd him with her a whole year, and who was famous for the transformations she made of all sorts of persons; the reader finds him at first with *Calypso* the daughter of wise *Atlas*, who bore up the vast pillars that reach'd from Earth to Heaven, and whose knowledge penetrated into the depths of the unfathomable Ocean: that is to say, who was ignorant of nothing in Heaven, Earth, or Sea. And as the first product and principal part of so high, so solid, and so profound a knowledge was to know how to conceal ones self; this wise man call'd his daughter by a name that signified a *secret* [Καλύπτειν]. The Poet makes his Heroe, whom he designed for a Politician, to stay seven whole years with this Nymph. She taught him so well, that afterwards he lost no opportunity of putting her lessons in practice: for he does no-

Of sacred *Troy*, and raz'd her heav'n-built wall,
Wand'ring from clime to clime, observant stray'd,   5
Their Manners noted, and their States survey'd.
On stormy seas unnumber'd toils he bore,
Safe with his friends to gain his natal shore:
Vain toils! their impious folly dar'd to prey

thing without a disguise. At his parting from *Ogygia* he is cast upon the Isle of
Phæacia: as kind as his reception was, yet he stays 'till the night before he went off
ere he wou'd discover himself. From thence he goes to *Ithaca*: the first adventure
that happen'd to him there was with *Minerva*, the most prudent among the Deities, as *Ulysses* was the most prudent among men. She says so expressly in that
very passage. Nor did they fail to disguise themselves. *Minerva* takes upon her the
shape of a shepherd, and *Ulysses* tells her he was oblig'd to fly from *Crete*, because
he had murder'd the son of King *Idomeneus*. The Goddess discovers her self first,
and commends him particularly, because these artifices were so easie and
natural to him, that they seem'd to be born with him. Afterwards the Heroe
under the form of a beggar deceives first of all *Eumæus*, then his son, and last of all
his wife, and every body else, till he found an opportunity of punishing his
Enemies, to whom he discover'd not himself 'till he kill'd them, namely on the
last night. After his discovering himself in the Palace, he goes the next day to
deceive his father, appearing at first under a borrow'd name; before he wou'd
give him joy of his return. Thus he takes upon him all manner of shapes, and
dissembles to the very last. But the Poet joins to this character a valour and a
constancy which render him invincible in the most daring and desperate
adventures.

3.   *Who, when his arms had wrought the destin'd fall*
            Of sacred Troy—
Whence is it that *Ulysses* is said to have overthrown *Troy*? and not *Achilles*, who
was of more remarkable courage than *Ulysses*? *Eustathius* tells us, that the destruction of *Troy* ought to be ascribed chiefly to *Ulysses*, as he not only took away the
Palladium, but was the inventor of the stratagem of the wooden horse, by which
that city was conquer'd. *Virgil* in his second book of the *Æneis* gives a noble
description of its destruction, by which we find that *Ulysses* was not only the con-
triver of its ruin, but bore a great share in the actions of the night in which that
City was overturn'd.

9. *Vain toils! their impious folly*, &c.] By this single trait, *Homer* marks an essential
difference between the *Iliad* and the *Odyssey*: namely, that in the former Poem
the people perish'd by the folly of their Kings:
        Quicquid delirant reges, plectuntur Achivi ⟨Horace, *Epist.* 1 ii 14⟩.
In this, the people perish by their own folly, while their Prince omits nothing to
procure their felicity. A plain reason why the *Odyssey* is more calculated for the
People, than the *Iliad. Dacier.*

On Herds devoted to the God of Day;   10
The God vindictive doom'd them never more
(Ah men unbless'd!) to touch that natal shore.
Oh snatch some portion of these acts from fate,
Celestial Muse! and to our world relate.

Now at their native realms the *Greeks* arriv'd;   15

13. *Oh snatch some portion of these acts from fate.*] It may be ask'd why the Poet invokes the Muse to recount only Part of the sufferings of *Ulysses*? and why those words, *To Us also*, are inserted? To the first it may be answer'd, that an heroic Poem dwells chiefly upon incidents of importance, and passes over every thing that does not contribute to raise our idea of the Heroe, or to the main design of the Poem: To the other *Eustathius* answers several ways; either, says he, the word καὶ is to be taken as an expletive, as it is in a thousand places in *Homer*; or it means that this is a subject so considerable, that it will be a theme to many Poets; or that being a true History it had spread over many nations of the world, and that *Homer* himself received the story of the Poem from *Ægypt*; and then the meaning will be, "Sing, oh Muse, to the *Greeks* as well as to other nations, the sufferings of *Ulysses*." I should prefer the first as being the most natural: the rest seem forced, and consequently improper for the opening of a Poem, where the utmost plainness is necessary; especially, if we consider that *Ulysses* was a *Grecian*, and it is not probable that the *Grecians* should be the least acquainted with the story, or the latest to celebrate the actions, of a *Grecian*.

15. *Now at their native realms the* Greeks *arriv'd.*] It is necessary for the better understanding of the Poem, to fix the period of Time from which it takes its beginning: *Homer*, as *Eustathius* observes, does not begin with the wandrings of *Ulysses*, he steps at once into the latter end of his actions, and leaves the preceding story to be told by way of narration. Thus in his *Iliad*, he dates his Poem from the anger of *Achilles*, which happen'd almost at the conclusion of the *Trojan* war. From hence *Horace* drew his observation in his *Ars Poet.* ⟨148–9⟩.

Semper ad eventum festinat; & in medias res,
Non secus ac notas, auditorem rapit.

There are but forty eight days from the departure of *Ulysses* from *Calypso*, to his discovery in *Ithaca*; he had been one year with *Circe*, and seven with *Calypso*, when the Gods dispatched *Mercury* to that Goddess; from which point of Time we are to date the *Odyssey*.

This observation gives a reason why the Poet invokes the Muse to recount the wandrings of this Heroe in part only; for *Ulysses*, as appears from the beginning of the ninth book, after he left the shores of *Troy*, was driven to *Ismarus* of the *Ciconians*. An Historian must have begun from the fall of *Troy*, and related his wandrings with truth and order; for History is chiefly for instruction: But a Poet takes another method, and disposes every circumstance arbitrarily; he chuses or

All who the Wars of ten long years surviv'd,
And 'scap'd the perils of the gulfy Main.
Ulysses, sole of all the victor train,
An exile from his dear paternal coast,
Deplor'd his absent Queen, and Empire lost.   20
Calypso in her caves constrain'd his stay,
With sweet, reluctant, amorous delay:
In vain—for now the circling years disclose
The day predestin'd to reward his woes.
At length his *Ithaca* is giv'n by Fate,   25
Where yet new labours his arrival wait;
At length their rage the hostile Pow'rs restrain,
All but the ruthless Monarch of the Main.
But now the God, remote, a heav'nly guest
In *Æthiopia* grac'd the genial feast,   30

rejects, as suits best with his principal design, and in such a manner as to give at once delight and instruction.

21. Calypso *in her Cave* ⟨sic⟩ *constrain'd his stay.*] To the Remark before cited of *Bossu*, upon the abode of *Ulysses* with *Calypso* ⟨above, p. 27⟩, may be added this of the Abbè *Fraguier*: that his residing seven years in the caves of *Calypso*, (the Goddess of Secrecy) may only be meant that he remain'd so long hid from the knowledge and enquiry of all men; or that whatever befel him in all that time was lost to History, or made no part in the Poem ⟨cited by Dacier, *Odyssey* (1716), 1 54⟩.

28. *All but the ruthless Monarch of the Main.*] It may be ask'd why *Neptune* is thus enraged against *Ulysses*? *Homer* himself tells us, it was because that Heroe had put out the eye of his son *Cyclops*. But if we take *Neptune* by way of Allegory for the Ocean, the passage implies, that the sufferings of *Ulysses* were chiefly by sea; and therefore Poetry, which adds a grandeur to the meanest circumstance, introduces the God of it as his greatest enemy. *Eustathius.*

30. *In* Æthiopia, *&c.*] *Strabo* ⟨1 ii 28⟩ in his first book delivers his opinion, that "the ancient *Grecians* included all those people who lived upon the southern Ocean, from east to west, in the general name of *Æthiopians*, and that it was not confined to those only who lay south of *Ægypt.*" *Ptolemy* says ⟨IV 6⟩, that "under the *Zodiac*, from east to west, inhabit the *Æthiopians*, black of colour." And elsewhere the same Geographer ⟨IV 8⟩ divides *Æthiopia* into the eastern and the western. These eastern and western *Æthiopians* were separated by the *Arabian* or *Ægyptian* Gulf; which tho' never mention'd by *Homer*, as *Aristarchus* remark'd ⟨Strabo, *loc. cit.*⟩, yet it is not probable (says *Strabo*) that he should be ignorant of it, it being but a thousand stadia distant from the *Mediterranean*, when he knew

(A race divided, whom with sloping rays
The rising and descending Sun surveys)
There on the world's extreamest verge rever'd,
With Hecatombs and pray'r in pomp prefer'd,
Distant he lay: while in the bright abodes   35
Of high *Olympus, Jove* conven'd the Gods:
Th' assembly thus the Sire supreme addrest;
Ægysthus' fate revolving in his breast,
Whom young *Orestes* to the dreary coast
Of *Pluto* sent, a blood-polluted Ghost.   40
    Perverse Mankind! whose Wills, created free,
Charge all their woes on absolute Decree;
All to the dooming Gods their guilt translate,
And Follies are miscall'd the crimes of Fate.
When to his lust *Ægysthus* gave the rein,   45

the *Ægyptian Thebes*, which was four times as far off. *Strab.* ⟨I ii 29⟩. *Plin.* ⟨VI xxxv⟩. *Spondan.* ⟨*Od.* p. 4⟩.

I will not repeat what was observ'd upon the Gods being gone to the *Æthiopians*, in the first book of the *Iliad*; 'tis sufficient in general to observe, that the *Æthiopians* were a people very religious towards the Gods, and that they held a pompous feast twelve days annually to their honour; and in particular, that the Poet very judiciously makes use of this solemnity to remove *Neptune* out of the way, who was the enemy of *Ulysses*, that he may with the greater security bring off his Heroe from *Calypso*'s Island. *Eustathius.*

41. Jupiter's speech.] The solemnity and sententiousness of this speech is taken notice of by *Eustathius*; and surely Poetry must be highly valuable, when it delivers such excellent instructions. It contain'd the whole of religion amongst the antients; and made Philosophy more agreeable. This passage is an instance of it, a passage worthy of a Christian; it shews us that the Supreme Being is sovereignly good; that he rewards the just, and punishes the unjust; and that the folly of man, and not the decree of Heaven, is the cause of human calamity.

45. Ægysthus.] It is difficult to find a reason why, in the original, *Jupiter* shou'd give such an honourable appellation to *Ægisthus*, as ἀμύμονος, *unblameable*, who had dishonoured the bed of *Agamemnon*, and taken his life away; especially in that very instant when he condemns the fact with so great solemnity: *Eustathius* says, that *Homer*, an enemy to censure and invective, introduces that God as having respect only to his good qualities, and commending him for his general character; and adds that it had been an indecency in the Poet to have given countenance to that base custom by the authority of *Jupiter*. *Dacier* is not satisfy'd with

Did Fate, or we, th' adult'rous act constrain?
Did Fate, or we, when great *Atrides* dy'd,
Urge the bold traitor to the Regicide?
Hermes I sent, while yet his soul remain'd

---

this reason, and tells us, that *Homer* gives *Ægisthus* this title, to vindicate *Jupiter* from the imputation of his crimes: He gives us to understand that Heaven is not the cause of man's failings; that he is by Creation able to act virtuously, and that it is thro' his own misconduct that he deviates into evil; and therefore the meaning is this; "*Jupiter* calling to mind *Ægisthus*, that *Ægisthus* "whom he had created wise and virtuous, and made capable to sustain that character." And this agrees admirably with the beginning of the speech of *Jupiter*, who there vindicates his own Divinity.

But if this shou'd seem too refin'd, it may be sufficient to take the word in that good sense which *Ægisthus* might have deserved for many good qualities: Thus *Achilles* is call'd the *swift of foot*, even while he stands, or sleeps; the first being his general character. It may be further confirm'd by a passage something resembling it in the holy Scriptures ⟨Ex. 1 : 15 ff⟩: The *Ægyptian* Midwives were guilty of a lye to *Pharaoh*, and yet God pardons it, and blesses them; He blesses them not because they lyed, but because they preserv'd the children of the *Israelites*.

49. Hermes *I sent*, &c.] It would be endless to observe every moral passage in the *Odyssey*, the whole of it being but one lesson of Morality. But surely it must be a pleasure to the Reader to learn what notions the antients had of a Deity, from the oldest book extant, except the book of *Moses*.

Jupiter here declares that he never fails to warn mankind from evil, and that he had sent *Mercury* for this purpose to *Ægisthus*. It may be ask'd what is this *Mercury* whom *Jupiter* sends? It is the light of Nature, which Heaven implants in the breast of every man: and which, as *Cicero* says, is not only more ancient than the world, but co-eval with the Master of the world himself. He writes to this effect. *There was from the beginning such a thing as Reason, a direct emanation from Nature it self, which prompted to good, and averted from evil. A Reason which did not then become a law, when it was first reduced to writing, but was so even from the moment it existed, and it existed from ever, of an equal date with the divine Intelligence: It is the true and primordial Law, proper to command and to forbid, it is the Reason of the great* Jupiter ⟨De Leg. II iv 10⟩.

That Reason of the supreme Being, is here call'd *Mercury*; that Reason flowing from God, which is constantly dictating to the most corrupted hearts, *this is good*, or, *this is evil*. Hence arose an ancient Proverb, recorded by *Simplicius* ⟨in his Commentary on Epictetus's *Encheiridion*, ch. lxxii⟩, *Reason is a* Mercury *to all men*. Epictetus [lib. 3 ⟨i 18⟩. Arrian] says, Apollo *knew that* Laius *would not obey his Oracle*. Apollo *nevertheless did not neglect to prophecy to* Laius *those evils that threaten'd him. The goodness of the Divinity never fails to advertise mankind; that source of truth is ever open and free: but men are ever incredulous, disobedient and rebellious*. Dacier.

Sincere from royal blood, and faith profan'd;   50
To warn the wretch, that young *Orestes* grown
To manly years shou'd re-assert the throne.
Yet impotent of mind, and uncontrol'd,
He plung'd into the gulf which Heav'n foretold.
    Here paus'd the God, and pensive thus replies   55
Minerva graceful with her azure eyes.
O thou! from whom the whole creation springs,
The source of pow'r on earth deriv'd to Kings!
His death was equal to the direful deed;
So may the Man of blood be doom'd to bleed!   60
But grief and rage alternate wound my breast
For brave *Ulysses*, still by fate opprest.
Amid'st an Isle, around whose rocky shore
The forests murmur, and the surges roar,
The blameless heroe from his wish'd-for home   65
A Goddess guards in her enchanted dome.
(*Atlas* her sire, to whose far-piercing eye

---

57. Minerva's *Speech*.] It may be ask'd what relation *Ulysses* has to *Ægisthus*, that the mention of the one should immediately give occasion for the remembrance of the other? and it may appear unnatural in the Poet to give rise to his Poem by so unexpected a transition from *Ægisthus* to *Ulysses*. *Eustathius* vindicates *Homer*, by shewing that it is not only beautiful but natural, to take rise from what offers it self to our immediate observation. What can be more natural, when *Jupiter* is relating how he punishes the wicked, than for Wisdom or *Minerva* to suggest, that the good ought to be rewarded? There is no forced introduction; no artful preparation, but the whole arises from the occasion, which is a great beauty. *Eustathius.*

63. *Amidst an Isle*, &c.] There was, according to true History, such an Island of *Calypso*, of which *Strabo* ⟨i ii 18⟩ writes; that *Solon* gives an account of the Island *Atlantis* bordering upon *Ægypt*, and that he went thither to make enquiry, and learn'd that an Island was once there, but by time was vanished ⟨cf. also Plutarch, *Solon* xxvi 1⟩. *Eustathius.*

67.   Atlas *her Sire, to whose far-piercing eye*
          The wonders of the Deep expanded lie:
          Th' eternal Columns which on earth he rears
          End in the starry vault, and prop the Spheres.]
Atlas is here said to understand all the depths of the Sea: but the Epithet ὀλοό-φρονος apply'd to him, has two different significations. It implies either, *one whose*

C

The wonders of the Deep expanded lye;
Th' eternal columns which on earth he rears
End in the starry vault, and prop the sphears.)   70
By his fair daughter is the chief confin'd,
Who sooths to dear delight his anxious mind:
Successless all her soft caresses prove,
To banish from his breast his Country's love;
To see the smoke from his lov'd palace rise,   75
While the dear isle in distant prospect lyes,
With what contentment could he close his eyes?

---

thoughts are full of terrible and dismal things, or, *one who has infinite knowledge and unbounded views*, and 'tis doubtful which of them *Homer* means. To reconcile both, may we not think our Author had heard something of the ancient tradition which makes *Atlas* the same person with *Enoch*, and represents him as a great Astronomer, who prophecy'd of the universal deluge, and exhorted mankind to repentance? Therefore he nam'd his son *Methuselah*, to show that after his death the waters shou'd overspread the face of the earth. His continual lamentations on this occasion caus'd him to be call'd the *Weeper*, for the world is always an enemy to melancholy predictions. Thus *Homer* upon the credit of this Tradition might very well call *Atlas*, *one whose thoughts ran upon dismal things*, or *one whose views and cares were vastly extended*.

I insist no otherwise upon this but as a conjecture, yet it is further strengthen'd by what follows in the next lines: *That* Atlas *sustains those Columns which being fixed upon the earth support the Heavens*. This is generally interpreted of his great skill in Astronomy and Geography. But may not the reason be more particular? Since *Atlas* or *Enoch* had prophecy'd of the Deluge, and since that prediction was looked upon as the effect of his skill in Astronomy; might it not be said he knew the abysses of the Sea, and sustain'd the pillars of Heaven, to express that he knew how the fountains of the deep and the waters above the Heavens shou'd unite to drown the earth?

As to the image of the *pillars of Heaven*, it is frequent in the sacred books, and used to express the height of vast mountains. (*Pindar* calls *Ætna* the οὐρανίαν κίονα ⟨*Pyth.* 1 19⟩:) and there might probably be something more particular that furnished *Homer* with this idea; I mean the pillars of *Hercules*, well-known in his time, and neighbouring to the mountain he describes. *Dacier.*

See the description of this mountain in the 4th book of *Virgil* ⟨246 f⟩, where the same image is preserv'd without any hint of allegory: As indeed it is no more than a poetical manner of expressing the *great height* and *extensive prospect* of the mountain.

75. *To see the smoke from his lov'd palace rise.*] There is an agreeable tenderness in this Image, and nothing can better paint the ardent desire a man naturally has

And will Omnipotence neglect to save
The suffering virtue of the wise and brave?
Must he, whose altars on the *Phrygian* shore   80
With frequent rites, and pure, avow'd thy pow'r,
Be doom'd the worst of human ills to prove,
Unbless'd, abandon'd to the wrath of *Jove*?

    Daughter! what words have pass'd thy lips unweigh'd?
(Reply'd the Thund'rer to the Martial Maid)   85
Deem not unjustly by my doom opprest
Of humane race the wisest, and the best.
Neptune, by pray'r repentant rarely won,
Afflicts the chief, t'avenge his Giant son

---

to review his native country after a long absence. This is still stronger than that which *Cicero* extols in several places of his works ⟨e.g. *De Domo Sua*, XLI 109; *De Reditu, passim*⟩, that *Ulysses* preferr'd the sight of *Ithaca* to the Immortality proffer'd him by *Calypso*. He here desires to purchase, at the price of his life, the pleasure, not of returning to his country, but even of seeing at a distance the very smoke of it. *Dacier.*

    There are some things dispers'd in this speech of *Pallas*, which I shall lay together; as that *Minerva* makes it an aggravation to the calamity of *Ulysses*, to be detain'd by a Goddess that loves him; that he is enclosed in an Island; and she adds, round which the Seas flow; as if that was not common to all Islands; but these expressions are used to shew the impossibility of the escape of *Ulysses*, without the interposition of *Jupiter*.

    In the conclusion she observes, that *Ulysses* never neglected to sacrifice before *Troy*: this is said to shew the great piety of *Ulysses*, who not only paid his sacrifices in *Ithaca*, where he abounded in riches, but amongst strangers in an enemy's country, where there might be a scarcity of offerings. *Eustathius.*

    84. *Daughter! what words*, &c.] This verse is frequently repeated both in the *Iliad* and the *Odyssey*; it has here a particular energy. *Jupiter* reproves *Minerva* for supposing he could ever be unmindful of an Heroe so pious as *Ulysses*. It is spoken with vehemence; an instance, says *Eustathius*, that it is not only equitable, but an attribute of Divinity, for rulers to remember those who serve them faithfully.

    89. *T'avenge his Giant son*.] It is artful in the Poet to tell the Reader the occasion of the sufferings of *Ulysses* in the opening of the Poem; 'tis a justice due to his character, to shew that his misfortunes are not the consequence of his crimes, but the effect of *Neptune*'s anger.

    It is observable, that *Homer* does not stop to explain how *Ulysses* put out the eye of the *Cyclops*; he hastens forward into the middle of his Poem, and leaves that for the future narration of *Ulysses*.

Whose visual orb *Ulysses* robb'd of light;   90
Great *Polypheme*, of more than mortal might!
Him young *Thoösa* bore, (the bright increase
Of *Phorcys*, dreaded in the sounds and seas:)
Whom *Neptune* ey'd with bloom of beauty blest,
And in his cave the yielding nymph comprest.   95
For this, the god constrains the *Greek* to roam,
A hopeless exile from his native home,
From death alone exempt—but cease to mourn;
Let all combine t'atchieve his wish'd return:
Neptune aton'd, his wrath shall now refrain,   100
Or thwart the synod of the gods in vain.
    Father and King ador'd! *Minerva* cry'd,
Since all who in th' *Olympian* bow'r reside
Now make the wand'ring *Greek* their public care,
Let *Hermes* to th' *Atlantic* isle ⟨*⟩ repair;   105
Bid him, arriv'd in bright *Calypso*'s court,
The Sanction of th' assembled pow'rs report:
That wise *Ulysses* to his native land
Must speed, obedient to their high command.
Mean time *Telemachus*, the blooming heir   110

* *Ogygia*

110. *Mean time* Telemachus—*demands my care*, &c.] *Rapin* has rais'd several
objections against this piece of conduct in *Homer* ⟨Comparaison V, 1 114–15⟩:
He tells us that the action of the *Odyssey* is imperfect, that it begins with the
voyages of *Telemachus*, and ends with those of *Ulysses*: That the four first books
are all concerning *Telemachus*: That his voyage bears no proportion to that of
Ulysses, that it contributes nothing to his return, which is brought about by
Jupiter, and the assistance of the *Phæacians*; that this gave occasion to *Beni* ⟨Paolo
Beni, *Comparatione di Homero, Virgilio e Torquato* (Padua, 1607), Seventh Dis-
course⟩ in his *academical discourses* to assert, that the Fable of the *Odyssey* is double,
that the four first books of it are neither Episode, nor part of an action, nor have
any connexion with the rest of the work.
    I am of opinion, that these objections are made with too great severity; The
destruction of the Suitors is the chief hinge upon which the Poem turns, as it contributes chiefly to the re-establishment of *Ulysses* in his country and regality; and
whatever contributes to this end, contributes to the principal action, and is of a

Of sea-girt *Ithaca*, demands my care:
'Tis mine, to form his green, unpractis'd years,
In sage debates, surrounded with his Peers,
To save the state; and timely to restrain
The bold intrusion of the Suitor-train;   115
Who crowd his palace, and with lawless pow'r
His herds and flocks in feastful rites devour.
To distant *Sparta* and the spacious waste

piece with the rest of the Poem; and that this voyage does so is evident, in that it gives a defeat to the Suitors, and controuls their insolence; it preserves *Ulysses*'s throne and bed inviolate, in that it gives *Telemachus* courage to resist their attempts: It sets his character in a fair point of light, who is the second personage of the Poem, and is to have a great share in the future actions of it.

Eustathius judiciously observes, that *Homer* here prepares the way for the defeat of the Suitors, the chief design of his Poem; and lays the ground-work of probability on which he intends to build his Poem, and reconcile it to the rules of credibility.

If it be ask'd for what end this voyage of *Telemachus* is made; the answer is, to enquire after *Ulysses*: So that whatever Episodes are interwoven, *Ulysses* is still in view; and whatever *Telemachus* acts, is undertaken solely upon his account; and consequently, whatever is acted, contributes to the principal design, the restoration of *Ulysses*. So that the Fable is entire, and the Action not double.

'Tis to be remember'd also, that the sufferings of *Ulysses* are the subject of the Poem; his personal calamities are not only intended, but his domestic misfortunes; and by this conduct *Homer* shews us the extent of his misfortunes: His Queen is attempted, his Throne threaten'd, and his Wealth consumed in riot; *Ulysses* suffers in *Telemachus*, and in every circumstance of life is unhappy.

112. *'Tis mine, to form his green, unpractis'd years*, &c.] In this the Poet draws the out-lines of what he is to fill up in the four subsequent books: and nothing can give us a greater idea of his unbounded invention, than his building upon so plain a foundation such a noble superstructure: He entertains us with variety of Episodes, historical relations, and manners of those ancient times. It must be confess'd, that the Characters in the *Odyssey*, and the number of the chief Actors, are but few; and yet the Poet never tires, he varies and diversifies the story so happily, that he is continually opening new scenes to engage our attention. He resembles his own *Proteus*, he is capable of all shapes, yet in all shapes the same Deity.

118. *To distant* Sparta *and the spacious waste Of sandy Pyle.*] *Rapin* is very severe upon this conduct ⟨Comparaison VI, I 118⟩. When *Telemachus*, says he, is to search for his father in the Courts of *Greece*, he cannot make the least progress without *Minerva*; 'tis she who inspires his thoughts, and assists in the execution.

Of sandy *Pyle*, the royal Youth shall haste.
There, warm with filial love, the cause enquire   120
That from his realm retards his god-like Sire:
Deliv'ring early to the voice of Fame
The promise of a great, immortal name.
She said: the sandals of cælestial mold
Fledg'd with Ambrosial plumes, and rich with gold,   125
Surround her feet; with these sublime she sails
Th' aerial space, and mounts the winged gales:
O'er earth and ocean wide prepar'd to soar,
Her dreaded arm a beamy jav'lin bore,
Pond'rous and vast; which when her fury burns   130
Proud Tyrants humbles, and whole hosts o'erturns.
From high *Olympus* prone her flight she bends,
And in the realm of *Ithaca* descends.
Her lineaments divine the grave disguise
Of *Mentes'* form conceal'd from human eyes: 135
(*Mentes*, the Monarch of the *Taphian* land)

Could not honour, duty, or nature, have moved his heart toward an absent
father? The Machine, adds he, has not the least appearance of probability, in-
as much as the Goddess conducts him to every place, except only where *Ulysses*
resides; of which she ought by no means to be ignorant, upon the account of her
Divinity.

But surely nothing can be more natural, than for a son, in order to gain
intelligence of an absent father, to enquire in those places, and of those persons,
where and from whom he is most likely to have information. Such is the conduct
of *Telemachus*: And Poetry, which delights in the Wonderful, because this conduct agrees with wisdom, ascribes it to *Minerva* the Goddess of it. No doubt but
Minerva knew where *Ulysses* resided: but men must act as men: such an immediate interposition as *Rapin* requires, had stopp'd at once the fountain of the
Poet's invention. If what a Poet invents be natural, it is justifiable; and he may
give the rein to his imagination, if he restrain it from running into extravagance
and wildness.

136. Mentes, *the Monarch of the* Taphian *land.*] We are told by tradition, that
Homer was so sensible of friendship, that to do honour to his particular friends, he
immortalized their names in his Poems. In the *Iliad* he has shewn his gratitude
to *Tychius*; and in the *Odyssey*, to *Mentes*, *Phemius*, and *Mentor*. This *Mentes* was
a famous Merchant of the isle of *Leucade*, who received *Homer* at *Smyrna*, and made
him his companion in all his voyages. It is to this *Mentes* we owe the two Poems

A glitt'ring spear wav'd awful in her hand.
There in the portal plac'd, the heav'n-born maid
Enormous riot and mis-rule survey'd.
On hides of Beeves, before the palace gate, 140
(Sad spoils of luxury) the Suitors fate.
With rival art, and ardor in their mien,
At Chess they vie, to captivate the Queen,
Divining of their loves. Attending nigh,
A menial train the flowing bowl supply: 145

of *Homer*, for the Poet in all probability had never wrote them without those lights and informations he receiv'd, and the discoveries he was enabled to make, by those travels. *Homer* is not contented to give his name to the King of the *Taphians*, but feigns also that the Goddess of Wisdom chose to appear in his shape, preferably to that of all the Kings who were nearer neighbours to *Ithaca*. *Eustathius* thinks there might have been a real King of *Taphos* of this name, who was a friend to *Ulysses*. This may possibly be; but I would chuse to adhere rather to the old tradition, as it does honour to friendship. *Dacier*.

139. *Enormous riot and mis-rule.*] This is the first appearance of the Suitors; and the Poet has drawn their pictures in such colours, as are agreeable to their characters thro' the whole Poem. They are, as *Horace* expresses it ⟨*Epist.* 1 ii 27–8⟩,
—Fruges consumere nati,
Sponsi Penelopes, Nebulones—
The Poet gives a fine contrast between them and *Telemachus*; he entertains himself with his own thoughts, weighs the sum of things, and beholds with a virtuous sorrow the disorders of the Suitors: He appears, (like *Ulysses* among his transform'd companions in the tenth book,) a wise man, among brutes.

143. *At Chess they vie, to captivate the Queen,*
Divining of their loves—
There are great disputes what this Game was, at which the Suitors play'd? *Athenæus* relates it ⟨1 16 f⟩ from *Appian* the Grammarian, who had it from *Cteson* a native of *Ithaca*, that the sport was in this manner. The number of the Suitors being 108, they equally divided their men, or balls; that is to say, 54 on each side; these were placed on the board opposite to each other. Between the two sides was a vacant space, in the midst of which was the main mark, or *Queen*, the point which all were to aim at. They took their turns by lot; he who took or displac'd that mark, got his own in its place; and if by a second man, he again took it, without touching any of the others, he won the game; and it pass'd as an omen of obtaining his mistress. This principal mark, or *Queen*, was called by whatever name the Gamesters pleas'd; and the Suitors gave it the name of *Penelope*.

'Tis said, this Game was invented by *Palamedes* during the siege of *Troy*. [*Sophocles in Palam.* ⟨Pearson, frag. 479⟩.] *Eustath. Spondan.* ⟨*Od.* pp. 7–8⟩. *Dacier*.

Others apart, the spacious hall prepare,
And form the costly feast with busy care.
There young *Telemachus*, his bloomy face
Glowing cælestial-sweet with godlike grace,
Amid the Circle shines: but hope and fear   150
(Painful vicissitude!) his bosom tear.
Now, imag'd in his mind, he sees restor'd ⎫
In peace and joy, the people's rightful Lord; ⎬
The proud Oppressors fly the vengeful sword. ⎭
While his fond soul these fancied triumphs swell'd,   155
The stranger Guest the royal Youth beheld.
Griev'd that a Visitant so long shou'd wait
Unmark'd, unhonour'd, at a Monarch's gate;
Instant he flew with hospitable haste,
And the new friend with courteous air embrac'd.   160
Stranger! whoe'er thou art, securely rest
Affianc'd in my faith, a friendly guest:
Approach the dome, the social banquet share,
And then the purpose of thy soul declare.
    Thus affable and mild, the Prince precedes,   165
And to the dome th' unknown Cælestial leads.
The spear receiving from her hand, he plac'd
Against a column, fair with sculpture grac'd;
Where seemly rang'd in peaceful order stood
Ulysses' Arms, now long disus'd to blood.   170
He led the Goddess to the sovereign seat,
Her feet supported with a stool of state;
(A purple carpet spread the pavement wide)
Then drew his seat, familiar, to her side:

---

157. *Griev'd that a Visitant so long should wait.*] The Reader will lose much of the pleasure of this Poem, if he reads it without the reflection, that he peruses one of the most ancient books in the world; it sets before him persons, places, and actions that existed three thousand years ago: Here we have an instance of the humanity of those early ages: *Telemachus* pays a reverence to this stranger, only because he is a stranger: He attends him in person, and welcomes him with all the openness of ancient hospitality.

Far from the Suitor-train, a brutal crowd,   175
With insolence, and wine, elate and loud;
Where the free guest, unnoted, might relate
If haply conscious, of his Father's fate.
The golden ew'r a maid obsequious brings,
Replenish'd from the cool, translucent springs;   180
With copious water the bright vase supplies
A silver Laver, of capacious size:
They wash. The tables in fair order spread,
They heap the glitt'ring Canisters with bread:
Viands of various kinds allure the taste,   185

185, &c. *The Feast describ'd.*] There is nothing that has drawn more ridicule
upon *Homer,* than the frequent descriptions of his entertainments: It has been
judged, that he was more than ordinarily delighted with them, since he omits no
opportunity to describe them; nay, his temperance has not been unsuspected,
according to that verse of *Horace* ⟨*Epist.* 1 xix 6⟩,

Laudibus arguitur vini vinosus Homerus.

But we must not condemn, without stronger evidence: a man may commend a
sumptuous entertainment, or good wines, without being either a drunkard or a
glutton. But since there are so many entertainments describ'd in the Poem, it
may not be improper to give this some explanation.

They wash before the feast; perhaps, says *Eustathius,* because they always at the
feast made libations to the Gods. The Ewer was of gold, the vessel from whence
the water was pour'd of silver, and the cups out of which they drank were of gold.

A damsel attends *Mentes,* but heralds wait upon the Suitors: *Eustathius* observes
a decency in this conduct; the Suitors were lewd debauchees, and consequently
a woman of modesty would have been an improper attendant upon such a company. Beautiful Youths attended the company in quality of cup-bearers.

A Matron who has charge of the houshold (ταμίη) brings in the bread and the
cold meats, for so *Eustathius* interprets εἴδατα; an Officer, whose employ it was to
portion out the victuals, brings in the meats that furnish'd out the rest of the
entertainment; and after the feast, a Bard diverts them with vocal and instru-
mental music.

Dacier is in great pain about the cold victuals; she is afraid lest the Reader
should think them the leavings of a former day: and tells us they might possibly
be in the nature of our cold *Tongues, Jambons,* &c. But I think such fears to be
groundless: We must have reference to the customs of those early ages; and if it
was customary for cold meats to be serv'd up, (neither is it necessary to suppose
them the leavings of the former entertainment) it can be no disgrace to the
hospitality of *Telemachus.*

C*

Of choicest sort and savour, rich repast!
Delicious wines th' attending herald brought;
The gold gave lustre to the purple draught.
Lur'd with the vapour of the fragrant feast,
In rush'd the Suitors with voracious haste: 190
Marshal'd in order due, to each a Sew'r
Presents, to bathe his hands, a radiant ew'r.
Luxurious then they feast. Observant round
Gay, stripling youths the brimming goblets crown'd.
The rage of hunger quell'd, they all advance,   195
And form to measur'd airs the mazy dance:
To *Phemius* was consign'd the chorded Lyre,
Whose hand reluctant touch'd the warbling wire:
Phemius, whose voice divine cou'd sweetest sing
High strains, responsive to the vocal string.   200
  Mean while, in whispers to his heav'nly guest
His indignation thus the Prince exprest.
  Indulge my rising grief, whilst these (my friend)
With song and dance the pompous revel end.
Light is the dance, and double sweet the lays,   205
When, for the dear delight, another pays.
His treasur'd stores these Cormorants consume,
Whose bones, defrauded of a regal tomb
And common turf, lie naked on the plain,
Or doom'd to welter in the whelming main.   210

---

197. *To* Phemius *was consign'd the chorded Lyre.*] In ancient times, Princes entertain'd in their families certain learned and wise men, who were both Poets and
Philosophers, and not only made it their business to amuse and delight, but to
promote wisdom and morality. *Ulysses*, at his departure for *Troy*, left one of these
with *Penelope*: and it was usual to consign, in this manner, the care of their wives
and families to the Poets of those days, as appears from a signal passage in the
third book, verse (of the original) 267, &c. To this man *Homer* gives the name of
Phemius; to celebrate one of his friends, who was so call'd, and who had been his
Præceptor (says *Eustathius*). I must add one remark, that tho' he places his
Master here in no very good company, yet he guards his character from any
imputation, by telling us, that he attended the Suitors by compulsion. This is
not only a great instance of his gratitude, but also of his tenderness and delicacy.

Shou'd he return, that troop so blithe and bold,
With purple robes inwrought, and stiff with gold,
Precipitant in fear, wou'd wing their flight,
And curse their cumbrous pride's unwieldy weight.
But ah I dream!—th' appointed hour is fled, 215
And Hope, too long with vain delusion fed,
Deaf to the rumour of fallacious fame,
Gives to the roll of death his glorious name!
With venial freedom let me now demand
Thy name, thy lineage, and paternal land: 220
Sincere, from whence began thy course, recite,
And to what ship I owe the friendly freight?
Now first to me this visit dost thou daign,
Or number'd in my Father's social train?
All who deserv'd his choice, he made his own, 225
And curious much to know, he far was known.
    My birth I boast (the blue-ey'd Virgin cries)
From great *Anchialus*, renown'd and wise:
Mentes my name; I rule the *Taphian* race,
Whose bounds the deep circumfluent waves embrace. 230
A duteous people, and industrious Isle,
To naval arts inur'd, and stormy toil.
Freighted with Iron from my native land,
I steer my voyage to the *Brutian* strand;

225. *All who deserv'd his choice*—] 'Tis evident, from this and many places in the *Iliad*, that Hospitality was hereditary; an happiness and honour peculiar to these heroic ages. And surely nothing can set the character of *Ulysses* in a more agreeable point of light, than what *Telemachus* here delivers of it; "He was the friend of all mankind." *Eustathius* observes that ἐπίστροφος has a middle signification; that it implies that *Ulysses* behav'd benevolently to all men; or that all men behaved benevolently to *Ulysses*; either sense makes *Ulysses* a very amiable person: He must be a friend to all men, to whom all men are friends.

234. *I steer my voyage to the* Brutian *strand*.] In the country of the *Brutians*, in the lower part of *Italy*, was a town call'd *Temese*. That *Homer* here meant this city, and not one of the same name in *Cyprus*, appears not only because this was famous for works of brass, but because (as *Strabo* observes) *Ithaca* lay in the direct way from *Taphos* to this city of the *Brutii*; whereas it was considerably out of the way to pass

To gain by commerce, for the labour'd mass,   235
A just proportion of refulgent Brass.
Far from your Capital my ship resides
At *Reithrus*, and secure at anchor rides;
Where waving groves on airy *Neion* grow,
Supremely tall, and shade the deeps below.   240
Thence to re-visit your imperial dome,
An old hereditary Guest I come:
Your Father's friend. *Laertes* can relate
Our faith unspotted, and its early date;
Who prest with heart-corroding grief and years,   245
To the gay Court a rural shed prefers,
Where sole of all his train, a Matron sage

---

by *Ithaca* to that of *Cyprus*. The same Author says, that the rooms for preparing of brass were remaining in his time, tho' then out of use ⟨VI i 5⟩. *Ovid, Met.* 15 ⟨707⟩.
     Hippotadæque domos regis, Temesesque metalla.
And *Statius, Silv.* ⟨1 i 42⟩.
     —se totis Temese dedit hausta metallis.
Bochart is of opinion, that the name of *Temese* was given to this town by the *Phœnicians*, from the brass it produced, *Temes* in their language signifying Fusion of Metals ⟨Pt. II : I xxxiii, p. 657⟩: an Art to which the *Phœnicians* much apply'd themselves. *Eustat. Dacier.*

   245. Laertes'*s Retirement.*] This most beautiful passage of *Laertes* has not escap'd the censure of the Critics; they say he acts an unmanly part, he forgets that he is a King, and reduces himself unworthily into the condition of a servant. *Eustathius* gives two reasons for his retirement, which answer those objections; the first is, that he could not endure to see the outrage and insolence of the Suitors; the second, that his Grief for *Ulysses* makes him abandon society, and prefer his vineyard to his Court. This is undoubtedly the picture of human nature under affliction; for sorrow loves solitude. Thus it is, as *Dacier* well observes, that *Menedemus* in *Terence* laments his lost Son ⟨*Heaut. Tim.* 121 ff⟩: *Menedemus* is the Picture of *Laertes*. Nor does it make any difference, that the one is a King, the other a person of private station: Kings are but enobled humanity, and are liable, as other men, to as great, if not greater, sensibility.

   The word ἑρπύζοντα (*creeping* about his vineyard) has also given offence, as it carries an idea of meanness with it; but *Eustathius* observes, that it excellently expresses the melancholy of *Laertes*, and denotes no meanness of spirit: The same word is apply'd to the great *Achilles* in the *Iliad*, when he laments at the Obsequies of *Patroclus* ⟨XXIII 225⟩; and *Horace* no doubt had it in his view ⟨*Epist.* I iv 4⟩,
     —Tacitum silvas inter reptare salubres.

Supports with homely food his drooping age,
With feeble steps from marshalling his Vines
Returning sad, when toilsome day declines.   250
     With friendly speed, induc'd by erring fame,
To hail *Ulysses'* safe return I came:
But still the frown of some cælestial pow'r
With envious joy retards the blissful hour.
Let not your soul be sunk in sad despair;   255
He lives, he breathes this heav'nly vital air,
Among a savage race, whose shelfy bounds
With ceaseless roar the foaming deep surrounds.
The thoughts which rowl within my ravish'd breast,
To me, no Seer, th' inspiring Gods suggest;   260
Nor skill'd, nor studious, with prophetic eye
To judge the winged Omens of the sky.
Yet hear this certain speech, nor deem it vain;
Though Adamantine bonds the chief restrain,
The dire restraint his wisdom will defeat,   265
And soon restore him to his regal seat.
But, gen'rous youth! sincere and free declare,
Are you, of manly growth, his royal heir?
For sure *Ulysses* in your look appears,
The same his features, if the same his years.   270
Such was that face, on which I dwelt with joy

---

257. *Among a savage race*, &c.] It is the observation of *Eustathius*, that what *Minerva* here delivers bears resemblance to the Oracles, in which part is false, part true: That *Ulysses* is detain'd in an Island, is a truth; that he is detain'd by Barbarians, a falshood: This is done by the Goddess, that she may be thought to be really a man, as she appears to be; she speaks with the dubiousness of a man, not the certainty of a Goddess; she raises his expectation, by shewing she has an insight into futurity; and to engage his belief, she discovers in part the truth to *Telemachus*. Neither was it necessary or convenient for *Telemachus* to know the whole truth: for if he had known that *Ulysses* inhabited a desart, detain'd by a Goddess, he must of consequence have known of his return, (for he that could certify the one, could certify the other,) and so had never gone in search of him; and it would hence have happen'd, that *Homer* had been depriv'd of giving us those graces of Poetry which arise from the voyage of *Telemachus*. *Eustathius*.

Ere *Greece* assembled stem'd the tydes to *Troy*;
But parting then for that detested shore,
Our eyes, unhappy! never greeted more.
　　To prove a genuine birth (the Prince replies)　　275
On Female truth assenting faith relies;
Thus manifest of right, I build my claim
Sure-founded on a fair Maternal fame,
Ulysses' Son: but happier he, whom fate
Hath plac'd beneath the storms which toss the great!　280
Happier the son, whose hoary sire is blest
With humble affluence, and domestic rest!
Happier than I, to future empire born,
But doom'd a Father's wretched fate to mourn!
　　To whom, with aspect mild, the Guest divine.　　285
Oh true descendent of a scepter'd line!

---

275. *To prove a genuine birth*, &c.] There is an appearance of something very
shocking in this speech of *Telemachus*. It literally runs thus: *My mother assures me
that I am the son of* Ulysses, *but I know it not*. It seems to reflect upon his mother's
chastity, as if he had a doubt of his own legitimacy. This seeming simplicity in
Telemachus, says *Eustathius*, is the effect of a troubled spirit; it is grief that makes
him doubt if he can be the son of the great, the generous *Ulysses*; it is no reflection
upon *Penelope*, and consequently no fault in *Telemachus*: It is an undoubted truth
that the mother only knows the legitimacy of the child: Thus *Euripides* ⟨quoted
from Menander, Spondanus, *Od.* p. 10⟩,

'Η μὲν γὰρ αὐτῆς οἶδεν ὄντ' ὁ δ' οἴεται.

that is, The mother knows the child, the father only believes it.
　　Thus also *Menander* ⟨Dindorf, p. 40⟩,

Αὐτὸν γὰρ οὐδεὶς οἶδε τοῦ πότ' ἐγένετο
'Αλλ' ὑπονοοῦμεν πάντες ἢ πιστεύομεν.

that is, No man knows assuredly who begot him, we only guess it, and believe it.
　　Aristotle in his *Rhetoric* is also of this opinion ⟨II 23⟩;

Ἄριστα περὶ τῶν τέκνων κρίνουσιν αἱ γυναῖκες.

What I have here said, is translated literally from *Eustathius*, and if it edifies the
Reader I am content. But the meaning of the passage is this, *Mentes* asks *Telemachus* if he be the son of *Ulysses*; he replies, "*So my mother assures me; but nothing
sure so wretched as I am could proceed from that great man.*"
　　But however this may be reconciled to truth, I believe few Ladies would take
it as a compliment, if their sons shou'd tell them there was some room to doubt
of their legitimacy: there may be abundance of truth in it, and yet very little
decency.

The Gods, a glorious fate from anguish free
To chaste *Penelope*'s increase decree.
But say, yon' jovial Troop so gaily drest,
Is this a bridal, or a friendly feast? 290
Or from their deed I rightlier may divine,
Unseemly flown with insolence and wine?
Unwelcome revellers, whose lawless joy
Pains the sage ear, and hurts the sober eye.

    Magnificence of old, (the Prince reply'd,) 295
Beneath our roof with Virtue cou'd reside;
Unblam'd abundance crown'd the royal board,
What time this dome rever'd her prudent Lord;
Who now (so heav'n decrees) is doom'd to mourn,
Bitter constraint! erroneous and forlorn. 300
Better the Chief, on *Ilion*'s hostile plain
Had fall'n surrounded with his warlike train;
Or safe return'd, the race of glory past,
New to his friends embrace, had breath'd his last!
Then grateful *Greece* with streaming eyes wou'd raise 305
Historic Marbles, to record his praise;
His praise, eternal on the faithful stone,
Had with transmissive honour grac'd his Son.
Now snatch'd by Harpies to the dreary coast,
Sunk is the Hero, and his glory lost! 310
Vanish'd at once! unheard of, and unknown!
And I, his Heir in misery alone.
Nor for a dear, lost Father only flow
The filial tears, but woe succeeds to woe:
To tempt the spouseless Queen with am'rous wiles, 315

---

309. *Now snatch'd by Harpies,* &c.] The meaning of this expression is, that
Ulysses has not had the rites of sepulture. This among the Ancients was esteem'd
the greatest of calamities, as it hinder'd the Shades of the deceased from entering
into the state of the happy.

315. *To tempt the spouseless Queen—resort the Nobles.*] It is necessary to reconcile
the conduct of the Suitors to probability, since it has so great a share in the process of the *Odyssey*. It may seem incredible that *Penelope*, who is a Queen, in whom

Resort the Nobles from the neighb'ring Isles;
From *Samos*, circled with th' *Ionian* main,
Dulichium, and *Zacynthus'* sylvan reign:
Ev'n with presumptuous hope her bed t'ascend,
The Lords of *Ithaca* their right pretend.   320
She seems attentive to their pleaded vows,
Her heart detesting what her ear allows.
They, vain expectants of the bridal hour,
My stores in riotous expence devour,
In feast and dance the mirthful months employ,   325
And meditate my doom, to crown their joy.
　　With tender pity touch'd, the Goddess cry'd:
Soon may kind heav'n a sure relief provide,
Soon may your Sire discharge the vengeance due,
And all your wrongs the proud oppressors rue!   330
Oh! in that portal shou'd the Chief appear,
Each hand tremendous with a brazen spear,
In radiant Panoply his limbs incas'd;
(For so of old my father's court he grac'd,
When social mirth unbent his serious soul,   335
O'er the full banquet, and the sprightly bowl)
He then from *Ephyré*, the fair domain
Of *Ilus* sprung from *Jason*'s royal strain,
Measur'd a length of seas, a toilsome length, in vain.
For voyaging to learn the direful art   340
To taint with deadly drugs the barbed dart;

the supreme power is lodg'd, should not dismiss such unwelcome intruders, especially since many of them were her own subjects: Besides, it seems an extraordinary way of courtship in them, to ruin the person to whom they make their addresses.

　　To solve this objection we must consider the nature of the *Grecian* governments: The chief men of the land had great authority; Tho' the government was monarchical, it was not despotic; *Laertes* was retir'd, and disabled with age: *Telemachus* was yet in his minority; and the fear of any violence either against her own person, or against her son, might deter *Penelope* from using any endeavours to remove men of such insolence, and such power. *Dacier.*

　　341. *To taint with deadly drugs the barbed dart.*] It is necessary to explain this

Observant of the Gods, and sternly just,
Ilus refus'd t'impart the baneful trust:
With friendlier zeal my father's soul was fir'd,
The drugs he knew, and gave the boon desir'd.   345
Appear'd he now with such heroic port,
As then conspicuous at the *Taphian* court;
Soon shou'd yon' boasters cease their haughty strife,
Or each atone his guilty love with life.
But of his wish'd return the care resign;   350
Be future vengeance to the pow'rs divine.
My sentence hear: With stern distaste avow'd,
To their own districts drive the Suitor-crowd:
When next the morning warms the purple east,
Convoke the Peerage, and the Gods attest;   355
The sorrows of your inmost soul relate;
And form sure plans to save the sinking state.
Shou'd second love a pleasing flame inspire,
And the chaste Queen connubial rites require;
Dismiss'd with honour let her hence repair   360

---

passage. It seems at first view, as if *Ulysses* had requested what a good man could
not grant. *Ilus*, says *Mentes*, deny'd the Poison, because he fear'd the anger of the
Gods; and the poison it self is call'd by *Homer* Ἀνδροφόνον, as if it were design'd
against mankind. *Eustathius* defends *Ulysses* variously: He intended, says he, to
employ it against beasts only, that infested his country, or in hunting. He assigns
another reason, and says that the Poet is preparing the way to give an air of
probability to the destruction of the Suitors. He poisons his arrows, that every
wound may be mortal; on this account the poison may be call'd ἀνδροφόνον;
for it is certain in the wars of *Troy*, poison'd arrows were not in use, for many
persons who were wounded recover'd; so that of necessity they must be reserv'd
for domestic occasions. From what has been said we may collect the reason why
Anchialus granted the poison to *Ulysses*, and *Ilus* deny'd it; *Anchialus* was the
friend of *Ulysses*, and knew that he would not employ it to any ill purpose; but
Ilus, who was a stranger to him, was afraid lest he should abuse it. *Eustathius*.

360. *Dismiss'd with honour let her hence repair*.] I will lay before the reader literally
what *Eustathius* observes upon these words. There is a Solœcism, says he, in these
verses or words, that cannot be reduc'd to the rules of construction. It should be
μήτηρ, not μητέρα ἄψ' ἴτω. How then comes the accusative case to be used
instead of the nominative? *Mentes*, adds he, may be suppos'd to have intended to

To great *Icarius*, whose paternal care
Will guide her passion, and reward the choice
With wealthy dow'r, and bridal gifts of price.
Then let this dictate of my love prevail:
Instant, to foreign realms prepare to sail,   365
To learn your Father's fortunes: Fame may prove
Or omen'd Voice (the messenger of *Jove*)
Propitious to the search. Direct your toil
Thro' the wide Ocean first to sandy *Pyle*,
Of *Nestor*, hoary Sage, his doom demand;   370
Thence speed your voyage to the *Spartan* strand,
For young *Atrides* to th' *Achaian* coast
Arriv'd the last of all the victor host.
If yet *Ulysses* views the light, forbear,
'Till the fleet hours restore the circling year.   375
But if his soul hath wing'd the destin'd flight,
Inhabitant of deep disastrous Night,
Homeward with pious speed repass the main,

---

have said ἀποπέμψον (send thy Mother away;) but considering, in the midst of
the Sentence, that such advice was not suitable to be given to *Telemachus*, he
checks himself, and suppresses ἀποπέμψον; and no other word immediately
occurring, that requir'd an accusative case, he falls into a Solœcism.

But perhaps this is more ingenious than true; tho' *Mentes* was in haste when he
spoke it, *Homer* was not when he compos'd it. Might not an errour creep into
the original by the negligence of a Transcriber, who might write Μητέρα for
Μήτηρ? This is the more probable, because the one stands in the Verse in every
respect as well as the other.

What *Eustathius* adds is very absurd: he says that *Telemachus* must observe both
the interpretations, either send thy Mother away, or let thy Mother retire. So
that the advice was double, send thy Mother away if thou dost not love her; but
if thou art unwilling to grieve her, let her recess be voluntary.

367. *Omen'd Voice—of* Jove.] There is a difficulty in this Passage. In any case
of enquiry, any Words that were heard by accident were call'd by the *Latins*,
Omens; by *Homer, the voice of Jupiter*; and he stiles them so, because it is thro' his
providence that those words come to our knowledge: κλέος signifies *fame* or
rumour; and the Ancients refer'd all voices or sounds to *Jupiter*; and stil'd him
Ζεὺς πανομφαῖος. So that the *voice of Jove* implies any words that we hear by
chance, from whence we can draw any thing that gives light to our concerns
or enquiries. *Dacier. Eustathius.*

To the pale Shade funereal rites ordain,
Plant the fair Column o'er the vacant grave,   380
A Hero's honours let the Hero have.
With decent grief the royal dead deplor'd,
For the chaste Queen select an equal Lord.
Then let revenge your daring mind employ, ⎫
By fraud or force the Suitor-train destroy, ⎬   385
And starting into manhood, scorn the boy. ⎭
Hast thou not heard how young *Orestes* fir'd
With great revenge, immortal praise acquir'd?
His virgin sword *Ægysthus'* veins imbru'd;
The murd'rer fell, and blood aton'd for blood.   390
O greatly bless'd with ev'ry blooming grace!
With equal steps the paths of glory trace;
Join to that royal youth's, your rival name,
And shine eternal in the sphere of fame—
But my Associates now my stay deplore,   395
Impatient on the hoarse-resounding shore.
Thou, heedful of advice, secure proceed;
My praise the precept is, be thine the deed.
    The counsel of my friend (the Youth rejoin'd)
Imprints conviction on my grateful mind.   400
So Fathers speak (persuasive speech and mild!)
Their safe experience to the fav'rite child.
But since to part, for sweet refection due

---

387. *Hast thou not heard*, &c.] It may seem that this example of *Orestes* does not
come fully up to the purpose intended: There is a wide difference in the circumstances; *Orestes* slew an adulterer, and a single person, with an adulteress. The
designs of *Telemachus* are not against one, but many enemies; neither are they
adulterers, nor have they slain the father of *Telemachus*, as is the case of *Orestes*:
nor is *Penelope* an adulteress. The intent therefore of the Goddess is only to shew
what a glorious act it is to defend our parents: *Orestes*, says *Mentes*, is every where
celebrated for honouring his father, and thou shalt obtain equal honour by
defending thy mother.
    The sense that πατροφονεύς here bears is remarkable, it signifies not only a
person who kills his own father, but who kills the father of any other person.
Eustathius.

The genial viands let my train renew;
And the rich pledge of plighted faith receive,   405
Worthy the heir of *Ithaca* to give.

Defer the promis'd boon, (the Goddess cries,
Celestial azure brightning in her eyes)
And let me now regain the *Reithrian* port:
From *Temesé* return'd, your royal court   410
I shall revisit; and that pledge receive,
And gifts, memorial of our friendship, leave.

Abrupt, with eagle-speed she cut the sky;
Instant invisible to mortal eye.
Then first he recognis'd th' Ætherial guest;   415
Wonder and joy alternate fire his breast:
Heroic thoughts infus'd his heart dilate,
Revolving much his father's doubtful fate:
At length compos'd, he join'd the suitor-throng,
Hush'd in attention to the warbled song.   420

---

413.   *—With eagle-speed she cut the sky;*
                        Instant invisible—.]

I pass over the several interpretations that have been given to the word ἀνοπαῖα; some say it implies she flew up the chimney, *&c.* In reality it signifies a species of an eagle; but it may also signifie the same as ἀφανὴς (invisible,) either of the latter senses are natural, or both together, *like an eagle she disappear'd. Eustathius.*

420. *Hush'd in attention to the warbled song.*] There may be two reasons why this is inserted; either the Suitors were pleas'd with the sweetness of the song, or the subject of it; they sate attentive to hear the death of *Ulysses,* in the process of his story. This gives us a reason why immediately *Penelope* descended to stop the song; she fear'd lest he might touch upon the story of *Ulysses,* and say that he dy'd in his return. This would have reduc'd her to the utmost necessity, and she could not have deferr'd to marry. *Phemius* would have certainly found credit, for Poets were believ'd to be inspir'd by the Gods: they were look'd upon as Prophets, and to have something of divinity in them, as appears from *Demodocus* in the 8th book of the *Odyssey.* Besides there was a further necessity to put a stop to the song. If *Phemius* had declar'd him to be dead, *Penelope* could not have avoided marriage; if alive, the Suitors might have desisted, or arm'd themselves against *Ulysses,* and then their Deaths, one of the principal incidents of the Poem, could not have follow'd; neither could *Telemachus* have gone in search of his father, if he had foreknown his death, or sudden return. It is therefore artful in the Poet to cut the song short, he reserves the story of *Ulysses* for future narration, and brings all this

His tender theme the charming Lyrist chose
Minerva's anger, and the direful woes
Which voyaging from *Troy* the Victors bore,
While storms vindictive intercept the shore.
The shrilling airs the vaulted roof rebounds,   425
Reflecting to the Queen the silver sounds.
With grief renew'd the weeping fair descends;
Their sovereign's step a virgin train attends:
A veil of richest texture wrought, she wears,
And silent, to the joyous hall repairs.   430
There from the portal, with her mild command
Thus gently checks the minstrel's tuneful hand.
    Phemius! let acts of Gods, and Heroes old,
What ancient bards in hall and bow'r have told,
Attemper'd to the Lyre, your voice employ;   435
Such the pleas'd ear will drink with silent joy.
But oh! forbear that dear, disastrous name,
To sorrow sacred, and secure of fame:
My bleeding bosom sickens at the sound,
And ev'ry piercing note inflicts a wound.   440
    Why, dearest object of my duteous love,
(Reply'd the Prince) will you the Bard reprove?
Oft, *Jove*'s ætherial rays (resistless fire)

---

about by a very probable method, by the interposition of *Penelope*, who requests
that some other story may be chosen, a story that she can hear without sorrow.

  It is very customary for women to be present at the entertainments of men; as
appears from the conduct of *Helen, Arete, Nausicaa,* and *Penelope* in divers parts of
the *Odyssey*: She is here introduced with the greatest decency; she enters not the
room, but stands with tears at the threshold; and even at that distance appears
with her face shaded by a veil. *Eustathius.*

  443. *Oft,* Jove's *ætherial rays,* &c.] *Telemachus* here reproves his mother for commanding *Phemius* to desist, or not to make *Ulysses* the subject of his song: by saying,
that it was not in the Poet's own power to chuse his subject, which was frequently
dictated and inspired by the Gods. This is a particular instance of the opinion
the Ancients held as to the immediate inspiration of their Poets. The words in the
original evidently bear this sense. *If the subject displease you, 'tis not the Poet but*
Jupiter *is to blame, who inspires men of invention, as he himself pleases.* And Mad.

The chanter's soul and raptur'd song inspire;
Instinct divine! nor blame severe his choice, 445
Warbling the *Grecian* woes with harp and voice:
For novel lays attract our ravish'd ears;
But old, the mind with inattention hears.
Patient permit the sadly-pleasing strain;
Familiar now with grief, your tears refrain, 450
And in the publick woe forget your own;
You weep not for a perish'd Lord, alone.
What *Greeks*, now wand'ring in the *Stygian* gloom,
With your *Ulysses* shar'd an equal doom!
Your widow'd hours, apart, with female toil 455
And various labours of the loom, beguile;
There rule, from palace-cares remote and free,
That care to man belongs, and most to me.
    Mature beyond his years the Queen admires
His sage reply, and with her train retires. 460
Then swelling sorrows burst their former bounds,
With echoing grief afresh the dome resounds;
'Till *Pallas*, piteous of her plaintive cries,
In slumber clos'd her silver-streaming eyes.
    Mean-time rekindl'd at the royal charms, 465
Tumultuous love each beating bosom warms;

Dacier strangely mistakes this passage, in rendring it, *'tis not the Poet but* Jupiter
*who is the cause of our misfortunes, for 'tis he who dispenses to wretched mortals good or evil
as he pleases.* At the same time she acknowledges the word ἀλφησταί, which she
here renders *laborious*, or *wretched*, to signify *persons of wit*, in the beginning of
lib. 6 ⟨line 8⟩ and *persons of skill and ability in their art*, in *lib.* 1 1 ⟨XIII 261⟩.
    455. *Your widow'd hours, apart, with female toil*, &c.] These verses are taken
literally from the 6th book of the *Iliad*, except that μῦθος is inserted instead of
πόλεμος ⟨490–3⟩; *Eustathius* explains the passage thus: *Women are not forbid
entirely to speak, for women are talking animals,* λαλητὸν ζῶον, *they have the faculty of
talking, and* indeed *are rational creatures*; but they must *not give too much liberty to that
unruly member, in the company of men. Sophocles* advises well ⟨*Ajax* 293⟩,
Γύναι, γυναιξὶ κόσμον ἡ σιγὴ φέρει.
O woman, silence is the ornament of thy sex. Madam *Dacier*, tho' she plunders almost
every thing, has spared this observation.

Intemp'rate rage a wordy war began;
But bold *Telemachus* assum'd the man.
Instant (he cry'd) your female discord end,
Ye deedless boasters! and the song attend: 470
Obey that sweet compulsion, nor profane
With dissonance, the smooth melodious strain.
Pacific now prolong the jovial feast;
But when the dawn reveals the rosy East,
I, to the Peers assembled, shall propose 475
The firm resolve I here in few disclose.
No longer live the cankers of my court;
All to your several states with speed resort;
Waste in wild riot what your land allows,
There ply the early feast, and late carouse. 480
But if, to honour lost, 'tis still decreed
For you my bowl shall flow, my flocks shall bleed,
Judge and revenge my right, impartial *Jove!*
By him, and all th' immortal thrones above,
(A sacred oath) each proud oppressor slain 485
Shall with inglorious gore this marble stain.
 Aw'd by the Prince, thus haughty, bold, and young,
Rage gnaw'd the lip, and wonder chain'd the tongue.
Silence at length the gay *Antinous* broke,
Constrain'd a smile, and thus ambiguous spoke. 490
 What God to your untutor'd youth affords

491. *The speech of* Antinous.] *Antinous* and *Eurymachus* are *Ithacensians*, and are
call'd the chief of the Suitors. It is therefore necessary to distinguish their characters; *Antinous* is violent, and determin'd against *Ulysses*; *Eurymachus* more
gentle and subtle: *Antinous* derides, *Eurymachus* flatters.
 This speech of *Antinous* is a conceal'd raillery; he tells *Telemachus*, that *Jove*
inspires his soul with wisdom, but means that his education has been such, that
he had learn'd nothing from man; he wishes (out of a seemingly kind concern for
him) that he may never reign in *Ithaca*, because the weight of a crown is a
burthen; and concludes with mentioning his hereditary title to it, to insinuate
that is his by descent only, and not by merit.
 Telemachus, in his answer, wisely dissembles the affront of *Antinous*, he takes it
in the better sense, and seems to differ only in opinion about the Regality. Think

This headlong torrent of amazing words?
May *Jove* delay thy reign, and cumber late
So bright a genius with the toils of state!
   Those toils (*Telemachus* serene replies)   495
Have charms, with all their weight, t'allure the wise.
Fast by the Throne obsequious *Fame* resides,
And *Wealth* incessant rolls her golden tides.
Nor let *Antinous* rage, if strong desire
Of wealth and fame a youthful bosom fire: 500
Elect by *Jove* his Delegate of sway,
With joyous pride the summons I'd obey.
Whene'er *Ulysses* roams the realm of Night,
Shou'd factious pow'r dispute my lineal right,
Some other *Greeks* a fairer claim may plead;   505
To your pretence their title wou'd precede.
At least, the sceptre lost, I still shou'd reign
Sole o'er my vassals, and domestic train.
   To this *Eurymachus*. To heav'n alone
Refer the choice to fill the vacant Throne.   510
Your patrimonial stores in peace possess;
Undoubted all your filial claim confess:
Your private right shou'd impious pow'r invade,
The peers of *Ithaca* wou'd arm in aid.

---

you, says he, that to be a King is to be miserable? To be a King, in my judgment,
is to enjoy affluence and honour. He asserts his claim to the succession of his
father, yet seems to decline it, to lay the suspicions of the Suitors asleep, that they
may not prevent the measures he takes to obtain it. *Eustathius*.

The speech of *Eurymachus* confirms the former observation, that this Suitor is
of a more soft and moderate behaviour than *Antinous*: He cloaths ill designs with
a seeming humanity, and appears a friend, while he carries on the part of an
enemy: *Telemachus* had said, that if it was the will of *Jupiter*, he would ascend the
Throne of *Ithaca*: *Eurymachus* answers, that this was as the Gods shou'd determine; an insinuation that they regarded not his claim from his father. *Telemachus* said he would maintain himself in the possession of his present inheri-
tance: *Eurymachus* wishes that no one may arrive to dispossess him; the latent
meaning of which is, "we of your own country are sufficient for that design".
If these observations of *Eustathius* be true, *Eurymachus* was not a less enemy than
Antinous, but a better dissembler.

But say, that Stranger-guest who late withdrew,   515
What, and from whence? his name and lineage shew.
His grave demeanour, and majestic grace
Speak him descended of no vulgar race:
Did he some loan of antient right require,
Or came fore-runner of your scepter'd Sire?   520
    Oh son of *Polybus!* the Prince replies,
No more my Sire will glad these longing eyes:
The Queen's fond hope inventive rumour cheers,
Or vain diviners' dreams divert her fears.
That stranger-guest the *Taphian* realm obeys,   525
A realm defended with incircling seas:
Mentes, an ever-honour'd name, of old
High in *Ulysses'* social list inroll'd.
    Thus he, tho' conscious of th' ætherial Guest,
Answer'd evasive of the sly request.   530
Mean time the Lyre rejoins the sprightly lay;
Love-dittied airs, and dance, conclude the day.
But when the Star of Eve, with golden light
Adorn'd the matron-brow of sable Night;
The mirthful train dispersing quit the court,   535
And to their several domes to Rest resort.
A tow'ring structure to the palace join'd;
To this his steps the thoughtful Prince inclin'd;
In his pavilion there to sleep repairs;
The lighted torch the sage *Euryclea* bears.   540
(Daughter of *Ops,* the just *Pisenor*'s son,

---

540. *The sage* Euryclea.] *Eurycleia* was a very aged person; she was bought by
Laertes, to nurse *Ulysses*; and in her old age attends *Telemachus*: She cost *Laertes*
twenty oxen; that is, a certain quantity of money (ὕλης μεταλλικῆς) which
would buy twenty oxen: or perhaps the form of an ox was stamp'd upon the
metal, and from thence had its appellation.

The simplicity of these Heroic times is remarkable; an old woman is the only
attendant upon the son of a King: She lights him to his apartment, takes care of
his cloaths, and hangs them up at the side of his bed. Greatness then consisted not
in shew, but in the mind: this conduct proceeded not from the meanness of
poverty, but from the simplicity of manners. *Eustathius.*

For twenty beeves by great *Laertes* won;
In rosy prime with charms attractive grac'd,
Honour'd by him, a gentle Lord and chaste,
With dear esteem: too wise, with jealous strife   545
To taint the joys of sweet, connubial life.
Sole with *Telemachus* her service ends,
A child she nurs'd him, and a man attends.)
Whilst to his couch himself the Prince addrest,
The duteous dame receiv'd the purple vest: 550
The purple vest with decent care dispos'd,
The silver ring she pull'd, the door re-clos'd;
The bolt, obedient to the silken cord,
To the strong staple's inmost depth restor'd,
Secur'd the valves. There, wrap'd in silent shade,   555
Pensive, the rules the Goddess gave, he weigh'd;
Stretch'd on the downy fleece, no rest he knows,
And in his raptured soul the Vision glows.

Having now gone thro' the first book, I shall only observe to the Reader, that
the whole of it does not take up the compass of an entire day: When *Minerva*
appears to *Telemachus* the Suitors were preparing to sit down to the banquet at
noon; and the business of the first book concludes with the day. It is true, that
the Gods hold a debate before the descent of *Minerva*, and some small time must
be allow'd for that transaction. It is remarkable, that there is not one Simile in
this book except we allow those three words to be one, ὄρνις δ' ὡς ἀνοπαῖα.
The same observation is true of the first book of the *Iliad*. See the Notes on that
place.

THE
SECOND BOOK
OF THE
ODYSSEY.

The ARGUMENT.
The Council of *Ithaca.*

Telemachus, *in the assembly of the Lords of* Ithaca, *complains of the injustice done him by the Suitors, and insists upon their departure from his Palace; appealing to the Princes, and exciting the people to declare against them. The Suitors endeavour to justify their stay, at least till he shall send the Queen to the Court of* Icarius *her father; which he refuses. There appears a prodigy of two Eagles in the sky, which an Augur expounds to the ruin of the Suitors.* Telemachus *then demands a vessel, to carry him to* Pylos *and* Sparta, *there to enquire of his father's fortunes.* Pallas *in the shape of* Mentor (*an ancient friend of* Ulysses) *helps him to a ship, assists him in preparing necessaries for the voyage, and embarks with him that night; which concludes the* second *day from the Opening of the Poem.*

The SCENE continues in the Palace of *Ulysses* in *Ithaca.*

N ow red'ning from the dawn, the Morning ray
Glow'd in the front of Heav'n, and gave the Day.
The youthful Hero, with returning light,
Rose anxious from th' inquietudes of Night.

This book opens with the first appearance of *Telemachus* upon the stage of action. And *Bossu* observes the great judgment of the Poet, in beginning with the transactions of *Ithaca* in the absence of *Ulysses* ⟨II xii⟩: By this method he sets the conduct of *Telemachus, Penelope,* and the Suitors, in a strong point of light; they all have a large share in the story of the Poem, and consequently ought to have distinguishing characters. It is as necessary in Epic Poetry, as it is on the Theatre, to let us immediately into the character of every person whom the Poet introduces: This adds perspicuity to the story, and we immediately grow acquainted

A royal robe he wore with graceful pride,   5
A two-edg'd faulchion threaten'd by his side,
Embroider'd sandals glitter'd as he trod,
And forth he mov'd, majestic as a God.
Then by his Heralds, restless of delay,
To council calls the Peers: the Peers obey.   10
Soon as in solemn form th' assembly sate,
From his high dome himself descends in state.
Bright in his hand a pond'rous javelin shin'd;
Two Dogs, a faithful guard, attend behind;

---

with each personage, and interest our selves in the good or ill fortune that attends them thro' the whole relation.

Telemachus is now about twenty years of age: In the eleventh book, the Poet tells us, he was an infant in the arms of his mother when *Ulysses* sail'd to *Troy*; that Heroe was absent near twenty years, and from hence we may gather the exact age of *Telemachus*. He is every where describ'd as a person of piety to the Gods, of duty to his parents, and as a lover of his country: he is prudent, temperate, and valiant: and the Poet well sets off the importance of this young Heroe, by giving him the Goddess of War and Wisdom for his constant attendant.

13. —*In his hand a pond'rous javelin shin'd.*] The Poet describes *Telemachus* as if he were marching against an enemy, or going to a council of war, rather than to an assembly of Peers in his own country: Two reasons are assign'd for this conduct; either this was the common usage of Princes in those times, or *Telemachus* might look upon the Suitors as enemies, and consequently go to council in arms as against enemies. *Eustathius.*

14. *Two Dogs, a faithful guard, attend behind.*] This passage has not escap'd the raillery of the Critics; they look upon it as a mean description of a Heroe and a Prince, to give him a brace of dogs only for his guards or attendants: But such was the simplicity of ancient Princes, that except in war they had rarely any attendants or equipage. And we may be confident, *Homer* copies after the custom of the time, unless we can be so absurd as to suppose, he would feign low circumstances unnecessarily, thro' a want of judgment.

Virgil judg'd otherwise, and thought this circumstance worthy of his imitation ⟨VIII 461–2⟩.

> *Quin etiam gemini custodes limine ab alto*
> *Procedunt, gressumque canes comitantur herilem.*

Achilles is describ'd in the *Iliad* with the same attendants.

> —*Nine large dogs domestic at his board.* B. 23 ⟨210⟩.

Poetry, observes *Dacier*, is like Painting, which draws the greatest beauties from the simplest customs: and even in history, we receive a sensible pleasure from the least circumstance that denotes the customs of ancient times. It may be

Pallas with grace divine his form improves,   15
And gazing crowds admire him as he moves.
   His Father's throne he fill'd: while distant stood
The hoary Peers, and Aged Wisdom bow'd.
    'Twas silence all: at last *Ægyptius* spoke;
Ægyptius, by his age and sorrows broke: 20
A length of days his soul with prudence crown'd,
A length of days had bent him to the ground.
His eldest *hope in arms to *Ilion* came,
By great *Ulysses* taught the path to fame;
But (hapless youth) the hideous *Cyclops* tore   25
His quiv'ring limbs, and quaff'd his spouting gore.
Three sons remain'd: To climb with haughty fires
The royal bed, *Eurynomus* aspires;
The rest with duteous love his griefs asswage,
And ease the Sire of half the cares of age.   30
Yet still his *Antiphus* he loves, he mourns,
And as he stood, he spoke and wept by turns.
   Since great *Ulysses* sought the *Phrygian* plains,

---

* *Antiphus*

---

added, that the Poet, as well as the Painter, is obliged to follow the customs of the
age of which he writes, or paints: a modern dress would ill become *Achilles* or
Ulysses, such a conduct would be condemned as an absurdity in painting, and
ought to be so in poetry.

31. *Yet still his* Antiphus *he loves, he mourns.*] *Homer*, says *Eustathius*, inserts these
particularities concerning the family of *Ægyptius*, to give an air of truth to his
story. It does not appear that *Ægyptius* knew the certainty of the death of *Antiphus*;
(for it is the Poet who relates it, and not the father;) whence, as *Dacier* observes,
should he learn it? he only laments him, according to the prevailing opinion that
all the companions of *Ulysses* were lost with *Ulysses*.

33. *Since great* Ulysses, *&c.*] We are here told, that there never had been any
council conven'd in *Ithaca*, since the departure of *Ulysses*. The general design and
moral of the *Odyssey*, is to inform us of the mischievous effects which the Absence
of a King and Father of a family produces: We deprive, as *Bossu* observes ⟨1 xv⟩,
the Poem of its very soul, and spoil the Fable, if we retrench from it the disorders
which the Suitors create in the absence of *Ulysses*, both in his family and dominions. Nothing can give us a greater image of those disorders, than what is here
related: What must a kingdom suffer in twenty years, without a Ruler, without

Within these walls inglorious silence reigns.
Say then, ye Peers! by whose commands we meet?   35
Why here once more in solemn council sit?
Ye young, ye old, the weighty cause disclose:
Arrives some message of invading foes?
Or say, does high necessity of state
Inspire some Patriot, and demand debate!   40
The present Synod speaks its author wise;
Assist him, *Jove!* thou regent of the skies!

He spoke. *Telemachus* with transport glows,
Embrac'd the omen, and majestic rose:
(His royal hand th' imperial scepter sway'd)   45
Then thus, addressing to *Ægyptius*, said.

Rev'rend old man! lo here confest he stands
By whom ye meet; my grief your care demands.
No story I unfold of public woes,
Nor bear advices of impending foes: 50
Peace the blest land, and joys incessant crown;
Of all this happy realm, I grieve alone.
For my lost Sire continual sorrows spring,
The great, the good; your Father, and your King.

---

a Council to make Laws or punish enormities? Such is the condition of *Ithaca*:
Laertes is superannuated; *Penelope* oppress'd by the violence of the Suitors; and
Telemachus to this time, in his minority.

It is very artful in the Poet to open the assembly by *Ægyptius*: *Telemachus* was
the person who conven'd it; and being the greatest personage present, it might
be expected that he should open the design of it: But to give *Telemachus* courage,
who was young and inexperienc'd, *Ægyptius* first rises, and by praising the person
who had summon'd them (of whom he seems ignorant) gives *Telemachus* to
understand he has friends among the assembly: This he could no other way so
safely have done, considering the power of the Suitors. By this means, *Telemachus* is encouraged to speak boldly, and arraign the disorders of the Suitors
with the utmost freedom.

54. *Your Father, and your King.*] *Telemachus* here sets the character of *Ulysses*, as
a King, in the most agreeable point of light: He rul'd his people with the same
mildness as a father rules his children. This must needs have a very happy effect
upon the audience; not only as it shews *Ulysses* to have been a good Governour;
but as it recalls the memory of the happiness they receiv'd from that mild

Yet more; our house from its foundation bows, 55
Our foes are pow'rful, and your sons the foes:
Hither, unwelcome, to the Queen they come;
Why seek they not the rich *Icarian* dome?
If she must wed, from other hands require
The dowry; Is *Telemachus* her Sire? 60
Yet thro' my court the noise of Revel rings,
And wastes the wise frugality of Kings.
Scarce all my herds their luxury suffice;
Scarce all my wine their midnight hours supplies.
Safe in my youth, in riot still they grow, 65

government, and obliquely condemns them of ingratitude who had forgot it. By this method also the Poet interests us deeply in the sufferings of *Ulysses*; we cannot see a good man and good King in distress, without the most tender emotions.

55. *Yet more—our house*, &c.] What *Telemachus* here says has given offence to the Critics; they think it indecent for a son to say, that he bears with more regret the disorder of his family than the loss of his father; yet this objection will vanish if we weigh *Penelope*, *Telemachus*, and his whole posterity, against the single person of *Ulysses*.

But what chiefly takes away this objection is, that *Telemachus* was still in hopes of his father's return: for ἀπώλεσα does not imply necessarily his death, but absence: and then both with justice and decency, *Telemachus* may say that he grieves more for the destruction of his family, than for the absence of *Ulysses*.

63. *Scarce all my herds their luxury suffice*.] This passage is ridicul'd by the Critics; they set it in a wrong light, and then grow very pleasant upon it: *Telemachus* makes a sad outcry because the Suitors eat his sheep, his beeves, and fatted goats; and at last falls into tears. The truth is, the riches of Kings and Princes, in those early ages, consisted chiefly in flocks and cattle; thus *Æneas* and *Paris* are describ'd as tending their flocks, &c. and *Abraham* in the scriptures, as abounding in this kind of wealth.

These Critics would form a different idea of the state and condition of *Telemachus*, if they consider'd that he had been capable to maintain no fewer than an hundred and eight persons in a manner very expensive for many years; for so many (with their attendants) were the Suitors, as appears from the 16th book; and at the same time he kept up the dignity of his own court, and liv'd with great hospitality.

But it is a sufficient answer to the objections against this passage, to observe, that it is not the expence, but manner of it, that *Telemachus* laments: This he expresly declares by the word μαψιδίως; and surely a sober man may complain against luxury, without being arraigned of meanness; and against profusion, without being condemned for parsimony.

Nor in the helpless Orphan dread a foe.
But come it will, the time when manhood grants
More pow'rful advocates than vain complaints.
Approach that hour! unsufferable wrong
Cries to the Gods, and vengeance sleeps too long.   70
Rise then ye Peers! with virtuous anger rise!
Your fame revere, but most th' avenging skies.
By all the deathless pow'rs that reign above,
By righteous *Themis* and by thund'ring *Jove*,
(*Themis*, who gives to councils, or denies   75
Success; and humbles, or confirms the wise)
Rise in my aid! suffice the tears that flow
For my lost Sire, nor add new woe to woe.
If e'er he bore the sword to strengthen ill,
Or having pow'r to wrong, betray'd the will;   80
On me, on me your kindled wrath asswage,
And bid the voice of lawless riot rage.
If ruin to our royal race ye doom,
Be You the spoilers, and our wealth consume.

75. Themis, *who gives to councils, or denies Success.*] *Eustathius* observes, that there
was a custom to carry the statue of *Themis* to the assemblies in former ages, and
carry it back again when those assemblies were dissolv'd; and thus *Themis* may
be said to form, and dissolve an assembly. *Dacier* dislikes this assertion, as having
no foundation in antiquity; she thinks that the assertion of *Telemachus* is general,
that he intimates it is Justice alone that establishes the councils of mankind,
and that Injustice confounds and brings the wicked designs of men to confusion.

I have follow'd this interpretation, not only as it suits best with the usual
morality of *Homer*, but also as *Jupiter* is mention'd with *Themis*; and no such
custom is pretended concerning his statue. He is expresly stil'd by the ancients
Ζεῦς ἀγοραῖος. In *Sicily* there was an Altar of Ζεῦς ἀγοραῖος, or of *Jupiter who
presides over Councils. Eustathius* from *Herodotus* ⟨v 46⟩.

84. *Be You the spoilers, and our wealth consume.*] To understand this passage, we
must remember, as *Eustathius* remarks, that *Telemachus* is pleading his cause
before the *Ithacensians*; them he constitutes the Judges of his cause: He therefore
prevents an answer which they might make, *viz. We are not the men that are guilty
of these outrages*; *Telemachus* rejoins, "It were better for me to suffer from your
hands; for by your quiescence you make my affairs desperate:" an intimation
that they should rise in his defence.

Then might we hope redress from juster laws,   85
And raise all *Ithaca* to aid our cause:
But while your Sons commit th' unpunish'd wrong,
You make the Arm of Violence too strong.
　　While thus he spoke, with rage and grief he frown'd,
And dash'd th' imperial sceptre to the ground.   90
The big round tear hung trembling in his eye:
The Synod griev'd, and gave a pitying sigh,
Then silent sate—at length *Antinous* burns
With haughty rage, and sternly thus returns.
　　O insolence of youth! whose tongue affords   95
Such railing eloquence, and war of words.
Studious thy country's worthies to defame,
Thy erring voice displays thy Mother's shame.
Elusive of the bridal day, she gives

---

91. *The big round tear hung trembling in his eye.*] This passage is not one of those, where the Poet can be blam'd for causing a Heroe to weep. If we consider the youth of *Telemachus*, together with the tenderness agreeable to that time of life; the subjects that demand his concern; the apprehension of the loss of a father; and the desolate state of his mother and kingdom: All these make his readiness to burst into tears an argument, not of any want of spirit in him, but of true sense, and goodness of nature: and is a great propriety, which shews the right judgment of the Poet.

95. *Oh insolence of youth,* &c.] We find *Antinous* always setting himself in the strongest opposition to *Telemachus*; and therefore, he is the first that falls by the spear of *Ulysses*; the Poet observes justice, and as *Antinous* is the first in guilt, he is the first in punishment. What *Antinous* says in this speech concerning the treachery of the female servant of *Penelope*, prepares the way for the punishment *Ulysses* inflicts on some of the maids in the conclusion of the Poem: This is an act of Poetical justice; and it is as necessary in Epic as in Tragic Poetry to reward the just, and punish the guilty. *Eustathius.*

99.　　　　　*Elusive of the bridal day, she gives*
　　　　　　Fond hopes to all, and all with hopes deceives.]
It will be necessary to vindicate the character of *Penelope* the Heroine of the Poem, from the aspersions of *Antinous*. It must be confest that she has a very hard game to play, she neither dares consent, nor deny; if she consents, she injures *Ulysses* whom she still expects to return: if she denies, she endangers the Throne, and the life of *Telemachus*, from the violence of the Suitors; so that no other method is left but to elude their addresses.

D

Fond hopes to all, and all with hopes deceives.   100
Did not the sun, thro' heav'n's wide azure roll'd,
For three long years the royal fraud behold?
While she, laborious in delusion, spread
The spacious loom, and mix'd the various thread:
Where as to life the wond'rous figures rise,   105
Thus spoke th' inventive Queen, with artful sighs.
"Tho' cold in death *Ulysses* breathes no more,
"Cease yet a while to urge the bridal hour;
"Cease, 'till to great *Laertes* I bequeath
"A task of grief, his ornaments of death.   110

I must not conceal, what *Eustathius* has mention'd from some Authors, as *Lycophron* ⟨772⟩, *&c.* who say that *Penelope* was κασωρίδα, in plain *English*, an *Harlot*; and he quotes *Herodotus* ⟨II 145⟩, as affirming that she had a son, named *Pan*, by *Hermes*; but the Bishop declares it is all a scandal; and every body must conclude the same, from her conduct, as describ'd in *Homer*.

To vindicate her in this place, we must consider who it is that speaks: *Antinous*, an unsuccessful Lover: and what he blames as a crime, is really her glory; he blames her because she does not comply with their desires; and it had been an act of guilt to have comply'd. He himself sufficiently vindicates her in the conclusion of his speech, where he extols her above all the race of womankind: so that the seeming inconsistence of *Penelope* must be imputed to the necessity of her affairs: she is artful, but not criminal.

The original says, she deceiv'd the Suitors by her messages; a plain intimation, that she us'd no extraordinary familiarities with her Admirers; and thro' the whole course of the Poem she seldom appears in their Assemblies.

109.   *Cease, 'till to great* Laertes *I bequeath*
        A task of grief, his ornaments of death.]

It was an ancient custom to dedicate the finest pieces of Weaving and Embroidery, to honour the funerals of the dead: and these were usually wrought by the nearest relations in their life-time. Thus in the 22d *Iliad*, *Andromache* laments, that the body of *Hector* must be exposed to the air, without those ornaments ⟨510–11⟩.

—ἀτάρ τοι εἵματ' ἐνὶ μεγάροισι κέονται,
Λεπτά τε καὶ χαρίεντα τετυγμένα χερσὶ γυναικῶν.

And the mother of *Euryalus* in *Virgil*, to her son ⟨IX 486–9⟩.

—*Nec te tua funera mater*
Produxi, pressive oculos, aut vulnera lavi,
Veste tegens, tibi quam noctes festina diesque
Urgebam, & tela curas solabar aniles.

"Lest when the Fates his royal ashes claim,
"The *Grecian* matrons taint my spotless fame;
"When he, whom living mighty realms obey'd,
"Shall want in death a shroud to grace his shade."
  Thus she: at once the gen'rous train complies,   115
Nor fraud mistrusts in virtue's fair disguise.
The work she ply'd; but studious of delay,
By night revers'd the labour of the day.
While thrice the sun his annual journey made,
The conscious lamp the midnight fraud survey'd;   120
Unheard, unseen, three years her arts prevail;
The fourth, her maid unfolds th' amazing tale.
We saw, as unperceiv'd we took our stand,
The backward labours of her faithless hand.
Then urg'd, she perfects her illustrious toils;   125
A wond'rous monument of female wiles!
  But you oh Peers! and thou oh Prince! give ear:
(I speak aloud, that ev'ry *Greek* may hear)
Dismiss the Queen; and if her sire approves,
Let him espouse her to the Peer she loves: 130
Bid instant to prepare the bridal train,
Nor let a race of Princes wait in vain.
Tho' with a grace divine her soul is blest,
And all *Minerva* breathes within her breast,
In wond'rous arts than woman more renown'd,   135
And more than woman with deep wisdom crown'd;
Tho' *Tyro* nor *Mycene* match her name,
Nor great *Alcmena*, (the proud boasts of Fame)
Yet thus by heav'n adorn'd, by heav'n's decree
She shines with fatal excellence, to thee: 140

---

140. *She shines with fatal excellence, to thee.*] *Eustathius* observes, that *Antinous* in
the opening of his Speech throws the fault upon *Penelope*, to engage the favour of
the multitude: But being conscious that he had said things which *Penelope* would
resent, he extols her in the conclusion of it. He ascribes an obstinacy of virtue
to her, and by this double conduct endeavours to make both *Penelope* and the
multitude his friends.

With thee, the bowl we drain, indulge the feast,
'Till righteous heav'n reclaim her stubborn breast.
What tho' from pole to pole resounds her name?
The son's destruction waits the mother's fame:
For 'till she leaves thy court, it is decreed,   145
Thy bowl to empty, and thy flock to bleed.
While yet he speaks, *Telemachus* replies.

147. Telemachus's *reply*.] *Telemachus* every where speaks with an openness and
bravery of spirit; this speech is a testimony of it, as well as his former; he answers
chiefly to the dismission of *Penelope*, says it would be an offence against Heaven
and Earth; and concludes with a vehemence of expression, and tells *Antinous* that
such a word, μῦθον, shall never fall from his tongue.

The Critics have found fault with one part of the speech, as betraying a spirit
of avarice and meanness in *Telemachus*:

> How to Icarius *in the bridal hour*
> Shall I, *by waste undone, refund the dow'r?*

They think it unworthy of *Telemachus* to make the Dower of *Penelope* an argument
against her dismission, and consequently ascribe his detention of her, not to duty,
but to covetousness. To take away this objection they point the verses in a
different manner, and place a stop after ἀποτίνειν, and then the sense runs thus;
"I cannot consent to dismiss her who bore me, and nurs'd me in my infancy,
while her husband is absent, or perhaps dead; besides, hard would be the
Punishment I should suffer, if I should voluntarily send away *Penelope* to *Icarius*."

Dacier dislikes this solution, and appeals to the customs of those Ages, to justify
her opinion: If a son forc'd away his mother from his house, he was obliged to
restore her dower, and all she brought in marriage to her husband: But if she
retir'd voluntarily to engage in a second marriage, the dower remain'd with the
son as lawful heir. This opinion of *Dacier* may be confirm'd from *Demosthenes*
in his orations, καὶ μετὰ ταῦτα ἀνδρὸς αὐτῇ τελευτήσαντος, ἀπολιποῦσα
τὸν οἶκον, καὶ κομισαμένη τὴν προῖκα ⟨XL 6⟩. *Afterwards upon the decease of her
husband, leaving his family, and receiving back her portion,* &c. The same Author adds,
that the reason why the Suitors are so urgent to send away *Penelope*, is that she
may chuse to marry some one of them, rather than return to *Icarius*; so that *Telemachus* only takes hold of their argument for her dismission, in order to detain her.
They address'd *Penelope* more for the sake of her riches than her beauty, (for she
must be about forty years old) and he tells them, that if he sends her away against
her consent, he must restore those riches, which they covet more than the person
of *Penelope*. This I confess is very refin'd; and perhaps it may be sufficient to take
off the objection of covetousness in *Telemachus*, to understand no more than what
the words at the first view seem to imply, *viz.* an abhorrence of their riots,
describ'd by *Telemachus* to have risen to such a degree as to have almost ruin'd his
kingdom, and made their demands impossible. I see nothing unnatural or mean

Ev'n Nature starts, and what ye ask denies.
Thus, shall I thus repay a mother's cares,
Who gave me life, and nurs'd my infant years? 150
While sad on foreign shores *Ulysses* treads,
Or glides a ghost with unapparent shades.
How to *Icarius* in the bridal hour
Shall I, by waste undone, refund the dow'r?
How from my father should I vengeance dread? 155
How would my mother curse my hated head?
And while in wrath to vengeful Fiends she cries,
How from their hell would vengeful Fiends arise?
Abhorr'd by all, accurs'd my name would grow,

in this interpretation, especially if we remember that the prodigious disorders of his family enter into the essence of the Poem. The greater the disorders are, the greater are the sufferings of *Ulysses*.

155. *How from my father should I vengeance dread*.] There is an ambiguity in the word Father; it may either signify *Icarius* or *Ulysses*, as *Eustathius* observes: but I think the context determines the person to be *Ulysses*; for *Telemachus* believes him to be yet living, and consequently might fear his vengeance, if he offer'd any indignity to *Penelope*.

157. *And while in wrath to vengeful Fiends she cries,*
How from their hell would vengeful Fiends arise?]
In the ninth *Iliad* we are told that the father of *Phœnix* imprecated the Furies against his son,

My sire with curses loads my hated head,
And cries "Ye Furies! barren be his bed.
Infernal Jove, *the vengeful Fiends below,*
And ruthless Proserpine, *confirm'd his vow* ⟨582–5⟩.

In the same book the Furies hear the curses of *Althea* upon her son,

She beat the ground, and call'd the Pow'rs beneath,
On her own son to wreak her brother's death.
Hell heard her curses from the realms profound,
And the fell Fiends who walk the nightly round.
⟨683–6, but for *fell* read *red* and for *who* read *that*⟩

These passages shew the opinion the Ancients had of the honour due from children to parents, to be such, that they believ'd there were Furies particularly commission'd to punish those who fail'd in that respect, and to fulfil the imprecations made against 'em by their offended parents. There is a greatness in this Idea, and it must have had an effect upon the obedience of the youth. We see *Telemachus* is full of the sense of it. *Dacier.*

The earth's disgrace, and Humankind my foe.   160
If this displease, why urge ye here your stay?
Haste from the court, ye spoilers, haste away:
Waste in wild riot what your land allows,
There ply the early feast, and late carouse.
But if, to honour lost, 'tis still decreed   165
For you my bowl shall flow, my flocks shall bleed;
Judge and assert my right, impartial *Jove!*
By him, and all th' immortal host above,
(A sacred oath) if heav'n the pow'r supply,
Vengeance I vow, and for your wrongs ye die.   170
    With that, two Eagles from a mountain's height
By *Jove's* command direct their rapid flight;
Swift they descend with wing to wing conjoin'd,
Stretch their broad plumes, and float upon the wind.
Above th' assembled Peers they wheel on high,   175
And clang their wings, and hovering beat the sky;
With ardent eyes the rival train they threat,
And shrieking loud denounce approaching fate.
They cuff, they tear, their cheeks and necks they rend,
And from their plumes huge drops of blood descend. 180
Then sailing o'er the domes and tow'rs they fly,

171, *&c. The Prodigy of the two Eagles.*] This prodigy is usher'd in very magnificently, and the verses are lofty and sonorous. The Eagles are *Ulysses* and *Telemachus; By Jove's command* they fly *from a mountain's height*: this denotes that the
two Heroes are inspir'd by *Jupiter*, and come from the country to the destruction
of the Suitors: The eagles fly *with wing to wing conjoyn'd*; this shews, that they act in
concert, and unity of councils: At first they *float upon the wind*; this implies the
calmness and secresy of the approach of those Heroes: At last they *clang their
wings and hovering beat the skies*; this shews the violence of the assault: *With ardent
eyes the rival train they threat.* This, as the Poet himself interprets it, denotes the
approaching fate of the Suitors. *Then sailing o'er the domes and tow'rs they fly Full
toward the east*; this signifies that the Suitors alone are not doom'd to destruction,
but that the men of *Ithaca* are involv'd in danger, as *Halitherses* interprets it.

    Nor to the Great alone is death decreed;
    We, and our guilty Ithaca *must bleed.*

    See here the natural explication of this prodigy, which is very ingenious!
Eustathius, verbatim.

Full tow'rd the east, and mount into the sky.
  The wondring Rivals gaze with cares opprest,
And chilling horrours freeze in every breast.
'Till big with knowledge of approaching woes   185
The Prince of Augurs, *Halitherses*, rose:
Prescient he view'd th' aerial tracts, and drew
A sure presage from ev'ry wing that flew.
  Ye sons (he cry'd) of *Ithaca* give ear,
Hear all! but chiefly you, oh Rivals! hear.   190
Destruction sure o'er all your heads impends;
Ulysses comes, and death his steps attends.
Nor to the Great alone is death decreed;
We, and our guilty *Ithaca* must bleed.
Why cease we then the wrath of heav'n to stay?   195
Be humbled all, and lead ye Great! the way.
For lo! my words no fancy'd woes relate:
I speak from science, and the voice is Fate.
  When great *Ulysses* sought the *Phrygian* shores
To shake with war proud *Ilion*'s lofty tow'rs,   200
Deeds then undone my faithful tongue foretold;
Heav'n seal'd my words, and you those deeds behold.
I see (I cry'd) his woes, a countless train;
I see his friends o'erwhelm'd beneath the main;
How twice ten years from shore to shore he roams;   205
Now twice ten years are past, and now he comes!

203.   *I see (I cry'd) his woes—*
                I see his friends o'erwhelm'd, &c.]
In three lines (observes *Eustathius*) the Poet gives us the whole *Odyssey* in Minia-
ture: And it is wonderful to think, that so plain a subject should produce such
variety in the process of it. *Aristotle* observes the simplicity of *Homer*'s platform
⟨*Poetics* XVII 10–11⟩; which is no more than this: A Prince is absent from his
country; *Neptune* destroys his companions; in his absence his family is disorder'd
by many Princes that address his wife, and plot against the life of his only son:
but at last after many storms he returns, punishes the Suitors, and re-establishes
his affairs: This is all that is essential to the Poem, the rest of it is made up of
Episodes. And yet with what miracles of Poetry, (*speciosa miracula*, as *Horace* stiles
them ⟨*Ars Poet.* 144⟩,) has he furnish'd out his Poem?

  To whom *Eurymachus*—Fly Dotard, fly!
With thy wise dreams, and fables of the sky.
Go prophecy at home; thy sons advise:
Here thou art sage in vain—I better read the skies. 210
Unnumber'd Birds glide thro' th' aerial way,
Vagrants of air, and unforeboding stray.
Cold in the tomb, or in the deeps below
Ulysses lies: oh wert thou lay'd as low!
Then would that busy head no broils suggest, 215
Nor fire to rage *Telemachus* his breast.
From him some bribe thy venal tongue requires,
And Int'rest, not the God, thy voice inspires.
His guide-less youth, if thy experienc'd age
Mis-lead fallacious into idle rage, 220
Vengeance deserv'd thy malice shall repress,
And but augment the wrongs thou would'st redress.
Telemachus may bid the Queen repair
To great *Icarius*, whose paternal care
Will guide her passion, and reward her choice, 225
With wealthy dow'r, and bridal gifts of price.
'Till she retires, determin'd we remain,
And both the Prince and Augur threat in vain:
His pride of words, and thy wild dream of fate,
Move not the brave, or only move their hate. 230
Threat on, oh Prince! elude the bridal day,
Threat on, till all thy stores in waste decay.
True, *Greece* affords a train of lovely dames,
In wealth and beauty worthy of our flames:

---

207. *The speech of* Eurymachus.] It has been observ'd, that *Homer* is the father of Oratory as well as Poetry; and it must be confess'd, that there is not any one branch of it that is not to be found in his Poetry. The Invective, Persuasive, Ironical, *&c.* may all be gather'd from it. Nothing can be better adapted to the purpose than this speech of *Eurymachus*: He is to decry the credit of the predictions of *Halitherses*: he derides, he threats, and describes him as a venal Prophet. He is speaking to the multitude, and endeavours to bring *Halitherses* into contempt, and in order to it he uses him contemptuously.

But never from this nobler suit we cease;   235
For wealth and beauty less than virtue please.
    To whom the Youth. Since then in vain I tell
My num'rous woes, in silence let them dwell.
But heav'n, and all the *Greeks*, have heard my wrongs:
To heav'n, and all the *Greeks*, redress belongs.   240
Yet this I ask (nor be it ask'd in vain)
A bark to waft me o'er the rolling main;
The realms of *Pyle* and *Sparta* to explore,
And seek my royal sire from shore to shore:
If, or to *Fame* his doubtful fate be known,   245
Or to be learn'd from *Oracles* alone?
If yet he lives, with patience I forbear
'Till the fleet hours restore the circling year;
But if already wand'ring in the train
Of empty shades, I measure back the main;   250
Plant the fair column o'er the mighty dead,
And yield his consort to the nuptial bed.
    He ceas'd; and while abash'd the Peers attend,
Mentor arose, *Ulysses'* faithful friend:

---

239. —*All the* Greeks *have heard my wrongs.*] It is necessary for the Reader to carry in his mind, that this Assembly consists not only of the Peers, but of the People of *Ithaca*: For to the People *Telemachus* here appeals.

It is evident, that the place of the Assembly was at least open to the Air in the upper parts: for otherways how should the Eagles be visible to the Suitors? and so very plainly as to be discover'd to threat them with their eyes? There was no doubt a place set apart for Council, usually in the market: For *Telemachus* is said to seat himself in his Father's throne, in the beginning of this book: But *Ulysses* had been absent twenty years; and therefore it is evident, that his throne had stood in the same place for the space of twenty years. It is past contradiction, that in *Athens* and other cities of *Greece* there were Βουλευτήρια, public Halls for the consultation of affairs.

254. Mentor *arose*, Ulysses' *faithful friend.*] The name of *Mentor* is another instance of the gratitude of our Poet's temper, it being the same which belong'd to a friend of his by whom he was entertain'd in *Ithaca*, during a defluxion on his eyes which seiz'd him in his voyages: and at whose house he is said to have laid the plan of this Poem. This character of *Mentor* is well sustain'd by his speech, and by the assistance he gratefully gives to young *Telemachus* on all occasions.

D*

[When fierce in arms he sought the scenes of war,   255
"My friend (he cry'd) my palace be thy care;
"Years roll'd on years my god-like sire decay,
"Guard thou his age, and his behests obey.]
Stern as he rose, he cast his eyes around
That flash'd with rage; and as he spoke, he frown'd. 260
     O never, never more! let King be just,
Be mild in pow'r, or faithful to his trust!
Let Tyrants govern with an iron rod,
Oppress, destroy, and be the scourge of God;
Since he who like a father held his reign,   265
So soon forgot, was just and mild in vain!
True, while my friend is griev'd, his griefs I share;
Yet now the Rivals are my smallest care:
They, for the mighty mischiefs they devise,
Ere long shall pay—their forfeit lives the price.   270
But against you, ye *Greeks!* ye coward train,
Gods! how my soul is mov'd with just disdain?
Dumb ye all stand, and not one tongue affords
His injur'd Prince the little aid of words.
     While yet he spoke, *Leocritus* rejoyn'd: 275
O pride of words, and arrogance of mind!
Would'st thou to rise in arms the *Greeks* advise?
Join all your pow'rs! in arms ye *Greeks* arise!
Yet would your pow'rs in vain our strength oppose;
The valiant few o'ermatch an host of foes.   280
Should great *Ulysses* stern appear in arms,

258. *Guard thou my Sire* ⟨sic⟩, *and his behests obey.*] The original says only, "*Obey the old man.*" *Eustathius* rightly determines, that the expression means *Laertes.* The Poet loses no opportunity of giving *Ulysses* an excellent character; this is as necessary as continually to repeat the disorders of the Suitors.
                    —*Servetur ad imum*
      Qualis ab incepto processerit, & sibi constet. ⟨Horace, *Ars Poet.* 126–7⟩
This conduct contributes admirably to the design of the Poem; and when the Poet in the unravelling of his Fable comes to reward and punish the chief actors, we acknowledge his justice in the death of the Suitors, and re-establishment of *Ulysses.*

While the bowl circles, and the banquet warms;
Tho' to his breast his spouse with transport flies,
Torn from her breast, that hour, *Ulysses* dies.
But hence retreating to your domes repair;   285
To arm the vessel, *Mentor!* be thy care,
And *Halitherses!* thine: be each his friend;
Ye lov'd the father; go, the son attend.
But yet, I trust, the boaster means to stay
Safe in the court, nor tempt the watry way.   290
      Then, with a rushing sound, th' Assembly bend
Diverse their steps: The rival rout ascend
The royal dome; while sad the Prince explores

---

282. *While the bowl circles, and the banquet warms.*] The original is not without
obscurity: it says, περὶ Δαιτὶ: or, *in the time of the banquet. Eustathius* interprets it,
τοῦ οἴνου στρατηγοῦντος αὐτοῖς, *The Wine as it were fighting on their side*; and
this agrees with what follows.

The design of this speech is to deter the people of *Ithaca* from rising in the cause
of *Ulysses*: *Mentor* speaks justly; *Leocritus* insolently: *Mentor* sets before them the
worth of *Ulysses*; *Leocritus* the power of the Suitors: *Mentor* speaks like a brave
man; *Leocritus* (observes *Eustathius*) like a coward, who wanting true courage flies
to the assistance of wine to raise a false one.

Perhaps it may be objected, that there is not a sufficient distinction in the
characters of the several Suitors; they are all describ'd as insolent voluptuaries.
But tho' they agree in this general character, yet there is something distinguishing
in the particular persons: Thus *Antinous* derides, *Eurymachus* covers villany with
mildness; *Antinous* is ever foremost in outrage, *Eurymachus* generally his second:
A greater distinction is neither necessary, nor possible to be represented. What the
Poet is to describe, is the insolence of the Suitors, and the disorders they create in
his family and kingdom; he is oblig'd to dwell upon these circumstances, because
they are essential to his design: and consequently that general resemblance of
their characters, is not a fault in the Poet.

291. *Then, with a rushing sound*, &c.] The Assembly which was conven'd by
Telemachus, is broke up in a riotous manner by *Leocritus*, who had no right to
dissolve it. This agrees with the lawless state of the country in the absence of its
King, and shews (says *Eustathius*) that the Suitors had usurp'd the chief Authority.

There is a fine contraste between the behaviour of *Telemachus* and that of the
Suitors. They return to repeat their disorders and debauches; *Telemachus* retires
to supplicate the Goddess of Wisdom, to assist him in his enterprizes. Thus the
Poet raises the character of *Telemachus*; he has shew'd him to be a youth of a brave
spirit, a good Speaker, and here represents him as a person of piety.

The neighb'ring main, and sorrowing treads the shores.
There, as the waters o'er his hands he shed,　　295
The royal suppliant to *Minerva* pray'd.

O Goddess! who descending from the skies
Vouchsaf'd thy presence to my wond'ring eyes,
By whose commands the raging deeps I trace,
And seek my sire thro' storms and rolling seas!　　300
Hear from thy heav'ns above, oh warrior-maid!
Descend once more, propitious to my aid.
Without thy presence vain is thy command;
Greece, and the rival train thy voice withstand.

Indulgent to his pray'r, the Goddess took　　305
Sage *Mentor*'s form, and thus like *Mentor* spoke.

O Prince, in early youth divinely wise,
Born, the *Ulysses* of thy age to rise!
If to the son the father's worth descends,
O'er the wide waves success thy ways attends:　　310
To tread the walks of death he stood prepar'd,
And what he greatly thought, he nobly dar'd.
Were not wise sons descendent of the wise,
And did not Heroes from brave Heroes rise,
Vain were my hopes: few sons attain the praise　　315
Of their great sires, and most their sires disgrace.
But since thy veins paternal virtue fires,
And all *Penelope* thy soul inspires,
Go, and succeed! the rivals' aims despise;
For never, never, wicked man was wise.　　320
Blind they rejoice, tho' now, ev'n now they fall;
Death hastes amain: one hour o'erwhelms them all!
And lo, with speed we plow the watry way;

---

307. *The speech of* Minerva.] This speech of *Minerva* is suited to encourage a
young man to imitate the virtue of his father, and not to suffer himself to be overcome by any appearance of difficulties. She sets his father before his eyes, and
tells him, there was never any danger which he durst not encounter; if he should
suffer himself to be discouraged, he would prove himself an unworthy son of a
brave Father. *Dacier. Eustathius.*

My pow'r shall guard thee, and my hand convey:
The winged vessel studious I prepare,   325
Thro' seas and realms companion of thy care.
Thou to the court ascend; and to the shores
(When night advances) bear the naval stores;
Bread, that decaying man with strength supplies,
And gen'rous wine, which thoughtful sorrow flies.   330
Mean-while the Mariners by my command
Shall speed aboard, a valiant chosen band.
Wide o'er the bay, by vessel vessel rides;
The best I chuse, to waft thee o'er the tides.

   She spoke: to his high dome the Prince returns,   335
And as he moves with royal anguish mourns.
'Twas riot all among the lawless train;
Boar bled by boar, and goat by goat lay slain.
Arriv'd, his hand the gay *Antinous* prest,
And thus deriding, with a smile addrest.   340

    Grieve not, oh daring Prince! that noble heart:
Ill suits gay youth the stern, heroic part.
Indulge the genial hour, unbend thy soul,
Leave thought to Age, and drain the flowing bowl.
Studious to ease thy grief, our care provides   345
The bark, to waft thee o'er the swelling tides.

341. Antinous's *speech.*] This speech must be understood ironically: ἔργον τε
ἔπος τε is us'd as before, and has relation to the preceding harangues of *Telemachus*
to the people, and his intended voyage; by way of derision *Antinous* bids him not
trouble his brave Spirit in contriving any more Orations, or in any bold attempt
to find out *Ulysses*; or to act the Orator, or Heroe's part.

The Critics have almost generally condemn'd these pieces of gayety and
raillery, as unworthy of heroic Poetry: if ever they are proper, they must be so
in the mouths of these Suitors; persons of no serious, or noble characters: Mirth,
wine, and feasting is their constant employment; and consequently if they fall
into absurdities, they act suitably to their characters. *Milton*, the best and
greatest imitator of *Homer*, has followed him unworthily in this respect; I mean,
has debased even this low raillery into greater lowness, by playing upon words
and syllables. But in this place the raillery is not without its effect, by shewing the
utmost contempt of *Telemachus*; and surely it is the lowest degree of calamity to
be at once oppress'd and despis'd.

Is this (returns the Prince) for mirth a time?
When lawless gluttons riot, mirth's a crime;
The luscious wines dishonour'd lose their taste,
The song is noise, and impious is the feast.   350
Suffice it to have spent with swift decay
The wealth of Kings, and made my youth a prey.
But now the wise instructions of the sage,
And manly thoughts inspir'd by manly age,
Teach me to seek redress for all my woe,   355
Here, or in *Pyle.*—in *Pyle* or here, your foe.
Deny your vessels; ye deny in vain;
A private voyager I pass the main.
Free breathe the winds, and free the billows flow,
And where on earth I live, I live your foe.   360

He spoke and frown'd, nor longer deign'd to stay,
Sternly his hand withdrew, and strode away.

Mean time, o'er all the dome, they quaff, they feast,
Derisive taunts were spread from guest to guest,
And each in jovial mood his mate addrest.

Tremble ye not, oh friends! and coward fly,   366
Doom'd by the stern *Telemachus* to dye?
To *Pyle* or *Sparta* to demand supplies,
Big with revenge, the mighty warrior flies:
Or comes from *Ephyré* with poisons fraught,   370
And kills us all in one tremendous draught?

Or who can say (his gamesome mate replies)
But while the dangers of the deeps he tries,
He, like his sire, may sink depriv'd of breath,
And punish us unkindly by his death?   375
What mighty labours would he then create,

---

368. *To* Pyle *or* Sparta *to demand supplies.*] It is observable, says *Eustathius,* that the Poet had in his choice several expedients to bring about the destruction of the Suitors, but he rejects them, and chuses the most difficult method, out of reverence to truth, being unwilling to falsify the Histories of *Sparta* and *Pylos.* This has a double effect; it furnishes the Poet with a series of noble incidents; and also gives an air of probability to the story of *Ulysses* and *Telemachus.*

To seize his treasures, and divide his state,
The royal Palace to the Queen convey,
Or him she blesses in the bridal day!
 Meantime the lofty rooms the Prince surveys,   380
Where lay the treasures of th' *Ithacian* race:
Here ruddy brass and gold refulgent blaz'd;
There polish'd chests embroider'd vestures grac'd;
Here jars of oil breath'd forth a rich perfume;
There casks of wine in rows adorn'd the dome.   385

---

378. *The royal Palace to the Queen convey.*] The Suitors allot the Palace to *Penelope*: it being, says *Eustathius*, the only thing that they cannot consume; and adds, that the expression of the Suitors concerning the labour they should undergo in dividing the substance of *Ulysses*, shews the wealth and abundance of that Heroe. *Dacier* has found out an allusion between φόνον in the first speech, and πόνον in the second; they differing only in one letter: She calls this a beauty, which she laments she cannot preserve in her translation. She is the only Commentator that ever was quick-sighted enough to make the discovery. The words have no relation; they stand at a sufficient distance; and I believe *Homer* would have thought such trifling unworthy of his Poetry. So that all the honour which accrues from that observation must be ascrib'd (in this case, as in many others) to the Commentator, and not the Author.

381. *Where lay the treasures of th'* Ithacian *race.*] Such passages as these have ever furnish'd Critics with matter of raillery: They think such houshold cares unworthy of a King, and that this conduct suits better with vulgar persons of less fortune. I confess, such descriptions now would be ridiculous in a Poet, because unsuitable to our manners. But if we look upon such passages as pictures and exact representations of the old world, the Reader will find a sensible pleasure in them.

It is a true observation, that the *Iliad* is chiefly suitable to the condition of Kings and Heroes; and consequently fill'd with circumstances in which the greatest part of mankind can have no concern or interest: The *Odyssey* is of more general use; the story of it is a series of calamities, which concern every man, as every man may feel them. We can bring the sufferings of *Ulysses* in some degree home to our selves, and make his condition our own; but what private person can ever be in the circumstances of *Agamemnon* or *Achilles*? What I would infer from this is, that the Reader ought not to take offence at any such descriptions, which are only mean as they differ from the fashions of the latter ages. In the *Iliad*, *Achilles* when he acts in the common offices of life, and not as an Heroe, is liable to the same objection. But if the manners of the antient ages be consider'd, we shall be reconcil'd to the actions of the antient Heroes; and consequently to *Homer*.

(Pure flav'rous wine, by Gods in bounty giv'n,
And worthy to exalt the feasts of heav'n.)
Untouch'd they stood, 'till his long labours o'er
The great *Ulysses* reach'd his native shore.
A double strength of bars secur'd the gates: 390
Fast by the door the wise *Euryclea* waits;
Euryclea, who, great *Ops!* thy lineage shar'd,
And watch'd all night, all day; a faithful guard.
     To whom the Prince. O thou whose guardian care
Nurs'd the most wretched King that breathes the air!
Untouch'd and sacred may these vessels stand,   396
'Till great *Ulysses* views his native land.
But by thy care twelve urns of wine be fill'd,
Next these in worth, and firm those urns be seal'd;
And twice ten measures of the choicest flour   400
Prepar'd, ere yet descends the evening hour.
For when the fav'ring shades of night arise,
And peaceful slumbers close my mother's eyes,
Me from our coast shall spreading sails convey,
To seek *Ulysses* thro' the wat'ry way.   405
     While yet he spoke, she fill'd the walls with cries,
And tears ran trickling from her aged eyes.
Oh whither, whither flies my son? she cry'd,
To realms, that rocks and roaring seas divide?
In foreign lands thy father's days decay'd,   410
And foreign lands contain the mighty dead.
The watry way, ill-fated if thou try,

394.   —*Oh thou whose guardian care*
                Nurs'd the most wretched King.]
Euryclea was not properly the Nurse of *Telemachus*, but of *Ulysses*; so that she is
call'd so not in a strict sense, but as one concern'd in his education from his
infancy, and as a general appellation of honour. *Telemachus* here reserves the best
wines for *Ulysses*; a lesson, (observes *Eustathius*) that even in the smallest matters
we ought to pay a deference to our parents. These occasional and seemingly-
trivial circumstances are not without their use, if not as poetical ornaments, yet
as moral instructions.

All, all must perish, and by fraud you die!
Then stay, my child! Storms beat, and rolls the main;
Oh beat those storms, and roll the seas in vain!   415
   Far hence (reply'd the Prince) thy fears be driv'n:
Heav'n calls me forth; these counsels are of heav'n.
But by the pow'rs that hate the perjur'd, swear,
To keep my voyage from the royal ear,
Nor uncompell'd the dang'rous truth betray,   420
'Till twice six times descends the lamp of day:
Lest the sad tale a mother's life impair,
And grief destroy what time a while would spare.
   Thus he. The matron with uplifted eyes
Attests th' all-seeing Sovereign of the skies.   425
Then studious she prepares the choicest flour,
The strength of wheat, and wines, an ample store.
   While to the rival train the Prince returns,
The martial Goddess with impatience burns;
Like thee *Telemachus*, in voice and size,   430
With speed divine from street to street she flies.
She bids the Mariners prepar'd to stand,

---

421. '*Till twice six times descends the lamp of day.*] It may be demanded how it was probable, (if possible) that the departure of *Telemachus* could be conceal'd twelve days from the knowledge of so fond a mother as *Penelope*? It must be allow'd, that this would not be possible except in a time of such great disorder as the Suitors created: *Penelope* confin'd herself almost continually within her own apartment, and very seldom appear'd publickly; so that there is no improbability in this relation. *Dacier*.

It may be added, that tho' *Telemachus* enjoyn'd secrecy for twelve days, yet he intended a very speedy return: and we find that he actually return'd in a much shorter space than twelve days; so that the strictness of the injunction proceeds solely from filial love, and was only cautionary against accidents that might detain him longer. ⟨*12° omits this paragraph*⟩

Eustathius makes a criticism upon the words ἀπομνύναι and ἐπομνύναι, the former is used negatively, the latter affirmatively; namely, the former in swearing *not to perform* a thing, the latter *to perform it*.

432. *She bids the Mariners*, &c.] It is probable that this passage of *Minerva* preparing the Mariners, &c. is thus to be understood: The men of *Ithaca*, retaining in memory the speech of *Telemachus*, and believing that what he then said, and

When Night descends, embodyed on the strand.
Then to *Noemon* swift she runs, she flies,
And asks a bark: the chief a bark supplies.   435
  And now, declining with his sloping wheels,
Down sunk the Sun behind the western hills.
The Goddess shov'd the vessel from the shores,
And stow'd within its womb the naval stores.
Full in the openings of the spacious main   440
It rides; and now descends the sailor train.
  Next, to the court, impatient of delay
With rapid step the Goddess urg'd her way;
There every eye with slumbrous chains she bound,
And dash'd the flowing goblet to the ground.   445
Drowzy they rose, with heavy fumes opprest,
Reel'd from the palace, and retir'd to rest.

---

now requests, was agreeable to justice; and having as it were his image graven upon their hearts; voluntarily resolve to lend him assistance: So that *Minerva* is to be taken allegorically, to imply that it was every person's own Reason that induced him to assist *Telemachus*. *Eustathius*.

435. Noemon—*the* ⟨sic⟩ *Bark supplies*.] It may be ask'd why this particularity is necessary, and may it not be thought that such a little circumstance is insignificant? The answer is, that a great deal depends upon this particularity; no less than the discovery of the voyage of *Telemachus* to the Suitors; and consequently, whatever the Suitors act in order to intercept him takes its rise from this little incident; the fountain is indeed small, but a large stream of Poetry flows from it.

444. *There every eye with slumbrous chains she bound*.] The words in the original are εὕδειν and ὕπνος, which are not to be taken for being *asleep*, but *drowzy*; this is evident from the usage of καθεύδειν, in the conclusion of the first book of the *Iliads*, where the signification has been mistaken by most translators: They make *Jupiter* there to be asleep; tho' two lines afterwards, in the second book, *Homer* expresly says,

> *Th' Immortals slumber'd on their thrones above:*
> *All, but the ever-waking eyes of* Jove.
>   ⟨3–4, but for *ever-waking* read *ever-wakeful*⟩

It may be ask'd how *Minerva* can be said to occasion this drowziness in the Suitors, and make them retire sooner than usual? *Eustathius* replies, that the person who furnish'd the wine supply'd it in greater quantities than ordinary, thro' which wine they contracted a drowziness: In this sense *Minerva*, or Wisdom, may be said to assist the designs of *Telemachus*.

Then thus, in *Mentor*'s reverend form array'd,
Spoke to *Telemachus* the martial Maid.
Lo! on the seas prepar'd the vessel stands;   450
Th' impatient mariner thy speed demands.
Swift as she spoke, with rapid pace she leads.
The footsteps of the Deity he treads.
Swift to the shore they move: Along the strand
The ready vessel rides, the sailors ready stand.   455
    He bids them bring their stores: th' attending train
Load the tall bark, and launch into the main.
The Prince and Goddess to the stern ascend;
To the strong stroke at once the rowers bend.
Full from the west she bids fresh breezes blow;   460
The sable billows foam and roar below.
The Chief his orders gives; th' obedient band
With due observance wait the chief's command;
With speed the mast they rear, with speed unbind
The spacious sheet, and stretch it to the wind.   465
High o'er the roaring waves the spreading sails
Bow the tall mast, and swell before the gales;
The crooked keel the parting surge divides,
And to the stern retreating roll the tides.
And now they ship their oars, and crown with wine   470

460. *She bids fresh breezes blow.*] This also is an allegory, and implies that the
sailors had the experience and art to guide the ship before the winds; but Poetry,
that delights to raise every circumstance, exalts it into the marvellous, and
ascribes it to the Goddess of Wisdom. *Eustathius.*

464. *With speed the mast they rear*, &c.] It is observable, that *Homer* never passes
by an opportunity of describing the sea, or a ship under sail; (and in many other
places, as well as in this, he dwells largely upon it:) I take the reason to be, not
only because it furnish'd him with variety of poetical images, but because he
himself having made frequent voyages, had a full Idea of it, and consequently
was delighted with it: This is evident from his conduct in the *Iliad*, where variety
of allusions and similitudes are drawn from the Sea, and are not the smallest
ornaments of his Poetry.

470.   *—And crown with wine*
          The holy Goblet to the Pow'rs divine.]
This custom of libations was frequent upon all solemn occasions, before meat,

The holy Goblet to the pow'rs divine:
Imploring all the Gods that reign above,
But chief, the blue-ey'd Progeny of *Jove*.
Thus all the night they stem the liquid way,
And end their voyage with the morning ray.   475

---

before sleep, voyages, journies; and in all religious rites, sacrifices, &c. They were always made with wine, pure and unmix'd, whence ἄκρατον is a word frequent in antient Authors. Sometimes they used mixed wine in Sacrifices; but *Eustathius* says, that this mixture was of wine with wine, and not of wine with water; hence came the distinction of ἔνσπονδον, and ἄσπονδον, the unlawful and lawful libation; wine unmix'd was lawful, the mix'd unlawful. *Homer* in this place uses κρητῆρας ἐπιστεφέας, or *Goblets crown'd with wine*; that is, fill'd 'till the wine stood above the brim of the Goblet: they esteem'd it an irreverence to the Gods not to fill the cups full, for then only they esteem'd the libation *whole* and *perfect*, ὅλον καὶ τέλειον, and then only worthy of the Gods. ⟨*12°* omits and . . . Gods⟩

This Book takes up the space of one day and one night: it opens with the morning; the speeches in the Council, with the preparations for the voyage of *Telemachus*, are the subject of the day; and the voyage is finish'd by the next morning. By this last circumstance we may learn that *Ithaca* was distant from *Pylos* but one night's voyage, nay something less, there being some time spent after the setting of the Sun, in carrying the provisions from the Palace to the vessel.

The book consists chiefly in the speeches of *Telemachus* and his friends, against those of the Suitors. It shews the great judgment of the Poet in chusing this method: hence we see the causes preceding the effects; and know from what spring every action flow'd: we are never at a loss for a reason for every incident; the speeches are as it were the ground-work upon which he builds all that relates to the adventures of *Telemachus*.

In the *Iliad*, after the dissolution of the Council in the first book, and the dissension between *Agamemnon* and *Achilles*, we immediately see upon what hinge the fable turns. So in the *Odyssey*, after the Poet has laid before us the warm debates between the Suitors and *Telemachus*, we immediately expect them to act as enemies: The war is declar'd, and we become judges as well as spectators of the scenes of action. Thus *Homer* adds the perspicuity of History to the ornaments of Poetry.

THE
THIRD BOOK
OF THE
ODYSSEY.

The ARGUMENT.
The Interview of *Telemachus* and *Nestor*.

Telemachus, *guided by* Pallas *in the shape of* Mentor, *arrives in the morning at* Pylos; *where* Nestor *and his sons are sacrificing on the sea-shore to* Neptune. Telemachus *declares the occasion of his coming, and* Nestor *relates what past in their return from* Troy, *how their fleets were separated, and he never since heard of* Ulysses. *They discourse concerning the death of* Agamemnon, *the revenge of* Orestes, *and the injuries of the* Suitors. Nestor *advises him to go to* Sparta *and enquire further of* Menelaus. *The sacrifice ending with the night,* Minerva *vanishes from them in the form of an Eagle :* Telemachus *is lodged in the Palace. The next morning they sacrifice a Bullock to* Minerva, *and* Telemachus *proceeds on his journey to* Sparta, *attended by* Pisistratus.

The Scene lies on the sea-shore of *Pylos*.

T HE sacred Sun, above the waters rais'd,
Thro' Heav'ns eternal, brazen portals blaz'd;
And wide o'er earth diffus'd his chearing ray,

The Scene is now remov'd from *Ithaca* to *Pylos*, and with it a new vein of Poetry is opened: Instead of the riots of the Suitors, we are entertain'd with the wisdom and piety of *Nestor*. This and the following book are a kind of Supplement to the *Iliad*; the nature of Epic poetry requires that something should be left to the imagination of the Reader, nor is the picture to be entirely drawn at full length. *Homer* therefore, to satisfie our curiosity, gives an account of the fortunes of those great men, who made so noble a figure at the siege of *Troy*. This conduct also shews his art: Variety gives life and delight; and it is much more necessary in Epic than in Comic or Tragic Poetry sometimes to shift the Scenes, to diversify and embellish the story. But as on the stage the Poet ought not to step at once

To Gods and men to give the golden day.
Now on the coast of *Pyle* the vessel falls,   5
Before old *Neleus'* venerable walls.
There, suppliant to the Monarch of the flood,
At nine green Theatres the *Pylians* stood,

---

from one part of the world to a too remote country, (for this destroys credibility, and the auditor cannot fancy himself this minute here, and the next a thousand miles distant) so in Epic Poetry, every removal must be within the degrees of probability. We have here a very easy transition; the Poet carries his Heroe no further than he really might sail in the compass of time he allots for his voyage. If he had still dwelt upon the disorders of the Suitors without interruption, he must grow tiresome; but he artfully breaks the thread of their History with beautiful incidents and Episodes, and reserves the further recital of their disorders for the end of his Poem: By this method we sit down with fresh appetite to the entertainment, and rise at last not cloy'd, but satisfied.

2. *Thro' Heav'ns eternal, brazen portals*—] The original calls Heaven πολύ-χαλκον, or *brazen*; the reason of it arises either from the Palaces of the Gods being built of brass by *Vulcan*; or rather the word implies no more than the Stability of Heaven, which for the same reason is in other places call'd σιδήρειον, or *fram'd of iron*. Eustathius.

8. *At nine green Theatres*.] It may be ask'd why the Poet is so very particular as to mention that the *Pylians* were divided into nine assemblies? and may it not seem a circumstance of no importance? *Eustathius* answers from the Antients, that there were nine cities subject to the power of *Nestor*: five in *Pylos*, the rest in *Bæotia*; the Poet therefore allots one Bank or Theatre to every city, which consisted of 500 men, the whole number amounting to 4500: These cities furnish'd the like complement of men to *Nestor* for the war at *Troy*: He sail'd in ninety vessels, and allowing fifty men to each vessel, they amount to that number. Hence it appears that this was a national sacrifice, every city furnish'd nine bulls, and by consequence the whole nation were partakers of it.

Ibid. *The sacrifice of the* Pylians.] This was a very solemn sacrifice of the *Pylians*; How comes it then to pass, that *Homer* passes it over in one line? *Eustathius* answers, that the occasion disallows a longer description, and *Homer* knows when to speak, and when to be silent. He chuses to carry on the adventures of *Telemachus*, rather than amuse himself in descriptions that contribute nothing to the story; he finds a time of more leisure in the latter part of this book, and there he describes it at length.

They taste the entrails; that is, every person eat a small portion of the sacrifice, and by this method every person became partaker of it.

There is nothing in *Homer* that shews where this sacrifice was offer'd, whether in a Temple, or in the open air. But *Eustathius* tells us from *Strabo*⟨VIII iii 16⟩, that it was in the Temple of *Samian Neptune*, ἐν ἱερῷ Σαμίου Ποσειδῶνος.

Each held five hundred, (a deputed train)
At each, nine oxen on the sand lay slain.   10
They taste the entrails, and the altars load
With smoaking thighs, an offering to the God.
Full for the port the *Ithacensians* stand,
And furl their sails, and issue on the land.
Telemachus already prest the shore;   15
Not first, the Pow'r of Wisdom march'd before,
And ere the sacrificing throng he join'd,
Admonish'd thus his well-attending mind.
   Proceed my son! this youthful shame expel;
An honest business never blush to tell.   20
To learn what fates thy wretched sire detain,
We past the wide, immeasurable main.
Meet then the Senior, far renown'd for sense,
With rev'rent awe, but decent confidence:
Urge him with truth to frame his fair replies;   25
And sure he will: For Wisdom never lies.
   Oh tell me *Mentor!* tell me faithful guide,
(The Youth with prudent modesty reply'd)
How shall I meet, or how accost the Sage,
Unskill'd in speech, nor yet mature of age?   30
Awful th' approach, and hard the task appears,
To question wisely men of riper years.
   To whom the martial Goddess thus rejoyn'd.
Search, for some thoughts, thy own suggesting mind;
And others, dictated by heav'nly pow'r,   35

---

25.   *Urge him with truth to frame his fair replies;*
           And sure he will: For Wisdom never lies.]
This sentiment is truly noble, and as nobly expressed: the simplicity of the diction corresponds with that of the thought. *Homer* in many places testifies the utmost abhorrence of a Lye. This verse is twice repeated in the present book, as well as in some others; and nothing can be stronger in the same view than that of *Achilles* in the 9th *Iliad*,
        Who dares think one thing and another tell,
        My heart detests him as the gates of hell. ⟨412–13⟩

Shall rise spontaneous in the needful hour.
For nought unprosp'rous shall thy ways attend,
Born with good omens, and with heav'n thy friend.
   She spoke, and led the way with swiftest speed:
As swift, the youth pursu'd the way she led;   40
And join'd the band before the sacred fire,
Where sate, encompast with his sons, the Sire.
The youth of *Pylos*, some on pointed wood
Transfix'd the fragments, some prepar'd the food.
In friendly throngs they gather, to embrace   45
Their unknown guests, and at the banquet place.
Pisistratus was first, to grasp their hands,
And spread soft hydes upon the yellow sands;

---

38. *Born with good omens, and with heav'n thy friend.*] There is some obscurity in the *Greek* expression, and the antient Critics have made it more obscure by their false interpretations; they imagine that the Poet only meant to say that *Tele-machus* was the legitimate son of *Penelope* and *Ulysses. Eustathius.*

Dacier very justly condemns this explication, as unworthy of *Homer*; and gives us a more plain and natural interpretation: *viz.* "You were not born in despight of the Gods, that is, you are well made, and of a good presence, you have good inclinations, and in a word, your birth is happy." She explains τραφέμεν after the same manner: "You were not educated in despight of the Gods;" that is, "the Gods have blessed your education:" This explication seems to be just, and an-swers perfectly the design of *Minerva*; which was to give a decent assurance to *Telemachus*. You are a person, says the Goddess, of a good presence, and happy education, why then should you be ashamed to appear before *Nestor*?

48. *And spread soft hydes upon the yellow sands.*] It is with pleasure that I read such passages in an Author of so great antiquity, as are pictures of the simplicity of those heroic ages: It is the remark of *Eustathius*, that *Pisistratus* the son of a King does not seat these strangers upon purple Tapestry, or any other costly furniture, but upon the Skins of beasts, that had nothing to recommend them but their softness; being spread upon the sand of the sea-shores.

This whole passage pleases me extremely; there is a spirit of true Devotion, Morality and good Sense in it; and the decency of behaviour between *Nestor* and *Telemachus* is describ'd very happily: *Nestor* shews great benevolence to *Tele-machus*; *Telemachus* great reverence to *Nestor:* the modesty of the one, and the humanity of the other, are worthy of our observation. We see the same picture of *Nestor* in the *Odyssey* that was drawn of him in the *Iliads*, with this only difference, that there he was a Counsellor of War, here he is painted in softer colours, ruling his people in peace, and diffusing a spirit of piety thro' his whole territories. He

Along the shore th' illustrious pair he led,
Where *Nestor* sate with youthful *Thrasymed.* 50
To each a portion of the Feast he bore,
And held the golden goblet foaming o'er;
Then first approaching to the elder guest,
The latent Goddess in these words addrest.

    Whoe'er thou art, whom fortune brings to keep 55
These rites of *Neptune*, monarch of the deep,
Thee first it fits, oh stranger! to prepare
The due libation and the solemn prayer:
Then give thy friend to shed the sacred wine; ⎫
Tho' much thy younger, and his years like mine, ⎬ 60
He too, I deem, implores the pow'rs divine: ⎭
For all mankind alike require their grace,
All born to want; a miserable race!

    He spake, and to her hand preferr'd the bowl:
A secret pleasure touch'd *Athena*'s soul, 65
To see the pref'rence due to sacred age
Regarded ever by the just and sage.
Of Ocean's King she then implores the grace.
Oh thou! whose arms this ample globe embrace,
Fullfil our wish, and let thy glory shine 70
On *Nestor* first, and *Nestor*'s royal line;
Next grant the *Pylian* states their just desires,
Pleas'd with their Hecatomb's ascending fires;
Last deign *Telemachus* and me to bless,

---

had now surviv'd the war of *Troy* almost ten years; and the Gods reward the old
age of this wise and religious Prince with peace and happiness.

    74. *Last deign* Telemachus *and me to bless*—] Since *Minerva* here mentions the
name of *Telemachus* in her prayer; how comes it to pass, that *Nestor* is at a loss to
know *Telemachus*? *Minerva* sate close by *Nestor*; he must therefore be suppos'd to
hear the prayer; and yet in the following lines he enquires who these strangers
are? We can scarce imagine *Nestor* ignorant that the son of *Ulysses* was named
Telemachus, there being so strict a friendship between *Nestor* and *Ulysses*. Perhaps
therefore *Minerva* pray'd in secret mentally; or perhaps *Nestor* might not take
notice of what was not addrest immediately to him, and consequently make
enquiry about it for the greater certainty.

And crown our voyage with desir'd success.   75
  Thus she; and having paid the rite divine,
Gave to *Ulysses'* son the rosie wine.
Suppliant he pray'd. And now the victims drest
They draw, they part, and celebrate the feast.
The banquet done, the Narrative old man   80
Thus mild, the pleasing conference began.
  Now, gentle guests! the genial banquet o'er,
It fits to ask ye, what your native shore,
And whence your race? on what adventure, say,
Thus far ye wander thro' the watry way?   85
Relate, if business, or the thirst of gain
Engage your journey o'er the pathless main?
Where savage Pyrates seek thro' seas unknown
The lives of others, vent'rous of their own.
  Urg'd by the precepts by the Goddess giv'n,   90
And fill'd with confidence infus'd from heav'n,
The Youth, whom *Pallas* destin'd to be wise,
And fam'd among the sons of men, replies.
Enquir'st thou, father! from what coast we came?
(Oh grace and glory of the *Grecian* name!)   95
From where high *Ithaca* o'erlooks the floods,
Brown with o'er-arching shades and pendent woods,

---

86. *Relate, if business or the thirst of gain*, &c.] If we form our images of persons
and actions in antient times, from the images of persons and actions in modern
ages, we shall fall into great mistakes: Thus in the present passage, if we annex
the same idea of Piracy, as it was practis'd three thousand years past, to Piracy
as it is practis'd in our ages; what can be a greater affront than this enquiry of
Nestor? But, says *Eustathius*, Piracy was formerly not only accounted lawful, but
honourable. I doubt not but *Thucydides* had this passage in view when he says,
that the antient Poets introduce men enquiring of those who frequent the sea, if
they be pirates, as a thing no way ignominious ⟨I v⟩. *Thucydides* tells us in the
same place that all those who liv'd on the sea-coast, or in the Islands, maintain'd
themselves by frequent inrodes upon unfortify'd towns, and if such piracies were
nobly perform'd they were accounted glorious. *Herodotus* ⟨II 167⟩ also writes, that
many of the antients, especially about *Thrace*, thought it ignominious to live by
labouring the ground, but to live by piracy and plunder was esteem'd a life of
honour. *Eustathius*.

Us to these shores our filial duty draws,
A private sorrow, not a publick cause.
My sire I seek, where-e'er the voice of fame   100
Has told the glories of his noble name,
The great *Ulysses*; fam'd from shore to shore
For valour much, for hardy suff'ring more.
Long time with thee before proud *Ilion*'s wall
In arms he fought; with thee beheld her fall.   105
Of all the Chiefs, this Heroe's fate alone
Has *Jove* reserv'd, unheard of, and unknown;
Whether in fields by hostile fury slain,
Or sunk by tempests in the gulphy main?
Of this to learn, opprest with tender fears   110
Lo at thy knee his suppliant son appears.
If or thy certain eye, or curious ear,
Have learnt his fate, the whole dark story clear:
And oh! whate'er heav'n destin'd to betide
Let neither flatt'ry smooth, nor pity hide.   115
Prepar'd I stand: he was but born to try
The lot of man; to suffer, and to die.
Oh then, if ever thro' the ten years war
The wise, the good *Ulysses* claim'd thy care;
If e'er he join'd thy council, or thy sword,   120
True in his deed, and constant to his word;
Far as thy mind thro' backward time can see, ⎫
Search all thy stores of faithful memory: ⎬
'Tis sacred truth I ask, and ask of thee.   ⎭
    To him experienc'd *Nestor* thus rejoin'd.   125

125. *The speech of* Nestor.] *Eustathius* observes the modesty of *Nestor: Tele-machus* had ascrib'd the fall of *Troy* in a great measure to *Nestor*; but *Nestor* speaks not in particular of himself, but is content with his share of glory in common with other warriors; he speaks in the plural number, and joyns all the *Greeks* as in the war, so in the glory of it. *Nestor* speaks of the sufferings of the *Greeks* by sea, as well as by land, during the siege of *Troy:* To understand this, it is necessary to re-member, that the *Greeks* made many expeditions against other places during the war both by sea and land, as appears from many passages in the *Iliads*, particu-larly from what *Achilles* says in the ninth book.

O friend! what sorrows dost thou bring to mind?
Shall I the long, laborious scenes review,
And open all the wounds of *Greece* anew?
What toils by sea! where dark in quest of prey
Dauntless we rov'd; *Achilles* led the way: 130
What toils by land! where mixt in fatal fight
Such numbers fell, such Heroes sunk to night:
There *Ajax* great, *Achilles* there the brave,
There wise *Patroclus*, fill an early grave:
There too my son—ah once my best delight,   135
Once swift of foot, and terrible in fight,
In whom stern courage with soft virtue join'd,
A faultless body, and a blameless mind:
Antilochus—what more can I relate?
How trace the tedious series of our fate?   140
Not added years on years my task could close,
The long historian of my country's woes:
Back to thy native Islands might'st thou sail,
And leave half-heard the melancholy tale.
Nine painful years, on that detested shore   145
What stratagems we form'd, what toils we bore?
Still lab'ring on, 'till scarce at last we found
Great *Jove* propitious, and our conquest crown'd.

---

133. *There* Ajax *great,* Achilles *there the brave.*] I have observ'd that the Poet
inserts into the *Odyssey* several incidents that happen'd after the fall of *Troy,* and
by that method agreeably diversifies his Poetry, and satisfies the curiosity of the
Reader: *Eustathius* remarks here, that he gives a title of honour to all the Heroes
he mentions but only to *Achilles. Achilles* had been the occasion of the sufferings
and death of many of the *Greeks* by his anger, and obstinacy in refusing to obey
Agamemnon; therefore while *Nestor* is lamenting the calamities of the *Greeks,* he
passes over *Achilles* without any honourable mention, who had so greatly added
to their sufferings. But I think this remark chimerical: one may as well say
Achilles needed no Epithet to distinguish him. ⟨*12° has* except *for* but *in l. 5*⟩

It is with pleasure I see the old man dwell upon the praise of *Antilochus:* The
father enlarges upon the fame of the son; he gives him four epithets of glory; and
while *Ajax* is only praised as a warrior, *Antilochus* is great and good, excellent in
the standing fight, or swift to pursue an enemy. *Longinus* has observ'd upon the
beauty of this passage ⟨IX 12⟩.

Far o'er the rest thy mighty father shin'd,
In wit, in prudence, and in force of mind.   150
Art thou the son of that illustrious sire?
With joy I grasp thee, and with love admire:
So like your voices, and your words so wise,
Who finds thee younger must consult his eyes.
Thy Sire and I were one; nor vary'd aught   155
In publick sentence, or in private thought;
Alike to Council or th' Assembly came,
With equal souls, and sentiments the same.
But when (by wisdom won) proud *Ilion* burn'd,
And in their ships the conqu'ring *Greeks* return'd;   160
'Twas God's high will the victors to divide,
And turn th' event, confounding human pride:
Some he destroy'd, some scatter'd as the dust,
(Not all were prudent, and not all were just)
Then *Discord*, sent by *Pallas* from above,   165

---

149. *Far o'er the rest thy mighty father shin'd.*] *Nestor* speaks of *Ulysses* as an inseparable friend; and it shews an excellent disposition in them both, to be rivals, and yet without envy. But the art of *Nestor* is remarkable, he first gives the character to *Ulysses* of being superior in wisdom to all the *Greeks*; and yet at last he finds a way secretly to set himself on a level with him, if not above him; We ever, says he, thought the same thoughts, and were ever of the same sentiments: which tho' it may imply that they were of equal wisdom; yet there is room left for it to signify, that *Ulysses* always assented to the wisdom of *Nestor*. *Eustathius.*

157. *The Council or the Assembly.*] There is a remarkable difference between βουλή and ἀγορά. The former denotes a select number of men assembled in council; the latter a public assembly where all the people were present. *Eustathius.*

165. *Sent by* Pallas—] *Nestor* in modesty conceals the reason of the anger of the Goddess; out of respect to *Ajax* the *Locrian* who was then dead: The crime of *Ajax* was the violation of *Cassandra* even in the Temple of *Minerva* before her image. But why should the Goddess be angry at others for the crime of *Ajax*? this is because they omitted to punish the offender. If *Ajax* was criminal in offending, others are criminal for not punishing the offence. *Eustathius.*

The crime of *Ajax* is mentioned in *Virgil. Æn.* 1 ⟨39–41⟩.

Pallasne exurere classem
Argivum, atque ipsos potuit submergere ponto,
Unius ob noxam, & furias Ajacis Oilei? &c.

Could angry *Pallas* with revengeful spleen

(Stern daughter of the great Avenger *Jove*)
The Brother-Kings inspir'd with fell debate;
Who call'd to council all th'*Achaian* state,
But call'd untimely (not the sacred rite
Observ'd, nor heedful of the setting light,   170
Nor herald sworn, the session to proclaim)
Sour with debauch, a reeling tribe, they came.
To these the cause of meeting they explain,
And *Menelaus* moves to cross the main;
Not so the King of Men: he will'd to stay;   175
The sacred rites and hecatombs to pay,
And calm *Minerva*'s wrath. Oh blind to fate!
The Gods not lightly change their love, or hate.
With ire-full taunts each other they oppose,
'Till in loud tumult all the *Greeks* arose: 180
Now diff'rent counsels ev'ry breast divide,
Each burns with rancour to the adverse side.
Th' unquiet night strange projects entertain'd;

> The *Græcian* navy burn, and drown the men;
> She for the fault of one offending foe,
> The bolts of *Jove* himself presum'd to throw.   *Dryden* ⟨60–3⟩.

Virgil borrow'd the description of the punishment of *Ajax* from the 4th of the *Odyssey*.

168, &c.   *Who call'd to council—*
                       But call'd untimely, &c.]

It may seem at first view, that the Poet affirms the night to be an improper season to convene a Council. This is not his meaning; In the *Iliad*, there are several councils by night; nay, ἐν νυκτὶ βουλὴ is used proverbially to express the best-concerted councils. What therefore *Nestor* here condemns is the calling not a select, but public assembly of the soldiers in the night; when they are in no danger of an enemy, and when they are apt to fly into insolence thro' wine, and the joy of victory. The night is then undoubtedly an ill chosen season; because the licence of the soldier cannot be so well restrain'd by night as by day. *Eustathius*.

177. *Oh blind to fate!*] It may be ask'd why *Nestor* condemns so solemnly this Heroe, calling him Νήπιος, when he describes him in so pious an action? this is not because the Gods are implacable, for as *Homer* himself writes ⟨*Il.* IX 497⟩, Στρεπτοὶ δέ τε καὶ θεοὶ αὐτοί; but because he vainly imagin'd that they would so soon be appeas'd, without any justice done upon the offender: Θεὸν ῥᾳδίως παλίντροπον are the words of *Eustathius*.

(So *Jove*, that urg'd us to our fate, ordain'd.)
We, with the rising morn our ships unmoor'd,   185
And brought our captives and our stores aboard;
But half the people with respect obey'd
The King of Men, and at his bidding stay'd.
Now on the wings of winds our course we keep,
(For God had smooth'd the waters of the deep)   190
For *Tenedos* we spread our eager oars,
There land, and pay due victims to the pow'rs:
To bless our safe return we join in pray'r,
But angry *Jove* dispers'd our vows in air,
And rais'd new discord. Then (so Heav'n decreed)   195
Ulysses first and *Nestor* dis-agreed:
Wise as he was, by various Counsels sway'd,
He there, tho' late, to please the Monarch, stay'd.
But I, determin'd, stem the foamy floods,
Warn'd of the coming fury of the Gods.   200
With us *Tydides* fear'd, and urg'd his haste:
And *Menelaus* came, but came the last.
He join'd our vessels in the *Lesbian* bay,
While yet we doubted of our watry way;
If to the right to urge the pilot's toil,   205
(The safer road) beside the *Psyrian* isle;
Or the strait course to rocky *Chios* plow,

197.   *Wise as he was, by various Counsels sway'd,*
            He there, tho' late, to please the Monarch, stay'd.]
It is with great address that *Nestor* relates the return of *Ulysses* to *Agamemnon*; he
ascribes it not directly to *Ulysses*, but to his associates in the voyage; he mollifies
it, in complaisance to *Telemachus*. But *Nestor*, according to *Dacier*, conceals the
true reason of his return; it was not to please *Agamemnon*, but out of fear of the
Goddess *Minerva*, whose statue he had taken by force from *Troy*: to appease that
Goddess, he returns to joyn in sacrifice with *Agamemnon*. *Eustathius*.
    200. *Warn'd of the coming fury of the Gods.*] It may be ask'd how *Nestor* attain'd
this knowledge of the evils which the Gods were preparing? *Eustathius* ascribes it
to his great Wisdom, which gave him an insight into futurity. *Dacier* with more
reason tells us, that *Nestor* knew that *Minerva* had been offended, and might consequently apprehend a punishment was to be inflicted for the offence.

And anchor under *Mimas'* shaggy brow?
We sought direction of the pow'r divine:
The God propitious gave the guiding sign;   210
Thro' the mid seas he bids our navy steer,
And in *Eubea* shun the woes we fear.
The whistling winds already wak'd the sky;
Before the whistling winds the vessels fly,
With rapid swiftness cut the liquid way,   215
And reach *Gerestus* at the point of day.
There hecatombs of bulls to *Neptune* slain
High-flaming please the monarch of the main.
The fourth day shone, when all their labours o'er
Tydides' vessels touch'd the wish'd-for shore: 220
But I to *Pylos* scud before the gales,
The God still breathing on my swelling sails;
Sep'rate from all, I safely landed here;
Their fates or fortunes never reach'd my ear.
Yet what I learn'd, attend; as here I sate, ⎫   225
And ask'd each voyager each Hero's fate; ⎬
Curious to know, and willing to relate. ⎭
    Safe reach'd the *Mirmydons* their native land,
Beneath *Achilles'* warlike son's command.

---

   221. *But I to* Pylos, &c.] *Eustathius* observes from the Antients, that the Poet
with great judgment suspends, and breaks off this relation of *Nestor*; by this
method he has an opportunity to carry *Telemachus* to other countries, and insert
into his Poem the story of *Menelaus* and *Helen*: This method likewise gives an air
of probability to what he writes; the Poet seems afraid to deceive, and when he
sends *Telemachus* to other parts for better intelligence, he seems to consult truth
and exactness.
   229. Achilles' *warlike son*.] The son of *Achilles* was nam'd *Neoptolemus*, by others
Pyrrhus; his story is this: When he had reach'd *Thessaly* with the *Myrmidons* of
Achilles, by the advice of *Thetis* he set fire to his vessels: And being warn'd by
Helenus, from the Oracles, to fix his habitation where he found a house whose
foundations were iron, whose walls were wood, and whose roof was wool; he took
his journey on foot, and coming to a certain lake of *Epirus*, he found some persons
fixing their spears with the points downwards into the earth, and covering the
tops of them with their cloaks, and after this manner making their tents: he
look'd upon the Oracle as fulfill'd, and dwelt there. Afterwards having a son by

Those, whom the heir of great *Apollo*'s art   230
Brave *Philoctetes*, taught to wing the dart;
And those whom *Idomen* from *Ilion*'s plain
Had led, securely crost the dreadful main.
How *Agamemnon* touch'd his *Argive* coast,
And how his life by fraud and force he lost,   235
And how the Murd'rer pay'd his forfeit breath;
What lands so distant from that scene of death
But trembling heard the Fame? and heard, admire
How well the son appeas'd his slaughter'd sire!
Ev'n to th' unhappy, that unjustly bleed,   240
Heav'n gives Posterity, t'avenge the deed.
So fell *Ægysthus*; and may'st thou, my friend,
(On whom the virtues of thy sire descend)
Make future times thy equal act adore,
And be, what brave *Orestes* was before!   245
    The prudent youth reply'd. Oh thou, the grace
And lasting glory of the *Grecian* race!
Just was the vengeance, and to latest days
Shall long posterity resound the praise.
Some God this arm with equal prowess bless!   250
And the proud Suitors shall its force confess:
Injurious men! who while my soul is sore
Of fresh affronts, are meditating more.
But heav'n denies this honour to my hand,

Andromache the wife of *Hector*, he nam'd him *Molossus*; from whom the region took
the name of *Molossia*. From this country are the *Molossi canes*, mention'd by
Virgil ⟨*Geo.* iii 403–4⟩. *Eustathius.*

242. *So fell Ægysthus; and may'st thou, my friend,* &c.] *Nestor* introduces the mention of *Ægisthus* very artfully; it is to raise an emulation in *Telemachus* to revenge
Ulysses, as *Orestes* had *Agamemnon*; it has the intended effect, and we find that
Telemachus dwells upon his story with a virtuous envy; yet at the same time with
great modesty: *Eustathius* gives us a different reading in
    —ἐσσομένοισι πυθέσθαι, or,
    —ἐσσομένοισιν ἀοιδήν.
both the expressions are used in *Homer*, the preference is therefore submitted to
the Reader.

E

Nor shall my father repossess the land: 255
The father's fortune never to return,
And the sad son's, to suffer and to mourn!

Thus he, and *Nestor* took the word: My son,
Is it then true, as distant rumours run,
That crowds of rivals for thy mother's charms   260
Thy Palace fill with insults and alarms?
Say, is the fault, thro' tame submission, thine? ⎫
Or leagu'd against thee, do thy people join,   ⎬
Mov'd by some Oracle, or voice divine?   ⎭
And yet who knows, but ripening lies in fate   265
An hour of vengeance for th' afflicted state;
When great *Ulysses* shall suppress these harms,
Ulysses singly, or all *Greece* in arms.

264. *Mov'd by some Oracle, or voice divine.*] The words in the original are, *follow-ing the voice of some God,* that is, some Oracle: *Homer* does not confine the expression either to a good or bad sense, but the context plainly shews, that they must be understood in a bad sense; namely to imply, that the people had recourse to pre-tended Oracles to justify their rebellion. This is evident from what follows, where *Nestor* encourages *Telemachus* to expect that *Ulysses* may punish them for their crimes, ἀποτίσεται ἐλθών—if there had been no crime, there ought to be no punishment.

268. Ulysses *singly, or all* Greece *in arms.*] The Poet shews his great judgment in preparing the Reader for the destruction of the Suitors: that great Catastrophe is manag'd by few hands, and it might seem incredible that so few could destroy so many: the Poet therefore to give an air of truth to his action, frequently incul-cates the assistance of *Pallas,* which must at least shew that such a great exploit is not impossible to be executed by stratagems and valour: It is by art, not strength, that *Ulysses* conquers.

All Greece *in arms.*

This is spoken in a general sense, and comprehends not only the subjects of *Ulysses,* or even the *Pylians* and *Spartans,* but implies that all the *Greeks* would rise in the cause of *Ulysses.* What the Suitors had spoken scoffingly in the preceding book, *viz.* that *Telemachus* was sailing to *Pyle* or *Sparta* for *supplies,* appears in this not to be impracticable; so that it was choice and not necessity that determin'd the Poet to make use of no such easy expedients for the destruction of the Suitors. *Eustathius.*

It may be added, that the very nature of Epic Poetry, and of the *Odyssey* in par-ticular, requires such a conduct: In the *Iliad Achilles* is the chief agent, and per-forms almost all the great actions; *Æneas* is painted after the same manner by

But if *Athena*, War's triumphant maid,
The happy son, will, as the father, aid, 270
(Whose fame and safety was her constant care
In ev'ry danger and in ev'ry war:
Never on man did heav'nly favour shine
With rays so strong, distinguish'd, and divine,
As those with which *Minerva* mark'd thy sire) 275
So might she love thee, so thy soul inspire!
Soon shou'd their hopes in humble dust be laid,
And long oblivion of the bridal bed.
　　Ah! no such hope (the Prince with sighs replies)
Can touch my breast; that blessing heav'n denies. 280
Ev'n by celestial favour were it giv'n,
Fortune or fate wou'd cross the will of heav'n.

Virgil; the one kills *Hector*, the other *Turnus*, both which are the decisive actions: It was equally necessary to exalt the character of *Ulysses*, by bringing him into difficulties from which he is personally to extricate himself: This the Poet sufficiently brings about by refusing all the easy methods for his re-establishment, because the more difficult ways are most conducive to the honour of his Heroe: Thus as *Achilles* and *Æneas* kill *Hector* and *Turnus* with their own hands, so the Suitors fall chiefly by the hand of *Ulysses*: It is necessary for the Heroe of the Poem to execute the decisive action, for by this method the Poet compleats his character, his own greatness surmounts all difficulties, and he goes off the stage with the utmost advantage, by leaving a noble character upon the mind of the spectators.

　　282. *Fortune or fate wou'd cross the will of heav'n.*] It may be ask'd how an expression so near blasphemy, as *Eustathius* observes, could escape a person of such piety as *Telemachus*? 'Tis true, the Poet makes *Minerva* herself correct it; but yet the objection remains, *viz.* how could *Telemachus* speak it? I think since the Poet himself condemns it, we may give it up as an indecency in *Telemachus*; it is natural for men in despair (and that was the condition of *Telemachus*) to use a vehemence of expression, and this might transport *Telemachus* beyond the bounds of prudence. The only possible way that occurs to me to take off the impiety is to have recourse to Destiny: It was the opinion of the Antients, that the Gods could not alter Destiny: and then *Telemachus* may mean no more, than that it was decreed by the Destinies that *Ulysses* shall return no more, so the Gods themselves could not restore him.

　　Thus in the 15th of the *Metamorphoses*, *Venus* in vain applies to the Gods to preserve *Julius Cæsar* ⟨780-1⟩.

　　　　—*Superosque movet, qui rumpere quamquam*

What words are these, and what imprudence thine?
(Thus interpos'd the Martial maid divine)
Forgetful youth! but know, the Pow'r above   285
With ease can save each object of his love;
Wide as his will, extends his boundless grace;
Nor lost in time, nor circumscrib'd by place.
Happier his lot, who, many sorrows past,
Long-lab'ring gains his natal shore at last;   290
Than who too speedy, hastes to end his life
By some stern ruffian, or adultrous wife.
Death only is the lot which none can miss,
And all is possible to heav'n, but this.
The best, the dearest fav'rite of the sky   295
Must taste that cup, for man is born to die.

  Thus check'd, reply'd *Ulysses'* prudent heir:
Mentor, no more—the mournful thought forbear;
For he no more must draw his country's breath,
Already snatch'd by Fate, and the black doom of death!
Pass we to other subjects; and engage   301

Ferrea non possunt veterum decreta sororum, &c.
And a little lower *Jupiter* says to *Venus* ⟨807-8⟩,
            —*Sola insuperabile fatum,*
         Nata, movere paras?
  289. ⟨For Pope's note on this line see p. 460 below.⟩
  294. *And all is possible to heav'n, but this.*] What *Minerva* here says justifies the
remark I made, that what *Telemachus* seem'd to have spoken rashly, may be
soften'd if not vindicated by having recourse to Destiny: It is evident from this
passage that Destiny was superior to the power of the Gods; otherwise *Minerva*
speaks as blasphemously as *Telemachus*: For what difference is there between
saying, that the Gods cannot preserve even these they love from death, and saying that the Gods could not save *Ulysses*? Why therefore may not the words of
Telemachus be thought to have respect to Destiny?
  I am of opinion, that the Poet had something further in view by putting these
words into the mouth of *Minerva*: The words of *Telemachus*, if taken grosly, might
appear shocking to so pious a person as *Nestor*, and make an ill impression upon
him to the disadvantage of *Telemachus*; *Minerva* therefore artfully explains it, and
softens the horrour of it by reconciling it to the Theology of those ages.
  301. *Pass we to other subjects*—] *Telemachus* here puts several questions, as it were

On themes remote the venerable Sage:
(Who thrice has seen the perishable kind
Of men decay, and thro' three Ages shin'd,
Like Gods majestic, and like Gods in mind.)   305
For much he knows, and just conclusions draws
From various precedents, and various laws.
O son of *Neleus*! awful *Nestor*, tell
How he, the mighty, *Agamemnon* fell?
By what strange fraud *Ægysthus* wrought, relate,   310
(By force he could not) such a Heroe's fate?
Liv'd *Menelaus* not in *Greece?* or where
Was then the martial brother's pious care?
Condemn'd perhaps some foreign shore to tread;
Or sure *Ægysthus* had not dar'd the deed.   315
   To whom the Full of Days. Illustrious youth,

---

in a breath, to *Nestor*; and *Plutarch* observes upon this passage, that he who enquires any thing of an old man, tho' the old man himself has no concern in the story, wins his heart at once; and incites a person, who is upon all occasions very willing to discourse. He introduces this as an instance of the art *Telemachus* uses, in adapting himself by his questions to the temper of the person with whom he converses: He puts together, continues he, several questions upon several subjects, which is more judicious than to confine his answer to a single interrogatory, and by that method deprive *Nestor* of one of the most pleasant enjoyments of old age, I mean the pleasure of talking. *Plutarch Symposiac.* ⟨*Quaest. Conviv.* II i 3 (631)⟩.

   303.   *Who thrice has seen the perishable kind*
                         Of men decay—]
The Poet here tells us that *Nestor* was now in his fourth generation: *Ovid* took the word γένεα to signify an hundred years ⟨*Metam.* XII 186-7⟩; but then *Nestor* must have been above 300 years old. Others with more probability understand it to signify a generation, or such a portion of time in which any race of men flourish together, which is computed to be about thirty years. I refer the Reader to the Note upon the 333d verse in the first book of the *Iliad*, for the particular age of *Nestor*. According to that computation, he must now be about ninety five years of age.

   309. *How he, the mighty,* Agamemnon *fell?*] *Telemachus* does not ask this question out of curiosity, but with great judgment; he knows there were designs against his life, as well as there had been against *Agamemnon*; he therefore asks it, that he may learn how to defeat them; chiefly to instruct himself how best to assist his father upon his return, by aiding him in escaping the snares of the Suitors. *Dacier.*

Attend (tho' partly thou hast guest) the truth.
For had the martial *Menelaus* found
The ruffian breathing yet on *Argive* ground;
Nor earth had hid his carcase from the skies,   320
Nor *Grecian* virgins shriek'd his obsequies,
But fowls obscene dismember'd his remains,
And dogs had torn him on the naked plains.
While us the works of bloody *Mars* employ'd,
The wanton youth inglorious peace enjoy'd;   325
He, stretch'd at ease in *Argos*' calm recess,
(Whose stately steeds luxuriant pastures bless)
With flattery's insinuating art
Sooth'd the frail Queen, and poyson'd all her heart.
At first with worthy shame and decent pride,   330
The royal dame his lawless suit deny'd.
For Virtue's image yet possest her mind,
Taught by a Master of the tuneful kind:
Atrides, parting for the *Trojan* war,
Consign'd the youthful Consort to his care;   335

---

333. *Taught by a Master of the tuneful kind.*] *Homer* thro' the whole *Odyssey* speaks much in honour of the Art which he himself loved, and in which he so eminently excell'd: From these and other passages, we may learn the state of Poetry in those ages: "Poets (says *Eustathius*) were rank'd in the class of Philosophers; and the Ancients made use of them as Præceptors in Music and Morality." *Strabo* ⟨1 ii 3⟩ quotes this very passage as an instance of the excellence of Poetry in forming the soul to worthy actions: *Ægisthus* could not debauch *Clytemnestra*, 'till he banish'd the Poet, who was her guide and instructor.

Various are the conjectures of the Ancients about the name of the Bard here celebrated: Some, says *Eustathius*, tell us, it was *Chariades*, some *Demodocus*, some *Glaucus*, &c. but I pass them over, because they are conjectures.

There were many degrees of these ἀοιδοὶ; some were ἀοιδοὶ θρήνων, others ἀοιδοὶ περὶ γάμους: But such Bards as are here mention'd were of an higher station, and retain'd as instructors by Kings and Princes.

I cannot omit one remark of *Eustathius*: he tells us, that some persons write that these ἀοιδοὶ had their names from hence, ὡς αἰδοῖα μὴ ἔχοντες; exactly resembling the modern *Italian* singers: Madam *Dacier* is not to be forgiven for passing over a remark of such importance; if this be true, it makes a great difference between the antient and modern Poets, and is the only advantage I know we have over them.

True to his charge, the Bard preserv'd her long
In honour's limits (such the pow'r of Song)
But when the Gods these objects of their hate
Dragg'd to destruction, by the links of fate;
The bard they banish'd from his native soil,   340
And left all helpless in a desart Isle:
There he, the sweetest of the sacred train,
Sung dying to the rocks, but sung in vain.
Then Virtue was no more (her guard away)
She fell, to lust a voluntary prey.   345
Ev'n to the temple stalk'd th' adult'rous spouse,
With impious thanks and mockery of vows,
With images, with garments, and with gold,
And od'rous fumes from loaded altars roll'd.

Mean time from flaming *Troy* we cut the way,   350
With *Menelaus*, thro' the curling sea.
But when to *Sunium*'s sacred point we came,
Crown'd with the temple of th' *Athenian* dame;
Atrides' pilot, *Phrontes*, there expir'd;
(*Phrontes*, of all the sons of men admir'd   355
To steer the bounding bark with steddy toil,
When the storm thickens, and the billows boil)
While yet he exercis'd the steerman's art,

344.   *Then Virtue was no more (her guard away)*
              She fell,— &c.]
There is a fine moral couch'd in the story of the Bard and *Clytemnestra*; it admirably paints the advantage we draw from wise companions for the improvement
of our Virtues: *Clytemnestra* was chaste because her instructor was wise: His wisdom was an insuperable guard to her modesty. It was long before she yielded;
virtue and honour had a long contest: but she no sooner yielded to adultery, but
she assisted in the murder of her husband; from whence we may draw another
moral, that one vice betrays us into another, and when once the fences of honour
are thrown down, we become a prey to every passion. *Dacier.*

346. *Ev'n to the temple stalk'd th' adult'rous spouse.*] Here is a surprizing mixture of
religion and impiety: *Ægisthus*, upon the accomplishment of so great a crime as
adultery, returns thanks to the Gods by oblations, as if they had assisted him in
the execution of it. *Nestor* dwells upon it at large, to shew that *Ægisthus* greatly
aggravated his guilt by such a piece of impious devotion. *Dacier.*

Apollo touch'd him with his gentle dart;
Ev'n with the rudder in his hand, he fell.   360
To pay whose honours to the Shades of hell
We check'd our haste, by pious office bound,
And laid our old companion in the ground.
And now, the rites discharg'd, our course we keep
Far on the gloomy bosom of the deep: 365
Soon as *Malæa*'s misty tops arise,
Sudden the Thund'rer blackens all the skies,
And the winds whistle, and the surges roll
Mountains on mountains, and obscure the pole.
The tempest scatters, and divides our fleet;   370
Part, the storm urges on the coast of *Creet*,
Where winding round the rich *Cydonian* plain,
The streams of *Jardan* issue to the main.
There stands a rock, high eminent and steep,
Whose shaggy brow o'erhangs the shady deep,   375
And views *Gortyna* on the western side;
On this, rough *Auster* drove th' impetuous tyde:

---

359. Apollo *touch'd him with his gentle dart*.] *Homer* calls the darts of *Apollo* ἀγανά, or gentle; to signify that those who dye thus suddenly, dye without pain. *Eustathius.*

Dacier complains that some Critics think *Homer* worthy of blame for enlarging upon so mean a person as a pilot, and giving us his genealogy. It is a sufficient answer to observe, that arts were in high esteem in those times, and men that were eminent in them were in great honour. Neither were arts then confin'd as in these ages to mean personages: no less a person than *Ulysses* builds a vessel in the sequel of the *Odyssey*; so that this is a false piece of delicacy. If *Homer* be culpable, so is *Virgil*; he gives the genealogy of *Palinurus* ⟨v 843⟩, as well as *Homer* of *Phrontis*. *Virgil*'s description is censur'd as too long, *Homer* concludes his in seven lines; and lastly, *Virgil*'s Episode has been judg'd by the Critics to be an unnecessary ornament, and to contribute nothing to the Poem: *Homer* relates the death of *Phrontis*, to introduce the dispersion of the fleet of *Menelaus*; the fleet might well be scatter'd, when it wanted so excellent a pilot.

371. *Part, the storm urges on the coast of* Crete.] *Homer* does not amuse us by relating what became of these companions of *Menelaus*; he omits this judiciously, and follows the thread of his story: *Menelaus* is the person whom the Poet has in view; he therefore passes over the story of his companions, to carry on the fable of the Poem by leading us directly to *Menelaus*.

With broken force the billows rowl'd away,
And heav'd the fleet into the neighb'ring bay.
Thus sav'd from death they gain'd the *Phæstan* shores,
With shatter'd vessels, and disabled oars: 381
But five tall barks the winds and waters tost
Far from their fellows, on th' *Ægyptian* coast.
There wander'd *Menelaus* thro' foreign shores,
Amassing gold, and gath'ring naval stores;   385
While curst *Ægysthus* the detested deed
By fraud fulfill'd, and his great brother bled.
Sev'n years, the traytor rich *Mycenæ* sway'd,
And his stern rule the groaning land obey'd;
The eighth, from *Athens* to his realm restor'd,   390
Orestes brandish'd the revenging sword,
Slew the dire pair, and gave to fun'ral flame
The vile assassin, and adult'rous dame.
That day, ere yet the bloody triumphs cease,
Return'd *Atrides* to the coast of *Greece*,   395
And safe to *Argos*' port his navy brought,
With gifts of price and pond'rous treasure fraught.

---

383. —*On th' Ægyptian coast.*] In the original it is, *The wind and water carry'd them to Ægyptus. Homer* by *Ægyptus* means the river *Nile*, and then it is always used in the masculine gender; the region about it took its name from the river *Ægyptus*, this is always used in the feminine gender; but the country had not receiv'd that name in the days of *Homer*. *Eustathius.*

What *Dacier* adds to this observation, may assist in determining the dispute concerning the priority of *Homer* and *Hesiod: Hesiod* makes mention of the river *Nilus* ⟨*Theogony* 338⟩; if therefore it be true that *Ægyptus* had not been called by the name of *Nilus* in the times of *Homer*, it is a demonstration that *Hesiod* was posterior to *Homer*; otherwise he could not have been acquainted with any other name but that of *Ægyptus*.

390. *From* Athens *to his realm*—.] There is a different reading in this place: instead of ἀπ' ᾿Αθηνάων, some write ἀπὸ Φωκήων; for *Orestes* was educated by *Strophius* King of *Phocis*, and father of *Pylades*: The Ancients reconcile the difference, by saying that *Orestes* might be sent from *Phocis* to *Athens* for his education, and returning thence to his own country, might revenge the death of his father *Agamemnon*; so that although he was first bred up in *Phocis*, he was afterwards a sojourner in *Athens*. *Eustathius.*

E*

Hence warn'd, my son beware! nor idly stand
Too long a stranger to thy native land;
Lest heedless absence wear thy wealth away,   400
While lawless feasters in thy palace sway;
Perhaps may seize thy realm, and share the spoil; ⎞
And thou return, with disappointed toil,   ⎟
From thy vain journey, to a rifled Isle.   ⎠
Howe'er, my friend, indulge one labour more,   405
And seek *Atrides* on the *Spartan* shore.
He, wand'ring long, a wider circle made,
And many-languag'd nations has survey'd;
And measur'd tracts unknown to other ships,
Amid the monstrous wonders of the deeps;   410
(A length of Ocean and unbounded sky,
Which scarce the sea-fowl in a year o'erfly)
Go then; to *Sparta* take the watry way,
Thy ship and sailors but for orders stay;
Or if by land thou chuse thy course to bend,   415
My steeds, my chariots, and my sons attend:
Thee to *Atrides* they shall safe convey,

411.   *A length of Ocean and unbounded sky,*
            Which scarce the sea-fowl in a year o'erfly.]
It must be confest, that *Nestor* greatly exaggerates this description: *Homer* himself tells us, that a ship may sail in five days from *Crete* to *Ægypt*; wherefore then this Hyperbole of *Nestor*? It might perhaps be to deter *Telemachus* from a design of sailing to *Crete*, and he through his inexperience might believe the description. It may be added, that what *Nestor* speaks concerning the flight of birds, may be only said to shew the great distance of that sea: Nay, by a favourable interpretation it may be reconcil'd to truth; the meaning then must be this: Should a person observe that sea a whole year, he would not see one bird flying over it, both because of the vastness and dreadfulness of it; and perhaps the whole of this might arise from the observation, that this sea is not frequented by birds. This is wholly and almost literally taken from *Eustathius*; and if we add to this the ignorance of the sea and sea-affairs in those ages, we shall the less wonder to hear so wise a man as *Nestor* describing it with so much terror; Navigation is now greatly improv'd, and the Moderns sail further in a month, than the Ancients could in a year; their whole art consisting chiefly in coasting along the shores, and consequently they made but little way.

Guides of thy road, companions of thy way.
Urge him with truth to frame his free replies,
And sure he will, for *Menelas* is wise.   420
　　　Thus while he speaks, the ruddy sun descends,
And twilight gray her evening shade extends.
Then thus the blue-ey'd Maid: O full of days!
Wise are thy words, and just are all thy ways.
Now immolate the Tongues, and mix the wine,   425
Sacred to *Neptune* and the pow'rs divine.
The lamp of day is quench'd beneath the deep,
And soft approach the balmy hours of sleep:
Nor fits it to prolong the heav'nly feast
Timeless, indecent, but retire to rest.   430

---

425. *Now immolate the Tongues*—.] Various are the reasons which *Eustathius* reports concerning this oblation of the tongues at the conclusion of the sacrifice. It was to purge themselves from any evil words they might have utter'd; or because the tongue was reckon'd the best part of the sacrifice, and so reserv'd for the completion of it; or they offer'd the tongue to the Gods, as witnesses to what they had spoken. I omit the rest as superfluous. They had a custom of offering the tongues to *Mercury*, because they believ'd him the giver of Eloquence. *Dacier* expatiates upon this custom: The people, says she, might fear, lest thro' wine and the joy of the festival they might have utter'd some words unbecoming the sanctity of the occasion: by this sacrifice of the tongues, they signify'd that they purged away whatever they had spoken amiss during the festival; and ask'd in particular pardon of *Mercury*, who presided over discourse; to the end they might not carry home any uncleanness which might stop the blessings expected from the sacrifice.

429. 　　　　　*Nor fits it to prolong the heav'nly feast,*
　　　　　　　Timeless, indecent, &c.—]

Eustathius shews the difference between ἑορταί festivals, and θυσίαι, or sacrifices: in the former it was customary to spend the whole night in wine and rejoicing: In the latter, this was reckon'd an unlawful custom, thro' the fear of falling into any indecencies through wine. He likewise gives another reason of this injunction, by telling us that it was the custom to offer sacrifices to the celestial Powers in the time of the day, and even to finish them about the setting of the sun; and that those who dealt in incantations perform'd their sacrifices to the infernal powers by night, and finish'd them before sun-rising. Either of these reasons sufficiently explains the words of the Goddess; and the former carries in it an excellent moral, that particular care should be taken in our acts of devotion, not to turn religion into impiety. ⟨*12° omits* time of the *in l. 8 of this note*⟩

So spake *Jove*'s daughter, the celestial maid.
The sober train attended and obey'd.
The sacred heralds on their hands around
Pour'd the full urns; the youths the goblets crown'd:
From bowl to bowl the holy bev'rage flows;   435
While to the final sacrifice they rose.
The tongues they cast upon the fragrant flame,
And pour, above, the consecrated stream.
And now, their thirst by copious draughts allay'd,
The youthful Hero and th' *Athenian* maid   440
Propose departure from the finish'd rite,
And in their hollow bark to pass the night:
But this the hospitable Sage denied.
Forbid it, *Jove*! and all the Gods! he cried,
Thus from my walls the much-lov'd son to send   445
Of such a heroe, and of such a friend?
Me, as some needy peasant, would ye leave,
Whom heav'n denies the blessing to relieve?
Me would ye leave, who boast imperial sway,
When beds of royal state invite your stay?   450

---

450. *When beds of royal state invite your stay?*] This passage gives us a full insight
into the manners of these hospitable ages; they not only kept a treasury for bowls
or vases of gold or silver, to give as ξεινήϊα, or gifts of hospitality, but also a wardrobe of various habits and rich furniture, to lodge and bestow upon strangers.
Eustathius relates, that *Tellias* of *Agrigentum* was a person of so great hospitality,
that five hundred horsemen coming to his house in the winter season, he entertain'd them, and gave every man a cloak and a tunic. This laudable custom prevailed, and still prevails, in the eastern countries: it was the practice of *Abraham*
of old ⟨Gen. 18 : 2 ff⟩, and is at this day of the *Turks*, as we may learn from their
Caravansaries, erected for the reception of travellers. And yet *Dacier* observes,
that a *French* Critic has shew'd so ill a taste as to ridicule this passage. "*Telemachus* (says the Author) being entertain'd by *Nestor*, intimates his intention of
returning to lodge on shipboard with his companions: but *Nestor* detains him, by
asking if he thought he had not quilts or coverlets to give him a night's lodging?
Upon this *Telemachus* goes to bed in a resounding gallery, and *Nestor* in a bed
which his wife made ready for him" ⟨Perrault: cf. his *Parallèle* (ed. Paris, 1693),
ii 52⟩. The noblest things are most liable to burlesque, by perverting their meaning; as some pictures, by varying the position, represent a man or a monster. He

No—long as life this mortal shall inspire,
Or as my children imitate their sire,
Here shall the wand'ring stranger find his home,
And hospitable rites adorn the dome.
    Well hast thou spoke (the blue-ey'd maid replies) 455
Belov'd old man! benevolent as wise.
Be the kind dictates of thy heart obey'd,
And let thy words *Telemachus* persuade:
He to thy palace shall thy steps pursue; ⎫
I to the ship, to give the orders due,   ⎬   460
Prescribe directions, and confirm the crew. ⎭
For I alone sustain their naval cares,
Who boast experience from these silver hairs;
All Youths the rest, whom to this journey move
Like years, like tempers, and their Prince's love. 465
There in the vessel shall I pass the night;
And soon as morning paints the fields of light,
I go to challenge, from the *Caucons* bold,
A debt, contracted in the days of old.

---

is very severe upon the resounding gallery, which in truth means no more than very lofty or elevated, and by consequence very noble and magnificent.

    468. *I go to challenge, from the* Caucons.] The Poet makes a double use of these words of the Goddess; she gives an air of probability to her excuse, why she should not be press'd to stay; and at the same time *Homer* avoids the absurdity of introducing that Goddess at *Sparta*, where *Menelaus* and *Helen* are celebrating the nuptials of their son and daughter: *Minerva* is a Virgin Deity, and consequently an enemy to all nuptial ceremonies. *Eustathius*.

    But it may be necessary to observe who these *Caucons* are: we find in the tenth book the *Caucons* mention'd as auxiliaries to *Troy:* There *Dolon* says

        The Carians, Caucons, *the* Pelasgian *host,*
        And Leleges *encamp along the coast.*

Are these *Caucons* the same with those here mention'd? *Eustathius* informs us, that there was a people of *Triphylia*, between *Elis* and *Pylos*, named *Caucons:* But *Strabo* says ⟨VIII iii 11, 17⟩, that the whole race is now extinct, and that these here mention'd are of *Dymæa*, and take their name from the river *Caucon:* whereas those in the *Iliads* are *Paphlagonians:* they were a wandring nation, and consequently might be the same people originally, and retain the same name in different countries.

> But this thy guest, receiv'd with friendly care,   470
> Let thy strong coursers swift to *Sparta* bear;
> Prepare thy chariot at the dawn of day,
> And be thy son companion of his way.
>   Then turning with the word, *Minerva* flies,
> And soars an Eagle thro' the liquid skies.   475
> Vision divine! The throng'd spectators gaze
> In holy wonder fixt, and still amaze.
> But chief the rev'rend Sage admir'd; he took
> The hand of young *Telemachus*, and spoke.
>   O happy Youth! and favour'd of the skies,   480
> Distinguish'd care of guardian deities!

478. *But chief the rev'rend Sage admir'd—*] It may be ask'd why *Nestor* is in such a surprize at the discovery of the Goddess: It is evident from the *Iliad*, that he had been no stranger to such intercourses of the Deities; nay, in this very book *Nestor* tells us, that *Ulysses* enjoy'd almost the constant presence of *Minerva*; insomuch that *Sophocles*, the great imitator of *Homer*, relates, that he knew the Goddess by her voice, without seeing her ⟨*Ajax* 14–17⟩. *Eustathius* answers, that the wonder of *Nestor* arose not from the discovery of that Deity, but that she should accompany so young a person as *Telemachus*: After her departure, the old man stood amaz'd, and look'd upon that Heroe as some very extraordinary person, whom in such early years the Goddess of War and Wisdom had vouchsafed to attend. This interpretation agrees perfectly with what *Nestor* speaks to *Telemachus*.

481. *Distinguish'd care of guardian deities.*] I will take this opportunity to obviate an objection that may be made against all interposition of the Gods in assisting the Heroes of the *Odyssey*: It has been thought by some Critics a disparagement to them to stand in continual need of such supernatural succour: If two persons were engaged in combat, and a third person should immediately step in to the assistance of one of the parties and kill the adversary, would it not reflect upon the valour of his friend who was so weak as to want such assistance? Why, for instance, should *Jupiter* help *Æneas* to kill *Turnus*? Was not he brave enough to fight, and strong enough to conquer his enemy by his own prowess? and would not *Turnus* have kill'd *Æneas* with the same assistance? It is therefore a disparagement to the actors, thus continually to supply the defects of a Heroe, by the power of a Deity.

But this is a false way of arguing, and from hence it might be infer'd that the love and favour of a Deity serves only to make those whom he assists, and those who depend upon such assistance, appear weak, impotent, cowardly, and unworthy to be conquerors. Can any doubt arise whether the love and favour of a God be a disparagement or honour to those whom he favours? According to

Whose early years for future worth engage,
No vulgar manhood, no ignoble age.
For lo! none other of the court above,
Than she, the daughter of almighty *Jove*,   485
Pallas herself, the War-triumphant Maid,
Confest, is thine, as once thy father's aid.
So guide me, Goddess! so propitious shine
On me, my consort, and my royal line!
A yearling bullock to thy name shall smoke,   490
Untam'd, unconscious of the galling yoke;
With ample forehead, and yet tender horns
Whose budding honours ductile gold adorns.
        Submissive thus the hoary Sire preferr'd
His holy vow: the fav'ring Goddess heard.   495
Then slowly rising, o'er the sandy space

these Critics, we should find the character of a perfect Heroe in an impious *Mezentius*, who acknowledges no God but his own arm and his own sword: 'Tis true, the objection would be just if the Heroe himself perform'd nothing of the action; or if when he were almost conquer'd by the superior valour of his enemy, he ow'd his life and victory to Gods and Miracles: But the Heroe always behaves himself in all his actions, as if he were to gain success without the assistance of the Deity; and the presence of the Gods is so order'd, that we may retrench every thing that is miraculous, without making any alteration in the action or character of the human personages. Thus in the instance of *Æneas* and *Turnus*, tho' *Jupiter* favours *Æneas*, yet *Æneas* is painted in stronger colours of fortitude, he appears superior, as a man unassisted, and able to conquer *Turnus*; and consequently the favour of *Jupiter* makes no alteration in the action or character of *Æneas*.

There is likewise a wide difference between the assistance of a Man, and of a God. The actions of men belong only to the performers of those actions, but when a Deity assists us by inspiring us with strength and courage, the actions we perform are really our own, and the more he favours us the more glory he gives us: so that the assistance of man eclipses, but the assistance of a God exalts, our glory. Thus for instance, when *Achilles* is pursuing *Hector*, he charges the *Greeks* to keep off from *Hector*; their assistance might lessen his glory: but when *Pallas* offers her assistance he immediately embraces it as an honour, and boasts of it as such to *Hector*. I have been large upon this objection, because the Reader ought to carry it in his memory thro' the whole Poem, and apply it to every action, in which any share is ascribed to any Deity. See *Bossu* more at large concerning this objection ⟨v vi⟩.

Precedes the father, follow'd by his race,
(A long procession) timely marching home
In comely order to the regal dome.
There then arriv'd, on thrones around him plac'd,   500
His sons and grand-sons the wide circle grac'd.
To these the hospitable Sage, in sign
Of social welcome, mix'd the racy wine,
(Late from the mellowing cask restor'd to light,
By ten long years refin'd, and rosy-bright.)   505
To *Pallas* high the foaming bowl he crown'd,
And sprinkled large Libation on the ground.
Each drinks a full oblivion of his cares,
And to the gifts of balmy sleep repairs.
Deep in a rich Alcove the Prince was laid,   510
And slept beneath the pompous Colonnade;
Fast by his side *Pisistratus* lay spread,
(In age his equal) on a splendid bed:
But in an inner court, securely clos'd,
The rev'rend *Nestor* with his Queen repos'd.   515
    When now *Aurora*, daughter of the dawn,
With rosie lustre purpled o'er the lawn;
The old man early rose, walk'd forth, and sate
On polish'd stone before his Palace gate:
With unguents smooth the lucid marble shone,   520

---

518. *And sate On polish'd stone before his Palace gate.*] We have here an ancient
custom recorded by the Poet; a King places himself before the gate of his Palace
upon a seat of marble, worn smooth by long use, says *Eustathius*, or perhaps
smooth'd exquisitely by the hand of the workman. What I would chiefly observe
is, that they placed themselves thus in public for the dispatch of justice: We read
in the scripture of Judges *sitting in the gate* ⟨Deut. 21 : 19; 22 : 15⟩; and that this
procedure of *Nestor* was for that purpose is probable from the expression, *He sate
in the seat where* Neleus [μήστωρ, or *Consiliarius*,] *used to sit*, (which seems to express his wisdom in the discharge of justice.) *Nestor* is also describ'd as bearing his
sceptre in his hand, which was never used but upon some act of regality, in the
dispatch of justice, or other solemn occasions. Perhaps, says *Dacier*, these seats or
thrones might be consecrated with oil, to draw a reference to the seats of Justice,
as by an act of religion; but I rather judge (adds she) that no more is meant than
to express the shining of these thrones, they being undoubtedly made of marble.

Where antient *Neleus* sate, a rustic throne;
But he descending to th' infernal shade,
Sage *Nestor* fill'd it, and the sceptre sway'd.
His sons around him mild obeysance pay,
And duteous take the orders of the day.   525
First *Echephron* and *Stratius* quit their bed;
Then *Perseus*, *Aretus*, and *Thrasymed*;
The last *Pisistratus* arose from rest:
They came, and near him plac'd the stranger-guest.
To these the Senior thus declar'd his will: 530
My sons! the dictates of your sire fulfil.
To *Pallas*, first of Gods, prepare the feast,
Who grac'd our rites, a more than mortal guest.
Let one, dispatchful, bid some swain to lead
A well-fed bullock from the grassy mead;   535
One seek the harbour where the vessels moor,
And bring thy friends, *Telemachus!* a-shore,
(Leave only two the gally to attend)
Another to *Laerceus* must we send,

---

528. *Pisistratus*.] Would I indulge my fancy in a conjecture, I might suppose
that the famous tyrant *Pisistratus* was descended, or borrow'd his name, from this
son of *Nestor*. *Herodotus* informs us ⟨v 65⟩, as *Eustathius* observes, that all the
Pisistrati were originally *Pylians*. If this be true, we have a very strong evidence
that *Homer* is not all fiction, but that he celebrates the great men of those ages
with reality, and only embellishes the true story with the ornaments of Poetry.

539. Laerceus—*Artist divine*, &c.] The Author of the *Parallel* ⟨Perrault (edn.
Paris, 1693), ii 53⟩ quotes this passage to prove that *Homer* was ignorant of the
Mechanic arts: We have here, says he, a Gilder with his anvil and hammer; but
what occasion has he for an anvil and hammer in the art of a Gilder? *Boileau* has
excellently vindicated *Homer* from this objection, in his reflections upon *Longinus*
⟨*Réflexions Critiques* iii, *Œuvres Complètes*, Paris, 1942, v 69–70⟩; this Gilder was a
gold-beater; *Nestor* we see furnish'd the gold, and he beat it into leaves, so that he
had occasion to make use of his anvil and hammer; the anvil was portable, because the work was not laborious. Our modern travellers assure us, that it is at
this day the practice in the eastern regions, as in *Persia*, &c. for the artists in
metals to carry about with them the whole implements of trade, to the house of
the persons where they find employment; it is therefore a full vindication of
Homer, to observe that the gold this artist used in gilding, was nothing but gold
beat into fine leaves.

Artist divine, whose skilful hands infold   540
The victim's horn with circumfusile gold.
The rest may here the pious duty share,
And bid the handmaids for the feast prepare,
The seats to range, the fragrant wood to bring,
And limpid waters from the living spring.   545
    He said, and busy each his care bestow'd;
Already at the gates the bullock low'd,
Already came the *Ithacensian* crew,
The dextrous smith the tools already drew:
His pond'rous hammer, and his anvil sound,   550
And the strong tongs to turn the metal round.
Nor was *Minerva* absent from the rite,
She view'd her honours, and enjoy'd the sight.
With rev'rent hand the King presents the gold, ⎫
Which round th' intorted horns the gilder roll'd; ⎬ 555
So wrought, as *Pallas* might with pride behold. ⎭
Young *Aretus* from forth his bridal bow'r ⎫
Brought the full laver, o'er their hands to pour, ⎬
And canisters of consecrated flour. ⎭

552. *Nor was* Minerva *absent*—] It may be ask'd in what sense *Minerva* can be said to come to the sacrifice? *Eustathius* answers, that the Ancients finding the inclinations of men to be bent incontinently upon pleasures, to oblige them to use them moderately, distinguish'd times, ordain'd sacrifices, and representing the Gods in the forms of men, brought them to use those pleasures with discretion; they taught them that the Gods came down to their libations and sacrifices, to induce them to govern their conversation with reverence and modesty: Thus *Jupiter* and the other Gods in the *Iliads*, and *Neptune* in the *Odyssey*, are said to feast with the *Æthiopians*.

If I might be pardon'd a conjecture, I would suppose, that *Minerva* may in another sense be said to come to the sacrifice; I mean by her Image or statue: and what may seem to confirm this opinion, is what *Diodorus* relates in his third book ⟨III ii 3⟩ concerning the above-mention'd *Æthiopians*; they carry'd about the statues of *Jupiter* and the other Gods twelve days, during which time the Gods were said to be gone to the *Æthiopians*: and if the Gods may be said to come to the *Æthiopians* by their statues; why may not the same be said of *Minerva*, from the introduction of her statue among the *Pylians*? So that the appearance of the Goddess may possibly mean the appearance of her statue.

Stratius and *Echephron* the victim led;   560
The axe was held by warlike *Thrasymed*,
In act to strike: Before him *Perseus* stood,
The vase extending to receive the blood.
The King himself initiates to the Pow'r;
Scatters with quiv'ring hand the sacred flour,   565
And the stream sprinkles: From the curling brows
The hair collected in the fire he throws.
Soon as due vows on ev'ry part were pay'd,
And sacred wheat upon the victim lay'd,
Strong *Thrasymed* discharg'd the speeding blow   570
Full on his neck, and cut the nerves in two.
Down sunk the heavy beast: the females round
Maids, wives, and matrons, mix a shrilling sound.

560. Stratius *and* Echephron, &c.] *Nestor* here makes use only of the ministry of his sons; the reason of it is, because it was reckon'd honourable to serve in the performance of sacrifice, this being in some sense an attending upon the Gods: or because it was the practice of those ages for great persons to do those offices with their own hands, which in the latter have been perform'd by servants.

Eustathius reports a saying of *Antigonus*, who observing his son behaving himself imperiously to his subjects, "Know'st thou not, says he, that Royalty it self is but illustrious servitude!" an intimation that he himself was but a servant of the public, and therefore should use his servants with moderation.

But the true reason of *Nestor*'s assisting in the sacrifice is, because Kings anciently had the inspection of religion, and Priesthood was joyn'd to Royalty, according to that of *Virgil* ⟨III 80⟩,

Rex Anius, rex idem hominum Phœbique sacerdos.

573. *Maids, wives, and matrons, mix a shrilling sound.*] I have kept the meaning of the word in the original, which signifies prayers made with loud cries, ὀλόλυξαν. ὀλολυγή, says *Hesychius* ⟨*Lexicon, s.v.*⟩, is, φωνὴ γυναικῶν ἣν ποιοῦνται ἐν τοῖς ἱεροῖς εὐχόμεναι, *the voice of women, which they make at sacrifices in their prayers.* But there is still something in it more to the present purpose; the Scholiast upon *Æschylus* remarks, that this word is not used properly but when apply'd to the prayers offer'd to *Minerva*; for *Minerva* is the only Goddess to whom prayers are made with loud cries, she being the Goddess of War; to other Deities they offer prayer with thanksgiving; καὶ γὰρ μόνῃ τῇ Ἀθηνᾷ δαίμονι οὔσῃ πολεμικῇ ὀλολύζουσι, τοῖς δ' ἄλλοις θεοῖς παιωνίζουσι ⟨cited in Mme. Dacier's *L'Odyssée* (Paris, 1716), I 272⟩.

Thus also in the 6th book of the *Iliad*, verse 301.

Αἱ δ' ὀλολυγῇ πᾶσαι Ἀθήνῃ χεῖρας ἀνέσχον.

Nor scorn'd the Queen the holy Choir to join,
(The first-born she, of old *Clymenus'* line;   575
In youth by *Nestor* lov'd, of spotless fame,
And lov'd in age, *Eurydicé* her name)
From earth they rear him, struggling now with death;
And *Nestor's* Youngest stops the vents of breath.
The soul for ever flies: on all sides round   580
Streams the black blood, and smokes upon the ground.
The beast they then divide, and dis-unite
The ribs and limbs, observant of the rite:
On these, in double cawls involv'd with art,
The choicest morsels lay from ev'ry part.   585
The sacred Sage before his altar stands,
Turns the burnt-off'ring with his holy hands,
And pours the wine, and bids the flames aspire:
The youth with instruments surround the fire.
The thighs now sacrific'd, and entrails drest,   590
Th' assistants part, transfix, and broil the rest.
While these officious tend the rites divine,
The last fair branch of the *Nestorean* line
Sweet *Polycaste*, took the pleasing toil

They fill the dome with supplicating cries ⟨375⟩.
And in the present passage in the *Odyssey*,
—αἱ δ' ὀλόλυξαν
Θυγατέρες τε νυοί τε, &c. *Dacier.*

594.   *Sweet* Polycaste, *took the pleasing toil*
              To bathe the Prince, &c.]

It is very necessary to say something about this practice of women bathing and
anointing men; it frequently occurs thro' the whole *Odyssey*, and is so contrary to
the usage of the moderns as to give offence to modesty; neither is this done by
women of inferior quality, but we have here a young Princess, bathing, anointing, and cloathing the naked *Telemachus. Eustathius* indeed tells us, it was undoubtedly by her father's command: but if it was a piece of immodesty, it does
not solve the objection, whoever commanded it. I confess it would be immodest
in these ages of the world, and the only excuse that occurs to me is, to say that
Custom establish'd it. It is in manners, in some degree, as in dress; if a fashion
never so indecent prevails, yet no person is ridiculous, because it is fashionable;
so in manners, if a practice prevails universally, tho' not reconcilable to real

To bathe the Prince, and pour the fragrant oil.   595
O'er his fair limbs a flow'ry vest he threw,
And issu'd, like a God to mortal view.
His former seat beside the King he found,
(His people's Father with his Peers around)
All plac'd at ease the holy banquet join,   600
And in the dazling goblet laughs the wine.
    The rage of thirst and hunger now supprest,
The Monarch turns him to his royal guest;
And for the promis'd journey bids prepare
The smooth-hair'd horses, and the rapid car,   605
Observant of his word. The word scarce spoke,
The sons obey, and join them to the yoke.
Then bread and wine a ready handmaid brings,
And presents, such as suit the state of Kings.
The glitt'ring seat *Telemachus* ascends;   610
His faithful guide *Pisistratus* attends:
With hasty hand the ruling reins he drew:
He lash'd the coursers, and the coursers flew.
Beneath the bounding yoke alike they held
Their equal pace, and smoak'd along the field.   615
The tow'rs of *Pylos* sink, its views decay,
Fields after fields fly back, till close of day:
Then sunk the Sun, and darken'd all the way.
    To *Pheræ* now, *Diocleus'* stately seat,
(Of *Alpheus'* race) the weary youths retreat.   620

modesty, yet no person can be said to be immodest who comes into it, because it is agreeable to the custom of the times and countries.

    610. &c. *The conclusion of the book*] I shall lay together what I have further to observe on the conclusion of this book: It is remarkable that the Poet does not amuse himself in describing the present he receiv'd from *Nestor*, or the provisions for the journey, or even the journey it self at large; he dispatches the whole in a few lines very judiciously; he carries his Heroe directly to *Menelaus*, who is to furnish many incidents that contribute to the design of the Poem, and passes over other matters as unnecessary.

    We have here likewise a piece of poetical Geography, and learn that it is exactly two days journey from *Pylos* to *Lacedæmon*.

His house affords the hospitable rite,
And pleas'd they sleep (the blessing of the night.)
But when *Aurora*, daughter of the dawn,
With rosy lustre purpled o'er the lawn;
Again they mount, their journey to renew,   625
And from the sounding portico they flew.
Along the waving fields their way they hold,
The fields receding as the chariot roll'd:
Then slowly sunk the ruddy globe of light,
And o'er the shaded landscape rush'd the night.   630

This book takes up three days; the first is spent in the enquiries *Telemachus* makes of *Nestor* concerning *Ulysses*; the two last in the morning sacrifice at *Pylos*, and in the journey of *Telemachus* to *Lacedæmon*; so that five days have now pass'd since the opening of the Poem. I have said nothing about the sacrifice, tho' it be the most exact description of the sacrifices as practis'd by the Ancients, perhaps extant in any Author; I refer to the observations upon the first book of the *Iliad*.

I would here remark that the three first books are written with the utmost simplicity, there has been no room for such exalted strokes of Poetry as are to be found in the *Iliad*, or in the future parts of the *Odyssey*: But this is not owing to the decay of genius in *Homer*, as some Critics have affirm'd, (who look upon the *Odyssey* as bearing marks of his declining years,) but to the nature of the subject. The characters of *Achilles* and *Ulysses* are both very great, but very different. The *Iliad* consists of battles, and a continual commotion; the *Odyssey* in Patience and Wisdom: and consequently the style of the two Poems must be as different as the characters of the two Heroes. A noble fountain of Poetry opens in the next book, and flows with an uninterrupted course almost through the whole *Odyssey*.

The Fourth Book of Homer's Odyssey.   Bb. p.4 (28

180

Now with their wheels imperial Sparta sounds,
^ whose limits high, defensive rock surrounds,
At the fair dome their rapid labour ends.
When ~~fully regent~~ sate Atrides midst of his bridal friends,
5   Atrides ~~sate~~ with double vows, invoking Hymen's pow'r,
    To bless his Sons & daughters
    ~~Both such vows, to bless the~~ nuphal hour.
    ~~He That day,~~
    ~~For him~~ to great Achilles's Son resign'd
    Hermione (the fairest of her kind)
    was sent
    ~~He had~~ to crown the long-protracted joy,
    The
10 Espous'd before the final doom of Troy:
    with steeds, and gilded cars, a gorgeous train
    Attend the Nymph to Phthia's distant reign.
    Meanwhile at home, to ~~Megapenthes~~
    And, ~~Megapenthes, to my~~ bed
    The virgin-choir Alector's daughter led.
15   Brave Megapenthes, ~~sprung~~ from a stol'n Amour
    ~~Thou the brave product of a stoln amour~~
    to great Atrides',
    whom to the Monarch's age his hand-maid bore:
    To Helen's bed the Gods alone assign
    Hermione, t'extend the regal Line;
    On whom a radiant pomp of Graces wait
20 Resembling Venus in attractive state.
          While thy gay friendly hoop y° King surrounds,
    with festival and mirth the ~~domestic~~ roofs sound.

THE
FOURTH BOOK
OF THE
ODYSSEY.

The ARGUMENT.

Telemachus *with* Pisistratus *arriving at* Sparta, *is hospitably receiv'd by* Menelaus, *to whom he relates the cause of his coming, and learns from him many particulars of what befel the* Greeks *since the destruction of* Troy. *He dwells more at large upon the Prophecies of* Proteus *to him in his return, from which he acquaints* Telemachus, *that* Ulysses *is detain'd in the Island of* Calypso.

In the mean-time the Suitors consult to destroy Telemachus *in his voyage home.* Penelope *is appriz'd of this, but comforted in a dream by* Pallas, *in the shape of her sister* Iphthima.

AND now proud *Sparta* with their wheels resounds,
 Sparta, whose walls a range of hills surrounds:
 At the fair dome their rapid labour ends;
Where sate *Atrides* 'midst his bridal friends,
With double vows invoking *Hymen*'s pow'r,   5
To bless his sons and daughters nuptial hour.

Aristotle in his Poetics reports ⟨xxv 24–5⟩, that certain ancient Critics reproached *Homer* for an indecency in making *Telemachus* take his abode with *Menelaus,* and not with his own grandfather *Icarius*: this *Monsieur Dacier* sufficiently answers, by shewing that *Icarius* had settled himself in *Acarnania,* and not in *Lacedæmon* ⟨*La Poëtique d'Aristote . . . avec des Remarques,* Paris, 1692, p. 461⟩.

5. —*invoking* Hymen's *pow'r.*] *Athenæus* ⟨v 180c–182⟩ has been very severe upon this passage, as *Eustathius* observes, and *Dacier* from *Eustathius.*

Aristarchus, says *Athenæus,* misguides us, the words τὸν δ' εὗρον δαινύντα, led him into an error; whereas the marriage is compleated, the wedded couples gone away from *Menelaus,* and he and *Helen* are alone at *Lacedæmon.* The five verses, continues he, (the fifteenth to the twentieth inclusively) are taken from the 18th book of the *Iliads,* and inserted very improperly in this place by *Aristarchus.* *Athenæus* gives several reasons for his opinion, as that music and dancing were very contrary to the severe manners of the *Lacedæmonians;* besides the dance was

That day, to great *Achilles'* son resign'd
Hermione, (the fairest of her kind)
Was sent to crown the long-protracted joy,

a *Cretan* dance, how then could it be practis'd among the *Spartans*? The Poet mentions neither the name of the Bard, nor one word of the subject of the songs: neither can the words μολπῆς ἐξάρχοντες, be apply'd at all to the Dancers, but to the Musicians; and lastly, it is not to be imagin'd that *Telemachus* and *Pisistratus* should be so unpolite, as not to be at all affected with the music, had there been any, and yet break out into such wonder at the sight of the beauty of the Palace of *Menelaus*. *Aristarchus*, adds he, thought the description of the wedding of the son and daughter of a King was too meanly and concisely describ'd, and therefore made this addition.

But it is easy to refute *Athenæus*, and vindicate *Aristarchus*. *Athenæus* understood πέμπε and ἤγετο in the wrong tense, they are of the imperfect, *he was sending*, or *about to send*, and not *had sent*, &c. If the marriage had been absolutely finish'd, why should *Minerva* absent her self from *Menelaus*, when the celebration of the nuptials is the only reason of the absence of that Goddess? and as for music and dancing being contrary to the severe manners of the *Lacedæmonians*, this is all conjecture: *Menelaus* lived more than three hundred years before *Lycurgus*; and because such diversions were forbid in *Sparta* in the days of *Lycurgus*, must it follow that they were not used in those of *Menelaus*? And should it be granted that music and dancing were not used in his times, might he not relax a little from the severity of his times, upon such an occasion of joy as the marriage of a son and daughter? I am sure these diversions are not more contrary to the severity of the *Spartans*, than the magnificence of the Palace of *Menelaus* was to their simplicity. "But he does not name the Bard, or the subject of his songs": But is this a reason why the verses are spurious? we should rather admire the judgment of the Poet, who having so fair an opportunity to describe these nuptials, yet rejects the temptation, dismisses the whole in a few lines, and follows where his subject leads him. The objection about the dance being *Cretan* is not more valid: *Menelaus* (as we learn from the preceding book) had been in *Crete*, and might bring it thence to *Lacedæmon*. And as for the Criticism upon ἐξάρχοντες it is but a fallacy; *Casaubon* has shewn beyond contradiction, that ἐξάρχειν is apply'd indifferently to all those who give example to others ⟨Isaac Casaubon, *Commentary on Athenaeus* (1597), Bk IV, xxvii⟩; and consequently may be apply'd to Dancers as well as Musicians. It may be further added, that although it should be allow'd that the word ἐξάρχειν is only properly apply'd to music, yet in this place the word would not be improperly apply'd to dancers; for the dancers, without usurping upon the province of the singer, might μολπῆς ἐξάρχειν, or chuse those songs, to which they desired to dance; as is the usage at this day.

Diodorus ⟨on the authority of Eustathius 1480 146⟩ is of opinion, that the whole twelve lines after the second to the fifteenth are not genuine; but what has been said of *Athenæus*, may be apply'd to *Diodorus*.

Espous'd before the final doom of *Troy:*   10
With steeds, and gilded cars, a gorgeous train
Attend the nymph to *Phthia*'s distant reign.
Mean-while at home, to *Megapenthes*' bed
The virgin-choir *Alector*'s daughter led.
Brave *Megapenthes*, from a stol'n amour   15
To great *Atrides*' age his hand-maid bore:
To *Helen*'s bed the Gods alone assign
Hermione, t'extend the regal line;
On whom a radiant pomp of Graces wait,
Resembling *Venus* in attractive state.   20
　While this gay friendly troop the King surround,
With festival and mirth the roofs resound:
A Bard amid the joyous circle sings
High airs, attemper'd to the vocal strings;
Whilst warbling to the varied strain, advance   25
Two sprightly youths to form the bounding dance.
'Twas then that issuing thro' the palace gate
The splendid car roll'd slow in regal state:
On the bright eminence young *Nestor* shone,
And fast beside him great *Ulysses*' son: 30
Grave *Eteoneus* saw the pomp appear,
And speeding, thus address'd the royal ear.
　Two youths approach, whose semblant features prove
Their blood devolving from the source of *Jove.*
Is due reception deign'd, or must they bend   35
Their doubtful course to seek a distant friend?
　Insensate! with a sigh the King replies,

---

37. Menelaus *blames* Eteoneus.] This is the first appearance of *Menelaus*; and
surely nothing can more reconcile him to the favour of the spectators, than those
amiable colours in which the Poet paints him. There is an overflow of humanity
and gratitude in his expressions, like that of *Dido* in *Virgil* ⟨1 630⟩,
　　　　　Non ignara mali, miseris succurrere disco.
They contain a fine piece of morality, and teach that those men are more tender-
hearted and humane who have felt the reverse of fortune, than those who have
only liv'd in a condition of prosperity.

Too long, mis-judging, have I thought thee wise:
But sure relentless folly steels thy breast,
Obdurate to reject the stranger-guest;   40
To those dear hospitable rites a foe,
Which in my wand'rings oft reliev'd my woe:
Fed by the bounty of another's board,
'Till pitying *Jove* my native realm restor'd—
Strait be the coursers from the car releast,   45
Conduct the youths to grace the genial feast.
    The Seneshal rebuk'd in haste withdrew;
With equal haste a menial train pursue:
Part led the coursers, from the car enlarg'd,
Each to a crib with choicest grain surcharg'd;   50
Part in a portico, profusely grac'd
With rich magnificence, the chariot plac'd:
Then to the dome the friendly pair invite,
Who eye the dazling roofs with vast delight;
Resplendent as the blaze of summer-noon,   55
Or the pale radiance of the midnight moon.
From room to room their eager view they bend;
Thence to the bath, a beauteous pile, descend;
Where a bright damsel-train attend the guests
With liquid odors, and embroider'd vests.   60
Refresh'd, they wait them to the bow'r of state,
Where circled with his Peers *Atrides* sate:
Thron'd next the King, a fair attendant brings
The purest product of the chrystal springs;
High on a massy vase of silver mold,   65
The burnish'd laver flames with solid gold;
In solid gold the purple vintage flows,
And on the board a second banquet rose.
When thus the King with hospitable port:—
Accept this welcome to the *Spartan* court;   70
The waste of nature let the feast repair,
Then your high lineage and your names declare:
Say from what scepter'd ancestry ye claim,

Recorded eminent in deathless fame?
For vulgar parents cannot stamp their race   75
With signatures of such majestic grace.
   Ceasing, benevolent he strait assigns
The royal portion of the choicest chines
To each accepted friend: with grateful haste
They share the honours of the rich repast.   80
Suffic'd, soft-whispering thus to *Nestor*'s son,
His head reclin'd, young *Ithacus* begun.
   View'st thou un-mov'd, O ever-honour'd most!
These prodigies of art, and wond'rous cost?
Above, beneath, around the Palace shines   85
The sumless treasure of exhausted mines:
The spoils of elephants the roofs inlay,
And studded amber darts a golden ray:
Such, and not nobler, in the realms above
My wonder dictates is the dome of *Jove*.   90
   The Monarch took the word, and grave reply'd.

---

81. *Soft-whisp'ring thus to* Nestor's *son.*] This may be thought a circumstance of no importance, and very trivial in *Telemachus*; but it shews his address and decency: He whispers, to avoid the appearance of a flatterer, or to conceal his own inexperience, in shewing too much surprize at the magnificence of the Palace of *Menelaus. Eustathius.*

91. *The Monarch took the word,* &c.] The ancients, says *Eustathius*, observe the prudence of *Menelaus* in his reply to *Telemachus*; and the prudence of *Telemachus* in his behaviour to *Menelaus*: *Menelaus* denies not his riches and magnificence, but to take off the envy which they might attract, he throws the calamities he has undergone into the contrary scale, and balances his felicity with his misfortunes: And *Telemachus* coming into the Palace at the time of an entertainment, chuses to satisfie his curiosity rather than his appetite. *Plutarch* I confess condemns *Telemachus* of inexperience; who when he saw the Palace of *Nestor* furnish'd only with things useful to life, as beds, tables, &c. is seiz'd with no admiration; but the superfluities of *Menelaus*, his ivory, amber and gold, &c. carry him into transports: whereas a *Socrates* or a *Diogenes* would have exclaim'd, What heaps of vanities have I beheld ⟨*De Cupiditate Divitiarum* 9 (527e)⟩! 'Tis true, such a judgment might become Philosophers; but who, as *Dacier* observes, can think the character of a *Socrates* or a *Diogenes* suitable to young *Telemachus*? What is decent in a Prince, and a young man, would ill become the gravity and wisdom of a Philosopher.

Presumptuous are the vaunts, and vain the pride
Of man, who dares in pomp with *Jove* contest,
Unchang'd, immortal, and supremely blest!
With all my affluence when my woes are weigh'd,   95
Envy will own, the purchase dearly paid.
For eight slow-circling years by tempests tost,
From *Cyprus* to the far *Phœnician* coast,
(*Sidon* the Capital) I stretch'd my toil
Thro' regions fatten'd with the flows of *Nile*.   100
Next, *Æthiopia*'s utmost bound explore,
And the parcht borders of th' *Arabian* shore:
Then warp my voyage on the southern gales,
O'er the warm *Libyan* wave to spread my sails:
That happy clime! where each revolving year   105

100.   *Thro' regions fatten'd with the flows of* Nile.
                Next, Æthiopia, *&c.*]
The words are in the original Αἰγυπτίους ἐπαληθείς, others read them Αἰγυπτίους ἐπ' ἀληθεῖς, from their veracity in oracles, for which they were very
famous; and indeed the word ἐπαληθείς is not necessary, it being used in the very
same sentence, tho' it must be confess'd such repetitions are frequent in *Homer*.
There is also a different reading of the word Ἐρεμβούς; some have it Ἐρεμνούς,
or *Blacks*; others, Σιδονίους Ἄραβας τε; but the common reading is thought the
best. The *Erembi* are the *Arabian* Troglodytes. *Strabo* ⟨ɪ ii 31 ff⟩ informs us, that
in former ages the bounds of the *Æthiopians* lay near to *Thebes* in *Ægypt*, so that
Menelaus travelling to *Thebes*, might with ease visit the *Æthiopians*. Others have
without any foundation imagin'd that he pass'd the streights of *Gibraltar*, and
sail'd to the *Indies. Sidon* is the capital of the *Phœnicians. Eustathius.*

105.   *—Where each revolving year*
                The teeming Ewes, &c.]
These sheep, as describ'd by *Homer*, may be thought the creation of the Poet, and
not the production of nature: But *Herodotus* ⟨ɪᴠ 29⟩, says *Eustathius*, writes, that
in *Scythia* the oxen have no horns thro' the extremity of the cold: He quotes this
very verse, rightly intimating, adds *Herodotus*, that in hot regions the horns of
cattle shoot very speedily. *Aristotle* directly asserts, that in *Libya* the young ones
of horned cattle have horns immediately after they are brought into the world
⟨*Hist. Animal.* ᴠɪɪɪ 28⟩. So that *Aristotle* and *Herodotus* vindicate *Homer*. The Poet
adds, that the sheep breed three times in the year; these words may have a different interpretation, and imply that they breed in three seasons of the year, and
not only in the spring as in other countries; or that the sheep have at once three
lambs; but the first is the better interpretation. *Athenæus* ⟨ᴠɪɪɪ 331⟩ upon this pas-

The teeming Ewes a triple offspring bear;
And two fair crescents of translucent horn
The brows of all their young increase adorn:
The shepherd swains with sure abundance blest,
On the fat flock and rural dainties feast; 110
Nor want of herbage makes the dairy fail,
But ev'ry season fills the foaming pail.
Whilst heaping unwish'd wealth, I distant roam;
The best of brothers, at his natal home,
By the dire fury of a traitress wife, 115
Ends the sad evening of a stormy life:
Whence with incessant grief my soul annoy'd,
These riches are possess'd, but not enjoy'd!
My wars, the copious theme of ev'ry tongue,

sage writes, that there are things in other countries no less strange than what *Homer* relates of these sheep of *Libya*. Thus in *Lusitania* a country of *Spain*, now *Portugal*, there is a wonderful fruitfulness in all cattle, by reason of the excellent temper of the air; the fruits there never rot, and the roses, violets and asparagus, never fail above three months in the year. *Eustathius*.

114. *The best of brothers,—*
—a traitress wife.]

Menelaus neither mentions *Agamemnon*, *Clytemnestra*, nor *Ægisthus* by name: a just indignation and resentment is the occasion of his suppressing the names of *Clytemnestra* and *Ægisthus*. Thro' the whole *Iliad Menelaus* is describ'd as a very affectionate brother, and the love he bears *Agamemnon* is the reason why he passes by his name in silence. We see that he dispatches the whole in one verse and a half; *Nestor* had told the story pretty largely in the preceding book, and as he was a person less nearly concern'd, might speak of it with more ease and better temper than *Menelaus*; the Poet avoids a needless repetition, and a repetition too of a story universally known to all the *Greeks*. The death of *Agamemnon* is distri- buted into four places in the *Odyssey*; *Nestor*, *Menelaus*, *Proteus*, and the shade of *Agamemnon* in the 11th book, all relate it, and every one very properly. *Proteus* as a prophet more fully than *Nestor* or *Menelaus*, and *Agamemnon* more fully than them all, as being best acquainted with it. *Eustathius*.

119. *My wars, the copious theme*, &c.] In the original *Menelaus* says, *I have destroy'd a house*, &c. There is an ambiguity in the expression, as *Eustathius* observes: for it may either signify the *house of* Priam, or his own in *Argos*; if it be understood of his own, then the meaning is, "I have indeed great wealth, but have purchas'd it with the loss of my people: I could be content with the third part of it, if I could restore those to life who have perish'd before *Troy*." If it be

To you, your fathers have recorded long: 120
How fav'ring heav'n repaid my glorious toils
With a sack'd Palace, and barbaric spoils.
Oh! had the Gods so large a boon deny'd,
And Life, the just equivalent, supply'd
To those brave warriors, who, with glory fir'd,   125
Far from their country in my cause expir'd!
Still in short intervals of pleasing woe,
Regardful of the friendly dues I owe,
I to the glorious dead, for ever dear!
Indulge the tribute of a grateful tear.   130
But oh! *Ulysses*—deeper than the rest
That sad Idea wounds my anxious breast!
My heart bleeds fresh with agonizing pain;
The bowl, and tasteful viands tempt in vain,
Nor sleep's soft pow'r can close my streaming eyes,   135
When imag'd to my soul his sorrows rise.
No peril in my cause he ceas'd to prove,

---

understood of the kingdom of *Priam*, the regret he shews will still appear the
greater. He is enumerating his domestic happiness, and his foreign conquest of
Troy; but he throws the destruction of so many brave men who fell before it, in
the contrary scale; and it so far outweighs both his wealth and his glory, that they
both are joyless to him. Either of these interpretations shew an excellent temper
of humanity in *Menelaus*, who thinks the effusion of blood too dear a price for
glory. At the same time the Poet gives an admirable picture of human nature,
which is restless in the pursuit of what it miscalls happiness, and when in possession of it, neglects it. But the disquiet of *Menelaus* arises not from inconstancy of
temper, but wisdom; it shews that all happiness is unsatisfactory.

131. *But oh!* Ulysses—*&c.*] It is with admirable address that the Poet falls into
his subject; it is art, but yet it seems to be nature: This conduct has a double
effect, it takes away all suspicion of flattery, for *Menelaus* is ignorant that the person with whom he discourses is *Telemachus*, this gives him a manifest evidence of
the love he bears to *Ulysses*; the young man could not but be pleased with the
praise of his father, and with the sincerity of it. It is also observable, that *Menelaus*
builds his friendship for *Ulysses* upon a noble foundation; I mean the sufferings
which *Ulysses* underwent for his friend: *Menelaus* ascribes not their affection to
any familiarity or Intercourse of entertainments, but to a more sincere cause, to
the hazards which brave men undertake for a friend. In short, the friendship of
Menelaus and *Ulysses* is the friendship of Heroes. *Eustathius.*

His labours equal'd only by my love:
And both alike to bitter fortune born,
For him, to suffer, and for me, to mourn!   140
Whether he wanders on some friendless coast,
Or glides in *Stygian* gloom a pensive ghost,
No fame reveals; but doubtful of his doom,
His good old Sire with sorrow to the tomb
Declines his trembling steps; untimely care   145
Withers the blooming vigour of his heir;
And the chaste partner of his bed and throne,
Wastes all her widow'd hours in tender moan.
   While thus pathetic to the Prince he spoke,
From the brave youth the streaming passion broke: 150
Studious to veil the grief, in vain represt,
His face he shrowded with his purple vest:
The conscious Monarch pierc'd the coy disguise,
And view'd his filial love with vast surprize;
Dubious to press the tender theme, or wait   155
To hear the youth enquire his father's fate.
   In this suspence bright *Helen* grac'd the room;

157. —*Bright* Helen *grac'd the room.*] *Menelaus* conjectur'd that the person he
had entertain'd was the son of *Ulysses*, from the tears he shed at the name of his
father, and from the resemblance there was between *Ulysses* and *Telemachus*; it
might therefore have been expected that *Menelaus* should immediately have
acknowledg'd *Telemachus*, and not delay'd a full discovery one moment, out of
regard to his absent friend; but *Menelaus* defers it upon a twofold account, to give
some time to *Telemachus* to indulge his sorrow for his father, and recover himself
from it, and also to avoid the repetition of a discovery upon the appearance of
Helen, who would be curious to know the condition of the strangers.
  It may be necessary to say something concerning *Helen*, that fatal beauty that
engag'd *Greece* and *Asia* in arms; she is drawn in the same colours in the *Odyssey*
as in the *Iliad*; it is a vicious character, but the colours are so admirably soften'd
by the art of the Poet, that we pardon her infidelity. *Menelaus* is an uncommon
instance of conjugal affection, he forgives a wife who had been false to him, and
receives her into a full degree of favour. But perhaps the Reader might have been
shock'd at it, and prejudiced against *Helen* as a person that ought to be forgot, or
have her name only mention'd to disgrace it: The Poet therefore, to reconcile her
to his Reader, brings her in as a penitent, condemning her own infidelity in very

Before her breath'd a gale of rich perfume.
So moves, adorn'd with each attractive grace,
The silver-shafted Goddess of the Chace!   160
The seat of majesty *Adraste* brings,
With art illustrious, for the pomp of Kings.
To spread the pall beneath the regal chair
Of softest woof, is bright *Alcippe*'s care.
A silver canister divinely wrought,   165
In her soft hands the beauteous *Phylo* brought:
To *Sparta*'s Queen of old the radiant vase
Alcandra gave, a pledge of royal grace:
For *Polybus* her Lord, (whose sov'reign sway
The wealthy tribes of *Pharian Thebes* obey)   170
When to that court *Atrides* came, carest
With vast munificence th' imperial guest:
Two lavers from the richest ore refin'd,
With silver tripods, the kind host assign'd;
And bounteous, from the royal treasure told   175
Ten equal talents of refulgent gold.
Alcandra, consort of his high command,
A golden distaff gave to *Helen*'s hand;
And that rich vase, with living sculpture wrought,
Which heap'd with wool the beauteous *Phylo* brought:
The silken fleece impurpl'd for the loom,   181
Rival'd the hyacinth in vernal bloom.
The sovereign seat then *Jove*-born *Helen* press'd,
And pleasing thus her sceptred Lord address'd.
    Who grace our palace now, that friendly pair,   185
Speak they their lineage, or their names declare?

strong expressions; she shews true modesty, when she calls herself impudent, and
by this conduct we are inclined, like *Menelaus*, to forgive her.
    161, &c. Adraste, Alcippe, Helen's Maids.] It has been observ'd, that *Helen*
has not the same attendants in the *Odyssey* as she had in the *Iliad*; they perhaps
might be *Trojans*, and consequently be left in their own country; or rather, it was
an act of prudence in *Menelaus*, not to suffer those servants about her who had
been her attendants and confidents in her infidelity. *Eustathius*.

Uncertain of the truth, yet uncontroul'd
Hear me the bodings of my breast unfold.
With wonder rapt, on yonder cheek I trace
The feature of the *Ulyssean* race: 190
Diffus'd o'er each resembling line appear,
In just similitude, the grace and air
Of young *Telemachus!* the lovely boy,
Who bless'd *Ulysses* with a father's joy,
What time the *Greeks* combin'd their social arms,   195
T'avenge the stain of my ill-fated charms!
　　Just is thy thought, the King assenting cries,
Methinks *Ulysses* strikes my wond'ring eyes:
Full shines the father in the filial frame,
His port, his features, and his shape the same: 200
Such quick regards his sparkling eyes bestow;
Such wavy ringlets o'er his shoulders flow!
And when he heard the long disastrous store
Of cares, which in my cause *Ulysses* bore;
Dismay'd, heart-wounded with paternal woes,   205
Above restraint the tide of sorrow rose:
Cautious to let the gushing grief appear,
His purple garment veil'd the falling tear.
　　See there confess'd, *Pisistratus* replies,
The genuine worth of *Ithacus* the wise!   210
Of that heroic sire the youth is sprung,
But modest awe hath chain'd his tim'rous tongue.
Thy voice, O King! with pleas'd attention heard,

192.
　　　　　　　—The grace and air
　　　　　　　Of young Telemachus!]
It may seem strange that *Helen* should at first view recollect the features of
Ulysses in *Telemachus*; and that *Menelaus*, who was better acquainted with him,
and his constant friend, should not make the same observation. But *Athenæus*, to
reconcile this to probability, says, that women are curious and skilful observers
of the likeness of children to parents, for one particular reason, that they may,
upon finding any dissimilitude, have the pleasure of hinting at the Unchastity of
others ⟨v 190E⟩.

F

Is like the dictates of a God rever'd.
With him at *Nestor*'s high command I came,   215
Whose age I honour with a parent's name.
By adverse destiny constrain'd to sue
For counsel and redress, he sues to you.
Whatever ill the friendless orphan bears,
Bereav'd of parents in his infant years,   220
Still must the wrong'd *Telemachus* sustain,
If hopeful of your aid, he hopes in vain:
Affianc'd in your friendly pow'r alone,
The youth wou'd vindicate the vacant throne.

    Is *Sparta* blest, and these desiring eyes   225
View my friend's son? (the King exulting cries)
Son of my friend, by glorious toils approv'd,
Whose sword was sacred to the man he lov'd:
Mirror of constant faith, rever'd, and mourn'd!—
When *Troy* was ruin'd, had the chief return'd,   230
No *Greek* an equal space had e'er possest
Of dear affection, in my grateful breast.
I, to confirm the mutual joys we shar'd,
For his abode a Capital prepar'd;
Argos the seat of sovereign rule I chose;   235
Fair in the plan the future palace rose,
Where my *Ulysses* and his race might reign,
And portion to his tribes the wide domain.
To them my vassals had resign'd a soil,
With teeming plenty to reward their toil.   240
There with commutual zeal we both had strove,
In acts of dear benevolence, and love:
Brothers in peace, not rivals in command,
And death alone dissolv'd the friendly band!

---

234. *For his abode a Capital prepar'd.*] The Poet puts these words in the mouth of
Menelaus, to express the sincerity of his friendship to *Ulysses*; he intended him all
advantage, and no detriment: we must therefore conclude, that *Ulysses* was still
to retain his sovereignty over *Ithaca*, and only remove to *Argos*, to live with so
sincere a friend as *Menelaus*. *Eustathius*.

Some envious pow'r the blissful scene destroys;   245
Vanish'd are all the visionary joys:
The soul of friendship to my hope is lost,
Fated to wander from his natal coast!

He ceas'd; a gust of grief began to rise:
Fast streams a tide from beauteous *Helen*'s eyes;   250
Fast for the Sire the filial sorrows flow;
The weeping Monarch swells the mighty woe:
Thy cheeks, *Pisistratus*, the tears bedew,
While pictur'd to thy mind appear'd in view
Thy martial *Brother; on the *Phrygian* plain   255
Extended pale, by swarthy *Memnon* slain!
But silence soon the son of *Nestor* broke,
And melting with fraternal pity spoke.

Frequent, O King, was *Nestor* wont to raise
And charm attention, with thy copious praise: 260
To crown thy various gifts, the sage assign'd
The glory of a firm capacious mind:
With that superior attribute controul
This unavailing impotence of soul.
Let not your roof with echoing grief resound,   265

* *Antilochus*

---

249. —*A gust of grief began to rise.* &c.] It has been observ'd thro' the *Iliad*, and may be observ'd through the whole *Odyssey*, that it was not a disgrace to the greatest Heroes to shed tears; and indeed I cannot see why it should be an honour to any man, to be able to divest himself of humane nature so far as to appear insensible upon the most affecting occasions; No man is born a Stoic; it is art, not nature; tears are only a shame, when the cause from whence they flow is mean or vicious. Here *Menelaus* laments a friend, *Telemachus* a father, *Pisistratus* a brother: but from what cause arise the tears of *Helen*? It is to be remember'd that *Helen* is drawn in the softest colours in the *Odyssey*; the character of the adultress is lost in that of the penitent; the name of *Ulysses* throws her into tears, because she is the occasion of all the sufferings of that brave man; the Poet makes her the first in sorrow, as she is the cause of all their tears.

265.   *Let not your roof with echoing grief resound,*
             Now for the feast the friendly bowl is crown'd.
It may be ask'd why sorrow for the dead should be more unseasonable in the

Now for the feast the friendly bowl is crown'd:
But when from dewy shade emerging bright,
Aurora streaks the sky with orient light,
Let each deplore his dead: the rites of woe
Are all, alas! the living can bestow: 270
O'er the congenial dust injoin'd to shear
The graceful curl, and drop the tender tear.
Then mingling in the mournful pomp with you,
I'll pay my brother's ghost a warrior's due,
And mourn the brave *Antilochus*, a name   275
Not unrecorded in the rolls of fame:
With strength and speed superior form'd, in fight
To face the foe, or intercept his flight:
Too early snatch'd by fate ere known to me!
I boast a witness of his worth in thee.   280

    Young and mature! the Monarch thus rejoins,
In thee renew'd the soul of *Nestor* shines:
Form'd by the care of that consummate sage,
In early bloom an Oracle of age.
When-e'er his influence *Jove* vouchsafes to show'r   285
To bless the natal, and the nuptial hour;
From the great sire transmissive to the race,
The boon devolving gives distinguish'd grace.
Such, happy *Nestor!* was thy glorious doom;
Around thee full of years, thy offspring bloom,   290
Expert of arms, and prudent in debate;
The gifts of heav'n to guard thy hoary state.

evening than the morning? *Eustathius* answers, lest others should look upon our
evening tears as the effect of wine, and not of love to the dead.
       Intempestivus venit inter pocula fletus.
       Nec lacrimas dulci fas est miscere falerno ⟨unidentified⟩.
I fancy there may be a more rational account given of this expression; The time
of feasting was ever look'd upon as a time of joy, and thanksgiving to the Gods;
it bore a religious veneration among the Ancients, and consequently to shed
tears when they should express their gratitude to the Gods with joy, was esteem'd
a prophanation.

But now let each becalm his troubled breast,
Wash, and partake serene the friendly feast.
To move thy suit, *Telemachus*, delay,   295
'Till heav'n's revolving lamp restores the day.
    He said, *Asphalion* swift the laver brings;
Alternate all partake the grateful springs:
Then from the rites of purity repair,
And with keen gust the sav'ry viands share.   300
Mean-time with genial joy to warm the soul,
Bright *Helen* mix'd a mirth-inspiring bowl:

---

302. *Bright* Helen *mix'd a mirth-inspiring bowl*, &c.] The conjectures about this cordial of *Helen* have been almost infinite. Some take *Nepenthes* allegorically, to signify History, Music, or Philosophy. *Plutarch* in the first of the *Symposiacs* affirms it to be, discourse well suiting the present passions and conditions of the hearers ⟨*Quaest. Conviv.* 1 i 4⟩. *Macrobius* is of the same opinion, *Delinimentum illud quod Helena vino miscuit, non herba fuit, non ex India succus, sed narrandi opportunitas, quæ hospitem mæroris oblitum flexit ad gaudium* ⟨*De Sat.* VII i⟩. What gave a foundation to this fiction of *Homer*, as *Dacier* observes, might be this. *Diodorus* writes that in *Ægypt*, and chiefly at *Heliopolis*, the same with *Thebes* where *Menelaus* sojourn'd, as has been already observ'd, there lived women who boasted of certain potions which not only made the unfortunate forget all their calamities, but drove away the most violent sallies of grief or anger ⟨1 xcvii 7⟩. *Eusebius* directly affirms, that even in his time the women of *Diospolis* were able to calm the rage of grief or anger by certain potions ⟨*Praepar. Evang.* x viii 11⟩. Now whether this be truth or fiction, it fully vindicates *Homer*, since a Poet may make use of a prevailing, tho' false, opinion.
    Milton mentions this *Nepenthes* in his excellent Masque of *Comus* ⟨672-3, 675-8⟩.

> —*Behold this cordial Julep here,*
> *That flames and dances in his chrystal bounds!*
> *Not that* Nepenthes *which the wife of* Thone
> *In* Ægypt *gave to* Jove-born *Helena,*
> *Is of such pow'r as this to stir up joy,*
> *To life so friendly, or so cool to thirst.*

But that there may be something more than fiction in this is very probable, since the *Ægyptians* were so notoriously skill'd in physick; and particularly since this very *Thon*, or *Thonis*, or *Thoon*, is reported by the ancients to have been the inventor of physic among the *Ægyptians*. The description of this *Nepenthes* agrees admirably with what we know of the qualities and effects of *Opium*.
    It is further said of *Thon*, that he was King of *Canopus*, and entertain'd *Menelaus* hospitably before he had seen *Helen*; but afterwards falling in love with her, and offering violence, he was slain by *Menelaus*. From his name the *Ægyptians*

Temper'd with drugs of sov'reign use, t'assuage
The boiling bosom of tumultuous Rage;
To clear the cloudy front of wrinkled Care,   305
And dry the tearful sluices of Despair:
Charm'd with that virtuous draught, th' exalted mind
All sense of woe delivers to the wind.
Though on the blazing pile his parent lay,
Or a lov'd brother groan'd his life away,   310
Or darling son oppress'd by ruffian-force
Fell breathless at his feet, a mangled corse,
From morn to eve, impassive and serene,
The man entranc'd wou'd view the deathful scene.
These drugs, so friendly to the joys of life,   315
Bright *Helen* learn'd from *Thone*'s imperial wife;
Who sway'd the sceptre, where prolific *Nile*
With various simples cloaths the fat'ned soil.
With wholsome herbage mix'd, the direful bane
Of vegetable venom, taints the plain;   320
From *Pæon* sprung, their patron-god imparts
To all the *Pharian* race his healing arts.
The beverage now prepar'd t'inspire the feast,
The circle thus the beauteous Queen address'd.
    Thron'd in omnipotence, supremest *Jove*   325

gave the name of *Thoth* to the first month of their year, and also to a city the
name of *Thonis*. *Ælian* writes that *Menelaus* when he travell'd to the *Æthiopians*,
committed *Helen* to the protection of *Thonis*; that she fell in love with him, that
Polydamna growing jealous confin'd her to the Island *Pharos*, but gave her an herb
to preserve her from the poison of serpents there frequent, which from *Helen* was
call'd *Helenium* ⟨*De Nat. Anim.* IX 21⟩. *Strabo* writes, that at *Canopus* on the mouth
of *Nile* there stands a city named *Thonies*, from King *Thonis*, who receiv'd *Helen*
and *Menelaus* ⟨XVII i 16⟩. *Herodotus* relates, that *Thonis* was Governor of *Canopus*,
that he represented the injury which *Paris* had done to *Menelaus*, to *Proteus* who
reign'd in *Memphis* ⟨II 113-14⟩. *Eustathius.*
    This last remark from *Herodotus* is sufficient to shew, that *Homer* is not so
fictitious as is generally imagined, that there really was a King named *Proteus*,
that the Poet builds his fables upon truth, and that it was truth that originally
determin'd *Homer* to introduce *Proteus* into his Poetry; but I intend to explain this
more largely in the story of *Proteus*.

Tempers the fates of human race above;
By the firm sanction of his sov'reign will,
Alternate are decreed our good and ill.
To feastful mirth be this white hour assign'd,
And sweet discourse, the banquet of the mind.   330
My self assisting in the social joy,
Will tell *Ulysses'* bold exploit in *Troy*:
Sole witness of the deed I now declare;
Speak you, (who saw) his wonders in the war.
    Seam'd o'er with wounds, which his own sabre gave,

---

331.   *My self—*
               Will tell Ulysses' *bold exploit—*]
What is here related shews the necessity of the introduction of *Helen*, and the use
the Poet makes of it: she is not brought in merely as a *muta Persona*, to fill up the
number of persons; but she relates several incidents, in which she her self was
concern'd, and which she could only know; and consequently not only diversifies, but carries on the design of the story. *Eustathius.*

    335. *Seam'd o'er with wounds*, &c.] The Poet here shews his judgment in passing
over many instances of the sufferings of *Ulysses*, and relating this piece of conduct,
not mention'd by any other Author. The art of *Ulysses* in extricating himself from
difficulties is laid down as the groundwork of the Poem, he is πολύτροπος, and
this is an excellent example of it. This further shews the necessity of the appearance of *Helen*, no other person being acquainted with the story. If this stratagem
be not a reality, yet it bears the resemblance of it; and *Megabyzus* the *Persian* (as
Eustathius observes) practis'd it, as we learn from history. We may reasonably
conjecture that *Ulysses* was committed to *Helen*, in hopes that he would discover
the affairs of the army more freely to her than any other person: for what could
be more agreeable to a *Greek*, than to be committed to the care of a *Greek*, as
Ulysses was to *Helen*? By the same conduct the Poet raises the character of *Helen*,
by making her shew her repentance by an act of generosity to her countryman.
The original says she gave an oath to *Ulysses* not to discover him before he was in
Safety in the *Grecian* army: Now this does not imply that she ever discover'd to the
Trojans that *Ulysses* had enter'd *Troy*: the contrary opinion is most probable; or
it cannot be imagin'd but all *Troy* must have been incens'd greatly against her,
had they known that she had conceal'd one of their mortal enemies, and dismiss'd him in safety: It was sufficient for *Ulysses* to take her oath that she would
not discover him, 'till he was in security: he left her future conduct to her own
discretion. It is probable that she furnish'd *Ulysses* with a sword, for in his return
he slew many *Trojans*: He came to *Troy*, observes *Eustathius*, in rags, and like a
slave; and to have conceal'd a sword, would have endanger'd his life upon a discovery of it, and given strong suspicions of an impostor.

In the vile habit of a village slave,   336
The foe deceiv'd, he pass'd the tented plain,
In *Troy* to mingle with the hostile train.
In this attire secure from searching eyes,
'Till haply piercing thro' the dark disguise   340
The chief I challeng'd; he, whose practis'd wit
Knew all the serpent-mazes of deceit,
Eludes my search: but when his form I view'd
Fresh from the bath with fragrant oils renew'd,
His limbs in military purple dress'd;   345
Each brightning grace the genuine *Greek* confess'd.
A previous pledge of sacred faith obtain'd,
'Till he the lines and *Argive* fleet regain'd
To keep his stay conceal'd; the chief declar'd
The plans of war against the town prepar'd.   350
Exploring then the secrets of the state,
He learn'd what best might urge the *Dardan* fate:
And safe returning to the *Grecian* host,
Sent many a shade to *Pluto*'s dreary coast.
Loud grief resounded thro' the tow'rs of *Troy*,   355
But my pleas'd bosom glow'd with secret joy:
For then with dire remorse, and conscious shame,

351. *Exploring then the secrets of the state.*] The word φρόνις is here used in a large sense: it takes in all the observations *Ulysses* made during his continuance in *Troy*; it takes in the designs and counsels of the enemy, his measuring the gates, the height of the walls, the easiest place for an assault or ambush, the taking away the *Palladium*, or whatever else a wise man may be suppos'd to observe, or act, in execution of such a stratagem. *Eustathius.*

357. *For then with dire remorse,* &c.] The conclusion of this speech is very artful: *Helen* ascribes her seduction to *Venus*, and mentions nothing of *Paris*. Instead of naming *Troy*, she conceals it, and only says she was carry'd thither, leaving *Troy* to the imagination of *Menelaus*; she suffers not herself to mention names so odious now to herself, and ever to *Menelaus*, as *Paris* and *Troy*. She compliments *Menelaus* very handsomely, and says, that he wanted no accomplishment either in mind or body: It being the nature of man not to resent the injuries of a wife so much upon the account of her being corrupted, but of the preference she gives to another person; he looks upon such a preference as the most affecting part of the injury. *Eustathius.*

I view'd th' effects of that disastrous flame,
Which kindled by th' imperious Queen of love,
Constrain'd me from my native realm to rove: 360
And oft in bitterness of soul deplor'd
My absent daughter, and my dearer Lord;
Admir'd among the first of human race,
For ev'ry gift of mind, and manly grace.

Right well, reply'd the King, your speech displays   365
The matchless merit of the chief you praise:
Heroes in various climes my self have found,
For martial deeds, and depth of thought renown'd;
But *Ithacus*, unrival'd in his claim,
May boast a title to the loudest fame: 370
In battel calm he guides the rapid storm,
Wise to resolve, and patient to perform.
What wond'rous conduct in the chief appear'd,
When the vast fabric of the Steed we rear'd!
Some Dæmon anxious for the *Trojan* doom,   375

---

365. *Menelaus's answer.*] The judgment of the Poet in continuing the story concerning *Ulysses* is not observ'd by any Commentator. *Ulysses* is the chief Heroe of the Poem, every thing should have a reference to him, otherwise the narration stands still without any advance towards the conclusion of it. The Poet therefore to keep *Ulysses* in our minds, dwells upon his sufferings and adventures: he supplies his not appearing in the present scene of Action, by setting his character before us, and continually forcing his prudence, patience, and valour upon our observation. He uses the same art and judgment with relation to *Achilles* in the *Iliads*: The Heroe of the Poem is absent from the chief scenes of action during much of the time which that Poem comprises, but he is continually brought into the mind of the Reader, by recounting his exploits and glory.

375. *Some Dæmon anxious for the* Trojan *doom.*] It is the observation of *Eustathius*, that these words are very artfully introduced to vindicate *Helen*; They imply that what she acted was by compulsion, and to evidence this more clearly, *Deiphobus* is given her for an attendant as a spy upon her actions, that she might not conceal any thing that should happen, but act her part well by endeavouring to deceive the *Greeks* in favour of *Troy*. It is the Dæmon, not *Helen*, that is in fault; this, continues *Eustathius*, answers many objections that lye against *Helen*; for if she was a real penitent, as she her self affirms, how comes she to endeavour to deceive the *Greeks*, by the disguise of her voice, into more misery than had yet arisen from a ten years war? Or indeed is it credible that any person could modulate her voice

F*

so artfully as to resemble so many voices? And how could the *Greeks* enclosed in the wooden horse believe that their wives who were in *Greece*, could be arriv'd in so short a space as they had been conceal'd there, from the various regions of *Greece*, and meet together in *Troy*? Would the wives of these Heroes come into an enemy's country, when the whole army, except these latent Heroes, were retir'd from it? this is ridiculous and impossible. I must confess there is great weight in these objections: But *Eustathius* answers all by the interposition of the Dæmon; and by an idle tradition that *Helen* had the name of *Echo*, from the faculty of mimicking sounds; and that this gift was bestow'd upon her by *Venus* when she married *Menelaus*, that she might be able to detect him if he should prove false to her bed, by imitating the voice of the suspected person: (but *Menelaus* had more occasion for this faculty than *Helen*.) As for the excuse of the Dæmon, it equally excuses all crimes: For instance, was *Helen* false to *Menelaus*? The Dæmon occa-sion'd it: Does she act an imposture to destroy all her *Grecian* friends, and even *Menelaus*? The Dæmon compells her to it: The Dæmon compells her to go with *Deiphobus*, to surround the horse thrice, to sound the sides of it, to endeavour to surprize the latent *Greeks* by an imitation of the voices of their wives, and in short, to act like a person that was very sincere in mischief.

Dacier takes another course, and gives up *Helen*, but remarks the great address of *Menelaus*. *Helen* had, said she, long desired nothing so much as to return to *Lacedæmon*; and her heart had long been wholly turn'd to *Menelaus*: *Menelaus* is not at all convinc'd of this pretended sincerity; but it would have been too gross, after he had taken her again to his bed, to convict her of falshood: He therefore contents himself barely to reply that some Dæmon, an enemy to the *Greeks*, had forc'd her to a conduct disagreeable to her sincerity. This (continues *Dacier*) is an artful, but severe Irony.

As for the objection concerning the impossibility of the *Greeks* believing their wives could be in *Troy*; she answers, that the Authors of this objection have not sufficiently consider'd human nature. The voice of a belov'd person might of a sudden, and by surprize, draw from any person a word involuntary, before he has time to make reflection. This undoubtedly is true, where circumstances make an imposture probable; but here is an impossibility; it is utterly impossible to believe the wives of these Heroes could be in *Troy*. Besides, *Menelaus* himself tells us, that even he had fallen into the snare, but *Ulysses* prevented it; this adds to the incredibility of the story, for if this faculty of mimickry was given upon his mar-riage with *Helen*, it was nothing new to him, he must be suppos'd to be acquainted with it, and consequently be the less liable to surprize: Nay it is not impossible, but the experiment might have been made upon him before *Helen* fled away with *Paris*.

In short, I think this passage wants a further vindication: the circumstances are low, if not incredible. *Virgil*, the great imitator of *Homer*, has given us a very different and more noble description of the destruction of *Troy*: he has not thought fit to imitate him in this description.

If we allow *Helen* to act by compulsion, to have fear'd the *Trojans*, and that *Deiphobus* was sent as a spy upon her actions; yet this is no vindication of her con-

Urg'd you with great *Deiphobus* to come,
T'explore the fraud: with guile oppos'd to guile,
Slow-pacing thrice around th' insidious pile;
Each noted leader's name you thrice invoke,
Your accent varying as their spouses spoke: 380
The pleasing sounds each latent warrior warm'd,
But most *Tydides'* and my heart alarm'd:
To quit the steed we both impatient press,
Threat'ning to answer from the dark recess.
Unmov'd the mind of *Ithacus* remain'd, 385
And the vain ardors of our love restrained:
But *Anticlus* unable to controul,
Spoke loud the languish of his yerning soul:
Ulysses strait with indignation fir'd,
(For so the common care of *Greece* requir'd) 390
Firm to his lips his forceful hands apply'd,
'Till on his tongue the flutt'ring murmurs dy'd:
Mean-time *Minerva* from the fraudful horse,
Back to the Court of *Priam* bent your course.
    Inclement fate! *Telemachus* replies, 395
Frail is the boasted attribute of wise:
The leader, mingling with the vulgar host,
Is in the common mass of matter lost!
But now let sleep the painful waste repair
Of sad reflection, and corroding care. 400
    He ceas'd; the menial fair that round her wait,
At *Helen*'s beck prepare the room of state:
Beneath an ample Portico, they spread
The downy fleece to form the slumbrous bed;
And o'er soft palls of purple grain unfold 405
Rich tapistry, stiff with inwoven gold:

---

duct: she still acts a mean part, and thro' fear becomes an accomplice in endeavouring to betray and ruin the *Greeks*.
    I shall just add, that after the death of *Paris*, *Helen* married *Deiphobus*; that the
story of the wooden horse is probably founded upon the taking of *Troy* by an
engine call'd a Horse, as the like engine was call'd a Ram by the *Romans*.

Then thro' th' illumin'd dome, to balmy rest
Th' obsequious Herald guides each princely guest:
While to his regal bow'r the King ascends,
And beauteous *Helen* on her Lord attends.   410
   Soon as the morn, in orient purple drest,
Unbarr'd the portal of the roseate east
The Monarch rose: magnificent to view,
Th' imperial mantle o'er his vest he threw;
The glitt'ring zone athwart his shoulder cast   415
A starry fauchion low-depending grac'd,
Clasp'd on his feet th' embroider'd sandals shine,
And forth he moves, majestic and divine:
Instant to young *Telemachus* he press'd,
And thus benevolent his speech address'd.   420
   Say, royal youth, sincere of soul report
What cause hath led you to the *Spartan* court?
Do public or domestic cares constrain
This toilsom voyage o'er the surgy main?
   O highly favour'd delegate of *Jove!*   425
(Replies the Prince) inflam'd with filial love,
And anxious hope, to hear my parent's doom,
A suppliant to your royal court I come.
Our sovereign seat a lewd usurping race
With lawless riot, and mis-rule disgrace;   430
To pamper'd insolence devoted fall
Prime of the flock, and choicest of the stall:
For wild ambition wings their bold desire,
And all to mount th' imperial bed aspire.
But prostrate I implore, oh King! relate   435
The mournful series of my father's fate:
Each known disaster of the Man disclose,
Born by his mother to a world of woes!
Recite them! nor in erring pity fear
To wound with storied grief the filial ear: 440
If e'er *Ulysses*, to reclaim your right,
Avow'd his zeal in council or in fight,

If *Phrygian* camps the friendly toils attest,
To the sire's merit give the son's request.

　　Deep from his inmost soul *Atrides* sigh'd,　　　　445
And thus indignant to the Prince reply'd:
Heav'ns! wou'd a soft, inglorious, dastard train
An absent heroe's nuptial joys profane!
So with her young, amid the woodland shades
A tim'rous hind the lion's court invades,　　　　　450
Leaves in that fatal laire the tender fawns,
Climbs the green cliff, or feeds the flow'ry lawns:
Mean-time return'd, with dire remorseless sway
The monarch-savage rends the trembling prey.
With equal fury, and with equal fame,　　　　　　455
Ulysses soon shall re-assert his claim.
O *Jove*, supreme, whom Gods and men revere!

---

447. *Heav'ns! would a soft, inglorious, dastard train.*] *Menelaus* is fir'd with indignation at the injuries offer'd his friend by the Suitors: he breaks out into an exclamation, and in a just contempt vouchsafes not to mention them: he thinks he fully distinguishes whom he intends, by calling them ἀνάλκιδες αὐτοὶ *those cowards*. The comparison which he introduces is very just, they are the Fawns, *Ulysses* is the Lion.

This is the first Simile that *Homer* has inserted in the *Odyssey*; but I cannot think it proceeded from a barrenness of invention, or thro' phlegm in the declension of his years, as some have imagin'd. The nature of the Poem requires a difference of stile from the *Iliad*: The *Iliad* rushes along like a torrent; the *Odyssey* flows gently on like a deep stream, with a smooth tranquility: *Achilles* is all fire, *Ulysses* all wisdom.

The Simile in *Homer* is really beautiful; but in *Hobbs* ridiculous ⟨329–32⟩.

As when a stag and hind ent'ring the den
Of th' absent Lion, lulls his whelps with tales,
Of hills and dales; the Lion comes agen,
And tears them into pieces with his nails.

Can any thing be more foreign to the sense of *Homer*, or worse translated? He construes κρημνοὺς ἐξερέῃσι, by telling stories of hills and dales to the Lion's whelps, instead of *Juga investigat* ⟨quoted from the Latin version accompanying the Greek text in Joshua Barnes's *Odyssey*, IV 337 (Cambridge, 1711)⟩: but such mistakes are so frequent in *Hobbs*, that one would almost suspect his learning in *Greek*: he has disgraced the best Poet, and a very great Historian; *Homer*, and *Thucydides* ⟨*Eight bookes of the Peloponnesian warre*, 1629⟩.

And *thou, to whom 'tis giv'n to gild the sphere!
With pow'r congenial join'd, propitious aid
The chief adopted by the martial maid!   460
Such to our wish the warrior soon restore,
As when contending on the *Lesbian* shore
His prowess *Philomelides* confess'd,
And loud-acclaiming *Greeks* the victor bless'd:
Then soon th' invaders of his bed and throne,   465
Their love presumptuous shall with life atone.
With patient ear, oh royal youth, attend
The storied labours of thy father's friend:
Fruitful of deeds, the copious tale is long,
But truth severe shall dictate to my tongue: 470
Learn what I heard the sea-born Seer relate,
Whose eye can pierce the dark recess of fate.
    Long on th' *Ægyptian* coast by calms confin'd,
Heav'n to my fleet refus'd a prosp'rous wind:
No vows had we prefer'd, nor victim slain!   475
For this the Gods each fav'ring gale restrain:
Jealous, to see their high behests obey'd,
Severe, if men th' eternal rights evade!
High o'er a gulphy sea, the *Pharian* Isle

* *Apollo.*

462. *As when contending on the* Lesbian *shore.*] The Poet here gives an account of one of *Ulysses*'s adventures. *Philomelides* was King of *Lesbos*, and *Eustathius* observes, that there was a tradition that *Ulysses* and *Diomedes* slew him, and turn'd a stately monument he had rais'd for himself into a public place for the reception of strangers.

479. —*The* Pharian *Isle.*] This description of *Pharos* has given great trouble to the Critics and Geographers; it is generally concluded, that the distance of *Pharos* is about seven Stadia from *Alexandria*; *Ammianus Marcellinus* mentions this very passage thus, *lib.* 22 ⟨xxii xvi 10⟩. *Insula Pharos, ubi Protea cum Phocarum gregibus diversatum Homerus fabulatur inflatius, a civitatis litore mille passibus disparata,* or, *about a mile distant from the shores.* How then comes *Homer* to affirm it to be distant a full day's sail? *Dacier* answers, that *Homer* might have heard that the *Nile*, continually bringing down much earthy substance, had enlarg'd the continent: and knowing it not to be so distant in his time, took the liberty of a Poet, and describ'd

Fronts the deep roar of disemboguing *Nile:*   480
Her distance from the shore, the course begun
At dawn, and ending with the setting sun,
A gally measures; when the stiffer gales
Rise on the poop, and fully stretch the sails.
There anchor'd vessels safe in harbour lye,   485
Whilst limpid springs the failing cask supply.
And now the twentieth sun descending, laves
His glowing axle in the western waves;
Still with expanded sails we court in vain
Propitious winds, to waft us o'er the main: 490
And the pale mariner at once deplores
His drooping vigour, and exhausted stores.

---

it as still more distant in the days of *Menelaus.* But *Dacier* never sees a mistake in *Homer.* Had his Poetry been worse if he had describ'd the real distance of *Pharos*? It is allowable in a Poet to disguise the truth, to adorn his story; but what ornament has he given his Poetry by this enlargement? *Bochart* ⟨Pt. 1: IV xxiv (pp. 296–7)⟩ has fully prov'd that there is no accession to the Continent from any substance that the *Nile* brings down with it: the violent agitation of the seas prohibit it from lodging, and forming it self into solidity. *Eratosthenes* ⟨in Strabo 1 ii 22⟩ is of opinion, that *Homer* was ignorant of the mouths of *Nile*: but *Strabo* ⟨*ibid.*⟩ answers that, his silence about them is not an argument of his ignorance, for neither has he ever mention'd where he was born. But *Strabo* does not enter fully into the meaning of *Eratosthenes*: *Eratosthenes* does not mean that *Homer* was ignorant of the mouths of *Nile* from his silence, but because he places *Pharos* at the distance of a whole day's sail from the Continent. The only way to unite this inconsistence is to suppose, that the Poet intended to specify the *Pelusiac* mouth of *Nile*, from which *Pharos* stands about a day's sail: but this is submitted to the Critics.

I can't tell whether one should venture to make use of the word *Nile* in the translation, it is doubtless an Anachronism; that name being unknown in the times of *Homer* and *Menelaus*, when the *Nile* was call'd *Ægyptus. Homer* in this very book

—Αἰγύπτοιο, διιπετέος ποταμοῖο. ⟨477⟩

Yet on the other hand, this name of *Ægyptus* is so little known, that a common Reader would scarce distinguish the river from the country; and indeed universal custom has obtain'd for using the *Latin* name instead of the *Grecian*, in many other instances which are equally anachronisms. Witness all the names of the Gods and Goddesses throughout *Homer. Jupiter* for *Zeus*, *Juno* for *Hera*, *Neptune* for *Poseidon*, &c.

When lo! a bright cærulean form appears,
The fair *Eidothea!* to dispel my fears;
Proteus her sire divine. With pity press'd,   495
Me sole the daughter of the deep address'd;
What-time, with hunger pin'd, my absent mates
Roam the wild Isle in search of rural cates,
Bait the barb'd steel, and from the fishy flood
Appease th' afflictive fierce desire of food.   500
   Whoe'er thou art, (the azure Goddess cries,)
Thy conduct ill deserves the praise of wise:
Is death thy choice, or misery thy boast,
That here inglorious on a barren coast
Thy brave associates droop, a meagre train   505
With famine pale, and ask thy care in vain?
   Struck with the kind reproach, I strait reply;
Whate'er thy title in thy native sky,
A Goddess sure! for more than mortal grace
Speaks thee descendent of etherial race: 510
Deem not, that here of choice my fleet remains;
Some heav'nly pow'r averse my stay constrains:
O, piteous of my fate, vouchsafe to shew,
(For what's sequester'd from celestial view?)

---

499. *Bait the barb'd steel, and from the fishy flood.*] *Menelaus* says, hunger was so violent among his companions that they were compell'd to eat fish. *Plutarch* in his *Symposiacs* ⟨*Quaest. Conviv.* VIII viii 3 (340 C–D)⟩ observes, that among the *Ægyptians*, *Syrians*, and *Greeks*, to abstain from fish was esteem'd a piece of sanctity; that tho' the *Greeks* were encamp'd upon the *Hellespont*, there is not the least intimation that they eat fish, or any sea-provision; and that the companions of *Ulysses*, in the 12th book of the *Odyssey*, never sought for fish till all their other provisions were consum'd, and that the same necessity compell'd them to eat the herds of the Sun which induced them to taste fish. No fish is ever offer'd in sacrifice: The *Pythagoreans* in particular command fish not to be eaten more strictly than any other animal: Fish afford no excuse at all for their destruction, they live as it were in another world, disturb not our air, consume not our fruits, or injure the waters; and therefore the *Pythagoreans*, who were unwilling to offer violence to any animals, fed very little, or not at all on fishes. I thought it necessary to insert this from *Plutarch*, because it is an observation that explains other passages in the sequel of the *Odyssey*.

What pow'r becalms th' innavigable seas?   515
What guilt provokes him, and what vows appease?
  I ceas'd, when affable the Goddess cry'd;
Observe, and in the truths I speak confide:
Th' oraculous Seer frequents the *Pharian* coast,
From whose high bed my birth divine I boast;   520
Proteus, a name tremendous o'er the main,
The delegate of *Neptune*'s watry reign.
Watch with insidious care his known abode;
There fast in chains constrain the various God:
Who bound, obedient to superior force,   525

---

521. Proteus, *a name tremendous o'er the main.*] *Eustathius* enumerates various opinions concerning *Proteus*; some understand *Proteus* allegorically to signify the first matter which undergoes all changes; others make him an emblem of true friendship, which ought not to be settled till it has been try'd in all shapes: others make *Proteus* a picture of a flatterer, who takes up all shapes, and suits himself to all forms, in compliance to the temper of the person whom he courts. The *Greeks* (observes *Diodorus* ⟨1 lxii 4⟩) imagin'd all these metamorphoses of *Proteus* to have been borrow'd from the practices of the *Ægyptian* Kings, who were accustom'd to wear the figures of Lions, Bulls or Dragons in their diadems, as emblems of Royalty, and sometimes that of Trees, &c. not so much for ornament as terror. Others took *Proteus* to be an enchanter; and *Eustathius* recounts several that were eminent in this art, as *Cratisthenes* the *Phliasian,* (which *Dacier* renders by mistake *Callisthenes* the *Physician*) who when he pleased could appear all on fire, and assume other appearances to the astonishment of the spectators: such also was *Xenophon, Scymnus* of *Tarentum, Philippides* of *Syracuse, Heraclitus* of *Mitylene,* and *Nymphodorus,* all practisers of magical arts; and *Eustathius* recites that the *Phocæ* were made use of in their Incantations. Some write that *Proteus* was an *Ægyptian* tumbler, who could throw himself into variety of figures and postures; others, a Stage-player; others, that he was a great General, skill'd in all the arts and stratagems of war: *Dacier* looks upon him to have been an enchanter, or θαυματο-ποιός. 'Tis certain from *Herodotus* ⟨11 114 ff⟩, that there was in the times of *Menelaus* a King named *Proteus,* who reign'd in *Memphis*; that *Ægypt* was always remarkable for those who excell'd in magical Arts; thus *Jannes* and *Jambres* chang'd, at least in appearance, a rod into a Serpent, and water into blood: It is not therefore improbable but that *Menelaus* hearing of him while he was in *Ægypt* went to consult him as an Enchanter, which kind of men always pretended to fore-know events; This perhaps was the real foundation of the whole story concerning *Proteus*; the rest is the fiction and embellishment of the Poet, who ascribes to his *Proteus* whatever the credulity of men usually ascribes to Enchanters.

Unerring will prescribe your destin'd course.
If studious of your realms, you then demand
Their state, since last you left your natal land;
Instant the God obsequious will disclose
Bright tracks of glory, or a cloud of woes.   530
    She ceas'd, and suppliant thus I made reply;
O Goddess! on thy aid my hopes rely:
Dictate propitious to my duteous ear,
What arts can captivate the changeful Seer?
For perilous th' assay, unheard the toil,   535
T'elude the prescience of a God by guile.
    Thus to the Goddess mild my suit I end.
Then she. Obedient to my rule, attend:
When thro' the Zone of heav'n the mounted sun
Hath journey'd half, and half remains to run;   540
The Seer, while Zephyrs curl the swelling deep,
Basks on the breezy shore, in grateful sleep,
His oozy limbs. Emerging from the wave,
The *Phocæ* swift surround his rocky cave,
Frequent and full; the consecrated train   545
Of *her, whose azure trident awes the main:
There wallowing warm, th' enormous herd exhales
An oily steam, and taints the noon-tide gales.
To that recess, commodious for surprize,
When purple light shall next suffuse the skies,   550
With me repair; and from thy warrior band
Three chosen chiefs of dauntless soul command:
Let their auxiliar force befriend the toil,
For strong the God, and perfected in guile.
Stretch'd on the shelly shore, he first surveys   555
The flouncing herd ascending from the seas;
Their number summ'd, repos'd in sleep profound
The scaly charge their guardian God surround:
So with his batt'ning flocks the careful swain

* *Amphitrite.*

Abides, pavilion'd on the grassy plain.   560
With pow'rs united, obstinately bold
Invade him, couch'd amid the scaly fold:
Instant he wears, elusive of the rape,
The mimic force of every savage shape:
Or glides with liquid lapse a murm'ring stream,   565
Or wrapt in flame, he glows at every limb.
Yet still retentive, with redoubled might
Thro' each vain passive form constrain his flight.
But when, his native shape resum'd, he stands
Patient of conquest, and your cause demands;   570
The cause that urg'd the bold attempt declare,
And sooth the vanquish'd with a victor's pray'r.
The bands relax'd, implore the Seer to say
What godhead interdicts the wat'ry way?
Who strait propitious, in prophetic strain   575
Will teach you to repass th' unmeasur'd main.
She ceas'd, and bounding from the shelfy shore,
Round the descending nymph the waves redounding roar.
   High rapt in wonder of the future deed,
With joy impetuous, to the port I speed: 580
The wants of nature with repast suffice,
'Till night with grateful shade involv'd the skies,
And shed ambrosial dews. Fast by the deep,
Along the tented shore, in balmy sleep
Our cares were lost. When o'er the eastern lawn,   585
In saffron robes the Daughter of the dawn
Advanc'd her rosy steps; before the bay,
Due ritual honours to the Gods I pay:
Then seek the place the sea-born nymph assign'd,
With three associates of undaunted mind.   590
Arriv'd, to form along th' appointed strand

---

569. *But when, his native shape resum'd*, &c.] This is founded upon the practice
of Enchanters, who never give their answers, till they have astonish'd the imagination of those who consult them with their juggling delusions. *Dacier.*

For each a bed, she scoops the hilly sand:
Then from her azure car, the finny spoils
Of four vast *Phocæ* takes, to veil her wiles;
Beneath the finny spoils extended prone,   595
Hard toil! the prophet's piercing eye to shun;
New from the corse, the scaly frauds diffuse
Unsavoury stench of oil, and brackish ooze:
But the bright sea-maid's gentle pow'r implor'd,
With nectar'd drops the sick'ning sense restor'd.   600
    Thus 'till the sun had travel'd half the skies,
Ambush'd we lie, and wait the bold emprise:
When thronging thick to bask in open air,
The flocks of Ocean to the strand repair:
Couch'd on the sunny sand, the monsters sleep: 605
Then *Proteus* mounting from the hoary deep,
Surveys his charge, unknowing of deceit:
(In order told, we make the sum compleat.)
Pleas'd with the false review, secure he lies,
And leaden slumbers press his drooping eyes.   610
Rushing impetuous forth, we strait prepare
A furious onset with the sound of war.
And shouting seize the God: our force t'evade
His various arts he soon resumes in aid:
A Lion now, he curls a surgy mane;   615
Sudden, our bands a spotted Pard restrain:

---

613. *And shouting seize the God.*—] *Proteus* has, thro' the whole story, been describ'd as a God who knew all things; it may then be ask'd, how comes it that he did not fore-know the violence that was design'd against his own person? and is it not a contradiction, that he who knew *Menelaus* without information, should not know that he lay in ambush to seize him? The only answer that occurs to me is, that these enchanters never pretend to have an inherent fore-knowledge of events, but learn things by magical arts, and by recourse to the secrets of their profession; so that *Proteus* having no suspicion, had not consulted his art, and consequently might be surprized by *Menelaus*: So far is agreeable to the pretensions of such deluders: The Poet indeed has drawn him in colours stronger than life; but Poetry adds or detracts at pleasure, and is allow'd frequently to step out of the way, to bring a foreign ornament into the story.

Then arm'd with tusks, and lightning in his eyes,
A Boar's obscener shape the God belies:
On spiry volumes there a Dragon rides;
Here, from our strict embrace a Stream he glides: 620
And last, sublime his stately growth he rears,
A Tree, and well-dissembled foliage wears.
Vain efforts! with superior pow'r compress'd,
Me with reluctance thus the Seer address'd.
Say, son of *Atreus*, say what God inspir'd 625
This daring fraud, and what the boon desir'd?
    I thus: O thou, whose certain eye foresees
The fix'd event of fate's remote decrees;
After long woes, and various toil endur'd,
Still on this desert Isle my fleet is moor'd; 630
Unfriended of the gales. All-knowing! say
What Godhead interdicts the wat'ry way?
What vows repentant will the Pow'r appease,
To speed a prosp'rous voyage o'er the seas?
    To *Jove*, (with stern regard the God replies,) 635
And all th' offended synod of the skies;
Just hecatombs with due devotion slain,
Thy guilt absolv'd, a prosp'rous voyage gain.
To the firm sanction of thy fate attend!
An exile thou, nor cheering face of friend, 640
Nor sight of natal shore, nor regal dome
Shalt yet enjoy, but still art doom'd to roam.
Once more the *Nile*, who from the secret source

---

635. *To* Jove—*just Hecatombs*—&c.] *Homer* continually inculcates morality, and piety to the Gods; he gives in this place a great instance of the necessity of it. *Menelaus* cannot succeed in any of his actions, till he pays due honours to the Gods; the neglect of sacrifice is the occasion of all his calamity, and the performance of it opens a way to all his future prosperity.

643.   —Nile, *who from the secret source*
                    Of Jove's *high seat descends*—]

Homer, it must be confess'd, gives the epithet διιπετής generally to all rivers; if he had used it here peculiarly, there might have been room to have imagin'd that he had been acquainted with the true cause of the inundations of this famous

Of *Jove*'s high seat descends with sweepy force,
Must view his billows white beneath thy oar,   645
And altars blaze along his sanguine shore.
Then will the Gods, with holy pomp ador'd,
To thy long vows a safe return accord.

    He ceas'd: heart-wounded with afflictive pain,
(Doom'd to repeat the perils of the main,   650
A shelfy tract, and long!) O Seer, I cry,
To the stern sanction of th' offended sky
My prompt obedience bows. But deign to say,
What fate propitious, or what dire dismay
Sustain those Peers, the reliques of our host,   655
Whom I with *Nestor* on the *Phrygian* coast
Embracing left? Must I the warriors weep,
Whelm'd in the bottom of the monstrous deep?
Or did the kind domestic friend deplore
The breathless heroes on their native shore?   660

    Press not too far, reply'd the God; but cease
To know, what known will violate thy peace:
Too curious of their doom! with friendly woe
Thy breast will heave, and tears eternal flow.
Part live; the rest, a lamentable train!   665
Range the dark bounds of *Pluto*'s dreary reign.
Two, foremost in the roll of *Mars* renown'd,
Whose arms with conquest in thy cause were crown'd,
Fell by disastrous fate; by tempests tost,
A third lives wretched on a distant coast.   670
    By *Neptune* rescu'd from *Minerva*'s hate,

---

river: The word Διιπετής implies it: For it is now generally agreed, that these
prodigious inundations proceed from the vast rains and the melting of the snows
on the mountains of the Moon in *Æthiopia*, about the autumnal Æquinox; when
those rains begin to fall, the river by degrees increases, and as they abate, it de-
creases; the word Διιπετής is therefore peculiarly proper when apply'd to the
Nile, for tho' all rivers depend upon the waters that fall from the air, or ἐκ Διός,
yet the *Nile* more especially, for when the rain ceases, the *Nile* consists only of
seven empty channels.

On *Gyræ*, safe *Oilean Ajax* sate,
His ship o'erwhelm'd: but frowning on the floods,
Impious he roar'd defiance to the Gods:
To his own prowess all the glory gave,   675
The pow'r defrauding who vouchsaf'd to save.
This heard the raging Ruler of the main;
His spear, indignant for such high disdain,
He launch'd; dividing with his forky mace
Th' aerial summit from the marble base: 680
The rock rush'd sea-ward, with impetuous roar
Ingulf'd, and to th' abyss the boaster bore.
   By *Juno*'s guardian aid, the wat'ry Vast
Secure of storms, your royal brother past:
'Till coasting nigh the Cape, where *Malea* shrouds   685
Her spiry cliffs amid surrounding clouds;
A whirling gust tumultuous from the shore,
Across the deep his lab'ring vessel bore.
In an ill-fated hour the coast he gain'd,
Where late in regal pomp *Thyestes* reign'd;   690
But when his hoary honours bow'd to fate,
Ægisthus govern'd in paternal state.
The surges now subside, the tempest ends;
From his tall ship the King of men descends:
There fondly thinks the Gods conclude his toil!   695

---

682. *And to th' abyss the boaster bore.*] It is in the original, *He dy'd having drunk the salt water.* This verse has been omitted in many editions of *Homer*; and the Ancients, says *Eustathius*, blame *Aristarchus* for not marking it as a verse that ought to be rejected; the simplicity of it consists in the sense, more than in the terms, and it is unworthy of *Proteus* to treat the death of *Ajax* with pleasantry, as he seems to do, by adding *having drunk salt water*: But why may not *Proteus* be suppos'd to be serious, and the terms ἁλμυρὸν ὕδωρ, to imply no more than that he was drown'd in waves of the ocean? I know only one reason that can give any colour to the objection, *viz.* it's being possibly become a vulgar expression, and used commonly in a ludicrous sense; then indeed it is to be avoided in Poetry; but it does not follow, because perhaps it might be used in this manner in the days of these Critics, that therefore it was so used in the days of *Homer*. What was poetical in the time of the Poet might be grown vulgar in the time of the Critics.

Far from his own domain salutes the soil;
With rapture oft the verge of *Greece* reviews,
And the dear turf with tears of joy bedews.
Him thus exulting on the distant strand,
A Spy distinguish'd from his airy stand;   700
To bribe whose vigilance, *Ægisthus* told
A mighty sum of ill-persuading gold:
There watch'd this guardian of his guilty fear,
'Till the twelfth moon had wheel'd her pale career;
And now admonish'd by his eye, to court   705
With terror wing'd conveys the dread report.
Of deathful arts expert, his Lord employs
The ministers of blood in dark surprize:
And twenty youths in radiant mail incas'd,
Close ambush'd nigh the spacious hall he plac'd.   710
Then bids prepare the hospitable treat:
Vain shews of love to veil his felon hate!
To grace the victor's welcome from the wars,
A train of coursers, and triumphal cars
Magnificent he leads: the royal guest   715
Thoughtless of ill, accepts the fraudful feast.
The troop forth issuing from the dark recess,
With homicidal rage the King oppress!
So, whilst he feeds luxurious in the stall,
The sov'reign of the herd is doom'd to fall.   720
The partners of his fame and toils at *Troy*,
Around their Lord, a mighty ruin! lye:
Mix'd with the brave, the base invaders bleed;
Ægisthus sole survives to boast the deed.
    He said; chill horrors shook my shiv'ring soul,   725

---

719. *So, whilst he feeds luxurious in the stall,* &c.] *Dacier* translates βοῦν, by
taureau a bull; and misunderstands *Eustathius* who directly says, that in the 2d
Iliad the Poet compares *Agamemnon* to a bull, in this place to an oxe, ταύρῳ
εἴκασεν, νῦν δὲ βοΐ αὐτὸν ὡμοίωσεν. The one was undoubtedly design'd to
describe the courage and majestic port of a warrior, the other to give us an image
of a Prince falling in full peace and plenty, ὡς βοῦν ἐπὶ φάτνῃ.

Rack'd with convulsive pangs in dust I roul;
And hate, in madness of extreme despair,
To view the sun, or breathe the vital air.
But when superior to the rage of woe,
I stood restor'd, and tears had ceas'd to flow;   730
Lenient of grief, the pitying God began.—
Forget the brother, and resume the man:
To fate's supreme dispose the dead resign,
That care be fate's, a speedy passage thine.
Still lives the wretch who wrought the death deplor'd,
But lives a victim for thy vengeful sword;   736
Unless with filial rage *Orestes* glow,
And swift prevent the meditated blow:
You timely will return a welcome guest,
With him to share the sad funereal feast.   740
 He said: new thoughts my beating heart employ,
My gloomy soul receives a gleam of joy.
Fair hope revives; and eager I addrest
The prescient Godhead to reveal the rest.
The doom decreed of those disastrous Two   745
I've heard with pain, but oh! the tale pursue;
What third brave son of *Mars* the fates constrain
To roam the howling desart of the main:
Or in eternal shade if cold he lies,

749. *Or in eternal shade if cold he lyes.*] *Proteus* in the beginning of his relation had said, that *one person was alive, and remain'd enclosed by the ocean*: How then comes *Menelaus* here to say, Give me an account of that other person who is alive, or *dead*? Perhaps the sorrow which *Menelaus* conceived for his friend *Ulysses*, might make him fear the worst; and *Proteus* adding *enclos'd by the ocean* might give a suspicion that he was dead, the words being capable of ambiguity. However this be, it sets the friendship of *Menelaus* in a strong light: where friendship is sincere, a state of uncertainty is a state of fears, we dread even possibilities, and give them an imaginary certainty. Upon this, one of the finest compliments that a Poet ever made to a patron turns, that of *Horace* to *Mæcenas*, in the first of the *Epodes* ⟨15–22⟩.

It may not perhaps be disagreeable to the Reader to observe, that *Virgil* has borrow'd this story of *Proteus* from *Homer*, and translated it almost literally ⟨Geo.

Provoke new sorrow from these grateful eyes.   750
That chief (rejoin'd the God) his race derives
From *Ithaca*, and wond'rous woes survives;
Laertes' son: girt with circumfluous tides,
He still calamitous constraint abides.
Him in *Calypso*'s cave of late I view'd,   755
When streaming grief his faded cheek bedew'd.
But vain his pray'r, his arts are vain to move
Th' enamour'd Goddess, or elude her love:

IV 387 ff〉. *Rapin* says, that *Homer*'s description is more ingenious and fuller of invention, but *Virgil*'s more judicious 〈Comparaison xiii, 1 148〉. I wish that Critic had given his reasons for his opinion. I believe in general, the plan of the *Iliad* and *Odyssey* is allow'd by the best of Critics to be more perfect than that of the *Æneis*. *Homer* with respect to the unity of time, has the advantage very manifestly; *Rapin* confesses it 〈Comparaison xii, 1 136〉, and *Aristotle* proposes him as an example to all Epic Authors 〈*Poetics* xxvi 14–15〉. Where then is the superiority of judgment? Is it that there are more fabulous, I mean incredible, stories in *Homer* than *Virgil*? as that of the *Cyclops*, the ships of *Alcinous*, &c. *Virgil* has imitated most of these bold fables, and the story of the ships of *Alcinous* is not more incredible than the transformation of the ships of *Æneas* 〈IX 117 ff〉. But this is too large a subject to be discuss'd in the compass of these Annotations. In particular passages I freely allow the preference to *Virgil*, as in the descent of *Æneas* into hell, &c. but in this story of *Proteus*, I cannot see any superiority of judgment. *Virgil* is little more than a translator; to shew the particulars would be too tedious: I refer it to the Reader to compare the two Authors, and shall only instance in one passage 〈*Od*. IV 454–58〉.

Ἡμεῖς δὲ ἰάχοντες ἐπεσσύμεθ', ἀμφὶ δὲ χεῖρας.
Βάλλομεν. οὐδ' ὁ γέρων δολίης ἐπελήθετο τέχνης,
Ἀλλ' ἦ τοι πρώτιστα λέων γένετ' ἠυγένειος,
Αὐτὰρ ἔπειτα δράκων, καὶ πάρδαλις ἠδὲ μέγας σῦς·
Γίγνετο δ'ὑγρὸν ὕδωρ, καὶ δένδρεον ὑψιπέτηλον, &c.

Cum clamore ruit magno, manicisque jacentem
Occupat: ille suæ contra non immemor artis,
Omnia transformat sese in miracula rerum,
Ignemque, horribilemque feram, fluviumque liquentem. &c.
〈*Geo*. IV 439–42〉

Homer has a manifest advantage in the occasion of the story: The loss of a few bees seems to be a cause too trivial for an undertaking so great as the surprize of a Deity; whereas the whole happiness of *Menelaus* depends upon this consultation of *Proteus*: This is a far more important cause, and consequently in this respect something more is due to *Homer*, than the sole honour of an inventor.

His vessel sunk, and dear companions lost,
He lives reluctant on a foreign coast.   760
But oh belov'd by heav'n! reserv'd to thee
A happier lot the smiling fates decree:
Free from that law, beneath whose mortal sway
Matter is chang'd, and varying forms decay;
Elysium shall be thine; the blissful plains   765
Of utmost earth, where *Rhadamanthus* reigns.
Joys ever-young, unmix'd with pain or fear,
Fill the wide circle of th' eternal year:
Stern winter smiles on that auspicious clime:
The fields are florid with unfading prime: 770
From the bleak pole no winds inclement blow,
Mold the round hail, or flake the fleecy snow;
But from the breezy deep, the Blest inhale
The fragrant murmurs of the western gale.
This grace peculiar will the Gods afford   775
To thee the Son of *Jove*, and beauteous *Helen*'s Lord.
    He ceas'd, and plunging in the vast profound,
Beneath the God the whirling billows bound.
Then speeding back, involv'd in various thought,

765.   Elysium *shall be thine; the blissful plains*
            Of utmost earth, &c.—]
This is the only place in which the *Elysian* field is mention'd in *Homer*. The conjectures of the Ancients are very various about it: *Plato* in his *Phæd.* places it in
cælo stellato, or the region of the Stars ⟨247 c⟩; but since *Homer* fixes it, εἰς
πείρατα γαίης, or (as *Milton* expresses it) at the *earth's green end* ⟨Earth's green
Cape, *Par. Lost* VIII 631; green earth's end, *Comus* 1014⟩, I will pass over the conjectures of others, especially since the μακάρων Νῆσοι, by which others express
Elysium, confines it to this world.
    Strabo ⟨III ii 13⟩, says *Eustathius,* places it not far from *Maurusia,* that lies near
the Streights: It is suppos'd by *Bochart* ⟨Pt. II: I xxxiv, pp. 663–4)⟩, as *Dacier*
observes, that the fable is of *Phœnician* extraction, that *Alizuth* in *Hebrew* signifies *joy* or *exultation,* which word the *Greeks* adapting to their way of pronunciation, call'd *Elysius.* If this be true, I should come into an opinion that has much
prevail'd, that the *Greeks* had heard of *Paradise* from the *Hebrews*; and that the
Hebrews describing *Paradise* as a place of *Alizuth,* or *joy,* gave occasion to all the
fables of the *Grecian Elysium.*

My friends attending at the shore I sought.   780
Arriv'd, the rage of hunger we controll,
'Till night with silent shade invests the pole;
Then lose the cares of life in pleasing rest.—
Soon as the morn reveals the roseate east,
With sails we wing the masts, our anchors weigh,   785
Unmoor the fleet, and rush into the sea.
Rang'd on the banks, beneath our equal oars
White curl the waves, and the vex'd ocean roars.
Then steering backward from the *Pharian* Isle,
We gain the stream of *Jove*-descended *Nile*:   790
There quit the ships, and on the destin'd shore
With ritual hecatombs the Gods adore:
Their wrath aton'd, to *Agamemnon*'s name
A Cenotaph I raise of deathless fame.
These rites to piety and grief discharg'd,   795
The friendly Gods a springing gale inlarg'd:
The fleet swift tilting o'er the surges flew,
'Till *Grecian* cliffs appear'd, a blissful view!
      Thy patient ear hath heard me long relate
A story, fruitful of disastrous fate: 800
And now, young Prince, indulge my fond request;
Be *Sparta* honour'd with his royal guest,
'Till from his eastern goal, the joyous sun
His twelfth diurnal race begins to run.
Mean-time my train the friendly gifts prepare,   805
Three sprightly coursers, and a polish'd car:
With these, a goblet of capacious mold,
Figur'd with art to dignify the gold,
(Form'd for libation to the Gods,) shall prove
A pledge and monument of sacred love.   810
      My quick return, young *Ithacus* rejoin'd,

---

806. *Three sprightly coursers*.] How comes it to pass that *Menelaus* proffers *three*
horses to *Telemachus*? This was a compleat set among the Ancients, they used one
Pole-horse and two leaders. *Eustathius*.

Damps the warm wishes of my raptur'd mind:
Did not my fate my needful haste constrain,
Charm'd by your speech, so graceful and humane,
Lost in delight the circling year wou'd roll, 815
While deep attention fix'd my list'ning soul.
But now to *Pyle* permit my destin'd way,
My lov'd associates chide my long delay.
In dear remembrance of your royal grace,
I take the present of the promis'd Vase; 820
The coursers for the champian sports, retain;
That gift our barren rocks will render vain:

---

822. *That gift our barren rocks will render vain.*] This passage where *Telemachus* refuses the horses has been much observ'd, and turn'd to a moral sense, *viz.* as a lesson to men to desire nothing but what is suitable to their conditions. *Horace* has introduced it into his Epistles ⟨1 vii 40–3⟩.

> Haud male Telemachus proles patientis Ulixei;
> "*Non est aptus equis Ithace locus, ut neque planis
> Porrectus spatiis, nec multæ prodigus herbæ:
> Atride, magis apta tibi tua dona relinquam.*"

This is the reason why *Ulysses* (as *Eustathius* observes upon the 10th of the *Iliads*) leaves the horses of *Rhesus* to the disposal of *Diomedes*; so that the same spirit of Wisdom reign'd in *Telemachus*, that was so remarkable in *Ulysses*. This is the reason why *Menelaus* smil'd; it was not at the frankness or simplicity of *Telemachus*, but it was a smile of joy, to see the young Prince inherit his father's wisdom.

It is the remark of *Eustathius*, that *Telemachus* is far from exalting the nature of his country; he confesses it to be barren, and more barren than the neighbouring Islands; yet that natural and laudable affection which all worthy persons have for their country makes him prefer it to places of a more happy situation. This appears to me a replication to what *Menelaus* had before offer'd concerning the transplantation of *Ulysses* to *Sparta*; this is contain'd in ἱπποβότοιο; and then the meaning is, 'Tis true *Ithaca* is a barren region, yet more desirable than this country of *Lacedæmon*, this ἱππόβοτος γαῖα. It is the more probable from the offer of horses which *Menelaus* had then made, and is also another reason for the smile of *Menelaus*.

Eustathius remarks that *Menelaus*, tho' he has expressed the greatest friendship for *Ulysses*, yet makes no offer to restore the fortunes of his friend by any military assistance; tho' he had a most fair opportunity given him to repay the past kindness of *Ulysses* to his wife *Penelope*, and his son *Telemachus*; and how comes *Telemachus* not to ask it either of *Nestor* or *Menelaus*? He answers, that this depended

Horrid with cliffs, our meagre land allows
Thin herbage for the mountain-goat to browze,
But neither mead nor plain supplies, to feed   825
The sprightly courser, or indulge his speed:
To sea-surrounded realms the Gods assign
Small tract of fertile lawn, the least to mine.

His hand the King with tender passion press'd,
And smiling thus, the royal Youth address'd: 830
O early worth! a soul so wise, and young,
Proclaims you from the sage *Ulysses* sprung.
Selected from my stores, of matchless price
An urn shall recompence your prudent choice:
Not mean the massy mold, of silver grac'd   835
By *Vulcan*'s art, the verge with gold enchas'd:
A pledge the sceptred pow'r of *Sidon* gave,
When to his realm I plow'd the orient wave.

Thus they alternate; while with artful care
The menial train the regal feast prepare: 840
The firstlings of the flock are doom'd to dye;
Rich fragrant wines the cheering bowl supply;
A female band the gift of *Ceres* bring;
And the gilt roofs with genial triumph ring.

Mean-while, in *Ithaca*, the Suitor-powrs   845
In active games divide their jovial hours:
In *Areas* vary'd with mosaic art,
Some whirl the disk, and some the jav'lin dart.
Aside, sequester'd from the vast resort,
Antinous sate spectator of the sport;   850
With great *Eurymachus*, of worth confest, ⎫
And high descent, superior to the rest;   ⎬
Whom young *Noëmon* lowly thus addrest.   ⎭

upon the uncertainty they were yet under, concerning the life of *Ulysses*. But the
truer reason in my opinion is, that the nature of Epic Poetry requires a contrary
conduct: The Heroe of the Poem is to be the chief agent, and the re-establishment
of his fortunes must be owing to his own wisdom and valour. I have enlarg'd
upon this already, so that there is no occasion in this place to insist upon it.

My ship equip'd within the neighb'ring port,
The Prince, departing for the *Pylian* court,   855
Requested for his speed; but, courteous, say
When steers he home, or why this long delay?
For *Elis* I shou'd sail with utmost speed,
T'import twelve mares which there luxurious feed,
And twelve young mules, a strong laborious race,   860
New to the plow, unpractis'd in the trace.
    Unknowing of the course to *Pyle* design'd,
A sudden horror seiz'd on either mind:
The Prince in rural bow'r they fondly thought,
Numb'ring his flocks and herds, not far remote.   865
Relate, *Antinous* cries, devoid of guile,
When spread the Prince his sail for distant *Pyle*?
Did chosen chiefs across the gulphy main
Attend his voyage, or domestic train?
Spontaneous did you speed his secret course,   870
Or was the vessel seiz'd by fraud or force?
    With willing duty, not reluctant mind,
(*Noëmon* cry'd) the vessel was resign'd.
Who in the balance, with the great affairs
Of courts, presume to weigh their private cares?   875
With him, the peerage next in pow'r to you:
And *Mentor*, captain of the lordly crew,
Or some Celestial in his reverend form,
Safe from the secret rock and adverse storm,
Pilots their course: For when the glimm'ring ray   880
Of yester dawn disclos'd the tender day,
Mentor himself I saw, and much admir'd.—
Then ceas'd the Youth, and from the court retir'd.
    Confounded and appall'd, th' unfinish'd game
The Suitors quit, and all to council came: 885
Antinous first th' assembled Peers addrest,
Rage sparkling in his eyes, and burning in his breast.
    O shame to manhood! shall one daring boy
The scheme of all our happiness destroy?

Fly unperceiv'd, seducing half the flow'r   890
Of nobles, and invite a foreign pow'r?
The pond'rous engine rais'd to crush us all,
Recoiling, on his head is sure to fall.
Instant prepare me, on the neighb'ring strand,
With twenty chosen mates a vessel mann'd;   895
For ambush'd close beneath the *Samian* shore
His ship returning shall my spies explore:
He soon his rashness shall with life atone,
Seek for his father's fate, but find his own.

  With vast applause the sentence all approve;   900
Then rise, and to the feastful hall remove:
Swift to the Queen the Herald *Medon* ran,
Who heard the consult of the dire Divan:
Before her dome the royal matron stands,
And thus the message of his haste demands.   905
    What will the Suitors? must my servant train

896. *For ambush'd close*, &c.] We have here another use which the Poet makes of the voyage of *Telemachus*. *Eustathius* remarks that these incidents not only diversify but enliven the Poem. But it may be ask'd why the Poet makes not use of so fair an opportunity to insert a gallant action of *Telemachus*, and draw him not as eluding, but defeating his adversaries? The answer is easy; That the Suitors sail'd compleatly arm'd, and *Telemachus* unprovided of any weapons: and therefore *Homer* consults credibility, and forbears to paint his young Heroe in the colours of a Knight of Romance, who upon all disadvantages engages and defeats his opposers. But then to what purpose is this ambush of the Suitors, and what part of the design of the Poem is carry'd on by it? The very chief aim of it; To shew the sufferings of *Ulysses*: He is unfortunate in all relations of life, as a King, as an husband, and here very eminently as a father; these sufferings are laid down in the proposition of the *Odyssey* as essential to the Poem, and consequently this ambush laid by the Suitors against the life of *Telemachus* is an essential ornament.

906. *The speech of* Penelope.] *Longinus* ⟨xxvii 4⟩ in particular commends this speech as a true picture of a person that feels various emotions of soul, and is born by every gust of passion from sentiment to sentiment, with sudden and unexpected transitions. There is some obscurity in the *Greek*, this arises from the warmth with which she speaks, she has not leisure to explain her self fully, a circumstance natural to a person in anger.

Penelope gives a very beautiful picture of *Ulysses*: "The best of Princes are

Th' allotted labours of the day refrain,
For them to form some exquisite repast?
Heav'n grant this festival may prove their last!
Or if they still must live, from me remove   910
The double plague of luxury and love!
Forbear, ye sons of insolence! forbear,
In riot to consume a wretched heir.
In the young soul illustrious thought to raise,
Were ye not tutor'd with *Ulysses'* praise?   915
Have not your fathers oft my Lord defin'd,
Gentle of speech, beneficent of mind?
Some Kings with arbitrary rage devour,
Or in their tyrant-Minions vest the pow'r:
Ulysses let no partial favours fall,   920
The people's parent, he protected all:
But absent now, perfidious and ingrate!
His stores ye ravage and usurp his state.
    He thus; O were the woes you speak the worst!
They form a deed more odious and accurst;   925
More dreadful than your boding soul divines:
But pitying *Jove* avert the dire designs!
The darling object of your royal care
Is mark'd to perish in a deathful snare:
Before he anchors in his native port,   930

---

allow'd to have their favourites, and give a greater share of affection than ordinary to particular persons. But *Ulysses* was a father to all his people alike, and loved them all as his children; a father, tho' he bears a more tender affection to one child than to another, yet shews them all an equal treatment; thus also a good King is not sway'd by inclination, but justice, towards all his subjects." *Dacier.*

One circumstance is very remarkable, and gives us a full view of a person in anger; at the very sight of *Medon Penelope* flies out into passion, she gives him not time to speak one syllable, but speaks her self as if all the Suitors were present, and reproaches them in the person of *Medon*, tho' *Medon* is just to her and *Ulysses*; but anger is an undistinguishing passion. What she says of ingratitude, recalls to my memory what is to be found in *Laertius* ⟨v 18⟩: *Aristotle* being ask'd what thing upon earth soonest grew old? reply'd, *an Obligation*. Tí τάχιστα γηράσκει; *respondit*, χάρις.

G

From *Pyle* re-sailing and the *Spartan* court,
Horrid to speak! in ambush is decreed
The hope and heir of *Ithaca* to bleed!
   Sudden she sunk beneath the weighty woes;
The vital streams a chilling horror froze: 935
The big round tear stands trembling in her eye,
And on her tongue imperfect accents dye.
At length, in tender language interwove
With sighs, she thus express'd her anxious love.
Why rashly wou'd my son his fate explore,   940
Ride the wild waves, and quit the safer shore?
Did he, with all the greatly wretched, crave
A blank oblivion, and untimely grave?
   'Tis not, reply'd the Sage, to *Medon* giv'n
To know, if some inhabitant of heav'n,   945
In his young breast the daring thought inspir'd:
Or if along with filial duty fir'd,
The winds and waves he tempts in early bloom,
Studious to learn his absent father's doom.
   The Sage retir'd: Unable to controul   950
The mighty griefs that swell her lab'ring soul,
Rolling convulsive on the floor, is seen
The piteous object of a prostrate Queen.
Words to her dumb complaint a pause supplies,
And breath, to waste in unavailing cries.   955
Around their sov'reign wept the menial fair,
To whom she thus address'd her deep despair.
   Behold a wretch whom all the Gods consign

---

941. *Ride the wild waves*—] Were this passage to be render'd literally, it would run thus; *climb the swift ships, which are horses to men on the seas. Eustathius* observes the allusion is very just, and that the only doubt is, whether it be brought in opportunely by *Penelope*? it may be doubted, if the mind could find leisure to introduce such allusions? *Dacier* answers, that *Penelope* speaks thus thro' indignation: The grief that she conceives at the hardiness of men, in finding out a way to pass the seas as well as land, furnished her with these figures very naturally, for figures are agreeable to passion.

To woe! Did ever sorrows equal mine?
Long to my joys my dearest Lord is lost,   960
His country's buckler, and the *Grecian* boast:
Now from my fond embrace by tempests torn,
Our other column of the state is born:
Nor took a kind adieu, nor sought consent!—
Unkind confed'rates in his dire intent!   965
Ill suits it with your shews of duteous zeal,
From me the purpos'd voyage to conceal:
Tho' at the solemn midnight hour he rose,
Why did you fear to trouble my repose?
He either had obey'd my fond desire,   970
Or seen his mother pierc'd with grief expire.
Bid *Dolius* quick attend, the faithful slave
Whom to my nuptial train *Icarius* gave,
To tend the fruit-groves: With incessant speed
He shall this violence of death decreed,   975
To good *Laertes* tell. Experienc'd age
May timely intercept their ruffian rage,
Convene the tribes, the murd'rous plot reveal,
And to their pow'r to save his race appeal.
    Then *Euryclea* thus. My dearest dread!   980
Tho' to the sword I bow this hoary head,
Or if a dungeon be the pain decreed,
I own me conscious of th' unpleasing deed:
Auxiliar to his flight, my aid implor'd,
With wine and viands I the vessel stor'd: 985
A solemn oath impos'd the secret seal'd,
'Till the twelfth dawn the light of heav'n reveal'd.
Dreading th' effect of a fond mother's fear,
He dar'd not violate your royal ear.
But bathe, and in imperial robes array'd, ⎫   990
Pay due devotions to the *martial maid,   ⎬
And rest affianc'd in her guardian aid.   ⎭

* *Minerva.*

Send not to good *Laertes*, nor engage
In toils of state the miseries of age:
'Tis impious to surmize, the pow'rs divine   995
To ruin doom the *Jove*-descended line:
Long shall the race of just *Arcesius* reign,
And Isles remote enlarge his old domain.

    The Queen her speech with calm attention hears,
Her eyes restrain the silver-streaming tears: 1000
She bathes, and rob'd, the sacred dome ascends;
Her pious speed a female train attends:
The salted cakes in canisters are laid,
And thus the Queen invokes *Minerva*'s aid.

    Daughter divine of *Jove*, whose arm can wield   1005
Th' avenging bolt, and shake the dreadful shield!
If e'er *Ulysses* to thy fane prefer'd
The best and choicest of his flock and herd;
Hear, Goddess, hear, by those oblations won;
And for the pious sire preserve the son: 1010
His wish'd return with happy pow'r befriend,
And on the suitors let thy wrath descend.

---

   998. *And Isles remote enlarge his old domain.*] *Dacier* offers a Criticism upon these last words of *Euryclea*: It cannot be imagin'd that these fertile fields can be spoken of *Ithaca*, *Plutarch's* description ⟨*Bruta Ratione Uti* 3⟩ of it is entirely contradictory to this: "*Ithaca*, says he, is rough and mountainous, fit only to breed goats; upon cultivation it scarce yields any fruits, and these so worthless, as scarce to recompence the labour of gathering." *Homer* therefore by this expression intended the other dominions of *Ulysses*, such as *Cephallenia*, &c.

   But I question not that the whole dominions of *Ulysses* are included, *Ithaca* as well as *Cephallenia*; for tho' *Ithaca* was mountainous, yet the vallies were fruitful, according to the description of it in the 13th of the *Odyssey*.

> The rugged soil allows no level space
> For flying chariots, or the rapid race;
> Yet not ungrateful to the Peasant's pain,
> Suffices fulness to the swelling grain:
> The loaded trees their various fruits produce,
> And clustring grapes afford a gen'rous juice, &c. ⟨289–94⟩

As for her remark upon ἀπόπροθι, it is of no validity; the word stands in opposition to δώματα, and implies no more than *here*, or at a distance in general.

She ceas'd; shrill ecstasies of joy declare
The fav'ring Goddess present to the pray'r:
The Suitors heard, and deem'd the mirthful voice   1015
A signal of her Hymenæal choice:
Whilst one most jovial thus accosts the board;
"Too late the Queen selects a second lord:
"In evil hour the nuptial rite intends,
"When o'er her son disastrous death impends."   1020
Thus he, unskill'd of what the fates provide!
But with severe rebuke *Antinous* cry'd.
    These empty vaunts will make the voyage vain;
Alarm not with discourse the menial train:
The great event with silent hope attend;   1025
Our deeds alone our council must commend.
    His speech thus ended short, he frowning rose,
And twenty chiefs renown'd for valour chose:

1015.   *The Suitors heard, and deem'd the mirthful voice,*
        A signal of her hymenæal choice.]
It may be ask'd whence this conjecture of the Suitors arises? *Penelope* is describ'd as weeping grievously, and fainting away, and yet immediately the Suitors conclude she is preparing for the Nuptials. *Eustathius* answers, that undoubtedly the Suitors understood the Queen had purify'd her self with water, and supplicated the Goddess *Minerva*, tho' the Poet omits the relation of such little particularities. But whence is it that the Poet gives a greater share of wisdom to *Eurycleia* than to *Penelope*? *Penelope* commands a servant to fly with the news of the absence of *Telemachus* to *Laertes*, which could not at all advantage *Telemachus*, and only grieve *Laertes*: *Eurycleia* immediately diverts her from that vain intention, advises her to have recourse to heaven, and not add misery to the already miserable *Laertes*: This is Wisdom in *Eurycleia*. But it must be confess'd that the other is Nature in *Penelope*: *Eurycleia* is calm, *Penelope* in a passion: and *Homer* would have been a very bad painter of human Nature, if he had drawn *Penelope* thus heated with passion in the mild temper of *Eurycleia*; grief and resentment give *Penelope* no time to deliberate, whereas *Eurycleia* is less concern'd, and consequently capable of thinking with more tranquillity.

1022. *With rebuke severe* ⟨sic⟩ *Antinous cry'd.*] *Antinous* speaks thus in return to what had been before said by one of the Suitors concerning *Telemachus*, viz. "the Queen little imagines that her son's death approaches;" he fears lest *Penelope* should know their intentions, and hinder their measures by raising the subjects of *Ithaca* that still retain'd their fidelity. *Dacier.*

Down to the strand he speeds with haughty strides,
Where anchor'd in the bay the vessel rides;   1030
Replete with mail, and military store,
In all her tackle trim, to quit the shore.
The desp'rate crew ascend, unfurl the sails;
(The sea-ward prow invites the tardy gales)
Then take repast, 'till *Hesperus* display'd   1035
His golden circlet in the western shade.
        Mean-time the Queen without refection due,
Heart-wounded, to the bed of state withdrew:
In her sad breast the Prince's fortunes roul,
And hope and doubt alternate seize her soul.   1040
So when the wood-man's toyl her cave surrounds
And with the hunter's cry the grove resounds;
With grief and rage the mother-lion stung,
Fearless herself, yet trembles for her young.
        While pensive in the silent slumb'rous shade,   1045
Sleep's gentle pow'rs her drooping eyes invade;
Minerva, life-like on imbody'd air,

1041. *So when the wood-man's toyl*, &c.] The Poet, to shew the majesty and high
spirit of *Penelope*, compares her to a Lioness: He manages the allusion very artfully: he describes the Lioness not as exerting any dreadful act of violence, (for
such a comparison is only proper to be apply'd to a Heroe) but inclosed by her
enemies; which at once shews both her danger and nobleness of spirit under it:
It is in the *Greek* δόλιον κύκλον, which may signify either, a circle of toils or nets,
or a circle of enemies: The former is perhaps preferable, as corresponding best
with the condition of *Penelope*, who was surrounded with the secret ambushes and
snares of the Suitors. *Eustathius.*

1047.   *Minerva, life-like on imbody'd air,*
                        Impress'd the form, &c.]
We have here an imaginary Being introduc'd by the Poet: The whole is manag'd
with great judgment; It is short, because it has not a direct and immediate relation to the progress of the Poem, and because such imaginary entercourses have
ever been looked upon as sudden in appearance, and as sudden in vanishing
away. The use the Poet makes of it, is to relieve *Penelope* from the extremity of
despair, that she may act her part in the future scenes with courage and constancy. We see it is *Minerva* who sends this phantom to *Penelope* to comfort her:
Now this is an allegory to express that as soon as the violence of sorrow was over,

Impress'd the form of *Iphthima* the fair:
(*Icarius'* daughter she, whose blooming charms
Allur'd *Eumelus* to her virgin-arms;   1050
A sceptred Lord, who o'er the fruitful plain
Of *Thessaly* wide stretch'd his ample reign:)
As *Pallas* will'd, along the sable skies
To calm the Queen the Phantom-sister flies.
Swift on the regal dome descending right,   1055
The bolted Valves are pervious to her flight.
Close to her head the pleasing vision stands,
And thus performs *Minerva's* high commands.
 O why, *Penelope*, this causeless fear,
To render sleep's soft blessing unsincere?   1060
Alike devote to sorrow's dire extreme
The day reflection, and the midnight dream!
Thy son, the Gods propitious will restore,
And bid thee cease his absence to deplore.
 To whom the Queen, (whilst yet her pensive mind
Was in the silent gates of sleep confin'd)   1066
O sister, to my soul for ever dear,
Why this first visit to reprove my fear?
How in a realm so distant shou'd you know
From what deep source my ceaseless sorrows flow?   1070
To all my hope my royal Lord is lost,
His country's buckler, and the *Grecian* boast:
And with consummate woe to weigh me down,

---

the mind of *Penelope* return'd to some degree of tranquillity: *Minerva* is no more
than the result of her own reflection and wisdom, which banish'd from her breast
those melancholy apprehensions. The manner likewise of its introduction is not
less judicious; the mind is apt to dwell upon those objects in sleep which make a
deep impression when awake: This is the foundation of the Poet's fiction; it is
no more than a dream which he here describes, but he cloaths it with a body,
gives it a momentary existence, and by this method exalts a low circumstance
into dignity and Poetry.

 1073. *And with consummate woe*, &c.] In the original, *Penelope* says plainly, she is
more concern'd for her son than her husband. I shall translate *Dacier's* observation upon this passage. We ought not to reproach *Penelope* for this seemingly

The heir of all his honours, and his crown,
My darling son is fled! an easy prey   1075
To the fierce storms, or men more fierce than they:
Who in a league of blood associates sworn,
Will intercept th' unwary Youth's return.
  Courage resume, the shadowy form reply'd,
In the protecting care of heav'n confide: 1080
On him attends the blue-ey'd martial Maid;
What earthly can implore a surer aid?
Me now the guardian Goddess deigns to send,
To bid thee patient his return attend.
  The Queen replies: If in the blest abodes, 1085
A Goddess thou, hast commerce with the Gods;
Say, breathes my Lord the blissful realm of light,
Or lies he wrapt in ever-during night?
  Enquire not of his doom, the Phantom cries,
I speak not all the counsel of the skies: 1090
Nor must indulge with vain discourse, or long,

---

shocking declaration, in preferring a son to an husband: Her sentiment is natural and just; she had all the reason in the world to believe that *Ulysses* was dead, so that all her hopes, all her affection was entirely placed upon *Telemachus*: His loss therefore must unavoidably touch her with the highest degree of sensibility; if he is lost, she can have recourse to no second comfort. But why may we not allow the reason which *Penelope* her self gives for this superiority of sorrow for *Telemachus*? "*Telemachus*, says she, is unexperienc'd in the world, and unable to contend with difficulties; whereas *Ulysses* knew how to extricate himself upon all emergencies." This is a sufficient reason why she should fear more for *Telemachus* than *Ulysses*: Her affection might be greater for *Ulysses* than *Telemachus*, yet her fears might be stronger for the son than the husband, *Ulysses* being capable to surmount dangers by experience, *Telemachus* being new to all difficulties.

1089. *Enquire not of his doom*, &c.] It may be ask'd what is the reason of this conduct, and why should the Phantom refuse to relate any thing concerning the condition of *Ulysses*? *Eustathius* answers, that if the Phantom had related the full truth of the story, the Poem had been at an end; the very constitution of it requires that *Ulysses* should arrive unknown to all, but chiefly to his wife, as will appear in the prosecution of the story: The question is very natural for an affectionate wife to make concerning an absent husband; but this being an improper place for the discovery, the Poet defers the solution of it, 'till the unravelling of the whole in the conclusion of the Poem.

The windy satisfaction of the tongue.
    Swift thro' the valves the visionary fair
Repass'd, and viewless mix'd with common air.
The Queen awakes, deliver'd of her woes;   1095
With florid joy her heart dilating glows:
The vision, manifest of future fate,
Makes her with hope her son's arrival wait.
    Mean-time the Suitors plow the wat'ry plain,
Telemachus in thought already slain!   1100
When sight of less'ning *Ithaca* was lost,
Their sail directed for the *Samian* coast,
A small but verdant Isle appear'd in view,
And *Asteris* th' advancing Pilot knew:
An ample port the rocks projected form,   1105
To break the rowling waves, and ruffling storm:
That safe recess they gain with happy speed,
And in close ambush wait the murd'rous deed.

The action of this book takes up the space of two nights and one day, so that from the opening of the Poem to the introduction of *Ulysses* are six days compleated.

But how long a time *Telemachus* afterwards stay'd with *Menelaus*, is a question which has employ'd some modern *French* Critics; one of which maintains, that he stay'd no longer than these two nights at *Lacedæmon* ⟨evidently the anonymous author of *Chronologie de l'Odyssée*, refuted in Boivin de Villeneuve's discourse of the same title, in *Mémoires de littérature . . . de l'Académie des Inscriptions et Belles Lettres*, II (Paris, 1717), 386 ff⟩: But it is evident from the sequel of the *Odyssey*, that *Telemachus* arriv'd again at *Ithaca* two days after *Ulysses*; but *Ulysses* was twenty nine days in passing from *Ogygia* to *Ithaca*, and consequently during the whole time *Telemachus* must have been absent from *Ithaca*. The ground of that Critick's mistake was from the silence of *Homer* as to the exact time of his stay, which was of no importance, being distinguish'd by no action, and only in an Episodical part. The same thing led me into the like error in 421n of the second book, where it is said that *Telemachus* return'd to *Ithaca* in less than twelve days.

G*

THE

FIFTH BOOK

OF THE

ODYSSEY.

The ARGUMENT.

The Departure of *Ulysses* from *Calypso*.

Pallas *in a Council of the Gods complains of the Detention of* Ulysses *in the Island of* Calypso; *whereupon* Mercury *is sent to command his removal. The seat of* Calypso *describ'd. She consents with much difficulty, and* Ulysses *builds a vessel with his own hands, on which he embarks.* Neptune *overtakes him with a terrible tempest, in which he is shipwreck'd, and in the last danger of death;* 'till Leucothea *a Sea Goddess assists him, and after innumerable perils, he gets ashore on* Phæacia.

T HE saffron Morn, with early blushes spread,
Now rose refulgent from *Tithonus'* bed;
With new-born day to gladden mortal sight,

Ulysses makes his first entry in this book. It may be ask'd where properly is the beginning of the Action? It is not necessary that the beginning of the *Action* should be the beginning of the *Poem*; there is a natural, and an artificial order, and *Homer* makes use of the latter. The Action of the *Odyssey* properly begins neither with the Poem, nor with the appearance of *Ulysses* here, but with the relation he makes of his departure from *Troy* in the ninth book. *Bossu* ⟨1 x⟩ has very judiciously remark'd, that in the constitution of the fable, the Poet ought not to make the Departure of a Prince from his own country the foundation of his Poem, but his Return, and his stay in other places involuntary. For if the stay of *Ulysses* had been voluntary, he would have been guilty in some degree of all the disorders that happen'd during his absence. Thus in this book *Ulysses* first appears in a desolate Island, sitting in tears by the side of the Ocean, and looking upon it as the obstacle to his return.

This artificial order is of great use, it cuts off all languishing and un-entertaining incidents, and passes over those intervals of time that are void of action; it gives continuity to the story, and at first transports the Reader into the middle

Plate 4   William Kent's headpiece for *Odyssey* v in Pope's quarto

And gild the courts of heav'n with sacred light.
Then met th' eternal Synod of the sky,
Before the God who thunders from on high,
Supreme in might, sublime in majesty.
Pallas, to these, deplores th' unequal fates
Of wise *Ulysses*, and his toils relates;
Her heroe's danger touch'd the pitying Pow'r,
The Nymph's seducements, and the magic bow'r.
 Thus she began her plaint. Immortal *Jove!*
And you who fill the blissful seats above!
Let Kings no more with gentle mercy sway,
Or bless a people willing to obey,
But crush the nations with an iron rod,
And ev'ry Monarch be the scourge of God:
If from your thoughts *Ulysses* you remove,

5

10

15

of the subject. In the beginning of the *Odyssey*, the Gods command *Mercury* to go down to the Island of *Ogygia*, and charge *Calypso* to dismiss *Ulysses*: one would think the Poem was to end in the compass of a few lines, the Poet beginning the action so near the end of the story; and we wonder how he finds matter to fill up his Poem, in the little space of time that intervenes between his first appearance and his re-establishment.

 This book, as well as the first, opens with an Assembly of the Gods. This is done to give an importance to his Poem, and to prepare the mind of the Reader to expect every thing that is great and noble, when Heaven is engag'd in the care and protection of his Heroes. Both these Assemblies are placed very properly, so as not to interrupt the series of action: The first assembly of the Gods is only pre-paratory to introduce the action; and this second is no more than a bare transi-tion from *Telemachus* to *Ulysses*; from the recital of the transactions in *Ithaca*, to what more immediately regards the person of *Ulysses*.

 In the former council, both the Voyage of *Telemachus* and the Return of *Ulysses* were determin'd at the same time: The day of that assembly is the first day both of the *principal action*, (which is the return of *Ulysses*) and of the *incident*, which is the voyage of *Telemachus*; with this difference, that the incident was immediately put in practice, by the descent of *Minerva* to *Ithaca*; and the execu-tion of it takes up the four preceding books; whereas the principal action was only then prepared, and the execution deferr'd to the present book, where *Mercury* is actually sent to *Calypso*.

 Eustathius therefore judges rightly when he says, that, in the first council, the safety alone of *Ulysses* was propos'd; but the means how to bring it about are here under consultation, which makes the necessity of the second council.

Who rul'd his subjects with a father's love.
Sole in an isle, encircled by the main,   20
Abandon'd, banish'd from his native reign,
Unblest he sighs, detain'd by lawless charms,
And press'd unwilling in *Calypso*'s arms.
Nor friends are there, nor vessels to convey,
Nor oars to cut th' immeasurable way.   25
And now fierce traytors, studious to destroy
His only son, their ambush'd fraud employ,
Who pious, following his great father's fame,
To sacred *Pylos* and to *Sparta* came.

What words are these (reply'd the Pow'r who forms   30
The clouds of night, and darkens heav'n with storms)
Is not already in thy soul decreed,
The chief's return shall make the guilty bleed?
What cannot Wisdom do? Thou may'st restore
The son in safety to his native shore;   35
While the fell foes who late in ambush lay,
With fraud defeated measure back their way.

Then thus to *Hermes* the command was giv'n.
Hermes, thou chosen messenger of heav'n!
Go, to the nymph be these our orders born;   40
'Tis *Jove*'s decree *Ulysses* shall return:
The patient man shall view his old abodes,
Nor help'd by mortal hand, nor guiding Gods;

43. *Nor help'd by mortal hand, nor guiding Gods.*] This passage is intricate: Why
should *Jupiter* command *Ulysses* to return without the guidance either of man or
God? *Ulysses* had been just declar'd the care of Heaven, why should he be thus
suddenly abandon'd? *Eustathius* answers, that it is spoken solely with respect to
the voyage which he immediately undertakes. This indeed shews a reason why
this command is given; if he had been under the guidance of a God, the shipwreck (that great incident which brings about the whole Catastrophe of the
Poem) must have been prevented by his power; and as for men, where were they
to be procur'd in a desolate island? What confirms this opinion is, that during
the whole shipwreck of *Ulysses*, there is no interposition of a Deity, not even of
Pallas who used to be his constant guardian; the reason is, because this command
of *Jupiter* forbids all assistance to *Ulysses*: *Leucothea* indeed assists him, but it is not

In twice ten days shall fertile *Scheria* find,
Alone, and floating to the wave and wind.   45
The bold *Phæacians*, there, whose haughty line

---

till he is shipwreck'd. It appears further, that this interdiction respects only the voyage from *Ogygia*, because *Jupiter* orders that there shall be no assistance from man, οὔτε θεῶν πομπή, οὔτ᾽ ἀνθρώπων; but *Ulysses* is transported from *Phæacia* to *Ithaca*, ἀνθρώπων πομπῇ, or by the assistance of the *Phæacians*, as *Eustathius* observes; and therefore what *Jupiter* here speaks has relation only to the present voyage. *Dacier* understands this to be meant of any *visible* assistance only: but this seems a collusion; for whether the Gods assist visibly or invisibly, the effects are the same; and a Deity unseen might have preserv'd *Ulysses* from storms, and directly guided him to his own country. But it was necessary for the design of *Homer*, that *Ulysses* should not sail directly home; if he had, there had been no room for the relation of his own adventures, and all those surprizing narrations he makes to the *Phæacians*; *Homer* therefore to bring about the shipwreck of *Ulysses*, withdraws the Gods.

45. *Alone, and floating to the wave.*] The word in the original is σχεδίης; νηός, as *Eustathius* observes, is understood: It signifies, continues he, a small vessel made of one entire piece of wood, or a vessel about which little wood is used; it is deriv'd from σχεδόν, from being αὐτοσχεδίως συμπεπῆχθαι, or its being compacted together with ease. *Hesychius* ⟨*Lexicon, s.v.*⟩ defines σχεδία to be, μικρὰ ναῦς ἢ ξύλα ἃ συνδέουσι, καὶ οὕτω πλέουσι: that is, a small bark, or float of wood which sailors bind together, and immediately use in navigation. This observation appear'd to me very necessary, to take off an objection made upon a following passage in this book: the Critics have thought it incredible that *Ulysses* should without any assistance build such a vessel, as *Homer* describes; but if we remember what kind of a vessel it is, it may be reconcil'd to probability.

46.   —*Whose haughty line*
                                            Is mixt with Gods.]

The *Phæacians* were the inhabitants of *Scheria*, sometimes call'd *Drepanè*, afterwards *Corcyra*, now *Corfu* in the possession of the *Venetians*. But it may be ask'd in what these people resemble the Gods? they are describ'd as a most effeminate nation; whence then this God-like Quality? *Eustathius* answers, that is either from their undisturb'd felicity, or from their divine quality of general benevolence: he prefers the latter; but from the general character of the *Phæacians*, I should prefer the former. *Homer* frequently describes the Gods as ἀεὶ ῥεῖα ζώοντες, *the Gods that live in endless ease*: This is suitable to the *Phæacians*, as will appear more fully in the sequel of the *Odyssey*. *Eustathius* remarks that the Poet here gives us in a few lines the heads of the eight succeeding books; and sure nothing can be a greater instance of *Homer*'s art, than his building so noble an edifice upon so small a foundation: The plan is simple and unadorn'd, but he embellishes it with all the beauties in nature.

Is mixt with Gods, half human, half divine,
The chief shall honour as some heav'nly guest,
And swift transport him to his place of rest.
His vessels loaded with a plenteous store   50
Of brass, of vestures, and resplendent Ore;
(A richer price than if his joyful Isle
Receiv'd him charg'd with *Ilion*'s noble spoil)
His friends, his country he shall see, tho' late;
Such is our sov'reign Will, and such is Fate.   55
     He spoke. The God who mounts the winged winds
Fast to his feet his golden pinions binds,
That high thro' fields of air his flight sustain
O'er the wide earth, and o'er the boundless main.
He grasps the wand that causes sleep to fly,   60
Or in soft slumber seals the wakeful eye:
Then shoots from heav'n to high *Pieria*'s steep,
And stoops incumbent on the rolling deep.
So wat'ry fowl, that seek their fishy food,

---

56. *The God who mounts the winged winds*.] This is a noble description of *Mercury*;
the verses are lofty and sonorous. *Virgil* has inserted them in his *Æneis, lib*. 4. 240.
          —*pedibus talaria nectit*
     Aurea: quæ sublimem alis, sive æquora supra,
     Seu terram, rapido pariter cum flamine portant.
     Tum virgam capit: hac animas ille evocat Orco
     Pallentes, alias sub tristia Tartara mittit;
     Dat somnos adimitque, & lumina morte resignat.
What is here said of the rod of *Mercury*, is, as *Eustathius* observes, an Allegory:
It is intended to shew the force of eloquence, which has a power to calm, or
excite, to raise a passion, or compose it: *Mercury* is the God of Eloquence, and he
may very properly be said θέλγειν, καὶ ἀγείρειν, to cool or inflame the passions,
according to the allegorical sense of these expressions.
     64. *So wat'ry fowl*.] *Eustathius* remarks, that this is a very just allusion; had the
Poet compar'd *Mercury* to an Eagle, tho' the comparison had been more noble,
yet it had been less proper; a sea-fowl most properly represents the passage of a
Deity over the seas; the comparison being adapted to the element.
     Some ancient Critics mark'd the last verse τῷ ἴκελος, *&c*. with an Obelisk, a
sign that it ought to be rejected: They thought that the word ὀχήσατο did not
sufficiently express the swiftness of the flight of *Mercury*; the word implies no more
than *he was carry'd*: But this expression is applicable to any degree of swiftness; for

With wings expanded o'er the foaming flood,   65
Now sailing smooth the level surface sweep,
Now dip their pinions in the briny deep.
Thus o'er the world of waters *Hermes* flew,
'Till now the distant Island rose in view:
Then swift ascending from the azure wave,   70
He took the path that winded to the cave.
Large was the Grot, in which the nymph he found,

where is the impropriety if we say, *Mercury* was borne along the seas with the utmost rapidity? The word is most properly apply'd to a chariot, ἐπὶ ὄχου, ὅ ἐστὶν ἄρματος. *Eustathius.*

72. *The nymph he found.*] *Homer* here introduces an Episode of *Calypso*; and as every Incident ought to have some relation to the main design of the Poem, it may be ask'd what relation this bears to the other parts of it? A very essential one: The sufferings of *Ulysses* are the subject of the *Odyssey*; here we find him inclos'd in an Island: all his calamities arise from his absence from his own country: *Calypso* then who detains him is the cause of all his calamities. It is with great judgment that the Poet feigns him to be restrain'd by a Deity, rather than a mortal. It might have appear'd somewhat derogatory from the prudence and courage of *Ulysses*, not to have been able by art or strength to have freed himself from the power of a mortal: but by this conduct the Poet at once excuses his Heroe, and aggravates his misfortunes: he is detain'd involuntarily, but it is a Goddess who detains him, and it is no disgrace for a man not to be able to over-power a Deity.

Bossu ⟨IV ix⟩ observes, that the art of Disguise is part of the character of *Ulysses*: Now this is imply'd in the name of *Calypso*, which signifies *concealment*, or *secret*. The Poet makes his Heroe stay seven whole years with this Goddess; she taught him so well, that he afterwards lost no opportunities of putting her instructions in practice, and does nothing without disguise.

Virgil has borrow'd part of his description of *Circe* in the 7th book of the *Æneis* ⟨11–14⟩, from this of *Calypso*.

> —*ubi Solis filia lucos*
> *Assiduo resonat cantu, tectisque superbis*
> *Urit odoratam nocturna in lumina cedrum,*
> *Arguto tenues percurrens pectine telas.*

What I have here said shews likewise the necessity of this machine of *Mercury*: It is an establish'd rule of *Horace* ⟨*Ars Poet.* 191–2⟩,

> *Nec deus intersit, nisi dignus vindice nodus*
> *Inciderit:—*

Calypso was a Goddess, and consequently all human means were insufficient to deliver *Ulysses*. There was therefore a necessity to have recourse to the Gods.

(The fair-hair'd nymph with ev'ry beauty crown'd)
She sate and sung; the rocks resound her lays:
The cave was brighten'd with a rising blaze: 75
Cedar and frankincense, an od'rous pile,
Flam'd on the hearth, and wide perfum'd the Isle;
While she with work and song the time divides,
And thro' the loom the golden shuttle guides.
Without the grot, a various sylvan scene   80
Appear'd around, and groves of living green;
Poplars and alders ever quiv'ring play'd,
And nodding cypress form'd a fragrant shade;
On whose high branches, waving with the storm,
The birds of broadest wing their mansion form,   85
The chough, the sea-mew, the loquacious crow,
And scream aloft, and skim the deeps below.
Depending vines the shelving cavern screen,
With purple clusters blushing thro' the green.
Four limpid fountains from the clefts distill, ⎫   90
And ev'ry fountain pours a sev'ral rill,   ⎬
In mazy windings wand'ring down the hill: ⎭
Where bloomy meads with vivid greens were crown'd,
And glowing violets threw odors round.

---

80. *The Bower of* Calypso.] It is impossible for a Painter to draw a more
admirable rural Landskip: The bower of *Calypso* is the principal figure, surrounded with a shade of different trees: Green meadows adorn'd with flowers,
beautiful fountains, and vines loaded with clusters of grapes, and birds hovering
in the air, are seen in the liveliest colours in *Homer*'s Poetry. But whoever observes the particular trees, plants, birds, &c. will find another beauty of propriety in this description, every part being adapted, and the whole scene drawn,
agreeable to a country situate by the sea.

89. *The* ⟨sic⟩ *purple clusters blushing thro' the green.*] *Eustathius* endeavours to fix
the season of the year when *Ulysses* departed from that Island; he concludes it to
be in the latter end of Autumn, or the beginning of Winter; for *Calypso* is describ'd
as making use of a fire, so is *Arete* in the sixth book, and *Eumæus* and *Ulysses* in
other parts of the *Odyssey*. This gives us reason to conclude, that the Summer
heats were past; and what makes it still more probable is, that a Vine is in this
place said to be loaded with grapes, which plainly confines the season of the year
to the Autumn.

A scene, where if a God shou'd cast his sight,   95
A God might gaze, and wander with delight!
Joy touch'd the Messenger of heav'n: he stay'd
Entranc'd, and all the blissful haunt survey'd.
Him, ent'ring in the cave, *Calypso* knew,
For pow'rs celestial to each other's view   100
Stand still confest, tho' distant far they lie
Or habitants of earth, or sea, or sky.
But sad *Ulysses* by himself apart,
Pour'd the big sorrows of his swelling heart;
All on the lonely shore he sate to weep,   105
And roll'd his eyes around the restless deep;
Tow'rd his lov'd coast he roll'd his eyes in vain,
'Till dimm'd with rising grief, they stream'd again.
   Now graceful seated on her shining throne,
To *Hermes* thus the nymph divine begun.   110
   God of the golden wand! on what behest
Arriv'st thou here, an unexpected guest?
Lov'd as thou art, thy free injunctions lay;
'Tis mine, with joy and duty to obey.
'Till now a stranger, in a happy hour   115
Approach, and taste the dainties of my bow'r.
   Thus having spoke, the nymph the table spread,

---

103. *But sad* Ulysses *by himself apart.*] *Eustathius* imagines, that the Poet describes *Ulysses* absent from *Calypso*, to the end that *Calypso* might lay a seeming obligation upon *Ulysses*, by appearing to dismiss him voluntarily: for *Ulysses* being absent, could not know that *Mercury* had commanded his departure; so that this favour appears to proceed from the sole kindness of the Goddess. *Dacier* dislikes this observation, and shews that decency requires the absence of *Ulysses*; if the Poet had describ'd him in the company of *Calypso*, it might have given suspicion of an amorous disposition, and he might seem content with his absence from his country; but the very nature of the Poem requires that he should be continually endeavouring to return to it: The Poet therefore with great judgment describes him agreeably to his character, his mind is entirely taken up with his misfortunes, and neglecting all the pleasures which a Goddess could confer, he entertains himself with his own melancholy reflections, sitting in solitude upon the sea-shores.

(Ambrosial cates, with Nectar rosie red)
Hermes the hospitable rite partook,
Divine refection! then recruited, spoke.   120
    What mov'd this journey from my native sky,
A Goddess asks, nor can a God deny:
Hear then the truth. By mighty *Jove*'s command
Unwilling, have I trod this pleasing land;
For who, self-mov'd, with weary wing wou'd sweep   125
Such length of ocean and unmeasur'd deep?
A world of waters! far from all the ways
Where men frequent, or sacred altars blaze.
But to *Jove*'s will submission we must pay;
What pow'r so great, to dare to disobey?   130
A man, he says, a man resides with thee,
Of all his kind most worn with misery:
The *Greeks*, (whose arms for nine long years employ'd
Their force on *Ilion*, in the tenth destroy'd)
At length embarking in a luckless hour,   135
With conquest proud, incens'd *Minerva*'s pow'r:
Hence on the guilty race her vengeance hurl'd
With storms pursu'd them thro' the liquid world.
There all his vessels sunk beneath the wave!
There all his dear companions found their grave!   140
Sav'd from the jaws of death by heav'n's decree,
The tempest drove him to these shores and thee.
Him, *Jove* now orders to his native lands
Strait to dismiss: so Destiny commands:
Impatient Fate his near return attends,   145
And calls him to his country, and his friends.
    Ev'n to her inmost soul the Goddess shook;
Then thus her anguish and her passion broke.
Ungracious Gods! with spite and envy curst!
Still to your own ætherial race the worst!   150
Ye envy mortal and immortal joy,
And love, the only sweet of life, destroy.
Did ever Goddess by her charms ingage

A favour'd mortal, and not feel your rage?
So when *Aurora* sought *Orion*'s love,   155
Her joys disturb'd your blissful hours above,
'Till in *Ortygia*, *Dian*'s winged dart
Had pierc'd the hapless hunter to the heart.
So when the covert of the thrice-ear'd field
Saw stately *Ceres* to her passion yield,   160
Scarce could *Iäsion* taste her heav'nly charms,
But *Jove*'s swift lightning scorch'd him in her arms.
And is it now my turn, ye mighty pow'rs!
Am I the envy of your blissful bow'rs?
A man, an outcast to the storm and wave,   165

---

155. *Orion.*] The love of *Calypso* to *Ulysses* might seem too bold a fiction, and
contrary to all credibility, *Ulysses* being a mortal, she a Goddess: *Homer* therefore
to soften the relation, brings in instances of the like passion, in *Orion* and *Iasion*;
and by this he fully justifies his own conduct, the Poet being at liberty to make use
of any prevailing story, tho' it were all fable and fiction.

But why should the death of *Orion* be here ascrib'd to *Diana*; whereas in other
places, she is said to exercise her power only over Women? The reason is, she
slew him for offering violence to her chastity; for tho' *Homer* be silent about his
crime, yet *Horace* relates it ⟨*Odes* III iv 70–2⟩.

—*Integræ*
Tentator Orion Dianæ
Virginea domitus sagitta.

Eustathius gives another reason why *Aurora* is said to be in love with *Orion*. He was
a great hunter, as appears from the eleventh book of the *Odyssey*; and the morning
or *Aurora* is most favourable to those diversions.

161. *Scarce could* Iasion, *&c.*] *Ceres* is here understood allegorically, to signify
the earth; *Iasion* was a great Husbandman, and consequently *Ceres* may easily be
feign'd to be in love with him: The thunderbolt with which he is slain signifies the
excess of heat, which frequently disappoints the hopes of the labourer. *Eustathius.*

165.   *A man, an outcast to the storm and wave,*
                    It was my crime to pity, and to save; &c.]

Homer in this speech of *Calypso* shews very naturally how passion misguides the
understanding. She views her own cause in the most advantageous, but false
light; and thence concludes that *Jupiter* offers a piece of injustice in commanding
the departure of *Ulysses*: She tells *Mercury*, that it is she who had preserv'd his
life, who had entertain'd him with affection, and offer'd him immortality; and
would *Jupiter* thus repay her tenderness to *Ulysses*? Would *Jupiter* force him from
a place where nothing was wanting to his happiness, and expose him again to the

It was my crime to pity, and to save;
When he who thunders rent his bark in twain,
And sunk his brave companions in the main.
Alone, abandon'd, in mid ocean tost,
The sport of winds, and driv'n from ev'ry coast,   170
Hither this Man of miseries I led,
Receiv'd the friendless, and the hungry fed;
Nay promis'd (vainly promis'd!) to bestow
Immortal life, exempt from age and woe.
'Tis past—and *Jove* decrees he shall remove;   175
Gods as we are, we are but slaves to *Jove*.
Go then he may (he must, if He ordain)
Try all those dangers, all those deeps, again.
But never, never shall *Calypso* send
To toils like these, her husband, and her friend.   180
What ships have I, what sailors to convey,
What oars to cut the long laborious way?
Yet, I'll direct the safest means to go:
That last advice is all I can bestow.
      To her, the Pow'r who bears the charming rod.   185
Dismiss the Man, nor irritate the God;
Prevent the rage of him who reigns above,
For what so dreadful as the wrath of *Jove?*
Thus having said, he cut the cleaving sky,
And in a moment vanish'd from her eye.   190
The Nymph, obedient to divine command,
To seek *Ulysses*, pac'd along the sand.
Him pensive on the lonely beach she found,
With streaming eyes in briny torrents drown'd,

---

like dangers from which she had preserv'd him? this was an act of cruelty. But on
the contrary, she speaks not one word concerning the truth of the cause: *viz.* that
she offer'd violence to the inclinations of *Ulysses*; that she made him miserable by
detaining him, not only from his wife, but from his whole dominions; and never
considers that *Jupiter* is just in delivering him from his captivity. This is a very
lively, tho' unhappy picture of human nature, which is too apt to fall into error,
and then endeavours to justify an error by a seeming reason. *Dacier*.

And inly pining for his native shore;   195
For now the soft Enchantress pleas'd no more:
For now, reluctant, and constrain'd by charms,
Absent he lay in her desiring arms,
In slumber wore the heavy night away,
On rocks and shores consum'd the tedious day;   200
There sate all desolate, and sigh'd alone,
With echoing sorrows made the mountains groan,
And roll'd his eyes o'er all the restless main,
'Till dimm'd with rising grief, they stream'd again.
  Here, on his musing mood the Goddess prest,   205
Approaching soft; and thus the chief addrest.
Unhappy man! to wasting woes a prey,
No more in sorrows languish life away:
Free as the winds I give thee now to rove—
Go, fell the timber of yon' lofty grove,   210
And form a Raft, and build the rising ship,
Sublime to bear thee o'er the gloomy deep.
To store the vessel let the care be mine,
With water from the rock, and rosie wine,

---

198. *Absent he lay in her desiring arms.*] This passage has fallen under the severe censure of the Critics, they condemn it as an act of conjugal infidelity, and a breach of Morality in *Ulysses*: It would be sufficient to answer, that a Poet is not oblig'd to draw a perfect character in the person of his Heroe: perfection is not to be found in human life, and consequently ought not to be ascribed to it in Poetry: Neither *Achilles* nor *Æneas* are perfect characters: *Æneas* in particular is as guilty, with respect to *Dido*, in the desertion of her, (for *Virgil* tells us they were married, *connubio jungam stabili* ⟨IV 126⟩) as *Ulysses* can be imagin'd to be by the most severe Critic, with respect to *Calypso*.

But those who have blam'd this passage, form their judgments from the morality of these ages, and not from the Theology of the Ancients: Polygamy was then allow'd, and even Concubinage, without being esteem'd any breach of conjugal fidelity: If this be not admitted, the heathen Gods are as guilty as the heathen Heroes, and *Jupiter* and *Ulysses* are equally criminals.

This very passage shews the sincere affection which *Ulysses* retain'd for his wife *Penelope*; even a Goddess cannot persuade him to forget her; his person is in the power of *Calypso*, but his heart is with *Penelope*. *Tully* had this book of *Homer* in his thought when he said of *Ulysses*, *Vetulam suam prætulit immortalitati* ⟨In *De Orat*. i. 44 and *De Leg*. ii. 1, Ulysses is said to prefer his *patria* (not *vetula*)⟩.

And life-sustaining bread, and fair array,   215
And prosp'rous gales to waft thee on thy way.
These, if the Gods with my desires comply,
(The Gods alas more mighty far than I,
And better skill'd in dark events to come)
In peace shall land thee at thy native home.   220
    With sighs, *Ulysses* heard the words she spoke,
Then thus his melancholy silence broke.
Some other motive, Goddess! sways thy mind,
(Some close design, or turn of womankind)
Nor my return the end, nor this the way,   225
On a slight Raft to pass the swelling sea
Huge, horrid, vast! where scarce in safety sails
The best-built ship, tho' *Jove* inspire the gales.
The bold proposal how shall I fulfill?
Dark as I am, unconscious of thy will.   230
Swear then, thou mean'st not what my soul forebodes;
Swear, by the solemn oath that binds the Gods.
    Him, while he spoke, with smiles *Calypso* ey'd,
And gently grasp'd his hand, and thus reply'd.
This shows thee, friend, by old experience taught,   235
And learn'd in all the wiles of human thought.
How prone to doubt, how cautious are the wise?
But hear, oh earth, and hear ye sacred skies!

---

222. *Then thus his melancholy silence broke.*] It may be ask'd what occasions this conduct in *Ulysses*? he has long been desirous to return to his country, why then is he melancholy at the proposal of it? This proceeds from his apprehensions of insincerity in *Calypso*: he had long been unable to obtain his dismission with the most urgent entreaties; this voluntary kindness therefore seems suspicious. He is ignorant that *Jupiter* had commanded his departure, and therefore fears lest his obstinate desire of leaving her should have provoked her to destroy him, under a shew of complying with his inclinations. This is an instance that *Ulysses* is not only wise in extricating himself from difficulties, but cautious in guarding against dangers.

238. *But hear, oh earth, and hear ye sacred skies!*] The oath of *Calypso* is introduc'd with the utmost solemnity. *Rapin* allows it to be an instance of true sublimity ⟨Comparaison xiii, 1 148⟩. The Ancients attested all nature in their oaths, that all

And thou oh *Styx!* whose formidable floods
Glide thro' the shades, and bind th' attesting Gods!   240
No form'd design, no meditated end
Lurks in the counsel of thy faithful friend;
Kind the persuasion, and sincere my aim;
The same my practice, were my fate the same.
Heav'n has not curst me with a heart of steel,   245
But giv'n the sense, to pity, and to feel.
  Thus having said, the Goddess march'd before:
He trod her footsteps in the sandy shore.
At the cool cave arriv'd, they took their state;
He fill'd the throne where *Mercury* had sate.   250
For him, the Nymph a rich repast ordains,
Such as the mortal life of man sustains:

---

nature might conspire to punish their perjuries. *Virgil* has imitated this passage,
but has not copy'd the full beauty of the original ⟨xii 176⟩.

Esto nunc sol testis & hæc mihi terra precanti.

It is the remark of *Grotius* ⟨*Annotata in Vetus Testamentum* (Paris, 1644), 1 173⟩ that
the like expression is found in *Deuteronomy, Hear oh ye heavens the words that I speak,
and let the earth hear the words of my mouth* ⟨32 : 1⟩. Which may almost literally be
render'd by this verse of *Homer,*

Ἴστω νῦν τόδε γαῖα, καὶ οὐρανὸς εὐρὺς ὕπερθεν. ⟨184⟩

251. *For him, the Nymph a rich repast ordains.*] The Passion of Love is no where
describ'd in all *Homer,* but in this passage between *Calypso* and *Ulysses;* and we
find that the Poet is not unsuccessful in drawing the tender, as well as the fiercer
passions. This seemingly-trifling circumstance is an instance of it; love delights
to oblige, and the least offices receive a value from the person who performs
them: This is the reason why *Calypso* serves *Ulysses* with her own hands; her
Damsels attend her, but love makes it a pleasure to her to attend *Ulysses. Eustathius.*

Calypso shews more fondness for *Ulysses,* than *Ulysses* for *Calypso:* Indeed
Ulysses had been no less than seven years in the favour of that Goddess; it was a
kind of matrimony, and husbands are not altogether so fond as lovers. But the
true reason is, a more tender behaviour had been contrary to the character of
Ulysses; it is necessary that his stay should be by constraint, that he should continually be endeavouring to return to his own country; and consequently to have
discover'd too great a degree of satisfaction in any thing during his absence, had
outrag'd his character. His return is the main hinge upon which the whole
Odyssey turns, and therefore no pleasure, not even a Goddess, ought to divert him
from it.

Before herself were plac'd the cates divine,
Ambrosial banquet, and celestial wine.
Their hunger satiate, and their thirst represt,   255
Thus spoke *Calypso* to her god-like guest.
　　Ulysses! (with a sigh she thus began)
Oh sprung from Gods! in wisdom more than man.
Is then thy home the passion of thy heart?
Thus wilt thou leave me, are we thus to part?   260
Farewel! and ever joyful may'st thou be,
Nor break the transport with one thought of me.
But ah *Ulysses!* wert thou giv'n to know
What fate yet dooms thee, yet, to undergo;
Thy heart might settle in this scene of ease,   265
And ev'n these slighted charms might learn to please.
A willing Goddess, and Immortal life,
Might banish from thy mind an absent wife.
Am I inferior to a mortal dame?
Less soft my feature, less august my frame?   270
Or shall the daughters of mankind compare
Their earth-born beauties with the heav'nly fair?
　　Alas! for this (the prudent man replies)
Against *Ulysses* shall thy anger rise?
Lov'd and ador'd, oh Goddess, as thou art,   275
Forgive the weakness of a human heart.
Tho' well I see thy graces far above

263.　　　　　*But ah* Ulysses! *wert thou giv'n to know*
　　　　　　　What fate yet dooms thee.]
This is another instance of the tyranny of the passion of love: *Calypso* had receiv'd
a command to dismiss *Ulysses*; *Mercury* had laid before her the fatal consequences
of her refusal, and she had promis'd to send him away; but her Love here again
prevails over her reason; she frames excuses still to detain him, and though she
dares not keep him, she knows not how to part with him. This is a true picture of
nature; Love this moment resolves, the next breaks these resolutions: She had
promis'd to obey *Jupiter*, in not detaining *Ulysses*; but she endeavours to persuade
Ulysses not to go away.

277.　　　　　*Tho' well I see thy graces far above*
　　　　　　　The dear, tho' mortal, object of my love.]

The dear, tho' mortal, object of my love,
Of youth eternal well the diff'rence know
And the short date of fading charms below;   280
Yet ev'ry day, while absent thus I roam,
I languish to return, and dye at home.
Whate'er the Gods shall destine me to bear
In the black ocean, or the wat'ry war,
'Tis mine to master with a constant mind;   285
Enur'd to perils, to the worst resign'd.
By seas, by wars, so many dangers run,
Still I can suffer; Their high will be done!
    Thus while he spoke, the beamy Sun descends,
And rising night her friendly shade extends.   290
To the close grot the lonely pair remove,
And slept delighted with the gifts of love.
When rosy morning call'd them from their rest,
Ulysses rob'd him in the cloak and vest.
The nymph's fair head a veil transparent grac'd,   295
Her swelling loins a radiant Zone embrac'd
With flow'rs of gold: an under robe, unbound,
In snowy waves flow'd glitt'ring on the ground.
Forth-issuing thus, she gave him first to wield
A weighty axe, with truest temper steel'd,   300
And double-edg'd; the handle smooth and plain,
Wrought of the clouded olive's easy grain;
And next, a wedge to drive with sweepy sway:
Then to the neighb'ring forest led the way.
On the lone Island's utmost verge there stood   305
Of poplars, pines, and firs, a lofty wood,
Whose leafless summits to the skies aspire,

Ulysses shews great address in this answer to *Calypso*; he softens the severity of it, by first asking a favourable acceptance of what he is about to say; he calls her his ador'd Goddess, and places *Penelope* in every degree below the perfections of *Calypso*. As it is the nature of woman not to endure a rival, *Ulysses* assigns the desire of his return to another cause than the love of *Penelope*, and ascribes it solely to the love he bears his country. *Eustathius.*

Scorch'd by the sun, or sear'd by heav'nly fire:
(Already dry'd.) These pointing out to view,
The Nymph just show'd him, and with tears withdrew.
  Now toils the Heroe; trees on trees o'erthrown 310
Fall crackling round him, and the forests groan:
Sudden, full twenty on the plain are strow'd,
And lopp'd, and lighten'd of their branchy load.
At equal angles these dispos'd to join,   315
He smooth'd, and squar'd 'em, by the rule and line.
(The wimbles for the work *Calypso* found)

311, &c. Ulysses *builds his ship*.] This passage has fallen under censure, as out-raging all probability: *Rapin* believes it to be impossible for one man alone to build so compleat a vessel in the compass of four days ⟨Comparaison xiii, 1 148⟩; and perhaps the same opinion might lead *Bossu* into a mistake, who allows twenty days to *Ulysses* in building it; he applies the word εἴκοσι, or *twenty*, to the days ⟨III xii⟩, which ought to be apply'd to the trees; δένδρεα is understood, for the Poet immediately after declares that the whole was compleated in the space of four days; neither is there any thing incredible in the description. I have ob-serv'd already that this vessel is but σχεδία, a *Float* or *Raft*; 'tis true, *Ulysses* cuts down twenty trees to build it; this may seem too great a provision of materials for so small an undertaking: But why should we imagine these to be large trees? the description plainly shews the contrary, for it had been impossible to have fell'd twenty large trees in the space of four days, much more to have built a vessel proportionable to such materials: but the vessel was but small, and con-sequently such were the trees. *Homer* calls these *dry trees*; this is not inserted with-out reason, for green wood is unfit for Navigation.

 Homer in this passage shews his skill in Mechanics; a shipwright could not have describ'd a vessel more exactly: but what is chiefly valuable, is the insight it gives us to what degree this art of shipbuilding was then arriv'd: We find likewise what use Navigators made of Astronomy in those ages; so that this passage deserves a double regard, as a fine piece of Poetry, and a valuable remain of Antiquity.

317.   *The wimbles for the work* Calypso *found*.   and
329.   *Thy Loom* Calypso *for the future sails*
     Supply'd the cloth.]

It is remarkable, that *Calypso* brings the tools to *Ulysses* at several times: this is another instance of the nature of Love; it seeks opportunities to be in the com-pany of the belov'd person. *Calypso* is an instance of it: she frequently goes away, and frequently returns; she delays the time, by not bringing all the implements at once to *Ulysses*; so that tho' she cannot divert him from his resolutions of leaving her, yet she protracts his stay.

 It may be necessary to make some observations in general upon this passage

With those he pierc'd 'em, and with clinchers bound.
Long and capacious as a shipwright forms
Some bark's broad bottom to out-ride the storms,   320
So large he built the Raft: then ribb'd it strong
From space to space, and nail'd the planks along;
These form'd the sides: the deck he fashion'd last;
Then o'er the vessel rais'd the taper mast,
With crossing sail-yards dancing in the wind;   325
And to the helm the guiding rudder join'd.
(With yielding osiers fenc'd, to break the force
Of surging waves, and steer the steady course)
Thy loom, *Calypso!* for the future sails
Supply'd the cloth, capacious of the gales.   330

of *Calypso* and *Ulysses*. Mr. *Dryden* has been very severe upon it. "What are the
tears," says he, "of *Calypso* for being left, to the fury and death of *Dido*? Where is
there the whole process of her passion, and all its violent effects to be found, in the
languishing Episode of the *Odysseis*?" ⟨*Dedication of the Aeneis, Essays*, ed. Ker, II
200⟩. Much may be said in vindication of *Homer*; there is a wide difference between the characters of *Dido* and *Calypso*, *Calypso* is a Goddess and consequently
not liable to the same passions, as an enrag'd woman: yet disappointed love
being always an outragious passion, *Homer* makes her break out into blasphemies
against *Jupiter* and all the Gods. "But the same process of love is not found in
Homer as in *Virgil*;" 'Tis true, and *Homer* had been very injudicious if he had
inserted it. The time allows it not; it was necessary for *Homer* to describe the conclusion of *Calypso*'s passion, not the beginning or process of it. It was necessary to
carry on the main design of the Poem, *viz.* the Departure of *Ulysses*, in order to
his re-establishment; and not amuse the Reader with the detail of a passion that
was so far from contributing to the end of the Poem, that it was the greatest
impediment to it. If the Poet had found an enlargement necessary to his design,
had he attempted a full description of the passion, and then fail'd, Mr. *Dryden*'s
Criticism had been judicious. *Virgil* had a fair opportunity to expatiate, nay the
occasion requir'd it, inasmuch as the love of *Dido* contributed to the design of the
Poem; it brought about her assistance to *Æneas*, and the preservation of his companions: and consequently the copiousness of *Virgil* is as judicious as the conciseness of *Homer*. I allow *Virgil*'s to be a masterpiece; perhaps no images are
more happily drawn in all that Poet; but the passages in the two Authors are not
similar, and consequently admit of no comparison: Would it not have been in-
sufferable in *Homer*, to have stepp'd seven years backward, to describe the process of *Calypso*'s passion, when the very nature of the Poem requires that *Ulysses*
should immediately return to his own country? ought the action to be suspended

With stays and cordage last he rigg'd the ship,
And roll'd on leavers, launch'd her in the deep.
    Four days were past, and now the work compleat
Shone the fifth morn: when from her sacred seat
The nymph dismist him, (od'rous garments giv'n,   335
And bath'd in fragrant oils that breath'd of heav'n)
Then fill'd two goat-skins with her hands divine,
With water one, and one with sable wine;
Of ev'ry kind provisions heav'd aboard,
And the full decks with copious viands stor'd.   340
The Goddess last a gentle breeze supplies,
To curl old Ocean, and to warm the skies.
    And now, rejoycing in the prosp'rous gales,
With beating heart *Ulysses* spreads his sails;
Plac'd at the helm he sate, and mark'd the skies,   345
Nor clos'd in sleep his ever-watchful eyes.
There view'd the *Pleiads*, and the northern Team,
And great *Orion*'s more refulgent beam,
To which, around the axle of the sky
The Bear revolving, points his golden eye;   350
Who shines exalted on th' etherial plain,
Nor bathes his blazing forehead in the main.

for a fine description? But an opposite conduct was judicious in both the Poets, and therefore *Virgil* is commendable for giving us the whole process of a love-passion in *Dido*, *Homer* for only relating the conclusion of it in *Calypso*. I will only add that *Virgil* has borrow'd his Machinery from *Homer*, and that the departure of *Æneas* and *Ulysses* is brought about by the command of *Jupiter*, and the descent of *Mercury*.

    344. —Ulysses *spreads his sails.*] It is observable that the Poet passes over the parting of *Calypso* and *Ulysses* in silence; he leaves it to be imagin'd by the Reader, and prosecutes his main action. Nothing but a cold compliment could have proceeded from *Ulysses*, he being overjoy'd at the prospect of returning to his country: it was therefore judicious in *Homer* to omit the relation; and not draw *Calypso* in tears, and *Ulysses* in a transport of joy. Besides, it was necessary to shorten the Episode: the commands of *Jupiter* were immediately to be obey'd; and the story being now turn'd to *Ulysses*, it was requisite to put him immediately upon action, and describe him endeavouring to re-establish his own affairs, which is the whole design of the *Odyssey*.

Far on the left those radiant fires to keep
The Nymph directed, as he sail'd the deep.
Full sev'nteen nights he cut the foamy way;   355
The distant land appear'd the following day:
Then swell'd to sight *Phæacia*'s dusky coast,
And woody mountains, half in vapours lost;
That lay before him, indistinct and vast,
Like a broad shield amid the watry waste.   360
    But him, thus voyaging the deeps below,
From far, on *Solymé's* aerial brow,

---

355. *Full sev'nteen nights he cut the foamy way.*] It may seem incredible that one person should be able to manage a vessel seventeen days without any assistance; but *Eustathius* vindicates *Homer* by an instance, that very much resembles this of *Ulysses*. A certain *Pamphylian* being taken prisoner, and carried to *Tamiathis* (afterwards *Damietta*) in *Ægypt*, continued there several years; but being continually desirous to return to his country, he pretends a skill in sea affairs; this succeeds, and he is immediately employ'd in Maritime business, and permitted the liberty to follow it according to his own inclination, without any inspection. He made use of this opportunity, and furnishing himself with a sail, and provisions for a long voyage, committed himself to the sea all alone; he cross'd that vast extent of waters that lies between *Ægypt* and *Pamphylia*, and arriv'd safely in his own country: In memory of this prodigious event he chang'd his name, and was called μονοναύτης, or the *sole-sailor*; and the family was not extinct in the days of *Eustathius*.

It may not be improper to observe, that this description of *Ulysses* sailing alone is a demonstration of the smallness of his vessel; for it is impossible that a large one could be managed by a single person. It is indeed said that twenty trees were taken down for the vessel, but this does not imply that all the trees were made use of, but only so much of them as was necessary to his purpose.

360. *Like a broad shield amid the watry waste.*] This expression gives a very lively idea of an Island of small extent, that is, of a form more long than large: *Aristarchus* ⟨Dindorf, p. 272⟩, instead of ῥινόν, writes ἐρινόν, or resembling a *Fig*; others tell us, that ῥινόν is used by the *Illyrians* to signify ἀχλύς, or a *Mist*; this likewise very well represents the first appearance of land to those that sail at a distance: it appears indistinct and confus'd, or as it is here express'd, like a Mist. *Eustathius.*

362. *From* ⟨. . .⟩ *Solymé's aerial brow.*] There is some difficulty in this passage. *Strabo*, as *Eustathius* observes, affirms that the expression of *Neptune*'s seeing *Ulysses* from the mountains of *Solyma*, is to be taken in a general sense, and not to denote the *Solymæan* mountains in *Pisidia*; but other eastern mountains that bear the same appellation ⟨1 ii 10, 28⟩. In propriety, the *Solymæans* inhabit the summits of

The King of Ocean saw, and seeing burn'd,
(From *Æthiopia*'s happy climes return'd)
The raging Monarch shook his azure head,   365
And thus in secret to his soul he said.
     Heav'ns! how uncertain are the Pow'rs on high?
Is then revers'd the sentence of the sky,
In one man's favour? while a distant guest
I shar'd secure the *Æthiopian* feast.   370
Behold how near *Phæacia*'s land he draws!
The land, affix'd by Fate's eternal laws
To end his toils. Is then our anger vain?
No, if this sceptre yet commands the main.
     He spoke, and high the forky Trident hurl'd,   375
Rolls clouds on clouds, and stirs the wat'ry world,
At once the face of earth and sea deforms,
Swells all the winds, and rouzes all the storms.
Down rush'd the night. East, west, together roar,
And south, and north, roll mountains to the shore.   380
Then shook the Heroe, to despair resign'd,
And question'd thus his yet-unconquer'd mind.
     Wretch that I am! what farther Fates attend
This life of toils, and what my destin'd end?
Too well alas! the island Goddess knew,   385
On the black sea what perils shou'd ensue.
New horrors now this destin'd head enclose;

mount *Taurus*, from *Lycia* even to *Pisidia*; these were very distant from the passage
of *Neptune* from the *Æthiopians*, and consequently could not be the mountains
intended by *Homer*; we must therefore have recourse to the preceding assertion
of *Strabo*, for a solution of the difficulty. *Dacier* endeavours to explain it another
way: Who knows, says she, but that the name of *Solymæan* was antiently extended to all very elevated mountains? *Bochart* ⟨Pt. II: I vi (p. 379)⟩ affirms,
that the word *Solymi* is deriv'd from the *Hebrew Selem*, or *Darkness*; why then
might not this be a general appellation? But this is all conjecture, and it is much
more probable that such a name should be given to some mountains by way of
distinction and emphatically, from some peculiar and extraordinary quality;
than extend it to all very lofty mountains, which could only introduce confusion
and error.

Unfill'd is yet the measure of my woes.
With what a cloud the brows of heav'n are crown'd?
What raging winds? what roaring waters round?   390
'Tis *Jove* himself the swelling tempest rears;
Death, present death on ev'ry side appears.
Happy! thrice happy! who in battle slain
Prest in *Atrides'* cause the *Trojan* plain:
Oh! had I dy'd before that well-fought wall,   395
Had some distinguish'd day renown'd my fall;
(Such as was that, when show'rs of jav'lins fled

---

393.   *Happy! thrice happy! who in battle slain,*
              Prest in Atrides' *cause the* Trojan *plain.*]
Plutarch in his *Symposiacs* ⟨*Quaest. Conviv.* IX i 2 (737 A)⟩ relates a memorable story
concerning *Memmius*, the *Roman* General: When he sack'd the City *Corinth*, and
made slaves of those who surviv'd the ruin of it, he commanded one of the youths
of a liberal education to write down some sentence in his presence, according to
his own inclinations. The youth immediately wrote this passage from *Homer*,
              Happy! thrice happy! who in battle slain,
              Prest in Atrides' *cause the* Trojan *plain.*
Memmius immediately burst into tears, and gave the youth and all his relations
their liberty.

Virgil has translated this passage in the first book of his *Æneis* ⟨94 ff⟩. The
storm, and the behaviour of *Æneas*, are copy'd exactly from it. The storm, in
both the Poets, is describ'd concisely, but the images are full of terror; *Homer*
leads the way, and *Virgil* treads in his steps without any deviation. *Ulysses* falls
into lamentation, so does *Æneas*: *Ulysses* wishes he had found a nobler death, so
does *Æneas*: this discovers a bravery of spirit, they lament not that they are to
die, but only the inglorious manner of it. This fully answers an objection that has
been made both against *Homer* and *Virgil*, who have been blam'd for describing
their Heroes with such an air of mean-spiritedness. Drowning was esteem'd by
the Ancients an accursed death, as it depriv'd their bodies of the rites of Sepulture; it is therefore no wonder that this kind of death was greatly dreaded, since
it barr'd their entrance into the happy regions of the dead for many hundreds of
years.

397.   *Such as was that, when show'rs of jav'lins fled*
              From conqu'ring Troy *around* Achilles *dead.*]
These words have relation to an Action, no where describ'd in the *Iliad* or *Odyssey*.
When *Achilles* was slain by the treachery of *Paris*, the *Trojans* made a sally to gain
his body, but *Ulysses* carried it off upon his shoulders, while *Ajax* protected him
with his shield. The war of *Troy* is not the subject of the *Iliad*, and therefore
Homer relates not the death of *Achilles*; but, as *Longinus* remarks, he inserts many

From conqu'ring *Troy* around *Achilles* dead)
All *Greece* had paid my solemn fun'rals then,
And spread my glory with the sons of men.   400
A shameful fate now hides my hapless head,
Un-wept, un-noted, and for ever dead!
    A mighty wave rush'd o'er him as he spoke,
The Raft it cover'd, and the mast it broke;
Swept from the deck, and from the rudder torn,   405
Far on the swelling surge the chief was born:
While by the howling tempest rent in twain
Flew sail and sail-yards ratling o'er the main.
Long press'd he heav'd beneath the weighty wave,
Clogg'd by the cumbrous vest *Calypso* gave: 410
At length emerging, from his nostrils wide
And gushing mouth, effus'd the briny tyde.
Ev'n then, not mindless of his last retreat,
He seis'd the Raft, and leapt into his seat,
Strong with the fear of death. The rolling flood   415
Now here, now there, impell'd the floating wood.
As when a heap of gather'd thorns is cast
Now to, now fro, before th' autumnal blast;
Together clung, it rolls around the field;
So roll'd the Float, and so its texture held: 420
And now the south, and now the north, bear sway, ⎫
And now the east the foamy floods obey,   ⎬
And now the west-wind whirls it o'er the sea.   ⎭
    The wand'ring Chief, with toils on toils opprest,

Actions in the *Odyssey* which are the sequel of the story of the *Iliad* ⟨IX 12⟩. This
conduct has a very happy effect; he aggrandizes the character of *Ulysses* by these
short histories, and has found out the way to make him praise himself, without
vanity.
    424.   *The wand'ring Chief, with toils on toils opprest,*
                     Leucothea saw, and pity touch'd her breast.]
It is not probable that *Ulysses* could escape so great a danger by his own strength
alone; and therefore the Poet introduces *Leucothea* to assist in his preservation.
But it may be ask'd, if this is not contradictory to the command of *Jupiter* in the

Leucothea saw, and pity touch'd her breast:					425
(Herself a mortal once, of *Cadmus*' strain,
But now an azure sister of the main)
Swift as a Sea-mew springing from the flood,
All radiant on the Raft the Goddess stood:
Then thus address'd him. Thou, whom heav'n decrees
To *Neptune*'s wrath, stern Tyrant of the Seas,					431
(Unequal contest) not his rage and pow'r,
Great as he is, such virtue shall devour.
What I suggest thy wisdom will perform;
Forsake thy float, and leave it to the storm:					435
Strip off thy garments; *Neptune*'s fury brave
With naked strength, and plunge into the wave.
To reach *Phæacia* all thy nerves extend,
There Fate decrees thy miseries shall end.
This heav'nly Scarf beneath thy bosom bind,					440

beginning of this book? *Ulysses* is there forbid all assistance either from men or
Gods; whence then is it that *Leucothea* preserves him? The former passage is to be
understood to imply an interdiction only of all assistance 'till *Ulysses* was shipwreck'd; he was to suffer, not to die: Thus *Pallas* afterwards calms the storm: she
may be imagin'd to have a power over the winds, as she is the daughter of
Jupiter, who denotes the Air, according to the observation of *Eustathius*: Here
Leucothea is very properly introduced to preserve *Ulysses*; she is a Sea-Goddess,
and had been a mortal, and therefore interests her self in the cause of a mortal.

440. *This heav'nly Scarf beneath thy bosom bind.*] This passage may seem extraordinary, and the Poet be thought to preserve *Ulysses* by incredible means. What
virtue could there be in this Scarf against the violence of storms? *Eustathius* very
well answers this objection. It is evident that the belief of the power of Amulets or
Charms prevailed in the times of *Homer*; thus *Moly* is used by *Ulysses* as a preservative against Fascination, and some charm may be supposed to be imply'd in
the *Zone* or *Cestus* of *Venus*. Thus *Ulysses* may be imagin'd to have worn a scarf,
or cincture, as a preservative against the perils of the sea. They consecrated
antiently *Votiva*, as tablets, *&c.* in the temples of their Gods: So *Ulysses*, wearing a
Zone consecrated to *Leucothea*, may be said to receive it from the hands of that
Goddess. *Eustathius* observes, that *Leucothea* did not appear in the form of a Bird,
for then how should she speak, or how bring this cincture or scarf? The expression
has relation only to the manner of her rising out of the sea, and descending into
it; the Action, not the Person, is intended to be represented. Thus *Minerva* is said
in the *Odyssey*, *to fly away*, ὄρνις ὡς ἀνοπαῖα, not in the *form* but with the *swiftness*

H

And live; give all thy terrors to the wind.
Soon as thy arms the happy shore shall gain,
Return the gift, and cast it in the main;
Observe my orders, and with heed obey,
Cast it far off, and turn thy eyes away.   445
  With that, her hand the sacred veil bestows,
Then down the deeps she div'd from whence she rose:
A moment snatch'd the shining form away,
And all was cover'd with the curling sea.
  Struck with amaze, yet still to doubt inclin'd,   450
He stands suspended, and explores his mind.
What shall I do? Unhappy me! who knows
But other Gods intend me other woes?
Whoe'er thou art, I shall not blindly join
Thy pleaded reason, but consult with mine: 455
For scarce in ken appears that distant Isle
Thy voice foretells me shall conclude my toil.
Thus then I judge: while yet the planks sustain

---

of an Eagle. Most of the Translators have render'd this passage ridiculously, they
describe her in the real form of a sea-fowl, tho' she speaks, and gives her Scarf. So
the version of *Hobbs* ⟨316, but conflated⟩:

She spoke, in figure of a Water-hen.

454.   *—I shall not blindly joyn*

Thy pleaded reason.—]

Eustathius observes, that this passage is a lesson to instruct us, that second reflections are preferable to our first thoughts; and the Poet maintains the character of
Ulysses by describing him thus doubtful and cautious. But is not *Ulysses* too incredulous, who will not believe a Goddess? and disobedient to her, by not com-
mitting himself to the seas? *Leucothea* does not confine *Ulysses* to an immediate
compliance with her injunctions; she indeed commands him to forsake the Raft,
but leaves the Time to his own discretion: And *Ulysses* might very justly be somewhat incredulous, when he knew that *Neptune* was his enemy, and contriving his
destruction. The doubts therefore of *Ulysses* are the doubts of a wise man: But
then, is not *Ulysses* describ'd with a greater degree of prudence, than the Goddess?
she commands him to leave the Raft, he chuses to make use of it 'till he arrives
nearer the shores. *Eustathius* directly ascribes more wisdom to *Ulysses* than to
Leucothea. This may appear too partial; it is sufficient to observe, that the command of *Leucothea* was general and left the manner of the execution of it to his own
prudence.

The wild waves fury, here I fix'd remain:
But when their texture to the tempest yields,   460
I launch adventrous on the liquid fields,
Join to the help of Gods the strength of man,
And take this method, since the best I can.
　　While thus his thoughts an anxious council hold,
The raging God a wat'ry mountain roll'd;   465
Like a black sheet the whelming billow spread,
Burst o'er the float, and thunder'd on his head.
Planks, Beams, dis-parted fly: the scatter'd wood
Rolls diverse, and in fragments strows the flood.
So the rude *Boreas*, o'er the field new shorn,   470
Tosses and drives the scatter'd heaps of corn.
And now a single beam the Chief bestrides;
There, poiz'd a while above the bounding tydes,
His limbs dis-cumbers of the clinging vest,
And binds the sacred cincture round his breast: 475
Then prone on Ocean in a moment flung,
Stretch'd wide his eager arms, and shot the seas along.
All naked now, on heaving billows laid,
Stern *Neptune* ey'd him, and contemptuous said:
　　Go, learn'd in woes, and other woes essay!   480
Go, wander helpless on the wat'ry way:
Thus, thus find out the destin'd shore, and then
(If *Jove* ordains it) mix with happier men.
Whate'er thy Fate, the ills our wrath could raise
Shall last remember'd in thy best of days.   485
　　This said, his sea-green steeds divide the foam,
And reach high *Ægæ* and the tow'ry dome.
　　Now, scarce withdrawn the fierce Earth-shaking pow'r,
Jove's daughter *Pallas* watch'd the fav'ring hour.
Back to their caves she bad the winds to fly,   490
And hush'd the blust'ring brethren of the sky.
The dryer blasts alone of *Boreas* sway,
And bear him soft on broken waves away;
With gentle force impelling to that shore,

Where Fate has destin'd he shall toil no more.   495
And now two nights, and now two days were past,
Since wide he wander'd on the wat'ry waste;
Heav'd on the surge with intermitting breath,
And hourly panting in the arms of death.
The third fair morn now blaz'd upon the main;   500
Then glassy smooth lay all the liquid plain,
The winds were hush'd, the billows scarcely curl'd,
And a dead silence still'd the wat'ry world.
When lifted on a ridgy wave, he spies
The land at distance, and with sharpen'd eyes.   505
As pious children joy with vast delight
When a lov'd Sire revives before their sight,
(Who ling'ring long has call'd on death in vain,
Fixt by some Dæmon to his bed of pain,

---

496. *And now two nights, and now two days were past.*] It may be thought incredible that any person should be able to contend so long with a violent storm, and at last survive it: It is allow'd that this could scarce be done by the natural strength of *Ulysses*; but the Poet has soften'd the narration, by ascribing his preservation to the cincture of *Leucothea*. The Poet likewise very judiciously removes *Neptune*, that *Ulysses* may not appear to be preserv'd against the power of that God; and to reconcile it entirely to credibility, he introduces *Pallas*, who calms the winds and composes the waves, to make way for his preservation.

506. *As pious children joy with vast delight.*] This is a very beautiful comparison, and well adapted to the occasion. We mistake the intention of it, as *Eustathius* observes, if we imagine that *Homer* intended to compare the person of *Ulysses* to these children: It is introduc'd solely to express the joy which he conceives at the sight of land; if we look upon it in any other view, the resemblance is lost, for the children suffer not themselves, but *Ulysses* is in the utmost distress. These Images drawn from common life are particularly affecting; they have relation to every man, as every man may possibly be in such circumstances: other Images may be more noble, and yet less pleasing; They may raise our admiration, but those engage our affections.

509. *Fixt by some Dæmon to his bed of pain.*] It was a prevailing opinion among the Ancients, that the Gods were the authors of all diseases incident to mankind. *Hippocrates* himself confesses ⟨*De Morbo Sacro* 1⟩ that he had found some distempers, in which the hand of the Gods was manifest, θεῖόν τι, as *Dacier* observes. In this place this assertion has a peculiar beauty, it shews that the malady was not contracted by any vice of the father, but inflicted by an evil Dæmon. Nothing is

'Till heav'n by miracle his life restore)   510
So joys *Ulysses* at th' appearing shore;
And sees (and labours onward as he sees)
The rising forests, and the tufted trees.

And now, as near approaching as the sound
Of human voice the list'ning ear may wound,   515
Amidst the rocks he hears a hollow roar
Of murm'ring surges breaking on the shore:
Nor peaceful port was there, nor winding bay,
To shield the vessel from the rowling sea;
But cliffs, and shaggy shores, a dreadful sight!   520
All rough with rocks, with foamy billows white.
Fear seiz'd his slacken'd limbs and beating heart;
As thus he commun'd with his soul apart.

Ah me! when o'er a length of waters tost,
These eyes at last behold th' unhop'd-for coast,   525
No port receives me from the angry main,

---

more evident, than that every person was suppos'd by the Ancients to have a good
and a bad Dæmon attending him; what the *Greeks* call'd a Dæmon, the *Romans*
named a *Genius*. I confess that this is no where directly affirm'd in *Homer*, but as
Plutarch observes ⟨*De Iside et Osiride* 26⟩, it is plainly intimated. In the second
book of the *Iliad* the word is used both in a good and bad sense; when *Ulysses*
addresses himself to the Generals of the army ⟨II 190⟩, he says δαιμόνιε, in the
better sense; and immediately afterwards he uses it to denote a coward,

Δαιμόνι' ἀτρέμας ἧσο ⟨II 200⟩.

This is a strong evidence, that the notion of good and bad Dæmons was believ'd
in the days of *Homer*.

524. *Ah me! when o'er a length of waters tost.*] *Ulysses* in this place calls as it were
a council in his own breast; considers his danger, and how to free himself from it.
But it may be ask'd if it be probable that he should have leisure for such a consultation, in the time of such imminent danger? The answer is, that nothing
could be more happily imagin'd, to exalt his character: He is drawn with a great
presence of mind, in the most desperate circumstances; fear does not prevail over
his reason; his wisdom dictates the means of his preservation; and his bravery of
spirit supports him in the accomplishment of it.

The Poet is also very judicious in the management of the speech; it is concise,
and therefore proper to the occasion, there being no leisure for prolixity; every
Image is drawn from the situation of the place, and his present condition; he
follows Nature, and Nature is the foundation of true Poetry.

But the loud deeps demand me back again.
Above, sharp rocks forbid access; around
Roar the wild waves; beneath, is sea profound!
No footing sure affords the faithless sand,   530
To stem too rapid, and too deep to stand.
If here I enter, my efforts are vain,
Dash'd on the cliffs, or heav'd into the main;
Or round the Island if my course I bend,
Where the ports open, or the shores descend,   535
Back to the seas the rowling surge may sweep,
And bury all my hopes beneath the deep.
Or some enormous whale the God may send,
(For many such on *Amphitrite* attend)
Too well the turns of mortal chance I know,   540
And hate relentless of my heav'nly foe.
    While thus he thought, a monst'rous wave up-bore
The Chief, and dash'd him on the craggy shore:
Torn was his skin, nor had the ribs been whole,
But instant *Pallas* enter'd in his soul.   545
Close to the cliff with both his hands he clung,
And stuck adherent, and suspended hung:
'Till the huge surge roll'd off. Then backward sweep
The refluent tydes, and plunge him in the deep.
As when the *Polypus* from forth his cave   550

---

550. *As when the* Polypus.] It is very surprizing to see the prodigious variety
with which *Homer* enlivens his Poetry: he rises or falls as his subject leads him, and
finds allusions proper to represent an Heroe in battle, or a person in calamity.
We have here an instance of it; he compares *Ulysses* to a *Polypus*; the similitude is
suited to the element, and to the condition of the person. It is observable, that
this is the only full description of a person shipwreck'd in all his Poems: he therefore gives a loose to his imagination, and enlarges upon it very copiously. There
appears a surprizing fertility of invention thro' the whole of it: In what a variety
of attitudes is *Ulysses* drawn, during the storm and at his escape from it? his
soliloquies in the turns of his condition, while he is sometimes almost out of
danger, and then again involv'd in new difficulties, engage our hopes and fears.
He ennobles the whole by his machinery, and *Neptune*, *Pallas* and *Leucothea*
interest themselves in his safety or destruction. He has likewise chosen the most

Torn with full force, reluctant beats the wave,
His ragged claws are stuck with stones and sands;
So the rough rock had shagg'd *Ulysses'* hands.
And now had perish'd, whelm'd beneath the main,
Th' unhappy man; ev'n Fate had been in vain: 555
But all-subduing *Pallas* lent her pow'r,
And Prudence sav'd him in the needful hour.
Beyond the beating surge his course he bore,
(A wider circle, but in sight of shore)
With longing eyes, observing, to survey   560
Some smooth ascent, or safe-sequester'd bay.
Between the parting rocks at length he spy'd
A falling stream with gentler waters glide;
Where to the seas the shelving shore declin'd,
And form'd a bay, impervious to the wind.   565
To this calm port the glad *Ulysses* prest,
And hail'd the river, and its God addrest.
      Whoe'er thou art, before whose stream unknown
I bend, a suppliant at thy wat'ry throne,
Hear, azure King! nor let me fly in vain   570
To thee from *Neptune* and the raging main.
Heav'n hears and pities hapless men like me,
For sacred ev'n to Gods is Misery:

---

proper occasion for a copious description; there is leisure for it. The proposition
of the Poem requires him to describe a man of sufferings in the person of *Ulysses*:
he therefore no sooner introduces him, but he throws him into the utmost
calamities, and describes them largely, to shew at once the greatness of his distress, and his wisdom and patience under it. In what are the sufferings of *Æneas*
in *Virgil* comparable to these of *Ulysses*? *Æneas* suffers little personally in comparison of *Ulysses*, his incidents have less variety, and consequently less beauty.
Homer draws his Images from Nature, but embellishes those Images with the
utmost Art, and fruitfulness of invention.

   573. *For sacred ev'n to Gods is Misery.*] This expression is bold, yet reconcileable
to truth: Heav'n in reality has regard to the misery and affliction of good men,
and at last delivers them from it. *Res est sacra miser,* as *Dacier* observes; and *Seneca,*
in his dissertation on Providence ⟨ii 9⟩, speaks to this purpose, *Ecce spectaculum
dignum ad quod respiciat, intentus operi suo, deus! Ecce par deo dignum, vir fortis cum*

Let then thy waters give the weary rest,
And save a suppliant, and a man distrest.   575
    He pray'd, and strait the gentle stream subsides,
Detains the rushing current of his tydes,
Before the wand'rer smooths the wat'ry way,
And soft receives him from the rowling sea.
That moment, fainting as he touch'd the shore,   580
He dropt his sinewy arms: his knees no more
Perform'd their office, or his weight upheld:
His swoln heart heav'd; his bloated body swell'd:
From mouth and nose the briny torrent ran;
And lost in lassitude lay all the man,   585
Depriv'd of voice, of motion, and of breath;
The soul scarce waking, in the arms of death.
Soon as warm life its wonted office found,
The mindful chief *Leucothea*'s scarf unbound;
Observant of her word, he turn'd aside   590

---

mala fortuna compositus! Misery is not always a punishment, but sometimes a tryal:
This is agreeable to true Theology.

    578. *Before the wand'rer smooths the wat'ry way.*] Such passages as these are bold,
yet beautiful. Poetry animates every thing, and turns Rivers into Gods. But what
occasion is there for the intervention of this River-God to smooth the waters,
when *Pallas* had already compos'd both the seas and the storms? The words in
the original solve the objection, πρόσθε δέ οἱ ποίησε γαλήνην; or *smooth'd the
way before him*, that is, his own current: the actions therefore are different; *Pallas*
gives a general calmness to the Sea, the River-God to his own current.

    581.   *He dropt his sinewy arms: his knees no more
                Perform'd their office.*]

Eustathius appears to me to give this passage a very forc'd interpretation; he
imagines that the Poet, by saying that *Ulysses* bent his knees and arms, spoke
philosophically, and intended to express that he contracted his limbs, that had
been fatigued with the long extension in swimming, by a voluntary remission;
lest they should grow stiff, and lose their natural faculty. But this is an impossibility: How could this be done, when he is speechless, fainting, without pulse
and respiration? Undoubtedly *Homer*, as *Dacier* observes, means by the expression
of ἔκαμψε γούνατα καὶ χεῖρας, no more than that his limbs fail'd him, or he
fainted. If the Action was voluntary, it implies that he intended to refresh them,
for γόνυ κάμπτειν is generally used in that sense by *Homer*; if involuntarily, it
signifies he fainted.

His head, and cast it on the rolling tyde.
Behind him far, upon the purple waves
The waters waft it, and the nymph receives.
    Now parting from the stream, *Ulysses* found
A mossy bank with pliant rushes crown'd;   } 595
The bank he press'd, and gently kiss'd the ground.
Where on the flow'ry herb as soft he lay,
Thus to his soul the Sage began to say.
    What will ye next ordain, ye Pow'rs on high!
And yet, ah yet, what fates are we to try?   600
Here by the stream if I the night out-wear,
Thus spent already, how shall nature bear
The dews descending, and nocturnal air?
Or chilly vapors breathing from the flood
When Morning rises? If I take the wood,   605
And in thick shelter of innum'rous boughs
Enjoy the comfort gentle sleep allows;
Tho' fenc'd from cold, and tho' my toil be past,
What savage beasts may wander in the waste?
Perhaps I yet may fall a bloody prey   610
To prowling bears, or lions in their way.
    Thus long debating in himself he stood:
At length he took the passage to the Wood,
Whose shady horrors on a rising brow
Wav'd high, and frown'd upon the stream below.   615
There grew two Olives, closest of the grove,
With roots intwin'd, and branches interwove;
Alike their leaves, but not alike they smil'd
With sister-fruits; one fertile, one was wild.
Nor here the sun's meridian rays had pow'r,   620
Nor wind sharp-piercing, nor the rushing show'r;
The verdant Arch so close its texture kept:
Beneath this covert, great *Ulysses* crept.
Of gather'd leaves an ample bed he made,
(Thick strown by tempest thro' the bow'ry shade) 625
Where three at least might winter's cold defy,
H*

Tho' *Boreas* rag'd along th' inclement sky.
This store, with joy the patient Heroe found,
And sunk amidst 'em heap'd the leaves around.
As some poor peasant, fated to reside   630
Remote from neighbours, in a forest wide,
Studious to save what human wants require,
In embers heap'd, preserves the seeds of fire:
Hid in dry foliage thus *Ulysses* lyes,
'Till *Pallas* pour'd soft slumbers on his eyes;   635
And golden dreams (the gift of sweet repose)
Lull'd all his cares, and banish'd all his woes.

---

630.   *As some poor peasant, fated to reside*
              Remote from neighbours.]

Homer is very happy in giving dignity to low Images. What can be more un-
promising than this comparison, and what more successfully executed? *Ulysses*,
in whom remains as it were but a spark of life, the vital heat being extinguish'd by
the shipwreck, is very justly compar'd to a brand, that retains only some small
remains of fire; the leaves that cover *Ulysses*, are represented by the embers; and
the preservation of the fire all night, paints the revival of his spirits by the repose
of the night; the expression,

              —Fated to reside
              Remote from neighbours,

is not added in vain; it gives, as *Eustathius* further observes, an air of credibility
to the allusion, as if it had really been drawn from some particular observation;
a person that lives in a desart being oblig'd to such circumstantial cares, where
it is impossible to have a supply, for want of neighbours. *Homer* literally calls these
remains *the seeds of fire*; *Æschylus* in his *Prometheus* ⟨109-10⟩ calls a spark of fire
πυρὸς πηγήν, or *a fountain of fire*; less happily in my judgment, the ideas of fire
and water being contradictory.

The Conclusion.] This book begins with the seventh day, and comprehends the
space of twenty five days; the first of which is taken up in the message of *Mercury*,
and interview between *Calypso* and *Ulysses*; the four following in the building of
the vessel; eighteen before the storm, and two after it. So that one and thirty days
are compleated, since the opening of the Poem.

Plate 5   Kent's tailpiece for *Odyssey* v in Pope's quarto

THE
SIXTH BOOK
OF THE
ODYSSEY.

The ARGUMENT.

Pallas *appearing in a dream to* Nausicaa, (*the daughter of* Alcinous *King of* Phæacia) *commands her to descend to the river, and wash the robes of State, in preparation to her nuptials.* Nausicaa *goes with her Handmaids to the river; where, while the garments are spread on the bank, they divert themselves in sports. Their Voices awake* Ulysses, *who addressing himself to the Princess, is by her relieved and cloathed, and receives directions in what manner to apply to the King and Queen of the Island.*

WHILE thus the weary Wand'rer sunk to rest,
   And peaceful slumbers calm'd his anxious breast;
   The martial Maid from heav'n's aereal height
Swift to *Phæacia* wing'd her rapid flight.
In elder times the soft *Phæacian* train   5
In ease possest the wide *Hyperian* plain;
'Till the *Cyclopean* race in arms arose,
A lawless nation of gygantic foes:
Then great *Nausithous* from *Hyperia* far
Thro' seas retreating from the sound of war,   10
The recreant nation to fair *Scheria* led,
Where never science rear'd her lawrel'd head:

---

12. *Where never science rear'd her lawrel'd head.*] The *Phæacians* having a great share in the succeeding parts of the *Odyssey*, it may not be improper to enlarge upon their character. *Homer* has here describ'd them very distinctly: he is to make use of the *Phæacians* to convey *Ulysses* to his country, he therefore by this short character, gives the Reader such an Image of them, that he is not surpriz'd at their credulity and simplicity, in believing all those fabulous recitals which *Ulysses* makes in the progress of the Poem. The place likewise in which he describes them is well chosen; it is before they enter upon Action, and by this

There round his tribes a strength of wall he rais'd,
To heav'n the glitt'ring domes and temples blaz'd;
Just to his realms, he parted grounds from grounds,   15
And shar'd the lands, and gave the lands their bounds.
Now in the silent grave the Monarch lay,
And wise *Alcinous* held the regal sway.

 To his high palace thro' the fields of air
The Goddess shot; *Ulysses* was her care.   20
There, as the night in silence roll'd away,
A heav'n of charms divine *Nausicaa* lay:
Thro' the thick gloom the shining portals blaze;
Two nymphs the portals guard, each nymph a Grace.

---

method we know what to expect from them, and see how every action is
naturally suited to their character.

 Bossu observes ⟨II xv⟩ that the Poet has inserted this verse with great judgment:
Ulysses, says he, knew that the *Phæacians* were simple and credulous; and that
they had all the qualities of a lazy people, who admire nothing so much as
romantic adventures: he therefore pleases them, by recitals suited to their own
humour: But even here the Poet is not unmindful of his more understanding
Readers, and the truth intended to be taught by way of moral is, that a soft and
effeminate life breaks the spirit, and renders it incapable of manly sentiments or
actions.

 Plutarch ⟨*De Exilio* 10⟩ seems to understand this verse in a different manner; he
quotes it in his dissertation upon Banishment, to shew that *Nausithous* made his
people happy tho' he left his own country, and settled them far from the commerce of mankind, ἑκὰς ἀνδρῶν ἀλφηστάων, without any particular view to the
Phæacians, which was undoubtedly intended by *Homer*; those words being a kind
of a Preface to their general character.

 This *Phæacia* of the ancients is the Island now called *Corfu*. The Inhabitants of
it were a Colony of the *Hyperians*: *Eustathius* remarks, that it has been a question
whether *Hyperia* were a City or an Island; he judges it to be a City: it was in-
vested by the *Cyclops*; but they had no shipping, as appears from the 10th of the
Odyssey, and consequently if it had been an Island, they could not have molested
the *Phæacians*; he therefore concludes it to be a City, afterwards call'd *Camarina*
in *Sicily*.

 Mr. *Barnes* has here added a verse that is not to be found in any other edition
⟨II 149 (line 8): ἀνθρώπων ἀπάνευθε πολυκλύστῳ ἐνὶ πόντῳ⟩; and I have
render'd it in the translation ⟨10⟩.

 24. *Two nymphs the portals guard, each nymph a Grace.*] The Poet, as *Eustathius*
observes, celebrates the beauty of these two attending Virgins to raise their char-

Light as the viewless air, the warrior Maid   25
Glides thro' the valves, and hovers round her head;
A fav'rite virgin's blooming form she took,
From *Dymas* sprung, and thus the vision spoke:
  Oh indolent! to waste thy hours away!
And sleep'st thou, careless of the bridal day?   30
Thy spousal ornament neglected lies;
Arise, prepare the bridal train, arise!

---

acters, that they may not be esteem'd common servants, or the Poet thought extravagant when he compares *Nausicaa* and her damsels to *Diana* and her nymphs.

The judgment with which he introduces the vision is remarkable: In the *Iliad*, when he is to give an air of importance to his vision, he cloathes it in the likeness of *Nestor*, the wisest person of the Army; a man of less consideration had been unsuitable to the greatness of the occasion, which was to persuade Kings and Heroes. Here the Poet sends a vision to a young Lady, under the resemblance of a young Lady: he adapts the circumstances to the person, and describes the whole with an agreeable propriety. *Eustathius.*

31.   The ⟨sic⟩ *spousal ornament neglected lies;*
                           Arise, prepare the bridal train.]
Here is a remarkable custom of Antiquity. *Eustathius* observes, that it was usual for the bride to give changes of dress to the friends of the bridegroom at the celebration of the marriage, and *Homer* directly affirms it. *Dacier* quotes a passage in *Judges* concerning *Sampson*'s giving changes of garments at his marriage feast ⟨14 : 12 ff⟩, as an instance of the like custom amongst the *Israelites*; but I believe, if there was such a custom at all amongst them, it is not evident from the passage alledg'd: Nothing is plainer than that *Sampson* had not given the garments, if his riddle had not been expounded: nay, instead of giving, he himself had receiv'd them, if it had not been interpreted. I am rather of opinion that what is said of *Sampson*, has relation to another custom amongst the Ancients, of proposing an Ænigma at festivals, and adjudging a reward to him that solv'd it. These the *Greeks* call'd γρίφους συμποτικούς, *griphos convivales*; *Athenæus* has a long dissertation about this practise in his 10th book ⟨448 ff⟩, and gives a number of instances of the Ænigmatical propositions in use at *Athens*, and of the forfeitures and rewards upon the solution, and non-solution of them; and *Eustathius* in the 10th book of the *Odyssey* comes into the same opinion. So that if it was a custom amongst the *Israelites* as well as *Greeks* to give garments, (as it appears to be to give other gifts) this passage is no instance of it: It is indeed a proof that the *Hebrews* as well as *Greeks* had a custom of entertaining themselves at their festivals, with these *griphi convivales*: I therefore believe that these changes of garments, were no more than rewards or forfeits, according to the success in the interpretation.

A just applause the cares of dress impart,
And give soft transport to a parent's heart.
Haste, to the limpid stream direct thy way,   35
When the gay morn unveils her smiling ray:
Haste to the stream! companion of thy care
Lo I thy steps attend, thy labours share.
Virgin awake! the marriage hour is nigh,
See! from their thrones thy kindred monarchs sigh!   40

---

33. *A just applause the cares of dress impart.*] It is very probable that *Quintilian* had this verse in his view when he wrote *cultus* ⟨ . . . ⟩ *magnificus addit hominibus, ut Græco versu testatum est, auctoritatem* ⟨*Inst. Orat.*: VIII, Proem. 20⟩. His words are almost a translation of it.

'Εκ γάρ τοι τούτων φάτις ἀνθρώπους ἀναβάινει
'Εσθλή.

What I would chiefly observe is the propriety with which this commendation of dress is introduc'd; it is put into the mouth of a young Lady (for so *Pallas* appears to be) to whose character it is suitable to delight in Ornament. It likewise agrees very well with the description of the *Phæacians*, whose chief happiness consisted in dancing, dressing, singing, &c. Such a commendation of ornament would have been improper in the mouth of a Philosopher, but beautiful when spoken by a young Lady to *Alcinous*.

35. *Haste, to the limpid stream.*] This passage has not escap'd the raillery of the Critics; *Homer*, say they, brings the Goddess of Wisdom down from heaven, only to advise *Nausicaa* to make haste to wash her cloaths against her wedding: what necessity is there for a conduct so extraordinary upon so trivial an occasion? *Eustathius* sufficiently answers the objection, by observing that the Poet very naturally brings about the safety of *Ulysses* by it; the action of the washing is the means, the protection of *Ulysses* the end of the descent of that Goddess; so that she is not introduced lightly, or without contributing to an important action: And it must be allow'd that the means made use of are very natural; they grow out of the occasion, and at once give the fable a poetical turn, and an air of probability.

It has been further objected, that the Poet gives an unworthy employment to *Nausicaa*, the daughter of a King; but such Critics form their idea of ancient, from modern greatness: It wou'd be now a meaness to describe a person of Quality thus employ'd, because custom has made it the work of persons of low condition: It would be now thought dishonourable for a Lady of high station to attend the flocks; yet we find in the most ancient history extant, that the daughters of *Laban* ⟨Gen. 29 : 6, 9⟩ and *Jethro* ⟨Ex. 2 : 16⟩, persons of power and distinction, were so employ'd, without any dishonour to their quality. In short, these passages are to be look'd upon as exact pictures of the old World, and consequently as valuable remains of Antiquity.

The royal car at early dawn obtain,
And order mules obedient to the rein;
For rough the way, and distant rolls the wave
Where their fair vests *Phæacian* virgins lave.
In pomp ride forth: for pomp becomes the great, 45
And Majesty derives a grace from State.
  Then to the Palaces of heav'n she sails,
Incumbent on the wings of wafting gales:
The seat of Gods, the regions mild of peace,
Full joy, and calm Eternity of ease. 50
There no rude winds presume to shake the skies,
No rains descend, no snowy vapours rise;

---

41. *The royal car* ⟨ . . . ⟩ *obtain*.] It would have been an impropriety to have render'd ἄμαξαν by the word chariot; *Homer* seems industriously to avoid ἅρμα, but constantly uses ἀπήνη, or ἄμαξα; this car was drawn by mules; whereas, observes *Eustathius*, the chariot or ἅρμα was proper only for horses. The word Car takes in the Idea of any other vehicle, as well as of a Chariot.

This passage has undergone a very severe censure, as mean and ridiculous, chiefly from the expressions to her father afterwards, ὑψηλήν, εὔκυκλον: which being render'd, *high, and round*, disgrace the Author: No person, I believe, would ask a father to lend his high and round Car; nor has *Homer* said it: *Eustathius* observes, that εὔκυκλος is the same as εὔτροχος; κύκλοι λέγονται οἱ τροχοί, or wheels; and that ὑπερτερία, is τὸ ἐπικείμενον τετράγωνον πλινθίον τῷ ἄξονι, or the quadrangular body of the Car that rests upon the axle of it; this fully answers the Criticism: *Nausicaa* describes the Car so particularly, to distinguish it from a Chariot, which had been improper for her purpose: The other part of the objection, concerning the roundness of the Car, is a mistake in the Critic; the word having relation to the wheels, and not to the body of it, which, as *Eustathius* observes, was quadrangular.

47. *Then to the Palaces of heav'n she sails*.] *Lucretius* has copy'd this fine passage, and equall'd, if not surpass'd the original ⟨III 18–22⟩.

> *Apparet divum numen, sedesque quietæ,*
> *Quas neque concutiunt venti, neque nubila nimbis*
> *Aspergunt, neque nix acri concreta pruina*
> *Cana cadens violat: semperque innubilus æther*
> *Integit, & large diffuso lumine ridet.*

The picture is the same in both Authors, but the colouring in my opinion is less beautiful in *Homer* than *Lucretius*: the three last lines in particular are fuller of ornament, and the very verses have an air of the serenity they were intended to paint.

But on immortal thrones the blest repose:
The firmament with living splendors glows.
Hither the Goddess wing'd th' aereal way,   55
Thro' heav'n's eternal gates that blaz'd with day.
    Now from her rosy car *Aurora* shed
The dawn, and all the orient flam'd with red.
Uprose the virgin with the morning light,
Obedient to the vision of the night.   60
The Queen she sought: the Queen her hours bestow'd
In curious works; the whirling spindle glow'd
With crimson threads, while busy damsels cull
The snowy fleece, or twist the purpled wool.
Mean-time *Phæacia*'s peers in council sate;   65
From his high dome the King descends in state,
Then with a filial awe the royal maid
Approach'd him passing, and submissive said;
    Will my dread Sire his ear regardful deign,
And may his child the royal car obtain?   70
Say, with thy garments shall I bend my way
Where thro' the vales the mazy waters stray?
A dignity of dress adorns the great,
And Kings draw lustre from the robe of state.
Five sons thou hast; three wait the bridal day,   75
And spotless robes become the young and gay:
So when with praise amid the dance they shine,
By these my cares adorn'd, that praise is mine.
    Thus she: but blushes ill-restrain'd betray
Her thoughts intentive on the bridal day: 80

---

61.   —*The Queen her hours bestow'd*
                      In curious works.]

This is another image of ancient life: We see a Queen amidst her attendants at
work at the dawn of day: *de nocte surrexit, & digiti ejus apprehenderunt fusum* ⟨cf.
Proverbs 31.15 and 31.19⟩. This is a practice as contrary to the manners of our
ages, as the other of washing the robes: 'Tis the more remarkable in this Queen,
because she liv'd amongst an idle effeminate people, that lov'd nothing but
pleasures. *Dacier.*

The conscious Sire the dawning blush survey'd,
And smiling thus bespoke the blooming maid.
My child, my darling joy, the car receive;
That, and whate'er our daughter asks, we give.
Swift at the royal nod th' attending train   85
The car prepare, the mules incessant rein.
The blooming virgin with dispatchful cares
Tunics, and stoles, and robes imperial bears.
The Queen, assiduous, to her train assigns
The sumptuous viands, and the flav'rous wines.   90
The train prepare a cruise of curious mold,
A cruise of fragrance, form'd of burnish'd gold;
Odour divine! whose soft refreshing streams
Sleek the smooth skin, and scent the snowy limbs.
Now mounting the gay seat, the silken reins   95

---

88. *Tunicks, and stoles, and robes imperial bears.*] It is not without reason that the Poet describes *Nausicaa* carrying the whole wardrobe of the family to the river: he inserts these circumstances so particularly, that she may be able to cloath *Ulysses* in the sequel of the story: he further observes the modesty and simplicity of these early times, when the whole dress of a King and his family (who reign'd over a people that delighted in dress) is without gold: for we see *Nausicaa* carries with her all the habits that were used at the greatest solemnities; which had they been wrought with gold could not have been washed. *Eustathius.*

95. *Now mounting the gay seat,* &c.] This Image of *Nausicaa* riding in her Car to the river, has exercis'd the pencils of excellent Painters. *Pausanias* in his fifth book ⟨xix 9⟩, which is the first of the *Eliacs*, speaks of a picture of two Virgins drawn by Mules, of which the one guides the reins, the other has her head cover'd with a veil: It is believ'd that it represents *Nausicaa*, the daughter of *Alcinous*, going with one of her virgins to the river. The words of *Pausanias* have caused some doubt with relation to the picture; he says, ἐπὶ ἡμιόνων, or *upon Mules*, but *Homer* describes her upon a Car; how then can *Nausicaa* be intended by the Painter? But *Romulus Amasæus* ⟨in his version of Pausanias (ed. 1613), v 325⟩, who comments upon *Pausanias*, solves the difficulty, by observing that ἐπὶ ἡμιόνων does not signify upon Mules, but a Car drawn by Mules, by a figure frequent in all Authors. *Pliny* is also thus to be understood in his 35th book ⟨xxxv xxxvi 101⟩; *Protogenes* the *Rhodian* painted at *Athens Paralus*, and likewise *Hemionida*, who is said to represent *Nausicaa*; *Hemionida* is used (as *Hermolaus Barbarus* observes upon that passage ⟨ad loc., in his *C. Plinii Secundi Naturae Historiarum* Libri xxxvii (1497)⟩) as a term of art to express a Virgin riding upon, or more properly drawn by Mules, or ἐπὶ ἡμιόνων. *Spondanus* ⟨*Od.* p. 83⟩.

Shine in her hand: Along the sounding plains
Swift fly the mules: nor rode the nymph alone,
Around, a beavy of bright damsels shone.
They seek the cisterns where *Phæacian* dames
Wash their fair garments in the limpid streams;   100
Where gathering into depth from falling rills,
The lucid wave a spacious bason fills.
The mules unharness'd range beside the main,

---

101.   *Where gathering into depth from falling rills,*
              The lucid wave a spacious bason fills.]
It is evident, that the Ancients had basons, or cisterns, continually supply'd by
the rivers for this business of washing; they were call'd, observes *Eustathius*,
πλυνοί, or βόθροι; and were sometimes made of marble, other times of wood.
Thus in the *Iliad*, book 22 ⟨201–4⟩,
              Each gushing fount a marble cistern fills,
              Whose polish'd bed receives the falling rills,
              Where Trojan *dames ere yet alarm'd by* Greece,
              Wash'd their fair garments in the days of peace.
The manner of washing was different from what is now in use: They trod them
with their feet, Στεῖβον, ἔτριβον τοῖς ποσί. *Eustathius.*

It may be thought that these customs are of small importance, and of little
concern to the present ages: It is true; but Time has stamp'd a value upon them:
like ancient Medals, their intrinsic worth may be small, but yet they are valuable,
because images of Antiquity.

Plutarch in his *Symposiacs* ⟨*Quaest. Conviv.* 1 ix (627A ff). Theon and Themistocles
are both characters in this dialogue.⟩ proposes this question, Why *Nausicaa*
washes in the river, rather than the sea, tho' it was more nigh, more hot, and consequently more fit for the purpose than the river? *Theon* answers from *Aristotle*
⟨*Meteorologica* II 3; *Problemata* XXIII 9⟩, that the sea-water has many gross, rough,
and earthy particles in it, as appears from its saltness, whereas fresh water is more
pure and unmixt, and consequently more subtle and penetrating, and fitter for
use in washing. *Themistocles* dislikes this reason, and affirms that sea-water being
more rough and earthy, than that of rivers, is therefore the most proper, for its
cleansing quality; this appears from observation, for in washing, ashes or some
such substance are thrown into the fresh water to make it effectual, for those
particles open the pores, and conduce to the effect of cleansing. The true reason
then is, that there is an unctuous nature in sea-water, (and *Aristotle* confesses all
salt to be unctuous ⟨*Meteorologica* II 3⟩) which hinders it from cleansing: whereas
river-water is pure, less mixt, and consequently more subtle and penetrating, and
being free from all oily substance, is preferable and more effectual than sea-
water.

Or crop the verdant herbage of the plain.

Then æmulous the royal robes they lave,   105
And plunge the vestures in the cleansing wave:
(The vestures cleans'd o'erspread the shelly sand,
Their snowy lustre whitens all the strand.)
Then with a short repast relieve their toil,
And o'er their limbs diffuse ambrosial oil;   110
And while the robes imbibe the solar ray,
O'er the green mead the sporting virgins play:
(Their shining veils unbound.) Along the skies
Tost, and retost, the ball incessant flies.
They sport, they feast; *Nausicaa* lifts her voice,   115
And warbling sweet, makes earth and heav'n rejoice.
   As when o'er *Erymanth Diana* roves,

---

117. *As when o'er* Erymanth Diana *roves*.] This is a very beautiful comparison,
(and when-ever I say any thing in commendation of *Homer*, I would always be
understood to mean the original.) *Virgil* was sensible to it, and inserted it in his
Poem ⟨1 498–502⟩,

> Qualis in Eurotæ ripis aut per juga Cynthi
> Exercet Diana choros: quam mille secutæ
> Hinc atque hinc glomerantur Oreades: illa pharetram
> Fert humero, gradiensque deas supereminet omnes:
> Latonæ tacitum pertentant gaudia pectus.

It has given occasion for various Criticisms, with relation to the beauty of the two
Authors. I will lay before the Reader what is said in behalf of *Homer* in *Aulus
Gellius*, and the answer by *Scaliger*.

   Gellius writes ⟨*Attic Nights* ix ix 12 ff⟩, that it was the opinion of *Valerius Probus*,
that no passage has been more unhappily copy'd by *Virgil* than this comparison.
Homer very beautifully compares *Nausicaa*, a Virgin, sporting with her damsels in
a solitary place, to *Diana*, a virgin Goddess, taking her diversion in a forest, in
hunting with her rural Nymphs. Whereas *Dido*, a widow, is drawn by *Virgil* in
the midst of a city, walking gravely with the *Tyrian* Princes, *Instans operi*,
regnisque futuris ⟨1 504⟩, a circumstance that bears not the least resemblance to the
sports of the Goddess. *Homer* represents *Diana* with her quiver at her shoulder,
but at the same time he describes her as an huntress: *Virgil* gives her a quiver, but
mentions nothing of her as an huntress, and consequently lays a needless burthen
upon her shoulder. *Homer* excellently paints the fulness of joy which *Latona* felt at
the sight of her daughter, γέγηθε δέ τε φρένα Λητώ; *Virgil* falls infinitely short
of it in the word *pertentant*, which signifies a light joy that sinks not deep into the

Or wide *Täygetus'* resounding groves;
A sylvan train the huntress Queen surrounds,
Her ratling quiver from her shoulder sounds: 120
Fierce in the sport, along the mountain brow
They bay the boar, or chase the bounding roe:
High o'er the lawn, with more majestic pace,
Above the nymphs she treads with stately grace;
Distinguish'd excellence the Goddess proves;   125
Exults *Latona* as the virgin moves.
With equal grace *Nausicaa* trod the plain,
And shone transcendent o'er the beauteous train.

heart. Lastly *Virgil* has omitted the strongest point and very flower of the comparison,

ʹΡεῖα δʹ ἀριγνώτη πέλεται, καλαὶ δέ τε πᾶσαι.

'Tis the last circumstance that compleats the comparison, as it distinguishes *Nausicaa* from her attendants, for which very purpose the allusion was introduced.

Scaliger ⟨v iii, p. 219 D 2⟩ (who never deserts *Virgil* in any difficulty) answers, that the persons, not the places, are intended to be represented by both Poets; otherwise *Homer* himself is blameable, for *Nausicaa* is not sporting on a mountain but a plain, and has neither bow nor quiver like *Diana*. Neither is there any weight in the objection concerning the gravity of the gait of *Dido*; for neither is *Nausicaa* describ'd in the act of hunting, but dancing: And as for the word *pertentant*, it is a Metaphor taken from musicians and musical instruments: it denotes a strong degree of joy, *per* bears an intensive sense, and takes in the perfection of joy. As to the quiver, it was an ensign of the Goddess, as ʹΑργυρότοξος was of *Apollo*, and is apply'd to her upon all occasions indifferently, not only by *Virgil*, but more frequently by *Homer*. Lastly, ῥεῖα δʹ ἀριγνώτη, *&c.* is superfluous, for the joy of *Latona* compleats the whole, and *Homer* has already said γέγηθε δέ τε φρένα Λητώ.

But still it must be allow'd, that there is a greater correspondence to the subject intended to be illustrated, in *Homer* than in *Virgil*. *Diana* sports, so does *Nausicaa*; *Diana* is a Virgin, so is *Nausicaa*; *Diana* is amongst her virgin Nymphs, *Nausicaa* among her virgin attendants: whereas in all these points there is the greatest dissimilitude between *Dido* and *Diana*: And no one I believe but *Scaliger* can think the verse above quoted superfluous, which indeed is the beauty and perfection of the comparison. There may, perhaps, be a more rational objection made against this line in both Poets.

Latonæ tacitum pertentant gaudia pectus.

This verse has no relation to the principal subject, the expectation is fully satisfy'd without it, and it alludes to nothing that either precedes or follows it, and consequently may be judg'd superfluous.

Mean time (the care and fav'rite of the skies)
Wrapt in embow'ring shade, *Ulysses* lies,   130
His woes forgot! But *Pallas* now addrest
To break the banks of all-composing rest.
Forth from her snowy hand *Nausicaa* threw
The various ball; the ball erroneous flew,
And swam the stream: Loud shrieks the virgin train,   135
And the loud shriek redoubles from the main.
Wak'd by the shrilling sound, *Ulysses* rose,

---

133.   *Forth from her snowy hand* Nausicaa *threw*
                The various ball.]
This Play with the Ball was called φεννίς, and ἐφετίνδα, by the Ancients; and
from the signification of the word, which is *deception*, we may learn the nature of
the Play: The ball was thrown to some one of the players unexpectedly, and he
as unexpectedly threw it to some other of the company to catch, from which surprize upon one another, it took the name of φεννίς. It was a sport much in use
amongst the Ancients, both men and women; it caus'd a variety of motions in
throwing, and running, and was therefore a very healthful exercise. The *Lacedæmonians* were remarkable for the use of it; *Alexander* the Great frequently
exercised at it; and *Sophocles* wrote a Play, call'd Πλύντριαι, or *Lotrices*; in which
he represented *Nausicaa* sporting with her damsels at this play: It is not now
extant.

  Dionysidorus ⟨on authority of Eustathius 250, 15⟩ gives us a various reading,
instead of σφαῖραν ἔπειτ᾽ ἔρριψε, he writes it, πάλλαν ἔπειτ᾽, which the *Latins*
render πῖλον, and *Suidas* ⟨on authority of Eustathius 1554, 33⟩ countenances the
alteration, for he writes that a damsel named *Larissa*, as she sported at this play,
(πίλῳ, not σφαίρῃ) was drowned in the river *Peneus. Eustathius.*

  What I would further observe is, the art of the Poet in carrying on the story:
He proceeds from incident to incident very naturally, and makes the sports of
these Virgins contribute to the principal design of the Poem, and promote the
re-establishment of *Ulysses*, by discovering him advantagiously to the *Phæacians.*
He so judiciously interweaves these sports into the texture of the story, that there
would be a chasm if they were taken away; and the sports of the Virgins are as
much of a piece with the whole, as any of the labours of *Ulysses.*

  The Poet reaps a further advantage from this conduct: it beautifies and enlivens the Poem with a pleasant and entertaining scene, and relieves the Reader's
mind by taking it off from a continual representation of horrour and sufferings in
the story of *Ulysses*: He himself seems here to take breath, and indulging his
fancy, lets it run out into several beautiful comparisons, to prepare the Reader to
hear with a better relish the long detail of the calamities of his Heroe. thro' the
sequel of the *Odyssey.*

And to the deaf woods wailing, breath'd his woes.
     Ah me! on what inhospitable coast,
On what new region is *Ulysses* tost?   140
Possest by wild barbarians fierce in arms,
Or men, whose bosom tender pity warms?
What sounds are these that gather from the shores?
The voice of nymphs that haunt the sylvan bow'rs?
The fair-hair'd *Dryads* of the shady wood,   145
Or azure daughters of the silver flood?
Or human voice? but issuing from the shades
Why cease I strait to learn what sound invades?
     Then, where the grove with leaves umbrageous bends,
With forceful strength a branch the Heroe rends;   150
Around his loins the verdant cincture spreads

---

139. *Ah me! on what inhospitable coast.*] This soliloquy is well adapted to the circumstances of *Ulysses*, and short, as is requisite in all soliloquies.

    Virgil has imitated it ⟨1 306–9⟩, and *Scaliger* in general prefers the copy to the
original ⟨v iii, p. 218 B2⟩.

> *Ut primum lux alma data est, exire; locosque*
> *Explorare novos, quas vento accesserit oras:*
> *Qui teneant (nam inculta videt) hominesne, feræne,*
> *Quærere constituit—*

But it may perhaps be true, that *Virgil* here falls short of *Homer*: There is not that
harmony of numbers, that variety of circumstances, and sentiments in the *Latin*,
as appears in the *Greek* Poet; and above all, the whole passage has more force and
energy by being put into the mouth of *Ulysses*, than when merely related by
Virgil.

    Dacier observes, that *Abraham* makes the very same reflections as *Ulysses*, upon
his arrival at *Gerar. Cogitavi mecum dicens, forsitan non est timor domini in loco isto*,
Gen. 20. 11. *I thought, surely the fear of God is not in this place;* which very well
answers to, καί σφιν νόος ἐστὶ θεουδής.

151.   *Around his loins the verdant cincture spreads*
                 A wreathy foliage and concealing shades.]
This passage has given great offence to the Critics. The interview between
Ulysses and *Nausicaa*, says *Rapin*, outrages all the rules of decency: She forgets her
modesty, and betrays her virtue, by giving too long an audience: she yields too
much to his complaints, and indulges her curiosity too far at the sight of a person
in such circumstances ⟨Comparaison vii, 1 123⟩. But perhaps *Rapin* is too severe;
Homer has guarded every circumstance with as much caution as if he had been
aware of the objection: He covers his loins with a broad foliage, (for *Eustathius*

A wreathy foliage, and concealing shades.
As when a Lion in the midnight hours

observes, that πτόρθος signifies κλάδος πλατύς, or *a broad branch*) he makes
Ulysses speak at a proper distance, and introduces *Minerva* to encourage her virgin
modesty. Is there here any outrage of decency? Besides, what takes off this objection of immodesty in *Nausicaa*, is, that the sight of a naked man was not unusual
in those ages; it was customary for Virgins of the highest quality to attend
Heroes to the bath, and even to assist in bathing them, without any breach of
modesty; as is evident from the conduct of *Polycaste* in the conclusion of the third
book of the *Odyssey*, who bathes and perfumes *Telemachus*. If this be true, the other
objections of *Rapin* about her yielding too much to his complaints, *&c.* are of no
weight; but so many testimonies of her virtuous and compassionate disposition,
which induces her to pity and relieve calamity. Yet it may seem that the other
damsels had a different opinion of this interview, and that thro' modesty they ran
away, while *Nausicaa* alone talks with *Ulysses*: But this only shews, not that she
had less modesty, but more prudence, than her retinue; the damsels fled not out
of modesty, but fear of an enemy: whereas *Nausicaa* wisely reflects that no such
person could arrive there, the country being an Island; and from his appearance,
she rightly concluded him to be a man in calamity. This Wisdom is the *Pallas* in
the Allegory, which makes her to stay when the other damsels fly for want of
equal reflection. *Adam* and *Eve* cover'd themselves after the same manner as
Ulysses.

153. *As when a Lion in the midnight hours.*] This is a very noble comparison, yet
has not escap'd censure; it has been objected that it is improper for the occasion,
as bearing images of too much terror, only to fright a few timorous Virgins, and
that the Poet is unseasonably sublime. This is only true in Burlesque poetry,
where the most noble images are frequently assembled to disgrace the subject,
and to shew a ridiculous disproportion between the allusion and the principal
subject; but the same reason will not hold in Epic Poetry, where the Poet raises
a low circumstance into dignity by a sublime comparison. The simile is not introduced merely to shew the impression it made upon the Virgins, but paints
Ulysses himself in very strong colours: *Ulysses* is fatigued with the tempests and
waves; the Lion with winds and storms: it is hunger that drives the Lion upon his
prey; an equal necessity compells *Ulysses* to go down to the Virgins: the Lion is
described in all his terrors, *Ulysses* arms himself as going upon an unknown
adventure; so that the comparison is very noble and very proper. This verse in
particular has something horrible in the very run of it.

Σμερδαλέος δ' αὐτῆσι φάνη κεκακωμένος ἅλμη.

Dionysius Halicarn. in his observations upon the placing of words ⟨*De Comp.
Verb.* xvi 98⟩ quotes it to this purpose; When *Homer*, says he, is to introduce a
terrible or unusual Image, he rejects the more flowing and harmonious vowels,
and makes choice of such mutes and consonants as load the syllables, and render
the pronunciation difficult.

Beat by rude blasts, and wet with wintry show'rs,
Descends terrific from the mountain's brow,   155
With living flames his rowling eye-balls glow;
With conscious strength elate, he bends his way
Majestically fierce, to seize his prey;
(The steer or stag:) or with keen hunger bold
Springs o'er the fence, and dissipates the fold.   160
No less a terror, from the neighb'ring groves
Rough from the tossing surge *Ulysses* moves;
Urg'd on by want, and recent from the storms;
The brackish ooze his manly grace deforms.
Wide o'er the shore with many a piercing cry   165
To rocks, to caves, the frighted virgins fly;
All but the Nymph: the nymph stood fix'd alone,
By *Pallas* arm'd with boldness not her own.
Mean-time in dubious thought the King awaits,
And self-considering, as he stands, debates;   170
Distant his mournful story to declare,
Or prostrate at her knee address the pray'r.
But fearful to offend, by wisdom sway'd,
At awful distance he accosts the maid.
If from the skies a Goddess, or if earth   175

Pausanias writes in his *Attics* ⟨1 xxii 6⟩, that the famous Painter *Polygnotus*
painted this subject in the gallery at *Athens*. Ἔγραψε δὲ καὶ πρὸς τῷ ποταμῷ
ταῖς ὁμοῦ πλυνούσαις ἐφιστάμενον 'Οδυσσέα; he painted *Ulysses* approaching *Nausicaa* and her damsels, as they were washing at the river. This is the same
Polygnotus who painted in the gallery called ποικίλη, the battle of *Marathon*
gain'd by *Miltiades* over the *Medes* and *Persians*.

175.   *If from the skies a Goddess, or if earth*
                        (Imperial Virgin) boast thy glorious birth,
                        To thee I bend!]

There never was a more agreeable and insinuating piece of flattery, than this
address of *Ulysses*; and yet nothing mean appears in it, as is usual in almost all
flattery. The only part that seems liable to any imputation, is that exaggeration
at the beginning, of calling her a Goddess; yet this is propos'd with modesty and
doubt, and hypothetically. *Eustathius* assigns two reasons why he resembles her to
Diana, rather than to any other Deity; either because he found her and her
damsels in a solitary place, such as *Diana* is suppos'd to frequent with her rural

(Imperial Virgin) boast thy glorious birth,
To thee I bend! if in that bright disguise

Nymphs; or perhaps *Ulysses* might have seen some statue or picture of that Goddess, to which *Nausicaa* bore a likeness. *Virgil* (who has imitated this passage) is more bold, when without any doubt or hesitation, before he knew *Venus*, he pronounces the person with whom he talks, *O dea, certe* ⟨I 327–9⟩.

Ovid has copy'd this passage in his *Metamorphoses*, book the 4th ⟨320–6, but with two half lines omitted after *felix*⟩.

> —*puer o dignissime credi*
> *Esse deus; seu tu deus es; potes esse cupido:*
> *Sive es mortalis; qui te genuere beati!*
> *Et frater felix, & quæ dedit ubera nutrix!*
> *Sed longe cunctis longeque potentior illa*
> *Si qua tibi sponsa est, si quam dignabere tæda!*

Scaliger prefers *Virgil*'s imitation to *Homer*;

> *O, quam te memorem virgo! namque haud tibi vultus*
> *Mortalis, nec vox hominem sonat. O dea, certe!*
> *An Phœbi soror, an Nympharum sanguinis una?* ⟨*Aen.* II 327–9⟩

See his reasons in the fifth book of his Poetics ⟨ch. iii, p. 217 A1⟩. But *Scaliger* brings ⟨v ii, p. 215 B2⟩ a much heavier charge against *Homer*, as having stoll'n the verses from *Musæus*, and disgraced them by his alterations. The verses are as follow.

> Κύπρι φίλη μετὰ Κύπριν, ᾿Αθηναίη μετ᾿ ᾿Αθηνὴν,
> Οὐ γὰρ ἐπιχθονίῃσιν ἴσην καλέω σε γυναιξίν.
> ᾿Αλλά σε θυγατέρεσσι Διὸς Κρονιώνος ἐΐσκω.
> ῎Ολβιος ὅς σ᾿ ἐφύτευσε, καὶ ὀλβίη ἣ τέκε μήτηρ,
> Γαστήρ θ᾿ ἣ σ᾿ ἐλόχευσε, μακαρτάτη.

Scaliger imagines this *Musæus* to be the same mention'd by *Virgil*, in the *Elysian* fields ⟨VI 667⟩,

> *Musæum ante omnes,* &c.

But I believe it is now agreed, that all the works of the ancient *Musæus* are perish'd, and that the person who wrote these verses liv'd many centuries after *Homer*, and consequently borrow'd them from him: *Scaliger* calls them fine and lively in *Musæus*, but abject, unnervate, and unharmonious in *Homer*. But his prejudice against *Homer* is too apt to give a wrong biass to his judgement. Is the similitude of sound in -ῃσιν ἴσην in the second verse of *Musæus*, harmonious? and is there not a tautology in the two last lines? *Happy is the mother that bore thee, and most happy the womb that brought thee forth*; as if the happy person in the former line, were not the same with the most happy in the latter! Whereas *Homer* still rises in his Images, and ends with a compliment very agreeable to a beautiful Woman.

> *But blest o'er all, the youth with heav'nly charms,*
> *Who clasps the bright perfection in his arms!*

But this is submitted to the Reader's better judgment.

Thou visit earth, a daughter of the skies,
Hail, *Dian*, hail! the huntress of the groves
So shines majestic, and so stately moves,   180
So breathes an air divine! But if thy race
Be mortal, and this earth thy native place,
Blest is the father from whose loins you sprung,
Blest is the mother at whose breast you hung,
Blest are the brethren who thy blood divide,   185
To such a miracle of charms ally'd:
Joyful they see applauding Princes gaze,
When stately in the dance you swim th' harmonious maze.
But blest o'er all, the youth with heav'nly charms,
Who clasps the bright perfection in his arms!   190
Never, I never view'd 'till this blest hour
Such finish'd grace! I gaze and I adore!
Thus seems the Palm with stately honours crown'd

---

187. *Joyful they see applauding Princes gaze.*] In the original, there is a false construction, for after σφισι θυμὸς ἰαίνεται, *Ulysses* uses λευσσόντων, whereas it
ought to be λεύσσουσι; but this disorder is not without its effect, it represents the
modest confusion with which he addresses *Nausicaa*; he is struck with a religious
awe at the sight of her, (for so σέβας properly signifies,) and consequently naturally falls into a confusion of expression: This is not a negligence, but a beauty.
Eustath.

193. *Thus seems the Palm.*] This allusion is introduced to image the stateliness,
and exactness of shape in *Nausicaa*, to the mind of the Reader; and so *Tully*, as
Spondanus observes ⟨*Od.* p. 87⟩, understands it. *Cicero*, 1. de legibus ⟨1 i 2⟩. *Aut
quod Homericus Ulysses Deli se proceram & teneram palmam vidisse dixit, hodie mon-
strant eandem.* *Pliny* also mentions this Palm, *lib.* 14. *Chap.* 44 ⟨xvi lxxxix 240⟩.
Nec non palma Deli ab ejusdem dei ætate conspicitur. The story of the Palm is this:
"When *Latona* was in travail of *Apollo* in *Delos*, the earth that instant produced a
large Palm, against which she rested in her labour." *Homer* mentions it in his
Hymns ⟨*To Apollo* 17–18⟩.

—κεκλιμένη—
Ἀγχοτάτω φοίνικος.
And also *Callimachus* ⟨Hymn iv 209–10, ii 4–5⟩.
Λύσατο δὲ ζωνὴν ἀπὸ δ' ἐκλίθη ἔμπαλιν ὤμοις
Φοίνικος ποτὶ πρέμνον. And again.
—ἐπένευσεν ὁ Δήλιος ἁδύ τι φοίνιξ
Ἐξαπίνης.

By *Phœbus'* altars; thus o'erlooks the ground;
The pride of *Delos*. (By the *Delian* coast   195
I voyag'd, leader of a warrior host,
But ah how chang'd! from thence my sorrow flows;
O fatal voyage, source of all my woes!)
Raptur'd I stood, and as this hour amaz'd,
With rev'rence at the lofty wonder gaz'd: 200
Raptur'd I stand! for earth ne'er knew to bear
A plant so stately, or a nymph so fair.
Aw'd from access, I lift my suppliant hands;

This allusion is after the oriental manner. Thus in the *Psalms*, how frequently are persons compar'd to *Cedars*? and in the same Author, children are resembled to *Olive branches*.

This Palm was much celebrated by the Ancients, the superstition of the age had given it a religious veneration, and even in the times of *Tully* the natives esteem'd it immortal; (for so the above-mention'd words imply;) This gives weight and beauty to the address of *Ulysses*, and it could not but be very acceptable to a young Lady, to hear herself compar'd to the greatest wonder in Creation.

Dionysius Halicarn. ⟨*De Comp. Verb.* xvi 98⟩ observes the particular beauty of these two verses.

Δήλῳ δή ποτε τοῖον Ἀπόλλωνος παρὰ βωμῷ,
Φοίνικος νέον ἔρνος ἀνερχόμενον ἐνόησα ⟨162–3⟩.

When *Homer*, says he, would paint an elegance of beauty, or represent any agreeable object, he makes use of the smoothest vowels and most flowing semivowels, as in the lines last recited: He rejects harsh sounds, and a collision of rough words; but the lines flow along with a smooth harmony of letters and syllables, without any offence to the ear by asperity of sound.

198. *O fatal voyage, source of all my woes.*] There is some obscurity in this passage: *Ulysses* speaks in general, and does not specify what voyage he means. It may therefore be ask'd how is it to be understood? *Eustathius* answers, that the voyage of the *Greeks* to the *Trojan* expedition is intended by the Poet; for *Lycophron* writes, that the *Greeks* sail'd by *Delos* in their passage to *Troy* ⟨on authority of Eustathius 1557, 52⟩.

Homer passes over the voyage in this transient manner without a further explanation: *Ulysses* had no leisure to enlarge upon that story, but reserves it more advantagiously for a future discovery before *Alcinous* and the *Phæacian* rulers. By this conduct he avoids a repetition, which must have been tedious to the Reader, who would have found little appetite afterwards, if he had already been satisfied by a full discovery made to *Nausicaa*. The obscurity therefore arises from choice, not want of judgment.

For Misery, oh Queen, before thee stands!
Twice ten tempestuous nights I roll'd, resign'd   205
To roaring billows, and the warring wind;
Heav'n bad the deep to spare! but heav'n my foe
Spares only to inflict some mightier woe!
Inur'd to cares, to death in all its forms,
Outcast I rove, familiar with the storms!   210
Once more I view the face of humankind:
Oh let soft pity touch thy gen'rous mind!
Unconscious of what air I breathe, I stand
Naked, defenceless on a foreign land.
Propitious to my wants, a Vest supply   215
To guard the wretched from th' inclement sky:
So may the Gods who heav'n and earth controul,
Crown the chaste wishes of thy virtuous soul,
On thy soft hours their choicest blessings shed,
Blest with a husband be thy bridal bed,   220
Blest be thy husband with a blooming race,
And lasting union crown your blissful days.
The Gods, when they supremely bless, bestow
Firm union on their Favourites below;
Then Envy grieves, with inly-pining Hate;   225
The good exult, and heav'n is in our state.
     To whom the Nymph: O stranger cease thy care,
Wise is thy soul, but man is born to bear:
Jove weighs affairs of earth in dubious scales,

---

229.   Jove *weighs affairs of earth in dubious scales,*
                    And the good suffers, while the bad prevails.]
The morality of this passage is excellent, and very well adapted to the present
occasion. *Ulysses* had said,
                    Heav'n bade the deep to spare! but heav'n my foe
                    Spares only to inflict some mightier woe.
Nausicaa makes use of this expression to pay her address to *Ulysses*, and at the
same time teaches, conformably to truth, that the afflicted are not always the
objects of divine hate: The Gods (adds she) bestow good and evil indifferently,
and therefore we must not judge of men from their conditions, for good men are
frequently wretched, and bad men happy. Nay sometimes affliction distinguishes

And the good suffers, while the bad prevails:　230
Bear, with a soul resign'd, the will of *Jove*;
Who breathes, must mourn: thy woes are from above.
But since thou tread'st our hospitable shore,
'Tis mine to bid the wretched grieve no more,
To cloath the naked, and thy way to guide—　235
Know, the *Phæacian* tribes this land divide;
From great *Alcinous'* royal loins I spring,
A happy nation, and an happy King.
　　Then to her maids—Why, why, ye coward train
These fears, this flight? ye fear, and fly in vain.　240
Dread ye a foe? dismiss that idle dread,
'Tis death with hostile step these shores to tread;
Safe in the love of heav'n, an ocean flows
Around our realm, a barrier from the foes;

---

a man of goodness, when he bears it with a greatness of spirit. *Sophocles* puts a very beautiful expression into the mouth of *Oedipus*, κάλλος κακῶν ⟨*Oed. Tyr.* 1396⟩, the *beauty and ornament of calamities. Eustathius.*

　Longinus is of opinion, that when great Poets and Writers sink in their vigour, and cannot reach the Pathetic, they descend to the Moral ⟨ix 12–13⟩. Hence he judges the *Odyssey* to be the work of *Homer*'s declining years, and gives that as a reason of its morality: He speaks not this out of derogation to *Homer*, for he compares him to the Sun, which tho' it has not the same warmth as when in the Meridian, is always of the same bigness: This is no dishonour to the *Odyssey*; the most useful, if not the most beautiful circumstance is allow'd it, I mean Instruction: In the *Odyssey Homer* appears to be the better Man, in the *Iliad* the better Poet.

　242. '*Tis death with hostile step these shores to tread.*] This I take to be the meaning of the word διερός, which *Eustathius* explains by ζῶν καὶ ἐρρωμένος, *vivus & valens*; or, *he shall not be long-liv'd*. But it may be ask'd how this character of valour in destroying their enemies, can agree with the *Phæacians*, an effeminate, unwarlike nation? *Eustathius* answers, that the protection of the Gods is the best defence, and upon this *Nausicaa* relies. But then it is necessary that man should co-operate with the Gods; for it is in vain to rely upon the Gods for safety, if we our selves make not use of means proper for it; whereas the *Phæacians* were a people wholly given up to luxury and pleasures. The true reason then of *Nausicaa*'s praise of the *Phæacians* may perhaps be drawn from that honourable partiality, and innate love which every person feels for his country. She knew no people greater than the *Phæacians*, and having ever liv'd in full security from enemies, she concludes that it is not in the power of enemies to disturb that security.

'Tis ours this son of sorrow to relieve,   245
Chear the sad heart, not let affliction grieve.
By *Jove* the stranger and the poor are sent,
And what to those we give, to *Jove* is lent.
Then food supply, and bathe his fainting limbs
Where waving shades obscure the mazy streams.   250
   Obedient to the call, the chief they guide
To the calm current of the secret tyde;
Close by the stream a royal dress they lay,
A vest and robe, with rich embroid'ry gay:
Then unguents in a vase of gold supply,   255
That breath'd a fragrance thro' the balmy sky.
   To them the King. No longer I detain
Your friendly care: retire, ye virgin train!
Retire, while from my weary'd limbs I lave
The foul pollution of the briny wave: 260
Ye Gods! since this worn frame refection knew,
What scenes have I survey'd of dreadful view?
But, nymphs, recede! safe chastity denies

---

247.   *By* Jove *the stranger and the poor are sent,*
          And what to those we give, to Jove *is lent.*]
This is a very remarkable passage, full of such a pious generosity as the wisest
teach, and the best practise. I am sensible it may be understood two ways; and
in both, it bears an excellent instruction. The words are, *the poor and stranger
are from* Jove, *and a small gift is acceptable to them*, or *acceptable to* Jupiter, Διï
φίλη. I have chosen the latter, in conformity to the eastern way of thinking:
He that hath pity upon the poor lendeth unto the Lord, as it is expressed in the *Proverbs*
⟨19 : 17⟩.

   263. *But,* Nymphs, *recede!* &c.] This place seems contradictory to the practice of
Antiquity, and other passages in the *Odyssey*: Nothing is more freqent than for
Heroes to make use of the ministry of damsels in bathing, as appears from *Polycaste* and *Telemachus*, &c. Whence is it then that *Ulysses* commands the attendants
of *Nausicaa* to withdraw while he bathes? *Spondanus* is of opinion, that the Poet
intended to condemn an indecent custom of those ages solemnly by the mouth of
so wise a person as *Ulysses* ⟨*Od.* p. 87⟩: but there is no other instance in all his
works to confirm that conjecture. I am at a loss to give a better reason, unless the
difference of the places might make an alteration in the action. It is possible that
in baths prepared for public use, there might be some convenience to defend the

To raise the blush, or pain the modest eyes.

The nymphs withdrawn, at once into the tide   265
Active he bounds; the flashing waves divide:
O'er all his limbs his hands the wave diffuse,
And from his locks compress the weedy ooze;
The balmy oil, a fragrant show'r, he sheds,
Then drest in pomp magnificently treads.   270
The warrior Goddess gives his frame to shine

---

person who bath'd in some degree from observation, which might be wanting in
an open river, so that the action might be more indecent in the one instance than
in the other, and consequently occasion these words of *Ulysses*: But this is a conjecture, and submitted as such to the Reader's better judgment.

265.   *—At once into the tide*
                               Active he bounds.]
It may be ask'd why *Ulysses* prefers the river-waters in washing, to the waters of
the sea, in the *Odyssey*; whereas in the tenth book of the *Iliad*, after the death of
Dolon, Diomed and *Ulysses* prefer the sea-waters to those of the river? There is a
different reason for this different regimen: In the *Iliad*, *Ulysses* was fatigued, and
sweated with the labours of the night, and in such a case the sea-waters being
more rough are more purifying and corroborating: But here *Ulysses* comes from
the seas, and (as *Plutarch* in his *Symposiacs* ⟨*Quaest. Conviv.* 1 ix 4 (677 E–F)⟩ observes
upon this passage), the more subtle and light particles exhale by the heat of
the sun, but the rough and saline stick to the body, 'till wash'd away by fresh
waters.

271. *The warrior Goddess gives his frame to shine.*] Poetry delights in the Marvellous, and ennobles the most ordinary subjects by dressing them with poetical
ornaments, and giving them an adventitious dignity. The foundation of this fiction, of *Ulysses* receiving beauty from *Pallas*, is only this: The shipwreck and
sufferings of *Ulysses* had changed his face and features, and his long fasting given
him a pale and sorrowful aspect; but being bath'd, perfum'd, and dress'd in
robes, he appears another man, full of life and beauty. This sudden change gave
Homer the hint to improve it into a miracle; and he ascribes it to *Minerva*, to give a
dignity to his Poetry. He further embellishes the description by a very happy
comparison. *Virgil* has imitated it ⟨1 589–93⟩.

> *Os humerosque deo similis; namque ipsa decoram*
> *Cæsariem nato genetrix, lumenque juventæ*
> *Purpureum, & lætos oculis afflarat honores.*
> *Quale manus addunt ebori decus, aut ubi flavo*
> *Argentum Pariusve lapis circumdatur auro.*

Scaliger, in the fifth book of his Poetics ⟨ch. iii, pp. 219 c2–220 a2⟩, prefers *Virgil*
before *Homer*; and perhaps his opinion is just: *Manus* he says is more elegant than

With majesty enlarg'd, and air divine;
Back from his brows a length of hair unfurls,
His hyacinthine locks descend in wavy curls.
As by some artist to whom *Vulcan* gives   275
His skill divine, a breathing statue lives;
By *Pallas* taught, he frames the wond'rous mold,
And o'er the silver pours the fusile gold.
So *Pallas* his heroic frame improves
With heav'nly bloom, and like a God he moves.   280
A fragrance breathes around: majestic grace
Attends his steps: th' astonish'd virgins gaze.
Soft he reclines along the murm'ring seas,
Inhaling freshness from the fanning breeze.
    The wond'ring Nymph his glorious port survey'd,   285
And to her damsels, with amazement, said.
    Not without Care divine the stranger treads
This land of joy: his steps some Godhead leads:
Would *Jove* destroy him, sure he had been driv'n
Far from this realm, the fav'rite Isle of heav'n: 290
Late a sad spectacle of woe, he trod
The desart sands, and now he looks a God.

---

vir; and *addunt ebori decus*, than χαρίεντα δὲ ἔργα τελείει. *Os humerosque deo similis*, carries a nobler idea than *Homer's* μείζονα καὶ πάσσονα; and above all,

> —*Lumenque juventæ*
> *Purpureum, & lætos oculis afflarat honores*,

is inexpressibly beautiful.

It is said that this image is made by the assistance of *Vulcan* and *Minerva*: Why by two Deities? *Eustathius* answers, the first rudiments and formation of it in the fire is proper to *Vulcan*, and *Minerva* is the president of arts; *Minerva* gives the Artificer Wisdom in designing, and *Vulcan* skill in labouring and finishing the work.

283. *He reclines along the murm'ring seas.*] This little circumstance, *Eustathius* observes is not without its effect; the Poet withdraws *Ulysses*, to give *Nausicaa* an opportunity to speak freely in his praise without a breach of modesty: She speaks apart to her damsels, and by this conduct, *Ulysses* neither hears his own commendation, which is a pain to all worthy spirits, nor does *Nausicaa* betray an indecent sensibility, because she speaks only to her own sex and attendants.

O heav'n! in my connubial hour decree
This man my spouse, or such a spouse as he!
But haste, the viands and the bowl provide—   295
The maids the viand, and the bowl supply'd:
Eager he fed, for keen his hunger rag'd,
And with the generous vintage thirst asswag'd.
   Now on return her care *Nausicaa* bends,
The robes resumes, the glittering car ascends,   300
Far blooming o'er the field: and as she press'd
The splendid seat, the list'ning chief address'd.
   Stranger arise! the sun rolls down the day,
Lo, to the Palace I direct thy way:
Where in high state the nobles of the land   305
Attend my royal sire, a radiant band.
But hear, tho' wisdom in thy soul presides,
Speaks from thy tongue and ev'ry action guides;
Advance at distance, while I pass the plain
Where o'er the furrows waves the golden grain: 310
Alone I re-ascend—With airy mounds

---

293.   *Oh heav'n! in my connubial hour decree*
       This man my spouse, or such a spouse as he!]

This passage has been censur'd as an outrage against Modesty and Credibility; Is it probable that a young Princess should fall in love with a stranger at the first sight? and if she really falls in love, is it not an indecent passion? I will lay before the Reader the observations of *Plutarch* upon it. "If *Nausicaa*, upon casting her eyes upon this stranger, and feeling such a passion for him as *Calypso* felt, talks thus out of wantonness, her conduct is blameable; but if perceiving his wisdom by his prudent address, she wishes for such an husband, rather than a person of her own country, who had no better qualifications than singing, dancing and dressing; she is to be commended ⟨*De Aud. Poet.* 8 (27 A–B)⟩." This discovers no weakness but prudence, and a true judgment. She deserves to be imitated by the fair sex, who ought to prefer a good understanding, before a fine coat, and a man of worth, before a good dancer.

   Besides, it may be offer'd in vindication of *Nausicaa*, that she had in the morning been assured by a vision from Heaven, that her nuptials were at hand; this might induce her to believe that *Ulysses* was the person intended by the vision for her husband; and his good sense and prudent behaviour, as *Dacier* observes, might make her wish it, without any imputation of immodesty.

I

A strength of wall the guarded city bounds:
The jutting land two ample bays divides;
Full thro' the narrow mouths descend the tides:
The spacious basons arching rocks enclose,   315
A sure defence from every storm that blows.
Close to the bay great *Neptune*'s fane adjoins:
And near, a Forum flank'd with marble shines,
Where the bold youth, the num'rous fleets to store,
Shape the broad sail, or smooth the taper oar;   320
For not the bow they bend, nor boast the skill
To give the feather'd arrow wings to kill,
But the tall mast above the vessel rear,
Or teach the fluttering sail to float in air;
They rush into the deep with eager joy,   325

313. *The jutting land two ample bays divides,*
       Full thro' the narrow mouths descend the tides.]
This passage is not without its difficulty: But the Scholiast upon *Dionysius Periegetes* ⟨*Schol. Dion.*, l. 493⟩ gives us a full explication of it. Δυὸ λιμένας ἔχει ἡ Φαιακίς, τὸν μὲν Ἀλκινόου, τὸν δὲ Ὑλλοῦ, διὸ φησὶ Καλλίμαχος ἀμφίδυμος φαίαξ. The Island of *Phæacia* has two ports, the one called the port of *Alcinous*, the other of *Hyllus*; thus *Callimachus* ⟨Fragment 15 (Pfeiffer)⟩ calls it the place of two ports. And *Apollonius* ⟨*Arg.* iv 983⟩ for the same reason calls it ἀμφιλαφής, or the place which is enter'd by two ports. *Dacier.*

325. *They rush into the deep with eager joy.*] It is very judicious in the Poet to let us thus fully into the character of the *Phæacians*, before he comes to show what relation they have to the story of the *Odyssey*: He describes *Alcinous* and the people of better rank, as persons of great hospitality and humanity, this gives an air of probability to the free and benevolent reception which *Ulysses* found: He describes the vulgar as excellent navigators; and he does this not only because they are Islanders; but, as *Eustathius* observes, to prepare the way for the return of *Ulysses*, who was to be restored by their conduct to his country, even against the inclination of *Neptune*, the God of the Ocean. But it may be ask'd, is not *Homer* inconsistent with himself, when he paints the *Phæacians* as men of the utmost humanity, and immediately after calls them a proud unpolish'd race; and given up to censoriousness? It is easy to reconcile the seeming contradiction, by applying the character of humanity to the higher rank of the nation, and the other to the vulgar and the mariners. I believe the same character holds good to this day amongst any people, who are much addicted to sea-affairs; they contract a roughness, by being secluded from the more general converse of mankind, and consequently are strangers to that affability which is the effect of a more enlarg'd

Climb the steep surge, and thro' the tempest fly;
A proud, unpolish'd race—To me belongs
The care to shun the blast of sland'rous tongues;
Lest malice, prone the virtuous to defame,
Thus with vile censure taint my spotless name.   330
   "What stranger this, whom thus *Nausicaa* leads?
"Heav'ns! with what graceful majesty he treads?
"Perhaps a native of some distant shore,
"The future consort of her bridal hour;
"Or rather, some descendant of the skies;   335
"Won by her pray'r, th' aereal bridegroom flies.
"Heav'n on that hour its choicest influence shed,
"That gave a foreign spouse to crown her bed!
"All, all the god-like worthies that adorn
"This realm, she flies: *Phæacia* is her scorn.   340

conversation. But what is it that inclines the *Phæacians* to be censorious? It is to be remember'd, that they are every where describ'd as a people abandon'd to idleness; To idleness therefore that part of their character is to be imputed. When the thoughts are not employed upon *things*, it is usual to turn them upon *persons*: A good man has not the inclination, an industrious man not the leisure, to be censorious, so that censure is the property of idleness. This I take to be the moral, intended to be drawn from the character of the *Phæacians*.

331. *What stranger this, whom thus* Nausicaa *leads?*] This is an instance of the great art of *Homer*, in saying every thing properly. *Nausicaa* had conceiv'd a great esteem for *Ulysses*, and she had an inclination to let him know it; but modesty forbad her to reveal it openly: How then shall *Ulysses* know the value she has for his person, consistently with the modesty of *Nausicaa*? Homer with great address puts her compliments into the mouth of the *Phæacians*, and by this method she speaks her own sentiments, as the sentiments of the *Phæacians*: *Nausicaa*, as it were, is withdrawn, and a whole nation introduced for a more general praise of *Ulysses*.

335. *Or rather, some descendant of the skies.*] *Eustathius* remarks, that the compliments of *Nausicaa* answer the compliments made to her by *Ulysses*: he resembled her to *Diana*, she him to the Gods. But it may be ask'd, are not both these extravagancies? and is it not beyond all credibility that *Nausicaa* should be thought a Goddess, or *Ulysses* a God? In these ages it would be judg'd extravagant, but it is to be remember'd that in the days of *Homer* every grove, river, fountain, and oak-tree were thought to have their peculiar Deities; this makes such relations as these more reconcilable, if not to truth, at least to the opinions of Antiquity, which is sufficient for Poetry.

And just the blame: for female innocence
Not only flies the guilt, but shuns th' offence:
Th' unguarded virgin as unchaste I blame,
And the least freedom with the sex is shame,
'Till our consenting sires a spouse provide   345
And public nuptials justify the bride.
But would'st thou soon review thy native plain?

---

344.   —*The least freedom with the sex is shame,*
              'Till our consenting sires a spouse provide.]

This is an admirable picture of ancient female-life among the Orientals; the
Virgins were very retir'd, and never appear'd amongst men but upon extraordinary occasions, and then always in the presence of the father or mother: But
when they were married, says *Eustathius*, they had more liberty. Thus *Helen* converses freely with *Telemachus* and *Pisistratus*, and *Penelope* sometimes with the
suitors. *Nausicaa* delivers her judgment sententiously, to give it more weight;
what can be more modest than these expressions? And yet they have been greatly
traduc'd by Monsieur *Perrault*, a *French* Critic; he translates the passage so as to
imply that "*Nausicaa* disapproves of a Virgin's lying with a man without the permission of her father, before marriage ⟨π 55⟩;" ἀνδράσι μίσγεσθαι led him
into this mistake, which is sometimes used in such a signification, but here it only
means *Conversation*: if the word μίσγεσθαι signified more than keeping company,
it would be more ridiculous, as *Boileau* observes upon *Longinus*, than *Perrault*
makes it: for it is join'd to ἀνδράσι, and then it would infer that *Nausicaa* disapproves of a young woman's lying with *several men* before she was married, without the licence of her father ⟨*Réflexions Critiques* iii, *Œuvres Complètes*, Paris, 1942,
v 70–1⟩. The passage, continues *Boileau*, is full of honour and decency: *Nausicaa*
has a design to introduce *Ulysses* to her father, she tells him she goes before to prepare the way for his reception, but that she must not be seen to enter the city in his
company, for fear of giving offence, which a modest woman ought not to give:
A virtuous woman is obliged not only to avoid immodesty, but the appearance
of it; and for her part she could not approve of a young woman keeping company
with men without the permission of her father or mother, before she was married.
Thus the indecency is not in *Homer*, but the Critic; it is indeed in *Homer* an excellent lecture of Modesty and Morality.

347. *But wou'dst thou soon review thy native plain?*] *Eustathius* and *Dacier* are both
of opinion, that *Nausicaa* had conceiv'd a passion for *Ulysses*: I think this passage
is an evidence that she rather admir'd and esteem'd, than lov'd him; for it is contrary to the nature of that passion to give directions for the departure of the person belov'd, but rather to invent excuses to prolong his stay. 'Tis true *Nausicaa* had wish'd in the foregoing parts of this book, that she might have *Ulysses*
for her husband, or such an husband as *Ulysses*: but this only shews that she

Attend, and speedy thou shalt pass the main:
Nigh where a grove, with verdant poplars crown'd
To *Pallas* sacred, shades the holy ground,   350
We bend our way: a bubling fount distills
A lucid lake, and thence descends in rills:
Around the grove a mead with lively green
Falls by degrees, and forms a beauteous scene;
Here a rich juice the royal vineyard pours;   355
And there the garden yields a waste of flow'rs.
Hence lies the town as far, as to the ear
Floats a strong shout along the waves of air.
There wait embowr'd, while I ascend alone
To great *Alcinous* on his royal throne.   360
    Arriv'd, advance impatient of delay,
And to the lofty palace bend thy way:
The lofty palace overlooks the town,
From ev'ry dome by pomp superior known;
A child may point the way. With earnest gait   365
Seek thou the Queen along the rooms of state;
Her royal hand a wond'rous work designs,
Around, a circle of bright damsels shines,
Part twist the threads, and part the wool dispose,
While with the purple orb the spindle glows.   370
High on a throne, amid the *Scherian* pow'rs,
My royal father shares the genial hours;
But to the Queen thy mournful tale disclose,

---

admir'd his accomplishments, nor could she have added *such a spouse as he*, at all,
if her affections had been engag'd and fix'd upon *Ulysses* only. This likewise
takes off the objection of a too great fondness in *Nausicaa*; for it might have
appeared too great a fondness to have fall'n in love at the first with an absolute
stranger.

    373. *But to the Queen thy mournful tale disclose.*] This little circumstance, seemingly
of small importance, is not without its beauty. It is natural for a daughter to
apply to the mother, rather than the father: Women are likewise generally of a
compassionate nature, and therefore the Poet first interests the Queen in the
cause of *Ulysses*. At the same time he gives a pattern of conjugal affection, in the
union between *Arete* and *Alcinous*.

With the prevailing eloquence of woes:
So shalt thou view with joy thy natal shore,   375
Tho' mountains rise between, and oceans roar.
    She added not, but waving as she wheel'd
The silver scourge, it glitter'd o'er the field:
With skill the virgin guides th' embroider'd rein,
Slow rowls the car before th' attending train.   380
Now whirling down the heav'ns, the golden day
Shot thro' the western clouds a dewy ray;
The grove they reach, where from the sacred shade
To *Pallas* thus the pensive Heroe pray'd.
    Daughter of *Jove!* whose arms in thunder wield   385
Th' avenging bolt, and shake the dreadful shield;
Forsook by thee, in vain I sought thy aid
When booming billows clos'd above my head:
Attend, unconquer'd maid! accord my vows,
Bid the Great hear, and pitying heal my woes.   390
    This heard *Minerva*, but forbore to fly
(By *Neptune* aw'd) apparent from the sky:
Stern God! who rag'd with vengeance unrestrain'd,
'Till great *Ulysses* hail'd his native land.

391.   —*But forbore to fly*
          (*By* Neptune *aw'd*) *apparent from the sky.*]
We see the Ancients held a subordination amongst the Deities, and tho' different in inclinations, yet they act in harmony: One God resists not another Deity. This is more fully explain'd, as *Eustathius* observes, by *Euripides*, in his *Hippolytus* ⟨1328–30⟩; where *Diana* says, it is not the custom of the Gods to resist one the other, when they take vengeance even upon the favourites of other Deities. The late tempest that *Neptune* had rais'd for the destruction of *Ulysses*, was an instance of *Neptune*'s implacable anger: this makes *Minerva* take such measures as to avoid an open opposition, and yet consult the safety of *Ulysses*: She descends, but it is secretly.

    This book takes up part of the night, and the whole thirty second day; the vision of *Nausicaa* is related in the preceding night, and *Ulysses* enters the city a little after the Sun sets in the following evening. So that thirty two days are compleated since the opening of the Poem.
    This book in general is full of life and variety: It is true, the subject of it is

simple and unadorn'd, but improved by the Poet, and render'd entertaining and noble. The Muse of *Homer* is like his *Minerva*, with respect to *Ulysses*, who from an object of commiseration improves his Majesty, and gives a grace to every feature.

THE
SEVENTH BOOK
OF THE
ODYSSEY.

The ARGUMENT.
The Court of Alcinous.

The Princess Nausicaa *returns to the city, and* Ulysses *soon after follows thither. He is met by* Pallas *in the form of a young Virgin, who guides him to the Palace, and directs him in what manner to address the Queen* Arete. *She then involves him in a mist, which causes him to pass invisible. The Palace and Gardens of* Alcinous *described.* Ulysses *falling at the feet of the Queen, the mist disperses, the* Phæacians *admire, and receive him with respect. The Queen enquiring by what means he had the garments he then wore, he relates to her and* Alcinous *his departure from* Calypso, *and his arrival on their dominions.*

The same day continues, and the book ends with the night.

THE patient, heav'nly man thus suppliant pray'd;
While the slow mules draw on th' imperial maid:
Thro' the proud street she moves, the publick gaze;

This book opens with the Introduction of *Ulysses* to *Alcinous*; every step the Poet takes carries on the main design of the Poem, with a progress so natural, that each incident seems really to have happen'd, and not to be invention. Thus *Nausicaa* accidentally meets *Ulysses*, and introduces him to *Alcinous* her father, who lands him in *Ithaca*: It is possible this might be true History; the Poet might build upon a real foundation, and only adorn the truth with the ornaments of Poetry. It is to be wish'd, that a faithful History of the *Trojan* war, and the voyages of *Ulysses*, had been transmitted to posterity; it would have been the best comment upon the *Iliad* and *Odyssey*. We are not to look upon the Poems of *Homer* as meer romances, but as true stories, heighten'd and beautify'd by Poetry: Thus the *Iliad* is built upon a real dissention, that happen'd in a real war between *Greece* and *Troy*; and the *Odyssey* upon the real voyages of *Ulysses*, and the disorders that happen'd thro' his absence in his own country. Nay, it is not

The turning wheel before the Palace stays.
With ready love her brothers gath'ring round,   5
Receiv'd the vestures, and the mules unbound.
She seeks the bridal bow'r: A matron there
The rising fire supplies with busy care,
Whose charms in youth her father's heart inflam'd,
Now worn with age, *Eurymedusa* nam'd: 10
The captive dame *Phæacian* rovers bore,
Snatch'd from *Epirus*, her sweet native shore,
(A grateful prize) and in her bloom bestow'd
On good *Alcinous*, honour'd as a God:

impossible but that many of those incidents that seem most extravagant in *Homer*, might have an appearing truth, and be justify'd by the opinions, and mistaken credulity of those ages. What is there in all *Homer* more seemingly extravagant, than the story of the race of the *Cyclops*, with one broad eye in their foreheads? and yet, as Sir *Walter Raleigh* very judiciously conjectures ⟨*History of the World*, Pt I, Bk 5, ch. I⟩, this may be built upon a seeming truth: They were a people of *Sicily* remarkable for savageness and cruelty, and perhaps might in their wars make use of a headpiece or Vizor, which had but one sight in it, and this might give occasion to sailors who coasted those shores to mistake the single sight of the Vizor, for a broad eye in the forehead, especially when they before look'd upon them as monsters for their barbarity. I doubt not but we lose many beauties in *Homer* for want of a real history, and think him extravagant, when he only complies with the opinions of former ages. I thought it necessary to make this observation, as a general vindication of *Homer*; especially in this place, immediately before he enters upon the relation of those stories which have been thought most to outrage credibility: if then we look upon the *Odyssey* as all fiction, we consider it unworthily; it ought to be read as a story founded upon truth, but adorn'd with the embellishments of Poetry, to convey instruction with pleasure the more effectually.

10. Eurymedusa *nam'd*.] *Eustathius* remarks, that the *Phæacians* were people of great commerce, and that it was customary in those ages to exchange slaves in traffic; or perhaps *Eurymedusa* might be a captive, pyracy then being honourable, and such seizures of cattle or slaves frequent. The passage concerning the brothers of *Nausicaa* has not escaped the censure of the Critics; *Homer* in the original calls them *like Gods*, and yet in the same breath gives them the employment of slaves, they unyoke the Mules, and carry into the Palace the burthens they brought. A twofold answer may be given to this objection, and this conduct might proceed from the general custom of the age, which made such actions reputable; or from the particular love the brothers bore their sister, which might induce them to act thus, as an instance of it.

I*

Nurse of *Nausicaa* from her infant years,   15
And tender second to a mother's cares.
Now from the sacred thicket where he lay,
To town *Ulysses* took the winding way.
Propitious *Pallas*, to secure her care,
Around him spread a veil of thicken'd air;   20

---

20. *Around him spread a veil of thicken'd air.*] It may be ask'd what occasion there
is to make *Ulysses* invisible? *Eustathius* answers, not only to preserve him from
insults as he was a stranger, but that he might raise a greater surprize in *Alcinous*
by his sudden appearance. But, adds he, the whole is an allegory; and *Ulysses*
wisely chusing the evening to enter unobserv'd, gave occasion to the Poet to
bring in the Goddess of Wisdom to make him invisible.

Virgil ⟨*Aen.* I 411–14⟩ has borrow'd this passage from *Homer*, and *Venus* renders
Æneas invisible in the same manner as *Minerva Ulysses. Scaliger* compares the two
Authors, and prefers *Virgil* infinitely before *Homer*, in the fifth book of his *Poetics*
⟨ch. iii, p. 219 A2⟩.

> *At Venus obscuro gradientes aere saepsit*
> *Et multo nebulæ circum dea fudit amictu;*
> *Cernere ne quis eos, neu quis contingere posset,*
> *Molirive moram, aut veniendi poscere causas.*

Scaliger says the verses are more sonorous than *Homer's*, and that it was more
necessary to make *Æneas* invisible than *Ulysses*, he being amongst a perfidious
nation. But was not the danger as great from the rudeness of the *Phæacians*, as from
the perfidiousness of the *Carthaginians*? Besides, *Virgil* does not mention the perfidiousness of the *Carthaginians*; so that it is the reason of *Scaliger*, not *Virgil*: and
whether the verses be more sonorous, is submitted to the ear of the Reader. He is
chiefly delighted with

> *Et multo nebulæ circum dea fudit amictu.*

Qui solus versus, says he, *deterreat Græcos ab ea sententia, qua suum contendunt pre-
ferendum.* He allows κερτομέοι τ' ἐπέεσσι, &c. to be a tolerably smooth verse,
Commodus & rasilis, but yet far inferior to this of *Virgil*.

> *Molirive moram, & veniendi poscere causas.*

It is but justice to lay the verses of *Homer* before the Reader.

> Καὶ τότ' Ὀδυσσεὺς ὦρτο πόλινδ' ἴμεν', ἀμφὶ δ' Ἀθήνη,
> Πολλὴν ἠέρα χεῦε φίλα φρονέουσ' Ὀδυσῆι.
> Μή τις Φαιήκων μεγαθύμων ἀντιβολήσας,
> Κερτομέοι τ' ἐπέεσσι, καὶ ἐξερέοιθ' ὅτις εἴη.

I determine not which Author has the greater beauty, but undoubtedly *Homer*
is more happy in the occasion of the fiction than *Virgil; Homer* drew his description from the wisdom of *Ulysses* in entering the town in the evening, he was really
invisible to the *Phæacians*, and *Homer* only heighten'd the truth by Poetry; but
Virgil is more bold, and has no such circumstance to justify his relation; for *Æneas*
went into *Carthage* in the open day.

To shun th' encounter of the vulgar crowd,
Insulting still, inquisitive, and loud.
When near the fam'd *Phæacian* walls he drew,
The beauteous city opening to his view,
His step a Virgin met, and stood before: 25
A polish'd Urn the seeming Virgin bore,
And youthful smil'd; but in the low disguise
Lay hid the Goddess with the azure eyes.
  Show me, fair daughter, (thus the chief demands)
The house of him who rules these happy lands.   30
Thro' many woes and wand'rings, lo! I come
To good *Alcinous'* hospitable dome.
Far from my native coast, I rove alone,
A wretched stranger, and of all unknown!
  The Goddess answer'd. Father, I obey,   35
And point the wand'ring traveller his way:
Well known to me the palace you enquire,
For fast beside it dwells my honour'd sire.
But silent march, nor greet the common train
With question needless, or enquiry vain.   40
A race of rugged mariners are these;
Unpolish'd men, and boistrous as their seas:
The native Islanders alone their care,
And hateful he that breathes a foreign air.
These did the Ruler of the deep ordain   45
To build proud navies, and command the main;
On canvas wings to cut the wat'ry way;
No bird so light, no thought so swift as they.

---

26. —*The seeming Virgin*, &c.] It may be ask'd why *Minerva* does not appear as
a Goddess, but in a borrow'd form? The Poet has already told us, that she dreaded the wrath of *Neptune*; one Deity could not openly oppose another Deity, and
therefore she acts thus invisibly.

47. *On canvas wings to cut the wat'ry way*.] This circumstance is not inserted without a good effect: It could not but greatly encourage *Ulysses* to understand that
he was arriv'd amongst a people that excell'd in navigation; this gave him a prospect of being speedily convey'd to his own country, by the assistance of a nation
so expert in maritime affairs. *Eustathius.*

Thus having spoke, th' unknown celestial leads:
The footsteps of the Deity he treads,   50
And secret moves along the crowded space,
Unseen of all the rude *Phæacian* race.
(So *Pallas* order'd, *Pallas* to their eyes
The mist objected, and condens'd the skies)
The chief with wonder sees th' extended streets,   55
The spreading harbours, and the riding fleets;
He next their princes lofty domes admires,
In sep'rate Islands crown'd with rising spires;
And deep intrenchments, and high walls of stone,
That gird the city like a marble zone.   60
At length the kingly palace gates he view'd:
There stopp'd the Goddess, and her speech renew'd.
My task is done; the mansion you enquire

---

53. —Pallas *to their eyes The mist condenses* ⟨sic⟩.] *Scaliger* in his *Poetics* ⟨v iii,
p. 219 a2⟩ calls this an impertinent repetition, and commends *Virgil* for not
imitating it, for *Homer* dwells upon it no less than three times; and indeed one
would almost imagine that *Virgil* was of the same opinion, for he has follow'd the
turn of this whole passage, and omitted this repetition: yet he treads almost step
by step in the path of *Homer*, and *Æneas* and *Ulysses* are drawn in the same
colours ⟨1 421-2⟩;

> Miratur molem *Æneas, magalia quondam:*
> Miratur portas, strepitumque & strata viarum.
> Θαύμαζεν δ' Ὀδυσεὺς λιμένας καὶ νῆας ἐίσας,
> Αὐτῶν θ' Ἡρώων ἀγορὰς καὶ τείχεα μακρὰ
> Ὑψηλά, σκολόπεσσιν ἀρηρότα.

Homer poetically inserts the Topography of this city of the *Phæacians*: Tho' they
were an unwarlike nation, yet they understand the art of Fortification; their city
is surrounded with a strong wall, and that wall guarded with palisades. But
whence this caution? since *Homer* tells us in the preceding book, that they were
in no danger of an enemy? It might arise from their very fears, which naturally
suggest to cowards, that they cannot be too safe; this would make them practise
the art of Fortification more assiduously than a more brave people, who usually
put more confidence in valour than in walls, as was the practice of the *Spartans*.

63. *My task is done*, &c.] As Deities ought not to be introduced without a
necessity, so when introduced, they ought to be employed in acts of importance,
and worthy of their divinity: It may be ask'd if *Homer* observes this rule in this
Episode, where a Goddess seems to appear only to direct *Ulysses* to the Palace of
Alcinous, which, as he himself tells us, a child could have done? But the chief

Appears before you: enter, and admire.
High-thron'd, and feasting, there thou shalt behold   65
The sceptred Rulers. Fear not, but be bold:
A decent boldness ever meets with friends,
Succeeds, and ev'n a stranger recommends.
First to the Queen prefer a suppliant's claim, ⎞
Alcinous' Queen, *Arete* is her name, ⎬   70
The same her parents, and her pow'r the same. ⎠
For know, from Ocean's God *Nausithous* sprung,
And *Peribæa*, beautiful and young:
(*Eurymedon's* last hope, who rul'd of old
The race of Giants, impious, proud and bold;   75
Perish'd the nation in unrighteous war,
Perish'd the Prince, and left this only heir.)
Who now by *Neptune's* am'rous pow'r comprest,
Produc'd a Monarch that his people blest,
Father and Prince of the *Phæacian* name: 80
From him *Rhexenor* and *Alcinous* came.
The first, by *Phœbus'* burning arrows fir'd,
New from his nuptials, hapless youth! expir'd.
No son surviv'd; *Arete* heir'd his state,

design of *Minerva* was to advise *Ulysses* in his present exigencies: and (as *Eustathius* remarks) she opens her speech to him with great and noble sentiments. She informs him how to win the favour of *Alcinous*, upon which depends the whole happiness of her Heroe; and by which she brings about his re-establishment in his kingdom, the aim of the whole *Odyssey*. *Virgil* makes use of the same method in his *Æneis*, and *Venus* there executes the same office for her son, as *Minerva* for her favourite, in some degree as a Guide, but chiefly as a Counsellor.

74. *Eurymedon*, &c.] This passage is worthy of observation, as it discovers to us the time when the race of the ancient Giants perish'd; this *Eurymedon* was grandfather to *Nausithous*, the father of *Alcinous*; so that the Giants were extirpated forty or fifty years before the war of *Troy*. This exactly agrees with ancient story, which informs us, that *Hercules* and *Theseus* purg'd the earth from those monsters. *Plutarch* in his life of *Theseus* ⟨vi, viii⟩ tells us, that they were men of great strength, and public robbers, one of whom was called the *Bender of Pines*. Now *Theseus* stole away *Helen* in her infancy, and consequently these Giants were destroy'd some years before the *Trojan* expedition. *Dacier, Plutarch.*

84, &c. *Arete*.] It is observable that this *Arete* was both wife and neice to

And her, *Alcinous* chose his royal mate.   85
With honours yet to womankind unknown,
This Queen he graces, and divides the throne;
In equal tenderness her sons conspire,
And all the children emulate their sire.
When thro' the street she gracious deigns to move,   90
(The publick wonder, and the publick love)
The tongues of all with transport sound her praise,
The eyes of all, as on a Goddess, gaze.
She feels the triumph of a gen'rous breast; ⎫
To heal divisions, to relieve th' opprest;   ⎬   95
In virtue rich; in blessing others, blest.   ⎭
Go then secure, thy humble suit prefer,
And owe thy country and thy friends to her.
    With that the Goddess deign'd no longer stay,

Alcinous, an instance that the *Græcians* married with such near relations: The same appears from *Demosthenes* ⟨e.g. XLVI 18–19⟩ and other *Greek* Orators. But what then is the notion of incest amongst the Ancients? The collateral branch was not thought incestuous, for *Juno* was the wife and sister of *Jupiter*. Brothers likewise married their brother's wives, as *Deiphobus Helen*, after the death of *Paris*: the same was practis'd amongst the *Jews*, and consequently being permitted by *Moses* was not incestuous. So that the only incest was in the ascending, not collateral or descending branch; as when parents and children married; thus when *Myrrha* lay with her father, and *Lot* with his daughters, this was accounted incest. The reason is very evident, a child cannot pay the duty of a child to a parent, and at the same time of a wife or husband; nor can a father act with the authority of a father towards a person who is at once his wife and daughter. The relations interfere, and introduce confusion, where the law of nature and reason requires regularity.

95. *To heal divisions*, &c.] This office of *Arete* has been look'd upon as somewhat extraordinary, that she should decide the quarrels of the subjects, a province more proper for *Alcinous*; and therefore the Ancients endeavour'd to soften it by different readings; and instead of οἶσιν τ᾽ εὖ φρονέῃσι, they inserted ᾗσιν τ᾽ εὖ φρονέῃσι, or *she decides amongst women*: *Eustathius* in the text reads it in a third way, ᾗσιν τ᾽ ἐϋφροσύνῃσι, or *by her Wisdom*. *Spondanus* believes, that the Queen had a share in the government of the *Phæacians* ⟨*Od.* p. 90⟩; but *Eustathius* thinks the Poet intended to set the character of *Arete* in a fair point of light, she bearing the chief part in this book, and a great share in the sequel of the *Odyssey*: by this method he introduces her to the best advantage, and makes her a person of importance, and worthy to have a place in heroic Poetry; and indeed he has given her a very amiable character.

But o'er the world of waters wing'd her way: 100
Forsaking *Scheria*'s ever-pleasing shore,
The winds to *Marathon* the Virgin bore;
Thence, where proud *Athens* rears her tow'ry head,
With opening streets and shining structures spread,
She past, delighted with the well-known seats;   105
And to *Erectheus'* sacred dome retreats.

    Mean-while *Ulysses* at the Palace waits,   ⎫
There stops, and anxious with his soul debates, ⎬
Fix'd in amaze before the royal gates.   ⎭

---

109. *Fixt in amaze before the royal gates.*] The Poet here opens a very agreeable scene, and describes the beauty of the Palace and Gardens of *Alcinous*. *Diodorus Siculus* ⟨II 55 ff⟩ adapts this passage to the Island *Taprobane*, *Justin Martyr* to *Paradise* ⟨*Cohortatio ad Graecos* 28в (*Patrologia Graeca*, v. 6)⟩; Τοῦ Παραδείσου δὲ εἰκόνα τὸν 'Αλκινόου κῆπον σῴζειν πεποίηκε. He transcribes this whole passage into his Apology, but with some variation from the common Editions, for instead of

$$\text{—ἀλλὰ μάλ' αἰεὶ}$$
$$\text{Ζεφυρίη πνείουσα,—}$$

he reads ἀλλ' ἀεὶ αὔρη Ζεφυρίη, &c. perhaps more elegantly. *Eustathius* observes that *Homer* suits his Poetry to the things he relates, for in the whole *Iliad* there is not a description of this nature, nor an opportunity to introduce it in a Poem that represents nothing but objects of terror and blood. The Poet himself seems to go a little out of the way to bring it into the *Odyssey*; for it has no necessary connection with the Poem, nor would it be less perfect if it had been omitted: but as *Mercury* when he survey'd the bower of *Calypso*, ravish'd with the beauty of it, stood awhile in a still admiration, so *Homer* delighted with the scenes he draws, stands still a few moments, and suspends the story of the Poem, to enjoy the beauties of these gardens of *Alcinous*. But even here he shews his judgment, in not letting his fancy run out into a long description: He concludes the whole in the compass of twenty verses, and resumes the thread of his story. *Rapin* I confess censures this description of the gardens: he calls it *Puerile* and too light for Eloquence, that it is spun out to too great a length, and is somewhat affected, has no due coherence with, nor bears a just proportion to the whole, by reason of its being too glittering ⟨*Comparaison* x, I 130⟩. This is spoken with too great severity: it is necessary to relieve the mind of the Reader sometimes with gayer scenes, that it may proceed with a fresh appetite to the succeeding entertainment: In short, if it be a fault, it is a beautiful fault; and *Homer* may be said here, as he was upon another occasion by St. *Augustin* ⟨*Confessions* I xiv⟩, to be *dulcissime vanus*. The admiration of the gold and silver is no blemish to *Ulysses*: for, as *Eustathius* remarks, it proceeds not out of avarice, but from the beauty of the work, and use-

The front appear'd with radiant splendors gay,   110
Bright as the lamp of night, or orb of day.
The walls were massy brass: the cornice high
Blue metals crown'd, in colours of the sky:
Rich plates of gold the folding doors incase;
The pillars silver, on a brazen base;   115
Silver the lintels deep-projecting o'er,
And gold, the ringlets that command the door.
Two rows of stately dogs, on either hand,
In sculptur'd gold and labour'd silver stand.
These *Vulcan* form'd with art divine, to wait   120
Immortal guardians at *Alcinous'* gate;
Alive each animated frame appears,
And still to live, beyond the pow'r of years.
Fair thrones within from space to space were rais'd,
Where various carpets with embroidry blaz'd,   125

fulness and magnificence of the buildings. The whole description, continues he, suits the character of the *Phæacians*, a proud, luxurious people, delighted with show and ostentation.

118. *Two rows of stately dogs*, &c.] We have already seen that dogs were kept as a piece of state, from the instance of those that attended *Telemachus*: Here *Alcinous* has images of dogs in gold, for the ornament of his Palace; *Homer* animates them in his Poetry; but to soften the description, he introduces *Vulcan*, and ascribes the wonder to the power of a God. If we take the poetical dress away, the truth is, that these dogs were form'd with such excellent art, that they seem'd to be alive, and *Homer* by a liberty allowable to Poetry describes them as really having that life, which they only have in appearance. In the *Iliad* he speaks of living Tripods with greater boldness. *Eustathius* recites another opinion of some of the Ancients, who thought these Κύνες not to be animals, but a kind of large nails (ἥλους) or pins, made use of in buildings, and to this day the name is retain'd by builders, as Dogs of iron, &c. It is certain the words will bear this interpretation, but the former is more after the spirit of *Homer*, and more noble in Poetry. Besides, if the latter were intended, it would be absurd to ascribe a work of so little importance to a Deity.

124. *Fair thrones within*, &c.] The Poet does not say of what materials these thrones were made, whether of gold or silver, to avoid the imputation of being thought fabulous in his description; it being almost incredible, remarks *Eustathius*, that such quantities of gold and silver could be in the possession of such a King as *Alcinous*; tho' if we consider that his people were greatly given to navigation, the relation may come within the bounds of credibility.

The work of matrons: These the Princes prest,
Day following day, a long-continu'd feast.
Refulgent pedestals the walls surround,
Which boys of gold with flaming torches crown'd;
The polish'd Ore, reflecting ev'ry ray,   130
Blaz'd on the banquets with a double day.
Full fifty handmaids form the household train;
Some turn the mill, or sift the golden grain,
Some ply the loom; their busy fingers move
Like poplar-leaves when *Zephyr* fans the grove.   135
Not more renown'd the men of *Scheria*'s Isle,

128.   *Refulgent pedestals the walls surround,*
                Which boys of gold with flaming torches crown'd.]
This is a remarkable piece of grandeur: Lamps, as appears from the 18th of the
Odyssey, were not at this time known to the *Grecians*, but only Torches: these were
held by Images in the shape of beautiful youths, and those Images were of gold.
Lucretius has translated these verses ⟨II 24–6⟩.
                —*Aurea sunt juvenum simulacra per aedes,*
                Lampadas igniferas manibus retinentia dextris,
                Lumina nocturnis epulis ut suppeditentur.
It is admirable to observe with what propriety *Homer* adapts his Poetry to the
characters of his persons: *Nestor* is a wise man; when he is first seen in the *Odyssey*,
it is at a sacrifice, and there is not the least appearance of pomp or luxury in his
palace or entertainments. The *Phæacians* are of an opposite character, and the
Poet describes them consistently with it; they are all along a proud, idle, effeminate people; tho' such a pompous description would have ill suited the wise
Nestor, it excellently agrees with the vain *Alcinous*.
   135. *Like poplar-leaves when* Zephyr *fans the grove.*] There is some obscurity in
this short allusion, and some refer it to the work, others to the damsels employ'd
in work: *Eustathius* is of the opinion that it alludes to the damsels, and expresses
the quick and continued motion of their hands: I have follow'd this interpretation, and think that *Homer* intended to illustrate that quick and intermingled
motion, by comparing them to the branches of a Poplar agitated by winds, all at
once in motion, some bending this, some that way. The other interpretations are
more forc'd, and less intelligible ⟨Line 106 in Homer; on 107, see following note⟩.
   107. [*of the original.*] Καιροσέων δ' ὀθονέων ἀπολείβεται ὑγρον ἔλαιον.]
This passage is not without difficulty: some of the Ancients understood it to
signify the thickness and closeness of the texture, which was so compactly wrought
that Oil could not penetrate it; others thought it expressed the smoothness and
softness of it, as if Oil seem'd to flow from it; or lastly, that it shone with such a

For sailing arts and all the naval toil,
Than works of female skill their women's pride,
The flying shuttle thro' the threads to guide:
Pallas to these her double gifts imparts,   140
Inventive genius, and industrious arts.
  Close to the gates a spacious Garden lies,

---

glossy colour as look'd like oil. *Dacier* renders the verse according to the opinion first recited.

> *So close the work, that oil diffus'd in vain,*
> *Glides off innoxious and without a stain.*

Any of these interpretations make the passage intelligible, (tho' I think the description does better without it). It is left to the judgment of the Reader which to prefer; they are all to be found in *Eustathius*.

138. —*Works of female skill their women's pride.*] We may gather from what *Homer* here relates concerning the skill of these *Phæacian* damsels, that they were fam'd for these works of curiosity: The *Corcyrians* were much given to traffic, and perhaps they might bring slaves from the *Sidonians*, who instructed them in these manufactures. *Dacier.*

142. *Close to the gates a spacious Garden lies.*] This famous Garden of *Alcinous* contains no more than four acres of ground, which in those times of simplicity was thought a large one even for a Prince. It is laid out, as *Eustathius* observes, into three parts: a grove for fruits and shade, a vineyard, and an allotment for olives and herbs. It is water'd with two fountains; the one supplies the palace and town, the other the garden and the flowers. But it may be ask'd what reality there is in the relation, and whether any trees bear fruit all the year in this Island? *Eustathius* observes, that experience teaches the contrary, and that it is only true of the greatest part of the year; *Homer*, adds he, disguises the true situation of the *Phæacians*, and here describes it as one of the happy Islands; at once to enrich his Poetry, and to avoid a discovery of his Poetical exaggeration. The relation is true of other places, if *Pliny* and *Theophrastus* deserve credit, as *Dacier* observes; thus the Citron bears during the whole year fruits and flowers. *Arbos ipsa omnibus horis pomifera, aliis cadentibus, aliis maturescentibus, aliis vero subnascentibus* ⟨H.P. IV iv 3⟩. The same is related of other trees by *Pliny: novusque fructus in his cum annotino pendet;* he affirms the like of the Pine, *habet fructum maturescentem, habet proximo anno ad maturitatem venturum, ac deinde tertio, &c.* ⟨XVI xliv 107⟩. So that what *Homer* relates is in it self true, tho' not entirely of *Phæacia.* Or perhaps it might be only intended for a more beautiful and poetical manner of describing the constant succession of one fruit after another in a fertile climate.

> ——*Figs on figs arise.*

Aristotle ⟨Fragment 617 (Bekker)⟩ apply'd this Hemistic scoffingly to the Sycophants of *Athens*: he was about to leave that city upon its rejoicing at the death of *Socrates*; and quoting this verse, he said he would not live in a place where

From storms defended, and inclement skies:
Four acres was th' allotted space of ground,
Fenc'd with a green enclosure all around.   145
Tall thriving trees confess'd the fruitful mold;
The red'ning apple ripens here to gold,
Here the blue fig with luscious juice o'erflows,
With deeper red the full pomegranate glows,
The branch here bends beneath the weighty pear,   150
And verdant olives flourish round the year.
The balmy spirit of the western gale
Eternal breathes on fruits untaught to fail:
Each dropping pear a following pear supplies,
On apples apples, figs on figs arise: 155
The same mild season gives the blooms to blow,
The buds to harden, and the fruits to grow.

—Γηράσκει σῦκον δ' ἐπὶ σύκῳ.
alluding to the derivation of the word Sycophant. *Eustathius.*
Some dry the black'ning clusters in the sun.
To understand this passage aright, it is necessary to know the manner of
ordering the vintage amongst the *Greeks*: First, they carried all the grapes they
gather'd into an house for a season; afterwards they exposed them ten days to the
sun, and let them lye abroad as many nights in the freshness of the air; then they
kept them five days in cool shades, and on the sixth they trod them, and put the
wine into vessels: This we learn from *Hesiod*: ἔργων, verse 229 ⟨*Works and Days*
611–14⟩.

—Πάντας ἀπόδρεπε οἴκαδε βότρυς
Δεῖξαι δ' ἠελίῳ δέκα τ' ἤματα καὶ δέκα νύκτας
Πέντε δὲ συσκίασαι, ἕκτῳ δ' εἰς ἄγγε' ἀφύσσαι
Δῶρα Διωνύσου πολυγηθέος.—

Homer distinguishes the whole into three orders: First, the grapes that have
already been expos'd to the sun are trod; the second order is of the grapes that are
exposed, while the others are treading; and the third, of those that are ripe to be
gathered, while the others are thus ordering. *Homer* himself thus explains it, by
saying, that while some vines were loaded with black and mature grapes, others
were green, or but just turning to blackness. *Homer* undoubtedly founds this
poetical relation upon observing some vines that bore fruit thrice annually.
Pliny affirms this to be true, *lib.* 16. *chap.* 27 ⟨xvi xlix 115⟩. *Vites quidem & triferæ
sunt, quas ob id insanas vocant, quoniam in iis alia maturescunt, alia turgescunt, alia
florent. Dacier.*

  Here order'd vines in equal ranks appear,
With all th' united labours of the year;
Some to unload the fertile branches run,   160
Some dry the black'ning clusters in the sun,
Others to tread the liquid harvest join,
The groaning presses foam with floods of wine.
Here are the vines in early flow'r descry'd, ⎫
Here grapes discolour'd on the sunny side, ⎬ 165
And there in autumn's richest purple dy'd. ⎭
  Beds of all various herbs, for ever green,
In beauteous order terminate the scene.
  Two plenteous fountains the whole prospect crown'd; ⎫
This thro' the gardens leads its streams around, ⎬
Visits each plant, and waters all the ground: ⎭
While that in pipes beneath the palace flows, 172
And thence its current on the town bestows;
To various use their various streams they bring,
The People one, and one supplies the King. 175
  Such were the glories which the Gods ordain'd
To grace *Alcinous*, and his happy land.
Ev'n from the Chief who men and nations knew,
Th' unwonted scene surprize and rapture drew;
In pleasing thought he ran the prospect o'er, 180
Then hasty enter'd at the lofty door.
Night now approaching, in the palace stand
With goblets crown'd, the Rulers of the land;
Prepar'd for rest, and off'ring to the * God
Who bears the virtue of the sleepy rod. 185

* *Mercury.*

184.   *Prepar'd for rest, and offering to the God*
     That ⟨sic⟩ bears the virtue of the sleepy rod.]
I have already explain'd from *Athenæus* ⟨1 16B⟩ this custom of offering to *Mercury*
at the conclusion of entertainments: he was thought by the Ancients to preside
over sleep: *dat somnos adimitque*, according to *Horace* ⟨actually, Virgil, *Aen.* IV
244⟩, as *Dacier* observes: In following ages this practice was alter'd, and they
offer'd not to *Mercury*, but to *Jove* the Perfecter, or to Ζεῦς τέλειος.

Unseen he glided thro' the joyous crowd,
With darkness circled, and an ambient cloud.
Direct to great *Alcinous'* throne he came,
And prostrate fell before th' Imperial dame.
Then from around him drop'd the veil of night;   190
Sudden he shines, and manifest to sight.
The Nobles gaze, with awful fear opprest;
Silent they gaze, and eye the god-like guest.
      Daughter of great *Rhexenor!* (thus began
Low at her knees, the much-enduring man)   195
To thee, thy consort, and this royal train,
To all that share the blessings of your reign,
A suppliant bends: oh pity human woe!
'Tis what the happy to th' unhappy owe.
A wretched exile to his country send,   200

190. *Then from around him drop'd the veil of night.*] If this whole story of the veil of air had been told simply and nakedly, it would imply no more than that *Ulysses* arriv'd without being discover'd; and the breaking of the veil denotes his first coming into sight, in the presence of the Queen. But *Homer* steps out of the vulgar road of an Historian, and cloaths it with a sublimity worthy of heroic Poetry. In the same manner *Virgil* discovers his *Æneas* to *Dido* ⟨1 586–7⟩;
      —*Cum circumfusa repente*
   Scindit se nubes, & in aethera purgat apertum.
Scaliger ⟨v iii, p. 219 B2⟩ prefers these verses to those of *Homer*, and perhaps with good reason: he calls the last part of the second verse a divine addition; and indeed it is far more beautiful than the θέσφατος ἀήρ of *Homer*.
   196. *To thee, thy consort, and this royal train.*] *Minerva* commanded *Ulysses* to supplicate the Queen: Why then does he exceed the directions of the Goddess, and not only address himself to *Alcinous*, but to the rest of the assembly? *Spondanus* answers ⟨*Od.* p. 92⟩, that *Ulysses* adapts himself to the present circumstances, and seeing the King and other Peers in the same assembly, he thought it improper not to take notice of them: he therefore addresses himself to all, that he may make all his friends. But then does not *Minerva* give improper directions? and is not *Ulysses* more wise than the Goddess of Wisdom? The true reason therefore may perhaps be, that *Ulysses* really complies with the injunctions of the Goddess: she commands him to address himself to the Queen; and he does so: this I take to mean chiefly or primarily, but not exclusively of the King: If the passage be thus understood, it solves the objection.
   200. *A wretched exile to his country send.*] *Ulysses* here speaks very concisely; and

Long worn with griefs, and long without a friend.
So may the Gods your better days increase,
And all your joys descend on all your race,
So reign for ever on your country's breast,
Your people blessing, by your people blest!   205
Then to the genial hearth he bow'd his face,
And humbled in the ashes took his place.
Silence ensu'd. The eldest first began,
Echeneus sage, a venerable man!

---

he may seem to break abruptly into the subject of his petition, without letting the audience either into the knowledge of his condition or person. Was this a proper method to prevail over an assembly of strangers? But his gesture spoke for him, he threw himself into the posture of a suppliant, and the persons of all suppliants were esteem'd to be sacred: He declar'd himself to be a man in calamity, and reserves his story to be told more at large, when the surprize of the *Phæacians* at the sudden appearance of a stranger was over: this conciseness therefore is not blameable, but rather an instance of *Homer*'s judgment, who knows when to be short, and when to be copious.

207. *And humbled in the ashes took his place.*] This was the custom of Suppliants: they betook themselves to the hearth as sacred, and a place of refuge. It was particularly in the protection of *Vesta*: Thus *Tully, lib.* 2 ⟨xxvii 67⟩ *de Natura Deorum*; *Nomen Vestæ sumptum est a Græcis, ea est enim quæ illis* ἑστία *dicitur, jusque ejus ad aras, & focos pertinet. Apollonius* ⟨*Arg.* IV 693–4⟩ likewise, as *Spondanus* observes ⟨*Od.* p. 94⟩, takes notice of this custom of Suppliants.

Τὼ δ' ἄνεῳ, καὶ ἄναυδοι ἐφ' ἑστίῃ ἀίξαντες
Ἵζανον, ἧτε δίκη λυγροῖς ἱκέτῃσι τέτυκται.

That is, they betook themselves to the hearth, and there sate mute, which is the custom of all unhappy Suppliants. If it was a custom, as *Apollonius* observes, to sit mute, this gives another reason why *Ulysses* used but few words in his supplication: he had greatly outrag'd a practice that was establish'd as sacred amongst the *Greeks*, and had not acted in the character of a Suppliant, if he had launch'd out into a long oration.

This was the most sure and effectual way of supplication; thus when *Themistocles* fled to *Admetus* King of the *Molossians*, he placed himself before the hearth, and was receiv'd, tho' that King had formerly vow'd his destruction ⟨*Life of Themistocles* xxiv⟩. *Plutarch* indeed calls it an unusual way of supplication, but that proceeded from his carrying a child in his arms to move the greater compassion, not from his throwing himself into the protection of the Household-Gods.

209. *Echeneus sage. &c.*] The expression in the original, as *Dacier* observes, is remarkable: Echeneus *an old man, who knew many ancient, and great variety of things*;

Whose well-taught mind the present age surpast,   210
And join'd to that th' experience of the last.
Fit words attended on his weighty sense,
And mild persuasion flow'd in eloquence.
   Oh sight (he cry'd) dishonest and unjust!
A guest, a stranger, seated in the dust!   215
To raise the lowly suppliant from the ground
Befits a Monarch. Lo! the Peers around
But wait thy word, the gentle guest to grace
And seat him fair in some distinguish'd place.
Let first the herald due libation pay   220
To *Jove*, who guides the wand'rer on his way;
Then set the genial banquet in his view,
And give the stranger-guest a stranger's due.
   His sage advice the list'ning King obeys;
He stretch'd his hand the prudent chief to raise,   225
And from his seat *Laodamas* remov'd,
(The monarch's offspring, and his best belov'd)
There next his side the god-like hero sate;
With stars of silver shone the bed of state.
The golden ew'r a beauteous handmaid brings,   230
Replenish'd from the cool translucent springs,
Whose polish'd vase with copious streams supplies
A silver laver, of capacious size.
The table next in regal order spread,
The glitt'ring canisters are heap'd with bread: 235
Viands of various kinds invite the taste,
Of choicest sort and savour, rich repast!

---

he was wise by long experience, and by being conversant in ancient story: The
Author of the book of Wisdom ⟨of Solomon⟩ speaks almost in the same expressions: *Scit præterita & de futuris æstimat* ⟨8 : 8⟩.
   226. *And from his seat* Laodamas *remov'd.*] *Plutarch* in his *Symposiacs* ⟨*Quaest.
Conviv.* 1 ii 4 (617A–B)⟩ discusses a question, whether the Master of the feast should
place his guests, or let them seat themselves promiscuously: He there commends
this conduct of *Alcinous*, as an instance of a courteous disposition and great
humanity, who gave a place of dignity to a stranger and suppliant.

Thus feasting high, *Alcinous* gave the sign
And bad the herald pour the rosy wine.
Let all around the due libation pay   240
To *Jove*, who guides the wand'rer on his way.
    He said. *Pontonous* heard the King's command;
The circling goblet moves from hand to hand:
Each drinks the juice that glads the heart of man.
Alcinous then, with aspect mild, began.   245
    Princes and Peers, attend! while we impart
To you, the thoughts of no inhuman heart.
Now pleas'd and satiate from the social rite
Repair we to the blessings of the night:
But with the rising day, assembled here,   250
Let all the Elders of the land appear,
Pious observe our hospitable laws,
And heav'n propitiate in the stranger's cause:
Then join'd in council, proper means explore
Safe to transport him to the wish'd-for shore: 255
(How distant that, imports not us to know,
Nor weigh the labour, but relieve the woe)
Mean-time, nor harm nor anguish let him bear;
This interval, Heav'n trusts him to our care,
But to his native land our charge resign'd,   260
Heav'n's is his life to come, and all the woes behind.
Then must he suffer what the Fates ordain;
For Fate has wove the thread of life with pain,
And twins ev'n from the birth, are misery and man!
    But if descended from th' *Olympian* bow'r,   265
Gracious approach us some immortal pow'r;
If in that form thou com'st a guest divine:
Some high event the conscious Gods design.

---

240. —*The due libation pay To* Jove.] We have already seen that the whole
assembly was about to pour libations to *Mercury*, whence is it then that they now
offer to *Jupiter*? *Eustathius* observes, it was because of the arrival of this stranger,
and *Jupiter* presides over all strangers, and is frequently stil'd Ζεὺς ξένιος and
Ζεὺς ἑστιοῦχος.

As yet, unbid they never grac'd our feast,
The solemn sacrifice call'd down the guest; 270
Then manifest of heav'n the vision stood,
And to our eyes familiar was the God.
Oft with some favour'd traveller they stray,
And shine before him all the desart way:
With social intercourse, and face to face, 275
The friends and guardians of our pious race.
So near approach we their celestial kind,
By justice, truth, and probity of mind;
As our dire neighbours of *Cyclopean* birth
Match in fierce wrong, the Giant-sons of earth. 280
    Let no such thought (with modest grace rejoin'd
The prudent *Greek*) possess the royal mind.
Alas! a mortal, like thy self, am I;

---

277. *So near approach we their celestial kind*, &c.] There is some intricacy in this
passage, and much labour has been used to explain it. Some would have it to
imply that, "we are as nearly ally'd to the Gods, as the *Cyclops* and Giants, who
are descended from them; and if the Gods frequently appear to these Giants who
defy them; how much more may it be expected by the *Phæacians* to enjoy that
favour, who reverence and adore them?" *Eustathius* explains it after another
method; *Alcinous* had conceiv'd a fix'd hatred against the race of the *Cyclops*, who
had expell'd the *Phæacians* from their country, and forc'd them to seek a new
habitation; he here expresses that hatred, and says, that the *Phæacians* resemble
the Gods as much in goodness, as the *Cyclops* and Giants one the other in impiety:
He illustrates it, by shewing that the expression has the same import as we should
say that *Socrates* comes as near to *Plato* in virtue, as *Anytus* and *Melitus* to one
another in wickedness; and indeed the construction will be easy, by understanding ᾿Αλλήλοις in the second verse.

—Σφισιν ἐγγύθεν εἰμέν,
῾Ὡς περ Κύκλωπές τε καὶ ἄγρια φῦλα Γιγάντων.
Subaudi, ἐγγύθεν ἀλλήλοις εἰσιν·

I have already spoken of the presence of the Gods at the sacrifices, in a former
note upon the *Odyssey*: This frequent intercourse of the Gods was agreable to the
Theology of the Ancients; but why then is *Alcinous* surpriz'd at the appearance of
Ulysses, whom he looks upon as a God, if such favours were frequent? *Spondanus*
replies ⟨*Od*. p. 95⟩, that it is the unusualness of the time, not the appearance, that
surprizes *Alcinous*; the Gods appear'd either at their sacrifices, or in their jour-
neys, and therefore he looks upon this visit as a thing extraordinary.

No glorious native of yon azure sky:
In form, ah how unlike their heav'nly kind?   285
How more inferior in the gifts of mind?
Alas, a mortal! most opprest of those
Whom Fate has loaded with a weight of woes;
By a sad train of miseries alone
Distinguish'd long, and second now to none!   290
By heav'n's high will compell'd from shore to shore;
With heav'n's high will prepar'd to suffer more.
What histories of toil could I declare?
But still long-weary'd nature wants repair;
Spent with fatigue, and shrunk with pining fast,   295
My craving bowels still require repaste.
Howe'er the noble, suff'ring mind, may grieve
Its load of anguish, and disdain to live;
Necessity demands our daily bread;
Hunger is insolent, and will be fed.   300
But finish, oh ye Peers! what you propose,
And let the morrow's dawn conclude my woes.
Pleas'd will I suffer all the Gods ordain,
To see my soil, my son, my friends, again.
That view vouchsaf'd, let instant death surprise   305
With ever-during shade these happy eyes!

---

305. *That view vouchsaf'd, let instant death,* &c.] It is very necessary to recall frequently to the Reader's mind the desire *Ulysses* has to reach his own country; and to shew that he is absent not by choice, but necessity, all the disorders in his kingdoms happen by reason of his absence: it is therefore necessary to set the desire of his return in the strongest point of light, that he may not seem accessory to those disorders, by being absent when it was in his power to return. It is observable that *Ulysses* does not here make any mention of *Penelope*, whom he scarce ever omits in other places, as one of the chief inducements to wish for his country; the reason of his silence, says *Eustathius*, is, because he is unwilling to abate the favour of *Alcinous*, by a discovery that would show it was impossible for him to marry his daughter; such a discovery might make the King proceed more cooly towards his transportation; whereas it would afterwards be less dangerous, when he has had an opportunity fully to engage him in his favour.

Th' assembled Peers with gen'ral praise approv'd
His pleaded reason, and the suit he mov'd.
Each drinks a full oblivion of his cares,
And to the gifts of balmy sleep repairs.   310
Ulysses in the regal walls alone   ⎫
Remain'd: Beside him, on a splendid throne, ⎬
Divine *Arete* and *Alcinous* shone.   ⎭
The Queen, on nearer view, the guest survey'd
Rob'd in the garments her own hands had made;   315
Not without wonder seen. Then thus began,
Her words addressing to the god-like man.

    Cam'st thou not hither, wond'rous stranger! say,
From lands remote, and o'er a length of sea?
Tell then whence art thou? whence that Princely air?
And robes like these, so recent and so fair?   321

    Hard is the task, oh Princess! you impose:
(Thus sighing spoke the Man of many woes)
The long, the mournful series to relate
Of all my sorrows, sent by heav'n and fate!   325

---

322. *Hard is the task, oh Princess!*] *Æneas* in *Virgil* speaks to *Venus* after the same
manner, as *Ulysses* to *Arete* ⟨1372-4⟩.

> *O dea, si prima repetens ab origine pergam,*
> *Et vacet annales nostrorum audire laborum,*
> *Ante diem clauso componet vesper Olympo.*

Scaliger observes ⟨v iii, p. 219 B1⟩ that *Virgil* so far exceeds the verses of *Homer*,
that they will not even bear a comparison; he is superior almost in every word:
for instance; he renders διηνεκέως, by *prima ab origine*, and adds the word *vacet*
beautifully; and still more beautifully he translates πολλὰ κήδεα, *annales nostro-*
rum audire laborum; and lastly he paraphrases the word ἀργαλέον by a most harmonious line,

> *Ante diem clauso componet vesper Olympo.*

which excellently describes the multitude of the sufferings of *Æneas*, which could
not be comprehended in the relation of a whole day.

    I will not deny but that *Virgil* excells *Homer* in this and many other passages
which he borrows from him; but then is it a just conclusion to infer, after the
manner of *Scaliger*, that *Virgil* is a better Poet than *Homer*? To conclude from particulars to generals is a false way of arguing. It is as if in a comparison of two
persons, a man should from single features give a superiority of beauty, which is
only to be gather'd from the symmetry of the whole body.

Yet what you ask, attend. An Island lies
Beyond these tracts, and under other skies,
Ogygia nam'd, in *Ocean*'s wat'ry arms:
Where dwells *Calypso*, dreadful in her charms!
Remote from Gods or men she holds her reign,   330

326. *Yet what you ask, attend*—] *Homer* here gives a summary of the subject of the two preceding books: this recapitulation cannot indeed be avoided, because it is necessary to let *Alcinous* into his story, and this cannot be done without a repetition; but generally all repetitions are tedious: The Reader is offended when that is related which he knows already, he receives no new instruction to entertain his judgment, nor any new descriptions to excite his curiosity, and by these means the very soul of Poetry is extinguish'd, and it becomes unspirited and lifeless. When therefore repetitions are absolutely necessary, they ought always to be short; and I may appeal to the Reader if he is not tir'd with many in *Homer*, especially when made in the very same words? Here indeed *Ulysses* tells his story but in part; the Queen ask'd him who he was, but he passes over this without any reply, and reserves the greatest part of his story to a time of more *leisure*, that he may discover himself to a better advantage before the whole Peerage of the *Phæacians*. I do not always condemn even the verbal repetitions of *Homer*, sometimes as in embassies they may be necessary, because every word is stamp'd with authority, and perhaps they might be customary in *Homer*'s times; if they were not, he had too fruitful an invention not to have varied his thoughts and expressions. *Bossu* observes ⟨III vi⟩, that with respect to repetitions *Virgil* is more exact than *Homer*; for instance, in the first book of the *Æneis*, when *Æneas* is repeating his sufferings to *Venus*, she interrupts him to give him comfort ⟨385–6⟩;

—*Nec plura querentem*
Passa Venus, medio sic interfata dolore est.

and in the third book, where good manners oblig'd this Heroe to relate his story at the request of *Andromache*, the Poet prevents it by introducing *Helenus*, who hinders the repetition ⟨344 ff⟩.

330. *Remote from Gods or men she holds her reign.*] *Homer* has the secret art of introducing the best instructions, in the midst of the plainest narrations. He has describ'd the unworthy passion of the Goddess *Calypso*, and the indecent advances she made to detain him from his country. It is possible this relation might make some impressions upon the mind of the Reader, inconsistent with exact Morality; What antidote then does *Homer* administer to expell this poison? He does not content himself with setting the chastity of *Penelope* in opposition to the loose desires of *Calypso*, and showing the great advantage the Mortal has over the Goddess; but he here discovers the fountain from whence this weakness rises, by saying, that neither man nor Gods frequented this Island: on one hand the absence of the Gods, and on the other the infrequency of objects made her yield at the sight of the first that appears. Every object is dangerous in solitude,

Amid the terrors of the rowling main.
Me, only me, the hand of fortune bore
Unblest! to tread that interdicted shore:
When *Jove* tremendous in the sable deeps
Launch'd his red lightning at our scatter'd ships: 335
Then, all my fleet, and all my foll'wers lost,
Sole on a plank, on boiling surges tost,
Heav'n drove my wreck th' *Ogygian* Isle to find,
Full nine days floating to the wave and wind.
Met by the Goddess there with open arms,   340
She brib'd my stay with more than human charms;
Nay promis'd, vainly promis'd, to bestow
Immortal life, exempt from age and woe.
But all her blandishments successless prove,
To banish from my breast my country's love.   345
I stay reluctant sev'n continu'd years,
And water her ambrosial couch with tears.
The eighth, she voluntary moves to part,
Or urg'd by *Jove*, or her own changeful heart.
A Raft was form'd to cross the surging sea; ⎫   350
Her self supply'd the stores and rich array; ⎬
And gave the gales to waft me on the way. ⎭
In sev'nteen days appear'd your pleasing coast,
And woody mountains half in vapours lost.
Joy touch'd my soul: My soul was joy'd in vain,   355
For angry *Neptune* rouz'd the raging main:

---

especially, as *Homer* expresses it, if we have no commerce with the Gods. *Dacier.*

344. *But all her blandishments successless prove.*—] *Dacier*, from *Eustathius*, assigns the reason of the refusal of *Ulysses* to comply with the proffers of *Calypso*, to forsake his wife and country: It was, because he knew that women in love promise more than they either can, or intend to perform. An insinuation, that he would have comply'd if he had thought the Goddess would, or could, have perform'd her promises. But this is contrary to the character of *Ulysses*, whose greatest Glory it is, not to have listen'd even to a Goddess. In this view he ceases to be an Heroe, and his return is no longer a virtue, but he returns only because he found not a temptation sufficient to keep him from his country.

The wild winds whistle, and the billows roar; ⎫
The splitting Raft the furious tempest tore; ⎬
And storms vindictive intercept the shore. ⎭
Soon as their rage subsides, the seas I brave   360
With naked force, and shoot along the wave,
To reach this Isle: but there my hopes were lost,
The surge impell'd me on a craggy coast.
I chose the safer sea, and chanc'd to find
A river's mouth, impervious to the wind,   365
And clear of rocks. I fainted by the flood;
Then took the shelter of the neighb'ring wood.
'Twas night; and cover'd in the foliage deep,
Jove plung'd my senses in the death of sleep.
All night I slept, oblivious of my pain;   370
Aurora dawn'd, and *Phœbus* shin'd in vain,
Nor 'till oblique he slop'd his evening ray,
Had *Somnus* dry'd the balmy dews away.
Then female voices from the shore I heard:
A maid amidst them, Goddess-like, appear'd: 375
To her I su'd; she pity'd my distress;
Like thee in beauty, nor in virtue less.
Who from such youth cou'd hope consid'rate care?
In youth and beauty wisdom is but rare!

---

379. *In youth and beauty wisdom is but rare.*] In the preceding line *Ulysses* speaks of
Nausicaa, yet immediately changes the words into the Masculine gender, for
grammatically it ought to be νεωτέρην ἀντιάσασαν. *Homer* makes this alteration
to pay the greater compliment to *Nausicaa*, and he intends to express by it, that
neither woman nor man of her years could be expected to have such remarkable
discretion. *Eustathius.*

Such sentences being very frequent in the *Odyssey*; it may not be improper to
observe, of what beauty a sentence is in Epic Poetry. A Sentence may be defin'd,
a moral instruction couch'd in few words. *Rapin* asserts, that sentences are more
proper in Dramatic than Heroic Poetry: for Narration is the essential character
of it, and it ought to be one continued thread of discourse, simple and natural,
without an affectation of figures, or moral reflections: that energy which some
pretend to collect and inclose within a small compass of words, is wont extremely
to weaken the rest of the discourse, and give it a forc'd air: it seems to jut out of

She gave me life, reliev'd with just supplies   380
My wants, and lent these robes that strike your eyes.
This is the truth: And oh ye pow'rs on high!
Forbid that want shou'd sink me to a lye.
    To this the King. Our daughter but exprest
Her cares imperfect to our god-like guest.   385
Suppliant to her, since first he chose to pray, ⎫
Why not her self did she conduct the way,   ⎬
And with her handmaids to our court convey? ⎭
    Heroe and King! (*Ulysses* thus reply'd)
Nor blame her faultless, nor suspect of pride: 390
She bade me follow in th' attendant train;

---

the structure of the Poem, and to be independent of it: he blames *Homer* for scattering his sentences too plentifully thro' his Poesy, and calls it an affectation and imperfection ⟨Comparaison xiii, 1 150⟩.

These objections would undoubtedly be of weight, if the sentences were so introduc'd as to break the thread of narration, as *Rapin* rightly observes. But is this the case with relation to *Homer*? He puts them into the mouth of the Actors themselves, and the narration goes on without the least interruption: It is not the Poet who speaks, nor does he suspend the narration to make a refin'd reflection, or give us a sentence of Morality. Is his Poetry the worse because he makes his agents speak weightily and sententiously? It is true, sentences used without moderation are absurd in Epic Poetry; they give it a seriousness that is more becoming the gravity of Philosophers, than the Spirit and Majesty of Poetry. *Bossu* judiciously observes ⟨vi iv⟩, that such thoughts have in their very nature a certain kind of calm Wisdom that is contrary to the passions; but says he, sentences make a Poem useful, and it seems natural to imagine, that the more a work is embellish'd with them, the more it deserves that general approbation which *Horace* promises to those who have the art to mix the profitable with the pleasant ⟨*Ars Poet.* 343–6⟩. In short, sentences are not only allowable but beautiful in Heroic Poetry, if they are introduc'd with propriety, and without affectation.

391.   *She bade me follow—*
                       But fear and rev'rence, &c.]
This is directly contrary to what is before asserted in the preceding book, where *Nausicaa* forbids *Ulysses* to attend her, to avoid suspicion and slander: Is not *Ulysses* then guilty of falshood, and is not falshood beneath the character of a Heroe? *Eustathius* confesses that *Ulysses* is guilty φανερῶς ψεύδεται, and he adds, that a wise man may do so sometimes opportunely. Ὅπερ ἂν ποιήσειε ἐν καιρῷ ὁ σοφός. I fear this concession of the Bishop's would not pass for good casuistry

But fear and rev'rence did my steps detain,
Lest rash suspicion might alarm thy mind:
Man's of a jealous and mistaking kind.
  Far from my soul (he cry'd) the Gods efface   395
All wrath ill-grounded, and suspicion base!
Whate'er is honest, Stranger, I approve.
And would to *Phœbus, Pallas,* and to *Jove,*
Such as thou art, thy thought and mine were one,
Nor thou unwilling to be call'd my son.   400
In such alliance could'st thou wish to join,
A Palace stor'd with treasures shou'd be thine.
But if reluctant, who shall force thy stay?   ⎫
Jove bids to set the stranger on his way,   ⎬
And ships shall wait thee with the morning ray. ⎭ 405
'Till then, let slumber close thy careful eyes; ⎫
The wakeful mariners shall watch the skies, ⎬
And seize the moment when the breezes rise: ⎭

---

in these ages. *Spondanus* ⟨*Od.* p. 97⟩ is of the same opinion as *Eustathius*; *Vir prudens certo loco & tempore mendaciis officiosissimis uti novit.* *Dacier* confesses that he somewhat disguises the truth. It will be difficult to vindicate *Ulysses* from the imputation, if the notions of truth and falshood were as strict in former, as in these ages; but we must not measure by this standard: It is certain that anciently Lying was reckon'd no crime by a whole nation; and it still bears a dispute, *An omne falsi-loquium sit mendacium?* Some Casuists allow of the *officiosum mendacium,* and such is this of *Ulysses,* entirely complemental and officious.

 400. *Nor thou unwilling to be call'd my son*—] The Ancients observe, that *Alcinous* very artfully inserts this proposition to *Ulysses,* to prove his veracity. If he had embraced it without hesitation, he would have concluded him an impostor; for it is not conceivable that he should reject all the temptations to marriage made him by *Calypso,* a Goddess, and yet immediately embrace this offer of *Alcinous* to marry his daughter. But if we take the passage in another sense, and believe that *Alcinous* spoke sincerely without any secret suspicions, yet his conduct is justifiable. It has I confess appear'd shocking, that *Alcinous,* a King, should at the very first interview offer his daughter to a stranger, who might be a vagrant and impostor: But examples are frequent in Antiquity of marriages thus concluded between strangers, and with as little hesitation: Thus *Bellerophon, Tydeus,* and *Polynices* were married. Great Personages regarded not riches, but were only sollicitous to procure worthy Husbands for their daughters, and birth and virtue were the best recommendations.

Plate 6 Frontispiece of the *Iliad*: the Farnese bust

HOMERVS De aereo capite olim penes illustrifs. Comitem Arundellium, nunc in Mufaeo
celeberrimi Viri, Richardi Mead. M.D.   Antiquifsima Homeri Statua egregij operis, ut deseribit
Cedrenus, Constantinopoli, Iustiniano Imperante, incendio periisse dicitur: Statuae autem illius hoc
efse Caput, ex Incendij ruinis feliciter servatum, cum ex oris figura et lineamentis, tum ex manifestis
liquefacti metalli indicijs conjectari licet.

Vid. Cedren. Histor. Compend. Cap. 340.

Plate 7   Frontispiece of the *Odyssey*: the Arundel bust

Then gently waft thee to the pleasing shore,
Where thy soul rests, and labour is no more.   410
Far as *Eubæa* tho' thy country lay,
Our ships with ease transport thee in a day.
Thither of old, Earth's * Giant-son to view,
On wings of winds with *Rhadamanth* they flew:
This land, from whence their morning course begun, 415

---

* *Tityus.*

It is observable that in the original there is a Chasm, an Infinitive mood without any thing to govern it; we must therefore supply the word ἐθέλοις to make it right construction. *Eustath.*

411. *Far as* Eubæa *tho' thy country lay.*] *Eubæa,* as *Eustathius* observes, is really far distant from *Corcyra,* the country of the *Phæacians*: But *Alcinous* still makes it more distant, by placing it in another part of the world, and describing it as one of the fortunate Islands; for in the fourth book *Rhadamanthus* is said to inhabit the *Elysian* fields. *Alcinous* therefore endeavours to have it believ'd that his Isle is near those fields, by asserting that *Rhadamanthus* made use of *Phæacian* vessels in his voyage to *Tityus. Eustathius* further adds, that *Rhadamanthus* was a Prince of great justice, and *Tityus* a person of great impiety, and that he made this voyage to bring him over to more virtuous dispositions.

415.   *The* ⟨sic⟩ *land, from whence their morning course begun,*
            Saw them returning with the setting sun.]

If *Homer* had given the true situation of *Corcyra* as it really lies opposite to *Epirus,* yet the Hyperbole of sailing thence to *Eubæa* and returning in the same day, had been utterly an impossibility; for in sailing thither they must pass the *Ionian* and *Icarian* seas, and double the *Peloponnesus.* But the fiction is yet more extravagant, by the Poet's placing it still more distant near the *Fortunate Islands.* But what is impossible to vessels to effect, that are as swift as birds, and can sail with the rapidity of a thought? *Eustathius.*

But then is the Poet justifiable for relating such incredible amplifications? It may be answer'd, if he had put these extravagancies into the mouth of *Ulysses,* he had been unpardonable, but they suit well with the character of *Alcinous*: They let *Ulysses* into his disposition, and he appears to be ignorant, credulous, and ostentatious. This was necessary, that *Ulysses* might know how to adapt himself to his humour, and engage his assistance; and this he actually brings about by raising his wonder and esteem by stories, that could not fail to please such an ignorant and credulous person as *Alcinous.*

Dacier adds, that the *Phæacians* were so puff'd up with their constant felicity and the protection of the Gods, that they thought nothing impossible; upon this opinion all these Hyperboles are founded: And this agrees too well with human nature, the more happy men are, the more high and extravagantly they talk, and

K

Saw them returning with the setting sun.
Your eyes shall witness and confirm my tale,
Our youth how dex'trous, and how fleet our sail,
When justly tim'd with equal sweep they row,
And Ocean whitens in long tracts below.   420
    Thus he. No word th' experienc'd man replies,
But thus to heav'n (and heav'nward lifts his eyes)
O *Jove!* oh father! what the King accords
Do thou make perfect! sacred be his words!
Wide o'er the world *Alcinous'* glory shine!   425
Let Fame be his, and ah! my country mine!
    Mean-time *Arete*, for the hour of rest
Ordains the fleecy couch, and cov'ring vest;
Bids her fair train the purple quilts prepare,
And the thick carpets spread with busy care.   430
With torches blazing in their hands they past,
And finish'd all their Queen's command with haste:
Then gave the signal to the willing guest;
He rose with pleasure, and retir'd to rest.
There, soft-extended, to the murm'ring sound   435
Of the high porch, *Ulysses* sleeps profound:
Within, releas'd from cares *Alcinous* lies;
And fast beside, were clos'd *Arete*'s eyes.

---

are too apt to entertain themselves with wild Chimæra's which have no existence
but in the Imagination.

    The moral then of these fables of *Alcinous* is, that a constant series of happiness
intoxicates the mind, and that moderation is often learn'd in the school of
adversity.

    423. *The prayer of* Ulysses.] It is observable, that *Ulysses* makes no reply directly
to the obliging proposition which the King made concerning his daughter.
A refusal might have been disadvantagious to his present circumstances, yet an
answer is imply'd in this prayer, which shows the impatience he has to return to
his country, and the gratitude he feels for his promises to effect it: and consequently it discovers that he has no intentions of settling with his daughter
amongst the *Phæacians. Dacier.*

    437, 438. *The last lines.*] It may seem somewhat extraordinary, that *Alcinous* and
his Queen who have been describ'd as patterns of conjugal happiness should sleep

in distinct beds. *Jupiter* and *Juno*, as *Dacier* observes from the first of the *Iliad*, have the same bed. Perhaps the Poet design'd to shew the luxury and false delicacy of those too happy *Phæacians*, who liv'd in such softness that they shun'd every thing that might prove troublesome or incommodious.

This book takes up no longer time than the evening of the thirty second day.

THE
EIGHTH BOOK
OF THE
ODYSSEY.

The ARGUMENT.

Alcinous calls a Council, in which it is resolved to transport *Ulysses* into *his country. After which, splendid entertainments are made, where the celebrated Musician and Poet* Demodocus, *plays and sings to the guests. They next proceed to the games, the race, the wrestling, Discus, &c. where* Ulysses *casts a prodigious length, to the admiration of all the spectators. They return again to the banquet, and* Demodocus *sings the loves of* Mars *and* Venus. Ulysses, *after a compliment to the Poet, desires him to sing the introduction of the wooden horse into* Troy; *which subject provoking his tears,* Alcinous *enquires of his guest, his name, parentage, and fortunes.*

Now fair *Aurora* lifts her golden ray,
And all the ruddy Orient flames with day:
Alcinous, and the chief with dawning light,

This book has been more severely censur'd by the Critics than any in the whole *Odyssey*: It may therefore be thought necessary to lay before the Reader what may be offer'd in the Poet's vindication.

Scaliger in his *Poetics* is very warm against it ⟨v ii, p. 216 B2⟩. *Demodocus*, observes that Critic, sings the lusts of the Gods (*fœditates*) at the feast of *Alcinous*. And *Bossu*, tho' he vindicates the Poet, remarks that we meet with some offensive passages in *Homer*, and instances in the adultery of *Mars* and *Venus* ⟨v ii⟩.

To know (says *Aristotle* in his *Art of Poetry* ⟨xv 1–3⟩) whether a thing be well or ill spoken, we must not only examine the thing whether it be good or ill, but we must also have regard to him that speaks or acts, and to the person to whom the Poet addresses: for the character of the person who speaks, and of him to whom he speaks, makes that to be good, which would not come well from the mouth of any other person. 'Tis on this account we vindicate *Homer* with respect to the Immorality that is found in the fable of the Adultery of *Mars* and *Venus*: We must consider that it is neither the Poet, nor his Heroe, that recites that story: but a *Phæacian* sings it to *Phæacians*, a soft effeminate people, at a festival. Besides, it is allowable even in grave and moral writings to introduce vicious persons, who

Rose instant from the slumbers of the night;
Then to the Council seat they bend their way,   5
And fill the shining thrones along the bay.
   Mean-while *Minerva* in her guardian care
Shoots from the starry vault thro' fields of air;
In form a herald of the King she flies

---

despise the Gods; and is not the Poet oblig'd to adapt his Poetry to the characters
of such persons? And had it not been an absurdity in him to have given us a
Philosophical or Moral song before a people who would be pleas'd with nothing
but gaiety and effeminacy? The Moral that we are to draw from this story is, that
an idle and soft course of life is the source of all criminal pleasures; and that those
persons who lead such lives, are generally pleas'd to hear such stories, as make
their betters partakers in the same vices. This relation of *Homer* is a useful lesson
to them who desire to live virtuously; and it teaches, that if we would not be
guilty of such vices, we must avoid such a method of life as inevitably leads to the
practice of them.

   Rapin attacks this book on another side, and blames it not for its Immorality,
but Lowness ⟨Comparaison viii, 1 126⟩. *Homer*, says he, puts off that air of
grandeur and majesty which so properly belongs to his character, he debases himself into a Droll, and sinks into a familiar way of talking; he turns things into
ridicule, by endeavouring to entertain his Reader with something pleasant and
diverting: For instance, in the eighth book of the *Odyssey*, he entertains the Gods
with a Comedy, some of whom he makes buffoons: *Mars* and *Venus* are introduced
upon the stage, taken in a net laid by *Vulcan*, contrary to the gravity which is so
essential to Epic Poetry.

   It must be granted, that the Gods are here painted in colours unworthy of
Deities, yet still with propriety, if we respect the spectators, who are ignorant,
debauch'd *Phæacians*. *Homer* was oblig'd to draw them not according to his own
idea of the Gods, but according to the wild fancies of the *Phæacians*. The Poet is
not at liberty to ascribe the wisdom of a *Socrates* to *Alcinous*: He must follow
Nature, and like a painter he may draw Deities or monsters, and introduce as he
pleases either vicious or virtuous characters, provided he always makes them of
a piece, consistent with their first representation.

   This rule of *Aristotle* in general vindicates *Homer*, and 'tis necessary to carry it
in our minds, because it ought to be apply'd to all incidents that relate to the
Phæacians, in the sequel of the *Odyssey*.

   6. *And fill the shining thrones along the bay.*] This place of Council was between the
two ports, where the Temple of *Neptune* stood; probably, like that in the second
book, open to the air.

   9. *In form a herald—*.] It may be ask'd what occasion there is to introduce a
Goddess, to perform an action that might have been as well executed by a real
Herald? *Eustathius* observes, that this *Minerva* is either Fame, which informs the

From Peer to Peer, and thus incessant cries. 10
Nobles and Chiefs who rule *Phæacia*'s states,
The King in council your attendance waits:
A Prince of grace divine your aid implores,
O'er unknown seas arriv'd from unknown shores.
She spoke, and sudden with tumultuous sounds 15
Of thronging multitudes the shore rebounds;
At once the seats they fill: and every eye
Gaz'd, as before some brother of the sky.
Pallas with grace divine his form improves,

Phæacians that a stranger of uncommon figure is arriv'd, and upon this report they assemble; or it implies, that this assembly was made by the Wisdom of the Peers, and consequently a Poet may ascribe it to the Goddess of Wisdom, it being the effect of her inspiration.

The Poet by the introduction of a Deity warns us, that something of importance is to succeed; this is to be usher'd in with solemnity, and consequently the appearance of *Minerva* in this place is not unnecessary: The action of importance to be describ'd is no less than the change of the fortunes of *Ulysses*; it is from this assembly that his affairs take a new turn, and hasten to a happy re-establishment.

13. *A Prince of form* ⟨sic⟩ *divine*—] *Minerva* speaks thus in favour of *Ulysses*, to excite the curiosity of the *Phæacians*: and indeed the short speech is excellently adapted to this purpose. They were fond of strangers: The Goddess therefore tells them, that a stranger is arriv'd of a God-like appearance. They admir'd outward show, he is therefore describ'd as a man of extraordinary beauty, and *Minerva* for this reason immediately improves it. *Eustathius*.

19. Pallas *with grace divine his frame* ⟨sic⟩ *improves*.] This circumstance has been repeated several times almost in the same words, since the beginning of the *Odyssey*. I cannot be of opinion that such repetitions are beauties. In any other Poet, they might have been thought to proceed from a poverty of invention, tho' certainly not in *Homer*, in whom there is rather a superfluity than barrenness. Perhaps having once said a thing well, he despair'd of improving it, and so repeated it; or perhaps he intended to inculcate this truth, that all our accomplishments, as beauty, strength, *&c.* are the gifts of the Gods; and being willing to fix it upon the mind, he dwells upon it, and inserts it in many places. Here indeed it has a particular propriety, as it is a circumstance that first engages the *Phæacians* in the favour of *Ulysses*: his beauty was his first recommendation, and consequently the Poet with great judgment sets his Heroe off to the best advantage, it being an incident from which he dates all his future happiness; and therefore to be insisted upon with a particular solemnity. *Plato* in his *Theætetus* applies the latter part of this description to *Parmenides*. Αἰδοῖός τέ μοι φαίνεται εἶναι ἄμα δεινός τε ⟨183E⟩.

More high he treads, and more enlarg'd he moves: 20
She sheds celestial bloom, regard to draw,
And gives a dignity of mien, to awe,
With strength the future prize of fame to play,
And gather all the honours of the day.
　　Then from his glitt'ring throne *Alcinous* rose;   25
Attend, he cry'd, while we our will disclose,
Your present aid this godlike stranger craves,
Tost by rude tempest thro' a war of waves:
Perhaps from realms that view the rising day,
Or nations subject to the western ray.   30
Then grant, what here all sons of woe obtain,
(For here affliction never pleads in vain:)
Be chosen youths prepar'd, expert to try
The vast profound, and bid the vessel fly:
Launch the tall bark, and order ev'ry oar,   35

---

25. *From his glitt'ring throne* Alcinous *rose*.] It might be expected that *Ulysses*, upon whose account alone *Alcinous* calls this assembly, should have made his condition known, and spoken himself to the *Phæacians*; whereas he appears upon the stage as a mute person, and the multitude departs entirely ignorant of his name and fortunes. It may be answer'd, that this was not a proper time for a fuller discovery, the Poet defers it 'till *Ulysses* had distinguish'd himself in the games, and fully rais'd their curiosity. It is for the same reason that *Ulysses* is silent; if he had spoken he could not have avoided to let them into the knowledge of his condition, but the contrary method is greatly for his advantage, and assures him of success from the recommendation of a King.

But there is another, and perhaps a better reason, to be given for this silence of *Ulysses*: The Poet reserves the whole story of his sufferings for an entire and un-interrupted narration; if he had now made any discovery, he must afterwards either have fall'n into tautology, or broken the thread of the relation, so that it would not have been of a piece, but wanted continuity. Besides, it comes with more weight at once, than if it had been made at several times, and consequently makes a deeper impression upon the memory and passion of the auditors. *Virgil* ⟨1 544 ff⟩ has taken a different method in the discovery of *Æneas*; there was a necessity for it; his companions, to engage *Dido* in their protection, tell her they belong to no less a Heroe than *Æneas*, so that he is in a manner known before he appears; but *Virgil* after the example of *Homer* reserves his story for an entire narration.

35. *Launch the tall bark*—] The word in the original is πρωτόπλοος; which

Then in our court indulge the genial hour:
Instant you sailors to this task attend,
Swift to the palace, all ye Peers ascend:
Let none to strangers honours due disclaim;
Be there *Demodocus*, the Bard of fame,   40
Taught by the Gods to please, when high he sings
The vocal lay responsive to the strings.

   Thus spoke the Prince: th' attending Peers obey,
In state they move; *Alcinous* leads the way:
Swift to *Demodocus* the herald flies,   45
At once the sailors to their charge arise:
They launch the vessel, and unfurl the sails,
And stretch the swelling canvas to the gales;
Then to the palace move: A gath'ring throng,
Youth, and white age, tumultuous pour along: 50
Now all accesses to the dome are fill'd;
Eight boars, the choicest of the herd, are kill'd:
Two beeves, twelve fatlings from the flock they bring
To crown the feast, so wills the bounteous King.
The herald now arrives, and guides along   55
The sacred master of celestial song:
Dear to the Muse! who gave his days to flow

---

signifies not only a ship that makes its first voyage, but a ship that out-sails other
ships, as *Eustathius* observes. It is not possible for a translator to retain such singu-
larities with any beauty; it would seem pedantry and affectation, and not Poetry.

  41. *Taught by the Gods to please—*] *Homer* here insinuates, that all good and
great qualities are the gifts of God. He shews us likewise, that Music was constantly made use of in the Courts of all the Oriental Princes; we have seen
Phemius in *Ithaca*, a second in *Lacedæmon* with *Menelaus*, and *Demodocus* here with
Alcinous. The *Hebrews* were likewise of remarkable skill in Music; every one
knows what effect the harp of *David* had upon the spirit of *Saul* ⟨1 Sam. 16⟩.
Solomon tells us ⟨Eccles. 2 : 8⟩, that he sought out singing men and singing women
to entertain him, like these in *Homer*, at the time of feasting: Thus another oriental
Writer compares Music at feasts to an emerald enclos'd in gold: *as a signet of an
emerald set in a work of gold, so is the melody of music with pleasant wine.* Eccl⟨us⟩. xxxii
6. *Dacier*.

  57.   *Dear to the Muse! who gave his days to flow
                With mighty blessings, mix'd with mighty woe.*]

With mighty blessings, mix'd with mighty woe:
With clouds of darkness quench'd his visual ray,
But gave him skill to raise the lofty lay.   60
High on a radiant throne sublime in state,
Encircled by huge multitudes, he sate:
With silver shone the throne; his Lyre well strung
To rapturous sounds, at hand *Pontonous* hung:
Before his seat a polish'd table shines,   65
And a full goblet foams with gen'rous wines:
His food a herald bore: And now they fed;
And now the rage of craving hunger fled.
    Then fir'd by all the Muse, aloud he sings

It has been generally thought that *Homer* represents himself in the person of *Demodocus*: and *Dacier* imagines that this passage gave occasion to the Ancients to believe that *Homer* was blind. But that he really was blind is testify'd by himself in his Hymn to *Apollo* ⟨169–72⟩, which *Thucydides* asserts to be the genuine production of *Homer*, and quotes it as such in his history ⟨III civ 4–5⟩.

    'Ὡ κοῦραι τίς δ' ὕμμιν ἀνὴρ ἥδιστος ἀοιδῶν
    'Ενθάδε πωλεῖται καὶ τέῳ τέρπεσθε μάλιστα;
    'Υμεῖς δ' εὖ μάλα πᾶσαι ὑποκρίνασθε ἀφήμως
    Τυφλὸς ἀνὴρ—

That is, "O Virgins, if any person asks you who is he, the most pleasing of all Poets, who frequents this place, and who is he who most delights you? reply, he is a blind man, &c." 'Tis true, as *Eustathius* observes, that there are many features in the two Poets that bear a great resemblance; *Demodocus* sings divinely, the same is true of *Homer*; *Demodocus* sings the adventures of the *Greeks* before *Troy*, so does *Homer* in his *Iliads*.

    If this be true, it must be allow'd that *Homer* has found out a way of commending himself very artfully: Had he spoken plainly, he had been extravagantly vain; but by this indirect way of praise, the Reader is at liberty to apply it either solely to *Demodocus*, or obliquely to *Homer*.

    It is remarkable, that *Homer* takes a very extraordinary care of *Demodocus* his brother Poet; and introduces him as a person of great distinction. He calls him in this book the Heroe *Demodocus*: He places him on a throne studded with silver, and gives him an herald for his attendant; nor is he less careful to provide for his entertainment, he has a particular table, and a capacious bowl set before him to drink as often as he had a mind, as the original expresses it. Some merry wits have turn'd the last circumstance into raillery, and insinuate that *Homer* in this place as well as in the former means himself in the person of *Demodocus*, an intimation that he would not be displeas'd to meet with the like hospitality.

K*

> The mighty deeds of Demigods and Kings: 70
> From that fierce wrath the noble song arose,
> That made *Ulysses* and *Achilles* foes:
> How o'er the feast they doom the fall of *Troy*;
> The stern debate *Atrides* hears with joy:
> For heav'n foretold the contest, when he trod   75
> The marble threshold of the *Delphic* God,
> Curious to learn the counsels of the sky,
> Ere yet he loos'd the rage of war on *Troy*.
> Touch'd at the song, *Ulysses* strait resign'd

74. *The stern debate* Atrides *heard* ⟨sic⟩ *with joy.*] This passage is not without obscurity, but *Eustathius* thus explains it from *Athenaeus* ⟨on authority of Eustathius 1586 20⟩; In the *Iliads* the Generals sup with *Agamemnon* with sobriety and moderation, and if in the *Odyssey* we see *Achilles* and *Ulysses* in contention to the great satisfaction of *Agamemnon*; it is because these contentions are of use to his affairs, they contend whether force or stratagem is to be employed to take *Troy*; *Achilles* after the death of *Hector*, persuaded to assault it by storm, *Ulysses* by stratagem. There is a further reason given for the satisfaction which *Agamemnon* expresses at the contest of these two Heroes: Before the opening of the war of *Troy* he consulted the oracle concerning the issue of it; *Apollo* answer'd, that *Troy* should be taken when two Princes most renown'd for wisdom and valour should contend at a sacrifice of the Gods; *Agamemnon* rejoices to see the prediction fulfill'd, knowing that the destruction of *Troy* was at hand, the Oracle being accomplish'd by the contest of *Ulysses* and *Achilles*.

79. *Touch'd at the song.*—] Many objections may be made against this relation; it may seem to offend against probability, and appears somewhat incredible, that *Demodocus* should thus luckily pitch upon the war of *Troy* for the subject of his song, and still more happily upon the deeds of *Ulysses*; for instance, a man may die of an Apoplexy, this is probable; but that this should happen just when the Poet has occasion for it, is in some degree incredible. But this objection will cease, if we consider not only that the war of *Troy* was the greatest event of those ages, and consequently might be the common subject of entertainment; but also that it is not *Homer* or *Demodocus* who relates the story, but the Muse who inspires it: *Homer* several times in this book ascribes the song to immediate inspiration; and this supernatural assistance reconciles it to human probability, and the story becomes credible when it is suppos'd to be related by a Deity. *Aristotle* in his *Poetics* ⟨XVI 8⟩ commends this conduct as artful and judicious; *Alcinous*, says he, invites *Ulysses* to an entertainment to divert him, where *Demodocus* sings his actions, at which he cannot refrain from tears, which *Alcinous* perceives, and this brings about the discovery of *Ulysses*.

It may further be objected, that a sufficient cause for this violence of tears is not

To soft affliction all his manly mind: 80
Before his eyes the purple vest he drew,
Industrious to conceal the falling dew:
But when the music paus'd, he ceas'd to shed
The flowing tear, and rais'd his drooping head:
And lifting to the Gods a goblet crown'd,   85
He pour'd a pure libation to the ground.
   Transported with the song, the list'ning train
Again with loud applause demand the strain:
Again *Ulysses* veil'd his pensive head,
Again unmann'd a show'r of sorrow shed: 90
Conceal'd he wept: the King observ'd alone
The silent tear, and heard the secret groan:
Then to the Bard aloud: O cease to sing,
Dumb be thy voice, and mute th' harmonious string;
Enough the feast has pleas'd, enough the pow'r   95
Of heav'nly song has crown'd the genial hour!
Incessant in the games your strength display,
Contest, ye brave, the honours of the day!
That pleas'd th' admiring stranger may proclaim
In distant regions the *Phæacian* fame: 100
None wield the gauntlet with so dire a sway,

apparent; for why should *Ulysses* weep to hear his own brave achievements, especially when nothing calamitous is recited? This indeed would be improbable, if that were the whole of what the Poet sung: But *Homer* only gives us the heads of the song, a few sketches of a larger draught, and leaves something to be fill'd up by the imagination of the reader. Thus for instance the words of *Demodocus* recall'd to the mind of *Ulysses* all the hardships he had undergone during a ten years war, all the scenes of horror he had beheld, and the loss and sufferings of all his friends. And no doubt he might weep even for the calamities he brought upon *Troy*, an ingenuous nature cannot be insensible when any of its own species suffers; the *Trojans* were his enemies, but still they were men, and compassion is due even to unfortunate enemies. I doubt not but it will be allow'd, that there is here sufficient cause to draw tears from a heroe, unless a heroe must be supposed to be divested of humanity.

   101. *None wield the gauntlet with so dire a sway.*] *Eustathius* asks how *Alcinous* could make such an assertion, and give the preference to his people before all nations, when he neither knew, nor was known to, any heroes out of his own Island? He

Or swifter in the race devour the way:
None in the leap spring with so strong a bound,
Or firmer, in the wrestling, press the ground.
    Thus spoke the King; th' attending Peers obey: 105
In state they move, *Alcinous* leads the way:
His golden lyre *Demodocus* unstrung,
High on a column in the palace hung:
And guided by a herald's guardian cares,
Majestic to the lists of Fame repairs.   110
    Now swarms the populace; a countless throng,
Youth and hoar age; and man drives man along:
The games begin: Ambitious of the prize,
Acroneus, *Thoon*, and *Eretmeus* rise;
The prize *Ocyalus* and *Prymneus* claim,   115
Anchialus and *Ponteus*, chiefs of fame:
There *Proreus*, *Nautes*, *Eratreus* appear,
And fam'd *Amphialus*, *Polyneus'* heir:
Euryalus, like *Mars* terrific, rose,

---

answers that he speaks like a *Phæacian*, with ostentation and vanity; besides it is natural for all people to form, not illaudably, too favourable a judgment of their own country: And this agrees with the character of the *Phæacians* in a more particular manner, who call'd themselves ἀγχίθεοι, and the favourites of the Gods.

    113. *The games.*—] *Eustathius* remarks, that *Homer* very judiciously passes over these games in a few lines, having in the *Iliad* exhausted that subject; he there enlarg'd upon them, because they were essential ornaments, it being necessary that *Patroclus* should be honour'd by his friend with the utmost solemnity. Here they are only introduc'd occasionally, and therefore the Poet hastens to things more requisite, and carries on the thread of his story. But then it may be ask'd why are they mention'd at all, and what do they contribute to the re-establishment of *Ulysses*? It is evident that they are not without an happy effect, they give *Ulysses* an opportunity to signalize his character, to engage the King and the Peers in his favour, and this induces them to convey him to his own country, which is one of the most material incidents in the whole *Odyssey*.

    119. Euryalus, *like* Mars *terrific, rose*.] I was at a loss for a reason why this figure of terror was introduc'd amongst an unwarlike nation, upon an occasion contrary to the general description in the midst of games and diversions. *Eustathius* takes notice, that the Poet distinguishes the character of *Euryalus*, to force it upon our observation; he being the person who uses *Ulysses* with roughness and

When clad in wrath he withers hosts of foes: 120
Naubolides with grace unequall'd shone,
Or equal'd by *Laodamas* alone.
With these came forth *Ambasineus* the strong;
And three brave sons, from great *Alcinous* sprung.
    Rang'd in a line the ready racers stand,   125
Start from the goal, and vanish o'er the strand:
Swift as on wings of winds upborn they fly,
And drifts of rising dust involve the sky:
Before the rest, what space the hinds allow

---

inhumanity, and is the only Peer that is describ'd with a sword, which he gives to
Ulysses to repair his injury.

He further remarks, that almost all the names of the persons who are mention'd as candidates in these games are borrow'd from the sea, *Phæacia* being an
Island, and the people greatly addicted to navigation. I have taken the liberty to
vary from the order observ'd by *Homer* in the catalogue of the names, to avoid
the affinity of sound in many of them, as *Euryalus, Ocyalus,* &c. and too many
names being tedious at least in *English* Poetry, I pass'd over the three sons of
Alcinous, Laodamas, Halius, and *Clytoneus,* and only mention'd them in general as
the sons of *Alcinous.*

    I was surpriz'd to see *Dacier* render
        —υἱὸς Πολυνήου Τεκτονίδαο
The son of *Polyneus* the carpenter: it looks like Burlesque: it ought to be render'd,
The son of *Polyneus Tectonides,* a *Patronymic,* and it is so understood by all
Commentators.

129.   —*What space the hinds allow*
                       Between the mule and ox, from plow to plow.]
This image drawn from rural affairs is now become obsolete, and gives us no
distinct Idea of the distance between *Clytoneus* and the other racers: but this
obscurity arises not from *Homer*'s want of perspicuity, but from the change which
has happen'd in the method of tillage, and from a length of time which has
effaced the distinct image which was originally stamp'd upon it; so that what was
understood universally in the days of *Homer* is grown almost unintelligible to
posterity. *Eustathius* only observes, that the teams of Mules were placed at some
distance from the teams of Oxen; the Mule being more swift in his labour than
the Ox, and consequently more ground was allow'd to the Mule than the Ox by
the Husbandman. This gives us an Idea that *Clytoneus* was the foremost of the
racers, but how much is not to be discover'd with any certainty. *Aristarchus,* as
Didymus informs us ⟨Scholia to *Odyssey* (Dindorf), Oxford, 1855, 1 364–5⟩, thus
interprets *Homer.* "As much as a yoke of mules set to work at the same time with a
yoke of oxen, outgoes the oxen, (for mules are swifter than oxen) so much

Between the mule and ox, from plow to plow;   130
Clytonius sprung: he wing'd the rapid way,
And bore th' unrival'd honours of the day.
With fierce embrace the brawny wrestlers joyn;
The conquest, great *Euryalus*, is thine.
Amphialus sprung forward with a bound,   135
Superior in the leap, a length of ground:
From *Elatreus*' strong arm the Discus flies,
And sings with unmatch'd force along the skies.
And *Laodame* whirls high, with dreadful sway,
The gloves of death, victorious in the fray.   140
   While thus the Peerage in the games contends,
In act to speak, *Laodamas* ascends:
   O friends, he cries, the stranger seems well-skill'd
To try th' illustrious labours of the field:
I deem him brave; then grant the brave man's claim,   145
Invite the Hero to his share of fame.
What nervous arms he boasts! how firm his tread!
His limbs how turn'd! how broad his shoulders spread!
By age unbroke!—but all-consuming care

Clytoneus outwent his competitors." The same description occurs in the tenth book of the *Iliads*, verse 419, to which passage I refer the Reader for a more large and different explication.

   149. *By age unbroke!*] It is in the original literally, *he wants not youth*; this is spoken according to appearance only, for *Ulysses* must be suppos'd to be above forty, having spent twenty years in the wars of *Troy*, and in his return to his country. 'Tis true *Hesiod* ⟨*Works and Days* 441⟩ calls a person a youth, αἰζηόν, who was forty years of age, but this must be understood with some allowance, unless we suppose that the life of man was longer in the times of *Hesiod*, than in these later ages; the contrary of which appears from many places in *Homer*, where the shortness of man's life is compar'd to the leaves of trees, &c. But what the Poet here relates is very justificable, for the Youth which *Ulysses* appears to have, proceeds from *Minerva*; it is not a natural quality, but conferr'd by the immediate operation of a Goddess.

   This speech concludes with an address of great beauty; *Laodamas* invites *Ulysses* to act in the games, yet at the same time furnishes him with a decent excuse, to decline the invitation if it be against his inclinations; should he refuse, he imputes the refusal to his calamities, not to any want of skill, or personal inability.

Destroys perhaps the strength that time wou'd spare: 150
Dire is the Ocean, dread in all its forms!
Man must decay, when man contends with storms.
 Well hast thou spoke, (*Euryalus* replies)
Thine is the guest, invite him thou to rise.
Swift at the word advancing from the croud   155
He made obeysance, and thus spoke aloud.
 Vouchsafes the rev'rend stranger to display
His manly worth, and share the glorious day?
Father, arise! for thee thy port proclaims
Expert to conquer in the solemn games.   160
To fame arise! for what more fame can yield
Than the swift race, or conflict of the field?
Steal from corroding care one transient day,
To glory give the space thou hast to stay;
Short is the time, and lo! ev'n now the gales 165
Call thee aboard, and stretch the swelling sails.
 To whom with sighs *Ulysses* gave reply:
Ah why th' ill-suiting pastime must I try?
To gloomy care my thoughts alone are free;
Ill the gay sports with troubled hearts agree: 170
Sad from my natal hour my days have ran,
A much-afflicted, much-enduring man!
Who suppliant to the King and Peers, implores
A speedy voyage to his native shores.
 Wide wanders, *Laodame*, thy erring tongue, 175
The sports of glory to the brave belong,
(Retorts *Euryalus*:) He boasts no claim
Among the great, unlike the sons of Fame.

---

167. —Ulysses *gave reply.*] These are the first words spoken by *Ulysses* before the
Phæacians; and we cannot but be curious to know how he makes his address to
engage a people, in which he has not personal interest, in his favour. His speech
is excellently adapted to this purpose; he represents himself as a suppliant to the
King and all the assembly; and all suppliants being esteem'd sacred, he at once
makes it a duty in all the assembly to protect him; if they refuse to assist him,
they become guilty of no less a crime, than a violation of the laws of hospitality.

A wand'ring merchant he frequents the main,
Some mean sea-farer in pursuit of gain;   180
Studious of freight, in naval trade well skill'd,
But dreads th' athletic labours of the field.
   Incens'd *Ulysses* with a frown replies,
O forward to proclaim thy soul unwise!
With partial hands the Gods their gifts dispense;   185
Some greatly think, some speak with manly sense;
Here heav'n an elegance of form denies,
But wisdom the defect of form supplies:
This man with energy of thought controuls,
And steals with modest violence our souls,   190
He speaks reserv'dly, but he speaks with force,
Nor can one word be chang'd but for a worse;
In public more than mortal he appears,
And as he moves the gazing crowd reveres.

---

190.   *And steals with modest violence our souls,*
              He speaks reserv'dly, but he speaks with force.]
There is a difficulty in the *Greek* expression, ἀσφαλέως ἀγορεύει, αἰδοῖ μειλιχίη;
that is, "he speaks securely with a winning modesty". *Dionysius Halicarnassus* interprets it, in his *Examination of Oratory* ⟨*Opusc.* ii xi 8 (Teubner)⟩, to signify that the
Orator argues *per concessa*, and so proceeds with certainty, or ἀσφαλέως; without danger of refutation. The word properly signifies without *stumbling* ἀπρο-
σκόπως, as in the proverb cited by *Eustathius*, φορητότερον ποσὶν ἢ περ γλώττη
προσκόπτειν; that is, "it is better to stumble with the feet than with the
tongue." The words are concise, but of a very extensive comprehension, and take
in every thing, both in sentiments and diction, that enters into the character of a
compleat orator. *Dacier* concurs in the same interpretation; *He speaks reservedly,
or with caution; he hazards nothing that he would afterwards wish* (repentir) *to alter. And
all his words are full of sweetness and modesty.* These two lines are found almost
literally in *Hesiod*'s *Theogony*, ver. 92.
              Ἐρχόμενον δ' ἀνὰ ἄστυ, θεὸν ὡς ἱλάσκονται
              Αἰδοῖ μειλιχίη. μετὰ δὲ πρέπει ἀγρομένοισιν.
Whether *Homer* borrow'd these verses from *Hesiod*, or *Hesiod* from *Homer*, is not
evident. *Tully* in his book *de Senectute* ⟨xv 54⟩ is of opinion, that *Homer* preceded
Hesiod many ages, and consequently in his judgment the verses are *Homer*'s.
I question not but he had this very passage in view in his third book of his Orator ⟨*De Orat.* iii xiv 53⟩. *Quem stupefacti dicentem intuentur, quem deum, ut ita dicam,
inter homines putant*; which is almost a translation of *Homer*.

While others beauteous as th' æthereal kind, 195
The nobler portion want, a knowing mind.
In outward show heav'n gives thee to excell,
But heav'n denies the praise of thinking well.
Ill bear the brave a rude ungovern'd tongue,
And, youth, my gen'rous soul resents the wrong: 200
Skill'd in heroic exercise, I claim
A post of honour with the sons of Fame:
Such was my boast, while vigour crown'd my days,
Now care surrounds me, and my force decays;
Inur'd a melancholy part to bear, 205
In scenes of death, by tempest and by war.
Yet thus by woes impair'd, no more I wa⟨i⟩ve
To prove the heroe.—Slander stings the brave.
    Then striding forward with a furious bound,
He wrench'd a rocky fragment from the ground: 210
By far more pond'rous and more huge by far,

---

201.   *Skill'd in heroic exercise, I claim*
           A post of honour with the sons of Fame.]
It may be thought that *Ulysses*, both here and in his subsequent speech, is too
ostentatious, and that he dwells more than modesty allows upon his own accomplishments: But self-praise is sometimes no fault. *Plutarch* has wrote a dissertation,
how a man may praise himself without envy: What *Ulysses* here speaks is not a
boast but a justification. Persons in distress, says *Plutarch* ⟨*De Laude Ipsius* 5 (541
A–B)⟩, may speak of themselves with dignity: It shews a greatness of soul, and
that they bear up against the storms of fortune with bravery; they have too much
courage to fly to pity and commiseration, which betray despair and an hopeless
condition: Such a man struggling with ill fortune shews himself a champion, and
if by a bravery of speech he transforms himself from miserable and abject, into
bold and noble, he is not to be censur'd as vain or obstinate, but great and invincible.
    This is a full justification of *Ulysses*, he opposes virtue to calumny; and what
Horace applies to himself we apply to this Heroe ⟨*Odes* III xxx 14–15 (reversed)⟩.
           Quæsitam meritis, sume superbiam.
Besides, it was necessary to shew himself a person of figure and distinction, to
recommend his condition to the *Phæacians*: He was a stranger to the whole
nation, and he therefore takes a probable method to engage their assistance by
acquainting them with his worth; he describes himself as unfortunate, but yet as
a heroe in adversity.

Than what *Phæacia*'s sons discharg'd in air.
Fierce from his arm th' enormous load he flings;
Sonorous thro' the shaded air it sings;
Couch'd to the earth, tempestuous as it flies,   215
The crowd gaze upward while it cleaves the skies.
Beyond all marks, with many a giddy round
Down rushing, it up-turns a hill of ground.
   That instant *Pallas*, bursting from a cloud,
Fix'd a distinguish'd mark, and cry'd aloud.   220
   Ev'n he who sightless wants his visual ray,
May by his touch alone award the day:
Thy signal throw transcends the utmost bound
Of ev'ry champion, by a length of ground:
Securely bid the strongest of the train   225
Arise to throw: the strongest throws in vain.
   She spoke: and momentary mounts the sky:
The friendly voice *Ulysses* hears with joy;
Then thus aloud, (elate with decent pride)

---

219. *That instant* Pallas, *bursting from a cloud.*] There is not a passage in the whole
Odyssey, where a Deity is introduced with less apparent necessity: The Goddess of
Wisdom is brought down from heaven to act what might have been done as well
by any of the spectators, namely to proclaim what was self-evident, the victory of
Ulysses. When a Deity appears, our expectations are awaken'd for the introduction of something important, but what action of importance succeeds? 'Tis true,
her appearance encourages *Ulysses*, and immediately upon it he challenges the
whole *Phæacian* assembly. But he was already victor, and no further action is
perform'd. If indeed she had appear'd openly in favour of *Ulysses*, this would have
been greatly advantagious to him, and the *Phæacians* must have highly reverenc'd
a person who was so remarkably honour'd by a Goddess: but it is not evident that
the *Phæacians*, or even *Ulysses* knew the Deity, but took her for a man as she
appear'd to be; and *Ulysses* himself immediately rejoices that he had found a
friend in the assembly. If this be true, the descent of *Pallas* will prove very
unnecessary; for if she was esteem'd to be meerly human, she acts nothing in the
character of a Deity, and performs no more than might have been performed by
a man, and consequently gave no greater courage to *Ulysses* than a friend actually
gave, for such only he believ'd her to be. *Eustathius* appears to be of the same
opinion, for he says the place is to be understood allegorically, and what is
thus spoken by a *Phæacian* with Wisdom, is by the Poet apply'd to the Goddess
of it.

Rise ye *Phæacians*, try your force, he cry'd;   230
If with this throw the strongest Caster vye,
Still, further still, I bid the Discus fly.
Stand forth, ye champions, who the gauntlet wield,
Or you, the swiftest racers of the field!
Stand forth ye wrestlers who these pastimes grace!   235
I wield the gauntlet, and I run the race.
In such heroic games I yield to none,
Or yield to brave *Laodamas* alone:
Shall I with brave *Laodamas* contend?
A friend is sacred, and I stile him friend.   240
Ungen'rous were the man, and base of heart,
Who takes the kind, and pays th' ungrateful part;
Chiefly the man, in foreign realms confin'd,
Base to his friend, to his own interest blind:
All, all your heroes I this day defy: 245
Give me a man that we our might may try!
Expert in ev'ry art, I boast the skill
To give the feather'd arrow wings to kill;

---

239.   *Shall I with brave* Laodamas *contend?*
     A friend is sacred, and I stile him friend.]
Nothing can be more artful than this address of *Ulysses*; he finds a way, in the middle of a bold challenge, to secure himself of a powerful advocate, by paying an ingenious and laudable deference to his friend. But it may be ask'd if decency be observ'd, and ought *Ulysses* to challenge the father *Alcinous*, (for he speaks universally) and yet except his son *Laodamas*, especially when *Alcinous* was more properly his friend than *Laodamas*? and why should he be excepted rather than the other brothers? *Spondanus* answers ⟨*Od.* p. 104⟩, that the two brothers are included in the person of *Laodamas*, they all have the same relation to *Ulysses* as being equally a suppliant to them all, and consequently claim the same exemption from this challenge as *Laodamas*; and *Alcinous* is not concern'd in it: he is the judge and arbitrator of the games, not a candidate, like *Achilles* in the *Iliad*. But why is *Laodamas* nam'd in particular? He was the elder brother, and *Ulysses* might therefore be consign'd to his care in particular, by the right due to his seniority; besides he might be the noblest personage, having conquer'd his antagonist at the gauntlet, which was the most dangerous, and consequently the most honourable exercise, and therefore *Ulysses* might pay him peculiar honours. *Spondanus*.

Should a whole host at once discharge the bow,
My well-aim'd shaft with death prevents the foe: 250
Alone superior in the field of *Troy*,
Great *Philoctetes* taught the shaft to fly.
From all the sons of earth unrival'd praise
I justly claim; but yield to better days,
To those fam'd days when great *Alcides* rose,   255
And *Eurytus*, who bade the Gods be foes:
(Vain *Eurytus*, whose art became his crime,
Swept from the earth, he perish'd in his prime;
Sudden th' irremeable way he trod,
Who boldly durst defy the Bowyer God.)   260
In fighting fields as far the spear I throw,
As flies an arrow from the well-drawn bow.
Sole in the race the contest I decline,

---

249.   *Should a whole host at once discharge the bow,*
         My well-aim'd shaft with death prevents the foe.]
There is an ambiguity in the original, and it may imply either, that if *Ulysses* and
his friends were at the same time to aim their arrows against an enemy, his arrow
would fly with more certainty and expedition than that of his companions: Or
that if his enemies had bent all their bows at once against him, yet his shaft would
reach his adversary before they could discharge their arrows. *Eustathius* follows
the former, *Dacier* the latter interpretation. And certainly the latter argues the
greater intrepidity and presence of mind: It shews *Ulysses* in the extremity of
danger capable of acting with calmness and serenity, and shooting with the same
certainty and steddiness, tho' multitudes of enemies endanger his life. I have
follow'd this explication, as it is nobler, and shews *Ulysses* to be a consummate
Heroe.

257. Vain Eurytus.—] This *Eurytus* was King of *Oechalia*, famous for his skill in
Archery; he propos'd his daughter *Iöle* in marriage to any person that could
conquer him at the exercise of the bow. Later writers differ from *Homer*, as
Eustathius observes, concerning *Eurytus*. They write that *Hercules* overcame him,
and he denying his daughter, was slain, and his daughter made captive by
Hercules: Whereas *Homer* writes that he was kill'd by *Apollo*, that is, died a sudden
death, according to the import of that expression. The Antients differ much
about *Oechalia*; some place it in *Eubœa*, and some in *Messenia*, of which opinion
is *Pausanias* ⟨IV (Messenia) ii 2⟩. But *Homer* in the *Iliad* places it in *Thessaly*: For
he mentions with it *Tricca* and *Ithomè*, which as *Dacier* observes were Cities of
Thessaly.

263. *Sole in the race the contest I decline.*] This is directly contrary to his challenge

Stiff are my weary joints; and I resign
By storms and hunger worn: Age well may fail,   265
When storms and hunger both at once assail.
Abash'd, the numbers hear the god-like man,
'Till great *Alcinous* mildly thus began.
Well hast thou spoke, and well thy gen'rous tongue

---

in the beginning of the speech, where he mentions the race amongst the other games. How then is this difference to be reconcil'd? Very naturally. *Ulysses* speaks with a generous warmth and is transported with anger in the beginning of his oration: Here the heat of it is cool'd, and consequently reason takes place, and he has time to reflect, that a man so disabled by calamities is not an equal match for a younger and less fatigued antagonist. This is an exact representation of human nature; when our passions remit, the vehemence of our speech remits; at first he speaks like a man in anger, here like the wise *Ulysses*.

It is observable that *Ulysses* all along maintains a decency and reverence towards the Gods, even while his anger seems to be master over his reason; he gives *Eurytus* as an example of the just vengeance of Heaven, and shews himself in a very opposite light: He is so far from contending with the Gods, that he allows himself to be inferior to some other Heroes: an instance of modesty.

265.   *—Age well may fail,*
                  When storms and hunger—]
This passage appears to me to refer to the late storms and shipwreck, and the long abstinence *Ulysses* suffer'd in sailing from *Calypso* to the *Phæacian* Island; for when *Nausicaa* found him, he was almost dead with hunger, as appears from the sixth of the *Odyssey*. *Dacier* is of a different opinion, and thinks it relates to his abstinence and shipwreck upon his leaving *Circe*, before he came to *Calypso*. This seems very improbable; for *Ulysses* had liv'd seven years with that Goddess in great affluence, and consequently must be suppos'd to have recruited his loss of strength in so long a time, and with the particular care of a Goddess: besides, *Alcinous* was acquainted with his late shipwreck, and his daughter *Nausicaa* was in some degree witness to it: Is it not therefore more probable that he should refer to this latter incident, than speak of a calamity that happened seven years past, to which they were entirely strangers?

Dacier likewise asserts that *Eustathius* is guilty of a mistake, in making κομιδὴ or *provision*, to signify the ship it self; but in reality he makes an evident distinction: Οὐ γὰρ διὰ τὸ μὴ κομιδὴν ἐν βρώμασιν ἔχειν ἐδαμάσθη ᾿Οδυσσεὺς τοῖς κύμασιν, ἀλλ᾿ ὅτι ἐθραύσθη κύμασιν ἡ κομιδὴν ἔχουσα ναῦς; "*Ulysses* suffer'd not in the storm because he had no provisions to eat, but because the ship that bore the provision was broken by the storm;" which shews a wide difference between the vessel and the provisions: So that the expression really implies that the vessel was broken, but *Eustathius* is far from affirming that κομιδή and ναῦς (except in such an improper sense) have the same signification.

With decent pride refutes a public wrong: 270
Warm are thy words, but warm without offence;
Fear only fools, secure in men of sense:
Thy worth is known. Then hear our country's claim,
And bear to heroes our heroic fame;
In distant realms our glorious deeds display,   275
Repeat them frequent in the genial day;
When blest with ease thy woes and wand'rings end,
Teach them thy consort, bid thy sons attend;
How lov'd of *Jove* he crown'd our sires with praise,
How we their offspring dignify our race.   280
    Let other realms the deathful gauntlet wield,
Or boast the glories of th' athletic field;
We in the course unrival'd speed display,
Or thro' cærulean billows plow the way:
To dress, to dance, to sing our sole delight,   285
The feast or bath by day, and love by night:
Rise then ye skill'd in measures: let him bear
Your fame to men that breathe a distant air:
And faithful say, to you the pow'rs belong
To race, to sail, to dance, to chaunt the song.   290
    But, herald, to the palace swift repair,
And the soft Lyre to grace our pastimes bear.
    Swift at the word, obedient to the King
The herald flies the tuneful lyre to bring.

---

275. *In distant realms our glorious deeds display.*] From this extravagant preface, it
might be imagin'd that *Alcinous* was King of a nation of Heroes: Whereas when
he comes to explain the excellence of his subjects, he has scarce any thing to boast
of that is manly; they spend an idle life in singing, dancing, and feasting. Thus
the Poet all along writes consistently: We may know the *Phæacians* by their character, which is always to be voluptuous, or as *Horace* expresses it ⟨*Epist.* I ii 28–9⟩,
                    —*Alcinoique*
        In cute curanda plus æquo operata juventus.
And *Eustathius* rightly observes that the Poet does not teach that we ought to live
such lives, but only relates historically what lives were led by the *Phæacians*; he
describes them as a contemptible people, and consequently proposes them as
objects of our scorn, not imitation.

Up rose nine Seniors, chosen to survey 295
The future games, the judges of the day:
With instant care they mark a spacious round,
And level for the dance th' allotted ground;
The herald bears the Lyre: Intent to play,
The Bard advancing meditates the lay: 300
Skill'd in the dance, tall youths, a blooming band,
Graceful before the heav'nly minstrel stand;
Light-bounding from the earth, at once they rise,
Their feet half-viewless quiver in the skies:
Ulysses gaz'd, astonish'd to survey 305
The glancing splendors as their sandals play.
Mean-time the Bard alternate to the strings

---

301. *Skill'd in the dance*—] I beg leave to translate *Dacier*'s Annotation upon this
passage, and to offer a remark upon it. This description, says that Lady, is
remarkable, not because the dancers mov'd to the sound of the harp and the
song; for in this there is nothing extraordinary: but in that they danc'd, if I may
so express it, an History; that is, by their gestures and movements they express'd
what the music of the harp and voice described, and the dance was a representation of what was the subject of the Poet's song. *Homer* only says they danc'd
divinely, according to the obvious meaning of the words. I fancy Madam *Dacier*
would have forborn her observation, if she had reflected upon the nature of the
song to which the *Phæacians* danc'd: It was an intrigue between *Mars* and *Venus*;
and they being taken in some very odd postures, she must allow that these
dancers represented some very odd gestures, (or movements as she expresses it)
if they were now dancing an History, that is acting in their motions what was the
subject of the song. But I submit to the judgment of Ladies, and shall only add,
that this is an instance how a critical eye can see some things in an Author, that
were never intended by him; tho' to do her justice, she borrowed the general
remark from *Eustathius*.

The words μαρμαρυγὰς θηεῖτο ποδῶν are very expressive, they represent the
quick glancings of their feet in the dance, *Motus pedum coruscans* ⟨evidently
Broome's phrase⟩; or
    The glancing splendors as their sandals play.
307.   —*The Bard alternate to the strings*
    The loves of Mars *and* Cytherea *sings*.]
The Reader may be pleased to look back to the beginning of the book for a
general vindication of this story. *Scaliger* in his *Poetics* ⟨v ii, p. 216 B2⟩ prefers the
song of *Iöpas* in *Virgil* ⟨1 740–6⟩, to this of *Demodocus* in *Homer*; *Demodocus deorum
canit fœditates, noster Iopas res rege dignas*. Monsieur *Dacier* in his Annotations upon

The loves of *Mars* and *Citherea* sings;
How the stern God enamour'd with her charms

Aristotle's Poetics ⟨*La Poëtique d'Aristote . . . avec des Remarques*, Paris, 1692, p. 442⟩ refutes the objection. The song of *Demodocus*, says he, is as well adapted to the inclinations and relish of the *Phæacians*, as the song of *Iopas* is to Queen *Dido*. It may indeed be question'd whether the subject of *Virgil*'s song be well chosen, and whether the deepest points of Philosophy were entirely proper to be sung to a Queen, and her female attendants.

> *The various labours of the wandring Moon,*
> *And whence proceed th' eclipses of the Sun,*
> *Th' original of men and beasts, and whence*
> *The rains arise, and fires their warmth dispence,* &c.
>   Dryden ⟨1 1040–3⟩.

Nor is *Virgil* more reserv'd than *Homer*: In the fourth *Georgic* ⟨345 ff⟩ he introduces a Nymph, who in the Court of the Goddess *Cyrenè* with her Nymphs about her, sings this very song of *Demodocus*.

> *To these* Clymene *the sweet theft declares*
> *Of* Mars; *and* Vulcan's *unavailing cares;*
> *And all the rapes of Gods, and every love*
> *From antient* Chaos *down to youthful* Jove.
>   Dryden ⟨*Geo.* IV 488–91⟩.

So that if either of the Poets are to be blamed, 'tis certainly *Virgil*: but neither of them, adds that Critic, are culpable: *Virgil* understood what a chaste Queen ought to hear before strangers, and what women might say when alone amongst themselves; thus to the Queen he sings a philosophical song, the intrigues of *Mars* and *Venus* amongst Nymphs when they were alone.

   Plutarch ⟨*De Vita et Poesi Homeri* 102⟩ vindicates this story of *Homer*: There is a way of teaching by mute actions, and those very fables that have given most offence, furnish us with useful contemplations: Thus in the story of *Mars* and *Venus*, some have by an unnecessary violence endeavour'd to reduce it into allegory: When *Venus* is in conjunction with the Star called *Mars*, they have an adultrous influence, but time, or the sun, reveals it. But the Poet himself far better explains the meaning of his fable, for he teaches that light music and wanton songs debauch the manners, and incline men to an unmanly way of living in luxury and wantonness.

   In short, *Virgil* mentions this story, *Ovid* translates it ⟨*Metam.* IV 170 ff⟩, *Plutarch* commends it, and *Scaliger* censures it. I will add the judgment of a late Writer, Monsieur *Boileau*, concerning *Scaliger*, in his Notes upon *Longinus*. "That proud scholar, says he, intending to erect altars to *Virgil*, as he expresses it, speaks of *Homer* too prophanely; but it is a book which he calls in part *Hypercritical*, to shew that he transgressed the bounds of true Criticism: That piece was a dishonour to *Scaliger*, and he fell into such gross errors, that he drew upon him the ridicule of all men of letters, and even of his own son" ⟨*Réflexions Critiques*, Conclusion, *Œuvres Complètes*, Paris, 1942, V 113⟩.

Clasp'd the gay panting Goddess in his arms,   310
By bribes seduc'd: and how the Sun, whose eye
Views the broad heav'ns disclos'd the lawless joy.
Stung to the soul, indignant thro' the skies
To his black forge vindictive *Vulcan* flies:
Arriv'd, his sinewy arms incessant place   315
Th' eternal anvil on the massy base.
A wond'rous Net he labours, to betray
The wanton lovers, as entwin'd they lay,
Indissolubly strong! then instant bears
To his immortal dome the finish'd snares.   320
Above, below, around, with art dispread,
The sure enclosure folds the genial bed;
Whose texture ev'n the search of Gods deceives,
Thin, as the filmy threads the spider weaves.
Then as withdrawing from the starry bow'rs,   325
He feigns a journey to the *Lemnian* shores:
His fav'rite Isle! Observant *Mars* descries
His wish'd recess, and to the Goddess flies;
He glows, he burns: The fair-hair'd Queen of love
Descends smooth-gliding from the Courts of *Jove*,   330
Gay blooming in full charms: her hand he prest
With eager joy, and with a sigh addrest.
  Come, my belov'd! and taste the soft delights;
Come, to repose the genial bed invites:
Thy absent spouse neglectful of thy charms   335
Prefers his barb'rous *Sintians* to thy arms!
  Then, nothing loth, the enamour'd fair he led,

336. *Prefers his barb'rous* Sintians *to thy arms.*] The *Sintians* were the inhabitants
of *Lemnos*, by origin *Thracians*: *Homer* calls them barbarous of speech, because
their language was a corruption of the *Greek, Asiatic*, and *Thracian*. But there is a
concealed raillery in the expression, and *Mars* ridicules the ill taste of *Vulcan* for
leaving so beautiful a Goddess to visit his rude and barbarous *Sintians*. The Poet
calls *Lemnos* the favourite Isle of *Vulcan*; this alludes to the subterraneous fires
frequent in that Island, and he is feigned to have his forge there, as the God of
fire. This is likewise the reason why he is said to fall into the Island *Lemnos* when
Jupiter threw him from Heaven. *Dacier.*

And sunk transported on the conscious bed.
Down rush'd the toils, enwrapping as they lay
The careless lovers in their wanton play: 340
In vain they strive, th' entangling snares deny
(Inextricably firm) the pow'r to fly:
Warn'd by the God who sheds the golden day,
Stern *Vulcan* homeward treads the starry way:
Arriv'd, he sees, he grieves, with rage he burns;   345
Full horribly he roars, his voice all heav'n returns.
  O *Jove*, he cry'd, oh all ye pow'rs above,
See the lewd dalliance of the Queen of Love!
Me, aukward me she scorns, and yields her charms
To that fair Lecher, the strong God of arms.   350
If I am lame, that stain my natal hour
By fate impos'd; such me my parent bore:
Why was I born? see how the wanton lies!
O sight tormenting to an husband's eyes!
But yet I trust, this once ev'n *Mars* would fly   355
His fair ones arms—he thinks her, once, too nigh.
But there remain, ye guilty, in my pow'r,
'Till *Jove* refunds his shameless daughter's dow'r.

---

348. *See the lewd dalliance of the Queen of Love.*] The original seems to be corrupted; were it to be translated according to the present editions, it must be, *See
the ridiculous deeds of* Venus. I conceive, that few husbands who should take their
spouses in such circumstances would have any great appetite to laugh; neither
is such an interpretation consonant to the words immediately following, οὐκ
ἐπιεικτά. It is therefore very probable that the verse was originally
Δεῦθ' ἵνα ἔργ' ἀγέλαστα καὶ οὐκ ἐπιεικτὰ ἴδησθε.
Come ye Gods, behold the sad and unsufferable deeds of Venus; and this agrees with the
tenor of *Vulcan's* behaviour in this comedy, who has not the least disposition to be
merry with his brother Deities.

358. *'Till* Jove *refund* ⟨sic⟩ *his shameless daughter's dow'r.*] I doubt not but this
was the usage of antiquity: It has been observed that the bridegroom made presents to the father of the bride, which were call'd ἕδνα; and if she was afterwards
false to his bed, this dower was restored by the father to the husband. Besides this
restitution, there seems a pecuniary mulct to have been paid, as appears evident
from what follows.
—The God of arms,
Must pay the penalty for lawless charms ⟨371–2⟩.

Too dear I priz'd a fair enchanting face:
Beauty unchaste is beauty in disgrace.　　　360
　Mean-while the Gods the dome of *Vulcan* throng,
Apollo comes, and *Neptune* comes along,
With these gay *Hermes* trod the starry plain;
But modesty with-held the Goddess-train.
All heav'n beholds, imprison'd as they lye,　　365
And unextinguish'd laughter shakes the sky.
　Then mutual, thus they spoke: Behold on wrong
Swift vengeance waits: and Art subdues the strong!
Dwells there a God on all th' *Olympian* brow
More swift than *Mars*, and more than *Vulcan* slow?　　370
Yet *Vulcan* conquers, and the God of arms

Homer in this as in many other places seems to allude to the laws of *Athens*, where death was the punishment for adultery. *Pausanias* ⟨IX (Boeotia) xxvi 8⟩ relates that *Draco* the *Athenian* lawgiver granted impunity to any person that took revenge upon an adulterer. Such also was the institution of *Solon* ⟨quoted from Lysias I 49⟩; "If any one seize an adulterer, let him use him as he pleases, ἐάν τις μοιχὸν λάβῃ, ὅτι ἂν βούληται χρῆσθαι. And thus *Eratosthenes* ⟨Lysias I 26; but it is the defendant Euphiletus who speaks thus *to* Eratosthenes⟩ answer'd a person who begg'd his life after he had injur'd his bed, οὐκ ἐγώ σε ἀπο-κτενῶ, ἀλλ' ὁ τῆς πόλεως νόμος, "It is not I who slay thee, but the law of thy country." But still it was in the power of the injur'd person to take a pecuniary mulct by way of attonement; for thus the same *Eratosthenes* speaks in *Lysias* ⟨I 25⟩, ἠντιβόλει καὶ ἱκέτευε μὴ αὐτὸν κτεῖναι, ἀλλ' ἀργύριον πράξασθαι, "he en-treated me not to take his life, but exact a sum of money." Nay, such penalties were allow'd by way of commutation for greater crimes than adultery, as in the case of murder: *Iliad 9.*

　　　　　—If a brother bleed,
　　On just atonement, we remit the deed:
　　A sire the slaughter of his son forgives;
　　The price of blood discharg'd, the murd'rer lives ⟨743–6⟩.
367.　　　　*—Behold on wrong*
　　Swift vengeance waits—]
Plutarch in his dissertation upon reading the Poets ⟨*De Aud. Poet.* 4 (19 D)⟩, quotes this as an instance of *Homer*'s judgment, in closing a ludicrous scene with decency and instruction. He artfully inserts a sentence by which he discovers his own judg-ment, and lets the Reader into the moral of his fables; by this conduct he makes even the representation of evil actions useful, by shewing the shame and detri-ment they draw upon those who are guilty of them.

Must pay the penalty for lawless charms.
   Thus serious they: but he who gilds the skies,
The gay *Apollo* thus to *Hermes* cries.
Wou'dst thou enchain'd like *Mars*, oh *Hermes*, lye,   375
And bear the shame, like *Mars*, to share the joy?
   O envy'd shame! (the smiling Youth rejoin'd,)
Add thrice the chains, and thrice more firmly bind;
Gaze all ye Gods, and ev'ry Goddess gaze,
Yet eager would I bless the sweet disgrace.   380
   Loud laugh the rest, ev'n *Neptune* laughs aloud,
Yet sues importunate to loose the God:
And free, he cries, oh *Vulcan!* free from shame
Thy captives; I ensure the penal claim.
   Will *Neptune* (*Vulcan* then) the faithless trust?   385
He suffers who gives surety for th' unjust:

---

382. Neptune ⟨ . . . ⟩ *sues* ⟨ . . . ⟩ *to loose the God.*] It may be asked why *Neptune* in particular interests himself in the deliverance of *Mars*, rather than the other Gods? *Dacier* confesses she can find no reason for it; but *Eustathius* is of opinion, that *Homer* ascribes it to that God out of decency, and deference to his superior Majesty and Eminence amongst the other Deities: It is suitable to the character of that most ancient, and consequently honourable God, to interrupt such an indecent scene of mirth, which is not so becoming his personage, as those more youthful Deities *Apollo* and *Mercury*. Besides, it agrees well with *Neptune*'s gravity to be the first who is mindful of friendship; so that what is here said of *Neptune* is not accidental, but spoken judiciously by the Poet in honour of that Deity.

386. *He suffers who gives surety for th' unjust.*] This verse is very obscure, and made still more obscure by the explanations of Critics. Some think it implies, that it is wicked to be surety for a wicked person; and therefore *Neptune* should not give his promise for *Mars* thus taken in adultery. Some take it generally; suretyship is detrimental, and it is the lot of unhappy men to be sureties: the words then are to be constru'd in the following order, δειλαί τοι ἐγγύαι, καὶ δειλῶν ἀνδρῶν ἐγγυάασθαι. *Sponsiones sunt infelices, & hominum est infelicium sponsiones dare.* Others understand it very differently, *viz.* to imply that the sureties of men of inferior condition, should be to men of inferior condition; then the sentence will bear this import: If *Mars*, says *Vulcan*, refuses to discharge the penalty, how shall I compell *Neptune* to pay it, who is so greatly my superior? And therefore adds by way of sentence, that the sponsor ought to be of the same station with the person to whom he becomes surety; or in *Latin, simplicium hominum, simplices esse debent sponsores.* I have followed *Plutarch*, who in his banquet of the seven wise men

But say, if that lewd scandal of the sky
To liberty restor'd, perfidious fly,
Say wilt thou bear the Mulct? He instant cries,
The mulct I bear, if *Mars* perfidious flies.   390
    To whom appeas'd: No more I urge delay;
When *Neptune* sues, my part is to obey.
    Then to the snares his force the God applies;
They burst; and *Mars* to *Thrace* indignant flies:
To the soft *Cyprian* shores the Goddess moves,   395
To visit *Paphos* and her blooming groves,
Where to the pow'r an hundred altars rise,
And breathing odours scent the balmy skies.
Conceal'd she bathes in consecrated bow'rs,
The Graces unguents shed, ambrosial show'rs,   400
Unguents that charm the Gods! she last assumes
Her wond'rous robes; and full the Goddess blooms.
    Thus sung the Bard: *Ulysses* hears with joy,
And loud applauses rend the vaulted sky.
    Then to the sports his sons the King commands,   405
Each blooming youth before the monarch stands:
In dance unmatch'd! a wond'rous ball is brought,
(The work of *Polybus*, divinely wrought)
This youth with strength enormous bids it fly,

⟨*Sept. Sap. Conviv.* 21 (164 B)⟩, explains it to signify that it is dangerous to be surety for a wicked person, according to the ancient sentence, ἐγγύα, πάρα δ᾽ ἄτη. *Loss follows suretyship.* Agreeably to the opinion of a much wiser person, *He that is surety for a stranger shall smart for it; and he that hateth suretyship is sure.* Prov. xi. 15.

394.   —Mars *to* Thrace *indignant flies:*
          To the soft Cyprian *shores the Goddess moves.*]
There is a reason for this particularity: The *Thracians* were a warlike people; the Poet therefore sends the God of War thither: and the people of *Cyprus* being effeminate, and addicted to love and pleasures, he feigns the recess of the *Goddess of Love* to have been in that Island. It is further observable, that he barely mentions the retreat of *Mars*, but dwells more largely upon the story of *Venus*. The reason is, the *Phæacians* had no delight in the God of War, but the soft description of *Venus* better suited with their inclinations. *Eustathius.*

And bending backward whirls it to the sky; 410
His brother springing with an active bound
At distance intercepts it from the ground:
The ball dismiss'd, in dance they skim the strand,
Turn and return, and scarce imprint the sand.
Th' assembly gazes with astonish'd eyes, 415
And sends in shouts applauses to the skies.
   Then thus *Ulysses*; Happy King, whose name
The brightest shines in all the rolls of fame:
In subjects happy! with surprize I gaze;
Thy praise was just; their skill transcends thy praise. 420
   Pleas'd with his people's fame the Monarch hears,
And thus benevolent accosts the Peers.
Since Wisdom's sacred guidance he pursues,
Give to the stranger-guest a stranger's dues:
Twelve Princes in our realm dominion share, 425
O'er whom supreme, imperial pow'r I bear:
Bring gold, a pledge of love, a talent bring,

---

410. *And bending backward whirls it to the sky.*] This is a literal translation of ἰδνωθεὶς ὀπίσω; and it gives us a lively image of a person in the act of throwing towards the skies. *Eustathius* is most learnedly trifling about this exercise of the ball, which was called οὐρανία, or *aëreal*; it was a kind of a dance, and while they sprung from the ground to catch the ball, they play'd with their feet in the air after the manner of dancers. He reckons up several other exercises at the ball, ἀπόρραξις, φαινίνδα, ἐπίσκυρος, and θερμαυστρίς; and explains them all largely. *Homer* seems to oppose this aëreal dance to the common one, ποτὶ χθονί, or *on the ground*, which appears to be added to make an evident distinction between the sports; otherwise it is unnecessary; and to dance upon the ground is imply'd in ὠρχείσθην, for how should a dance be perform'd but upon the ground?

420. *Thy praise was just*—] The original says, You promis'd that your subjects were excellent dancers, ἀπείλησας; that is, *threaten'd*: *Minans* is used in the same sense by the *Latins*, as *Dacier* observes; thus *Horace* ⟨*Serm.* II iii 9⟩,
                    Multa & præclara minantem.
Eustathius remarks, that the address of *Ulysses* is very artful, he calls it a seasonable flattery: In reality to excel in dancing, is but to excel in trifles, but in the opinion of *Alcinous* it was a most noble qualification: *Ulysses* therefore pleases his vanity by adapting his praise to his notions; and that which would have been an affront in some nations, is esteem'd as the highest compliment by *Alcinous*.

A vest, a robe, and imitate your King:
Be swift to give; that he this night may share
The social feast of joy, with joy sincere.   430
And thou, *Euryalus*, redeem thy wrong:
A gen'rous heart repairs a sland'rous tongue.
    Th' assenting Peers, obedient to the King,
In haste their heralds send the gifts to bring.
Then thus *Euryalus*: O Prince, whose sway   435
Rules this blest realm, repentant I obey!
Be his this sword, whose blade of brass displays
A ruddy gleam; whose hilt, a silver blaze;
Whose ivory sheath inwrought with curious pride,
Adds graceful terror to the wearer's side.   440
    He said, and to his hand the sword consign'd;
And if, he cry'd, my words affect thy mind,
Far from thy mind those words, ye whirlwinds bear,
And scatter them, ye storms, in empty air!
Crown, oh ye heav'ns, with joy his peaceful hours,   445
And grant him to his spouse and native shores!
    And blest be thou my friend, *Ulysses* cries,
Crown him with ev'ry joy, ye fav'ring skies;
To thy calm hours continu'd peace afford,
And never, never may'st thou want this sword!   450
    He said, and o'er his shoulder flung the blade.
Now o'er the earth ascends the evening shade:
The precious gifts th' illustrious heralds bear,

---

450. *And never, never may'st thou want this sword.*] It can scarce be imagin'd how
greatly this beautiful passage is misrepresented by *Eustathius*. He would have it to
imply, *May I never want this sword*, taking τοὶ adverbially: The presents of enemies
were reckon'd fatal, *Ulysses* therefore to avert the omen, prays that he may never
have occasion to have recourse to this sword of *Euryalus*, but keep it amongst his
treasures as a testimony of this reconciliation. This appears to be a very forc'd
interpretation, and disagreeable to the general import of the rest of the sentence;
he addresses to *Euryalus*, to whom then can this compliment be naturally paid but
to *Euryalus*? *Thou hast given me a sword*, says he, *may thy days be so peaceable as never to
want it!* This is an instance of the polite address, and the forgiving temper, of
Ulysses.

And to the court th' embody'd Peers repair.
Before the Queen *Alcinous*' sons unfold   455
The vests, the robes, and heaps of shining gold;
Then to the radiant thrones they move in state:
Aloft, the King in pomp Imperial sate.
    Thence to the Queen. O partner of our reign,
O sole belov'd! command thy menial train   460
A polish'd chest and stately robes to bear,
And healing waters for the bath prepare:
That bath'd, our guest may bid his sorrows cease,
Hear the sweet song, and taste the feast in peace.
A bowl that flames with gold, of wond'rous frame,   465
Our self we give, memorial of our name:
To raise in off'rings to almighty *Jove*,
And every God that treads the courts above.
    Instant the Queen, observant of the King,
Commands her train a spacious vase to bring,   470
The spacious vase with ample streams suffice,
Heap high the wood, and bid the flames arise.
The flames climb round it with a fierce embrace,
The fuming waters bubble o'er the blaze.
Her self the chest prepares: in order roll'd   475
The robes, the vests are rang'd, and heaps of gold:
And adding a rich dress inwrought with art
A gift expressive of her bounteous heart,
Thus spoke to *Ithacus:* To guard with bands
Insolvable these gifts, thy care demands: 480
Lest, in thy slumbers on the watry main,
The hand of Rapine make our bounty vain.
    Then bending with full force, around he roll'd
A labyrinth of bands in fold on fold,
Clos'd with *Circæan* art. A train attends   485

485. *Clos'd with* Circæan *art*—] Such passages as these have more of nature than
art, and are too narrative, and different from modern ways of speaking, to be
capable of much ornament in Poetry. *Eustathius* observes that keys were not in

Around the bath: the bath the King ascends:
(Untasted joy, since that disastrous hour,
He sail'd ill-fated from *Calypso*'s bow'r)
Where happy as the Gods that range the sky,
He feasted ev'ry sense, with ev'ry joy.   490
He bathes: the damsels with officious toil,
Shed sweets, shed unguents, in a show'r of oil:
Then o'er his limbs a gorgeous robe he spreads,
And to the feast magnificently treads.
Full where the dome its shining valves expands,   495
Nausicaa blooming as a Goddess stands,
With wond'ring eyes the heroe she survey'd,
And graceful thus began the royal maid.
    Hail god-like stranger! and when heav'n restores
To thy fond wish thy long-expected shores,   500
This ever grateful in remembrance bear,
To me thou ow'st, to me, the vital air.
    O royal maid, *Ulysses* strait returns,
Whose worth the splendors of thy race adorns,
So may dread *Jove* (whose arm in vengeance forms   505
The writhen bolt, and blackens heav'n with storms,)
Restore me safe, thro' weary wand'rings tost,
To my dear country's ever-pleasing coast,

---

use in these ages, but were afterwards invented by the *Lacedæmonians*; but they used to bind their carriages with intricate knots: Thus the *Gordian* knot was famous in antiquity. And this knot of *Ulysses* became a proverb, to express any insolvable difficulty, ὁ τοῦ ᾽Οδυσσέως δεσμός: This is the reason why he is said to have learned it from *Circe*; it was of great esteem amongst the Ancients, and not being capable to be unty'd by human art, the invention of it is ascrib'd, not to a man, but to a Goddess.

    A Poet would now appear ridiculous if he should introduce a Goddess only to teach his Heroe such an art, as to tye a knot with intricacy: but we must not judge of what has been, from what now is; customs and arts are never at a stay, and consequently the ideas of customs and arts are as changeable as those arts and customs: This knot in all probability was in as high estimation formerly, as the finest watchwork or machines are at this day; and were a person fam'd for an uncommon skill in such works, it would be no absurdity in the language of poetry, to ascribe his knowledge in them to the assistance of a Deity.

L

As while the spirit in this bosom glows,
To thee, my Goddess, I address my vows,   510
My life, thy gift I boast! He said, and sate
Fast by *Alcinous* on a throne of state.
Now each partakes the feast, the wine prepares,
Portions the food, and each his portion shares.
The Bard an herald guides: the gazing throng   515
Pay low obeysance as he moves along:
Beneath a sculptur'd arch he sits enthron'd,
The Peers encircling form an awful round.
Then from the chine, *Ulysses* carves with art
Delicious food, an honorary part;   520
This, let the Master of the Lyre receive,
A pledge of love! 'tis all a wretch can give.
Lives there a man beneath the spacious skies,
Who sacred honours to the Bard denies?
The Muse the Bard inspires, exalts his mind;   525
The Muse indulgent loves th' harmonious kind:

510. *To thee, my Goddess, I address my vows.*] This may seem an extravagant compliment, especially in the mouth of the wise *Ulysses*, and rather prophane than polite. *Dacier* commends it as the highest piece of address and gallantry; but perhaps it may want explication to reconcile it to decency. *Ulysses* only speaks comparatively, and with relation to that one action of her saving his life: "As therefore, says he, I owe my thanks to the Heavens for giving me life originally, so I ought to pay my thanks to thee for preserving it; thou hast been to me as a Deity. To preserve a life, is in one sense to give it." If this appears not to soften the expression sufficiently, it may be ascribed to an overflow of gratitude in the generous disposition of *Ulysses*; he is so touch'd with the memory of her benevolence and protection, that his soul labours for an expression great enough to represent it, and no wonder if in this struggle of thought, his words fly out into an excessive but laudable boldness.

519. *—From the chine* Ulysses *carves with art.*] Were this literally to be translated, it would be, that *Ulysses* cut a piece from the chine of the white-tooth'd boar, round which there was much fat. This looks like Burlesque to a person unacquainted with the usages of Antiquity: But it was the highest honour that could be paid to *Demodocus*. The greatest Heroes in the *Iliad* are thus rewarded after victory, and it was esteem'd an equivalent for all dangers. So that what *Ulysses* here offers to the Poet, is offer'd out of a particular regard and honour to his Poetry.

The herald to his hand the charge conveys,
Not fond of flattery, nor unpleas'd with praise.
    When now the rage of hunger was allay'd,
Thus to the Lyrist wise *Ulysses* said.   530
O more than man! thy soul the Muse inspires,
Or *Phœbus* animates with all his fires:
For who by *Phœbus* uninform'd, could know
The woe of *Greece*, and sing so well the woe?
Just to the tale, as present at the fray,   535
Or taught the labours of the dreadful day:
The song recals past horrours to my eyes,
And bids proud *Ilion* from her ashes rise.
Once more harmonious strike the sounding string,
Th' *Epæan* fabric, fram'd by *Pallas*, sing: 540
How stern *Ulysses*, furious to destroy,
With latent heroes sack'd imperial *Troy*.
If faithful thou record the tale of fame,
The God himself inspires thy breast with flame:
And mine shall be the task, henceforth to raise   545

---

531.   *—Thy soul the Muse inspires,*
                   Or Phœbus *animates with all his fires.*]

Ulysses here ascribes the songs of *Demodocus* to immediate inspiration; and *Apollo* is made the patron of the Poets, as *Eustathius* observes, because he is the God of Prophecy. He adds, that *Homer* here again represents himself in the person of *Demodocus*: it is he who wrote the war of *Troy* with as much faithfulness, as if he had been present at it; it is he who had little or no assistance from former relations of that story, and consequently receives it from *Apollo* and the *Muses*. This is a secret but artful insinuation that we are not to look upon the *Iliad* as all fiction and fable, but in general as a real history, related with as much certainty as if the Poet had been present at those memorable actions.

    Plutarch in his chapter of reading Poems ⟨*De Aud. Poet.* 4 (20 A)⟩ admires the conduct of *Homer*, with relation to *Ulysses*: He diverts *Demodocus* from idle fables, and gives him a noble theme, the destruction of *Troy*. Such subjects suit well with the sage character of *Ulysses*. It is for the same reason that he here passes over in silence the amour of *Mars* and *Venus*, and commends the song at the beginning of this book, concerning the contention of the Worthies before *Troy*: An instruction, what songs a wise man ought to hear, and that Poets should recite nothing but what may be heard by a wise man.

In ev'ry land, thy monument of praise.
    Full of the God he rais'd his lofty strain,
How the *Greeks* rush'd tumultuous to the main:
How blazing tents illumin'd half the skies,
While from the shores the winged navy flies: 550
How ev'n in *Ilion*'s walls, in deathful bands,
Came the stern *Greeks* by *Troy*'s assisting hands:
All *Troy* up-heav'd the steed: of diff'ring mind,
Various the *Trojans* counsell'd; part consign'd
The monster to the sword, part sentence gave   555
To plunge it headlong in the whelming wave;
Th' unwise award to lodge it in the tow'rs,
An off'ring sacred to th' immortal pow'rs:
Th' unwise prevail, they lodge it in the walls,
And by the Gods decree proud *Ilion* falls;   560

---

554. *Various the* Trojans *counsell'd*—] It is observable that the Poet gives us only
the heads of this song, and though he had an opportunity to expatiate and introduce a variety of noble Images, by painting the fall of *Troy*, yet this being foreign
to his story, he judiciously restrains his fancy, and passes on to the more immediate actions of the *Odyssey*. *Virgil, lib.* 2 ⟨35–9⟩ of his *Æneis*, has translated these
verses.

> Scinditur incertum studia in contraria vulgus,
> At Capys, & quorum melior sententia menti,
> Aut Pelago Danaum insidias suspectaque dona
> Præcipitare jubent, subjectisque urere flammis:
> Aut terebrare cavas uteri & tentare latebras.

Scaliger ⟨v iii, p. 220 b2⟩ prefers these before those of *Homer*, and says, that
Homer trifles in describing so particularly the divisions of the *Trojan* councils:
That *Virgil* chuses to burn the horse, rather than describe it as thrown from the
rocks: For how should the *Trojans* raise it thither? Such objections are scarce
worthy of a serious answer, for it is no difficulty to imagine that the same men
who heaved this machine into *Troy*, should be able to raise it upon a rock: And as
for the former objection, *Virgil* recites almost the same divisions in council as
Homer, nay borrows them, with little variation.

Aristotle ⟨*Poetics* xvi 8⟩ observes the great art of *Homer*, in naturally bringing
about the discovery of *Ulysses* to *Alcinous* by this song. He calls this a Remembrance; that is, when a present object stirs up a past image in the memory, as a
picture recalls the figure of an absent friend; thus *Ulysses* hearing *Demodocus* sing
to the harp his former hardships, breaks out into tears, and these tears bring
about his discovery.

Destruction enters in the treach'rous wood,
And vengeful slaughter, fierce for human blood.
  He sung the *Greeks* stern-issuing from the steed,
How *Ilion* burns, how all her fathers bleed:
How to thy dome, *Deiphobus!* ascends   565
The *Spartan* King; how *Ithacus* attends,
(Horrid as *Mars*) and how with dire alarms
He fights, subdues: for *Pallas* strings his arms.
  Thus while he sung, *Ulysses'* griefs renew,
Tears bathe his cheeks, and tears the ground bedew: 570
As some fond matron views in mortal fight
Her husband falling in his country's right:
Frantic thro' clashing swords she runs, she flies,
As ghastly pale he groans, and faints, and dies;
Close to his breast she grovels on the ground,   575
And bathes with floods of tears the gaping wound;
She cries, she shrieks: the fierce insulting foe
Relentless mocks her violence of woe,
To chains condemn'd as wildly she deplores,
A widow, and a slave, on foreign shores!   580

---

571. *As some fond matron*—] This is undoubtedly a very moving and beautiful
comparison; but it may be ask'd if it be proper to compare so great a Heroe as
Ulysses to a woman, the weakness of whose sex justifies her tears? Besides she
appears to have a sufficient cause for her sorrows, as being under the greatest
calamities, but why should *Ulysses* weep? Nothing but his valour and success is
recorded, and why should this be an occasion of sorrow? *Eustathius* replies, that
they who think that *Ulysses* is compared to the matron, mistake the point of the
comparison: Whereas the tears alone of *Ulysses* are intended to be compared to
the tears of the matron. It is the sorrow of the two persons, not the persons themselves, that is represented in the comparison. But there appears no sufficient
cause for the tears of *Ulysses*; this objection would not have been made, if the
subject of the song had been consider'd; it sets before his eyes all the calamities of
a long war, all the scenes of slaughter of friends and enemies that he had beheld in
it: It is also to be remember'd, that we have only the abridgment of the song, and
yet we see spectacles of horror, blood, and commiseration. Tears discover a
tender, not an abject spirit. *Achilles* is not less a Heroe for weeping over the ashes
of *Patroclus*, nor *Ulysses* for lamenting the calamities and deaths of thousands of
his friends.

So from the sluices of *Ulysses'* eyes
Fast fell the tears, and sighs succeeded sighs:
Conceal'd he griev'd: the King observ'd alone
The silent tear, and heard the secret groan;
Then to the Bard aloud: O cease to sing,   585
Dumb be thy voice, and mute the tuneful string:
To ev'ry note his tears responsive flow,
And his great heart heaves with tumultuous woe;
Thy Lay too deeply moves: then cease the lay,
And o'er the banquet every heart be gay: 590
This social right demands: for him the sails
Floating in air, invite th' impelling gales:
His are the gifts of love: The wise and good
Receive the stranger as a brother's blood.
But, friend, discover faithful what I crave,   595
Artful concealment ill becomes the brave:
Say what thy birth, and what the name you bore,
Impos'd by parents in the natal hour?
(For from the natal hour distinctive names,
One common right, the great and lowly claims:)   600
Say from what city, from what regions tost,
And what inhabitants those regions boast?
So shalt thou instant reach the realm assign'd,
In wond'rous ships self-mov'd, instinct with mind;

---

604. *In wond'rous ships self-mov'd, instinct with mind.*] There is not a passage that
more outrages all the rules of credibility than the description of these ships of
Alcinous. The Poet inserts these wonders only to shew the great dexterity of the
Phæacians in navigation; and indeed it was necessary to be very full in the
description of their skill, who were to convey *Ulysses* home in despight of the very
God of the Ocean. It is for the same reason that they are describ'd as sailing
almost invisibly, to escape the notice of that God. Antiquity animated every
thing in Poetry; thus *Argo* is said to have had a mast made of *Dodonæan* oak,
indued with the faculty of speech. But this is defending one absurdity, by instan-
cing in a fable equally absurd; all that can be said in defence of it is, that such
extravagant fables were believ'd, at least by the vulgar, in former ages; and consequently might be introduced without blame in Poetry; if so, by whom could a
boast of this nature be better made, than by a vain *Phæacian*? Besides, these extra-

No helm secures their course, no pilot guides,   605
Like man intelligent, they plow the tides,
Conscious of every coast, and every bay,
That lies beneath the sun's all-seeing ray;
Tho' clouds and darkness veil th' encumber'd sky,
Fearless thro' darkness and thro' clouds they fly: 610
Tho' tempests rage, tho' rolls the swelling main,
The seas may roll, the tempests rage in vain.
Ev'n the stern God that o'er the waves presides,
Safe as they pass, and safe repass the tides,
With fury burns; while careless they convey   615
Promiscuous every guest to every bay.
These ears have heard my royal Sire disclose
A dreadful story big with future woes,
How *Neptune* rag'd, and how by his command

vagancies let *Ulysses* into the humour of the *Phæacians*, and in the following books
he adapts his story to it, and returns fable for fable. It must likewise certainly be
a great encouragement to *Ulysses* to find himself in such hands as could so easily
restore him to his country; for it was natural to conclude, that though *Alcinous*
was guilty of great amplification, yet that his subjects were very expert navigators.

619.   —*how by his command*
                        Firm-rooted in the surge a ship should stand.]
The Antients, as *Eustathius* observes, mark these verses with an Obelisk and
Asterism. The Obelisk shew'd that they judg'd what relates to the oracle was mis-
placed, the Asterism denoted that they thought the verses very beautiful. For
they thought it not probable that *Alcinous* would have call'd to memory this
prediction and the menace of *Neptune*, and yet persisted to conduct to his own
country the enemy of that Deity: Whereas if this oracle be supposed to be forgotten by *Alcinous*, (as it will, if these verses be taken away) then there will be an
appearance of truth, that he who was a friend to all strangers, should be persuaded to land so great and worthy a Heroe as *Ulysses* in his own dominions, and
therefore they reject them to the 13th of the *Odyssey*. But as *Eustathius* observes,
Alcinous immediately subjoins,
                        But this the Gods may frustrate or fulfill,
                        As suits the purpose of th' eternal will. ⟨623–4⟩
And therefore the verses may be very proper in this book, for *Alcinous* believes
that the Gods might be prevailed upon not to fulfill this denunciation. It has been
likewise remark'd that the conduct of *Alcinous* is very justifiable: The *Phæacians*

Firm-rooted in the surge a ship should stand   620
A monument of wrath: how mound on mound
Should bury these proud tow'rs beneath the ground.
But this the Gods may frustrate or fulfill,
As suits the purpose of th' eternal will.
But say thro' what waste regions hast thou stray'd,   625
What customs noted, and what coasts survey'd?
Possest by wild barbarians fierce in arms,
Or men, whose bosom tender pity warms?

---

had been warn'd by an oracle, that an evil threaten'd them for the care they
should shew to a stranger; yet they forbear not to perform an act of piety to
Ulysses, being persuaded that men ought to do their duty, and trust the issue to
the goodness of the Gods. This will seem to be more probable, if we remember
Alcinous is ignorant that *Ulysses* is the person intended by the prediction, so that
he is not guilty of a voluntary opposition to the Gods, but really acts with piety in
assisting his guest, and only complies with the common laws of hospitality.

It is but a conjecture, yet it is not without probability, that there was a rock
which look'd like a vessel, in the entrance of the haven of the *Phæacians*: the fable
may be built upon this foundation, and because it was environ'd by the ocean,
the transformation might be abscrib'd to the God of it.

621.   *—How mound on mound*
                        Should bury these proud tow'rs beneath the ground.]

The *Greek* word is ἀμφικαλύψειν, which does not necessarily imply that the city
should be buried actually, but that a mountain should surround it, or cover it
round; and in the 13th book we find that when the ship was transformed into a
rock, the city continues out of danger. *Eustathius* is fully of opinion, that the city
was threaten'd to be overwhelm'd by a mountain; the Poet, says he, invents this
fiction to prevent posterity from searching after this Isle of the *Phæacians*, and to
preserve his story from detection of falsification; after the same manner as he
introduces *Neptune* and the rivers of *Troy*, bearing away the wall which the *Greeks*
had rais'd as a fortification before their navy. But *Dacier*, in the omissions which
she inserts at the end of the second volume of her *Odyssey*, is of a contrary opinion,
for the mountain is not said to cover the city, but to threaten to cover it: as
appears from the 13th book of the *Odyssey*, where *Alcinous* commands a sacrifice to
the Gods to avert the execution of this denunciation.

But the difference in reality is small, the city is equally threaten'd to be buried
as the vessel to be transform'd; and therefore *Alcinous* might pronounce the same
fate to both, since both were threaten'd equally by the prediction; it was indeed
impossible for him to speak after any other manner, for he only repeats the words
of the oracle, and cannot foresee that the sacrifice of the *Phæacians* would appease
the anger of *Neptune*.

Say why the fate of *Troy* awak'd thy cares,
Why heav'd thy bosom, and why flow'd thy tears?   630
Just are the ways of heav'n : From heav'n proceed
The woes of man; heav'n doom'd the *Greeks* to bleed,
A theme of future song! Say then if slain
Some dear-lov'd brother press'd the *Phrygian* plain?
Or bled some friend? who bore a brother's part,   635
And claim'd by merit, not by blood, the heart.

635.   *Or bled some friend? who bore a brother's part,*
                And claim'd by merit, not by blood, the heart.]
This excellent sentence of *Homer* at once guides us in the choice, and instructs us
in the regard, that is to be paid to the person of a Friend. If it be lawful to judge
of a man from his writings, *Homer* had a soul susceptible of real friendship, and
was a lover of sincerity. It would be endless to take notice of every casual instruction inserted in the *Odyssey*; but such sentences show *Homer* to have been a man
of an amiable character, as well as excellent in Poetry: The great abhorrence he
had of Lies cannot be more strongly exprest than in those two passages in the
ninth *Iliad* ⟨312 ff⟩, and in the 14th *Odyssey* ⟨156 ff⟩: In the first of which he
makes the man of the greatest soul, *Achilles*, bear testimony to his aversion of them;
and in the latter declares, that "the poorest man, tho' compell'd by the utmost
necessity, ought not to stoop to such a practice". In this place he shews that worth
creates a kind of relation, and that we are to look upon a worthy friend, as a
brother.

   This book takes up the whole thirty third day, and part of the evening: for the
council opens in the morning, and at sun setting the *Phæacians* return to the
Palace from the games; after which *Ulysses* bathes and sups, and spends some
time of the evening in discoursing, and hearing the songs of *Demodocus*. Then
Alcinous requests him to relate his own story, which he begins in the next book,
and continues it thro' the four subsequent books of the *Odyssey*.

L*

THE

NINTH BOOK

OF THE

ODYSSEY.

The ARGUMENT.

The Adventures of the Cicones, Lotophagi, *and*
Cyclops.

Ulysses *begins the relation of his adventures; how after the destruction of*
Troy, *he made an incursion on the* Cicones, *by whom they were repuls'd;*
and meeting with a storm, were driven to the coast of the Lotophagi.
From thence they sail'd to the land of the Cyclops, *whose manners and*
situation are particularly characteris'd. The Giant Polyphemus *and his*
cave describ'd; the usage Ulysses *and his companions met there; and*
lastly, the method and artifice by which he escaped.

THEN thus *Ulysses*. Thou, whom first in sway
As first in virtue, these thy realms obey!
How sweet the products of a peaceful reign?

As we are now come to the Episodical part of the *Odyssey*, it may be thought
necessary to speak something of the nature of Episodes.

As the action of the Epic is always one, entire, and great Action; so the most
trivial Episodes must be so interwoven with it, as to be necessary parts, or convenient, as Mr. *Dryden* observes ⟨*Dedication of the Aeneis, Essays*, ed. Ker, II 154⟩,
to carry on the main design: either so necessary, as without them the Poem must
be imperfect, or so convenient, that no others can be imagin'd more suitable to
the place in which they stand: There is nothing to be left void in a firm building,
even the cavities ought not to be fill'd up with rubbish destructive to the strength
of it, but with materials of the same kind, tho' of less pieces, and fitted to the
main fabric.

Aristotle tells us, that what is comprehended in the first platform of the fable
is proper, the rest is Episode ⟨*Poetics* XVII 5–11⟩: Let us examine the *Odyssey* by
this rule: The groundwork of the Poem is, a Prince absent from his country
several years, *Neptune* hinders his return, yet at last he breaks thro' all obstacles,

Plate 8 Kent's headpiece for *Odyssey* IX in Pope's quarto

and returns, where he finds great disorders, the Authors of which he punishes, and restores peace to his kingdoms. This is all that is essential to the model; this the Poet is not at liberty to change; this is so necessary, that any alteration destroys the design, spoils the fable, and makes another Poem of it. But Episodes are changeable; for instance, tho' it was necessary that *Ulysses* being absent should spend several years with foreign Princes, yet it was not necessary that one of these Princes should be *Antiphates*, another *Alcinous*, or that *Circe* or *Calypso* should be the persons who entertain'd him: It was in the Poet's choice to have chang'd these persons and states, without changing his design or fable. Thus tho' these adventures or Episodes become parts of the subject after they are chosen, yet they are not originally essential to the subject. But in what sense then are they necessary? The reply is, Since the absence of *Ulysses* was absolutely necessary, it follows that not being at home, he must be in some other country; and therefore tho' the Poet was at liberty to make use of none of these particular adventures, yet it was not in his choice to make use of none at all; if these had been omitted, he must have substituted others, or else he would have omitted part of the matter contain'd in his model, *viz.* the adventures of a person long absent from his country; and the Poem would have been defective. So that Episodes are not actions, but parts of an action. It is in Poetry, as *Aristotle* observes ⟨*Poetics* VI 19–21⟩, as in Painting; a Painter puts many actions into one piece, but they all conspire to form one entire and perfect Action: A Poet likewise uses many Episodes, but all those Episodes taken separately finish nothing, they are but imperfect members, which all together make one and the same action, like the parts of a human body, they all conspire to constitute the whole man.

In a word, the Episodes of *Homer* are compleat Episodes; they are proper to the subject, because they are drawn from the ground of the fable; they are so joyn'd to the principal action, that one is the necessary consequence of the other, either truly or probably: and lastly, they are imperfect members which do not make a compleat and finish'd body; for an Episode that makes a compleat action, cannot be part of a principal action, as is essential to all Episodes.

An Episode may then be defin'd, "a necessary part of an action, extended by probable circumstances." They are part of an action, for they are not added to the principal action, but only dilate and amplify that principal action: Thus the Poet to shew the sufferings of *Ulysses* brings in the several Episodes of *Polyphemus*, *Scylla*, the *Sirens*, &c. But why should the words "extended by probable circumstances" enter the definition? Because the Sufferings of *Ulysses* are propos'd in the model of the Fable in general only, but by relating the circumstances, the manner how he suffer'd is discover'd, and this connects it with the principal action, and shews very evidently the necessary relation the Episode bears to the main design of the *Odyssey*. What I have said I hope plainly discovers the difference between the Episodic and Principal action, as well as the nature of Episodes. See *Bossu* more largely upon this subject ⟨II ii–vi⟩.

3. *How sweet the products of a peaceful reign*, &c.] This passage has given great joy to the Critics, as it has afforded them the ill-natur'd pleasure of railing, and the satisfaction of believing they have found a fault in a good Writer. It is fitter, say

they, for the mouth of *Epicurus* than for the sage *Ulysses*, to extol the pleasures of feasting and drinking in this manner: He whom the Poet proposes as the standard of human Wisdom, says *Rapin*, suffers himself to be made drunk by the *Phæacians* ⟨Comparaison vii, 1 123⟩. But it may rather be imagin'd, that the Critic was not very sober when he made the reflection; for there is not the least appearance of a reason for that imputation. *Plato* indeed in his third book *de Repub.* ⟨390 B⟩ writes, that what *Ulysses* here speaks is no very proper example of temperance: but every body knows that *Plato*, with respect to *Homer*, wrote with great partiality. *Athenæus* in his 12th book ⟨513 B–C⟩ gives us the following interpretation. *Ulysses* accommodates his discourse to the present occasion; he in appearance approves of the voluptuous lives of the *Phæacians*, and having heard *Alcinous* before say, that feasting and singing, &c. was their supreme delight: he by a seasonable flattery seems to comply with their inclinations: it being the most proper method to attain his desires of being convey'd to his own country. He compares *Ulysses* to the *Polypus*, which is fabled to assume the colour of every rock to which he approaches: Thus *Sophocles* ⟨Pearson, frag. 289⟩,

Νόει πρὸς ἀνδρὶ σῶμα ⟨χρῶμα⟩ πουλύπους, ὅπως
Πέτρᾳ τραπέσθαι γνησίου φρονήματος.

That is, "In your accesses to mankind observe the *Polypus*, and adapt your self to the humour of the person to whom you apply." *Eustathius* observes that this passage has been condemn'd, but he defends it after the very same way with *Athenæus*.

It is not impossible but there may be some compliance with the nature and manners of the *Phæacians*, especially because *Ulysses* is always describ'd as an artful man, not without some mixture of dissimulation: But it is no difficult matter to take the passage literally, and yet give it an irreproachable sense. *Ulysses* had gone thro' innumerable calamities, he had liv'd to see a great part of *Europe* and *Asia* laid desolate by a bloody war; and after so many troubles, he arrives among a nation that was unacquainted with all the miseries of war, where all the people were happy, and pass'd their lives in ease and pleasures: this calm life fills him with admiration, and he artfully praises what he found praise-worthy in it; namely, the entertainments and music, and passes over the gallantries of the people, as *Dacier* observes, without any mention. *Maximus Tyrius* fully vindicates *Homer*. It is my opinion, says that Author, that the Poet, by representing these guests in the midst of their entertainment, delighted with the song and music, intended to recommend a more noble pleasure than eating or drinking, such a pleasure as a wise man may imitate, by approving the better part, and rejecting the worse, and chusing to please the ear rather than the belly. 12 *Dissert.* ⟨*Diss.* xxii 2 (Teubner)⟩.

If we understand the passage otherwise, the meaning may be this. I am persauded, says *Ulysses*, that the most agreeable end which a King can propose, is to see a whole nation in universal joy, when music and feasting are in every house, when plenty is on every table, and wines to entertain every guest; This to me appears a state of the greatest felicity.

In this sense *Ulysses* pays *Alcinous* a very agreeable compliment; as it is cer-

The heav'n-taught Poet, and enchanting strain:
The well-fill'd palace, the perpetual feast,   5
A land rejoycing, and a people blest.
How goodly seems it, ever to employ
Man's social days in union, and in joy?
The plenteous board high-heap'd with cates divine,
And o'er the foaming bowl the laughing wine.   10
    Amid these joys, why seeks thy mind to know
Th' unhappy series of a wand'rer's woe?
Remembrance sad, whose image to review
Alas! must open all my wounds anew.
And oh, what first, what last shall I relate,   15
Of woes unnumber'd, sent by Heav'n and Fate?
    Know first the man (tho' now a wretch distrest)
Who hopes thee, Monarch! for his future guest.
Behold *Ulysses!* no ignoble name,

---

tainly the most glorious aim of a King to make his subjects happy, and diffuse an universal joy thro' his dominions: He must be a rigid Censor indeed who blames such pleasures as these, which have nothing contrary in them to Virtue and strict Morality; especially as they here bear a beautiful opposition to all the horrors which *Ulysses* had seen in the wars of *Troy,* and shew *Phæacia* as happy as *Troy* was miserable. I will only add, that this agrees with the oriental way of speaking; and in the Poetical parts of the Scriptures, the voice of melody, feasting, and dancing, are used to express the happiness of a nation.

19. *Behold* Ulysses!—] The Poet begins with declaring the name of *Ulysses*: the *Phæacians* had already been acquainted with it by the song of *Demodocus,* and therefore it could not fail of raising the utmost attention and curiosity (as *Eustathius* observes) of the whole assembly, to hear the story of so great an Heroe. Perhaps it may be thought that *Ulysses* is ostentatious, and speaks of himself too favourably; but the necessity of it will appear, if we consider that *Ulysses* had nothing but his personal qualifications to engage the *Phæacians* in his favour. It was therefore requisite to make those qualifications known, and this was not possible to be done but by his own relation, he being a stranger among strangers. Besides, he speaks before a vain-glorious people, who thought even boasting no fault. It may be question'd whether *Virgil* be so happy in these respects, when he puts almost the same words into the mouth of *Æneas* ⟨1 378–9⟩.

　　Sum pius Æneas, raptos qui ex hoste penates
　　Classe veho mecum, fama super æthera notus.

For his boast contributes nothing to the re-establishment of his affairs, for he

Earth sounds my wisdom, and high heav'n my fame.   20
My native soil is *Ithaca* the fair,
Where high *Neritus* waves his woods in air:
Dulichium, Samè, and *Zacynthus* crown'd

---

speaks to the Goddess *Venus*. Yet *Scaliger* ⟨*Poet.* v iii, p. 219 A1⟩ infinitely prefers
Virgil before *Homer*, tho' there be no other difference in the words, than *raptos qui
ex hoste penates*, instead of

— Ὅς πᾶσι δόλοισιν
'Ανθρώποισι μέλω.—

He questions whether Subtilties, or δόλοι, ever rais'd any person's glory to the
Heavens; whereas that is the reward of piety. But the word is to be understood
to imply Wisdom, and all the stratagems of war, &c. according to the first verse
of the *Odyssey*,

The Man for Wisdom's various arts renown'd.

He is not less severe upon the verses immediately preceding,

Σοὶ δ' ἐμὰ κήδεα θυμὸς ἐπετράπετο στονόεντα, &c.

which lines are undoubtedly very beautiful, and admirably express the number
of the sufferings of *Ulysses*; the multitude of them is so great, that they almost
confound him; and he seems at a loss where to begin, how to proceed, or where to
end; and they agree very well with the proposition in the opening of the *Odyssey*,
which was to relate the sufferings of a brave man. The verses which *Scaliger*
quotes are ⟨*Aen.* II 3–4⟩

*Infandum regina jubes renovare dolorem;
Trojanas ut opes, &c.*

Omnia sane non sine ⟨*illa*⟩ *sua divinitate* ⟨Scaliger, *loc. cit.*⟩, and he concludes, that
Virgil has not so much imitated *Homer*, as taught us how *Homer* ought to have
wrote.

21. —Ithaca *the fair*, *Where high* Neritus, &c.] *Eustathius* gives various interpretations of this position of *Ithaca*; some understand it to signify that it lies low;
others explain it to signify that it is of a low position, but high with respect to the
neighbouring Islands; others take πανυπερτάτη (*excellentissima*) in another sense
to imply the excellence of the country, which tho' it lies low, is productive of
brave inhabitants, for *Homer* immediately adds ἀγαθὴ κουροτρόφος. *Strabo*
⟨x ii 12⟩ gives a different exposition; *Ithaca* is χθαμαλή, as it lies near to the Continent, and πανυπερτάτη, as it is the utmost of all the Islands towards the North,
πρὸς ἄρκτον, for thus πρὸς ζόφον is to be understood. So that *Ithaca*, adds he, is
not of a low situation, but as it lies oppos'd to the Continent, nor the most lofty
(ὑψηλοτάτη) but the most extream of the northern Islands; for so πανυπερτάτη signifies. *Dacier* differs from *Strabo* in the explication of πρὸς ἠῶ τ' ἠέλιόν
τε, which she believes to mean the South; she applies the words to the East, or
South-east, and appeals to the maps which so describe it. It is the most northern
of the Islands, and joyns to the Continent of *Epirus*; it has *Dulichium* on the east,
and on the south *Samos* and *Zacynthus*.

With shady mountains, spread their isles around.
These to the north and night's dark regions run,   25
Those to *Aurora* and the rising sun.)
Low lies our Isle, yet blest in fruitful stores;
Strong are her sons, tho' rocky are her shores;
And none, ah none so lovely to my sight,
Of all the lands that heav'n o'erspreads with light!   30
In vain *Calypso* long constrain'd my stay,
With sweet, reluctant, amorous delay;
With all her charms as vainly *Circe* strove,
And added magick, to secure my love.
In pomps or joys, the palace or the grott,   35
My country's image never was forgot,
My absent parents rose before my sight,
And distant lay contentment and delight.
   Hear then the woes, which mighty *Jove* ordain'd
To wait my passage from the *Trojan* land.   40
The winds from *Ilion* to the *Cicons'* shore,

---

31. *In vain* Calypso—] *Eustathius* observes, that *Ulysses* repeats his refusal of the
Goddess *Calypso* and *Circe* in the same words, to shew *Alcinous*, by a secret denial,
that he could not be induc'd to stay from his country, or marry his daughter: He
calls *Circe* Δολόεσσα, because she is skill'd in magical Incantations: He describes
Ithaca with all its inconveniencies, to convince *Alcinous* of his veracity, and that he
will not deceive him in other circumstances, when he gives so disadvantagious
a character of a country for which he expresses so great a fondness; and lastly, in
relating the death of his friends, he seems to be guilty of a tautology, in θάνατόν
τε μόρον τε. But *Aulus Gellius* gives us the reason of it, *Atrocitatem rei bis idem
dicendo auxit, inculcavitque, non igitur illa ejusdem significationis repetitio, ignava &
frigida videri debet* ⟨*Attic Nights* XIII xxv 19–20⟩.

41. —*To the* Cicons' *shore*.] Here is the natural and true beginning of the
Odyssey, which comprehends all the sufferings of *Ulysses*, and these sufferings take
their date immediately after his leaving the shores of *Troy*; from that moment he
endeavours to return to his own country, and all the difficulties he meets with in
returning, enter into the subject of the Poem. But it may then be ask'd, if the
Odyssey does not take up the space of ten years, since *Ulysses* wastes so many in his
return; and is not this contrary to the nature of Epic Poetry, which is agreed must
not at the longest exceed the duration of one year, or rather Campaign? The
answer is, the Poet lets all the time pass which exceeds the bounds of Epic action,
before he opens the Poem; thus *Ulysses* spends some time before he arrives at the
Island of *Circe*, with her he continues one year, and seven with *Calypso*; he begins

Beneath cold *Ismarus*, our vessels bore.
We boldly landed on the hostile place,
And sack'd the city, and destroy'd the race,
Their wives made captive, their possessions shar'd,   45
And ev'ry soldier found a like reward.
I then advis'd to fly: not so the rest,
Who stay'd to revel, and prolong the feast:
The fatted sheep and sable bulls they slay,
And bowls flow round, and riot wastes the day.   50
Mean-time the *Cicons*, to their holds retir'd,
Call on the *Cicons*, with new fury fir'd;
With early morn the gather'd country swarms,
And all the Continent is bright with arms:
Thick, as the budding leaves or rising flow'rs   55
O'erspread the land, when spring descends in show'rs:
All expert soldiers, skill'd on foot to dare,
Or from the bounding courser urge the war.
Now Fortune changes (so the fates ordain)
Our hour was come, to taste our share of pain.   60
Close at the ships the bloody fight began,
Wounded they wound, and man expires on man.

---

artificially at the conclusion of the action, and finds an opportunity to repeat the most considerable and necessary incidents which preceded the opening of the *Odyssey*; by this method he reduces the duration of it into less compass than the space of two months. This conduct is absolutely necessary, for from the time that the Poet introduces his Heroe upon the stage, he ought to continue his action to the very end of it, that he may never afterwards appear idle or out of motion: This is verified in *Ulysses*; from the moment he leaves the Island *Ogygia* to the death of the Suitors, he is never out of view, never idle; he is always either in action, or preparing for it, 'till he is re-establish'd in his dominions. If the Poet had follow'd the natural order of the action, he, like *Lucan*, would not have wrote an Epic Poem, but an History in verse.

44. *And sack'd the city*—] The Poet assigns no reason why *Ulysses* destroys this City of the *Ciconians*, but we may learn from the *Iliad*, that they were auxiliaries of *Troy*, Book the second ⟨1026–7⟩.

> *With great* Euphemus *the* Ciconians *move,*
> *Sprung from* Trœzenian *Cœus, lov'd of* Jove.

And therefore *Ulysses* assaults them as enemies. *Eustathius*.

Long as the morning sun increasing bright
O'er heav'n's pure azure spread the growing light,
Promiscuous death the form of war confounds,   65
Each adverse battel gor'd with equal wounds:
But when his evening wheels o'erhung the main,
Then conquest crown'd the fierce *Ciconian* train.
Six brave companions from each ship we lost,
The rest escape in haste, and quit the coast.   70
With sails outspread we fly th' unequal strife,
Sad for their loss, but joyful of our life.
Yet as we fled, our fellows rites we pay'd,
And thrice we call'd on each unhappy Shade.

---

69. *Six brave companions from each ship we lost.*] This is one of the passages which
fell under the censure of *Zoilus*; it is very improbable, says that Critic ⟨on
authority of Eustathius, 1614, 46⟩, that each vessel should lose six men exactly,
this seems a too equal distribution to be true, considering the chance of battle.
But it has been answer'd, that *Ulysses* had twelve vessels, and that in this engage-
ment he lost seventy two soldiers; so that the meaning is, that taking the total of
his loss, and dividing it equally thro' the whole fleet, he found it amounted
exactly to six men in every vessel. This will appear to be a true solution, if we
remember that there was a necessity to supply the loss of any one ship out of the
others that had suffer'd less; so that tho' one vessel lost more than the rest, yet
being recruited equally from the rest of the fleet, there would be exactly six men
wanting in every vessel. *Eustathius.*

74. *And thrice we call'd on each unhappy Shade.*] This passage preserves a piece of
Antiquity: It was the custom of the *Grecians*, when their friends dy'd upon foreign
shores, to use this ceremony of recalling their souls, tho' they obtain'd not their
bodies; believing by this method, that they transported them to their own
country: *Pindar* mentions the same practice ⟨*Pyth.* IV 159–60⟩,

Κέλεται γὰρ ἐὰν
Ψυχὰν κομίξαι Φρίξος, &c.

That is, "*Phrixus* commands thee to call his soul into his own country." Thus the
Athenians when they lost any men at sea, went to the shores and calling thrice on
their names, rais'd a Cenotaph or empty monument to their memories; by per-
forming which solemnity, they invited the shades of the departed to return, and
perform'd all rites as if the bodies of the dead had really been buried by them in
their Sepulchres. *Eustathius.*

The *Romans* as well as the *Greeks* follow'd the same custom: thus *Virgil* ⟨VI 506⟩,

—*Et magna Manes ter voce vocavi.*

The occasion of this practice arose from the opinion, that the souls of the departed

Mean-while the God whose hand the thunder forms,
Drives clouds on clouds, and blackens heav'n with storms:
Wide o'er the waste the rage of *Boreas* sweeps,   77
And Night rush'd headlong on the shaded deeps.
Now here, now there, the giddy ships are born,
And all the rattling shrouds in fragments torn.   80
We furl'd the sail, we ply'd the lab'ring oar,
Took down our masts, and row'd our ships to shore.
Two tedious days and two long nights we lay,
O'erwatch'd and batter'd in the naked bay.
But the third morning when *Aurora* brings,   85
We rear the masts, we spread the canvas wings;
Refresh'd, and careless on the deck reclin'd,
We sit, and trust the pilot and the wind.
Then to my native country had I sail'd;
But, the cape doubled, adverse winds prevail'd.   90
Strong was the tyde, which by the northern blast
Impell'd, our vessels on *Cythera* cast.
Nine days our fleet th' uncertain tempest bore
Far in wide ocean, and from sight of shore:
The tenth we touch'd, by various errors tost,   95

were not admitted into the state of the happy, without the performance of the
sepulchral solemnities.

    95.   *The tenth we touch'd—*
                        The land of Lotos—]

This passage has given occasion for much controversy; for since the *Lotophagi* in
reality are distant from the *Malian* Cape twenty two thousand five hundred
stades, *Ulysses* must sail above two thousand every day, if in nine days he sail'd
to the *Lotophagi*. This objection would be unanswerable, if we place that nation
in the *Atlantic* Ocean, but *Dacier* observes from *Strabo* ⟨1 ii 17–18⟩, that *Polybius*
examin'd this point ⟨xxxiv iv⟩, and thus gives us the result of it. This great Historian maintains, that *Homer* has not placed the *Lotophagi* in the *Atlantic* Ocean,
as he does the Islands of *Circe* and *Calypso*, because it was improbable that in the
compass of ten days the most favourable winds could have carry'd *Ulysses* from
the *Malian* Cape into that Ocean; it therefore follows, that the Poet has given us
the true situation of this nation, conformably to Geography, and placed it as it
really lies in the Mediterranean; now in ten days a good wind will carry a vessel
from *Malia* into the Mediterranean, as *Homer* relates.

The land of *Lotos*, and the flow'ry coast.
We climb'd the beach, and springs of water found,
Then spread our hasty banquet on the ground.
Three men were sent, deputed from the crew,
(An herald one) the dubious coast to view, 100
And learn what habitants possest the place?
They went, and found a hospitable race:
Not prone to ill, nor strange to foreign guest,
They eat, they drink, and nature gives the feast;
The trees around them all their food produce, 105
Lotos the name, divine, nectareous juice!

This is an instance that *Homer* sometimes follows truth without fiction, at other times disguises it. But I confess I think *Homer*'s Poetry would have been as beautiful if he had describ'd all his Islands in their true positions: His inconstancy in this point, may seem to introduce confusion and ambiguity, when the truth would have been more clear, and as beautiful in his Poetry.

Nothing can better shew the great deference which former ages pay'd *Homer*, than these defences of the learned Ancients; they continually ascribe his deviations from truth, (as in the instance before us) to design, not to ignorance; to his art as a Poet, and not to want of skill as a Geographer. In a writer of less fame, such relations might be thought errors, but in *Homer* they are either understood to be no errors, or if errors, they are vindicated by the greatest names of Antiquity.

Eustathius adds, that the Ancients disagree about this Island: some place it about *Cyrene*, from *Maurusia* of the *African* Moors: It is also named *Meninx*, and lies upon the *African* coast, near the lesser *Syrtis*. It is about three hundred and fifty stades in length, and somewhat less in breadth: It is also nam'd *Lotophagitis*, from *Lotos*.

100. *An herald one.*] The reason why the Poet mentions the Herald in particular, is because his office was sacred; and by the common law of nations his person inviolable: *Ulysses* therefore joyns an Herald in this commission, for the greater security of those whom he sends to search the country. *Eustathius.*

106. Lotos.] *Eustathius* assures us, that there are various kinds of it. It has been a question whether it is a herb, a root, or a tree: He is of opinion, that *Homer* speaks of it as an herb; for he calls it ἄνθινον εἶδαρ, and that the word ἐρέπτεσθαι is in its proper sense apply'd to the grazing of beasts, and therefore he judges it not to be a tree, or root. He adds, there is an *Ægyptian Lotos*, which as *Herodotus* affirms ⟨II 92⟩, grows in great abundance along the *Nile* in the time of its inundations; it resembles (says that Historian in his *Euterpe*) a Lilly, the *Ægyptians* dry it in the sun, then take the pulp out of it, which grows like the head of a poppy, and bake it as bread; this kind of it agrees likewise with the ἄνθινον εἶδαρ of *Homer*.

(Thence call'd *Lotophagi*) which whoso tastes,
Insatiate riots in the sweet repasts,
Nor other home nor other care intends,
But quits his house, his country, and his friends: 110
The three we sent, from off th' inchanting ground
We dragg'd reluctant, and by force we bound:
The rest in haste forsook the pleasing shore,
Or, the charm tasted, had return'd no more.
Now plac'd in order, on their banks they sweep   115
The sea's smooth face, and cleave the hoary deep;
With heavy hearts we labour thro' the tyde,
To coasts unknown, and oceans yet untry'd.
     The land of *Cyclops* first; a savage kind,

Athenæus writes of the *Libyan Lotos* in the 14th book of his *Deipnosophist* ⟨651 D–E⟩;
he quotes the words of *Polybius* in the 12th book of his History, now not extant;
that Historian speaks of it as an eye-witness, having examin'd the nature of it.
"The *Lotos* is a tree of no great height, rough and thorny: it bears a green leaf,
somewhat thicker and broader than that of the bramble or briar; its fruit at first is
like the ripe berries of the myrtle, both in size and colour, but when it ripens it
turns to purple; it is then about the bigness of an olive, it is round, and contains a
very small kernel; when it is ripe they gather it, and bruising it among bread-
corn, they put it up into a vessel, and keep it as food for their slaves; they dress it
after the same manner for their other domestics, but first take out the kernel from
it: It has the taste of a fig, or dates, but is of a far better smell: They likewise make
a wine of it, by steeping and bruising it in water; it has a very agreeable taste, like
wine temper'd with honey. They drink it without mixing it with water, but it will
not keep above ten days, they therefore make it only in small quantities for
immediate use." Perhaps it was this last kind of *Lotos*, which the companions of
Ulysses tasted; and if it was thus prepar'd, it gives a reason why they were overcome with it; for being a wine, it had the power of intoxication.

     114. *The charm once tasted* ⟨sic⟩, *had return'd no more.*] It must be confess'd, that
the effects of this *Lotos* are extraordinary, and seem fabulous: How then shall we
reconcile the relation to credibility? The foundation of it might perhaps be no
more than this; The companions of *Ulysses* might be willing to settle among these
Lotophagi, being won by the pleasure of the place, and tired with a life of danger
and the perils of seas. Or perhaps it is only an Allegory, to teach us that those who
indulge themselves in pleasures, are with difficulty withdrawn from them, and
want an *Ulysses* to lead them by a kind violence into the paths of glory.

     119. *The land of* Cyclops *first*—] *Homer* here confines himself to the true Geo-
graphy of *Sicily*: for in reality, a ship may easily sail in one day from the land of the

Lotophagi to *Sicily*: These *Cyclops* inhabited the western part of that Island, about *Drepana* and *Lilybæum*. *Bochart* shews us ⟨Pt. II : I xxx (pp. 619–20)⟩, that they derive their name from the place of their habitation; for the *Phæacians* call them *Chek-lub*, by contraction for *Chek-lelub*; that is, the gulph of *Lilybæum*, or the men who dwell about the *Lilybæan* gulph. The *Greeks* (who understood not the *Phæacian* language) form'd the word *Cyclop*, from *Chek-lub*, from the affinity of sound; which word in the *Greek* language, signifying a circular eye, might give occasion to fable that they had but one large round eye in the middle of their foreheads. *Dacier*.

Eustathius tells us that the eye of *Cyclops* is an allegory, to represent that in anger, or any other violent passion, men see but one single object as that passion directs, or see but with one eye: εἰς ἕν τι, καὶ μόνον ἐφορᾷ: and that passion transforms us into a kind of savages, and makes us brutal and sanguinary, like this *Polyphemus*; and he that by reason extinguishes such a passion, may like *Ulysses* be said to put out that eye that made him see but one single object.

I have already given another reason of this fiction; namely their wearing a headpiece, or martial Vizor that had but one sight thro' it. The vulgar form their judgments from appearances; and a mariner who pass'd these coasts at a distance, observing the resemblance of a broad eye in the forehead of one of these *Cyclops*, might relate it accordingly, and impose it as a truth upon the credulity of the ignorant: it is notorious that things equally monstrous have found belief in all ages.

But it may be ask'd if there were any such persons who bore the name of *Cyclops*? No less an Historian than *Thucydides* informs us ⟨VI ii I⟩, that *Sicily* was at first possess'd and inhabited by Giants, by the *Laestrygones* and *Cyclops*, a barbarous and inhuman people: But he adds, that these savages dwelt only in one part of that Island.

Cedrenus ⟨*Historiarum Compendium* 132 C (*Patrologia Graeca*, V 121)⟩ gives an exact description of the *Cyclops*: Ἐκεῖθεν Ὀδυσσεὺς ἐμπίπτει Κύκλωπι ἐν Σικελίᾳ οὐχ ἑνὶ ὀφθαλμῷ, *&c*. "*Ulysses* fell among the *Cyclops* in *Sicily*, a people not one-ey'd according to the Mythologists, but men like other men, only of a more gigantic stature, and of a barbarous and savage temper." From this description, we may see what *Homer* writes as a Poet, and what as an Historian; he paints these people in general agreeably to their persons, only disguises some features, to give an ornament to his relation, and to introduce the Marvellous, which demands a place chiefly in Epic Poetry.

What *Homer* speaks of the fertility of *Sicily*, is agreeable to History: It was call'd anciently *Romani Imperii Horreum*. *Pliny*. lib. 10. cap. 10. ⟨XVIII xxi 95⟩ writes, that the *Leontine* plains bear for every grain of corn, an hundred. *Diodorus Siculus* relates in his History ⟨V ii 4⟩ what *Homer* speaks in Poetry, that the fields of *Leontium* yield wheat without the culture of the husbandman; he was an eye-witness, being a native of the Island. From hence in general it may be observ'd, that where-ever we can trace *Homer*, we find, if not historic truth, yet the resemblance of it; that is, as plain truth as can be related without converting his Poem into an History.

Nor tam'd by manners, nor by laws confin'd: 120
Untaught to plant, to turn the glebe and sow,
They all their products to free nature owe.
The soil untill'd a ready harvest yields,
With wheat and barley wave the golden fields,
Spontaneous wines from weighty clusters pour,   125
And *Jove* descends in each prolific show'r.
By these no statutes and no rights are known,
No council held, no Monarch fills the throne,
But high on hills or airy cliffs they dwell,

---

127.   *By these no statutes and no rights are known,*
No council held, no Monarch fills the throne.]

Plato (observes *Spondanus* ⟨*Od.* p. 120⟩)in his third book of laws ⟨*Laws* III 680B⟩, treats of Government as practis'd in the first ages of the world; and refers to this passage of *Homer*; "Mankind was originally independant, every Master of a family was a kind of a King of his family, and reign'd over his wife and children like these *Cyclopeans*," according to the expression of *Homer*,

Τοῖσιν δ' οὔτ' ἀγοραὶ βουληφόροι, οὔτε θέμιστες.

Aristotle likewise complains ⟨*Nic. Ethics* x 1180a 28⟩, that even in his times, in many places, men lived without laws, according to their own fancies, ζῆ ἕκαστος ὡς βούλεται, κυκλωπικῶς θεμιστεύων παίδων, ἡ ἀλόχου, referring likewise to this passage of *Homer*.

Dacier adds from *Plato* ⟨*Laws* III 677B ff⟩, that after the Deluge, three manners of life succeeded among mankind; the first was rude and savage; men were afraid of a second flood, and therefore inhabited the summits of mountains, without any dependance upon one another, and each was absolute in his own family: The second was less brutal; as the fear of the Deluge wore away by degrees, they descended toward the bottom of mountains, and began to have some intercourse: The third was more polish'd; when a full security from the apprehensions of a flood was establish'd by time, they then began to inhabit the plains, and a more general commerce by degrees prevailing, they enter'd into societies, and establish'd laws for the general good of the whole community. These *Cyclopeans* maintain'd the first state of life in the days of *Ulysses*; they had no intercourse with other societies, by reason of their barbarities, and consequently their manners were not at all polish'd by the general laws of humanity. This account agrees excellently with the holy Scriptures, and perhaps *Plato* borrow'd it from the writings of *Moses*; after the Deluge men retreated to mountains for fear of a second flood; their chief riches, like these *Cyclopeans*, consisted in flocks and herds; and every master of a family ruled his house without any controul or subordination.

129. *But high on hills,—Or deep in caves*] This is said, to give an air of probability

Or deep in caves whose entrance leads to hell.   130
Each rules his race, his neighbour not his care,
Heedless of others, to his own severe.
    Oppos'd to the *Cyclopean* coasts, there lay
An Isle, whose hills their subject fields survey;
Its name *Lachæa*, crown'd with many a grove,   135
Where savage goats thro' pathless thickets rove:
No needy mortals here, with hunger bold,
Or wretched hunters thro' the wintry cold
Pursue their flight, but leave them safe to bound
From hill to hill, o'er all the desart ground.   140
Nor knows the soil to feed the fleecy care,
Or feels the labours of the crooked share,
But uninhabited, untill'd, unsown
It lies, and breeds the bleating goat alone.
For there no vessel with vermilion prore,   145
Or bark of traffic, glides from shore to shore;   .
The rugged race of savages, unskill'd
The seas to traverse, or the ships to build,
Gaze on the coast, nor cultivate the soil,
Unlearn'd in all th' industrious arts of toil.   150
Yet here all products and all plants abound,
Sprung from the fruitful genius of the ground;

---

to the revenge which *Ulysses* takes upon this giant, and indeed to the whole story.
He describes his solitary life, to shew that he was utterly destitute of assistance;
and it is for the same reason, continues *Eustathius*, that the Poet relates that he left
his fleet under a desart neighbouring Island, namely to make it probable, that the
Cyclops could not seize it, or pursue *Ulysses*, having no shipping.

   134. *An Isle, whose hills,* &c.] This little Isle is now call'd *Ægusa*, which signifies
the Isle of goats. *Cluverius* ⟨*Sicilia Antiqua* (Leyden, 1619), II 423⟩ describes it
after the manner of *Homer, Prata mollia, & irrigua, solum fertile, portum commodum,
fontes limpidos.* It is not certain whether the Poet gives any name to it; perhaps it
had not received any in these ages, it being without inhabitants; tho' some take
λάχεια for a proper name, as is observ'd by *Eustathius.*

   144. *bleating goat.*] It is exactly thus in the original, Ver. 124. μηκάδας, *balantes;*
which *Pollux, lib.* 5. ⟨88⟩ observes not to be the proper term for the voice of goats,
which is φριμαγμός.

Fields waving high with heavy crops are seen,
And vines that flourish in eternal green,
Refreshing meads along the murm'ring main,   155
And fountains streaming down the fruitful plain.
    A port there is, inclos'd on either side,
Where ships may rest, unanchor'd and unty'd;
'Till the glad mariners incline to sail,
And the sea whitens with the rising gale.   160
High at its head, from out the cavern'd rock
In living rills a gushing fountain broke:
Around it, and above, for ever green
The bushing alders form'd a shady scene.
Hither some fav'ring God, beyond our thought,   165
Thro' all-surrounding shade our navy brought;
For gloomy Night descended on the main,
Nor glimmer'd *Phœbe* in th' ethereal plain:
• But all unseen the clouded Island lay,
And all unseen the surge and rowling sea,   170
'Till safe we anchor'd in the shelter'd bay:
Our sails we gather'd, cast our cables o'er,
And slept secure along the sandy shore.
Soon as again the rosy morning shone,
Reveal'd the landscape and the scene unknown,   175
With wonder seiz'd, we view the pleasing ground,
And walk delighted, and expatiate round.
Rows'd by the woodland nymphs, at early dawn,

---

165. *Hither some fav'ring God*—] This circumstance is inserted with great judgment, *Ulysses* otherwise might have landed in *Sicily*, and fall'n into the hands of the *Cyclopeans*, and consequently been lost inevitably: He therefore piously ascribes his safety by being driven upon this desolate Island, to the guidance of the Gods; he uses it as a retreat, leaves his navy there, and passes over into *Sicily* in one single vessel, undiscover'd by these gigantic savages; this reconciles the relation to probability, and renders his escape practicable. *Eustathius.*

178. *The woodland nymphs.*] This passage is not without obscurity, and it is not easy to understand what is meant by *the daughters of Jupiter. Eustathius* tells us, the Poet speaks allegorically, and that he means to specify the plants and herbs of the

The mountain goats came bounding o'er the lawn:
In haste our fellows to the ships repair,   180
For arms and weapons of the sylvan war;
Strait in three squadrons all our crew we part,
And bend the bow, or wing the missile dart;
The bounteous Gods afford a copious prey,
And nine fat goats each vessel bears away: 185
The royal bark had ten. Our ships compleat
We thus supply'd, (for twelve were all the fleet.)
    Here, till the setting sun rowl'd down the light,
We sate indulging in the genial rite:
Nor wines were wanting; those from ample jars   190
We drain'd, the prize of our *Ciconian* wars.
The land of *Cyclops* lay in prospect near;   ⎫
The voice of goats, and bleating flocks we hear,   ⎬
And from their mountains rising smokes appear.   ⎭

---

field. *Jupiter* denotes the air, not only in *Homer*, but in the *Latin* Poets. Thus
Virgil ⟨*Geo.* ii 325–6⟩,

> Tum pater omnipotens fecundis imbribus Æther
> Conjugis in gremium lætæ descendit—

and consequently the herbs and plants being nourish'd by the mild air and fruitful rains, may be said to be the daughters of *Jupiter*, or off-spring of the skies; and
these goats and beasts of the field being fed by these plants and herbs may be said
to be awaken'd by the daughters of *Jupiter*, that is, they awake to feed upon
the herbage early in the morning. Κοῦραι Διός, ἀλληγορικῶς αἱ τῶν φυτῶν
αὐξητικαὶ δυνάμεις, ἃς ὁ Ζεὺς ποιεῖ. Thus *Homer* makes Deities of the vegetative
faculties and virtues of the field. I fear such boldnesses would not be allow'd in
modern Poetry.

It must be confess'd that this interpretation is very refin'd: But I am sure it will
be a more natural explication to take these for the real mountain Nymphs
(*Oreades*) as they are in many places of the *Odyssey*; the very expression is found
in the sixth book ⟨105⟩,

> —νύμφαι κοῦραι Διός—

and there signifies the Nymphs attending upon *Diana* in her sports: Immediately
after, *Ulysses* being awaken'd by a sudden noise, mistakes *Nausicaa* and her damsels for Nymphs of the mountains or floods; and this conjecture will not be without probability, if we remember that these Nymphs were huntresses, as is evident
from their relation to *Diana*. Why then may not the other expression be meant of
the Nymphs that are fabled to inhabit the mountains?

Now sunk the sun, and darkness cover'd o'er   195
The face of things: along the sea-beat shore
Satiate we slept: But when the sacred dawn
Arising glitter'd o'er the dewy lawn,
I call'd my fellows, and these words addrest.
My dear associates, here indulge your rest: 200
While, with my single ship, adventurous I
Go forth, the manners of yon men to try;
Whether a race unjust, of barb'rous might,
Rude, and unconscious of a stranger's right;
Or such who harbour pity in their breast,   205
Revere the Gods, and succour the distrest?
    This said, I climb'd my vessel's lofty side;
My train obey'd me and the ship unty'd.
In order seated on their banks, they sweep
Neptune's smooth face, and cleave the yielding deep.   210
When to the nearest verge of land we drew,
Fast by the sea a lonely cave we view,
High, and with dark'ning lawrels cover'd o'er;
Where sheep and goats lay slumb'ring round the shore.
Near this, a fence of marble from the rock,   215
Brown with o'er-arching pine, and spreading oak.
A Giant-shepherd here his flock maintains
Far from the rest, and solitary reigns,
In shelter thick of horrid shade reclin'd;

---

201. *While, with my single ship, advent'rous I.*] The Reader may be pleas'd to
observe, that the Poet has here given the reins to his fancy, and run out into a
luxuriant description of *Ægusa* and *Sicily*: he refreshes the mind of the Reader
with a pleasing and beautiful scene, before he enters upon a story of so much
horror, as this of the *Cyclops*.

A very sufficient reason may be assign'd, why *Ulysses* here goes in person to
search this land: He dares not, as *Eustathius* remarks, trust his companions; their
disobedience among the *Ciconians*, and their unworthy conduct among the *Lotophagi*, have convinc'd him that no confidence is to be repos'd in them: This seems
probable, and upon this probability *Homer* proceeds to bring about the punishment of *Polyphemus*, which the wisdom of *Ulysses* effects, and it is an action of
importance, and consequently ought to be perform'd by the Heroe of the Poem.

And gloomy mischiefs labour in his mind. 220
A form enormous! far unlike the race
Of human birth, in stature, or in face;

---

221. *A form enormous! far unlike the race Of human birth.*] *Goropius Becanus*, an *Antwerpian*, has wrote a large discourse to prove, that there never were any such men as Giants ⟨Jean Becan ("Goropius"), 1518–72, author of *Gigantomachia*⟩; contrary to the testimony both of prophane and sacred History: Thus *Moses* speaks of the *Rephaims* of *Asteroth*, the *Zamzummims* of *Ham*, the *Emims* of *Moab*, and *Anakims* of *Hebron*. See *Deut.* ii. ver. 20. "That also was call'd a land of Giants, it was a great people, and tall as the *Zamzummims*." Thus *Goliath* must be allow'd to be a Giant, for he was six cubits and a span, that is, nine feet and a span in height; his coat of mail weigh'd five thousand shekels of brass, about one hundred and fifty pounds; (but I confess others understand the lesser Shekel:) the head of his spear alone weigh'd six hundred shekels of iron, that is about eighteen or nineteen pounds. We find the like relations in prophane History: *Plutarch* in his life of *Theseus* ⟨vi⟩ says, that age was productive of men of prodigious stature, Giants. Thus *Diodorus Siculus* ⟨1 xxxvi 6⟩; *Ægyptii scribunt, Isidis ætate, fuisse vasto corpore homines, quos Græci dixere Gigantes. Herodotus* affirms ⟨1 68⟩ that the body of *Orestes* was dug up, and appear'd to be seven cubits long; but *Aulus Gellius* ⟨*Attic Nights* III x 11⟩ believes this to be an error. *Josephus* writes, *l.* 18, *cap.* 6 ⟨(Teubner) XVIII 103⟩ that *Vitellius* sent a *Jew* named *Eleazar*, seven cubits in height, as a present from *Artabanus* King of the *Parthians*, to *Tiberius Cæsar*; this man was ten feet and a half high. *Pliny*, 7. 16. ⟨VII xvi 74⟩ speaks of a man that was nine feet nine inches high; and in another place, 6. 30. ⟨VII ii 31 (but misinterpreted)⟩ *Sybortas, gentem Æthiopum Nomadum, octona cubita longitudine excedere.*

Thus it is evident, that there have been men of very extraordinary stature in former ages. Tho' perhaps such instances were not frequent in any age or any nation. So that *Homer* only amplifies, not invents; and as there was really a people call'd *Cyclopeans*, so they might be men of great stature, or giants.

It may seem strange that in all ancient stories the first planters of most nations are recorded to be Giants; I scarce can persuade my self but such accounts are generally fabulous; and hope to be pardon'd for a conjecture which may give a seeming reason how such stories came to prevail. The *Greeks* were a people of very great antiquity; they made many expeditions, as appears from *Jason*, &c. and sent out frequent Colonies: Now the head of every Colony was call'd ἄναξ, and these adventurers being persons of great figure in story, were recorded as men of war, of might and renown, thro' the old world: It is therefore not impossible but the *Hebrews* might form their word *Anac*, from the *Greek* ἄναξ, and use it to denote persons of uncommon might and abilities. These they call'd *Anac*, and sons of *Anac*; and afterwards in a less proper sense used it to signify men of uncommon stature, or giants. So that in this sense, all nations may be said to be originally peopled by a son of *Anac*, or a Giant. But this is submitted as a conjecture to the Reader's judgment.

As some lone mountain's monstrous growth he stood,
Crown'd with rough thickets, and a nodding wood.
I left my vessel at the point of land,   225
And close to guard it, gave our crew command:
With only twelve, the boldest and the best,
I seek th' adventure, and forsake the rest.
Then took a goatskin fill'd with precious wine, ⎫
The gift of *Maron*, of *Evantheus'* line,   230
(The Priest of *Phœbus* at th' *Ismarian* shrine) ⎭
In sacred shade his honour'd mansion stood
Amidst *Apollo*'s consecrated wood;
Him, and his house, heav'n mov'd my mind to save,
And costly presents in return he gave;   235
Sev'n golden talents to perfection wrought,
A silver bowl that held a copious draught,
And twelve large vessels of unmingled wine,
Mellifluous, undecaying, and divine!
Which now some ages from his race conceal'd,   240
The hoary Sire in gratitude reveal'd.
Such was the wine: to quench whose fervent stream,
Scarce twenty measures from the living stream

---

229. *Precious wine, The gift of* Maron.] Such digressions as these are very frequent in *Homer*, but I am far from thinking them always beauties: 'Tis true, they
give variety to Poetry; but whether that be an equivalent for calling off the
attention of the Reader from the more important action, and diverting it with
small incidents, is what I much question. It is not indeed impossible but this
Maron might have been the friend of *Homer*, and this praise of him will then be a
monument of his grateful disposition; and in this view, a beauty. It must be
confess'd that *Ulysses* makes use of this wine to a very good effect, *viz.* to bring
about the destruction of *Polyphemus*, and his own deliverance; and therefore it was
necessary to set it off very particularly, but this might have been done in fewer
lines. As it now stands it is a little Episode; our expectations are rais'd to learn the
event of so uncommon an adventure, when all of a sudden *Homer* breaks the story,
and gives us a History of *Maron*. But I distrust my judgment much rather than
Homer's.

243.   *Scarce twenty measures from the living stream*
            To cool one cup suffic'd—]
There is no wine of so strong a body as to bear such a disproportionable quantity;

To cool one cup suffic'd: the goblet crown'd
Breath'd aromatic fragrancies around.   245
Of this an ample vase we heav'd a-board,
And brought another with provisions stor'd.
My soul foreboded I should find the bow'r
Of some fell monster, fierce with barb'rous pow'r,
Some rustic wretch, who liv'd in heav'n's despight,   250
Contemning laws, and trampling on the right.
The cave we found, but vacant all within,
(His flock the Giant tended on the green)
But round the grott we gaze, and all we view
In order rang'd, our admiration drew: 255
The bending shelves with loads of cheeses prest,
The folded flocks each sep'rate from the rest,
(The larger here, and there the lesser lambs,
The new-fall'n young here bleating for their dams;
The kid distinguish'd from the lambkin lies:)   260
The cavern ecchoes with responsive cries.
Capacious chargers all around were lay'd,
Full pails, and vessels of the milking trade.
With fresh provision hence our fleet to store
My friends advise me, and to quit the shore;   265
Or drive a flock of sheep and goats away,
Consult our safety, and put off to sea.

but *Homer* amplifies the strength of it to prepare the Reader for its surprising effects immediately upon *Polyphemus*.

250. *Some rustic wretch, who liv'd*, &c.] This whole passage must be consider'd as told by a person long after the adventure was past, otherwise how should *Ulysses* know that this cave was the habitation of a savage monster before he had seen him? and when he tells us that himself and twelve companions went to search, what people were inhabitants of this Island? *Eustathius* and *Dacier* seem both to have overlook'd this observation: for in a following note she condemns *Ulysses* for not flying from the Island, as he was advis'd by his companions. But if, on the other hand, we suppose that *Ulysses* was under apprehensions from the savageness of the place, of finding a savage race of people; it will be natural enough that his mind should forebode as much; and it appears from other passages, that this sort of instinctive presage was a favourite opinion of *Homer*'s.

Their wholsome counsel rashly I declin'd,
Curious to view the man of monstrous kind,
And try what social rites a savage lends: 270
Dire rites alas! and fatal to my friends!
    Then first a fire we kindle, and prepare
For his return with sacrifice and prayer.
The loaden shelves afford us full repast;
We sit expecting. Lo! he comes at last.   275
Near half a forest on his back he bore,
And cast the pond'rous burden at the door.
It thunder'd as it fell. We trembled then,
And sought the deep recesses of the den.
Now driv'n before him, thro' the arching rock,   280
Came tumbling, heaps on heaps, th' unnumber'd flock:
Big-udder'd ewes, and goats of female kind,
(The males were penn'd in outward courts behind)
Then, heav'd on high, a rock's enormous weight
To the cave's mouth he roll'd, and clos'd the gate.   285
(Scarce twenty four-wheel'd cars, compact and strong,
The massy load cou'd bear, or roll along)
He next betakes him to his evening cares,
And sitting down, to milk his flocks prepares;
Of half their udders eases first the dams,   290
Then to the mother's teats submits the lambs.
Half the white stream to hard'ning cheese he prest, ⎫
And high in wicker baskets heap'd: the rest   ⎬
Reserv'd in bowls, supply'd his nightly feast.   ⎭
His labour done, he fir'd the pyle that gave   295
A sudden blaze, and lighted all the cave:
We stand discover'd by the rising fires;
Askance the giant glares, and thus enquires.
    What are ye, guests? on what adventure, say,
Thus far ye wander thro' the wat'ry way?   300
Pyrates perhaps, who seek thro' seas unknown
The lives of others, and expose your own?
    His voice like thunder thro' the cavern sounds:

My bold companions thrilling fear confounds,
Appall'd at sight of more than mortal man!   305
At length, with heart recover'd, I began.
    From *Troy*'s fam'd fields, sad wand'rers o'er the main,
Behold the relicks of the *Grecian* train!
Thro' various seas by various perils tost,
And forc'd by storms, unwilling, on your coast;   310
Far from our destin'd course, and native land,
Such was our fate, and such high *Jove*'s command!
Nor what we are befits us to disclaim,
Atrides' friends, (in arms a mighty name)
Who taught proud *Troy* and all her sons to bow;   315
Victors of late, but humble suppliants now!
Low at thy knee thy succour we implore;
Respect us, human, and relieve us, poor.
At least some hospitable gift bestow;
'Tis what the happy to th' unhappy owe: 320
'Tis what the Gods require: Those Gods revere,
The poor and stranger are their constant care;
To *Jove* their cause, and their revenge belongs,
He wanders with them, and he feels their wrongs.
    Fools that ye are! (the Savage thus replies,   325
His inward fury blazing at his eyes)
Or strangers, distant far from our abodes,
To bid me rev'rence or regard the Gods.
Know then we *Cyclops* are a race above
Those air-bred people, and their goat-nurs'd *Jove*:   330

---

307. *From* Troy's *fam'd fields*, &c.] This speech is very well adapted to make an impression upon *Polyphemus*. *Ulysses* applies to move either his fears or his compassion; he tells him he is an unfortunate person, and comes as a suppliant; and if this prevails nothing, he adds he is a subject of the great *Agamemnon*, who had lately destroy'd a mighty kingdom: Which is spoken to make him afraid to offer violence to the subject of a King who had power to revenge any injuries offer'd his people. To intimidate him further, he concludes with the mention of the Gods, and in particular of *Jupiter*, as avengers of any breach of the laws of hospitality: These are arguments well chosen to move any person, but an inhuman *Polyphemus. Eustathius.*

And learn, our pow'r proceeds with thee and thine,
Not as He wills, but as our selves incline.
But answer, the good ship that brought ye o'er,
Where lies she anchor'd? near, or off the shore?
  Thus he. His meditated fraud I find,   335
(Vers'd in the turns of various humankind)
And cautious, thus. Against a dreadful rock,
Fast by your shore the gallant vessel broke.
Scarce with these few I scap'd; of all my train,
Whom angry *Neptune* whelm'd beneath the main; 340
The scatter'd wreck the winds blew back again.
  He answer'd with his deed. His bloody hand
Snatch'd two, unhappy! of my martial band;
And dash'd like dogs against the stony floor:
The pavement swims with brains and mingled gore. 345
Torn limb from limb, he spreads his horrid feast,
And fierce devours it like a mountain beast:
He sucks the marrow, and the blood he drains,
Nor entrails, flesh, nor solid bone remains.

---

344.   *And dash'd like dogs—*
              The pavement swims, &c.]
There is a great beauty in the versification in the original.
    Σὺν δὲ δύω μάρψας, ὥς τε σκύλακας ποτὶ γαίη
    Κόπτ'. ἐκ δ' ἐγκέφαλος χαμάδις ῥέε, δεῦε δὲ γαίαν.
Dionysius Halicarn. takes notice of it, in his Dissertation upon placing words ⟨*De Comp. Verb.* xvi 118⟩: When the companions of *Ulysses,* says that Author, are dash'd against the rock, to express the horror of the action *Homer* dwells upon the most inharmonious harsh letters and syllables: he no where uses any softness, or any run of verses to please the ear. *Scaliger*⟨*Poet.* v iii, p. 241 B1⟩ injudiciously condemns this description; "*Homer,* says he, makes use of the most offensive and loathsome expressions, more fit for a butcher's shambles than the majesty of Heroic Poetry". *Macrobius, lib.* 5. *cap.* 13. of his *Saturnalia,* commends these lines of *Homer,* and even prefers them before the same description in *Virgil* ⟨III 622 ff⟩; his words are, *Narrationem facti nudam Maro posuit, Homerus* πάθος *miscuit, & dolore narrandi invidiam crudelitatis æquavit.* And indeed he must be a strange Critic that expects soft verses upon a horrible occasion, whereas the verses ought if possible to represent the thought they are intended to convey; and every person's ear will inform him that *Homer* has not in this passage executed this rule unsuccessfully.

We see the death from which we cannot move,   350
And humbled groan beneath the hand of *Jove*.
His ample maw with human carnage fill'd,
A milky deluge next the giant swill'd;
Then stretch'd in length o'er half the cavern'd rock,
Lay senseless, and supine, amidst the flock.   355
To seize the time, and with a sudden wound
To fix the slumb'ring monster to the ground,
My soul impells me; and in act I stand
To draw the sword; but Wisdom held my hand.
A deed so rash had finish'd all our fate,   360
No mortal forces from the lofty gate
Could roll the rock. In hopeless grief we lay,
And sigh, expecting the return of day.
Now did the rosy-finger'd morn arise,
And shed her sacred light along the skies.   365
He wakes, he lights the fire, he milks the dams,
And to the mother's teat submits the lambs.
The task thus finish'd of his morning hours,
Two more he snatches, murders, and devours.
Then pleas'd and whistling, drives his flock before;   370
Removes the rocky mountain from the door,
And shuts again; with equal ease dispos'd,
As a light quiver's lid is op'd and clos'd.
His giant voice the ecchoing region fills:
His flocks, obedient, spread o'er all the hills.   375
    Thus left behind, ev'n in the last despair
I thought, devis'd, and *Pallas* heard my prayer.
Revenge, and doubt, and caution, work'd my breast;
But this of many counsels seem'd the best:
The monster's club within the cave I spy'd,   380
A tree of stateliest growth, and yet undry'd,
Green from the wood; of height and bulk so vast,
The largest ship might claim it for a mast.
This shorten'd of its top, I gave my train
A fathom's length, to shape it and to plain;   385

M

The narrow'r end I sharpen'd to a spire;
Whose point we harden'd with the force of fire,
And hid it in the dust that strow'd the cave.
Then to my few companions, bold and brave,
Propos'd, who first the vent'rous deed should try?   390
In the broad orbit of his monstrous eye
To plunge the brand, and twirl the pointed wood;
When slumber next should tame the man of blood.
Just as I wish'd, the lots were cast on four;
My self the fifth. We stand, and wait the hour.   395
He comes with evening: all his fleecy flock
Before him march, and pour into the rock:
Not one, or male or female, stay'd behind;
(So fortune chanc'd, or so some God design'd)
Then heaving high the stone's unwieldy weight,   400
He roll'd it on the cave, and clos'd the gate.
First down he sits, to milk the woolly dams,
And then permits their udder to the lambs.
Next seiz'd two wretches more, and headlong cast,
Brain'd on the rock; his second dire repast.   405
I then approach'd him reeking with their gore,
And held the brimming goblet foaming o'er:
Cyclop! since human flesh has been thy feast,

---

394. *The lots were cast*—] *Ulysses* bids his friends to cast lots; this is done to shew that he would not voluntarily expose them to so imminent danger. If he had made the choice himself, they whom he had chosen might have thought he had given them up to destruction, and they whom he had rejected might have judg'd it a stain upon them as a want of merit, and so have complain'd of injustice; but by this method he avoids these inconveniencies.

399. —*Or so some God design'd.*] *Ulysses* ascribes it to the influence of the Gods, that *Polyphemus* drives the whole flock into his den, and does not separate the females from the males as he had before done; for by this accident *Ulysses* makes his escape, as appears from the following part of the story. *Homer* here uses the word ὀϊσσάμενος, to shew the suspicion which *Polyphemus* might entertain that *Ulysses* had other companions abroad who might plunder his flocks; and this gives another reason why he drove them all into his cave, namely for the greater security.

Now drain this goblet, potent to digest:
Know hence what treasures in our ship we lost,   410
And what rich liquors other climates boast.
We to thy shore the precious freight shall bear,
If home thou send us, and vouchsafe to spare.
But oh! thus furious, thirsting thus for gore,   ⎫
The sons of men shall ne'er approach thy shore,   ⎬   415
And never shalt thou taste this Nectar more.   ⎭

    He heard, he took, and pouring down his throat
Delighted swill'd the large, luxurious draught.
More! give me more, he cry'd: the boon be thine,
Whoe'er thou art that bear'st celestial wine!   420
Declare thy name; not mortal is this juice,
Such as th' unblest *Cyclopean* climes produce,
(Tho' sure our vine the largest cluster yields,
And *Jove*'s scorn'd thunder serves to drench our fields)
But this descended from the b⟨l⟩est abodes,   425
A rill of Nectar, streaming from the Gods.

    He said, and greedy grasp'd the heady bowl,
Thrice drain'd, and pour'd the deluge on his soul.
His sense lay cover'd with the dozy fume;
While thus my fraudful speech I reassume.   430
Thy promis'd boon, O *Cyclop!* now I claim,
And plead my title: *Noman* is my name.

---

432. —Noman *is my name.*] I will not trouble the Reader with a long account of οὖτις to be found in *Eustathius*, who seems delighted with this piece of pleasantry; nor with what *Dacier* observes, who declares she approves of it extreamly, and calls it a very happy imagination. If it were modesty in me to dissent from *Homer*, and two Commentators, I would own my opinion of it, and acknowledge the whole to be nothing but a collusion of words, and fitter to have place in a Farce or Comedy, than in Epic Poetry. *Lucian* has thus used it ⟨*Cataplus* 636⟩, and apply'd it to raise laughter in one of his facetious dialogues. The whole wit or jest lies in the ambiguity of οὖτις, which *Ulysses* imposes upon *Polyphemus* as his own name, which in reality signifies *No Man*. I doubt not but *Homer* was well pleased with it, for afterwards he plays upon the word, and calls *Ulysses* οὐτιδανὸς οὖτις. But the faults of *Homer* have a kind of veneration, perhaps like old age, from their antiquity.

By that distinguish'd from my tender years,
'Tis what my parents call me, and my peers.
　　The Giant then. Our promis'd grace receive,   435
The hospitable boon we mean to give:
When all thy wretched crew have felt my pow'r,
Noman shall be the last I will devour.
　　He said; then nodding with the fumes of wine
Dropt his huge head, and snoring lay supine.   440
His neck obliquely o'er his shoulder hung,
Prest with the weight of sleep that tames the strong:
There belcht the mingled streams of wine and blood,
And human flesh, his indigested food.
　　Sudden I stir the embers, and inspire   445
With animating breath the seeds of fire;
Each drooping spirit with bold words repair,
And urge my train the dreadful deed to dare.
The stake now glow'd beneath the burning bed
(Green as it was) and sparkled fiery red.   450
Then forth the vengeful instrument I bring;
With beating hearts my fellows form a ring.
Urg'd by some present God, they swift let fall
The pointed torment on his visual ball.
My self above them from a rising ground   455
Guide the sharp stake, and twirl it round and round.
As when a shipwright stands his workmen o'er,
Who plye the wimble, some huge beam to bore;

Euripides has translated this whole passage in his Tragedy, call'd the *Cyclops*
⟨669–73⟩. The Chorus begins thus, *Why dost thou thus cry out*, Cyclops? Cyc. *I am
undone.* Cho. *You seem to be in a woful condition.* Cyc. *I am utterly miserable.* Cho. *You
have been drunk and fall'n into the embers?* Cyc. Noman *has undone me.* Cho. *Well then*
No man *has injur'd you.* Cyc. Noman *has blinded me.* Chor. *Then you are not blind.*
　　This appears to me more fit for the two *Sosia's* in *Plautus*, than for Tragic or
Epic Poetry; and I fancy an Author who should introduce such a sport of words
upon the stage, even in the Comedy of our days, would meet with small applause.
　　458. *Why plye the wimble.*] This and the following comparison are drawn from
low life, but enobled with a dignity of expression. Instead of ἑλόντες, *Aristarchus*
reads ἔχοντες ⟨Dindorf, p. 435⟩, as *Eustathius* informs us. The similitudes are

Urg'd on all hands it nimbly spins about,
The grain deep-piercing till it scoops it out: 460
In his broad eye so whirls the fiery wood;
From the pierc'd pupil spouts the boiling blood;
Sing'd are his brows; the scorching lids grow black;
The gelly bubbles, and the fibres crack.
And as when Arm'rers temper in the ford 465
The keen-edg'd pole-axe, or the shining sword,
The red-hot metal hisses in the lake,
Thus in his eyeball hiss'd the plunging stake.
He sends a dreaful groan: the rocks around
Thro' all their inmost-winding caves resound. 470
Scar'd we receded. Forth, with frantic hand
He tore, and dash'd on earth the goary brand:
Then calls the *Cyclops*, all that round him dwell,
With voice like thunder, and a direful yell.
From all their dens the one-ey'd race repair, 475
From rifted rocks, and mountains bleak in air.
All haste assembled, at his well-known roar,
Enquire the cause, and croud the cavern door.
    What hurts thee, *Polypheme?* what strange affright
Thus breaks our slumbers, and disturbs the night? 480
Does any mortal in th' unguarded hour
Of sleep, oppress thee, or by fraud or pow'r?
Or thieves insidious thy fair flock surprize?
Thus they: the *Cyclop* from his den replies.

natural and lively, we are made spectators of what they represent. *Sophocles* has imitated this, in the Tragedy where *Œdipus* tears out his own eyes ⟨1 275⟩; and *Euripides* has transferr'd this whole adventure into his *Cyclops* ⟨655 ff⟩ with very little alteration, and in particular the former comparison. But to instance in all that *Euripides* has imitated, would be to transcribe a great part of that Tragedy. In short, this Episode in general is very noble, but if the Interlude about *Outis* be at all allowable in so grave and majestic a Poem, it is only allowable because it is here related before a light and injudicious assembly, I mean the *Phæacians*, to whom any thing more great or serious would have been less pleasing, so that the Poet writes to his audience. I wonder this has never been offer'd in defence of this low entertainment.

Friends, *Noman* kills me; *Noman* in the hour   485
Of sleep, oppresses me with fraudful pow'r.
"If no man hurt thee, but the hand divine
"Inflict disease, it fits thee to resign:
"To *Jove* or to thy father *Neptune* pray."
The brethren cry'd, and instant strode away.   490
    Joy touch'd my secret soul, and conscious heart,
Pleas'd with th' effect of conduct and of art.
Mean-time the *Cyclop* raging with his wound,
Spreads his wide arms, and searches round and round:
At last, the stone removing from the gate,   495
With hands extended in the midst he sate;
And search'd each passing sheep, and felt it o'er,
Secure to seize us ere we reach'd the door.
(Such as his shallow wit, he deem'd was mine)
But secret I revolv'd the deep design: 500
'Twas for our lives my lab'ring bosom wrought;
Each scheme I turn'd, and sharpen'd ev'ry thought;
This way and that, I cast to save my friends,
'Till one resolve my varying counsel ends.
    Strong were the Rams, with native purple fair,   505
Well fed, and largest of the fleecy care.
These, three and three, with osier bands we ty'd,

---

495. —*The stone removing from the gate.*] This conduct of *Polyphemus* may seem
very absurd, and it looks to be improbable that he should not call the other Giants
to assist him, in the detection of the persons who had taken his sight from him;
especially when it was now day-light, and they at hand. *Eustathius* was aware of
the objection, and imputes it to his folly and dullness. *Tully*, 5. *Tuscul.* ⟨xxxix
115⟩ gives the same character of *Polyphemus*; and because it vindicates *Homer* for
introducing a speech of *Polyphemus* to his Ram, I will beg leave to transcribe it.
*Tiresiam, quem sapientem fingunt poetæ, nunquam inducunt deplorantem Cæcitatem suam;
at vero Polyphemum Homerus, cum immanem ferumque finxisset, cum ariete etiam collo-
quentem facit, ejusque laudare fortunas, quod qua vellet, ingredi posset, & quæ vellet
attingere: Recte hic equidem; nihilo enim erat ipse Cyclops quam aries ille prudentior.* This is
a full defence of *Homer*; but *Tully* has mistaken the words of *Polyphemus* to the
Ram, for there is no resemblance to *ejus laudare fortunas, quod qua vellet ingredi
posset, &c.* I suppose *Tully* quoted by memory.

(The twining bands the *Cyclop*'s bed supply'd)
The midmost bore a man; the outward two
Secur'd each side: So bound we all the crew.   510
One ram remain'd, the leader of the flock;
In his deep fleece my grasping hands I lock,
And fast beneath in woolly curls inwove
There cling implicite, and confide in *Jove*.
When rosy morning glimmer'd o'er the dales,   515
He drove to pasture all the lusty males:
The ewes still folded, with distended thighs
Unmilk'd, lay bleating in distressful cries.
But heedless of those cares, with anguish stung,

---

511. *One ram remain'd, the leader of the flock.*] This passage has been mis-understood, to imply that *Ulysses* took more care of himself than of his companions, in chusing the largest ram for his own convenience; an imputation unworthy of the character of an Heroe. But there is no ground for it, he takes more care of his friends than of his own person, for he allots them three sheep, and lets them escape before him. Besides this conduct was necessary; for all his friends were bound, and by chusing this ram, he keeps himself at liberty to unbind the rest after their escape. Neither was there any other method practicable; for he being the last, there was no person to bind him. *Eustathius.*

The care *Ulysses* takes of his companions agrees with the character of *Horace* ⟨*Epist.* 1 ii 21–2⟩.

> *Dum sibi, dum sociis reditum parat, aspera multa*
> *Pertulit—*

But it may seem improbable that a Ram should be able to carry so great a burthen as *Ulysses*; the generation of sheep, as well as men, may appear to have decreas'd since the days of *Ulysses*. *Homer* himself seems to have guarded against this objection, he describes these sheep as εὐτρεφέες, καλοί, μεγάλοι; the Ram is spoken of as μακρὰ βιβάς, (an expression apply'd to *Ajax*, as *Eustathius* observes, in the *Iliad* ⟨vii 213, xv 686⟩.) History informs us of sheep of a very large size in other countries, and a Poet is at liberty to chuse the largest, if by that method he gives his story a greater appearance of probability.

517.   *The Ewes still folded,—*
                                Unmilk'd, lay bleating.]

This particularity may seem of no importance, and consequently unnecessary: but it is in Poetry as in Painting; they both with very good effect use circumstances that are not absolutely necessary to the subject, but only appendages and embellishments; This particular has that effect, it represents Nature, and therefore gives an air of truth and probability to the story. *Dacier.*

He felt their fleeces as they pass'd along,   520
(Fool that he was) and let them safely go,
All unsuspecting of their freight below.
    The master Ram at last approach'd the gate,
Charg'd with his wool, and with *Ulysses'* fate.
Him while he past the monster blind bespoke: 525
What makes my ram the lag of all the flock?
First thou wert wont to crop the flow'ry mead,
First to the field and river's bank to lead,
And first with stately step at evening hour
Thy fleecy fellows usher to their bow'r.   530
Now far the last, with pensive pace and slow
Thou mov'st, as conscious of thy master's woe!
Seest thou these lids that now unfold in vain?
(The deed of *Noman* and his wicked train)
Oh! didst thou feel for thy afflicted Lord,   535
And wou'd but Fate the pow'r of speech afford!
Soon might'st thou tell me, where in secret here
The dastard lurks, all trembling with his fear:
Swung round and round, and dash'd from rock to rock,
His batter'd brains shou'd on the pavement smoke.   540
No ease, no pleasure my sad heart receives,
While such a monster as vile *Noman* lives.
    The Giant spoke, and thro' the hollow rock
Dismiss'd the Ram, the father of the flock.
No sooner freed, and thro' th' enclosure past,   545
First I release my self, my fellows last:
Fat sheep and goats in throngs we drive before,
And reach our vessel on the winding shore.
With joy the sailors view their friends return'd,
And hail us living whom as dead they mourn'd.   550
Big tears of transport stand in ev'ry eye:
I check their fondness, and command to fly.
Aboard in haste they heave the wealthy sheep,
And snatch their oars, and rush into the deep.
    Now off at sea, and from the shallows clear,   555

As far as human voice cou'd reach the ear;
With taunts the distant giant I accost,
Hear me, oh *Cyclop!* hear ungracious host!
'Twas on no coward, no ignoble slave,
Thou meditat'st thy meal in yonder cave;   560
But one, the vengeance fated from above
Doom'd to inflict; the instrument of *Jove*.
Thy barb'rous breach of hospitable bands,
The God, the God revenges by my hands.

    These words the *Cyclops'* burning rage provoke: 565
From the tall hill he rends a pointed rock;
High o'er the billows flew the massy load,
And near the ship came thund'ring on the flood.
It almost brush'd the helm, and fell before:

---

569. *It almost brush'd the helm,* &c.] The Ancients, remarks *Eustathius*, placed
an Obelisk and Asterism before this verse; the former, to note that they thought
it mis-placed; the latter, to shew that they look'd upon it as a beauty. Apparently
it is not agreeable to the description; for how is it possible that this huge rock
falling *before* the vessel should endanger the rudder, which is in the stern? Can a
ship sail with the stern foremost? Some ancient Criticks to take away the contradiction, have asserted that *Ulysses* turn'd his ship to speak to *Polyphemus*; but this
is absurd, for why could not *Ulysses* speak from the stern as well as from the prow?
It therefore seems that the verse ought to be entirely omitted, as undoubtedly it
may without any chasm in the Author. We find it inserted a little lower, and
there it corresponds with the description, and stands with propriety.

    But if we suppose that the ship of *Ulysses* lay at such a distance from the cave
of *Polyphemus*, as to make it necessary to bring it nearer, to be heard distinctly;
then indeed we may solve the difficulty, and let the verse stand: for if we suppose
Ulysses approaching toward *Polyphemus*, then the rock may be said to be thrown
before the vessel, that is, beyond it, and endanger the rudder, and this bears
some appearance of probability.

    This passage brings to my memory a description of *Polyphemus* in *Apollonius*;
Argonaut. I ⟨182–4⟩.

       Κεῖνος ἀνὴρ καὶ πόντου ἐπὶ γλαυκοῖο θέεσκεν
       Οἴδματος, οὐδὲ θοοὺς βάπτεν πόδας ἀλλ' ὅσον ἄκροις
       Ἴχνεσι τεγγόμενος διερῇ πεφόρητο κελεύθῳ.

If *Polyphemus* had really this quality of running upon the waves, he might have
destroy'd *Ulysses* without throwing this mountain; but *Apollonius* is undoubtedly
guilty of an absurdity, and one might rather believe that he would sink the earth
at every step, than run upon the waters with such lightness as not to wet his feet.

  M*

The whole sea shook, and refluent beat the shore.   570
The strong concussion on the heaving tyde
Roll'd back the vessel to the Island's side:
Again I shov'd her off; our fate to fly,
Each nerve we stretch, and ev'ry oar we ply.
Just 'scap'd impending death, when now again   575
We twice as far had furrow'd back the main,
Once more I raise my voice; my friends afraid
With mild entreaties my design dissuade.
What boots the god-less Giant to provoke?
Whose arm may sink us at a single stroke.   580
Already, when the dreadful rock he threw,
Old Ocean shook, and back his surges flew.
Thy sounding voice directs his aim again;
The rock o'erwhelms us, and we 'scap'd in vain.
But I, of mind elate, and scorning fear,   585
Thus with new taunts insult the monster's ear.
Cyclop! if any, pitying thy disgrace,
Ask who disfigur'd thus that eye-less face?
Say 'twas *Ulysses*; 'twas his deed, declare,
Laertes' son, of *Ithaca* the fair;   590
Ulysses, far in fighting fields renown'd,
Before whose arm *Troy* tumbled to the ground.
Th' astonisht Savage with a roar replies:
Oh heav'ns! oh faith of ancient prophecies!
This, *Telemus Eurymedes* foretold,   595

Virgil has more judiciously apply'd those lines to *Camilla* in his *Æneis* ⟨VII 810–11⟩.
          —*Mare per medium fluctu suspensa tumenti*
          Ferret iter, celeres nec tingeret æquore plantas.
    The Poet expresses the swiftness of *Camilla* in the nimble flow of the verse, which consists almost entirely of dactyles, and runs off with the utmost rapidity, like the last of those quoted from *Apollonius*.
    595. *This,* Telemus Eurymedes *foretold.*] This incident sufficiently shews the use of that dissimulation which enters into the character of *Ulysses*: If he had discover'd his name, the *Cyclops* had destroy'd him as his most dangerous enemy. *Plutarch* in his discourse upon Garrulity ⟨*De Garrulitate* 8 (506B)⟩, commends the fidelity of the companions of *Ulysses*, who when they were dragg'd by this Giant

(The mighty Seer who on these hills grew old;
Skill'd the dark fates of mortals to declare,
And learn'd in all wing'd omens of the air)
Long since he menac'd, such was Fate's command;
And nam'd *Ulysses* as the destin'd hand.　　600
I deem'd some godlike Giant to behold,
Or lofty Hero, haughty, brave, and bold;
Not this weak pigmy-wretch, of mean design,
Who not by strength subdu'd me, but by wine.
But come, accept our gifts, and join to pray　　605
Great *Neptune*'s blessing on the watry way:
For his I am, and I the lineage own;
Th' immortal father no less boasts the son.
His pow'r can heal me, and re-light my eye;
And only his, of all the Gods on high.　　610

and dash'd against the rock, confess'd not a word concerning their Lord, and scorn'd to purchase their lives at the expence of their honesty. *Ulysses* himself, adds he, was the most *eloquent* and most *silent* of men; he knew that a word spoken never wrought so much good, as a word conceal'd; Men teach us to speak, but the Gods teach us silence; for silence is the first thing that is taught us at our initiation into sacred mysteries; and we find these companions had profited under so great a Master in silence as *Ulysses*.

Ovid relates this prophecy in the story of *Polyphemus* and *Galatea* ⟨*Metam.* xiii 770–5⟩.

> *Telemus interea Siculum delatus in æquor,*
> *Telemus Eurymides, quem nulla fefellerat ales,*
> *Terribilem Polyphemon adit; lumenque quod unum*
> *Fronte geris media, rapiet tibi, dixit, Ulysses:*
> *Risit, &, o vatum stolidissime, falleris, inquit,*
> *Altera jam rapuit:—*

603. *Not this weak pigmy-wretch*—] This is spoken in compliance with the character of a Giant; the *Phæacians* wonder'd at the manly stature of *Ulysses*, *Polyphemus* speaks of him as a dwarf; his rage undoubtedly made him treat him with so much contempt. Nothing in nature can be better imagin'd than this story of the *Cyclops*, if we consider the assembly before which it was spoken, I mean the *Phæacians*, who had been driven from their habitation by the *Cyclopeans*, as appears from the sixth of the *Odyssey*, and compell'd to make a new settlement in their present country: *Ulysses* gratifies them by shewing what revenge he took upon one of their ancient enemies, and they could not decently refuse assistance to a person, who had punish'd those who had insulted their forefathers.

O! could this arm (I thus aloud rejoin'd)
From that vast bulk dislodge thy bloody mind,
And send thee howling to the realms of night!
As sure, as *Neptune* cannot give thee sight.
    Thus I: while raging he repeats his cries,   615
With hands uplifted to the starry skies.
Hear me, oh *Neptune!* thou whose arms are hurl'd
From shore to shore, and gird the solid world.
If thine I am nor thou my birth disown,
And if th' unhappy *Cyclop* be thy Son;   620
Let not *Ulysses* breathe his native air,
Laertes' son, of *Ithaca* the fair.
If to review his country be his fate,
Be it thro' toils and suff'rings, long and late;
His lost companions let him first deplore;   625
Some vessel, not his own, transport him o'er;
And when at home from foreign suff'rings freed,
More near and deep, domestic woes succeed!
    With Imprecations thus he fill'd the air,
And angry *Neptune* heard th' unrighteous pray'r.   630
A larger rock then heaving from the plain,
He whirl'd it round; it sung across the main:
It fell, and brush'd the stern: The billows roar,
Shake at the weight, and refluent beat the shore.
With all our force we kept aloof to sea,   635
And gain'd the Island where our vessels lay.
Our sight the whole collected navy chear'd,

---

617. *The prayer of the* Cyclops.] This is a masterpiece of art in *Ulysses*; he shews *Neptune* to be his enemy, which might deter the *Phæacians* from assisting in his transportation, yet brings this very circumstance as an argument to induce them to it. *O* Neptune, *says the* Cyclops, *destroy* Ulysses, *or if he be fated to return, may it be in a vessel not of his own!* Here he plainly tells the *Phæacians* that the prayer of *Cyclops* was almost accomplish'd, for his own ships were destroy'd by *Neptune*, and now he was ready to sail in a foreign vessel; by which the whole prayer would be compleated. By this he persuades them, that they were the people ordain'd by the Fates to land him in his own country.

Who, waiting long, by turns had hop'd and fear'd.
There disembarking on the green sea-side,
We land our cattle, and the spoil divide: 640
Of these due shares to ev'ry sailor fall;
The master Ram was voted mine by all:
And him (the guardian of *Ulysses'* fate)
With pious mind to Heav'n I consecrate.
But the great God, whose thunder rends the skies,   645
Averse, beholds the smoaking sacrifice;
And sees me wand'ring still from coast to coast;
And all my vessels, all my people, lost!
    While thoughtless we, indulge the genial rite, ⎫
As plenteous cates and flowing bowls invite;   ⎬   650
'Till evening *Phœbus* roll'd away the light: ⎭
Stretch'd on the shore in careless ease we rest,
'Till ruddy morning purpled o'er the east.
Then from their anchors all our ships unbind,
And mount the decks, and call the willing wind.   655
Now rang'd in order on our banks, we sweep
With hasty strokes the hoarse-resounding deep;
Blind to the future, pensive with our fears,
Glad for the living, for the dead in tears.

---

642. *The master Ram was voted mine.*] This perhaps might be a present of honour
and distinction: But I should rather take it with *Eustathius* to be the Ram which
brought *Ulysses* out of the den of *Polyphemus*. That Heroe immediately offers it in
sacrifice to *Jupiter*, in gratitude for his deliverance; an instance of piety to be
imitated in more enlighten'd ages.

The book concludes with a testimony of this Heroe's humanity; in the midst
of the joy for his own safety, his generous heart finds room for a tender sentiment
for the loss of his companions; both his joys and his sorrows are commendable
and virtuous.

Virgil has borrow'd this Episode of *Polyphemus*, and inserted it into the third of
the *Æneis* ⟨655 ff⟩. I will not presume to decide which Author has the greatest
success, they both have their peculiar excellencies. *Rapin* ⟨Comparaison xiii,
1 142⟩ confesses this Episode to be equal to any parts of the *Iliad*, that it is an
original, and that *Homer* introduced that monstrous character, to shew the
Marvellous, and paint it in a new set of colours. *Demetrius Phalereus* ⟨130⟩ calls it

a piece of Sublime strangely horrible: and *Longinus* ⟨ix 14⟩, even while he is condemning the *Odyssey*, allows this adventure of *Polyphemus* to be very great and beautiful; (for so Monsieur *Boileau* understands *Longinus*, tho' Monsieur *Dacier* differs from his judgment ⟨*A Treatise of the Sublime . . . With Critical Reflections, Remarks, and Observations. By M. Boileau, M. Dacier, and M. Boivin* (London, 1712), ch. vii & commentary⟩.) In *Homer* we find a greater variety of natural incidents than in *Virgil*, but in *Virgil* a greater pomp of verse: *Homer* is not uniform in his description, but sometimes stoops perhaps below the dignity of Epic Poetry; *Virgil* walks along with an even, grave, and majestic pace: They both raise our admiration, mix'd with delight and terror.

Plate 9   Kent's tailpiece for *Odyssey* ix in Pope's quarto

THE

TENTH BOOK

OF THE

ODYSSEY.

The ARGUMENT.

Adventures with Æolus, *the* Laestrygones, *and* Circe.

Ulysses *arrives at the Island of* Æolus, *who gives him prosperous winds, and incloses the adverse ones in a Bag, which his companions untying, they are driven back again, and rejected. Then they sail to the* Laestrygones, *where they lose eleven ships, and with one only remaining, proceed to the Island of* Circe. Eurylochus *is sent first with some Companions, all which, except* Eurylochus, *are transform'd into Swine.* Ulysses *then undertakes the adventure, and by the help of* Mercury, *who gives him the herb* Moly, *overcomes the Enchantress, and procures the restoration of his men. After a year's stay with her, he prepares at her instigation for his voyage to the infernal shades.*

A T length we reach'd *Æolia's* sea-girt shore,
    Where great *Hippotades* the scepter bore,
    A floating Isle! High-rais'd by toil divine,

Poetry is a mixture of History and Fable; the foundation is historical, because the Poet does not entirely neglect truth; the rest is fabulous, because naked truth would not be sufficiently surprizing; for the Marvellous ought to take place, especially in Epic Poetry. But it may be ask'd, does not *Homer* offend against all degrees of probability in these Episodes of the *Sirens, Scylla* and *Charybdis, Cyclops* and *Antiphates*? How are these incredible stories to be reduc'd into the bounds of probability? 'tis true, the Marvellous ought to be used in Epic Poetry; but ought it to transgress all power of belief? *Aristotle* in his *Art of Poetry* lays down a rule to justifie these incidents: *A Poet*, says that Author, *ought to prefer things impossible, provided they are probable, before things possible, that are nevertheless incredible.* Chap. 15 ⟨xxv 27–8⟩. This rule is not without obscurity; but Monsieur *Dacier* has explain'd it in his Annotations upon that Author ⟨*La Poëtique d'Aristote . . . avec des Remarques*, Paris, 1692, p. 408⟩: A thing may be impossible, and yet probable: Thus when the Poet introduces a Deity, any incident humanly impossible receives a full probability by being ascribed to the skill and power of a God: 'Tis thus we justifie the story of the transformation of the ship of the *Phæacians* into a rock, and the fleet of *Æneas* into Sea-nymphs. But such relations ought not to be too frequent in a Poem; for it is an established rule, that all incidents which require a divine probability only, should be so disengaged from the action, that they may be substracted from it, without destroying it; for instance, if we omit the transformation of the ship, the action of the *Odyssey* will retain the same perfection. And therefore those Episodes which are necessary, and make essential parts of the Poem, ought to be grounded upon human probability; now the Episodes of *Circe*, *Polyphemus*, the *Sirens*, *&c.* are necessary to the action of the *Odyssey*: But will any man say they are within the bounds of human probability? How then shall we solve this difficulty? *Homer* artificially has brought them within the degrees of it; he makes *Ulysses* relate them before a credulous and ignorant assembly; he lets us into the character of the *Phæacians*, by saying they were a very dull nation, in the sixth book,

> *Where never Science rear'd her laurel'd head.*

It is thus the Poet gives probability to his fables, by reciting them to a people who believ'd them, and who thro' a laziness of life were fond of romantic stories: he adapts himself to his audience, and yet even here he is not unmindful of his more intelligent Readers; he gives them (observes *Bossu* ⟨III vii⟩) in these fables all the pleasure that can be reap'd from physical or moral truths, disguis'd under miraculous Allegories, and by this method reconciles them to poetical probability.

There are several heads to which Probability may be reduced; either to Divinity, and then nothing is improbable, for everything is possible to a Deity; or to our Ideas of things whether true or false: thus in the descent of *Ulysses* into Hell, there is not one word of probability or historic truth, but if we examine it by the ideas that the old world entertain'd of Hell, it becomes probable; or lastly, we may have respect to vulgar opinion or fame; for a Poet is at liberty to relate a falshood, provided it be commonly believ'd to be true. We might have recourse to this last rule, which is likewise laid down by *Aristotle* ⟨*Poetics* XXV 29⟩, to vindicate the *Odyssey*, if there were occasion for it; for in all ages such fables have found belief.

I will only add, that *Virgil* has given a sanction to these stories, by inserting them in his *Æneis*; and *Horace* calls them by the remarkable epithet of *specious miracles* ⟨*Ars Poet.* 144–5⟩.

> *—Ut speciosa dehinc miracula promat,*
> *Antiphaten, Scyllamque & cum Cyclope Charybdin.*

Longinus ⟨XII 13–14⟩ calls these fables Dreams, but adds, that they are the dreams of *Jupiter*; he likewise blames these Episodes, because in all of them there is much more fable and narration than action: Which criticism may perhaps be too severe, if we consider that past adventures are here brought into present use, and tho' they be not actions, yet they are the representations of actions, agreeable to the nature of Episodes.

It may be question'd if *Virgil* is so happy in the choice of the audience, to which he relates many of these fables; the *Carthaginians* were not ignorant, like the *Phæacians*: From whence then do his stories receive their Probability? It is not so easy to answer this objection, unless we have recourse to common fame: *Virgil* was not the Author of them, *Homer* had establish'd them, and brought them into fame, so that *Virgil* had common opinion to vindicate him, joyn'd with *Homer*'s authority.

1. *We reach'd Æolia's ⟨ . . . ⟩ shore.*] It is difficult to distinguish what is truth from what is fiction in this relation: *Diodorus*, ⟨v iv 7⟩ who was a *Sicilian*, speaks of *Æolus*, and refers to this passage: "This is that *Æolus*, says he, who entertain'd *Ulysses* in his voyages: He is reported to have been a pious and just Prince, and given to hospitality, and therefore φίλος ἀθανάτοις, as *Homer* expresses it." But whence has the fable of his being the Governour of the Winds taken its foundation? *Eustathius* tells us, that he was a very wise man, and one who from long observation could foretell what weather was like to follow: others say he was an Astronomer, and studied chiefly the nature of the Winds; and as *Atlas* from his knowledge in Astrology was said to sustain the heavens; so *Æolus*, from his experience and observation, was fabled to be the ruler or disposer of the Winds. But what explication can be given of this bag, in which he is said to bind the Winds? *Eratosthenes*, continues *Eustathius*, said pleasantly ⟨cf. Strabo 1 24⟩, that we shall then find the places where *Ulysses* voyag'd, when we have discover'd the artist, or cobler, τὸν σκυτέα, who sew'd up this bag of the winds. But the reason of the fiction is suppos'd to be this: *Æolus* taught the use and management of sails, and having foretold *Ulysses* from what quarter the winds would blow, he may be said to have gather'd them into a kind of enclosure, and retain'd them as use should require. *Diodorus* explains it a little differently, *lib.* 5 ⟨v iv 7⟩. Πρὸς δὲ τούτοις τὴν τῶν ἱστίων χρείαν τοῖς ναυτικοῖς ἐπεισηγήσασθαι, καὶ ἀπὸ τῆς τοῦ πυρὸς προσημασίας παρατετηρηκότα, προλέγειν τοὺς ἐγχωρίους ἀνέμους εὐστόχως ἐξ οὗ ταμίαν ἀνέμων μῦθος ἀνέδειξε: that is, "He taught the use of sails, and having learn'd from observing the bearing of the smoke and fires (of those *Vulcanian* Islands) what winds would blow, he usually foretold them with exactness, and from hence he is fabled to be the disposer of the winds." The words of *Varro*, quoted by *Servius* ⟨Servius on *Aeneid* 1 52⟩, are to the same purpose: *Varro autem dicit hunc insularum regem fuisse, ex quarum nebulis & fumo Vulcaniæ insulæ prædicens futura flabra ventorum, ab imperitis visus est ventos sua potestate retinere.*

Polybius ⟨xxxiv ii 9⟩ will not admit that this story of *Æolus* is entirely fable; and *Strabo* ⟨1 ii 15⟩ is of the same opinion, that *Ulysses* was in the *Sicilian* seas; and that there was such a King as *Æolus*, he affirms to be truth, but that he met with such adventures is, in the main, fiction. There may another reason, as *Eustathius* observes, be given for the fiction of binding up the winds in a bag: they who practis'd the art of Incantation or charms, made use of the skin of a Dolphin, and pretended by certain ceremonies to bind or loose the winds as they pleased; and this practice is a sufficient ground to build upon in Poetry.

The solution also of *Bochart* ⟨Pt. II: 1 xxxiii (p. 658)⟩ is worth our notice: *Homer* borrow'd the word Αἴολος from the *Phœnician Aol*, which signifies a whirl-wind or tempest, from whence the *Greeks* form'd their word ἄελλα; the *Phœnicians* observing the King of this Island to be very expert in foretelling the winds, call'd him King *Aolin*, or King of the winds and storms; from hence *Homer* form'd a proper name, and call'd him Αἴολος. It must be confess'd, that this solution is ingenious, and not without an appearance of probability.

But having laid together what may be said in vindication of this story of *Æolus*: Justice requires that I should not suppress what has been objected against it by no less a Critic than *Longinus*: he observes that a genius naturally lofty sometimes falls into trifling; an instance of this, adds he, is what *Homer* says of the bag wherein *Æolus* inclosed the winds. *Cap.* 7 ⟨XII 14⟩. περὶ ὕψους.

3. *A floating Isle*—] The word in the original is πλωτῆ: some take it, as *Eustathius* remarks, for a proper name; but *Aristarchus* ⟨Dindorf, p. 445⟩ believes *Homer* intended to express by it a floating Island, that was frequently removed by concussions and earthquakes, for it is seen sometimes on the right, at other times on the left hand; the like has been said of *Delos*; and *Herodotus* ⟨II 91⟩ thus describes the Island *Echemis* ⟨Chemmis⟩ in the *Ægyptian* seas. *Dionysius*, in his περιήγησις ⟨*Geographii Graeca Minores* (ed. Müller, 1855–61), II 131⟩, affirms, that this Island is not call'd by the name of πλωτή, by reason of its floating, but because it is an Island of fame, and much sail'd unto, or πλωτή, by navigators; that is, πλεομένη, or ἐν τόποις πλεομένοις κειμένη, or lying in seas of great navigation: but perhaps the former opinion of *Aristarchus* may be preferable, as it best contributes to raise the wonder and admiration of the credulous ignorant *Phæacians*, which was the sole intention of *Ulysses*.

These Islands were seven in number, (but eleven at this day) *Strongyle, Hiera, Didyma, Hicesia, Lipara, Ericodes*, and *Phænicodes*, all lying in the *Sicilian* seas, as *Diodorus Siculus* testifies; but differs in the name of one of the Islands ⟨v vi 7; Diodorus' name for Hicesia is Euonymus⟩.

Strabo ⟨VI ii 11⟩ is of opinion, that the Island call'd by *Homer*, the *Æolian*, is *Strongyle*; Ἡ δὲ Στρογγύλη, ἐστὶ διάπυρος, τῷ φέγγει πλεονεκτοῦσα, ἐνταῦθα δὲ τὸν Αἴολον οἰκῆσαι φασί. "This Island *Strongyle* abounds with subterraneous fires, &c. and here *Æolus* is said to have reign'd." *Pliny* agrees with *Strabo, lib.* 3 ⟨III ix 94⟩ but *Dacier* understands it to be *Lipara*, according to *Virgil, Æn. lib.* 8 ⟨416–17⟩ but in reality the seven were all call'd the *Æolian* Islands.

Insula Sicanium juxta latus, Æoliamque
Erigitur Liparen, fumantibus ardua saxis.

But why is it fabled to be surrounded with a wall of brass? *Eustathius* says, that this may proceed from its being almost inaccessible; but this reason is not sufficient to give foundation to such a fiction. *Dacier* observes that it is thus described, because of the subterranean fires, which from time to time break out from the entrails of this Island. *Aristotle* speaking of *Lipara*, which is the most considerable of the *Æolian* Islands, thus describes it; "All night long the Island *Lipara* appears enlighten'd with fires" ⟨*On Marvellous Things Heard* 37⟩. The same relation agrees with *Strongyle*, call'd *Strombolo* at this day.

I will take the liberty to propose a conjecture, which may perhaps not unhappily give a reason of this fiction of the wall of brass, from this description of *Aristotle*: All night fires appear (says the Author) from this Island, and these fires

Strong walls of brass the rocky coast confine.
Six blooming youths, in private grandeur bred,   5
And six fair daughters, grac'd the royal bed:
These sons their sisters wed, and all remain
Their parent's pride, and pleasure of their reign.
All day they feast, all day the bowls flow round,

---

falling upon the seas, might cast a ruddy reflexion round the Island, which to navigators might look like a wall of brass enclosing it. This is but a conjecture drawn from appearances; but to write according to appearances is allowable in Poetry, where a seeming or a real truth may be used indifferently.

5. *Six blooming youths—And six fair daughters.*] *Diodorus Siculus* mentions the names of the six sons of *Æolus* ⟨v viii 1⟩, but is silent concerning his daughters; and therefore others, who can find mysteries in the plainest description, assure us, that this is not to be understood historically, but allegorically: *Æolus* represents the year, his twelve children are the twelve months, six of which are female, to denote those six months in which the earth brings forth her fruits; by his six sons the other months are understood, in which the seed is sown, or in which the herbs, fruits, &c. are nourish'd in order to production, these may therefore be call'd males. But this is to darken an Author into mystery, not to explain him. *Dacier* gives us another allegorical interpretation: The Poet makes him the governour of the winds, and gives him twelve children, these denote the twelve principal winds; half of which children are males, half females; the males denote the winter winds, which as it were brood upon the earth, and generate its increase; the females those warmer seasons of the year, when the more prolific winds blow, and make the earth teem with fruitfulness: These children of *Æolus* are in continual feasts in his Palace; that is, the winds are continually fed by the exhalations from the earth, which may be call'd their food or nourishment: The brothers and sisters inter-marry; this denotes the nature of the winds, which blow promiscuously, and one wind unites it self with another from all quarters of the world indifferently: The brothers and sisters are said to sleep by night together; that is, the winds are usually still and calm, and as it were rest together, at that season. But what occasion is there to have recourse to an uncertain Allegory, when such great names as *Polybius* ⟨xxxiv ii 9⟩, *Strabo* ⟨1 ii 9, 15⟩, and *Diodorus* assure us, that this relation is in part true History; and if there was really such a King as *Æolus*, why might he not be a father of six sons and as many daughters? I should prefer a plain History to a dark Allegory.

9.   *All day they feast,—*
                    —and musick thro' the Isle resounds.]
Homer was not unacquainted with the wonders related of this Island *Lipara*. "In this Island, says *Aristotle* ⟨*On Marvellous Things Heard* 101⟩, a monument is reported to be, of which they tell miracles: they assure us that they hear issuing from it the sound of timbrels or cymbals, plainly and distinctly." It is easy to per-

And joy and music thro' the Isle resound: 10
At night each pair on splendid carpets lay,
And crown'd with love the pleasures of the day.
    This happy port affords our wand'ring fleet
A month's reception, and a safe retreat.
Full oft the Monarch urg'd me to relate   15
The fall of *Ilion*, and the *Grecian* fate;
Full oft I told: at length for parting mov'd;
The King with mighty gifts my suit approv'd.
The adverse winds in leathern bags he brac'd,
Compress'd their force, and lock'd each struggling blast:
For him the mighty Sire of Gods assign'd   21
The tempest's Lord, and tyrant of the wind;
His word alone the list'ning storms obey,
To smooth the deep, or swell the foamy sea.
These in my hollow ship the Monarch hung,   25
Securely fetter'd by a silver thong.
But *Zephyrus* exempt, with friendly gales   ⎫
He charg'd to fill, and guide the swelling sails: ⎬
Rare gift! but oh, what gift to fools avails! ⎭
    Nine prosp'rous days we ply'd the lab'ring oar;   30
The tenth presents our welcome native shore:
The hills display the beacon's friendly light,

ceive that this is founded upon the noise the fires make which are enclosed in the
caverns of this Island, and that *Homer* alludes to the ancient name of it, which in
the *Phænician* language (*Meloginin*, as *Bochart* observes ⟨Pt. II: 1 xxvii (p. 572)⟩)
signifies the land of those who play upon instruments. We learn from *Callimachus*,
in his Hymn to *Diana* ⟨III 46 ff⟩, that *Lipara* was originally call'd *Meligounis*. She
(Diana) *went to find out the* Cyclops: *she found them in* Lipara, *for that is the name the
Isle now bears, but anciently it was call'd* Meligounis; *they were labouring a huge mass of
red hot iron*, &c. So that *Homer* is not all invention, but adapts his Poetry to tradition and ancient story. *Dacier.*
    32. *The hills display the beacon's friendly light.*] *Eustathius* observes that these fires
were a kind of beacons kept continually burning to direct Navigators; the smoke
gave notice by day, the light of the flame by night. *Ithaca* was environ'd with
rocks, and consequently there was a necessity for this care, to guide sea-faring
men to avoid those rocks, and to point out the places of landing with security.
    But is it not an imputation to the wisdom of *Ulysses*, to suffer himself to be sur-

And rising mountains gain upon our sight.
Then first my eyes, by watchful toils opprest,
Comply'd to take the balmy gifts of rest;   35
Then first my hands did from the rudder part,
(So much the love of home possess'd my heart)
When lo! on board a fond debate arose;
What rare device those vessels might enclose?
What sum, what prize from *Æolus* I brought?   40
Whilst to his neighbour each express'd his thought,
      Say whence, ye Gods, contending nations strive
Who most shall please, who most our Hero give?
Long have his coffers groan'd with *Trojan* spoils;
Whilst we, the wretched part'ners of his toils,   45
Reproach'd by want, our fruitless labours mourn,
And only rich in barren fame return.
Now *Æolus*, ye see, augments his store:
But come, my friends, these mystick gifts explore.
They said: and (oh curs'd fate!) the thongs unbound;   50

priz'd with sleep, when he was almost ready to enter the ports of his own country?
and is it not probable that the joy he must be suppos'd to receive at the sight of it,
should not induce him to a few hours watchfulness? It is easier to defend his
sleeping here, than in the 13th of the *Odyssey*: the Poet very judiciously tells us,
that *Ulysses* for nine days together almost continually wak'd and took charge of
the vessel, and the word κεκμηῶτα shews that nature was wearied out, and that
he fell into an involuntary repose; it can therefore be no diminution to his character to be forc'd to yield to the calls of nature, any more than it is to be hungry:
His prudence and love of his country sufficiently appear from the care he took
thro' the space of nine days to arrive at it; so that this circumstance must be
imputed to the infirmity of human nature, and not to a defect of care or wisdom
in *Ulysses*.

50. *They said: and (oh curs'd fate!) the thongs unbound.*] This relation has been
blam'd as improbable; what occasion was there to unbind the bag, when these
companions of *Ulysses* might have satisfy'd their curiosity that there was no
treasure in it from the lightness of it? But *Homer* himself obviates this objection,
by telling us that *Æolus* fasten'd it in the vessel, as *Eustathius* observes,

Νηῒ δ' ἐνὶ γλαφυρῇ κατέδει—⟨23⟩

Bossu gives us the moral of this fable or allegory, *cap.* 10. *lib.* 1. By the winds
inclosed in the bag, into which the companions of *Ulysses* were so unwise as to pry
is to be understood, that we ought not to intrude into those mysteries of govern-

The gushing tempest sweeps the Ocean round;
Snatch'd in the whirl, the hurried navy flew,
The Ocean widen'd, and the shores withdrew.
Rowz'd from my fatal sleep, I long debate
If still to live, or desp'rate plunge to Fate: 55
Thus doubting, prostrate on the deck I lay,
'Till all the coward thoughts of death gave way.

    Mean-while our vessels plough the liquid plain, ⎫
And soon the known *Æolian* coast regain: ⎬
Our groans the rocks re-murmur'd to the main.   ⎭   60
We leap'd on shore, and with a scanty feast
Our thirst and hunger hastily repress'd;
That done, two chosen heralds strait attend
Our second progress to my royal friend;
And him amidst his jovial sons we found,   65
The banquet steaming, and the goblets crown'd:
There humbly stopp'd with conscious shame and awe,
Nor nearer than the gate presum'd to draw.
But soon his sons their well-known guest descry'd,
And starting from their couches loudly cry'd,   70
Ulysses here! what Dæmon cou'dst thou meet
To thwart thy passage, and repel thy fleet?
Wast thou not furnish'd by our choicest care

---

ment which the Prince intends to keep secret: The tempests and confusions rais'd by the loosing the winds, represent the mischiefs and disorders that arise from such a vain curiosity in the subject: A wise people permit the winds to rest without molestation, and satisfie themselves with those that the Prince is pleas'd to release, and believe them to be the most proper and useful. But whatever judgment is pass'd upon this explication, it is certainly an instance of the ill consequences of avarice, and unseasonable curiosity.

55. *If still to live, or desp'rate plunge to Fate.*] We ought not to infer from this passage, that *Homer* thought a person might lawfully take away his own life to avoid the greatest dangers; what *Ulysses* here speaks arises from the violence of a sudden passion, and gives us a true picture of Human Nature: The wisest of men are not free from the infirmity of passion, but reason corrects and subdues it. This is the case in the instance before us; *Ulysses* has so much of the man in him as to be liable to the passion of man; but so much virtue and wisdom as to restrain and govern it.

For *Greece*, for home, and all thy soul held dear?
Thus they; in silence long my fate I mourn'd,   75
At length these words with accent low return'd.
Me, lock'd in sleep, my faithless crew bereft
Of all the blessings of your god-like gift!
But grant, oh grant our loss we may retrieve:
A favour you, and you alone can give.   80
    Thus I with art to move their pity try'd,
And touch'd the Youths; but their stern Sire reply'd,
Vile wretch, begone! this instant I command
Thy fleet accurs'd to leave our hallow'd land.
His baneful suit pollutes these bless'd abodes,   85
Whose fate proclaims him hateful to the Gods.
    Thus fierce he said: we sighing went our way,
And with desponding hearts put off to sea.
The sailors spent with toils their folly mourn,
But mourn in vain; no prospect of return.   90
    Six days and nights a doubtful course we steer, }
The next proud *Lamos'* stately tow'rs appear,
And *Læstrigonia's* gates arise distinct in air.
The shepherd quitting here at night the plain,

---

83. *Vile wretch, begone!*—] This unhospitable character of *Æolus* may seem contrary to the humane disposition which *Homer* before ascrib'd to him; he therefore
tells us, that *Ulysses* appear'd to him to be an object of divine vengeance, and that
to give him assistance would be to act against the will of the Gods. But, observes
Eustathius, is not this an ill-chosen relation to be made to the *Phæacians*, as the
Critics have remark'd, and might it not deter them from assisting a man whom
Æolus had rejected as an enemy to the Gods? He answers, that it was evident to
the *Phæacians*, that *Ulysses* was no longer under the displeasure of Heaven, that the
imprecations of *Polyphemus* were fulfill'd; he being to be transported to his own
country by strangers, according to his prayer in the ninth of the *Odyssey*, and consequently the *Phæacians* have nothing to fear from the assistance which they lend
Ulysses.

94. *The shepherd quitting here at night the plain,* &c.] This passage has been
thought to be very difficult; but *Eustathius* makes it intelligible: The land of the
Laestrygones was fruitful, and fit for pasturage; it was the practice to send the
sheep by day, and the oxen by night; for it was infested by a kind of fly that was
very grievous to the oxen by day, whereas the wool of the sheep defended them

from it; and therefore the shepherds drove their oxen to pasture by night. If the same shepherd who watched the sheep by day, could pass the night without sleep, and attend the oxen, he perform'd a double duty, and consequently merited a double reward. *Homer* says, that the ways of the night and day were near to each other, that is, the pastures of the sheep and oxen, and the ways that led to them were adjacent; for the shepherd that drove his flocks home, (or εἰσελάων, as *Homer* expresses it,) could call to the herdsman, who drove his herds to pasture, or ἐξελάων, and be heard with ease, and therefore the roads must be adjoining.

Crates ⟨on authority of Eustathius 1649, 30⟩ gives us a very different interpretation: He asserts that *Homer* intended to express the situation of the *Laestrygones*, and affirms that they lay under the head of the Dragon, (κεφαλὴν δράκοντος, which *Dacier* renders the tail of the Dragon) according to *Aratus* ⟨61–2⟩,

> —ἧχί περ (κεφαλῇ) ἄκραι
> Μίσγονται δύσιες, καὶ ἀντολαὶ ἀλλήλησιν.

which *Tully* thus translates ⟨*De Nat. Deor.* ii 42⟩,

> *Hoc caput hic paullum sese subitoque recondit*
> *Ortus ubi atque obitus partem admiscentur in unam.*

If this be true, the Poet intended to express that there was scarce any night at all among the *Laestrygones*, according to that of *Manilius* ⟨III 346⟩,

> *Vixque ortus, occasus erit—*

But how will this agree with the situation of the *Laestrygones*, who were undoubtedly *Sicilians*, according to the direct affirmation of *Thucydides, lib. 6.* of his History ⟨VI ii 1⟩? Besides, if *Laestrygonia* lay under the head of the Dragon, *Ulysses* must have spent seven months, instead of seven days, in sailing from the Æolian Islands to that country. Neither is there any necessity to have recourse to this solution; for what signifies the length or shortness of the day to the double wages of the shepherds, when it was paid to him who took upon him a double charge of watching the whole day and night, which comprehends the space of four and twenty hours; which alone whether the greater part of it was by night or day, entitled the shepherd to a double reward? I therefore should rather chuse the former interpretation, with which *Didymus* agrees ⟨cf. Spondanus, p. 135⟩. Νυκτεριναί, καὶ ἡμεριναὶ νομαὶ ἐγγύς εἰσι τῆς πόλεως; that is, "both the night pastures, and those of the day, are adjacent to the city."

It is evident that the *Laestrygones* also inhabited *Formiæ*, a city of *Campania* near *Cajeta*: Thus *Horace, lib. 3. Ode* 17 ⟨1–7⟩.

> *Æli vetusto nobilis ab Lamo—*
> *Auctore ab illo ducit originem*
> *Qui Formiarum mœnia dicitur*
> *Princeps—*

It was also call'd *Hormiæ*, according to *Strabo* ⟨v iii 6⟩, Φορμίαι, Λακωνικὸν κτίσμα, Ὁρμίαι λεγόμενον πρότερον διὰ τὸ εὔορμον; that is, "*Formiæ* was built by a *Laconian*, call'd also *Hormiæ*, from its being an excellent station for ships." *Tully* had this place in view in his epistle to *Atticus, lib. 2. Epist. 13. Si vero in hanc* Τηλέπυλον, *veneris* λαιστρυγονίην, *Formias dico*. And *Pliny* to the same purpose,

Calls, to succeed his cares, the watchful swain;   95
But he that scorns the chains of sleep to wear
And adds the herdsman's to the shepherd's care,
So near the pastures, and so short the way, ⎫
His double toils may claim a double pay, ⎬
And joyn the labours of the night and day. ⎭   100
    Within a long recess a bay there lies,
Edg'd round with cliffs, high-pointing to the skies;
The jutting shores that swell on either side
Contract its mouth, and break the rushing tide.
Our eager sailors seize the fair retreat,   105
And bound within the port their crowded fleet:
For here retir'd the sinking billows sleep,
And smiling calmness silver'd o'er the deep.
I only in the bay refus'd to moor,

---

lib. 3. *cap.* 5. *Oppidum Formiæ, Hormiæ ante dictum ut existimavere, antiqua Laestry-gonum sedes.* But how will this agree with *Homer*, who places them in *Sicily*, and *Tully* and *Pliny* in *Campania* in *Italy?*

   Dacier answers, that they were originally *Sicilians*, as appears from *Pliny, lib.* 3. *Chap.* 89. *flumina, Symæthum, Terias, intus Laestrygonii campi, oppida Leontini.* And why might not these *Laestrygones*, or a Colony of them, leave *Sicily* to settle in *Italy*, as it is evident the *Phæacians* had done, and fix'd in *Corcyra?* *Bochart's* opinion concerning this nation is not to be neglected ⟨Pt. II: 1 xxx (p. 621)⟩; the words *Laestrygones* and *Leontines* are of the same import; *Laestrygon* is a *Phoenician* name, *Lais tircam*, that is, *a devouring Lion*; this is render'd literally by the *Latin* word *Leontinum*, and both denote the savage and Leonine disposition of this people: the word *Lamus* is also of *Phoenician* extract: *Laham*, or *Lahama*, signi-fies *a Devourer*; from hence probably was deriv'd that *Lamia*, who devour'd young infants, mention'd by *Horace* in his *Art of Poetry* ⟨340⟩.

               Nec pransæ Lamiæ vivum puerum extrahat alvo.

We are inform'd that there was a Queen of *Libya* of that name, by *Diodorus Siculus* ⟨xx xli 2–6⟩; she was a person of great beauty, but of great barbarity.

   109. *I only in the bay refus'd to moor.*] It may appear at the first view, that *Ulysses* took more care of himself than of his companions; and it may be ask'd, why did he not restrain them from entering the bay, when his caution plainly shews that he was apprehensive of danger? had he more fear than the rest of the company? No; but a greater foresight; a wise man provides as far as lies within his power against all contingencies, and the event shews, that his companions were rash, and he wise to act with so much circumspection; they staid not for command,

And fix'd, without, my haulsers to the shore.   110
   From thence we climb'd a point, whose airy brow
Commands the prospect of the plains below:
No tracks of beasts, or signs of men we found,
But smoaky volumes rolling from the ground.
Two with our herald thither we command,   115
With speed to learn what men possess'd the land.
They went, and kept the wheel's smooth-beaten road
Which to the city drew the mountain wood;
When lo! they met, beside a crystal spring,
The daughter of *Antiphates* the King;   120
She to *Artacia*'s silver streams came down,
(*Artacia*'s streams alone supply the town:)
The damsel they approach, and ask'd what race
The people were? who monarch of the place?
With joy the Maid th' unwary strangers heard,   125

and therefore were justly punish'd for acting precipitately without the direction of their General and King.

   120. *The daughter of* Antiphates, &c.] It is not evident from whence *Ulysses* had the knowledge of these particulars; the persons whom he sent to search the land perish'd in the attempt, or were destroy'd with the fleet by the *Laestrygones*: How then could this relation be made to *Ulysses*? It is probable that he had his information from *Circe* or *Calypso*, for *Circe* in the sequel of the *Odyssey* tells *Ulysses*, that she was acquainted with all the sufferings that he had undergone by sea; and if she, as a Goddess, knew his adventures, why might she not relate to him these particulars? *Homer* a little lower tells us, that the *Laestrygones* transfix'd (πείροντες) the companions of *Ulysses*, and then carry'd them away on their weapons like so many fishes; others prefer εἴροντες, that is, connecting them together like a range of fishes; both which very well express the prodigious strength of these Giants: others chuse the word ἀσπαίροντας, or, "they eat them yet alive (*palpitantes*) like fishes." The preference is submitted to the Reader. *Eustathius*.

   I will only add, that possibly the relation of the barbarity of *Polyphemus*, and *Antiphates*, with respect to their eating the flesh of men, may not be entirely fabulous: Modern history assures us, that savages have been found in parts of the world lately discover'd, who eat the bodies of their enemies: It is therefore no wonder that the more polite and civiliz'd nations of Antiquity, look'd upon such men as monsters, and that their Poets painted them as such, or perhaps aggravated the *fierté*, or fierceness of their features, struck with horrour at their brutal inhumanity.

And shew'd them where the royal dome appear'd.
They went; but as they ent'ring saw the Queen
Of size enormous, and terrific mien,
(Not yielding to some bulky mountain's height)
A sudden horror struck their aking sight.   130
Swift at her call her husband scowr'd away
To wreak his hunger on the destin'd prey;
One for his food the raging glutton slew,
But two rush'd out, and to the navy flew.
   Balk'd of his prey, the yelling monster flies,   135
And fills the city with his hideous cries;
A ghastly band of Giants hear the roar,
And pouring down the mountains, crowd the shore.
Fragments they rend from off the craggy brow,
And dash the ruins on the ships below: 140
The crackling vessels burst; hoarse groans arise,
And mingled horrors eccho to the skies.
The men, like fish, they stuck upon the flood,
And cram'd their filthy throats with human food.
Whilst thus their fury rages at the bay,   145
My sword our cables cut, I call'd to weigh;
And charg'd my men, as they from fate wou'd flie,
Each nerve to strain, each bending oar to ply.
The sailors catch the word, their oars they seize,
And sweep with equal strokes the smoaky seas;   150
Clear of the rocks th' impatient vessel flies;
Whilst in the port each wretch encumber'd dies.
With earnest haste my frighted sailors press,
While kindling transports glow'd at our success;
But the sad fate that did our friends destroy   155
Cool'd ev'ry breast, and damp'd the rising joy.
   Now dropp'd our anchors in th' *Ææan* bay,
Where *Circe* dwelt, the daughter of the Day;

158. *Where* Circe *dwelt.*] *Hesiod* in his *Theogony* ⟨956-7⟩ agrees with *Homer* as to
the Genealogy of *Circe* and *Æetes.*

Her mother *Persè*, of old Ocean's strain,
Thus from the Sun descended, and the Main.   160
(From the same lineage stern *Æætes* came,
The far-fam'd brother of th' enchantress dame)
Goddess, and Queen, to whom the pow'rs belong
Of dreadful Magic, and commanding Song.
Some God directing, to this peaceful bay   165
Silent we came, and melancholy lay,
Spent and o'erwatch'd. Two days and nights roll'd on,
And now the third succeeding morning shone.
I climb'd a cliff, with spear and sword in hand,

Ἡελίῳ δ' ἀκάμαντι τέκεν κλυτὴ Ὠκεανίνη
Περσηῒς Κίρκην τε καὶ Αἰήτην βασιλῆα.

That is, "*Perseis* the daughter of *Oceanus* bore to *Phœbus*, *Circe* and King *Æetes*."
But why are they fabled to be the offspring of the sun? *Eustathius* answers, either
from their high birth, as the great personages of Antiquity were call'd Διογενεῖς,
or the sons of *Jupiter*, and the Sun in the ancient Mythology represented that
Deity; or from their extraordinary beauty, which might be compar'd to the Sun,
or from their illustrious actions. But perhaps the whole might be deriv'd from the
way of speaking among the Orientals; at this day we are inform'd from the best
Historians, that such language prevails in the eastern countries, and Kings and
great personages are call'd the brothers or offspring of the Sun.

This *Ææa* is a mountain or promontory in *Italy*: perhaps originally an Island,
and still keeping the resemblance of it. Thus *Procopius, Gothicorum, lib.* 1 ⟨v xi 2–3⟩;
but Broome quotes from the accompanying translation into Latin found in the
edition of Maltretus (Paris, 1661–3)⟩. *Circaeum haud modico tractu in mare porrectum
insulæ speciem fert, tam præternavigantibus quam terrestri itinere prætereuntibus:* and
Strabo, lib. 5 ⟨v iii 6⟩. Κιρκαῖον ὄρος νησίζον θαλάττη τε καὶ ἕλεσι. But is the
relation that *Homer* makes of this Island, and of *Circe*, agreeable to truth? Undoubtedly it is not; but *Homer* was very well acquainted with the story of *Medea*
and applies what was reported of that Enchantress to *Circe*, and gives the name of
Ææa to the Island of *Circe*, in resemblance to *Æa*, a city of *Colchis*, the country of
Medea and *Æetes*. That *Homer* was not a stranger to the story of *Medea* is evident,
for he mentions the ship *Argo* in the 12th *Odyssey*, in which *Jason* sail'd to *Colchis*,
where *Medea* fell in love with him; so that tho' *Circe* be a fabled Deity, yet what
Homer says of her, was applicable to the character of another person, and consequently a just foundation for a story in Poetry. With this opinion *Strabo* agrees
⟨1 ii 40⟩.

169. *I climb* ⟨sic⟩ *a cliff.*] *Scaliger, lib.* 5. of his *Poetics* ⟨cap. iii, p. 218 B2⟩
observes, that there is a general resemblance between *Ulysses* in *Homer*, and
Æneas in *Virgil*, and that *Æneas* acts in the same manner as *Ulysses* ⟨1 306–9⟩.

Whose ridge o'erlook'd a shady length of land;   170
To learn if aught of mortal works appear,
Or chearful voice of mortal strike the ear?
From the high point I mark'd, in distant view,
A stream of curling smoke ascending blue,
And spiry tops, the tufted trees above,   175
Of *Circe*'s Palace bosom'd in the grove.
    Thither to haste, the region to explore,
Was first my thought: but speeding back to shore
I deem'd it best to visit first my crew,
And send out spies the dubious coast to view.   180
As down the hill I solitary go,
Some pow'r divine who pities human woe
Sent a tall stag, descending from the wood,
To cool his fervor in the crystal flood;
Luxuriant on the wave-worn bank he lay,   185
Stretch'd forth, and panting in the sunny ray.
I lanc'd my spear, and with a sudden wound
Transpierc'd his back, and fix'd him to the ground.
He falls, and mourns his fate with human cries:
Thro' the wide wound the vital spirit flies.   190
I drew, and casting on the river side
The bloody spear, his gather'd feet I ty'd
With twining osiers which the bank supply'd.

—*exire, locosque*
Explorare novos, quas vento accesserit oras,
Qui teneant, (nam inculta videt) hominesne feræne
Quærere constituit.

That Critic remarks, that tho' the attitudes of the two Heroes are the same, yet they are drawn by *Virgil* with a more masterly hand: *Fusior & latior Homerus invenietur, pictior Virgilius, & numeris astrictior* ⟨218 D2 (slightly altered)⟩.

Ulysses himself here takes a general view of the Island, but sends his companions for a more particular information; this was necessary to introduce the following story, and give it an air of probability; if he had made the experiment in his own person, his virtue would have been proof against the sorceries of *Circe*, and consequently there could not have been room for a description of her enchantments. *Eustathius.*

An ell in length the pliant wisp I weav'd,
And the huge body on my shoulders heav'd: 195
Then leaning on the spear with both my hands,
Up-bore my load, and prest the sinking sands
With weighty steps, 'till at the ship I threw
The welcome burden, and bespoke my crew.

  Chear up my friends! it is not yet our fate   200
To glide with ghosts thro' *Pluto*'s gloomy gate.
Food in the desart land, behold! is giv'n,
Live, and enjoy the providence of heav'n.

  The joyful crew survey his mighty size,
And on the future banquet feast their eyes,   205
As huge in length extended lay the beast;
Then wash their hands, and hasten to the feast.
There, 'till the setting sun rowl'd down the light,
They sate indulging in the genial rite.

When evening rose, and darkness cover'd o'er   210
The face of things, we slept along the shore.
But when the rosy morning warm'd the east,
My men I summon'd, and these words addrest.

  Followers and friends! attend what I propose:
Ye sad companions of *Ulysses'* woes!   215
We know not here what land before us lies,
Or to what quarter now we turn our eyes,
Or where the sun shall set, or where shall rise?

---

218. *Or where the sun shall set, or where shall rise.*] The interpretations of this passage are various; some, says *Eustathius*, judge these words not to proceed from the ignorance of *Ulysses*, but that they are the language of despair suggested by his continual calamities: For how could *Ulysses* be ignorant of the east or west, when he saw the sun rise and set every day? others understand it to signifie, that he was ignorant of the clime of the world (ὅπη κοσμικοῦ κλίματος) in which this Island lay. *Strabo* ⟨x ii 12⟩ was of opinion, that the appearances of the heavenly bodies, as the stars, &c. were different in this Island from the position which he had ever before observ'd in any country, and therefore he might well confess his ignorance, and express his concern for his almost desperate condition. He understands by ἠώς all that region thro' which the Sun passes opposite to the North. It is true, that the four quarters of the world may be suppos'd to be here men-

Here let us think (if thinking be not vain)
If any counsel, any hope remain.   220
Alas! from yonder Promontory's brow,
I view'd the coast, a region flat and low;
An Isle incircled with the boundless flood;
A length of thickets, and entangled wood.
Some smoak I saw amid the forest rise,   225
And all around it only seas and skies!
 With broken hearts my sad companions stood, ⎞
Mindful of *Cyclops* and his human food,   ⎟
And horrid *Lestrygons*, the men of blood.   ⎠
Presaging tears apace began to rain;   230
But tears in mortal miseries are vain.
In equal parts I strait divide my band,
And name a chief each party to command;

tion'd by *Ulysses*, ἠώς may express the southern parts thro' which the sun passes, and ζόφος the opposite quarter, which may be said comparatively to be ζόφος, or dark: And then the rising and setting of the Sun, will undeniably denote the eastern and western regions. *Spondanus* ⟨*Od*. p. 137⟩ is of opinion, that *Homer* intended to express the four quarters of the world, otherwise the second verse is a tautology: *Dacier* calls it an explication of the first description. And indeed the mind of man is apt to dwell long upon any object, by which it is deeply affected, as *Ulysses* must here be supposed to be, and therefore he might enlarge upon the sentiment advanc'd in the former line. The meaning then will be this. I know not, says that Heroe, where this Island lies, whether east or west, where the Sun rises, or where he sets. I should therefore understand *Ulysses* to mean, that he knows not how this Island lies with respect to the rest of the world, and especially to *Ithaca* his own country. This is evident from his conduct when he sail'd from *Formiæ* the land of the *Laestrygones*; for instead of making toward the east where *Ithaca* lay, he bore to this Island of *Circe*, which lies on the west of *Formiæ*.

220. *If any counsel, any hope remain.*] This expression may be thought unworthy of the mouth of an Heroe, and serve only to cause his companions to despair; but in reality it has a double effect, it gives us a lively picture of Human Nature, which in the greatest men will show some degrees of sensibility, and at the same time it arms his friends against surprize, and sets the danger they are in full before their eyes, that they may proceed with due circumspection. We do not find that *Ulysses* abandons himself to despair, he still acts like a brave man, but joyns wisdom with bravery, and proceeds at once with the caution of a Philosopher, and the spirit of an Heroe.

I led the one, and of the other side
Appointed brave *Eurylochus* the guide.   235
Then in the brazen helm the lotts we throw,
And fortune casts *Eurylochus* to go:
He march'd, with twice eleven in his train:
Pensive they march, and pensive we remain.
    The Palace in a woody vale they found,   240
High rais'd of stone; a shaded space around:
Where mountain wolves and brindled lions roam,

236. *Then in the brazen helm the lotts we throw.*] *Dacier* is of opinion that *Ulysses* cast lotts out of an apprehension of being disobey'd if he had given positive commands; his companions being so greatly discourag'd by the adventures of *Polyphemus* and the *Laestrygones*. It will be a nobler reason, and more worthy of an Heroe to say, that *Ulysses* was so far from declining a common danger, that he submits himself to an equal chance with his companions to undertake it: This expedition appear'd very hazardous, and if he had directly commanded a select number of his men to attempt it, they might have thought he had exposed them to almost certain destruction; but the contrary conduct takes away this apprehension, and at the same time shews the bravery of *Ulysses*, who puts himself upon a level with the meanest of his soldiers, and is ready to expose his person to an equality of danger.

    Ulysses divides his men into two bodies; each contains two and twenty men: This is agreeable, observes *Eustathius*, to the former account of *Homer*; each vessel carried fifty men, six out of every one were destroy'd by the *Ciconians*, and therefore forty four is the exact number, inclusive of himself and the surviving company.

    242. *Where mountain wolves and brindled lions*, &c.] *Virgil* has borrow'd almost this whole description of *Circe* ⟨vii 15–17⟩, and as *Scaliger* judges ⟨*Poet.* v iii, p. 224 c1⟩, perhaps with good reason, greatly improved it.

     Hinc exaudiri gemitus iræque leonum
     Vincla recusantum, & sera sub nocte rudentum,
     Saetigerique sues, atque in præsepibus ursi, &c.

     From hence were heard rebellowing from ⟨to⟩ *the main,*
     The roars of lions that refuse the chain,
     The grunts of bristled boars, and groans of bears,
     And herds of howling wolves that stun the sailors ears:
     These from their caverns, at the close of night,
     Fill the sad Isle with horrour and affright:
     Darkling they mourn their fate, whom Circe's *pow'r,*
     That watch'd the Moon, and planetary hour,

With words and wicked herbs, from human kind
Had alter'd, and in brutal shapes confin'd.   Dryden ⟨vii 18–27⟩.

It must be confess'd that *Iræ leonum vincla recusantum*, and the epithets and short descriptions adapted to the nature of each savage, are beautiful additions. *Virgil* likewise differs from *Homer* in the manner of the description: *Homer* draws the beasts with a gentleness of nature; *Virgil* paints them with the fierceness of savages. The reason of *Homer*'s conduct is, because they still retain'd the sentiments of men, in the forms of beasts, and consequently their native tenderness.

There is a beautiful moral couch'd under this fable or allegory: *Homer* intended to teach, as *Eustathius* remarks, that pleasure and sensuality debase men into beasts. Thus *Socrates* understood it, as *Xenophon* informs us ⟨*Mem.* i iii 7⟩. Perhaps, adds *Dacier*, by the fawning wolves and lions that guard the portals of *Circe*'s Palace, the Poet means to represent the attendants of such houses of debauchery, which appear gentle and courteous, but are in reality of a brutal disposition, and more dangerous than lions. But upon what foundation is this fable built? Many writers inform us, that *Circe* was a famous Courtezan, and that her beauty drew her admirers as it were by enchantment. Thus *Horace* writes ⟨*Epist.* i ii 23–6⟩,

—Circes pocula nosti,
Quæ si cum sociis stultus, cupidusque bibisset,
Sub domina Meretrice *fuisset turpis & excors,*
Vixisset canis immundus, vel amica luto sus.

It is evident, that *Ulysses* had a very intimate commerce with *Circe*, for *Hesiod* writes ⟨*Theogony* 1011–13⟩ that he had two sons by her, *Agrius* and *Latinus*, who afterwards reign'd in *Tuscany*; other Authors call them *Nausithous* and *Telegonus*.

Κίρκη δ' Ἠελίου θυγάτηρ ὑπεριονίδαο
Γείνατ' Ὀδυσσῆος ταλισίφρονος ἐν φιλότητι
Ἄγριον ἠδὲ Λατῖνον.

Dionysius Halicarn. ⟨*Rom. Antiq.* iv xlv 1⟩ and *Aristotle* ⟨*Poetics* xiv 13⟩ mention *Telegonus* as the son of *Circe* and *Ulysses*, who afterwards slew his father with the bone of a fish inadvertently. Thus *Horace* ⟨*Odes* iii xxix 8⟩,

Telegoni juga Parricidæ.

But then is not this intrigue a breach of Morality, and conjugal fidelity in that Heroe? I refer the Reader to line 198n of the fifth book of the *Odyssey*: I shall only add, that the notions of Morality are now very different from what they were in former ages: Adultery alone was esteem'd criminal, and punish'd with death by the ancient Heathens: Concubinage was not only permitted, but thought to be honourable, as appears from the practice, not only of Heroes, but even of the Pagan Deities; and consequently this was the vice of the age, not in particular of *Ulysses*. But there is a stronger objection against *Ulysses*, and it may be ask'd, how is he to be vindicated for wasting no less space than a whole year in dalliance with an harlot? *Penelope* and his country seem both forgotten, and consequently he appears to neglect his own re-establishment, the chief design of the *Odyssey*: What adds some weight to this observation is, that his companions seem more sensible of his long absence from his country, and regret it more than that Heroe; for they awake him out of his dream, and intreat him to depart from

N

(By magic tam'd) familiar to the dome.
With gentle blandishment our men they meet,
And wag their tails, and fawning lick their feet.   245
As from some feast a man returning late,
His faithful dogs all meet him at the gate,
Rejoycing round, some morsel to receive,
(Such as the good man ever us'd to give.)
Domestick thus the griesly beasts drew near;   250
They gaze with wonder, not unmixt with fear.
Now on the threshold of the dome they stood,
And heard a voice resounding thro' the wood:
Plac'd at her loom within, the Goddess sung;

the Island. It is therefore necessary to take away this objection: for if it be unanswerable, *Ulysses* is guilty of all the miseries of his family and country, by neglecting to redress them by returning; and therefore he must cease to be an
Heroe, and is no longer to be propos'd as a pattern of Wisdom, and imitation, as
he is in the opening of the *Odyssey*. But the stay of *Ulysses* is involuntary, and consequently irreproachable; he is in the power of a Deity, and therefore not
capable of departing without her permission: this is evident: for upon the re-
monstrance made by his companions, he dares not undertake his voyage without
her dismission. His asking consent plainly shews that it was not safe, if practicable,
to go away without it; if he had been a free agent, her leave had been unnecessary: 'tis true, she tells him she will not detain him any longer against his inclinations; but this does not imply that his stay till then had been voluntary, or that he
never had intreated to be dismissed before, but rather intimates the contrary: it
only shews that now at last she is willing he should go away. But why should
Ulysses stand in need of being admonish'd by his companions? does not this
imply that he was unmindful of returning? This is only an evidence that they
were desirous to return as well as he; but he makes a wise use of their impatience,
and takes an occasion from their importunities to press for an immediate dismission.

In short, I am not pleading for perfection in the character of *Ulysses*: Human
Nature allows it not, and therefore it is not to be ascribed to it in Poetry. But if
Ulysses were here guilty, his character ceases to be of a piece; we no longer
interest our selves in his misfortunes, since they are all owing to his own folly; the
nature of the Poem requires, that he should be continually endeavouring to
restore his affairs: if then he be here sunk into a lethargy, his character is at once
lost, his calamities are a just punishment, and the moral of the *Odyssey* is destroy'd,
which is to shew Wisdom and Virtue rewarded, and Vice and Folly punished by
the death of the suitors, and re-establishment of *Ulysses*.

The vaulted roofs and solid pavement rung.   255
O'er the fair web the rising figures shine,
Immortal labour! worthy hands divine.
Polites to the rest the question mov'd,
(A gallant leader, and a man I lov'd.)
    What voice celestial, chaunting to the loom   260
(Or Nymph, or Goddess) ecchos from the room?
Say shall we seek access? With that they call;
And wide unfold the portals of the hall.
    The Goddess rising, asks her guests to stay,
Who blindly follow where she leads the way.   265
Eurylochus alone of all the band,
Suspecting fraud, more prudently remain'd.
On thrones around, with downy coverings grac'd,
With semblance fair th' unhappy men she plac'd.
Milk newly prest, the sacred flow'r of wheat,   270
And honey fresh, and *Pramnian* wines the treat:
But venom'd was the bread, and mix'd the bowl,

---

272. *But venom'd was the bread, and mix'd the bowl.*] It is an undoubted truth, that *Homer* ascribes more power to these magical drugs and incantations than they have in reality; but we are to remember that he is speaking before a credulous audience, who readily believed these improbabilities, and at the same time he very judiciously provides for the satisfaction of his more understanding Readers, by couching an excellent moral under his fables; *viz.* that by indulging our appetites we sink below the dignity of Human Nature, and degenerate into brutality.

I am not in the number of those who believe that there never were any Magicians who perform'd things of an uncommon nature: The story of *Jannes* and *Jambres*, of the Witch of *Endor*, and *Simon Magus*, are undeniable instances of the contrary. Magic is suppos'd to have been first practis'd in *Ægypt*, and to have spread afterwards among the *Chaldaeans*: It is very evident that *Homer* had been in *Ægypt*, where he might hear an account of the wonders perform'd by it. *Dacier* is of opinion, that these deluders, or Magicians, were mimics of the real miracles of *Moses*, and that they are describ'd with a wand, in imitation of that great Prophet.

But if any person thinks that Magic is mere fable, and never had any existence, yet establish'd fame and common opinion justifie a Poet for using it. What has been more ridicul'd than the winds being inclosed in a bag by *Æolus*, and committed to *Ulysses*? but as absurd as this appears, more countries than *Lapland*

With drugs of force to darken all the soul:
Soon in the luscious feast themselves they lost,
And drank oblivion of their native coast.   275
Instant her circling wand the Goddess waves,
To hogs transforms 'em, and the Sty receives.
No more was seen the human form divine,
Head, face and members bristle into swine:
Still curst with sense, their mind remains alone,   280
And their own voice affrights them when they groan.
Mean-while the Goddess in disdain bestows
The mast and acorn, brutal food! and strows

---

pretend to the power of selling a storm or a fair wind at this day, as is notorious
from travellers of credit: and perhaps a Poet would not even in these ages be
thought ridiculous, if speaking of *Lapland*, he should introduce one of these
Venefica's, and describe the ceremonies she used in the performance of her pretended incantations. *Milton* not unhappily has introduc'd the imagin'd power of
these *Lapland* Witches into his *Paradise Lost* ⟨II 662-6⟩.

> —*The night-hag, when call'd*
> *In secret, riding thro' the air she comes,*
> *Lur'd with the smell of infant blood, to dance*
> *With* Lapland *Witches, while the labouring Moon*
> *Eclipses at their charms.*—

In short, *Virgil* has imitated *Homer* in all these bold Episodes, and *Horace* ⟨*Ars
Poet.* 144⟩ calls them the Miracles of the *Odyssey*.

    278. *No more was seen the human form divine*, &c.] *Longinus* ⟨XII 14⟩ here reports
a Criticism of *Zoilus*; he is very pleasant upon this transformation of the companions of *Ulysses*, and calls them, *the squeaking pigs of* Homer: we may gather
from this instance the nature of his Criticisms, and conjecture that they tended to
turn the finest incidents of *Homer* into ridicule. Burlesque was his talent, and
instead of informing the reason by pointing out the errors of the Poem, his only
aim was to make his Readers laugh; but he drew upon himself the indignation of
all the learned world: he was known by the name of the vile *Thracian* slave, and
liv'd in great want and poverty; and posterity prosecutes his memory with the
same animosity. The man was really very learned, as *Dionysius Halicarn.* informs
us ⟨*Ad Pompeium* I 757⟩: His morals were never reproach'd, and yet, as *Vitruvius*
relates ⟨*De Architect.* VII, Pref. 8⟩, he was crucify'd by *Ptolemy*, or as others write,
ston'd to death, or burnt alive at *Smyrna*; so that his only crime was his defamation
of *Homer*: a tragical instance of the great value which was set upon his Poetry by
antiquity, and of the danger of attacking a celebrated Author with malice and
envy.

The fruits of cornel, as their feast, around;
Now prone, and groveling on unsav'ry ground.   285
   Eurylochus with pensive steps and slow,
Aghast returns; the messenger of woe,
And bitter fate. To speak he made essay,⎫
In vain essay'd, nor would his tongue obey,⎬
His swelling heart deny'd the words their way:⎭   290
But speaking tears the want of words supply,
And the full soul bursts copious from his eye.
Affrighted, anxious for our fellows fates,
We press to hear what sadly he relates.
   We went, *Ulysses!* (such was thy command)   295

295, &c. *We went*, Ulysses! (*such was thy command*)] We have here a very lively picture of a person in a great fright, which was admir'd, observes *Eustathius*, by the Ancients: There is not only a remarkable harmony in the flowing of the Poetry, but the very manner of speaking represents the disorder of the speaker; he is in too great an emotion to introduce his speech by any Preface, he breaks at once into it, without preparation, as if he could not soon enough deliver his thoughts. *Longinus* ⟨xix 2⟩ quotes these lines as an instance of the great judgment of *Homer*: there is nothing, says that Critic, which gives more life to a discourse, than the taking away the connections, and conjunctions; when the discourse is not bound together and embarrass'd, it walks and slides along of it self, and will want very little oftentimes of going faster even than the thought of the Orator: Thus in *Xenophon*, *Joyning their bucklers, they gave back, they fought, they slew, they dy'd together* ⟨*Hellenica* iv iii 19⟩; of the same nature is that of *Eurylochus*,

> *We went*, Ulysses—*such was thy command*—
> *Access we sought—nor was access deny'd:*
> *Radiant she came—the portals open'd wide*, &c.
> *I only wait behind—of all the train;*
> *I waited long—and ey'd the doors in vain:*
> *The rest are vanish'd—none repass'd the gate.*

These periods thus cut off, and yet pronounc'd with precipitation, are signs of a lively sorrow; which at the same time hinders, yet forces him to speak.
   Many such sudden transitions are to be found in *Virgil* ⟨ix 427⟩, of equal beauty with this of *Homer*:

> *Me, me, inquam qui feci, in me convertite tela.*

Here the Poet shews the earnestness of the speaker, who is in so much haste to speak, that his thoughts run to the end of the sentence almost before his tongue can begin it. Thus *Achæmenides* in his flight from the *Cyclops* ⟨iii 599–601⟩,

> *—Per sidera testor,*

Thro' the lone thicket, and the desart land.
A Palace in a woody vale we found
Brown with dark forests, and with shades around.
A voice celestial eccho'd from the doom,
Or Nymph, or Goddess, chaunting to the loom.   300
Access we sought, nor was access deny'd:
Radiant she came; the portals open'd wide:

Per superos, atque hoc cæli spirabile lumen,
Tollite me, Teucri.

Here the Poet makes no connection with the preceding discourse, but leaves out
the *inquit*, to express the precipitation and terror of *Achæmenides*.

But our countryman *Spenser* has equall'd if not surpass'd these great Poets of
Antiquity, in painting a figure of Terror in the ninth *Canto* of the *Fairy Queen* ⟨I
ix 24–6⟩, where Sir *Trevisan* flies from Despair.

He answer'd nought at all: but adding new
Fear to his first amazement, staring wide
With stony eyes, and heartless hollow hue,
Astonish'd stood, as one that had espy'd
Infernal furies, with their chains unty'd;
Him yet again, and yet again bespake
The gentle Knight; who nought to him reply'd,
But trembling every joynt did inly quake,
And falt'ring tongue at last, these words seem'd forth to shake.

For God's dear love, Sir Knight, do me not stay,
For lo! he comes, he comes, fast after me,
Eft looking back, would fain have run away.

The description sets the figure full before our eyes, he speaks short, and in broken
and interrupted periods, which excellently represent the agony of his thoughts;
and when he is a little more confirm'd and embolden'd, he proceeds,

And am I now in safety sure, quoth he,
From him who would have forced me to die?
And is the point of Death now turn'd from me?
Then I may tell this hapless History.

We see he breaks out into interrogations, which, as *Longinus* observes ⟨XIX 2⟩,
give great motion, strength, and action to discourse. If the Poet had proceeded
simply, the expression had not been equal to the occasion; but by these short
questions, he gives strength to it, and shews the disorder of the speaker, by the
sudden starts and vehemence of the periods. The whole *Canto* of Despair is a
piece of inimitable Poetry; the picture of Sir *Trevisan* has a general resemblance
to this of *Eurylochus*, and seems to have been copy'd after it, as will appear upon
comparison.

The Goddess mild invites the guests to stay:
They blindly follow where she leads the way.
I only wait behind, of all the train;   305
I waited long, and ey'd the doors in vain:
The rest are vanish'd, none repass'd the gate;
And not a man appears to tell their fate.

    I heard, and instant o'er my shoulders flung
The belt in which my weighty faulchion hung;   310
(A beamy blade) then seiz'd the bended bow,
And bade him guide the way, resolv'd to go.
He, prostrate falling, with both hands embrac'd
My knees, and weeping thus his suit address'd.

    O King belov'd of *Jove!* thy servant spare,   315
And ah, thy self the rash attempt forbear!
Never, alas! thou never shalt return,
Or see the wretched for whose loss we mourn.
With what remains, from certain ruin fly,
And save the few not fated yet to die.   320
    I answer'd stern. Inglorious then remain,

---

   313. *With both hands embrac'd My knees—*] The character of *Eurylochus*, who had
married *Clymene* the sister of *Ulysses*, is the character of a brave man, who being
witness to the dreadful fate of his companions is diffident of himself, and judges
that the only way to conquer the danger is to fly from it. To fear upon such an
occasion, observes *Dacier*, is not Cowardice, but Wisdom. But what is more
remarkable in this description, is the art of *Homer* in inserting the character of a
brave man under so great a consternation, to set off the character of *Ulysses*, who
knows how at once to be bold and wise; for the more terrible and desperate the
adventure is represented by *Eurylochus*, the greater appears the intrepidity of
Ulysses, who trusting to his own wisdom, and the assistance of the Gods, has the
courage to attempt it. What adds to the merit of the action is, that he undertakes
it solely for his companions, as *Horace* describes him ⟨*Epist.* I ii 21–2⟩:
> *Dum sibi, dum sociis reditum parat, aspera multa*
> *Pertulit, adversis rerum immersabilis undis.*

321.   —*Inglorious then remain,*
                Here feast and loiter.—]
This expression is used sarcastically by *Ulysses*, and in derision of his fears. *Dacier*
remarks, that *Ulysses* having not seen what is related by *Eurylochus*, believes his
refusal to return, proceeds from his faint-heartedness: An instance, adds she, that
we frequently form wrong judgments of mens actions, when we are ignorant of

Here feast and loiter, and desert thy train.
Alone, unfriended, will I tempt my way;
The laws of Fate compell, and I obey.
    This said, and scornful turning from the shore   325
My haughty step, I stalk'd the vally o'er.
'Till now approaching nigh the magic bow'r,
Where dwelt th' enchantress skill'd in herbs of pow'r;
A form divine forth issu'd from the wood,
(Immortal *Hermes* with the golden rod)   330
In human semblance. On his bloomy face
Youth smil'd celestial, with each opening grace.
He seiz'd my hand, and gracious thus began.
Ah whither roam'st thou? much-enduring man!
O blind to fate! what led thy steps to rove   335
The horrid mazes of this magic grove?
Each friend you seek in yon enclosure lies,
All lost their form, and habitants of styes.
Think'st thou by wit to model their escape?
Sooner shalt thou, a stranger to thy shape,   340
Fall prone their equal: First thy danger know,
Then take the antidote the Gods bestow.
The plant I give thro' all the direful bow'r
Shall guard thee, and avert the evil hour.
Now hear her wicked arts. Before thy eyes   345
The bowl shall sparkle, and the banquet rise;
Take this, nor from the faithless feast abstain,
For temper'd drugs and poysons shall be vain.

---

the motives of them. I confess I am of opinion, that there is some degree of cowardice in the character of *Eurylochus*: A man truly brave would not express such confusion and terror in any extremity; he is not to be inspirited either by *Ulysses,* or the example of his other companions, as appears from the sequel, insomuch that *Ulysses* threatens to kill him for a coward; this prevails over his first fears, and he submits to meet a future danger, merely to avoid one that is present. What makes this observation more just is, that we never see a brave man drawn by *Homer* or *Virgil* in such faint colours; but they always discover a presence of mind upon all emergencies.

Soon as she strikes her wand, and gives the word,
Draw forth and brandish thy refulgent sword,   350
And menace death: those menaces shall move
Her alter'd mind to blandishment and love.
Nor shun the blessing proffer'd to thy arms,
Ascend her bed, and taste celestial charms:
So shall thy tedious toils a respite find,   355
And thy lost friends return to humankind.
But swear her first by those dread oaths that tie
The pow'rs below, the blessed in the sky;
Lest to the⟨e⟩ naked secret fraud be meant,
Or magic bind thee, cold and impotent.   360
    Thus while he spoke, the sovereign plant he drew,

361.   —*The sovereign plant he drew,*
                Where on th' all-bearing earth unmark'd it grew, &c.]
This whole passage is to be understood allegorically. *Mercury* is Reason, he being
the God of Science: The plant which he gives as a preservative against incantation is instruction; the root of it is black, the flower white and sweet; the root
denotes that the foundation or principles of instruction appear obscure and
bitter, and are distasteful at first, according to that saying of *Plato*, *The beginnings
of instruction are always accompanied with reluctance and pain* ⟨cited in Mme. Dacier's
L'Odyssée (Paris, 1716), II 235–6⟩. The flower of *Moly* is white and sweet; this
denotes that the fruits of instruction are sweet, agreeable, and nourishing. *Mercury* gives this plant; this intimates, that all instruction is the gift of Heaven:
Mercury brings it not with him, but gathers it from the place where he stands, to
shew that Wisdom is not confin'd to places, but that every where it may be found,
if Heaven vouchsafes to discover it, and we are disposed to receive and follow it.
Thus *Isocrates* understands the Allegory of *Moly*; he adds, Πικρὰν εἶναι ῥίζαν
αὐτῆς τὸ δὲ Μώλυος ἄνθος λευκὸν κατὰ γάλα διὰ τὴν τοῦ τέλους παιδείας
λαμπρότητα, ἤδη καὶ τὸ ἡδὺ καὶ τρόφιμον ⟨on authority of Eustathius, 1658,
27⟩. The root of *Moly* is bitter, but the flower of it white as milk, to denote the
excellency of instruction, as well as the pleasure and utility of it in the end.
He further illustrates the Allegory, by adding καρποὺς τῆς παιδείας εἰ καὶ
μὴ γάλακτι ἰκέλους ἀλλὰ γλυκεῖς, &c. That is, "the fruits of instruction
are not only white as milk, but sweet, tho' they spring from a bitter root." *Eustathius.*
    Maximus Tyrius also gives this story an allegorical sense, *Dissert*. 16 ⟨*Diss*. xxvi
9 (Teubner citation, but Broome's text)⟩. Αὐτὸν μὲν τὸν Ὀδυσσέα ουχ ὁρᾶς,
ὡς παντοίαις συμφοραῖς ἀντιτεχνώμενος ἀρετῇ σώζει, τοῦτο αὐτῷ τὸ ἐκ
Κίρκης Μῶλυ, τοῦτο τὸ ἐν θαλάττη κρήδεμνον; that is, "Dost thou not observe
N*

Where on th' all-bearing earth unmark'd it grew,
And shew'd its nature and its wond'rous pow'r:
Black was the root, but milky white the flow'r;
Moly the name, to mortals hard to find,   365
But all is easy to th' ethereal kind.
This *Hermes* gave, then gliding off the glade
Shot to *Olympus* from the woodland shade.
     While full of thought, revolving fates to come,
I speed my passage to th' enchanted dome: 370
Arriv'd, before the lofty gates I stay'd;
The lofty gates the Goddess wide display'd:
She leads before, and to the feast invites;
I follow sadly to the magic rites.
Radiant with starry studs, a silver seat   375
Receiv'd my limbs; a footstool eas'd my feet.
She mixt the potion, fraudulent of soul;
The poison mantled in the golden bowl.

Ulysses, how by opposing virtue to adversity he preserves his life? This is the Moly that protects him from *Circe*, this is the Scarf that delivers him from the storm, from *Polyphemus*, from Hell," &c. See also *Dissert.* 19 ⟨*Diss.* xxix 6–7 (Teubner)⟩.

It is pretended that *Moly* is an *Ægyptian* plant, and that it was really made use of as a preservative against Enchantments: but I believe the *Moly* of *Mercury*, and the *Nepenthe* of *Helen*, are of the same production, and grow only in Poetical ground.

Ovid has translated this passage in his *Metamorphoses*, lib. 14 ⟨291–2⟩.

   Pacifer huic dederat florem Cyllenius album;
   Moly vocant Superi. nigra radice tenetur, &c.

There is a remarkable sweetness in the verse which describes the appearance of *Mercury* in the shape of a young man;

   —Νεηνίη ἀνδρὶ ἐοικώς
Πρῶτον ὑπηνήτῃ τοῦ περ χαριεστάτη ἥβη.
   —*On his bloomy face*
   Youth smil'd celestial—

Virgil was sensible of the beauty of it, and imitated it ⟨ix 181⟩.

   Ora puer prima signans intonsa juventa.

But in the opinion of *Macrobius*, he falls short of *Homer*, lib. 5. Saturn. *13. Præter-missa gratia incipientis pubertatis* τοῦ περ χαριεστάτῃ, *Minus gratam fecit latinam descriptionem.*

I took, and quaff'd it, confident in heav'n:
Then wav'd the wand, and then the word was giv'n. 380
Hence, to thy fellows! (dreadful she began)
Go, be a beast!—I heard, and yet was man.
    Then sudden whirling like a waving flame
My beamy faulchion, I assault the dame.
Struck with unusual fear, she trembling cries, 385
She faints, she falls; she lifts her weeping eyes.
    What art thou? say! from whence, from whom you
       came?
O more than human! tell thy race, thy name.
Amazing strength, these poysons to sustain!
Not mortal thou, nor mortal is thy brain. 390
Or art thou he? the man to come (foretold
By *Hermes* pow'rful with the wand of gold)
The man from *Troy*, who wander'd Ocean round;
The man, for Wisdom's various arts renown'd.
Ulysses? oh! thy threat'ning fury cease, 395
Sheath thy bright sword, and join our hands in peace;
Let mutual joys our mutual trust combine,
And Love and love-born confidence be thine.
    And how, dread *Circe!* (furious I rejoyn)
Can Love and love-born confidence be mine? 400
Beneath thy charms when my companions groan,

---

379. *I took, and quaff'd it, confident in heav'n.*] It may be ask'd if *Ulysses* is not as culpable as his companions, in drinking this potion? Where lies the difference? and how is the Allegory carried on, when *Ulysses* yields to the solicitation of *Circe*, that is Pleasure, and indulges, not resists his appetites? The moral of the fable is, that all pleasure is not unlawful, but the excess of it: We may enjoy, provided it be with moderation. *Ulysses* does not taste till he is fortify'd against it; whereas his companions yielded without any care or circumspection; they indulged their appetites only, *Ulysses* tastes merely out of a desire to deliver his associates: he makes himself master of *Circe*, or Pleasure, and is not in the power of it, and enjoys it upon his own terms; they are slaves to it, and out of a capacity ever to regain their freedom but by the assistance of *Ulysses*. The general moral of the whole fable of *Circe* is, that Pleasure is as dreadful an enemy as Danger, and a *Circe* as hard to be conquer'd as a *Polyphemus*.

Transform'd to beasts, with accents not their own.
O thou of fraudful heart! shall I be led
To share thy feast-rites, or ascend thy bed;
That, all unarm'd, thy vengeance may have vent,   405
And magic bind me, cold and impotent?
Celestial as thou art, yet stand deny'd:
Or swear that oath by which the Gods are ty'd,
Swear, in thy soul no latent frauds remain,
Swear, by the Vow which never can be vain.   410
 The Goddess swore: then seiz'd my hand, and led
To the sweet transports of the genial bed.
Ministrant to their Queen, with busy care
Four faithful handmaids the soft rites prepare;
Nymphs sprung from fountains, or from shady woods,
Or the fair offspring of the sacred floods.   416
One o'er the couches painted carpets threw,
Whose purple lustre glow'd against the view:
White linnen lay beneath. Another plac'd
The silver stands with golden flaskets grac'd: 420

---

403.   —*Shall I be led*
                        To share thy feast-rites.]

Eustathius observes, that we have here the picture of a man truly wise, who when Pleasure courts him to indulge his appetites, not only knows how to abstain, but suspects it to be a bait to draw him into some inconveniencies: A man should never think himself in security in the house of a *Circe*. It may be added, that these apprehensions of *Ulysses* are not without a foundation; from this intercourse with that Goddess, *Telegonus* sprung, who accidentally slew his father *Ulysses*.

414. *Four faithful handmaids*, &c.] This large description of the entertainment in the Palace of *Circe* is particularly judicious; *Ulysses* is in an house of pleasure, and the Poet dwells upon it, and shews how every circumstance contributes to promote and advance it. The attendants are all Nymphs, and the bath and perfumes usher in the feast and wines. The four verses that follow, are omitted by *Dacier*, and they are mark'd in *Eustathius* as superfluous; they are to be found in other parts of the *Odyssey*; but that, I confess, would be no argument why they should not stand here, (such repetitions being frequent in *Homer*) if they had a due propriety, but they contain a tautology; we see before a table spread for the entertainment of *Ulysses*, why then should that circumstance be repeated? If they are omitted, there will no chasm or incoherence appear, and therefore probably they were not originally inserted here by *Homer*.

With dulcet bev'rage this the beaker crown'd,
Fair in the midst, with gilded cups around:
That in the tripod o'er the kindled pyle
The water pours; the bubling waters boil:
An ample vase receives the smoking wave,   425
And in the bath prepar'd my limbs I lave;
Reviving sweets repair the mind's decay,
And take the painful sense of toil away.
A vest and tunick o'er me next she threw,
Fresh from the bath and dropping balmy dew.   430
Then led and plac'd me on the sov'reign seat,
With carpets spread; a footstool at my feet.
The golden ew'r a nymph obsequious brings,
Replenish'd from the cool, translucent springs;
With copious water the bright vase supplies   435
A silver laver of capacious size.
I wash'd. The table in fair order spread,
They heap the glittering canisters with bread;
Viands of various kinds allure the taste,
Of choicest sort and savour, rich repaste!   440
Circe in vain invites the feast to share;
Absent I ponder, and absorpt in care:
While scenes of woe rose anxious in my breast,
The Queen beheld me, and these words addrest.
    Why sits *Ulysses* silent and apart?   445
Some hoard of grief close harbour'd at his heart.
Untouch'd before thee stand the cates divine,
And unregarded laughs the rosy wine.
Can yet a doubt, or any dread remain,
When sworn that oath which never can be vain?   450
    I answer'd, Goddess! Human is my breast,
By justice sway'd, by tender pity prest:
Ill fits it me, whose friends are sunk to beasts,
To quaff thy bowls, or riot in thy feasts.
Me wou'dst thou please? for them thy cares imploy,   455
And them to me restore, and me to joy.

With that, she parted: In her potent hand
She bore the virtue of the magic wand.
Then hast'ning to the styes set wide the door,
Urg'd forth, and drove the bristly herd before;   460
Unwieldy, out They rush'd, with gen'ral cry,
Enormous beasts dishonest to the eye.
Now touch'd by counter-charms, they change agen,
And stand majestic, and recall'd to men.
Those hairs of late that bristled ev'ry part,   465
Fall off, miraculous effect of art:
'Till all the form in full proportion rise,
More young, more large, more graceful to my eyes.
They saw, they knew me, and with eager pace
Clung to their master in a long embrace: 470
Sad, pleasing sight! with tears each eye ran o'er,
And sobs of joy re-eccho'd thro' the bow'r:
Ev'n *Circe* wept, her adamantine heart
Felt pity enter, and sustain'd her part.

Son of *Laertes!* (then the Queen began)   475
Oh much-enduring, much-experienc'd man!
Haste to thy vessel on the sea-beat shore,
Unload thy treasures, and thy gally moor;
Then bring thy friends, secure from future harms,
And in our grotto's stow thy spoils and arms.   480

She said. Obedient to her high command
I quit the place, and hasten to the strand.
My sad companions on the beach I found,
Their wistful eyes in floods of sorrow drown'd.
As from fresh pastures and the dewy field   485

---

468. *More young,—more graceful to my eyes.*] *Homer* excellently carries on his allegory; he intends by this expression of the enlargement of the beauty of *Ulysses*'s companions, to teach that men who turn from an evil course, into the paths of Virtue, excel even themselves; having learn'd the value of Virtue from the miseries they suffer'd in pursuit of Vice, they become new men, and as it were enjoy a second life. *Eustathius.*

485. *As from fresh pastures and the dewy field,* &c.] If this simile were to be render'd

(When loaded cribs their evening banquet yield)
The lowing herds return; around them throng
With leaps and bounds their late-imprison'd young,
Rush to their mothers with unruly joy,
And ecchoing hills return the tender cry: 490
So round me press'd exulting at my sight,
With cries and agonies of wild delight,
The weeping sailors; nor less fierce their joy
Than if return'd to *Ithaca* from *Troy*.
Ah master! ever-honour'd, ever dear,   495
(These tender words on ev'ry side I hear)
What other joy can equal thy return?
Not that lov'd country for whose sight we mourn,
The soyl that nurs'd us, and that gave us breath:
But ah! relate our lost companions death.   500
    I answer'd chearful. Haste, your gally moor,

---

literally it would run thus; "as calves seeing the droves of cows returning at night
when they are fill'd with their pasturage, run skipping out to meet them; the
stalls no longer detain them, but running round their dams they fill the plain with
their lowings, *&c.*" If a similitude of this nature were to be introduced into
modern Poetry, I am of opinion it would fall under ridicule for a want of delicacy: but in reality, images drawn from Nature, and a rural life, have always a
very good effect; in particular, this before us enlivens a melancholy description
of sorrows, and so exactly expresses in every point the joy of *Ulysses*'s companions,
we see them in the very description. To judge rightly of comparisons, we are not
to examine if the subject from whence they are deriv'd be great or little, noble or
familiar, but we are principally to consider if the image produc'd be clear and
lively, if the Poet have skill to dignifie it by Poetical words, and if it perfectly paints
the thing it is intended to represent. This rule fully vindicates *Homer*; tho' he frequently paints low life, yet he never uses terms which are not noble; or if he uses
humble words and phrases, it is with so much art, that, as *Dionysius* observes
⟨*De Comp. Verb.* iii⟩, they become noble and harmonious: In short, a Top may be
used with propriety and elegance in a similitude by a *Virgil* ⟨vii 378–84⟩, and the
Sun may be dishonour'd by a *Mævius* ⟨of whom, however, nothing is known
apart from Virgil's reference in Eclogues iii⟩; a mean thought express'd in noble
terms being more tolerable, than a noble thought disgrac'd by mean expressions.
Things that have an intrinsic greatness need only to be barely represented to fill
the soul with admiration, but it shews the skill of a Poet to raise a low subject, and
exalt common appearances into dignity.

And bring our treasures and our arms a-shore:
Those in yon hollow caverns let us lay;
Then rise and follow where I lead the way.
Your fellows live: believe your eyes, and come   505
To taste the joys of *Circe*'s sacred dome.
    With ready speed the joyful crew obey:
Alone *Eurylochus* persuades their stay.
Whither (he cry'd) ah whither will ye run?
Seek ye to meet those evils ye shou'd shun?   510
Will you the terrors of the dome explore,
In swine to grovel, or in lions roar,
Or wolf-like howl away the midnight hour
In dreadful watch around the magic bow'r?
Remember *Cyclops*, and his bloody deed;   515
The leader's rashness made the soldiers bleed.
    I heard incens'd, and first resolv'd to speed
My flying faulchion at the rebel's head.
Dear as he was, by ties of kindred bound,
This hand had stretch'd him breathless on the ground;
But all at once my interposing train   521
For mercy pleaded, nor could plead in vain.
Leave here the man who dares his Prince desert,
Leave to repentance and his own sad heart,
To guard the ship. Seek we the sacred shades   525
Of *Circe*'s Palace, where *Ulysses* leads.
    This with one voice declar'd, the rising train
Left the black vessel by the murm'ring main.
Shame touch'd *Eurylochus* his alter'd breast,

---

515. *Remember* Cyclops, *&c.*] The Poet paints *Eurylochus* uniformly, under
great disorder of mind and terrible apprehensions; There is no similitude between *Circe* and *Cyclops*, with respect to the usage of the companions of *Ulysses*; but
Homer puts these expressions into his mouth, to represent the nature of Terror,
which confounds the thoughts, and consequently distracts the language of a
person who is possessed by it. The character therefore of *Eurylochus* is the imitation of a person confounded with fears, speaking irrationally and incoherently.
Eustathius.

He fear'd my threats, and follow'd with the rest.   530
  Mean-while the Goddess with indulgent cares
And social joys, the late-transform'd repairs:
The bath, the feast, their fainting soul renews;
Rich in refulgent robes, and dropping balmy dews:
Brightning with joy their eager eyes behold   535
Each others face, and each his story told:
Then gushing tears the narrative confound,
And with their sobs the vaulted roofs resound.
When hush'd their passion, thus the Goddess cries:
Ulysses, taught by labours to be wise,   540
Let this short memory of grief suffice.
To me are known the various woes ye bore,
In storms by sea, in perils on the shore;
Forget whatever was in Fortune's pow'r,
And share the pleasures of this genial hour.   545
Such be your minds as ere ye left your coast,
Or learn'd to sorrow for a country lost.
Exiles and wand'rers now, where-e're ye go,
Too faithful memory renews your woe;
The cause remov'd, habitual griefs remain,   550
And the soul saddens by the use of pain.
  Her kind intreaty mov'd the gen'ral breast;
Tir'd with long toil, we willing sunk to rest.
We ply'd the banquet and the bowl we crown'd,
'Till the full circle of the year came round.   555
But when the Seasons, following in their train,
Brought back the months, the days, and hours again;
As from a lethargy at once they rise,
And urge their chief with animating cries.
  Is this, *Ulysses*, our inglorious lot?   560
And is the name of *Ithaca* forgot?
Shall never the dear land in prospect rise,
Or the lov'd palace glitter in our eyes?
  Melting I heard; yet 'till the sun's decline
Prolong'd the feast, and quaff'd the rosy wine: 565

But when the shades came on at evening hour,
And all lay slumbring in the dusky bow'r;
I came a suppliant to fair *Circe*'s bed,
The tender moment seiz'd, and thus I said.

    Be mindful, Goddess, of thy promise made;   570
Must sad *Ulysses* ever be delay'd?
Around their lord my sad companions mourn,
Each breast beats homeward, anxious to return:
If but a moment parted from thy eyes,
Their tears flow round me, and my heart complies.   575
   Go then, (she cry'd) ah go! yet think, not I,
Not *Circe*, but the Fates your wish deny.
Ah hope not yet to breathe thy native air!
Far other journey first demands thy care;

---

579.   *Far other journey*—
             To tread th' uncomfortable paths beneath.]
There should in all the Episodes of Epic Poetry appear a Convenience, if not a
Necessity of every incident; it may therefore be ask'd what Necessity there is for
this descent of *Ulysses* into hell, to consult the shade of *Tiresias*? Could not *Circe*,
who was a Goddess, discover to him all the future contingencies of his life?
Eustathius excellently answers this objection; *Circe* declares to *Ulysses* the necessity
of consulting *Tiresias*, that he may learn from the mouth of that Prophet, that his
death was to be from the Ocean; she acts thus in order to dispose him to stay with
her, after his return from the regions of the dead: or if she cannot persuade him to
stay with her, that she may at least secure him from returning to her rival
Calypso; she had promis'd him Immortality, but by this descent, he will learn that
it is decreed that he should receive his death from the Ocean; for he dy'd by the
bone of a sea-fish call'd *Xiphias*. Her love for *Ulysses* induces her not to make the
discovery her self, for it was evident she would not find credit, but *Ulysses* would
impute it to her love, and the desire she had to deter him from leaving her Island.
This will appear more probable, if we observe the conduct of *Circe* in the future
parts of the *Odyssey*: she relates to him the dangers of *Scylla* and *Charybdis*, of the
Oxen of *Phœbus*, and the *Sirens*; but says nothing concerning his death: This likewise gives an air of probability to the relation. The Isle of *Circe* was adjoining to
Scylla and *Charybdis*, &c. and consequently she may be suppos'd to be acquainted
with those places, and give an account of them to *Ulysses* with exactness, but she
leaves the decrees of Heaven and the fate of *Ulysses* to the narration of the Prophet, it best suiting his character to see into futurity. By the descent of *Ulysses* into
Hell may be signify'd, that a wise man ought to be ignorant of nothing, that he
ought to ascend in thought into Heaven, and understand the heavenly appearances, and be acquainted with what is contain'd in the bowels of the earth, and

To tread th' uncomfortable paths beneath,   580
And view the realms of darkness and of death.
There seek the *Theban* Bard, depriv'd of sight,
Within, irradiate with prophetic light;
To whom *Persephone*, entire and whole,

---

bring to light the secrets of Nature: That he ought to know the nature of the
Soul, what it suffers, and how it acts after it is separated from the body. *Eustathius.*

584. *To whom* Persephone, *&c.*] *Homer* here gives the reason why *Tiresias*
should be consulted, rather than any other ghost, because

τοῦ τε φρένες ἔμπεδοί εἰσι.

This expression is fully explain'd, and the notion of the Soul after death, which
prevail'd among the Ancients, is set in a clear light, Verse 92, and 122, of the
23d book of the *Iliad*, to which passages I refer the Readers. But whence had
Tiresias this privilege above the rest of the dead? *Callimachus* ascribes it to
Minerva ⟨Hymn v 129–30⟩,

Καὶ μόνος εὖτε θάνῃ, πεπνυμένος ἐν νεκύεσσι
Φοιτάσει, μεγάλῳ τίμιος ᾿Αγεσίλᾳ.

Tully mentions this preheminence of *Tiresias* in his first book of *Divination* ⟨xl 88⟩.
Perhaps the whole fiction may arise from his great reputation among the
Antients for Prophecy; and in honour to his memory they might imagine that his
soul after death retain'd the same superiority. *Ovid* in his *Metamorphoses* ⟨III 316–
38⟩ gives us a very jocular reason, for the blindness and prophetic knowledge of
Tiresias, from a matrimonial contest between *Jupiter* and *Juno*. *Cato Major*, as
Plutarch in his *Political Precepts* ⟨*Praec. Gerendae Reipub.* 10 (805 A)⟩ informs us,
apply'd this verse to *Scipio*, when he was made Consul contrary to the *Roman*
Statutes,

Οἷος πέπνυται, τοὶ δὲ σκιαὶ ἀΐσσουσιν.

But I ought not to suppress what *Diodorus Siculus* relates concerning *Tiresias*.
Biblioth. lib. 4 ⟨IV lxvi 6⟩ he tells us, that he had a daughter nam'd *Daphne*, a
Priestess at *Delphi*. Παρ᾿ ἧς φασι καὶ τὸν ποιητὴν ῞Ομηρον πολλὰ τῶν ἐπῶν
σφετερισάμενον, κοσμῆσαι τὴν ἰδίαν ποίησιν. That is, "From whom it is said,
that the Poet *Homer* received many (of the *Sibyl's*) verses, and adorn'd his own
Poetry with them." If this be true, there lay a debt of gratitude upon *Homer*, and
he pays it honourably, by this distinguishing character, which he gives to the
father. An instance of a worthy disposition in the Poet, and it remains at once an
honour to *Tiresias*, and a monument of his own gratitude.

This descent of *Ulysses* into Hell has a very happy effect, it gives *Homer* an
opportunity to embellish his Poetry with an admirable variety, and to insert
Fables and Histories that at once instruct and delight: It is particularly happy
with respect to the *Phæacians*, who could not but highly admire a person whose
wisdom had not only deliver'd him from so many perils on earth, but had been
permitted by the Gods to see the regions of the dead, and return among the

Gave to retain th' unseparated soul: 585
The rest are forms of empty *Æther* made,
Impassive semblance, and a flitting shade.
    Struck at the word, my very heart was dead:
Pensive I sate; my tears bedew'd the bed;
To hate the light and life my soul begun,   590
And saw that all was grief beneath the sun.
Compos'd at length, the gushing tears supprest,
And my tost limbs now weary'd into rest,
How shall I tread (I cry'd) ah *Circe!* say,
The dark descent, and who shall guide the way?   595
Can living eyes behold the realms below?
What bark to waft me, and what wind to blow?
    Thy fated road (the magic Pow'r reply'd)
Divine *Ulysses!* asks no mortal guide.
Rear but the mast, the spacious sail display,   600
The northern winds shall wing thee on thy way.
Soon shalt thou reach old Ocean's utmost ends,

---

living: this relation could not fail of pleasing an audience, delighted with strange stories, and extraordinary adventures.

602. *Soon shalt thou reach old Ocean's utmost ends,* &c.] This whole scene is excellently imagin'd by the Poet, as *Eustathius* observes; the trees are all barren, the place is upon the shores where nothing grows; and all the rivers are of a melancholy signification, suitable to the ideas we have of those infernal regions. *Ulysses* arrives at this place, where he calls up the shades of the dead, in the space of one day; from whence we may conjecture, that he means a place that lies between *Cumæ* and *Baiæ*, near the lake *Avernus*, in *Italy*; which, as *Strabo* remarks ⟨v iv 5⟩, is the scene of the Necromancy of *Homer*, according to the opinion of Antiquity. He further adds, that there really are such rivers as *Homer* mentions, tho' not placed in their true situation, according to the liberty allowable to Poetry. Others write, that the *Cimmerii* once inhabited *Italy*, and that the famous cave of *Pausilypum* was begun by them about the time of the *Trojan* wars: Here they offer'd sacrifice to the *Manes*, which might give occasion to *Homer*'s fiction. The *Grecians*, who inhabited these places after the *Cimmerians*, converted these dark habitations into stoves, bathes, &c.

Silius Italicus writes, that the *Lucrine* lake was anciently call'd *Cocytus*, lib. 12 ⟨116–17⟩.

> *Ast hic Lucrino mansisse vocabula quondam*
> *Cocyti memorat.—*

Where to the main the shelving shore descends;
The barren trees of *Proserpine*'s black woods,
Poplars and willows trembling o'er the floods: 605
There fix thy vessel in the lonely bay,
And enter there the kingdoms void of day:

It is also probable, that *Acheron* was the ancient name of *Avernus*, because *Acherusia*, a large water near *Cumæ*, flows into it by conceal'd passages. *Silius Italicus* informs us, that *Avernus* was also called *Styx* ⟨XII 120–1⟩.

> *Ille olim populis dictum Styga, nomine verso*
> *Stagna inter celebrem nunc mitia monstrat Avernum.*

Here *Hannibal* offer'd sacrifice to the *Manes*, as it is recorded by *Livy* ⟨XXIV xii⟩; and *Tully* affirms it ⟨*Tusc. Disp.* I xvi 37⟩ from an ancient Poet, from whom he quotes the following fragment ⟨but Broome misquotes. The first line below belongs to Cicero's prose, not to the "ancient Poet"⟩;

> *Inde in vicinia nostra Averni lacus*
> *Unde animæ excitantur obscura umbra,*
> *Alti Acherontis aperto ostio.*

This may seem to justifie the observation that *Acheron* was once the name of *Avernus*, tho' the words are capable of a different interpretation.

If these remarks be true, it is probable that *Homer* does not neglect Geography, as most Commentators judge. *Virgil* describes *Æneas* descending into Hell by *Avernus* ⟨VI 201 ff⟩, after the example of *Homer*. *Milton* places these rivers in Hell, and beautifully describes their natures, in his *Paradise Lost* ⟨II 574–86⟩.

> *—Along the banks*
> *Of four Infernal rivers, that disgorge*
> *Into the burning lake their baleful streams,*
> *Abhorred* Styx, *the flood of deadly hate;*
> *Sad* Acheron, *of sorrow, black and deep:*
> Cocytus, *nam'd of lamentation loud*
> *Heard on the ruful stream: fierce* Phlegeton,
> *Whose waves of torrent fire inflame with rage;*
> *Far off from these a slow and silent stream,*
> Lethe *the river of oblivion, rouls*
> *Her watry Labyrinth, whereof who drinks*
> *Forthwith his former state and being forgets,*
> *Forgets both joy and grief, pleasure and pain.*

Thus also agreeably to the idea of Hell the offerings to the infernal powers are all black, the *Cimmerians* lie in a land of darkness; the Heifer which *Ulysses* is to offer is barren, like that in *Virgil* ⟨VI 251⟩,

> *—Sterilemque tibi, Proserpina, vaccam;*

to denote that the grave is unfruitful, that it devours all things, that it is a place where all things are forgotten.

Where *Phlegeton*'s loud torrents rushing down,
Hiss in the flaming gulf of *Acheron*;
And where, slow rolling from the *Stygian* bed,   610
Cocytus' lamentable waters spread;
Where the dark rock o'erhangs th' infernal lake,
And mingling streams eternal murmurs make.
First draw thy faulchion, and on ev'ry side
Trench the black earth a cubit long and wide: 615
To all the shades around libations pour,
And o'er th' ingredients strow the hallow'd flour:
New wine and milk, with honey temper'd, bring,
And living water from the chrystal spring.
Then the wan shades and feeble ghosts implore,   620
With promis'd off'rings on thy native shore;
A barren cow, the stateliest of the Isle,
And, heap'd with various wealth, a blazing pyle:
These to the rest; but to the *Seer* must bleed
A sable ram, the pride of all thy breed.   625
These solemn vows and holy off'rings paid
To all the Phantome-nations of the dead;
Be next thy care the sable sheep to place
Full o'er the pit, and hell-ward turn their face:
But from th' infernal rite thine eye withdraw,   630
And back to Ocean glance with rev'rend awe.
Sudden shall skim along the dusky glades
Thin airy shoals, and visionary shades.
Then give command the sacrifice to haste,
Let the flea'd victims in the flames be cast,   635
And sacred vows, and mystic song, apply'd
To griesly *Pluto*, and his gloomy bride.
Wide o'er the pool thy faulchion wav'd around
Shall drive the spectres from forbidden ground:
The sacred draught shall all the dead forbear,   640
'Till awful from the shades arise the *Seer*.
Let him, Oraculous, the end, the way
The turns of all thy future fate, display,   ⎫
Thy pilgrimage to come, and remnant of thy day.   ⎬
                                                                   ⎭

So speaking, from the ruddy orient shone 645
The morn conspicuous on her golden throne.
The Goddess with a radiant tunick drest
My limbs, and o'er me cast a silken vest.
Long flowing robes of purest white array
The nymph, that added lustre to the day: 650
A Tiar wreath'd her head with many a fold;
Her waste was circled with a zone of gold.
Forth issuing then, from place to place I flew;
Rouze man by man, and animate my crew.
Rise, rise my mates! 'tis *Circe* gives command; 655
Our journey calls us; haste, and quit the land.
All rise and follow, yet depart not all,
For fate decreed one wretched man to fall.
    A youth there was, *Elpenor* was he nam'd,
Nor much for sense, nor much for courage fam'd; 660
The youngest of our band, a vulgar soul
Born but to banquet, and to drain the bowl.
He, hot and careless, on a turret's height
With sleep repair'd the long debauch of night:
The sudden tumult stirr'd him where he lay, 665
And down he hasten'd, but forgot the way;
Full endlong from the roof the sleeper fell,
And snapt the spinal joint, and wak'd in hell.
    The rest crowd round me with an eager look;
I met them with a sigh, and thus bespoke. 670
Already, friends! ye think your toils are o'er,
Your hopes already touch your native shore:

---

659. *A youth there was,* Elpenor *was he nam'd.*] *Homer* dismisses not the description of this house of Pleasure and Debauch, without shewing the Moral of his Fable which is the ill consequences that attend those who indulge themselves in sensuality; this is set forth in the punishment of *Elpenor*. He describes him as a person of no worth, to shew that debauchery enervates our faculties, and renders both the mind and body incapable of thinking, or acting with greatness and bravery. At the same time these circumstantial relations are not without a good effect; for they render the story probable, as if it were spoken with the veracity of an History, not the liberty of Poetry.

Alas! far otherwise the nymph declares,
Far other journey first demands our cares.
To tread th' uncomfortable paths beneath,   675
The dreary realms of darkness and of death:
To seek *Tiresias'* awful shade below,
And thence our fortunes and our fates to know.
    My sad companions heard in deep despair;
Frantic they tore their manly growth of hair;   680
To earth they fell; the tears began to rain;
But tears in mortal miseries are vain.
Sadly they far'd along the sea-beat shore;
Still heav'd their hearts, and still their eyes ran o'er.
The ready victims at our bark we found,   685
The sable ewe, and ram, together bound.
For swift as thought, the Goddess had been there,
And thence had glided, viewless as the air:
The paths of Gods what mortal can survey?
Who eyes their motion, who shall trace their way?   690

I will conclude this book with a Paragraph from *Plutarch*'s *Morals*: It is a piece
of advice to the Fair Sex, drawn from this story of *Circe* and *Ulysses*. "They who
bait their hooks (says this Philosopher) with intoxicated drugs may catch fish
with little trouble; but then they prove dangerous to eat, and unpleasant to the
taste: Thus women who use arts to ensnare their admirers, become wives of fools
or madmen: They whom the sorceress *Circe* enchanted, were no better than
brutes; and she used them accordingly, enclosing them in styes; but she lov'd
Ulysses entirely, whose prudence avoided her intoxications, and made his conversation agreeable. Those women who will not believe that *Pasiphae* was ever
enamour'd of a bull, are yet themselves so extravagant, as to abandon the
society of men of sense and temperance, and to betake themselves to the embraces
of brutal and stupid fellows." *Plut. Conjugal Precepts* ⟨5⟩.

THE
ELEVENTH BOOK
OF THE
ODYSSEY.

The ARGUMENT.
The Descent into Hell

Ulysses *continues his Narration, How he arriv'd at the land of the* Cimmerians, *and what ceremonies he perform'd to invoke the dead. The manner of his descent, and the Apparition of the Shades; his conversation with* Elpenor, *and with* Tiresias, *who informs him in a prophetic manner of his fortunes to come. He meets his mother* Anticleia, *from whom he learns the state of his family. He sees the shades of the ancient* Heroines, *afterwards of the* Heroes, *and converses in particular with* Agamemnon *and* Achilles. Ajax *keeps at a sullen distance, and disdains to answer him. He then beholds* Tityus, Tantalus, Sysiphus, Hercules; *'till he is deterred from further curiosity by the apparition of horrid Spectres, and the cries of the wicked in torments.*

Now to the shores we bend, a mournful train,
Climb the tall bark, and launch into the main:
At once the mast we rear, at once unbind

The Ancients call'd this book Νεκυομαντεία, or Νέκυια, the book of Necromancy: because (says *Eustathius*) it contains an interview between *Ulysses*, and the shades of the dead.

Virgil has not only borrow'd the general design from *Homer*, but imitated many particular incidents: *L'Abbé Fraguier* in the *Memoirs of Literature* ⟨*Discours sur la Manière dont Virgile a imité Homère*, in *Mémoires de Littérature . . . de l'Académie Royale des Inscriptions et Belles Lettres*, II (Paris, 1717) 162⟩ gives his judgment in favour of the *Roman* Poet, and justly observes, that the end and design of the journey is more important in *Virgil* than in *Homer*. *Ulysses* descends to consult *Tiresias*, *Æneas* his father. *Ulysses* takes a review of the shades of celebrated persons that preceded his times, or whom he knew at *Troy*, who have no relation to the story of the *Odyssey*: *Æneas* receives the History of his own posterity; his father instructs him how to manage the *Italian* war, and how to conclude it with honour; that is, to lay the foundations of the greatest Empire in the world: and the Poet by a very happy address takes an opportunity to pay a noble compliment to his patron *Augustus*. In the *Æneid* there is a magnificent description of the descent and entrance into Hell; and the *diseases*, *cares*, and *terrors* that *Æneas* sees in his journey, are very happily imagin'd, as an introduction into the regions of Death: whereas in *Homer* there is nothing so noble, we scarce are able to discover the place where the Poet lays his scene, or whether *Ulysses* continues below or above the ground. Instead of a descent into hell, it seems rather a conjuring up, or an evocation of the dead from hell; according to the words of *Horace*, who undoubtedly had this passage of *Homer* in his thoughts, *Satyr 8. lib.* 1 ⟨26-9⟩.

> —*Scalpere terram*
> *Unguibus, & pullam divellere mordicus agnam*
> *Cœperunt; cruror in fossam confusus, ut inde*
> *Manes* elicerent, *animas responsa daturas*.

But if it be understood of an evocation only, how shall we account for several visions and descriptions in the conclusion of this book? *Ulysses* sees *Tantalus* in the waters of hell, and *Sisyphus* rowling a stone up an infernal mountain; these *Ulysses* could not conjure up, and consequently must be suppos'd to have enter'd at least the borders of those infernal regions. In short, *Fraguier* is of opinion, that *Virgil* profited more by the *Frogs* of *Aristophanes* than by *Homer*; and Mr. *Dryden* prefers the sixth book of the *Æneid* to the eleventh of the *Odyssey* ⟨*Dedication of The Aeneis, Essays*, ed. Ker, II 201⟩, I think with very great reason.

I will take this opportunity briefly to mention the original of all these fictions of infernal Rivers, Judges, &c. spoken of by *Homer*, and repeated and enlarged by *Virgil*. They are of *Ægyptian* extract, as Mr. *Sandys* (that faithful traveller, and judicious Poet) observes, speaking of the Mummies of *Memphis* ⟨*A Relation of a Journey*, II (1615)⟩, *p.* 134.

"These ceremonies perform'd, they laid the corps in a boat to be wafted over *Acherusia*, a lake on the south of *Memphis*, by one only person, whom they call'd *Charon*; which gave *Orpheus* the invention of his infernal ferriman; an ill-favoured slovenly fellow, as *Virgil* describes him, *Æneid 6*. About this lake stood the shady temple of *Hecate*, with the ports of *Cocytus* and *Oblivion*, separated by bars of brass, the original of like fables. When landed on the other side, the bodies were brought before certain Judges; if convinc'd of an evil life they were depriv'd of burial; if otherwise they suffer'd them to be interr'd." This explication shews the foundation of those ancient fables of *Charon, Rhadamanthus*, &c. And also that the Poets had a regard to truth in their inventions, and grounded even their fables upon some remarkable customs, which grew obscure and absurd only because the memory of the customs to which they allude is lost to posterity.

I will only add from *Dacier*, that this book is an evidence of the antiquity of the opinion of the Soul's Immortality. It is upon this that the most ancient of all divinations was founded, I mean that which was perform'd by the evocation of the dead: There is a very remarkable instance of this in the holy Scriptures, in an age not very distant from that of *Homer*. *Saul* consults one of these infernal agents to call up *Samuel*, who appears, or some evil spirit in his form, and predicts

The spacious sheet, and stretch it to the wind:
Then pale and pensive stand, with cares opprest,   5
And solemn horrour saddens every breast.
A freshning breeze the *Magic pow'r supply'd,
While the wing'd vessel flew along the tyde:
Our oars we shipp'd: all day the swelling sails
Full from the guiding pilot catch'd the gales.   10
    Now sunk the Sun from his aerial height,
And o'er the shaded billows rush'd the night:
When lo! we reach'd old Ocean's utmost bounds,
Where rocks controul his waves with ever-during mounds.
    There in a lonely land, and gloomy cells,   15

* *Circe.*

his impending death and calamities ⟨1 Sam. 28 : 7 ff⟩. This is a pregnant instance
of the antiquity of Necromancy, and that it was not of *Homer*'s invention; it prevailed long before his days among the *Chaldaeans*, and spread over all the oriental
world. *Æschylus* has a Tragedy intitled *Persæ*, in which the shade of *Darius* is call'd
up, like that of *Samuel*, and foretells Queen *Atossa* all her misfortunes ⟨681 ff⟩.
Thus it appears that there was a foundation for what *Homer* writes; he only
embellishes the opinions of Antiquity with the ornaments of Poetry.
    I must confess that *Homer* gives a miserable account of a future state; there is
not a person describ'd in happiness, unless perhaps it be *Tiresias*; the good and
the bad seem all in the same condition: Whereas *Virgil* has an Hell for the
wicked, and an *Elysium* for the just. Tho' perhaps it may be a vindication of
Homer to say, that the notions of *Virgil* of a future state were different from these
of *Homer*; according to whom Hell might only be a receptacle for the vehicles of
the dead, and that while they were in Hell, their φρὴν or Spirit might be in
Heaven, as appears from what is said of the εἴδωλον of *Hercules* in this 11th book
of the *Odyssey*.

15.   *There in a lonely land, and gloomy cells,*
                        The dusky nation of Cimmeria *dwells.*]
It is the opinion of many Commentators, that *Homer* constantly in these voyages
of *Ulysses* makes use of a fabulous Geography; but perhaps the contrary opinion
in many places may be true: In this passage, *Ulysses* in the space of one day sails
from the Island of *Circe* to the *Cimmerians*: Now it is very evident from *Herodotus*
⟨IV 12, 28, 100⟩ and *Strabo* ⟨I ii 9⟩, that they inhabited the regions near the
Bosphorus, and consequently *Ulysses* could not sail thither in the compass of a day;
and therefore, says *Strabo*, the Poet removes not only the *Cimmerians*, but their
climate and darkness, from the northern *Bosphorus* into *Campania* in *Italy*.
    But that there really were a people in *Italy* named *Cimmerians* is evident from
the testimony of many Authors. So *Lycophron* plainly understands this passage,

The dusky nation of *Cimmeria* dwells;
The Sun ne'er views th' uncomfortable seats,
When radiant he advances, or retreats:
Unhappy race! whom endless night invades,
Clouds the dull air, and wraps them round in shades.   20
The ship we moor on these obscure abodes;
Dis-bark the sheep, an offering to the Gods;
And hellward bending, o'er the beach descry
The dolesome passage to th' infernal sky.
The victims, vow'd to each *Tartarean* pow'r,   25
Eurylochus and *Perimedes* bore.
Here open'd Hell, all Hell I here implor'd,
And from the scabbard drew the shining sword;
And trenching the black earth on ev'ry side,
A cavern form'd, a cubit long and wide.   30
New wine, with honey-temper'd milk, we bring,

---

and relates these adventures as perform'd in *Italy* ⟨695 ff, 701–2⟩. He recapitulates all the voyages of *Ulysses*, and mentioning the descent into Hell and the *Cimmerians*, he immediately describes the infernal rivers, and adds, (speaking of the *Apennine*)

’Εξ οὗ τὰ πάντα χύτλα, καὶ πᾶσαι μυχῶν
Πηγαὶ κατ’ ’Αυσονῖτιν ἕλκονται χθόνα.

That is, "From whence all the rivers, and all the fountains flow thro' the regions of *Italy*." And these lines of *Tibullus* ⟨III vii 64–6⟩,

> *Cimmerion etiam obscuras accessit ad arces,*
> *Quis numquam candente dies apparuit ortu,*
> *Sive supra terras Phoebus, seu curreret infra.*

are understood by all interpreters to denote the *Italian Cimmerians*; who dwelt near *Baiæ* and the lake *Avernus*; and therefore *Homer* may be imagin'd not entirely to follow a fabulous Geography. It is evident from *Herodotus* ⟨I 15⟩ that these *Cimmerians* were anciently a powerful nation, for passing into *Asia* (says that Author in his *Clio*) they possess'd themeslves of *Sardis*, in the time of *Ardys*, the son of *Gyges*. If so, it is possible they might make several settlements in different parts of the world, and call those settlements by their original name, *Cimmerians*, and consequently there might be *Italian*, as well as *Scythian Cimmerians*.

It must be allow'd that this horrid region is well chosen, for the descent into Hell: It is describ'd as a land of obscurity and horrors, and happily imagin'd to introduce a relation concerning the realms of death and darkness.

31. *New wine, with honey-temper'd milk*.] The word in the original is, μελίκρατον,

Then living waters from the chrystal spring;
O'er these was strow'd the consecrated flour,
And on the surface shone the holy store.
   Now the wan shades we hail, th' infernal Gods,   35
To speed our course, and waft us o'er the floods,
So shall a barren heifer from the stall
Beneath the knife upon your altars fall;
So in our palace, at our safe return
Rich with unnumber'd gifts the Pyle shall burn;   40
So shall a Ram, the largest of the breed,
Black as these regions, to *Tiresias* bleed.
   Thus solemn rites and holy vows we paid
To all the Phantom nations of the dead.
Then dy'd the sheep; a purple torrent flow'd,   45
And all the cavern smok'd with streaming blood.
When lo! appear'd along the dusky coasts,

which (as *Eustathius* observes) the Ancients constantly understood to imply a mixture of honey and milk; but all writers who succeeded *Homer* as constantly used it to signify a composition of water mix'd with honey. The *Latin* Poets have borrow'd their magical rites from *Homer*: Thus *Ovid Metam.* 7. 243.

      Haud procul egesta scrobibus tellure duabus
      Sacra facit: cultrosque in guttura velleris atri
      Conjicit; & patulas perfundit sanguine fossas,
      Tum super invergens liquidi carchesia Bacchi,
      Æneaque invergens tepidi carchesia lactis, &c.

Thus also *Statius* ⟨*Theb.* IV 451–3⟩:
      —*Tellure cavata*
      Inclinat Bacchi latices, & munera verni,
      Lactis, & Actæos imbres, &c.

   This libation is made to all the departed shades; but to what purpose (objects *Eustathius*) should these rites be paid to the dead, when it is evident from the subsequent relation that they were ignorant of these ceremonies 'till they had tasted the libation? He answers from the Ancients, that they were merely honorary to the regents of the dead, *Pluto* and *Proserpina*; and used to obtain their leave to have an interview with the shades in their dominions.

   47.   *When lo! appear'd along the dusky coasts,*
           Thin, airy shoals of visionary ghosts.]

We are inform'd by *Eustathius*, that the Ancients rejected these six verses; for say they, these are not the shades of persons newly slain, but who have long been in these infernal regions: How then can their wounds be suppos'd still to be visible, especially thro' their armour, when the Soul was separated from the body? Neither is this the proper place for their appearance, for the Poet immediately subjoins, that the ghost of *Elpenor* was the first that he encounter'd in these regions of darkness. But these objections will be easily answer'd by having recourse to the notions which the Ancients entertain'd concerning the dead; we must remember that they imagin'd that the soul tho' freed from the body had still a vehicle, exactly resembling the body; as the figure in a mold retains the resemblance of the mold, when separated from it; the body is but as a case to this vehicle, and it is in this vehicle that the wounds are said to be visible; this was suppos'd to be less gross than the mortal body, and less subtile than the Soul; so that whatever wounds the outward body receiv'd when living, were believ'd to affect this inward Substance, and consequently might be visible after separation.

It is true that the Poet calls the ghost of *Elpenor* the first ghost, but this means the first whom he knew: *Elpenor* was not yet buried, and therefore was not yet receiv'd into the habitation of the dead, but wanders before the entrance of it. This is the reason why his shade is said to present it self the foremost; it comes not up from the realm of death, but descends towards it from the upper world.

But these shades of the warriors are said still to wear their armour in which they were slain, for the Poet adds that it was stain'd with blood: How is it possible for these ghosts, which are only a subtle substance, not a gross body, to wear the armour they wore in the other world? How was it convey'd to them in these infernal regions? All that occurs to me in answer to this objection is, that the Poet describes them suitably to the characters they bore in life; the warriors on earth are warriors in Hell; and that he adds these circumstances only to denote the manner of their death, which was in battle, or by the sword. No doubt but *Homer* represents a future state according to the notions which his age entertain'd of it, and this sufficiently justifies him as a Poet, who is not oblig'd to write severe truths, but according to fame and common opinions.

But to prove these verses genuine, we have the authority of *Virgil*: he was too sensible of their beauty not to adorn his Poems with them. *Georg.* 4. 470 ⟨actually, 471 ff omitting 473-4⟩.

> *At cantu commotæ Erebi de sedibus imis*
> *Umbræ ibant tenues, simulacraque luce carentum,*
> *Matres, atque viri, defunctaque corpora vita*
> *Magnanimum heroum, pueri, innuptæque puellæ,*
> *Impositique rogis juvenes,* &c.

It must be confess'd that the *Roman* Poet omits the circumstance of the armour in his translation, as being perhaps contrary to the opinions prevailing in his age; but in the sixth book he describes his Heroes with arms, horses, and infernal chariots; and in the story of *Deiphobus* we see his shade retain the wounds in Hell, which he received at the time of his death in *Troy* ⟨vi 495, slightly misquoted⟩.

> —*Lacerum crudeliter ora*
> *Deiphobum vidit,* &c.

Thin, airy shoals of visionary ghosts;
Fair, pensive youths, and soft-enamour'd maids,
And wither'd Elders, pale and wrinkled shades: 50
Ghastly with wounds the forms of warriors slain
Stalk'd with majestic port, a martial train:
These, and a thousand more swarm'd o'er the ground,
And all the dire assembly shriek'd around.
Astonish'd at the sight, aghast I stood,   55
And a cold fear ran shivering thro' my blood;
Strait I command the sacrifice to haste,
Strait the flea'd victims to the flames are cast,
And mutter'd vows, and mystic song apply'd
To griesly *Pluto*, and his gloomy bride.   60
    Now swift I wav'd my faulchion o'er the blood;
Back started the pale throngs, and trembling stood.
Round the black trench the gore untasted flows,
'Till awful, from the shades *Tiresias* rose.
    There, wand'ring thro' the gloom I first survey'd, 65
New to the realms of death, *Elpenor*'s shade:
His cold remains all naked to the sky
On distant shores unwept, unburied lye.
Sad at the sight I stand, deep fix'd in woe,
And ere I spoke the tears began to flow.   70
    O say what angry pow'r *Elpenor* led
To glide in shades, and wander with the dead?
How could thy soul, by realms and seas disjoyn'd,

---

73.   *How could thy soul, by realms and seas disjoyn'd,*
           Out-fly the nimble sail?]

Eustathius is of opinion, that *Ulysses* speaks pleasantly to *Elpenor*, for were his
words to be literally translated they would be, *Elpenor, thou art come hither on foot,*
sooner than I in a ship. I suppose it is the worthless character of *Elpenor* that led that
Critic into this opinion; but I should rather take the sentence to be spoken
seriously, not only because such railleries are an insult upon the unfortunate, and
levities perhaps unworthy of Epic Poetry, but also from the general conduct of
Ulysses, who at the sight of *Elpenor* bursts into tears, and compassionates the fate
of his friend. Is there any thing in this that looks like raillery? if there be, we must
confess that *Ulysses* makes a very quick transition from sorrow to pleasantry. The

Out-fly the nimble sail, and leave the lagging wind?
The Ghost reply'd: To Hell my doom I owe,   75

other is the more noble sense, and therefore I have follow'd it, and it excellently paints the surprize of *Ulysses* at the unexpected sight of *Elpenor*, and expresses his wonder that the Soul the moment it leaves the body, should reach the receptacle of departed shades.

But it may be ask'd what connection this story of *Elpenor* has to the subject of the Poem, and what it contributes to the end of it? *Bossu* very well answers ⟨II iv⟩ that the Poet may insert some incidents that make no part of the fable or action; especially if they be short, and break not the thread of it: this before us is only a small part of a large Episode, which the Poet was at liberty to insert or omit, as contributed most to the beauty of his Poetry: besides, it contains an excellent moral, and shews us the ill effects of drunkenness and debauchery. The Poet represents *Elpenor* as a person of a mean character, and punishes his crime with sudden death, and dishonour.

I will only add that *Virgil* treads in the footsteps of *Homer*, and *Misenus* in the *Æneid*, is the *Elpenor* of the *Odyssey:* There is indeed some difference; *Misenus* suffers for his presumption ⟨VI 162 ff⟩, *Elpenor* for his debauchery.

75.   —*To hell my doom I owe,*
                    Dæmons accurst, dire ministers of woe.]

The words in the original are, Ἄσέ με δαίμονος αἶσα. The identity of sound in ἄσε and αἶσα may perhaps appear a little inharmonious, and shock the ear. It is a known observation that the nice ears in the Court of *Augustus* could not pardon *Virgil* for a like similitude of cadence in this verse ⟨IV 504⟩.

                    At regina Pyra—

But these are rather negligences than errors; they are indeed to be avoided, but a great genius sometimes overlooks such niceties, and sacrifices sound to sense.

The words of *Quintilian* are very apposite to this purpose, *lib.* 8. *cap.* 3 ⟨50–1⟩. *Ejusdem verbi aut sermonis iteratio, quanquam non magnopere summis auctoribus vitata, interim vitium videri potest; in quod sæpe incidit etiam Cicero, securus tam parvæ observationis.* He brings an instance of it from his oration for *Cluentius* ⟨Cicero, *Pro Cluentio* XXXV 96⟩, *Non solum igitur illud judicium, judicii simile, judices, non fuit.* It must be confess'd, that the sense is not only darken'd, but the ear shock'd at the repetition of the same word in the same period.

This is a very pregnant instance, that the opinion of an evil Dæmon or Genius prevail'd in the days of *Homer:* but this excuse of *Elpenor*, in ascribing his calamity to a Dæmon, gives great offence to *Maximus Tyrius*, he being a Stoic Philosopher. He says ⟨*Diss.* xiii 8–9 (Teubner)⟩ *Elpenor* is guilty of falshood in this excuse to *Ulysses*; for *Dæmons, parcæ, &c.* are nothing but the idle pretext of wicked men, who are industrious to transfer their own follies to the Gods, according to those verses in the beginning of the *Odyssey.*

                    Why charge mankind on heav'n their own offence,
                    And call their woes the crime of providence?

Com'st thou, my son, alive, to realms beneath, 190
The dolesom realms of darkness and of death:
Com'st thou alive from pure, ætherial day?
Dire is the region, dismal is the way!
Here lakes profound, there floods oppose their waves,
There the wide sea with all his billows raves! 195
Or (since to dust proud *Troy* submits her tow'rs)
Com'st thou a wand'rer from the *Phrygian* shores?
Or say, since honour call'd thee to the field,
Hast thou thy *Ithaca*, thy bride, beheld?
    Source of my life, I cry'd, from earth I fly 200
To seek *Tiresias* in the nether sky,
To learn my doom: for tost from woe to woe,
In every land *Ulysses* finds a foe:
Nor have these eyes beheld my native shores,
Since in the dust proud *Troy* submits her tow'rs. 205
    But, when thy soul from her sweet mansion fled,
Say what distemper gave thee to the dead?

---

195. *There the wide sea with all his billows raves.*] If this passage were literally
translated, it would run thus: *My son, how didst thou arrive at this place of darkness,
when so many rivers, and the Ocean lie in the midway?* This (says *Eustathius*) plainly
shews that *Homer* uses a fabulous Geography; for whereas the places that are
mention'd in these voyages of *Ulysses* are really situated upon the *Mediterranean*,
Anticleia here says that they lie in the middle of the Ocean. But this is undoubtedly
an error: The whole of the observation depends upon the word μέσσῳ; But why
must this denote the *midway* so exactly? It is not sufficient to say, that *between*
Ithaca and this infernal region, rivers and the Ocean roul? And that this is the
real meaning is evident from this book, for *Ulysses* sails in the space of one day
from the Island of *Circe* to the place where he descends: How then could these
places where *Ulysses* touches in his voyage lie in the middle of the Ocean, unless
we can suppose he pass'd half the Ocean in one day? The Poet directly affirms,
that he descends at the extremity of it; but this extremity is no more than one
day's voyage from the Island of *Circe*, and consequently that Island could not lie
in the middle of the Ocean: Therefore this place is no evidence that *Homer* uses
a fabulous Geography.

    Eustathius very justly observes, that *Homer* judiciously places the descent into
Hell at the extremity of the Ocean: for it is natural to imagine, that to be the only
passage to it, by which the Sun and the Stars themselves appear to descend, and
sink into the realms of darkness.

Has life's fair lamp declin'd by slow decays,
Or swift expir'd it, in a sudden blaze?
Say if my sire, good old *Laertes*, lives?   210
If yet *Telemachus*, my son, survives?
Say by his rule is my dominion aw'd,
Or crush'd by traytors with an iron rod?
Say if my spouse maintains her royal trust,
Tho' tempted chaste, and obstinately just?   215
Or if no more her absent Lord she wails,
But the false woman o'er the wife prevails.
    Thus I, and thus the parent shade returns.
Thee, ever thee, thy faithful consort mourns;
Whether the night descends, or day prevails,   220
Thee she by night, and thee by day bewails.
Thee in *Telemachus* thy realm obeys;
In sacred groves celestial rites he pays,
And shares the banquet in superior state,

---

218. —*Thus the parent shade returns.*] The questions which *Ulysses* asks (remarks *Eustathius*) could not fail of having a very good effect upon his *Phæacian* audience: By them he very artfully (and as it seems undesignedly) lets them into the knowledge of his dignity, and shews the importance of his person; to induce them to a greater care to conduct him to his country. The process of the whole story is so artfully carried on, that *Ulysses* seems only to relate an accidental interview, while he tacitly recommends himself, and lets them know the person who asks their assistance is a King. It is observable that *Anticleia* inverts the order in her answer, and replies last to the first question. Orators always reserve the strongest argument for the conclusion, to leave it fresh upon the memory of their auditors: or rather, the Poet uses this method to introduce the sorrow of *Ulysses* for the death of his mother more naturally: He steals away the mind of the Reader from attending the main action, to enliven it with a scene of tenderness and affection in these regions of horror.

224. *And shares the banquet in superior state*, &c.] This passage is fully explain'd by *Eustathius*: he tells us, that it was an ancient custom to invite Kings and Legislators to all publick feasts; this was to do them honour: and the chief seat was always reserved for the chief Magistrate. Without this observation, the lines are unintelligible. It is evident that the words are not spoken of sacrifices or feasts made to the Gods, but social entertainments, for they are general, πάντες καλέουσι, "all the people of the realm invite *Telemachus* to their feasts;" And this seems to have been a right due to the chief Magistrate, for ἀλεγύνειν implies it,

Grac'd with such honours as become the Great.   225
Thy sire in solitude foments his care:
The court is joyless, for thou art not there!
No costly carpets raise his hoary head,
No rich embroid'ry shines to grace his bed:
Ev'n when keen winter freezes in the skies,   230
Rank'd with his slaves, on earth the Monarch lies:
Deep are his sighs, his visage pale, his dress
The garb of woe and habit of distress.
And when the Autumn takes his annual round,
The leafy honours scatt'ring on the ground;   235
Regardless of his years, abroad he lies,
His bed the leaves, his canopy the skies.
Thus cares on cares his painful days consume,
And bow his age with sorrow to the tomb!
     For thee, my son, I wept my life away;   240
For thee thro' hell's eternal dungeons stray:
Nor came my fate by ling'ring pains and slow,
Nor bent the silver-shafted Queen her bow;
No dire disease bereav'd me of my breath;
Thou, thou my son wert my disease and death;   245
Unkindly with my love my son conspir'd,
For thee I liv'd, for absent thee expir'd.
     Thrice in my arms I strove her shade to bind, ⎫
Thrice thro' my arms she slipt like empty wind, ⎬
Or dreams, the vain illusions of the mind.   ⎭
                                                   250

---

which word *Eustathius* explains by ἕν λόγῳ ποιεῖσθαι; "such an honour as
ought not to be neglected," or
          Grac'd with such honours as become the Great. ⟨225⟩
It gives us a very happy image of these ages of the world, when we observe such
an intercourse between the King and the subject: The Idea of power carries no
terror in it, but the Ruler himself makes a part of the public Joy.
     248.   *Thrice in my arms I strove her shade to bind,*
                          Thrice thro' my arms—]
This passage plainly shews that the vehicles of the departed were believ'd by the
Ancients to be of an aerial substance, and retain nothing of corporeal grossness.
     Virgil has borrow'd these verses ⟨II 792–4⟩.
     o*

Wild with despair, I shed a copious tyde
Of flowing tears, and thus with sighs reply'd.
    Fly'st thou, lov'd shade, while I thus fondly mourn?
Turn to my arms, to my embraces turn!
Is it, ye pow'rs that smile at human harms!   255
Too great a bliss to weep within her arms?
Or has hell's Queen an empty Image sent,
That wretched I might ev'n my joys lament?
    O son of woe, the pensive shade rejoyn'd,
Oh most inur'd to grief of all mankind!   260
'Tis not the Queen of Hell who thee deceives:
All, all are such, when life the body leaves;
No more the substance of the man remains,
Nor bounds the blood along the purple veins;
These the funereal flames in atoms bear,   265
To wander with the wind in empty air,
While the impassive soul reluctant flies
Like a vain dream to these infernal skies.
But from the dark dominions speed thy way,

Ter conatus ibi collo dare bracchia circum;
Ter frustra comprensa manus effugit imago,
Par levibus ventis, volucrique simillima somno.

Scaliger ⟨*Poet.* v iii, p. 222 B1⟩ gives the preference to the *Roman* Poet, because he uses three verses, at a time when the word *ter* occurs in the description, whereas *Homer* concludes in little more than two lines. But this is not criticizing, but trifling; and ascribing to an Author what the Author himself had no thought of. This puts me in mind of a story in *Lucian* ⟨*Ver. Hist.* II 20⟩, where a person of a strong imagination thinking there was a mystery in μῆνιν, the first word in the *Iliad*, is introduc'd enquiring of *Homer* in the regions of the dead, why he placed it in the beginning of his Poem? he answers, Because it first came into his head. I doubt not but the number of the lines in this place in both Poets was equally accidental; *Virgil* adds nothing to the thought of *Homer*, tho' he uses more words.

256. —*A bliss to weep within her arms*.] This is almost a literal translation; the words in the Greek are, τεταρπώμεσθα γόοιο, or, *that we may delight our selves with sorrow*, which *Eustathius* explains by saying, *there is a pleasure in weeping*: I should rather understand the words to signify, that in the instant while he is rejoycing at the sight of his mother, he is compell'd to turn his joy into tears, to find the whole scene a delusion.

And climb the steep ascent to upper day;   270
To thy chaste bride the wond'rous story tell,
The woes, the horrors, and the laws of Hell.
   Thus while she spoke, in swarms hell's Empress brings
Daughters and wives of Heroes and of Kings;
Thick, and more thick they gather round the blood,   275
Ghost throng'd on ghost (a dire assembly) stood!
Dauntless my sword I seize: the airy crew,
Swift as it flash'd along the gloom, withdrew;
Then shade to shade in mutual forms succeeds,
Her race recounts, and their illustrious deeds.   280
   Tyro began: whom great *Salmoneus* bred;
The royal partner of fam'd *Cretheus*' bed.

---

279. *Then shade to shade—succeeds.*] Nothing can better shew the invention of *Homer*, than his capacity of furnishing out a scene of such great variety in this infernal region: He calls up the Heroes of former ages from a state of inexistence to adorn and diversify his Poetry. If it be ask'd what relation this journey into hell has to the main action of the *Odyssey*? the answer is, it has an Episodic affinity with it, and shews the sufferings of *Ulysses* more than any of his voyages upon the Ocean, as It is more horrible and full of terrors. What a treasury of ancient History and fables has he open'd by this descent? he lets us into a variety of different characters of the most famous personages recorded in ancient story; and at the same time lays before us a supplement to the *Iliad*. If *Virgil* paid a happy piece of flattery to the *Romans*, by introducing the greatest persons of the best families in *Rome*, in his descent in the *Æneid*; *Homer* no less happily interests the *Grecians* in his story, by honouring the Ancestors of the noblest families who still flourish'd in *Greece*, in the *Odyssey*; a circumstance that could not fail of being very acceptable to a *Grecian* or *Roman* Reader, but perhaps less entertaining to us, who have no particular interest in these stories.

   281. Tyro—*whom great* Salmoneus *bred.*] *Virgil* ⟨vi 585–94⟩ gives a very different character of *Salmoneus* from this of *Homer*: he describes him as an impious person who presum'd to imitate the thunder of *Jupiter*, whereas *Homer* stiles him blameless, or ἀμύμων; an argument, says *Eustathius*, that the preceding story is a fable invented since the days of *Homer*. This may perhaps be true, and we may naturally conclude it to be true from his silence of it, but not from the epithet ἀμύμων; for in the first book of the *Odyssey*, *Jupiter* gives the same appellation to *Ægisthus*, even while he condemns him of murder and adultery. *Eustathius* adds, that *Salmoneus* was a great proficient in Mechanics, and inventor of a vessel call'd βροντεῖον, which imitated thunder by rouling stones in it, which gave occasion to the fictions of the Poets.

For fair *Enipeus*, as from fruitful urns
He pours his wat'ry store, the Virgin burns;
Smooth flows the gentle stream with wanton pride,   285
And in soft mazes rouls a silver Tide:
As on his banks the maid enamour'd roves,
The Monarch of the deep beholds and loves;
In her *Enipeus'* form and borrow'd charms,
The am'rous God descends into her arms: 290
Around, a spacious arch of waves he throws,
And high in air the liquid mountain rose;
Thus in surrounding floods conceal'd he proves
The pleasing transport, and compleats his loves.
Then softly sighing, he the fair addrest,   295
And as he spoke her tender hand he prest.
Hail happy nymph! no vulgar births are ow'd
To the prolific raptures of a God:
Lo! when nine times the moon renews her horn,
Two brother heroes shall from thee be born;   300

---

283.   *For fair* Enipeus, *as from fruitful urns*
                He pours his wat'ry store, the Virgin burns.]
There are no fables in the Poets that seem more bold than these concerning the
commerce between women, and river Gods; but *Eustathius* gives us a probable
solution: I will translate him literally. It was customary for young Virgins to
resort frequently to rivers to bathe in them; and the Ancients have very well
explain'd these fables about the intercourse between them and the water Gods:
Receive my Virginity O Scamander! says a Lady; but it is very apparent who this
Scamander was: Her lover *Cimon* lay conceal'd in the reeds. This was a good excuse
for female frailty, in ages of credulity: for such imaginary intercourse between the
fair Sex and Deities was not only believ'd, but esteem'd honourable. No doubt
the Ladies were frequently deceiv'd; their lovers personated the Deities, and they
took a *Cimon* to their arms in the disguise of a *Scamander.*
    It is uncertain where this *Enipeus* flows: *Strabo* ⟨VIII iii 32⟩ (says *Eustathius*)
imagines it to be a river of *Peloponnesus,* that disembogues its waters into the
Alpheus; for the *Thessalian* river is *Eniseus,* and not *Enipeus*: This rises from mount
Othrys, and receives into it the *Epidanus.* The former seems to be the river intended
by *Homer,* for it takes its source from a village call'd *Salmona*; and what strengthens
this conjecture is the neighbourhood of the Ocean (or *Neptune* in this fable) to
that river. *Lucian* has made this story of *Enipeus* the subject of one of his Dialogues
⟨*D. Mar.* xiii⟩.

Thy early care the future worthies claim,
To point them to the arduous paths of fame;
But in thy breast th' important truth conceal,
Nor dare the secret of a God reveal:
For know, thou *Neptune* view'st! and at my nod 305
Earth trembles, and the waves confess their God.
   He added not, but mounting spurn'd the plain,
Then plung'd into the chambers of the main.
   Now in the time's full process forth she brings
Jove's dread vicegerents, in two future Kings; 310
O'er proud *Iölcos Pelias* stretch'd his reign,
And god-like *Neleus* rul'd the *Pylian* plain:
Then fruitful, to her *Cretheus'* royal bed
She gallant *Pheres* and fam'd *Æson* bred:
From the same fountain *Amythaon* rose, 315
Pleas'd with the din of war, and noble shout of foes.
   There mov'd *Antiope* with haughty charms,
Who blest th' Almighty Thund'rer in her arms;
Hence sprung *Amphion*, hence brave *Zethus* came,

319. *Hence sprung* Amphion.—] The fable of *Thebes* built by the power of Music is not mention'd by *Homer*, and therefore may be supposed to be of later invention. *Homer* relates many circumstances in these short histories differently from his successors; *Epicaste* is call'd *Jocasta*, and the Tragedians have entirely varied the story of *Œdipus*: They tell us he tore out his eyes, that he was driven from *Thebes*, and being conducted by his daughter *Antigone*, arriv'd at *Athens*, where entering the Temple of the Furies, he dy'd in the midst of a furious storm, and was carried by it into Hell: Whereas *Homer* directly affirms, that he continued to reign in *Thebes* after all his calamities.

   It is not easy to give a reason why the mother, and not the father, is said to send the Furies to torment *Oedipus*, especially because he was the murderer of his father *Laius*: *Eustathius* answers, that it was by accident that he slew *Laius*; but upon the discovery of his wickedness in marrying his mother *Jocasta*, he used her with more barbarity and rigour than was necessary, and therefore she pursues him with her vengeance. *Jocasta* and *Dido* both die after the same manner by their own hands: I agree with *Scaliger* ⟨*Poet.* v iii, p. 231 c2⟩, that *Virgil* ⟨xii 603⟩ has describ'd hanging more happily than *Homer*. ⟨*Od.* xi 278⟩

   Informis Leti nodum trabe nectit ab alta.
   Ἁψαμένη βρόχον αἰπὺν ἀφ' ὑψηλοῖο μελάθρου.
There is nothing like the *informis Leti nodus* in *Homer*: and as that Critic observes,

Founders of *Thebes*, and men of mighty name;   320
Tho' bold in open field, they yet surround
The town with walls, and mound inject on mound;
Here ramparts stood, there tow'rs rose high in air,
And here thro' sev'n wide portals rush'd the war.

    There with soft step the fair *Alcmena* trod,   325
Who bore *Alcides* to the thund'ring God;
And *Megara*, who charm'd the son of *Jove*,
And soften'd his stern soul to tender love.

    Sullen and sow'r with discontented mien
Jocasta frown'd, th' incestuous *Theban* Queen;   330
With her own son she joyn'd in nuptial bands,
Tho' father's blood embru'd his murd'rous hands:
The Gods and men the dire offence detest,
The Gods with all their furies rend his breast:
In lofty *Thebes* he wore th' imperial crown,   335
A pompous wretch! accurs'd upon a throne.
The wife self-murder'd from a beam depends,
And her foul soul to blackest Hell descends;
Thence to her son the choicest plagues she brings,
And the fiends haunt him with a thousand stings.   340

    And now the beauteous *Chloris* I descry,
A lovely shade, *Amphion*'s youngest joy!

---

tam atrox res aliquo verborum ambitu studiosius comprehendenda fuit. The story of *Oedipus* is this: *Laius* being inform'd by the Oracle, that he should be slain by his son, caus'd *Oedipus* immediately to be expos'd by his shepherds to wild beasts; but the shepherds preserv'd him, and gave him education: When he came to years of maturity he went toward *Thebes* in search of his father, but meeting *Laius* by the way, and a quarrel arising, he slew him ignorantly, and married *Jocasta* his mother; This is the subject of two Tragedies in *Sophocles*.

341. —*The beauteous* Chloris *I descry*.] A Critic ought not only to endeavour to point out the beauties in the sense, but also in the versification of a Poet: *Dionysius Halicarn.* ⟨*De Comp. Verb.* xvi 98⟩ cites these two verses as peculiarly flowing and harmonious.

Καὶ Χλῶριν εἶδον περικαλλέα, τήν ποτε Νηλεὺς
Γῆμεν ἐὸν διὰ Κάλλος, ἐπεὶ πόρε μυρία ἕδνα.

There is not one elision, nor one rough vowel or consonant, but they flow along with the utmost smoothness, and the beauty of the Muse equals that of *Chloris*.

With gifts unnumber'd *Neleus* sought her arms,
Nor paid too dearly for unequal'd charms;
Great in *Orchomenos*, in *Pylos* great,   345
He sway'd the scepter with imperial state.
Three gallant sons the joyful Monarch told,
Sage *Nestor*, *Periclimenus* the bold,
And *Chromius* last; but of the softer race,
One nymph alone, a miracle of grace.   350
Kings on their thrones for lovely *Pero* burn,
The Sire denies, and Kings rejected mourn.
To him alone the beauteous prize he yields,
Whose arm should ravish from *Phylacian* fields
The herds of *Iphiclus*, detain'd in wrong;   355
Wild, furious herds, unconquerably strong!
This dares a Seer, but nought the Seer prevails,

345. *Great in* Orchomenos—] This is a very considerable city lying between
Bœotia and *Phocis*, upon the river *Cephisus*: *Homer* calls it the *Minyan Orchomenos*,
because the *Minyans* an ancient people inhabited it; it was the colony of these
Minyans that sail'd to *Iolcos*, and gave name to the *Argonauts*. *Eustathius*.

348. —Periclimenus *the bold*.] The reason why *Homer* gives this epithet to
Periclymenus may be learn'd from *Hesiod* ⟨*Catalogue of Women* 10⟩: *Neptune* gave
him the power to change himself into all shapes, but he was slain by *Hercules*:
Periclymenus assaulted that Heroe in the shape of a bee, or fly, who discovering
him in that disguise, by the means of *Pallas* slew him with his club. This is the person of whom *Ovid* speaks, but adds that he was slain in the shape of an eagle by
Hercules ⟨*Metam.* XII 556–8⟩.

        Mira Periclymeni mors est, cui posse figuras
        Sumere quas vellet, rursusque reponere sumptas,
        Neptunus dederat, &c.

Euphorion speaks of him in the shape of a bee or fly ⟨An error: the quotation is
from Hesiod (*ibid.* 14); ὄφις means snake, not fly⟩.

      —῎αλλοτε δ' αὖτε μελισσῶν ἀγλαὰ φῦλα
      ῎Αλλοτε δεινὸς ὄφις—

357. *This dares a Seer*, &c.] This story is related with great obscurity, but we
learn from the 15th book that the name of this Prophet was *Melampus*. *Iphiclus*
was the son of *Deioneus*, and Uncle to *Tyro*; he had seiz'd upon the goods of *Tyro*
the mother of *Neleus*, among which were many beautiful oxen: these *Neleus*
demands, but is unjustly deny'd by *Iphiclus*: *Neleus* had a daughter named *Pero*,
a great beauty who was courted by all the neighbouring Princes, but the father
refuses her, unless to the man who recovers these oxen from *Iphiclus*: *Bias* was in

In beauty's cause illustriously he fails:
Twelve moons the foe the captive youth detains
In painful dungeons, and coercive chains;   360
The foe at last from durance where he lay,
His art revering, gave him back to day;
Won by prophetic knowledge, to fulfill
The stedfast purpose of th' Almighty will.

    With graceful port advancing now I spy'd   365
Leda the fair, the god-like *Tyndar*'s bride:
Hence *Pollux* sprung who wields with furious sway
The deathful gauntlet, matchless in the fray;

---

love with *Pero*, and persuades his brother *Melampus* a Prophet to undertake the recovery; he attempts it, but being vanquish'd, is thrown into prison; but at last set at liberty, for telling *Iphiclus*, who was childless, how to procure issue. *Iphiclus* upon this gave him the oxen for a reward.

    Nothing can be more ridiculous than the explanation of this story in *Eustathius*, which I will lay before the Reader for his entertainment. *Melampus*, after he was made a prisoner, was trusted to the care of a man and a woman; the man used him with mercy, and the woman with cruelty: One day he heard a low noise, and a family of *worms* in conference. (He understood the language of all the animal creation, beasts and reptiles.) These worms were discoursing how they had eaten thro' a great beam that lay over the head of *Melampus*: He immediately provides for his own safety, feigns a sickness, and begs to be carried into the fresh air; The woman and the man immediately comply with his request; at which instant the beam falling, kills the woman: An account of this is forthwith carried to *Iphiclus*, who sending for *Melampus*, asks who he is? He tells him, a Prophet, and that he came for the Oxen of *Neleus*; *Iphiclus* commands him to declare how he may have an heir? *Melampus* kills an Ox, and calls all the birds of the air to feast on it; they all appear except the Vultur; he proposes the case to them, but they give no satisfactory answer; at last the Vultur appears, and gives *Melampus* a full information: Upon this *Iphiclus* obtains a child, and *Melampus* the Oxen of *Neleus*.

    364. *The stedfast purpose of th' Almighty will.*] These words, Διὸς δ' ἐτελείετο βουλή, seem to come in without any connection with the story, and consequently unnecessarily; but *Homer* speaks of it concisely, as an adventure well known in his times, and therefore not wanting a further explication: But *Apollodorus* relates the whole at large, *lib.* 1 ⟨1 ix 12 ff⟩. The reason why these words are inserted is, to inform us that there were ancient Prophecies concerning *Iphiclus*, that it was decreed by *Jupiter* he should have no children 'till he had recourse to a Prophet, who explaining these Prophecies to him should shew him how to obtain that blessing: In this sense the will of *Jupiter* may be said to be fulfill'd.

And *Castor* glorious on th' embattled plain
Curbs the proud steed, reluctant to the rein: 370
By turns they visit this etherial sky,
And live alternate, and alternate die:
In hell beneath, on earth, in heav'n above
Reign the Twin-gods, the fav'rite sons of *Jove*.

There *Ephimedia* trod the gloomy plain,   375
Who charm'd the Monarch of the boundless main;
Hence *Ephialtes*, hence stern *Otus* sprung,
More fierce than Giants, more than Giants strong;
The earth o'erburthen'd groan'd beneath their weight,
None but *Orion* e'er surpass'd their height: 380
The wond'rous youths had scarce nine winters told,
When high in air, tremendous to behold,
Nine ells aloft they rear'd their tow'ring head,

372. *And live alternate, and alternate die.*] *Castor* and *Pollux* are called Διόσκυροι,
or *the sons of* Jupiter; but what could give occasion to this fiction, of their living
and dying alternately? *Eustathius* informs us that it is a physical Allegory: They
represent the two Hemispheres of the world; the one of which is continually enlighten'd by the sun, and consequently the other is then in darkness: and these
being successively illuminated according to the order of the day and night, one
of these sons of *Jupiter* may be said to revive when one part of the world rises into
day, and the other to die, when it descends into darkness. What makes this
Allegory the more probable is, that *Jupiter* denotes in many allegories of *Homer*,
the Air, or the upper regions of it.

383. *Nine ells aloft they rear'd their* ⟨ . . . ⟩ *head.*] This is undoubtedly a very bold
fiction, and has been censur'd by some Critics as monstrous, and prais'd by others
as sublime. It may seem utterly incredible that any human creatures could be
nine ells, that is, eleven yards and a quarter in height, at the age of nine years.
But it may vindicate *Homer* as a Poet to say that he only made use of a fable, that
had been transmitted down from the earliest times of the world, for so early the
war between the Gods and Giants was supposed to be. There might a rational
account be given of these apparent incredibilities; if I might be allow'd to say
what many Authors of great name have conjectur'd, that these stories are only
traditional, and all founded upon the ejection of the fall'n Angels from Heaven,
and the wars they had with the good Angels to regain their stations. If this might
be allow'd, we shall then have real Giants, who endeavour'd to take Heaven by
assault; then nothing can be invented by a Poet so boldly, as to exceed what may
justly be believ'd of these beings: then the stories of heaping mountain upon

And full nine cubits broad their shoulders spread.
Proud of their strength and more than mortal size,   385
The Gods they challenge, and affect the skies;
Heav'd on *Olympus* tott'ring *Ossa* stood;

mountain will come within the bounds of credibility. But without having recourse to this solution, *Longinus* brings this passage as an instance of true sublimity, *Chap. 6* ⟨VIII 2⟩. He is proving that the Sublime is sometimes found without
the pathetic, for some passions are mean, as fear, sadness, sorrow, and consequently incapable of sublimity; and on the other hand, there are many things
great and sublime, in which there is no passion; of this kind is what *Homer* says
concerning *Otus*, and *Ephialtes*, with so much boldness.

> The Gods they challenge, and affect the skies ⟨386⟩.

And what he adds concerning the success of these Giants is still bolder.

> Had they to manhood grown, the bright abodes
> Of Heav'n had shook, and Gods been heap'd on Gods.
>
> ⟨389–90, but very differently rendered in the text⟩

Virgil was of the opinion of *Longinus*, for he has imitated *Homer* ⟨VI 582–4⟩.

> Hic & Aloidas geminos immania vidi
> Corpora, qui manibus magnum rescindere caelum
> Aggressi, superisque Jovem detrudere regnis.

Macrobius, lib. 5. Saturn. cap. 13, judges these verses to be inferior to *Homer*'s
in Majesty; in *Homer* we have the height and breadth of these Giants, and he
happily paints the very size of their limbs in the run of his Poetry; two words,
ἐννέωροι, and ἐννεαπήχεες, almost make one verse, designedly chosen to express
their bulk in the turn of the words; but *Virgil* says only *immania corpora*, and makes
no addition concerning the Giants, omitting entirely the circumstance of their
size; *Homer* relates the piling hill upon hill; *Virgil* barely adds, that they endeavour'd to storm the heavens.

Scaliger ⟨*Poet.* V iii, p. 240 c2⟩ is firm and faithful to *Virgil*, and vindicates his
favourite in the true spirit of criticism; I persuade my self he glances at *Macrobius*,
for he cavils at those instances which he produces as beauties in *Homer*; I give his
answer in his own words. *Admirantur Græculi pueriles mensuras; nimis sæpe cogor excla-
mare, aliud esse Græculum circulatorem, aliud regiæ orationis auctorem: Indignam censuit
sua majestate Virgilius hanc minutam superstitionem, &c.*

Eustathius remarks that the Ancients greatly admir'd the exact proportion of
these Giants, for the body is of a due symmetry, when the thickness is three degrees
less than the height of it: According to this account, these Giants grew one cubit
every year in bulk, and three in height. *Homer* says, that they fell by the shafts of
Apollo, that is they dy'd suddenly; but other writers relate, that as they were
hunting, *Diana* sent a stag between them, at which both at once aiming their
weapons and she withdrawing the stag, they fell by their own darts. *Eustathius.*

387. —*On* Olympus *tott'ring* Ossa *stood,* &c.] *Strabo* ⟨I ii 20⟩ takes notice of the

On *Ossa*, *Pelion* nods with all his wood:
Such were they Youths! had they to manhood grown,
Almighty *Jove* had trembled on his throne.   390
But ere the harvest of the beard began
To bristle on the chin, and promise man,
His shafts *Apollo* aim'd; at once they sound,
And stretch the Giant-monsters o'er the ground.

There mournful *Phædra* with sad *Procris* moves,   395
Both beauteous shades, both hapless in their loves;
And near them walk'd, with solemn pace and slow,
Sad *Ariadne*, partner of their woe;
The royal *Minos Ariadne* bred,
She *Theseus* lov'd; from *Crete* with *Theseus* fled;   400
Swift to the *Dian* Isle the Heroe flies,
And tow'rds his *Athens* bears the lovely prize;

---

judgment of *Homer*, in placing the mountains in this order; they all stand in *Macedonia*; *Olympus* is the largest, and therefore he makes it the basis upon which *Ossa* stands, that being the next to *Olympus* in magnitude, and *Pelion* being the least is placed above *Ossa*, and thus they rise pyramidically. *Virgil* follows a different regulation ⟨*Geo.* I 281–2⟩,

> *Ter sunt conati imponere Pelion Ossæ,*
> *Scilicet atque Ossæ frondosum imponere Olympum.*

Here the largest mountain is placed uppermost, not so naturally as in the order of *Homer*. There is a peculiar beauty in the former of these verses, in which *Virgil* makes the two vowels in *conati imponere* meet without an elision, to express the labour and straining of the Giants in heaving mountain upon mountain. I appeal to the ear of every Reader, if he can pronounce these two words without a pause and stop; the difficulty in the flow of the verse excellently represents the labour of the Giants straining to shove *Pelion* upon *Ossa*. *Dacier* remarks that *Virgil* follows the scituation of the mountains, without regarding the magnitude; thus *Pelion* lies first on the north of *Macedonia*, *Ossa* is the second, and the third *Olympus*; but she prefers *Homer*'s method as most rational.

402. *And tow'rds his* Athens *bears the lovely prize.*] *Homer* justifies *Theseus* from any crime with relation to *Ariadna*, he is guilty of no infidelity, as succeeding Poets affirm; she dy'd suddenly in *Dia*, or *Naxos* (an Island lying between *Thera* and *Crete*) *Diana* slew her at the instigation of *Bacchus*, who accused her to that Goddess, for prophaning her temple by too free an intercourse with *Theseus*; this *Homer* calls μαρτυρίη Διονύσου. *Clymene* was a daughter of *Mynias*, *Mæra* of *Prætus* and *Antæa*, who having made a vow to *Diana* of perpetual virginity, broke

There *Bacchus* with fierce rage *Diana* fires,
The Goddess aims her shaft, the Nymph expires.
 There *Clymenè*, and *Mæra* I behold,   405
There *Eriphylè* weeps, who loosely sold
Her lord, her honour, for the lust of gold.
But should I all recount, the night would fail,
Unequal to the melancholy tale:
And all-composing rest my nature craves,   410
Here in the court, or yonder on the waves;
In you I trust, and in the heav'nly pow'rs,
To land *Ulysses* on his native shores.
 He ceas'd: but left so charming on their ear
His voice, that list'ning still they seem'd to hear.   415
'Till rising up, *Aretè* silence broke,

---

it; and therefore fell by that Goddess. *Phædra* was wife to *Theseus*, and fell in love
with her son *Hippolytus*. *Eriphyle* was the daughter of *Taläus* and *Lysimache*, wife of
the Prophet *Amphiaraus*; who being brib'd with a collar of gold by *Polynices*,
oblig'd her husband to go to the war of *Thebes*, tho' she knew he was decreed to
fall before that city: she was slain by her son *Alcmæon*. *Eustathius*.

 Ulysses, when he concludes, says it is time to repose
     Here in the court, or yonder on the waves ⟨411⟩.
To understand this the Reader must remember, that in the beginning of the
eighth book all things were prepar'd for his immediate voyage, or as it is there
express'd,
     —*Ev'n now the gales*
   Call thee aboard, and stretch the swelling sails ⟨165-6⟩.
So that he desires to repose in the ship, that he may begin his voyage early in the
morning.

 414.   *He ceas'd: but left so charming on their ear*
      His voice—]
I cannot tell whether this pause, or break in the narration of *Ulysses*, has a good
effect or not; whether it gives a relief to the Reader, or is an unexpected dis-
appointment of the pursuit of the story? But certainly what is inserted during
this short interruption, is particularly well chosen; it unites the Episode with the
main action, and shews how it contributes to the end of the *Odyssey*, in influencing
the *Phæacians* not only to restore *Ulysses*, but restore him with wealth and honour;
which is the aim of the whole Poem.

 416. —*Aretè silence broke.*] *Eustathius* observes, that the two motives which the
Queen uses to move the *Phæacians* to liberality, is the relation *Ulysses* has to her,
as her peculiar guest, (for *Nausicaa* first recommended him to the Queen's pro-

Stretch'd out her snowy hand, and thus she spoke:
  What wond'rous man heav'n sends us in our guest!
Thro' all his woes the Hero shines confest;
His comely port, his ample frame express   420
A manly air, majestic in distress.
He, as my guest, is my peculiar care,
You share the pleasure,—then in bounty share;
To worth in misery a rev'rence pay,
And with a gen'rous hand reward his stay;   425
For since kind heav'n with wealth our realm has blest,
Give it to heav'n, by aiding the distrest.
  Then sage *Echeneus*, whose grave, rev'rend brow
The hand of Time had silver'd o'er with snow,
Mature in wisdom rose: Your words, he cries,   430
Demand obedience, for your words are wise.
But let our King direct the glorious way
To gen'rous acts; our part is to obey.
  While life informs these limbs, (the King reply'd)
Well to deserve, be all my cares employ'd: 435
But here this night the royal guest detain,
'Till the sun flames along th' etherial plain;

tection) and their own wealth: (for so he renders ἕκαστος δ' ἔμμορε τιμῆς, and
Dacier follows his interpretation) I have adventur'd to translate it differently, in
this sense: " 'Tis true, he is my peculiar guest, but you all share in the honour he
does us, and therefore it is equitable to joyn in his assistance;" then she closes her
speech with reminding them of their abilities; which in the other sense would be
tautology.

425. —*With a gen'rous hand reward his stay.*] This I am persuaded is the true
meaning of the passage; *Ulysses* had shew'd a desire immediately to go aboard,
and the Queen draws an argument from this to induce the *Phæacians* to a greater
contribution, and *Ulysses* to a longer stay; she persuades them to take time to
prepare their presents, which must occasion the stay of *Ulysses* 'till they are prepar'd. They might otherwise (observes *Dacier*) have pretended to comply with
the impatience of *Ulysses*, and immediately dismiss'd him with a small gratuity,
under the pretext of not having time to prepare a greater. It must be confess'd, to
the reproach of Human Nature, that this is but too just a picture of it; Self-
interest makes the Great very ready to gratify their petitioners with a dismission,
or to comply with them to their disadvantage.

Be it my task to send with ample stores
The stranger from our hospitable shores;
Tread you my steps: 'Tis mine to lead the race,   440
The first in glory, as the first in place.

    To whom the Prince: This night with joy I stay,
O Monarch great in virtue as in sway!
If thou the circling year my stay controul,
To raise a bounty noble as thy soul;   445
The circling year I wait, with ampler stores
And fitter pomp to hail my native shores:
Then by my realms due homage would be paid;
For wealthy Kings are loyally obey'd!

    O King! for such thou art, and sure thy blood   450
Thro' veins (he cry'd) of royal fathers flow'd;
Unlike those vagrants who on falshood live,
Skill'd in smooth tales, and artful to deceive,
Thy better soul abhors the liar's part,

---

444. *If thou the circling year*, &c.—] This speech of *Ulysses* has been condemn'd
by the Critics, as avaritious; and therefore *Eustathius* judges it to be spoken artfully and complimentally; *Didymus* ⟨Scholium in Barnes, II 298⟩, with a well-bred
urbanity, or χαριέντως: I see nothing mean in it, what *Ulysses* speaks proceeds
from the gratitude of his soul; the heart of a brave man is apt to overflow while it
acknowledges an obligation. *Spondanus* ⟨*Od.* p. 161⟩ imagines that *Ulysses* may
possibly speak jocosely, and asks if it is probable that he could be induc'd to stay
from his country out of a mean consideration of a few presents, who had already
preferr'd it to immortality? But in truth, *Ulysses* never behaves with levity; and it
would give us an ill idea of that Heroe, should he return the united kindness of the
Peers of *Phæacia* with scorn and derision: Besides, *Ulysses* values these presents no
otherwise than as they may contribute to his re-establishment in his country; for
he directly says,

        So by my realms due homage should be paid,
        A wealthy Prince is loyally obey'd.

                           ⟨448–9, but much altered in the text⟩
This is an evidence, that the words of *Ulysses* flow not from so base a fountain as
avarice, but that all his thoughts and actions center upon his country.

    454.   *Thy better soul abhors the liar's part,*
                       Wise is thy voice—]
This is an instance of the judgment of *Homer* in sustaining his characters; the
Phæacians were at first describ'd as a credulous people, and he gives us here an

Wise is thy voice, and noble is thy heart.   455
Thy words like music every breast controul,
Steal thro' the ear, and win upon the soul;
Soft, as some song divine, thy story flows,
Nor better could the Muse record thy woes.

But say, upon the dark and dismal coast,   460
Saw'st thou the Worthies of the *Grecian* Host?
The god-like leaders, who in battle slain,
Fell before *Troy*, and nobly prest the plain?
And lo! a length of night behind remains,
The evening stars still mount th' ethereal plains.   465
Thy tale with raptures I could hear thee tell,
Thy woes on earth, the wond'rous scenes in hell,
'Till in the vault of heav'n the stars decay,
And the sky reddens with the rising day.

O worthy of the pow'r the Gods assign'd,   470
(*Ulysses* thus replies) a King in mind!
Since yet the early hour of night allows
Time for discourse, and time for soft repose,
If scenes of misery can entertain,
Woes I unfold, of woes a dismal train.   475
Prepare to hear of murther and of blood;

---

instance of their credulity, for they swallow all these fables as so many realities.
The verse in the original is remarkable.

Σοὶ δ' ἔπι μὲν μορφὴ ἐπέων, ἔνι δὲ φρένες ἐσθλαί.

Which *Eustathius* thinks was used by *Alcinous*, to tell *Ulysses* that his fables were so
well laid together as to have the appearance of truths: *Dacier* follows him, and (as
usual) delivers his opinion as her own sentiment. But this cannot be *Homer*'s
intention, for it supposes *Alcinous* to look upon these relations as fables, contrary
to the universal character of their ignorant credulity; I therefore am persuaded
that μορφὴ ἐπέων signifies the pleasantness or beauty of his relation, and φρένες
ἐσθλαί the integrity of his heart in opposition to the character of a liar, or perhaps his wisdom in general: and this excellently agrees with his resembling him
to a Musician, (who always was a Poet in those ages, and sung the exploits of
Heroes, &c. to the lyre) In this view the sweetness of the music represents the
agreeableness of the narration, and the subject of the musician's song the story
of his adventures.

Of god-like Heroes who uninjur'd stood
Amidst a war of spears in foreign lands,
Yet bled at home, and bled by female hands.
    Now summon'd *Proserpine* to hell's black hall   480
The heroine shades; they vanish'd at her call.
    When lo! advanc'd the forms of Heroes slain ⎫
By stern *Ægysthus*, a majestic train,   ⎬
And high above the rest, *Atrides* prest the plain. ⎭
He quaff'd the gore: and strait his soldier knew,   485
And from his eyes pour'd down the tender dew;
His arms he stretch'd; his arms the touch deceive,
Nor in the fond embrace, embraces give:
His substance vanish'd, and his strength decay'd,
Now all *Atrides* is an empty shade.   490
    Mov'd at the sight, I for a space resign'd
To soft affliction all my manly mind,
At last with tears—O what relentless doom
Imperial Phantom, bow'd thee to the tomb?
Say while the sea, and while the tempest raves,   495
Has fate oppress'd thee in the roaring waves,
Or nobly seiz'd thee in the dire alarms
Of war and slaughter, and the clash of arms?
    The Ghost returns: O chief of humankind
For active courage, and a patient mind;   500
Nor while the sea, nor while the tempest raves,
Has Fate oppress'd me on the roaring waves!
Nor nobly seiz'd me in the dire alarms,
Of war and slaughter, and the clash of arms.
Stab'd by a murd'rous hand *Atrides* dy'd,   505
A foul adult'rer, and a faithless bride;
Ev'n in my mirth and at the friendly feast,
O'er the full bowl, the traitor stab'd his guest;
Thus by the goary arm of slaughter falls
The stately Oxe, and bleeds within the stalls.   510
But not with me the direful murther ends,
These, these expir'd! their crime, they were my friends;

Thick as the boars, which some luxurious lord
Kills for the feast, to crown the nuptial board.
When war has thunder'd with its loudest storms,   515
Death thou hast seen in all her ghastly forms;
In duel met her, on the listed ground,
When hand to hand they wound return for wound;
But never have thy eyes astonish'd view'd
So vile a deed, so dire a scene of blood.   520
Ev'n in the flow of joy, when now the bowl
Glows in our veins, and opens ev'ry soul,
We groan, we faint; with blood the dome is dy'd,
And o'er the pavement floats the dreadful tyde—
Her breast all gore, with lamentable cries,   525
The bleeding Innocent *Cassandra* dies!
Then tho' pale death froze cold in ev'ry vein,
My sword I strive to wield, but strive in vain;
Nor did my traitress wife these eyelids close,
Or decently in death my limbs compose.   530
O Woman, woman, when to ill thy mind
Is bent, all hell contains no fouler fiend:
And such was mine! who basely plung'd her sword
Thro' the fond bosom where she reign'd ador'd!
Alas! I hop'd, the toils of war o'ercome,   535
To meet soft quiet and repose at home;
Delusive hope! O wife, thy deeds disgrace
The perjur'd sex, and blacken all the race;
And should Posterity one virtuous find,

539.   *And should posterity one virtuous find,*
          Name Clytemnestra, *they will curse the kind.*]
There cannot be a greater satyr upon the fair sex than this whole conference
between *Ulysses* and *Agamemnon*. *Terence* has fall'n into the same sentiment with
Homer ⟨Hec. 274–5⟩.
          Edepol, næ nos æque sumus omnes invisæ viris
          Propter paucas, quæ omnes faciunt dignæ ut videamur malo.
But how is this to be reconciled to justice, and why should the innocent suffer for
the crimes of the guilty? We are to take notice, that *Agamemnon* speaks with anger,

Name *Clytemnestra*, they will curse the kind.   540
   O injur'd shade, I cry'd, what mighty woes
To thy imperial race from woman rose!
By woman here thou tread'st this mournful strand,
And *Greece* by woman lies a desart land.
   Warn'd by my ills beware, the Shade replies,   545
Nor trust the sex that is so rarely wise;
When earnest to explore thy secret breast,
Unfold some trifle, but conceal the rest.
But in thy consort cease to fear a foe,
For thee she feels sincerity of woe: 550

---

an undistinguishing passion, and his words flow from resentment, not reason; it must be confess'd that *Agamemnon* had received great provocation, his wife had dishonour'd his bed, and taken his life away, it is therefore no wonder if he flies out into a vehemence of language: a Poet is oblig'd to follow nature, and give a fierceness to the features, when he paints a person in such emotions, and add a violence to his colours.

It has been objected that *Homer*, and even *Virgil* were enemies to the fairest part of the creation; that there is scarce a good character of a woman in either of the Poets: But *Andromache* in the *Iliad*, and *Penelope*, *Arete*, and *Nausicaa* in the *Odyssey*, are instances to the contrary. I must own I am a little at a loss to vindicate *Ulysses* in this place; he is speaking before *Arete* and *Nausicaa*, a Queen and her daughter; and entertains them with a satyr upon their own sex, which may appear unpolite, and a want of decency; and be apply'd by *Alcinous* as a caution to beware of his spouse, and not to trust her in matters of importance with his secrets: for this is the moral that is naturally drawn from the fable. Madam *Dacier* gives up the cause, and allows the advice of not trusting women to be good; it comes from her indeed a little unwillingly, with *I will not say but the counsel may be right*. I for my part will allow *Ulysses* to be in an hundred faults, rather than lay such an imputation upon the Ladies; *Ulysses* ought to be consider'd as having suffer'd twenty years calamities for that sex in the cause of *Helen*, and this possibly may give a little acrimony to his language. He puts it indeed in the mouth of *Agamemnon*; but the objection returns, why does he chuse to relate such a story before a Queen and her daughter? In short, I think they ought to have torn him to pieces, as the Ladies of *Thrace* serv'd *Orpheus*.

541.   —*What mighty woes*
              To thy imperial race from woman rose?
Ulysses here means *Aërope* the wife of *Atreus*, and mother of *Agamemnon*, who being corrupted by *Thyestes*, involv'd the whole family in the utmost calamities. *Eustathius*.

When *Troy* first bled beneath the *Grecian* arms
She shone unrival'd with a blaze of charms,
Thy infant son her fragrant bosom prest,
Hung at her knee, or wanton'd at her breast;
But now the years a num'rous train have ran;   555
The blooming boy is ripen'd into man;
Thy eyes shall see him burn with noble fire,
The sire shall bless his son, the son his sire:
But my *Orestes* never met these eyes,
Without one look the murther'd father dies;   560
Then from a wretched friend this wisdom learn,
Ev'n to thy Queen disguis'd, unknown, return;
For since of womankind so few are just,
Think all are false, nor ev'n the faithful trust.

But say, resides my son in royal port,   565
In rich *Orchomenos*, or *Sparta*'s court?
Or say in *Pyle?* for yet he views the light,
Nor glides a Phantom thro' the realms of night.

Then I. Thy suit is vain, nor can I say
If yet he breathes in realms of chearful day;   570
Or pale and wan beholds these nether skies?
Truth I revere: For Wisdom never lies.

Thus in a tyde of tears our sorrows flow,
And add new horror to the realms of woe.
'Till side by side along the dreary coast   575
Advanc'd *Achilles*' and *Patroclus*' ghost,

---

565. *But say, resides my son*—] *Eustathius* gives us the reason why *Agamemnon* mentions *Pyle*, *Sparta*, and *Orchomenos*, as places where *Orestes* might make his residence: *Sparta* was under the dominion of his brother *Menelaus*: *Pyle*, of his old friend and faithful Counsellor *Nestor*; and *Orchomenos* was a city of great strength, and therefore of great security. We may evidently gather from this passage what notion the Ancients had concerning a future state: namely, that persons after death were entirely strangers to the affairs of this world: For *Orestes* his son had slain his murderer *Ægisthus*, and reign'd in peaceable possession of his dominions; when *Agamemnon* is ignorant of the whole transaction, and desires *Ulysses* to give him information.

576. —Achilles' *and* Patroclus' *ghost.*] *Homer* lets no opportunity pass of cele-

A friendly pair! near these the * *Pylian* stray'd,
And tow'ring *Ajax*, an illustrious shade!
War was his joy, and pleas'd with loud alarms,
None but *Pelides* brighter shone in arms.   580
  Thro' the thick gloom his friend *Achilles* knew,
And as he speaks the tears descend in dew.
  Com'st thou alive to view the *Stygian* bounds,
Where the wan Spectres walk eternal rounds;
Nor fear'st the dark and dismal waste to tread,   585
Throng'd with pale ghosts, familiar with the dead?
  To whom with sighs: I pass these dreadful gates
To seek the *Theban*, and consult the Fates:
For still distrest I rove from coast to coast,
Lost to my friends, and to my country lost.   590
But sure the eye of Time beholds no name
So blest as thine in all the rolls of Fame;
Alive, we hail'd thee with our guardian Gods,
And dead, thou rul'st a King in these abodes.
  Talk not of ruling in this dol'rous gloom,   595
Nor think vain words (he cry'd) can ease my doom;
Rather I chuse laboriously to bear
A weight of woes, and breath the vital air,
A slave to some poor hind that toils for bread;

---

* *Antilochus.*

---

brating his Heroe *Achilles*, he cannot fail of awakening our attention to hear the
story of this great man after death, of whom alive we saw such wonders. Besides,
the Poet pays an honour to true friendship: The person whom *Achilles* best loved
on earth, is his chief companion in the other world: a very strong argument to
cultivate friendship with sincerity. *Achilles* here literally fulfils what he promis'd
in the *Iliad* ⟨xxii 487–90; but for *melancholy shades* read *silent shades of Hell*⟩.

    If in the melancholy shades below
    The flames of friends and lovers cease to glow,
    Yet mine shall sacred last; mine undecay'd
    Burn on thro' death, and animate my shade.

 599.   *A slave to some poor hind who* ⟨sic⟩ *toils for bread,*
     Than reign the scepter'd monarch of the dead.]
Nothing sure can give us a more disadvantagious image of a future state, than this

Than reign the scepter'd monarch of the dead.   600
 But say, if in my steps my son proceeds,
And emulates his god-like father's deeds?
If at the clash of arms, and shout of foes,
Swells his bold heart, his bosom nobly glows?
Say if my sire, the rev'rend *Peleus* reigns   605
Great in his *Pthia*, and his throne maintains;
Or weak and old, my youthful arm demands,
To fix the scepter stedfast in his hands?
O might the lamp of life rekindled burn,
And death release me from the silent urn!   610

speech which *Homer* puts into the mouth of so great an Heroe as *Achilles*: If the
Poet intended to shew the vanity of that destructive glory which is purchas'd by
the sword, and read a lecture to all the disturbers of mankind, whom we absurdly
honour as Heroes, it must be allow'd he has done it effectually: If this was not his
design, the remark of *Plato* 3 *Repub.* ⟨386c ff⟩ is not without a foundation; he
there proscribes this whole passage as dangerous to morals, and blames the Poet
for making *Achilles* say he prefers misery and servitude to all the honours which
the dead are capable of enjoying. For what, says he, can make death more
terrible to young persons? and will it not dispose them to suffer all calamities to
avoid it, deter them from exposing themselves to danger, even in the defence of
their country, and teach them to be cowards and slaves? *Lucian* was of *Plato*'s
opinion, for he mentions this passage, and ridicules it in his dialogues. *Dacier*
gives a different turn to it, and endeavours to shew that there is no danger of such
consequences, as *Plato* draws from it: "*Achilles*, adds she, speaks directly contrary to his declared sentiments and actions, and therefore there is no danger he
should persuade mankind to prefer servitude before death, when he himself dy'd
rather than not revenge his friend *Patroclus.* Such words which are contradicted
both by the sentiments and actions of him that speaks, have on the contrary a
very good effect." But I cannot come into her opinion, I will let *Achilles* answer
for himself out of *Lucian*: "In the other world I was ignorant, says he, of the state
of the dead, I had not experienced the difference between the two states, when
I preferr'd a little empty glory to life" ⟨*Dia. of the Dead*, 26 (2 : 400)⟩. This is an
answer to what *Dacier* advances, for *Achilles* speaks with experience, and yet prefers misery and life before glory and death. I know not how to vindicate *Homer*,
unless it be a vindication to say, that he wrote according to the opinions that
anciently prevail'd in the world; or that like *Hercules*, while the vehicle of *Achilles*
is in this state of horrour, his soul may be in Heaven; especially since he received divine honours after death, as well as *Hercules. Tull. Nat. Deor.* 3 ⟨xviii 45⟩.
Astypalæa Achillem sanctissime colit, qui si deus est, & Orpheus, &c.

This arm that thunder'd o'er the *Phrygian* plain,
And swell'd the ground with mountains of the slain,
Should vindicate my injur'd Father's fame,
Crush the proud rebel, and assert his claim.
    Illustrious shade, (I cry'd) of *Peleus'* fates   615
No circumstance the voice of fame relates;
But hear with pleas'd attention the renown
The wars and wisdom of thy gallant son:
With me from *Scyros* to the field of fame
Radiant in arms the blooming Heroe came: 620
When *Greece* assembled all her hundred states
To ripen counsels, and decide debates,
Heav'ns! how he charmed us with a flow of sense,
And won the heart with manly Eloquence!
He first was seen of all the Peers to rise,   625
The third in wisdom where they all were wise;
But when to try the fortune of the day
Host mov'd tow'rd host in terrible array,
Before the van, impatient for the fight,
With martial port he strode, and stern delight;   630
Heaps strow'd on heaps beneath his fauchion groan'd,
And monuments of dead deform'd the ground.

---

626. *The third in wisdom*—] I have not ventured to render the *Greek* literally,
Ulysses says that *Neoptolemus* was so wise, that only he himself and *Nestor* were
wiser; a truth that would appear more graceful, if spoken by any other person
than *Ulysses*. But perhaps the Poet puts these words into his mouth, only because
he is speaking to the *Phæacians*, who loved themselves to boast, and were full of
vain-glory; and consequently they could not think self-praise a crime in *Ulysses*;
on the contrary, it could not fail of having a very good effect, as it sets him off as
a person of consummate wisdom.
    The Poet excellently sustains the character of *Achilles* in this interview: In the
Iliad he is describ'd a dutiful son, and always expressing a tender affection for his
father *Peleus*; in the *Odyssey* he is drawn in the same soft colours: In the *Iliad* he is
represented as a man of strong resentment; in the *Odyssey*, he first imagines that
his father suffers, and upon this imagination he immediately takes fire, and flies
into threats and fury.
    Dictys, lib. 6. ⟨VI vii–ix⟩ relates, that *Peleus* was expuls'd from his kingdom by
Acastus, but that *Pyrrhus* the son of *Achilles* afterwards reveng'd the injury.

The time would fail should I in order tell
What foes were vanquish'd, and what numbers fell;
How, lost thro' love, *Eurypylus* was slain,   635

---

635. *How, lost thro' love*, Eurypylus *was slain.*] It must be own'd that this passage
is very intricate: *Strabo* himself ⟨xiii i 69⟩ complains of its obscurity: The Poet
(says that Author) rather proposes an *Ænigma*, than a clear History: for who are
these *Cetæans*, and what are these *presents of women*? and adds, that the Gram-
marians darken, instead of clearing the obscurity. But it is no difficulty to solve
these objections from *Eustathius*.

It is evident from *Strabo* himself ⟨xiii i 70⟩, that *Eurypylus* reign'd near the river
Caicus, over the *Mysians*, and *Pliny* ⟨v xxxiii 125⟩ confines it to *Teuthrania*; this
agrees with what *Ovid* writes, *Metam. 2* ⟨243⟩.
                         —*Teuthranteusque Caïcus.*
And *Virgil* shews us that *Caïcus* was a river of *Mysia, Georg. 4* ⟨370⟩.
                  Saxosumque sonans Hypanis, Mysusque Caïcus.
But what relation has *Caicus* to the *Cetians*? *Hesychius* ⟨*Lexicon,* s.v.⟩ informs us,
that they are a people of *Mysia*, so call'd from the river *Cetium*, which runs thro'
their country; Κήτειοι, γένος Μυσῶν, ἀπὸ τοῦ παρρέοντος ποταμοῦ Κήτεος.
This river discharges it self into the *Caicus*, and consequently the *Cetians* were
Mysians, over whom *Eurypylus* reign'd. It would be endless to transcribe the
different opinions of writers cited by *Eustathius*; some read the verse thus:
               Χήτειοι κτείνοντο γυναικῶν, εἵνεκα δώρων.
Then the meaning will be, *How they fell far from their wives, for the sake of a reward*;
that is, for their pay from *Hector*, who, as it appears from the *Iliad*, tax'd the
Trojans to pay the auxiliaries, one of whom was *Eurypylus*. Others think the word
signifies, *Great of stature*, and in this sense we find it used in the first line of the
4th *Odyssey*.
                     —Λακεδαίμονα κητώεσσαν.
But I have follow'd the first opinion, as appearing most probable and natural.

But how are we to explain the second objection, or γυναικῶν εἵνεκα δώρων?
Some (says *Eustathius*) understand the expression as apply'd to *Neoptolemus*, and
not *Eurypylus*; namely, *Eurypylus* and his soldiers fell by means of the *gifts of
women*; that is, *Neoptolemus* was led to the war by the promise of having *Hermione*
in marriage, the daughter of *Menelaus*, which promise occasion'd the death of
Eurypylus, by bringing *Neoptolemus* to the siege of *Troy*. Others understand it to be
spoken of a golden vine, sent by *Priam* to his sister *Astyoche* the mother of *Eurypylus*,
to induce her to persuade her son to undertake this expedition to *Troy*, where he
was slain by the son of *Achilles*; this vine was said to be given to *Tros* the father
of *Priam* by *Jupiter*, as a recompense for his carrying away his son *Ganymede* to be
his cup-bearer; but this is too much a fable to be follow'd. Others more probably
assert, that *Priam* had promis'd one of his daughte⸱⸱ ⸱ *Eurypylus*, to engage his
assistance in the war; and this agrees very well with *Homer*'s manner of writing in

And round him bled his bold *Cetæan* train.
To *Troy* no Hero came of nobler line,
Or if of nobler, *Memnon*, it was thine.
    When *Ilion* in the horse receiv'd her doom,
And unseen armies ambush'd in its womb;   640
Greece gave her latent warriors to my care,
'Twas mine on *Troy* to pour th' imprison'd war:
Then when the boldest bosom beat with fear,
When the stern eyes of Heroes dropp'd a tear;
Fierce in his look his ardent valour glow'd,   645
Flush'd in his cheek, or sally'd in his blood;
Indignant in the dark recess he stands,
Pants for the battle, and the war demands;
His voice breath'd death, and with a martial air
He grasp'd his sword, and shook his glitt'ring spear.   650
And when the Gods our arms with conquest crown'd,
When *Troy*'s proud bulwarks smok'd upon the ground,
Greece to reward her soldier's gallant toils
Heap'd high his navy with unnumber'd spoils.
    Thus great in glory from the din of war   655
Safe he return'd, without one hostile scar;
Tho' spears in iron tempests rain'd around,
Yet innocent they play'd, and guiltless of a wound.
    While yet I spoke, the Shade with transport glow'd,
Rose in his majesty, and noblier trod;   660
With haughty stalk he sought the distant glades
Of warrior Kings, and joyn'd th' illustrious shades.

---

many places of the *Iliad*; and there is a great resemblance between *Eurypylus* in the *Odyssey* and *Othryoneus* in the *Iliad*, *lib*. 13. 461.
        Cassandra's love he sought, with boasts of pow'r,
        And promis'd conquest was the proffer'd dow'r.
  Spondanus cites ⟨*Od.* p. 165⟩ a passage from *Dictys*, *lib.* 4 ⟨IV xiv⟩, that very well explains these difficulties: *Inter quæ tam læta,* (*nimirum mortem Achillis, &c.*) *Priamo supervenit nuntius Eurypylum Telephi filium ex Mysia adventare, quem rex multis antea illectum præmiis, ad postremum oblatione Cassandræ confirmaverat, addiderat etiam auream vitem, & ob id per populos memorabilem.*

Now without number ghost by ghost arose,
All wailing with unutterable woes.
Alone, apart, in discontented mood   665
A gloomy shade, the sullen *Ajax* stood;
For ever sad with proud disdain he pin'd,
And the lost arms for ever stung his mind;
Tho' to the contest *Thetis* gave the laws,
And *Pallas*, by the *Trojans* judg'd the cause.   670
O why was I victorious in the strife!
O dear-bought honour with so brave a life!
With him the strength of war, the soldiers pride,
Our second hope to great *Achilles* dy'd!
Touch'd at the sight from tears I scarce refrain,   675
And tender sorrow thrills in ev'ry vein;

---

669.   *Tho' to the contest* Thetis *gave the laws,*
                        And Pallas, *by the* Trojans *judg'd the cause.*]
There are two particulars which want explication in these verses: How did
Thetis give the law to the contest between *Ajax* and *Ulysses*? and how could the
Trojans be made judges to determine between two *Grecian* Heroes? *Thetis* the
mother of *Achilles* was a Goddess, and out of honour to her, the Chiefs of the
Grecian army propos'd the arms of her son as a reward to the most worthy; and
Poetry, to give a magnificence to the story, introduces the Goddess as acting in
person what is done upon her account. *Thetis* may properly be said to be desirous
that the memory of her son should be honour'd; and *Homer* to express this desire
poetically, tells us it was the act of that Goddess, to propose the arms of *Achilles*
as a reward to the most worthy of the *Grecian* Heroes.

The second difficulty is fully explain'd by *Eustathius*: *Agamemnon* finding it an
invidious affair to give the preference to any one of the *Grecian* Heroes, and being
willing to avoid the reproach of partiality, commanded the *Trojan* prisoners to
be brought before the whole army, and ask'd from which of the two Heroes *Ajax*
or *Ulysses* they had received the greater detriment, they immediately reply'd
from *Ulysses*; thus the *Trojans* adjudg'd the cause. The Poet adds, that this was
done by *Minerva*; that is, the affair was conducted with wisdom, the result of
which in Poetry is usually ascrib'd to the Goddess of it; and no doubt but the
Goddess of Wisdom must always prefer Wisdom to mere Valour, or an *Ulysses* to
an *Ajax*. This decision is related in a very different manner by other Poets; in
particular, by *Ovid* in his *Metamorphoses* ⟨XIII 382 ff⟩; but *Lucian* in his Dialogues
⟨*D. Mort.* xxix⟩ agrees with *Homer* in every point very circumstantially; and
consequently, with some obscurity; but what I have here said fully explains that
dialogue of *Lucian*, as well as this passage of *Homer*.

P

Pensive and sad I stand, at length accost,
With accents mild, th' inexorable ghost.
　　Still burns thy rage? and can brave souls resent
Ev'n after death? relent, great Shade, relent!　　　680
Perish those arms which by the Gods decree
Accurs'd our army with the loss of thee!
With thee we fell; *Greece* wept thy hapless fates,
And shook astonish'd thro' her hundred states;
Not more, when great *Achilles* prest the ground,　　685
And breath'd his manly spirit thro' the wound.
O deem thy fall not ow'd to man's decree,
Jove hated *Greece*, and punish'd *Greece* in thee!
Turn then, oh peaceful turn, thy wrath controul,
And calm the raging tempest of thy soul.　　　690
　　While yet I speak, the shade disdains to stay,
In silence turns, and sullen stalks away.

691.　　　　　*—The shade disdains to stay,*
　　　　　　　In silence turns, and sullen stalks away.]
This silence of *Ajax* was very much admir'd by the Ancients, and *Longinus* ⟨IX 2⟩
proposes it as an instance of the true sublimity of thought, which springs from an
elevation of soul, and not from the diction; for a man may be truly sublime without speaking a word: Thus in the silence of *Ajax* there is something more noble,
than in any thing he could possibly have spoken. Mons. *Rapin* ⟨Comparaison xiii
I 149–50⟩ agrees with *Longinus*: The stubborn, untractable *Ajax* (says that
Author) could not have made a better return to the compliments full of submission which were paid him by *Ulysses*, than by a disdainful and contemptuous
silence: *Ajax* has more the air of grandeur and majesty, when he says nothing,
than when the Poet makes him speak. *Virgil* ⟨VI 469–76⟩ was sensible of the
beauty of it, and paints *Dido* in the attitude of *Ajax*. *Fraguier* ⟨above, XI, n. I⟩ infinitely prefers the silence of *Dido* to that of *Ajax*; she was a woman disappointed in
love, and therefore no wonder if she was greatly passionate, and sunk under the
weight of the calamity: but *Ajax* was a Heroe, and ought to have freed himself
by his courage from such an unworthy degree of resentment. But to me there
appears no weight in this objection: We must remember what an Heroe *Ajax* is,
a sow'r, stubborn, untractable Heroe; and upon all occasions given to taciturn-
ity; this is his universal and notorious character thro' the whole *Iliad*: The Poet
therefore adapts his description to it, and he is the same *Ajax* in the *Odyssey* as he
was in the *Iliad*: Had this been spoken of any other Heroe, the criticism had
been more just, but in *Ajax* this stubborn silence is proper and noble.

Touch'd at his sour retreat, thro' deepest night,
Thro' hell's black bounds I had pursu'd his flight,
And forc'd the stubborn spectre to reply;   695
But wond'rous visions drew my curious eye.
High on a throne, tremendous to behold,
Stern *Minos* waves a mace of burnish'd gold;
Around ten thousand thousand spectres stand
Thro' the wide dome of *Dis*, a trembling band.   700
Still as they plead, the fatal lots he rowls,
Absolves the just, and dooms the guilty souls.
  There huge *Orion* of portentous size,

---

701. *Still as they plead*—] The expression in the *Greek* is remarkable, ἥμενοι,
ἑστᾱότες τε; that is, "standing and sitting;" this is to be referr'd to different persons; the ἑστᾱότες were the συνδικασταί, or persons who pleaded the cause of
the guilty or innocent before the infernal judges: The ἥμενοι were the persons
for whom they pleaded, or those who were about to receive judgment. I doubt
not but this was a custom observ'd in the courts of Judicature in the days of
Homer. Eustath.

703.   —Orion *of portentous size,*
                  Swift thro' the gloom a Giant-hunter flies.]
The diversion of this infernal hunter may seem extraordinary in pursuing the
shades of beasts; but it was the opinion of the Ancients, that the same passions to
which men were subject on earth continued with them in the other world; and
their shades were liable to be affected in the same manner as their bodies: Thus
we frequently see them shedding tears, and *Sisyphus* sweats, in rolling the stone
up the mountain. *Virgil* ⟨VI 652–5⟩.
                  Stant terra defixæ hastæ, passimque soluti
                  Per campum pascuntur equi, . . . quæ cura nitentes
                  Pascere equos, eadem sequitur tellure repostos.
And again ⟨VI 444⟩,
                  —*Curæ non ipsa in morte relinquunt.*
I cannot but be of opinion that *Milton* has far surpass'd both the *Greek* and the
Roman Poet, in the description of the fall'n Angels in Hell, as the Ideas are more
noble and suitable to the characters he describes ⟨II 528–55⟩.
                  Part on the plain, or in the air sublime
                  Upon the wing, or in swift race contend,
                  *As at th'*Olympian *games or* Pythian *fields:*
                  Part curb the ⟨their⟩ fiery steeds, or shun the goal
                  With rapid wheels, or fronted brigades form.
                  Others with vast Typhœan *rage more fell*

Swift thro' the gloom a Giant-hunter flies;
A pond'rous mace of brass with direful sway   705
Aloft he whirls, to crush the savage prey;
Stern beasts in trains that by his truncheon fell,
Now griesly forms, shoot o'er the lawns of hell.
    There *Tityus* large and long, in fetters bound,

> *Rend up both rocks, and hills, and ride the air*
> *In whirlwind: Hell scarce holds the wild uproar*
>   *—Others more mild*
> *Retreated in a silent valley, sing*
> *With notes Angelical to many an harp,*
> *Their own heroic deeds—*
> *The ⟨Their⟩ song was partial, but the harmony*
> *Suspended Hell, and took with ravishment*
> *The thronging audience, &c.*

709. *There* Tityus—] It is needless to mention that *Virgil* has adorn'd his descent into Hell with most of these fables borrow'd from *Homer*; It is equally unnecessary to relate what antiquity says of these fabled persons, and their histories; but the moral of them all is observ'd by *Eustathius*, and fully explain'd by *Lucretius* ⟨III 978 ff⟩ which I will lay together from Mr. *Dryden*'s translation ⟨*The latter Part of the Third Book of Lucretius* 183–6, 189–91, 197–209⟩.

> *—The dismal tales that Poets tell*
> *Are verify'd on earth, and not in hell;*
> *No* Tantalus *looks with a fearful eye,*
> *Or dreads th' impending rock to crush him from on high;*
> *No* Tityus, *torn by Vulturs, lies in hell,*
> *Nor could the lobes of his rank liver swell*
> *To that prodigious mass, for their eternal meal.*
> *But he's the* Tityus, *who, by love oppress'd,*
> *Or tyrant passion preying on his breast,*
> *And ever anxious thoughts, is robb'd of rest.*
> *The* Sisyphus *is he, whom noise and strife*
> *Seduce from all the soft retreats of life,*
> *To vex the government, disturb the laws,*
> *Drunk with the fumes of popular applause,*
> *He courts the giddy croud to make him great,*
> *And sweats and toils in vain, to mount the sov'reign seat;*
> *For still to aim at pow'r, and still to fail,*
> *Ever to strive, and never to prevail,*
> *What is it, but in reason's true account,*
> *To heave the stone against the rising mount?*

I will only add the reason from *Eustathius*, why *Tityus* was fabled to be the son of

O'erspreads nine acres of infernal ground;   710
Two rav'nous vultures furious for their food
Scream o'er the fiend, and riot in his blood,
Incessant gore the liver in his breast,
Th' immortal liver grows, and gives th' immortal feast.
For as o'er *Panopé*'s enamel'd plains   715
Latona journey'd to the *Pythian* fanes,
With haughty love th' audacious monster strove
To force the Goddess, and to rival *Jove*.
  There *Tantalus* along the *Stygian* bounds
Pours out deep groans; (with groans all hell resounds)
Ev'n in the circling floods refreshment craves,   721
And pines with thirst amidst a sea of waves:
When to the water he his lip applies,
Back from his lip the treach'rous water flies.
Above, beneath, around his hapless head,   725
Trees of all kinds delicious fruitage spread;
There figs sky-dy'd, a purple hue disclose,
Green looks the olive, the pomegranate glows,
There dangling pears exalted scents unfold,
And yellow apples ripen into gold;   730
The fruit he strives to seize: but blasts arise,
Toss it on high, and whirl it to the skies.

---

the earth; it was from his being immers'd in worldly cares, and from his centring
all his affections upon the earth, as if he had sprung from it; this is alluded to by
the expression κείμενον ἐν δαπέδῳ. *Spondanus* ⟨*Od.* p. 168⟩ gives us another
reason; *Elara* being pregnant by *Jupiter*, he to avoid the jealousy of *Juno* conceal'd her in a cavern of the earth, where *Tityus* being born, is fabled to be the
son of the earth: He adds, that the fiction of his covering nine acres, arose from
that space of ground which was enclosed for his place of burial. Perhaps the story
of *Tantalus* was invented solely to paint the nature of a covetous person, who
starves amidst plenty, like *Tantalus* in the midst of water. Thus *Horace* applies it,
Satyr. 1. *v.* 70.

> *Tantalus a labris sitiens fugientia captat*
> *Flumina. quid rides? mutato nomine de te*
> *Fabula narratur. congestis undique saccis*
> *Indormis inhians, & tanquam parcere sacris*
> *Cogeris—*

p*

I turn'd my eye, and as I turn'd survey'd
A mournful vision! the *Sisyphyan* shade;
With many a weary step, and many a groan,   735
Up the high hill he heaves a huge round stone;
The huge round stone, resulting with a bound,
Thunders impetuous down, and smoaks along the ground.
Again the restless orb his toil renews,
Dust mounts in clouds, and sweat descends in dews.   740

---

736. *Up the high hill he heaves a huge round stone.*] This is a very remarkable instance of the beauty of *Homer*'s versification; it is taken notice of by *Eustathius*, but copiously explain'd by *Dionysius Halicarn.* in his treatise of placing of words ⟨*De Comp. Verb.* xx 139–40⟩.

Λᾶαν βαστάζοντα πελώριον ἀμφοτέρησιν.
Ἦ τοι ὁ μὲν σκηριπτόμενος χερσίν τε ποσίν τε,
Λᾶαν ἄνω ὤθεσκε—⟨594–6⟩

Here, (says *Dionysius*) we see in the choice and disposition of the words the fact which they describe; the weight of the stone, and the striving to heave it up the mountain: To effect this, *Homer* clogs the verse with Spondees or long syllables, and leaves the vowels open, as in λᾶαν, and in ἄνω ὤθεσκε, which two words it is impossible to pronounce without hesitation and difficulty; the very words and syllables are heavy, and as it were make resistance in the pronunciation, to express the heaviness of the stone, and the difficulty with which it is forced up the mountain. To give the *English* Reader a faint image of the beauty of the original in the translation, I have loaded the verse with monosyllables, and these almost all begin with *Aspirates.*

Up the high hill he heaves a huge round stone.

Homer is no less happy in describing the rushing down of the stone from the top of the mountain.

Αὖτις ἔπειτα πέδονδε κυλίνδετο λᾶας ἀναιδής.⟨598⟩

Is it not evident, (continues *Dionysius*) that the swiftness of the verse imitates the celerity of the stone in its descent; nay, that the verse runs with the greater rapidity? What is the cause of this? It is because there is not one monosyllable in the line, and but two dissyllables, ten of the syllables are short, and not one spondee in it, except one that could not be avoided at the conclusion of it; there is no hiatus or gap between word and word, no vowels left open to retard the celerity of it: the whole seems to be but one word, the syllables melt into one another, and flow away with the utmost rapidity in a torrent of Dactyls. I was too sensible of the beauty of this not to endeavour to imitate it, tho' unsuccessfully: I have therefore thrown it into the swiftness of an *Alexandrine*, to make it of a more proportionable number of syllables with the *Greek.*

I refer the Reader for a fuller explication of these verses to *Dionysius.*

Now I the strength of *Hercules* behold,
A tow'ring spectre of gigantic mold,
A shadowy form! for high in heav'n's abodes
Himself resides, a God among the Gods;
There in the bright assemblies of the skies,   745
He Nectar quaffs, and *Hebe* crowns his joys.
Here hovering ghosts, like fowl, his shade surround,
And clang their pinions with terrific sound;
Gloomy as night he stands, in act to throw
Th' aerial arrow from the twanging bow.   750
Around his breast a wond'rous Zone is rowl'd,
Where woodland monsters grin in fretted gold,
There sullen Lions sternly seem to roar,
The bear to growl, to foam the tusky boar:
There war and havoc and destruction stood,   755
And vengeful murther red with human blood.
Thus terribly adorn'd the figures shine,
Inimitably wrought with skill divine.

---

741. —Hercules, ⟨ . . . ⟩ *A shadowy form.*] This is the passage formerly referr'd
to in these annotations, to prove that *Hercules* was in Heaven, while his shade was
in the infernal regions; a full evidence of the partition of the human composition
into three parts: The body is buried in the earth; the image or εἴδωλον descends
into the regions of the departed; and the soul, or the divine part of man, is
receiv'd into Heaven: Thus the body of *Hercules* was consumed in the flames, his
image is in Hell, and his soul in Heaven. There is a beautiful moral couch'd in the
fable of his being married to *Hebe*, or *youth*, after death: to imply, that a perpetual
youth or a reputation which never grows old, is the reward of those Heroes, who
like *Hercules* employ their courage for the good of humankind.

758. *Inimitably wrought with skill divine.*] This verse is not without obscurity;
Eustathius gives us several interpretations of it.

Μὴ τεχνησάμενος, μηδ' ἄλλο τι τεχνήσαιτο.

The negative μή, by being repeated, seems to be redundant; and this in a great
measure occasions the difficulty; but in the *Greek* language two negatives more
strongly deny; this being premis'd, we may read the verse as if the former μὴ were
absent, and then the meaning will be, "He that made this zone, never made any
thing equal to it:" as if we should say that *Phidias* who made the statue of
Jupiter never made any other statue like it; that is, he employ'd the whole power
of his skill upon it. Others understand the verse as an execration: *Oh never, never
may the hand that made it, make any thing again so terrible as this Zone!* And this will give

The mighty ghost advanc'd with awful look,
And turning his grim visage, sternly spoke.   760
    O exercis'd in grief! by arts refin'd!
O taught to bear the wrongs of base mankind!
Such, such was I! still tost from care to care,
While in your world I drew the vital air;
Ev'n I who from the Lord of thunders rose,   765
Bore toils and dangers, and a weight of woes;
To a base Monarch still a slave confin'd,
(The hardest bondage to a gen'rous mind!)
Down to these worlds I trod the dismal way,
And drag'd the three-mouth'd dog to upper day;   770
Ev'n hell I conquer'd, thro' the friendly aid
Of *Maia*'s off-spring and the martial Maid.
    Thus he, nor deign'd for our reply to stay,
But turning stalk'd with giant strides away.
    Curious to view the Kings of ancient days,   775
The mighty dead that live in endless praise,

---

some reason for the repetition of the negative particles. *Dacier* approves of this latter explication, and moralizes upon it: It proceeds (says she) from a tender sentiment of humanity in *Ulysses*, who wishes that there may never more be occasion for such a design, as the artist executed in this belt of *Hercules*; that there may be no more giants to conquer, no more monsters to tame, or no more human blood be shed. I wish that such a pious and well-natur'd explication were to be drawn from the passage! But how is it possible that the artist who made this Zone should ever make another, when he had been in his grave some Centuries? (for such a distance there was between the days of *Hercules* and *Ulysses*;) and consequently it would be impertinent to wish it. I have therefore follow'd the former interpretation. I will only add, that this belt of *Hercules* is the reverse of the girdle of *Venus*; in that, there is a collection of every thing that is amiable, in this a variety of horrors; but both are master-pieces in their kind.

769. *Down to these worlds I trod the dismal way*.] Nothing can be more artfully inserted than the mention of this descent of *Hercules* into the regions of the dead: *Ulysses* shews by it at least that it was a vulgar opinion, and consequently within the degrees of poetical probability; a Poet being at liberty to follow common fame: In particular, it could not fail of having a full effect upon his *Phæacian* auditors, not only as it in some measure sets him upon a level with *Hercules*, but as it is an example of a like undertaking with this which he has been relating, and therefore a probable method to gain their belief of it. *Eustathius*.

Resolv'd I stand! and haply had survey'd
The god-like *Theseus*, and *Perithous*' shade;
But swarms of spectres rose from deepest hell,
With bloodless visage, and with hideous yell,   780
They scream, they shriek; sad groans and dismal sounds
Stun my scar'd ears, and pierce hell's utmost bounds.
No more my heart the dismal din sustains,
And my cold blood hangs shiv'ring in my veins;
Lest *Gorgon* rising from th' infernal lakes,   785
With horrors arm'd, and curls of hissing snakes,
Should fix me, stiffen'd at the monstrous sight,
A stony image, in eternal night!
Strait from the direful coast to purer air

777.   *—And haply had survey'd*
                        The God-like Theseus—]
Plutarch in his life of *Theseus* ⟨xx (2)⟩ informs us, that this verse has been thought
not genuine; but added to the *Odyssey* in honour of the *Athenians* by *Pisistratus*.
     The Poet shews us that he had still a noble fund of invention, and had it in his
power to open new scenes of wonder and entertainment; but that this infernal
Episode might not be too long, he shifts the scene: The invention of the Gorgon,
which terrifies him from a longer abode in these realms of darkness gives a
probable reason for his immediate return. *Eustathius* informs us from *Athenæus*
⟨v 221 b–e⟩ that *Alexander* the *Mydian* writes in his History of Animals, that there
really was a creature in *Libya*, which the *Nomades* call'd a Gorgon; it resembled a
wild Ram, or as some affirm a calf; whose breath was of such a poisonous nature,
as to kill all that approach'd it: In the same region the *Catoblepton* ⟨*Catoblepon*⟩
is found, a creature like a bull, whose eyes are so fix'd in the head as chiefly to look
downward; *Pliny* calls it *Catoblepas, lib.* 8. *cap.* 21 ⟨viii xxxii 77⟩, which is likewise
suppos'd to kill with its eyes: The Gorgon (proceeds *Athenæus*) has its hair hanging over its eyes down from the forehead, of such thickness that it scarce is able to
remove it, to guide it self from danger; but it kills not by its breath, but with
emanations darted from its eyes: The beast was well known in the time of
Marius, for certain of his soldiers seeing it, mistook it for a wild sheep, and pursued it to take it; but the hair being remov'd by the motion of its flying, it slew all
upon whom it look'd: at length the *Nomades*, who knew the nature of the beast,
destroy'd it with darts at a distance, and carried it to the General *Marius*. How-
soever little truth there be in this story, it is a sufficient ground for poetical
fictions, and all the fables that are ascrib'd to the Gorgon.
     789.   *—To purer air*
                        I speed my flight—]
It may not probably be unpleasant to the Reader to observe the manner how the

I speed my flight, and to my mates repair.   790
My mates ascend the ship; they strike their oars;
The mountains lessen, and retreat the shores;
Swift o'er the waves we fly; the fresh'ning gales
Sing thro' the shrouds, and stretch the swelling sails.

two great Poets *Homer* and *Virgil* close the scene of their infernal adventures, by restoring their Heroes to the earth. *Ulysses* returns by the same way he descended, of which we have a plain description in the beginning of this book: *Virgil* ⟨vi 893–8⟩ takes a different method, he borrows his conclusion from another part of *Homer*; in which he describes the two gates of sleep; the one is ivory, the other of horn: Thro' the ivory gate, issue falshoods, thro' the gate of horn truths: *Virgil* dismisses *Æneas* thro' the gate of falshood: Now what is this, but to inform us that all that he relates is nothing but a dream, and that dream a falshood? I submit it to the Critics who are more dispos'd to find fault than I am, to determine whether *Virgil* ought to be censur'd for such an acknowledgment, or prais'd for his ingenuity?

THE
TWELFTH BOOK
OF THE
ODYSSEY.

The ARGUMENT.
The Sirens, Scylla, *and* Charybdis

He relates, how after his return from the Shades, he was sent by Circe *on his voyage, by the coast of the* Sirens, *and by the streight of* Scylla *and* Charybdis : *The manner in which he escap'd those dangers : How being cast on the Island* Trinacria, *his companions destroy'd the Oxen of the Sun : The vengeance that follow'd ; how all perish'd by shipwreck except himself, who swimming on the mast of the ship, arriv'd on the Island of* Calypso. *With which his narration concludes.*

Thus o'er the rolling surge the vessel flies,
'Till from the waves th' *Ææan* hills arise.
Here the gay Morn resides in radiant bow'rs,

We are now drawing to a conclusion of the Episodic narration of the *Odyssey*; it may therefore not be unentertaining to speak something concerning the nature of it, before we dismiss it.

There are two ways of relating past subjects; the one, simply and methodically by a plain rehearsal, and this is the province of History; the other artificially, where the Author makes no appearance in person, but introduces Speakers, and this is the practice of Epic Poetry. By this method the Poet brings upon the stage those very persons who perform'd the action he represents : he makes them speak and act over again the words and actions they spoke or perform'd before, and in some sort transports his auditors to the time when, and the places where, the action was done. This method is of great use; it prevents the Poet from delivering his story in a plain simple way like an Historian, it makes the Auditors witnesses of it, and the action discovers it self. Thus for instance, it is not *Homer* but *Ulysses* who speaks; the Poet is withdrawn, and the Heroe whose story we hear is as it were rais'd from the grave, and relates it in person to the audience. *Aristotle* observes ⟨*Poetics* XXIV⟩, that the Epic Poem ought to be Dramatic, that is active; *Homer* (says that Author) ought to be especially commended for being the only

Poet who knew exactly what to do; he speaks little himself, but introduces some of his persons, a man or a woman, a God or a Goddess; and this renders his Poem active, or Dramatic. Narration is the very soul that animates the Poem, it gives an opportunity to the Poet to adorn it with different Episodes; it has, as it were, the whole world for its stage, and gives him liberty to search thro' the Creation for incidents or adventures for the employment of his Heroes: Thus for instance, he was at liberty to ascribe the several dangers of *Scylla* and *Charybdis*, of *Polyphemus* and *Antiphates* to *Ulysses*, tho' that Heroe had been as unacquainted with those dangers, as *Æneas* was in reality with *Dido*; the choice of the Episodes being not essential, but arbitrary.

In short, it is from this Episodic narration that the Poet could at all find room to place these Episodes in the *Odyssey*. *Aristotle*, I confess, has set no precise limits to the time of the action, but the Critics in general confine it to one Campaign; at least, they affirm this to be the most perfect duration, according to the model of the *Iliad* and *Odyssey*. Now this Episodic narration gives the Poet an opportunity to relate all that is contain'd in four books without breaking in upon the time of the action: for all that we read between the eighth book and the thirteenth comprehends only the space of one evening; namely, the evening of the thirty third day. The Poet inserts all the adventures that happen'd to *Ulysses* in almost ten years from his departure from *Troy*, into the compass of one evening by way of narration, and so maintains the Unity both of the time and action.

I speak not of the Narration in general; concerning which the curious may consult *Bossu* ⟨III⟩, or *Dryden*'s preface to the translation of the *Æneis*.

1. *Thus o'er the rolling surge*—] The words in the original are ποταμοῖο ῥόον 'Ὠκεανοῖο, which *Strabo* ⟨1 i 7⟩ judges to mean no more than a *part* of the ocean, for if it be otherwise understood it will be a tautology, and who would write that *he went out of the ocean into the ocean*, as it must be rendered if ποταμός be the same with θάλασσα in the next line. But it is perhaps better to understand the passage literally and plainly, only to denote the place from whence *Ulysses* return'd from his infernal voyage; that is, from the extremity of the Ocean. It is usual for the waves of the sea to bear violently and rapidly upon some shores, the waters being pent up by the nearness of the land, and therefore form a current, or ῥόον. So that the expression means no more than *Ulysses* surmounted this current, and then gain'd the wide Ocean.

It is likewise evident from the beginning of this book, that *Ulysses* pass'd only one night in Hell; for he arriv'd at the *Cimmerians* in one day, saw the visions of Hell in the following night, and in the space of the next day return'd from the *Cimmerians* in the evening to *Circe*'s Island, as appears from his going to repose immediately upon his landing.

It may be further prov'd that this was a Nocturnal interview, from the nature of the magical incantations which were always perform'd by night: all sacrifices were offer'd by night to the infernal powers, the offering it self was black, to represent the kingdom of darkness: Thus also in other Poets the Moon is said to turn pale at these magical rites, or as *Virgil* expresses it ⟨*Ecl.* VIII 69⟩,

       Carmina vel caelo possunt deducere lunam.

And indeed, as *Eustathius* observes (from whom this note is chiefly translated) it would have been absurd to have represented the realms of darkness survey'd by the light of the day.

3.   *Here the gay Morn resides in radiant bow'rs,*
                            Here keeps her revels—]

This passage is full of obscurity: For how is it possible to suppose this Island of *Circe* to be the residence of the Morning; that is, for the day to rise immediately upon it, when it is known to lie in a western scituation? Some have imagin'd that this is spoken solely with respect to *Ulysses*, who returning from the shades, might properly say that he arriv'd at the place where the day resides, that is to a place enlighten'd by the sun. Others understand it comparatively, with respect to the *Cimmerians*, or rather to the realms of death, which *Homer* places in the west; with regard to these, *Æxa* may be said to lie in the east, or in the poetical language, to be the residence of the morning. Besides the *Circæan* promontory is of an extraordinary altitude, and consequently the beams at sun-rising may fall upon it; nay, it is said to be illustrated by the Sun even by night. Others have conjectur'd, that what is here said implies no more than that *Ulysses* landed upon the eastern parts of the Island: And lastly, others not improbably refer the whole to the word *Ocean* in the former line, and then the whole passage will be clear, and agree with the fable of the Sun's rising and setting in the Ocean. This is what *Eustathius* remarks, who adds, that the Ancients understood χοροί not to signify *dances*, but χῶροι, the *regions of the morning.* I have translated it in the former sense, according to the consent of most interpreters: And I am persuaded it is used to denote the pleasure and gaiety which the Sun restores to the whole Creation, when dispelling the melancholy darkness, he restores light and gladness to the earth; which is imag'd to us by the playing or dancing of the first beams of the Sun; or rather of *Aurora*, who properly may be said to dance, being a Goddess. *Dacier* renders χοροί, dances; but judges that *Homer* here follows a fabulous Geography, and that as he transported the *Cimmerians* with all their darkness from the *Bosphorus* to *Campania*; so likewise he now removes *Æxa* with all its light from *Colchis* into *Italy*: and therefore the Poet gives the properties and scituation to the Island of *Circe*, which are only true of the eastern *Colchis*.

It is very evident, (continues she) that *Homer* was perfectly acquainted with the *Phœnician* story; he tells us that *Elpenor* was buried upon the promontory on the sea-shores, and that it was called by his name, *Elpenor*. Now the *Phœnicians*, who endeavour'd to naturalize all names in their own language, affirm'd, according to *Bochart* ⟨Pt. II: 1 xxxiii (pp. 654–5)⟩, that this promontory was not so call'd from *Elpenor*, but from their word *Hilbinor*, which signifies, *ubi albescit lux matutina;* that is, "where the dawning of the day begins to appear:" This Promontory being of great height, the rays of the morning might fall upon it; and this tradition might furnish *Homer* with his fiction of the bow'rs, and dances of it.

What may seem to confirm *Dacier*'s opinion of the transportation of *Colchis* into *Italy*, is the immediate mention the Poet makes of *Jason*, and *Ætes* King of *Colchis*: Besides the Ancients believ'd *Phasis*, a river of *Colchis*, to be the bounds of the habitable oriental world: and *Æxa* being the capital of it, lying upon the

Here keeps her revels with the dancing *Hours*;
Here *Phœbus* rising in th' etherial way,   5
Thro' heav'n's bright portals pours the beamy day.
At once we fix our haulsers on the land,
At once descend, and press the desart sand;
There worn and wasted, lose our cares in sleep
To the hoarse murmurs of the rowling deep.   10
    Soon as the morn restor'd the day, we pay'd
Sepulchral honours to *Elpenor*'s shade.
Now by the axe the rushing forest bends,
And the huge pyle along the shore ascends.
Around we stand, a melancholy train,   15
And a loud groan re-ecchoes from the main.
Fierce o'er the Pyre, by fanning breezes spread,
The hungry flame devours the silent dead.
A rising tomb, the silent dead to grace,
Fast by the roarings of the main we place;   20
The rising tomb a lofty column bore,
And high above it rose the tapering oar.
    Mean-time the *Goddess our return survey'd
From the pale ghosts, and hell's tremendous shade.
Swift she descends: A train of nymphs divine   25
Bear the rich viands and the generous wine:
In act to speak the *Pow'r of magic stands,
And graceful thus accosts the list'ning bands.
    O sons of woe! decreed by adverse fates

* *Circe.*

Phasis it might very rationally be mistaken for the place where the Sun rose; thus
Mimnermus writes ⟨ii 7⟩,

Αἰήταο πόλιν τόθι τ' ὠκέος ἠελίοιο
Ἀκτῖνες χρυσέῳ κείαται ἐν θαλάμῳ
Ὠκεανοῦ παρὰ χείλεσ' ἵν ᾤχετο θεῖος Ἰήσων.

That is, "the city of *Ætes* where the rays of the Sun appear in a bed of gold, above
the margin of the Ocean, where the divine *Jason* arriv'd:" This is an evidence
that the Poet was well acquainted with Antiquity, and that (as *Strabo* judges ⟨1
ii 9⟩) his astonishing fictions have truth for their foundation.

Alive to pass thro' hell's eternal gates! 30
All, soon or late, are doom'd that path to tread;
More wretched you! twice number'd with the dead!
This day adjourn your cares; exalt your souls,
Indulge the taste, and drein the sparkling bowls:
And when the morn unveils her safron ray, 35
Spread your broad sails, and plow the liquid way:
Lo I this night, your faithful guide, explain
Your woes by land, your dangers on the main.
    The Goddess spoke; in feasts we waste the day,
'Till *Phœbus* downward plung'd his burning ray; 40
Then sable Night ascends, and balmy rest
Seals ev'ry eye, and calms the troubled breast.
Then curious she commands me to relate
The dreadful scenes of *Pluto*'s dreary state.
She sate in silence while the tale I tell, 45
The wond'rous visions, and the laws of Hell.
    Then thus: The lot of man the Gods dispose;
These ills are past; now hear thy future woes.
O Prince attend! some fav'ring pow'r be kind,
And print th' important story on thy mind! 50
    Next, where the *Sirens* dwell, you plow the seas;

51. *Next, where the* Sirens *dwell*—] The Critics have greatly labour'd to explain what was the foundation of this fiction of the *Sirens*. We are told by some, that the *Sirens* were Queens of certain small Islands, named *Sirenusæ*, that lye near *Capreæ* in *Italy*, and chiefly inhabited the Promontory of *Minerva*, upon the top of which that Goddess had a Temple, as some affirm, built by *Ulysses*, according to this verse of *Seneca, Epist.* 77 ⟨2⟩.
Alta procelloso speculatur vertice Pallas.
Here, there was a renown'd Academy in the reign of these *Sirens*, famous for Eloquence and the liberal Sciences, which gave occasion for the invention of this fable of the sweetness of the voice, and attracting songs of the *Sirens*. But why then are they fabled to be destroyers, and painted in such dreadful colours? We are told that at last the Students abus'd their knowledge, to the colouring of wrong, the corruption of manners, and subversion of government; that is, in the language of Poetry, they were feign'd to be transform'd into monsters, and with their music to have entic'd passengers to their ruin, who there consum'd their patrimonies, and poison'd their virtues with riot and effeminacy. The place is now call'd

Their song is death, and makes destruction please.
Unblest the man, whom music wins to stay
Nigh the curst shore, and listen to the lay;
No more that wretch shall view the joys of life,   55
His blooming offspring, or his beauteous wife!
In verdant meads they sport, and wide around
Lie human bones, that whiten all the ground;
The ground polluted floats with human gore,
And human carnage taints the dreadful shore.   60

Massa. In the days of *Homer* the Sirens were fabled to be two only in number, as appears from his speaking of them in the dual, as ὅπα Σειρήνοιϊν, νῆσον Σειρήνοιϊν; their names (adds *Eustathius*) were *Thelxiepia*, and *Aglaophemè*. Other writers, in particular *Lycophron* ⟨712 ff⟩, mention three *Sirens*, *Ligia*, *Parthenope*, and *Leucosia*. Some are of opinion (continues the same Author ⟨Lycophron⟩) that they were ψαλτρίας καὶ ἑταιρίδας; that is, "singing women and harlots", who by the sweetness of their voices drew the unwary to ruin their health and fortune. Others tell us of a certain Bay contracted within winding streights and broken cliffs, which by the singing of the winds, and beating of the waters, returns a delightful harmony; that allures the passenger to approach, who is immediately thrown against the rocks, and swallow'd up by the violent eddies.

But others understand the whole passage allegorically, or as a fable containing an excellent moral, to shew that if we suffer our selves to be too much allur'd by the pleasures of an idle life, the end will be destruction: thus *Horace* moralizes it ⟨*Serm.* II iii 14–15⟩;

> —*Vitanda est improba Siren*
> *Desidia*—

But the fable may be apply'd to all pleasures in general, which if too eagerly pursued betray the uncautious into ruin; while wise men, like *Ulysses*, making use of their reason stop their ears against their insinuations.

57.   —*Around*
        Lie human bones, that whiten all the ground]

There is a great similitude between this passage and the words of *Solomon* in the *Proverbs*, where there is a most beautiful description of an harlot, in the eighth and ninth chapters ⟨7 : 7, 10, 21–2; 9 : 18⟩.

I beheld among the simple ones, I discern'd among the youths, a young man void of understanding; and behold there met him a woman with the attire of an harlot, and subtil of heart, &c. With her much fair speech she caused hm to yield, she forced him with the flattering of her lips: he goeth after her straightway, as an Ox goeth to the slaughter, but he knoweth not that the dead are there, and her guests are in the depths of Hell.

This may serve for a comment upon *Homer*, and it is an instance, that without any violence the nature of harlots may be conceal'd under the fable of the *Sirens*.

Fly swift the dang'rous coast; let ev'ry ear
Be stop'd against the song! 'tis death to hear!
Firm to the mast with chains thy self be bound,
Nor trust thy virtue to th' enchanting sound.
If mad with transport, freedom thou demand,   65
Be every fetter strain'd, and added band to band.
 These seas o'erpass'd, be wise! but I refrain
To mark distinct thy voyage o'er the main:
New horrors rise! let prudence be thy guide,
And guard thy various passage thro' the tyde.   70
 High o'er the main two Rocks exalt their brow,

71. *High o'er the main two Rocks*—] There is undoubtedly a great amplification in the description of *Scylla* and *Charybdis*; it may not therefore be unnecessary to lay before the Reader, what is truth and what fiction.

 Thucydides, lib. 4. ⟨IV xxiv 4⟩ thus describes it. "This streight is the sea that flows between *Rhegium* and *Messenè*, where at the narrowest distance, *Sicily* is divided from the Continent; and this is that part of the sea which *Ulysses* is said to have pass'd, and 'tis called *Charybdis*: This sea, by reason of the streights, and the concourse of the *Tyrrhene* and *Sicilian* seas breaking violently into it, and there raising great commotions, is with good reason call'd χαλεπή or destructive." *Charybdis* stands on the coast of *Sicily*; *Scylla* on the coast of *Italy*.

 Mr. *Sandys* ⟨*A Relation of a Journey*, IV (1615), p. 246⟩ examin'd these rocks and seas with a particular view to the descriptions of the Poets: Speaking of *Charybdis*, he writes, "When the winds begin to ruffle, especially from the south, it forthwith runs round with violent eddies, so that many vessels miscarry by it. The stream thro' the streight runs toward the *Ionian*, and part of it sets into the haven, which turning about, and meeting with other streams makes so violent an encounter that ships are glad to prevent the danger by coming to an anchor. *Scylla*, adds he, is seated in the midst of a bay, upon the neck of a narrow mountain, which thrusts it self into the sea, having at the uppermost end a steep high rock, so celebrated by the Poets, and hyperbolically describ'd by *Homer* as unaccessable. The fables are indeed well fitted to the place, there being divers little sharp rocks at the foot of the greater: These are the dogs that are said to bark there, the waters by their repercussion from them make a noise like the barking of dogs; and the reason why *Scylla* is said to devour the fishes, as *Homer* expresses it.

> *When stung with hunger she embroils the flood,*
> *The Sea-dog and the Dolphin are her food;*
> *She makes the huge Leviathan her prey,*
> *And all the monsters of the wat'ry way.* ⟨117–20⟩

The reason of this is, because these rocks are frequented by Lamprons,

The boiling billows thund'ring roll below;
Thro' the vast waves the dreadful wonders move,
Hence nam'd *Erratic* by the Gods above.

and greater fishes, that devour the bodies of the drown'd. But *Scylla* is now without danger, the current not setting upon it; and I much wonder at the proverb,

Incidit in Scyllam qui vult vitare Charybdim,

⟨cf. Walter of Lille (*Oxford Dict. Engl. Proverbs*): "Incidis in Scyllam cupiens vitare Charybdim"⟩ when they stand twelve miles distant: I rather conjecture, adds he, that there has been more than one *Charybdis*, occasion'd by the recoiling streams: As one there is between the south end of this bay of *Scylla*, and the opposite point of *Sicily*; there the waves justling make a violent eddy, which when the winds are rough, more than threaten destruction to ships, as I have heard from the *Sicilians*, when seeking perhaps to avoid the then more impetuous turning they have been driven by weather upon the not far distant *Scylla*."

Strabo ⟨1 ii 19⟩, (as *Eustathius* remarks) speaking of the *Leontines*, says, that they were an unhospitable people, *Cyclopeans* and *Laestrygones*: and adds, that *Scylla* and *Charybdis* were inhabited by robbers and murderers. From the terrible situation of those rocks, and the murders and depredation of the robbers these fictions might arise; they might murder six of the companions of *Ulysses*, and throw them into the sea from *Scylla*, which may be expressed in their being said to be swallow'd up by that monster.

Bochart ⟨Pt. II: 1 xxviii (p. 576)⟩ judges the names of *Scylla* and *Charybdis* are of *Phoenician* extract, the one deriv'd from *Sool*, which signifies loss and ruin, the other from *Chorobdam*, which implies the abyss of destruction.

It is highly probable that these rocks were more dangerous formerly than at these times, the violence of the waters may not only have enlarg'd their channel by time, but by throwing up banks and sands, have diverted their course from bearing upon these rocks with the same violence as anciently; add to this, that men by art may have contributed to render these seas more safe, being places of great resort and navigation. Besides, the unskilfulness of the Ancients in sea affairs, and the smallness and form of their vessels, might render those seas very dangerous to them, which are safe to modern navigators.

74. *Hence nam'd* Erratic—] It will reconcile the Reader in some measure to the boldness of these fictions, if he considers that *Homer*, to render his Poetry more marvellous, joyns what has been related of the *Symplegades*, to the description of *Scylla* and *Charybdis*: such a fiction of the justling of these rocks could not be shocking to the ears of the Ancients, who had before heard of the same property in the *Symplegades*. The whole fable is perhaps grounded upon appearance: Navigators looking upon these rocks at a distance, might in different views, according to the position of the ship, sometimes see them in a direct line, and then they would appear to joyn, and after they had pass'd a little further they might look upon them obliquely, and then they would be discover'd to be at some distance;

No bird of air, no dove of swiftest wing,   75
That bears *Ambrosia* to th' Ætherial King,
Shuns the dire rocks: In vain she cuts the skies,
The dire rocks meet, and crush her as she flies;
Not the fleet bark when prosp'rous breezes play,
Plows o'er that roaring surge its desp'rate way;   80
O'erwhelm'd it sinks: while round a smoke expires,
And the waves flashing seem to burn with fires.
Scarce the fam'd *Argo* pass'd these raging floods,
The sacred *Argo*, fill'd with demigods!
Ev'n she had sunk, but *Jove*'s imperial bride   85

and this might give occasion to the fable of their meeting and recoiling alternately. *Strabo* ⟨III ii 12⟩ agrees that *Homer* borrow'd his description of *Scylla* and
Charybdis from the *Symplegades*; *Homer* (says he) describes these, like the *Cyanean*
rocks; he continually lays the foundation of his fables upon some well known
History: Thus he feigns these rocks to be full of dangers and horrors, according to
the relations of the *Cyanean*, which from their justling are call'd *Symplegades*.

75.   *—No dove of swiftest wing,*
                That bears Ambrosia *to th' Ætherial King.*]
What might give *Homer* this notion, might be what is related of the *Symplegades*.
Phineus being ask'd by *Jason* if he could pass those rocks with safety, he desires to
know how swift the vessel was; *Jason* answers, as swift as a dove; Then, said
Phineus, send a dove between the rocks, and if she escapes, you may pass in safety:
Jason complies, and the pigeon in her passage lost only her tail; that Heroe
immediately sets sail, and escapes with the loss only of his rudder: This story
being reported of the *Symplegades*, might give *Homer* the hint of applying the
crushing of the doves to *Scylla* and *Charybdis*. You may find in *Eustathius* several
far-fetcht notions upon this passage, but I shall pass them over in silence.
Longinus blames it ⟨IX 14⟩, and I have ventur'd in the translation to omit that
particular which occasion'd his censure ⟨i.e. that Jupiter sends replacements
for the doves lost in flight⟩.

85.   *—Jove's imperial bride*
                Wing'd her fleet sail—]
A Poet should endeavour to raise his images and expressions as far as possible
above meanness and vulgarity: In this respect no Poet was ever more happy than
Homer: This place is an instance of it; it means no more than that while *Jason*
made his voyage he had favourable winds and serene air. As *Juno* is frequently
used in *Homer* to denote the air, he ascribes the prosperous wind to that Goddess,
who presides over the air: Thus in Poetry, *Juno*
            Wing'd her fleet sail, and push'd her o'er the tyde.
                                        Eustathius.

Wing'd her fleet sail, and push'd her o'er the tyde.
   High in the air the rock its summit shrouds,
In brooding tempests, and in rouling clouds;
Loud storms around and mists eternal rise,
Beat its bleak brow, and intercept the skies.   90
When all the broad expansion bright with day
Glows with th' autumnal or the summer ray,
The summer and the autumn glows in vain,
The sky for ever low'rs, for ever clouds remain.
Impervious to the step of man it stands,   95
Tho' born by twenty feet, tho' arm'd with twenty hands;
Smooth as the polish of the mirrour rise
The slippery sides, and shoot into the skies.
Full in the center of this rock display'd,
A yawning cavern casts a dreadful shade: 100
Nor the fleet arrow from the twanging bow
Sent with full force, cou'd reach the depth below.
Wide to the west the horid gulph extends,
And the dire passage down to hell descends.
O fly the dreadful sight! expand thy sails,   105
Ply the strong oar, and catch the nimble gales;
Here *Scylla* bellows from her dire abodes,
Tremendous pest! abhorr'd by man and Gods!
Hideous her voice, and with less terrors roar

---

104. *And the dire passage down to hell descends.*] *Homer* means by Hell, the regions
of Death, and uses it to teach us that there is no passing by this rock without
destruction, or in *Homer's* words it is a sure passage into the kingdom of death.
Eustathius.

109.   —*With less terrors roar*
                          The whelps of Lions—]
The words in the original are, σκύλακος νεογιλῆς, which in the proper and
immediate sense do not confine it to the whelps of a Lion, but to whelps in
general, and perhaps chiefly of the canine kind; νεογιλόν *Eustathius* interprets
νεωστὶ γιγνόμενον, or newly whelp'd, and in the latter sense the passage is
understood by that Author; for he writes, φωνὴ σκύλακος ὀλίγη, Σκύλλη δὲ
μεγὰ κακὸν; that is, "the voice of a whelp is low, but *Scylla* is describ'd as an huge
monster;" and the Poet uses it as we do this expression; *The voice of a wicked man is*

The whelps of Lions in the midnight hour.   110
Twelve feet deform'd and foul the fiend dispreads;
Six horrid necks she rears, and six terrific heads;
Her jaws grin dreadful with three rows of teeth;
Jaggy they stand, the gaping den of death:
Her parts obscene the raging billows hide;   115
Her bosom terribly o'erlooks the tyde.
When stung with hunger she embroils the flood,
The Sea-dog and the Dolphin are her food;
She makes the huge Leviathan her prey,
And all the monsters of the wat'ry way;   120
The swiftest racer of the azure plain
Here fills her sails and spreads her oars in vain;
Fell *Scylla* rises, in her fury roars,
At once six mouths expands, at once six men devours.
        Close by, a rock of less enormous height   125
Breaks the wild waves, and forms a dang'rous streight;

soft, but his deeds are mischievous and abominable. I have adventur'd to translate the
words in the other sense, after most interpreters, for *Homer* expresses the voice of
Scylla by δεινὸν λελακυῖα, or *uttering a dreadful noise*: Now what he calls her voice,
is nothing but the roaring of the waves in storms when they beat against that
rock; and this being very loud, is better represented by the roaring of a Lion,
than the complaining of a young whelp. *Chapman* ⟨XII 135⟩ follows *Eustathius*.

> For here the *whuling* Scylla *shrouds her face,*
> *That breathes a voice, at all parts, no more base*
> *Than are a newly-kitten'd kitling's cries.*

which is really burlesque enough. *Dacier* renders the words by *rugissement d'un
eune Lion*, or the roarings of a young Lion.

118. *The Sea-dog and the Dolphin are her food.*] *Polybius* ⟨XXXIV iii⟩ (as *Strabo*
remarks ⟨I ii 15⟩) contends, that *Homer* in all his fictions alludes to the customs of
Antiquity: For instance, *Scylla* was a famous fishery for taking such fishes as
Homer mentions: This was the manner of taking the Sea-dog; several small boats
went out only with two men in it, the one rowed, the other stood with his instrument ready to strike the fish; all the boats had one speculator in common, to give
notice when the fish approach'd, which usually swum with more than half of the
body above water: *Ulysses* is this speculator, who stands arm'd with his spear;
and it is probable, adds *Polybius*, that *Homer* thought *Ulysses* really visited *Sicily*,
since he ascribes to *Scylla* ⟨the monster⟩ that manner of fishing which is really
practis'd by the *Scyllians* ⟨natives of Scylla (cf. above), i.e. Scyllæum, in Sicily⟩.

Q*

Full on its crown a fig's green branches rise,
And shoot a leafy forest to the skies;
Beneath, *Charybdis* holds her boist'rous reign
'Midst roaring whirlpools, and absorbs the main,   130
Thrice in her gulphs the boiling seas subside,
Thrice in dire thunders she refunds the tyde.
Oh if thy vessel plow the direful waves
When seas retreating roar within her caves,
Ye perish all! tho' he who rules the main   135
Lend his strong aid, his aid he lends in vain.
Ah shun the horrid gulph! by *Scylla* fly,
'Tis better six to lose, than all to die.

---

127. *Full on its crown a fig's green branches rise.*] These particularities, which seem
of no consequence, have a very good effect in Poetry, as they give the relation an
air of truth and probability. For what can induce a Poet to mention such a tree,
if the tree were not there in reality? Neither is this fig-tree describ'd in vain, it is
the means of preserving the life of *Ulysses* in the sequel of the story. The Poet
describes the fig-tree loaded with leaves; even this circumstance is of use, for the
branches would then bend downward to the sea by their weight, and be reach'd
by *Ulysses* more easily. It shews likewise, that this shipwreck was not in winter, for
then the branches are naked. *Eustath.*

Dacier gathers from hence, that the season was Autumn, meaning the time
when *Ulysses* arriv'd among the *Phæacians*; but this is a mistake, for he was cast
upon the *Ogygian* coast by this storm, and there remain'd with *Calypso* many
years. The branch with which *Ulysses* girds his loins in the sixth book is describ'd
with leaves, and that is indeed a full proof that he was thrown upon the *Phæacian*
shores before the season in which trees shed their leaves, and probably in the
Autumn.

131.   *Thrice in her gulphs the boiling seas subside,*
                    Thrice in dire thunders she refunds the tyde.]
Strabo ⟨1 i 7, 1 ii 36⟩ quotes this passage to prove, that *Homer* understood the flux
and reflux of the Ocean. "An instance, says he, of the care that Poet took to
inform himself in all things is what he writes concerning the tydes, for he calls the
reflux ἄψορρον, or the *revolution of the waters*: He tells us, that *Scylla* (it should be
Charybdis) thrice swallows, and thrice refunds the waves; this must be understood
of regular tydes:" There are indeed but two tydes in a day, but this is the error of
the Librarians, who put τρίς for δίς. *Eustathius* solves the expression of the three
tydes differently, it ought to be understood of the νυχθήμερον, or the space of the
night and day, and then there will be a regular flux and reflux thrice in that time,
or eight hours periodically.

I then: O nymph propitious to my pray'r,
Goddess divine, my guardian pow'r, declare,   140
Is the foul fiend from human vengeance freed?
Or if I rise in arms, can *Scylla* bleed?
  Then she: O worn by toils, oh broke in fight,
Still are new toils and war thy dire delight?
Will martial flames for ever fire thy mind,   145
And never, never be to Heav'n resign'd?
How vain thy efforts to avenge the wrong?
Deathless the pest! impenetrably strong!
Furious and fell, tremendous to behold!
Ev'n with a look she withers all the bold!   150
She mocks the weak attempts of human might;
O fly her rage! thy conquest is thy flight.
If but to seize thy arms thou make delay, ⎫
Again the fury vindicates her prey, ⎬
Her six mouths yawn, and six are snatch'd away. ⎭   155
From her foul womb *Cratæis* gave the air
This dreadful Pest! To her direct thy pray'r,
To curb the monster in her dire abodes,
And guard thee thro' the tumult of the floods.
  Thence to *Trinacria*'s shore you bend your way,   160
Where graze thy herds, illustrious Source of day!

---

142. *Or if I rise in arms, can* Scylla *bleed?*] This short Question excellently
declares the undaunted spirit of this Heroe: *Circe* lays before him the most
affrighting danger; *Ulysses* immediately offers to encounter it, to revenge the
death of his friends, and the Poet artfully at the same time makes that Goddess
launch out into the praise of his Intrepidity; a judicious method to exalt the
character of his Heroe. *Dacier.*

156.   —Cratæis *gave to* ⟨sic⟩ *air*
                        This dreadful Pest—]

It is not evident who this *Cratæis* is whom the Poet makes the mother of *Scylla*:
Eustathius informs us that it is *Hecate,* a Goddess very properly recommended by
Circe; she, like *Circe* being the president over sorceries and enchantments. But why
should she be said to be the mother of *Scylla*? *Dacier* imagines that *Homer* speaks
ænigmatically, and intends to teach us that these monsters are merely the
creation or offspring of magic, or Poetry.

161. *Where graze thy herds*—] This fiction concerning the immortal herds of

Sev'n herds, sev'n flocks enrich the sacred plains,
Each herd, each flock full fifty heads contains:
The wond'rous kind a length of age survey,
By breed increase not, nor by death decay.   165
Two sister Goddesses possess the plain,
The constant guardians of the woolly train;
Lampetie fair, and *Phaethusa* young,
From *Phœbus* and the bright *Neæra* sprung;
Here watchful o'er the flocks, in shady bow'rs   170
And flow'ry meads they waste the joyous hours.
Rob not the God! and so propitious gales
Attend thy voyage, and impell thy sails;
    But if thy impious hands the flocks destroy,
The Gods, the Gods avenge it, and ye die!   175
'Tis thine alone (thy friends and navy lost)
Thro' tedious toils to view thy native coast.
    She ceas'd: And now arose the morning ray;
Swift to her dome the Goddess held her way.

Apollo, is bold, but founded upon truth and reality. Nothing is more certain than that in ancient times whole herds of cattle were consecrated to the Gods, and were therefore sacred and inviolable: These being always of a fix'd number, neither more nor less than at the first consecration, the Poet feigns that they never bred or increas'd: and being constantly supply'd upon any vacancy, they were fabled to be immortal, or never to decay; (for the same cause one of the most famous *legions* of Antiquity was call'd *immortal* ⟨Herodotus VII 83⟩.) *Eustathius* informs us, that they were labouring oxen employ'd in tillage, and it was esteem'd a particular prophanation to destroy a labouring ox, it was criminal to eat of it, nay it was forbid to be offer'd even in sacrifices to the Gods; and a crime punishable with death by the laws of *Solon*: so that the moral intended by *Homer* in this fable of the violation of the herds of *Apollo*, is, that in our utmost necessity we ought not to offend the Gods. As to the flocks of sheep, *Herodotus* informs us, that in *Apollonia* along the *Ionian* gulph, flocks of sheep were consecrated to that Deity, and were therefore inviolable ⟨IX 93⟩.

179. *Swift to her dome the Goddess held her way.*] It is very judicious in the Poet not to amuse us with repeating the compliments that pass'd between these two lovers at parting: The commerce *Ulysses* held with *Circe* was so far from contributing to the end of the *Odyssey*, that it was one of the greatest impediments to it; and therefore *Homer* dismisses that subject in a few words, and passes on directly to the great sufferings and adventures of his Heroe, which are essential to the Poem.

Then to my mates I measur'd back the plain,   180
Climb'd the tall bark, and rush'd into the main;
Then bending to the stroke, their oars they drew
To their broad breasts, and swift the galley flew.
Up sprung a brisker breeze; with freshning gales
The friendly Goddess stretch'd the swelling sails;   185
We drop our oars: at ease the pilot guides;
The vessel light along the level glides.
When rising sad and slow, with pensive look,
Thus to the melancholy train I spoke:
    O friends, oh ever partners of my woes,   190
Attend while I what Heav'n foredooms disclose.
Hear all! Fate hangs o'er all! on you it lies
To live, or perish! to be safe, be wise!
    In flow'ry meads the sportive *Sirens* play,
Touch the soft lyre, and tune the vocal lay;   195
Me, me alone, with fetters firmly bound,
The Gods allow to hear the dangerous sound.
Hear and obey: If freedom I demand,
Be ev'ry fetter strain'd, be added band to band.
    While yet I speak the winged gally flies,   200
And lo! the *Siren* shores like mists arise.
Sunk were at once the winds; the air above,
And waves below, at once forgot to move!
Some Demon calm'd the Air, and smooth'd the deep,
Hush'd the loud winds, and charm'd the waves to sleep.
Now every sail we furl, each oar we ply;   206
Lash'd by the stroke the frothy waters fly.
The ductile wax with busy hands I mold,

But it may not be unnecessary to observe how artfully the Poet connects this
Episode of *Circe* with the thread of it; he makes even the Goddess who detains him
from his country, contribute to his return thither, by the advice she gives him
how to escape the dangers of the Ocean, and how to behave in the difficult
emergencies of his voyages: 'Tis true, she detains him out of fondness, but yet this
very fondness is of use to him, since it makes a Goddess his instructor, and as it
were a guide to his country.

And cleft in fragments, and the fragments roll'd;
Th' aereal region now grew warm with day,   210
The wax dissolv'd beneath the burning ray;
Then every ear I barr'd against the strain,
And from access of phrenzy lock'd the brain.
Now round the mast my mates the fetters roll'd,
And bound me limb by limb, with fold on fold.   215
Then bending to the stroke, the active train
Plunge all at once their oars, and cleave the main.
    While to the shore the rapid vessel flies,
Our swift approach the *Siren* quire descries;
Celestial music warbles from their tongue,   220
And thus the sweet deluders tune the song.
    O stay, oh pride of *Greece! Ulysses* stay!
O cease thy course, and listen to our lay!
Blest is the man ordain'd our voice to hear,

---

222. *O stay, oh pride of* Greece! Ulysses *stay!*] There are several things remarkable in this short song of the *Sirens*: One of the first words they speak is the name
of *Ulysses*, this shews that they had a kind of Omniscience; and it could not fail of
raising the curiosity of a wise man, to be acquainted with persons of such extensive knowledge: The song is well adapted to the character of *Ulysses*; it is not
pleasure or dalliance with which they tempt that Heroe, but a promise of Wisdom, and a recital of the war of *Troy* and his own glory. *Cicero* was so pleased with
these verses, that he translated them, *lib.* 5. de *finibus bon. & mal.* ⟨xviii 49⟩.

> *O Decus Argolicum, quin puppim flectis, Ulysses,*
> *Auribus ut nostros possis agnoscere cantus?*
> *Nam nemo hæc unquam est transvectus cærula cursu,*
> *Quin prius adstiterit vocum dulcedine captus;*
> *Post, variis avido satiatus pectore Musis,*
> *Doctior ad patrias lapsus pervenerit oras.*
> *Nos grave certamen belli, clademque tenemus*
> *Græcia quam Trojæ divino numine vexit,*
> *Omniaque elatis rerum vestigia terris.*

Homer saw (says *Tully*) that his fable could not be approv'd, if he made his Heroe
to be taken with a mere song: The *Sirens* therefore promise Knowledge, the desire
of which might probably prove stronger than the love of his country: To desire to
know all things, whether useful or trifles, is a faulty curiosity; but to be led from
the contemplation of things great and noble, to a thirst of knowledge is an
instance of a greatness of soul.

The song instructs the soul, and charms the ear. 225
Approach! thy soul shall into raptures rise!
Approach! and learn new wisdom from the wise.
We know whate'er the Kings of mighty name
Atchiev'd at *Ilion* in the field of fame;
Whate'er beneath the sun's bright journey lies. 230
O stay, and learn new wisdom from the wise!
   Thus the sweet charmers warbled o'er the main;
My soul takes wing to meet the heav'nly strain;
I give the sign, and struggle to be free:
Swift row my mates, and shoot along the sea; 235
New chains they add, and rapid urge the way,
'Till dying off, the distant sounds decay:
Then scudding swiftly from the dang'rous ground,
The deafen'd ear unlock'd, the chains unbound.
   Now all at once tremendous scenes unfold; 240
Thunder'd the deeps, the smoking billows roll'd!
Tumultous waves embroil'd the bellowing flood,
All trembling, deafen'd, and aghast we stood!
No more the vessel plow'd the dreadful wave,
Fear seiz'd the mighty, and unnerv'd the brave; 245

---

241. —*The smoking billows roll'd*.] What is to be understood by the smoke of the
billows? Does the Poet mean a real fire arising from the rocks? Most of the
Critics have judg'd that the rock vomited out flames; for *Homer* mentions in the
beginning of this book.
          —Πυρός τ' ὀλοοῖο θύελλαι. ⟨68⟩
I have taken the liberty to translate both these passages in a different sense; by
the smoke I understand the mists that arise from the commotion and dashing of
the waters, and by the *storms of fire*, (as *Homer* expresses it) the reflections the
water casts in such agitations that resemble flames; thus in storms literally
          —*Ardescunt ignibus undæ* ⟨Ovid, *Metam.* XI 523⟩.
Scylla and *Charybdis* are in a continual storm, and may therefore be said to emit
flames. I have soften'd the expression in the translation by inserting the word
seem.
   Ulysses continues upon one of these rocks several hours; that is, from morning
till noon, as appears from the conclusion of this book; for leaping from the float,
he laid hold upon a fig-tree that grew upon *Charybdis*; but both the fig-tree and
Ulysses must have been consum'd, if the rock had really emitted flames.

Each drop'd his oar: But swift from man to man
With look serene I turn'd, and thus began.
O friends! Oh often try'd in adverse storms!
With ills familiar in more dreadful forms!
Deep in the dire *Cyclopean* den you lay,   250
Yet safe return'd—*Ulysses* led the way.
Learn courage hence! and in my care confide:
Lo! still the same *Ulysses* is your guide!
Attend my words! your oars incessant ply;
Strain ev'ry nerve, and bid the vessel fly.   255
If from yon justling rocks and wavy war

250.   *Deep in the dire* Cyclopean *den you lay,*
                Yet safe return'd—Ulysses *led the way.*]
Plutarch excellently explains this passage in his Dissertation, *How a man may praise
himself without blame or envy* ⟨*De Laude Ipsius* 16 (545 C)⟩: "*Ulysses* (says that Author)
speaks not out of vanity; he saw his companions terrify'd with the noise, tumult,
and smoke of the gulphs of *Scylla* and *Charybdis*; he therefore to give them courage,
reminds them of his wisdom and valour, which they found had frequently extricated them from other dangers: This is not vain-glory or boasting, but the dictate
of Wisdom; to infuse courage into his friends, he engages his virtue, prowess and
capacity for their safety, and shews what confidence they ought to repose in his
conduct." *Virgil* puts the words of *Ulysses* in the mouth of *Æneas* ⟨1 198–203⟩.
                O socii, neque enim ignari sumus ante malorum,
                O passi graviora; dabit deus his quoque finem.
                Vos & Scyllæam rabiem penitusque sonantes
                Accestis scopulos: vos & Cyclopea saxa
                Experti, revocate animos, mæstumque timorem
                Mittite. forsan & hæc olim meminisse juvabit.
It must be allow'd, that *Virgil* has improv'd what he borrows; it tends more to
confirm the courage of his friends than what *Ulysses* speaks: *Macrobius* is of this
opinion, *Saturn. lib.* 5. *cap.* 11. *Ulysses* lays before his companions only one
instance of his conduct in escaping dangers, *Æneas* mentions a second: there is
something more strong in
                —*Forsan & hæc olim meminisse juvabit,*
than in καί που τῶνδε μνήσεσθαι ὀίω; not only as it gives them hope to escape,
but as it is an assurance that this very danger shall be a pleasure, and add to their
future happiness: it is not only an argument of resolution but consolation.
Scaliger ⟨*Poet.* v iii, p. 218 D2⟩ agrees with *Macrobius, Ex ipsis periculis proponit
voluptatem: nihil enim jucundius ea memoria quæ periculorum evasionem, victoriamque
recordatione repræsentat.*

Jove safety grants; he grants it to your care.
And thou whose guiding hand directs our way,
Pilot, attentive listen and obey!
Bear wide thy course, nor plow those angry waves   260
Where rouls yon smoke, yon tumbling ocean raves;
Steer by the higher rock: lest whirl'd around
We sink, beneath the circling eddy drown'd.

While yet I speak, at once their oars they seize,
Stretch to the stroke, and brush the working seas.   265
Cautious the name of *Scylla* I supprest;
That dreadful sound had chill'd the boldest breast.

Mean-time, forgetful of the voice divine,
All dreadful bright my limbs in armour shine;
High on the deck I take my dang'rous stand,   270
Two glitt'ring javelins lighten in my hand;
Prepar'd to whirl the whizzing spear I stay,
'Till the fell fiend arise to seize her prey.
Around the dungeon, studious to behold
The hideous pest, my labouring eyes I roll'd;   275
In vain! the dismal dungeon dark as night
Veils the dire monster, and confounds the sight.

Now thro' the rocks, appal'd with deep dismay,
We bend our course, and stem the desp'rate way;
Dire *Scylla* there a scene of horror forms,   280

268.   —*Forgetful of the voice divine,*
              All dreadful bright my limbs in armour shine.]
This seemingly small circumstance is not without a good effect: It shews that
Ulysses, even by the injunctions of a Goddess, cannot lay aside the Heroe. It is not
out of a particular care of his own safety that he arms himself, for he takes his
stand in the most open and dangerous part of the vessel. It is an evidence likewise
that the death of his companions is not owing to a want of his protection; for it is
plain that, as *Horace* expresses it ⟨*Epist.* 1 ii 21–2⟩,
              Dum sibi, dum sociis reditum parat, aspera multa
              Pertulit—
By this conduct we see likewise, that all the parts of the *Odyssey* are consistent, and
that the same care of his companions, which *Homer* ascribes to *Ulysses* in the first
lines of it, is visible thro' the whole Poem.

And here *Charybdis* fills the deep with storms.
When the tyde rushes from her rumbling caves
The rough rock roars; tumultuous boil the waves;
They toss, they foam, a wild confusion raise,
Like waters bubbling o'er the fiery blaze;   285
Eternal mists obscure th' aereal plain,
And high above the rock she spouts the main:
When in her gulphs the rushing sea subsides,
She dreins the ocean with the refluent tides:
The rock rebellows with a thund'ring sound;   290
Deep, wond'rous deep, below appears the ground.
      Struck with despair, with trembling hearts we view'd
The yawning dungeon, and the tumbling flood;
When lo! fierce *Scylla* stoop'd to seize her prey,
Stretch'd her dire jaws and swept six men away;   295
Chiefs of renown! loud echoing shrieks arise;
I turn, and view them quivering in the skies;
They call, and aid with out-stretch'd arms implore:
In vain they call! those arms are stretch'd no more.
As from some rock that overhangs the flood,   300
The silent fisher casts th' insidious food,

---

283. *The rough rock roars*—] I doubt not every Reader who is acquainted with *Homer*, has taken notice in this book, how he all along adapts his verses to the horrible subject he describes, and paints the roarings of the Ocean in words as sonorous as that element. Δεινὸν ἀνερροίβδησε—τρὶς ἀναροιβδεῖ—ἀναβρόξειε —βόμβησεν, &c. *Subjicit rem oculis, & aurium nostrarum dominus est*, says *Scaliger* ⟨*Poet.* v iii, p. 222 D2⟩. It is impossible to preserve the beauty of *Homer*, in a language so much inferior; but I have endeavour'd to imitate what I could not equal. I have clog'd the verse with the roughness and identity of a letter, which is the harshest our language affords; and clogg'd it with Monosyllables, that the concourse of the rough letters might be more quick and close in the pronuntia-tion, and the most open and sounding vowel occurs in every word.

300.   *As from some rock that overhangs the flood,*
                  The silent fisher—]
These tender and calm similitudes have a peculiar beauty, when introduc'd to illustrate such images of terror as the Poet here describes: they set off each the other by an happy contrast, and become both more strong by opposition. *Eustathius* remarks, that there is always a peculiar sweetness in allusions that are borrow'd from calm life, as fishing, hunting, and rural affairs.

With fraudful care he waits the finny prize,
And sudden lifts it quivering to the skies:
So the foul monster lifts her prey on high,
So pant the wretches, struggling in the sky,   305
In the wide dungeon she devours her food,
And the flesh trembles while she churns the blood.
Worn as I am with griefs, with care decay'd;
Never, I never, scene so dire survey'd!
My shiv'ring blood congeal'd forgot to flow,   310
Aghast I stood, a monument of woe!
    Now from the rocks the rapid vessel flies,
And the hoarse din like distant thunder dies;
To *Sol*'s bright Isle our voyage we pursue,
And now the glitt'ring mountains rise to view.   315
There sacred to the radiant God of day
Graze the fair herds, the flocks promiscuous stray;
Then suddenly was heard along the main
To low the ox, to bleat the woolly train.
Strait to my anxious thoughts the sound convey'd   320
The words of *Circe* and the *Theban* Shade;
Warn'd by their awful voice these shores to shun,
With cautious fears opprest, I thus begun.
    O friends! oh ever exercis'd in care!
Hear heav'n's commands, and rev'rence what ye hear!
To fly these shores the prescient *Theban* Shade   326
And *Circe* warns! O be their voice obey'd:
Some mighty woe relentless heav'n forbodes:
Fly the dire regions, and revere the Gods!
    While yet I spoke, a sudden sorrow ran   ⎫   330
Thro' every breast, and spread from man to man,   ⎬
'Till wrathful thus *Eurylochus* began.   ⎭

314. *To* Sol's *bright Isle*—] This Isle is evidently *Sicily*; for he has already
inform'd us, that these herds were on *Trinacria*, (so anciently call'd from the three
promontories of *Lilybæum*, *Pelorus*, and *Pachynus*.)

332. '*Till wrathful thus* Eurylochus *began*.] *Homer* has found out a way to turn
reproach into praise. What *Eurylochus* speaks in his wrath against *Ulysses*, as a
fault, is really his glory; it shews him to be indefatigable, patient in adversity, and

O cruel thou! some fury sure has steel'd
That stubborn soul, by toil untaught to yield!
From sleep debarr'd, we sink from woes to woes;   335
And cruel, enviest thou a short repose?
Still must we restless rove, new seas explore,
The sun descending, and so near the shore?
And lo! the night begins her gloomy reign,
And doubles all the terrors of the main.   340
Oft in the dead of night loud winds arise,
Lash the wild surge, and bluster in the skies;
Oh should the fierce south-west his rage display,
And toss with rising storms the wat'ry way,
Tho' Gods descend from heav'n's aereal plain   345
To lend us aid, the Gods descend in vain:
Then while the night displays her awful shade,
Sweet time of slumber! be the night obey'd!
Haste ye to land! and when the morning ray
Sheds her bright beam, pursue the destin'd way.   350
A sudden joy in every bosom rose;
So will'd some Demon, minister of woes!

To whom with grief—O swift to be undone,
Constrain'd I act what wisdom bids me shun.
But yonder herds, and yonder flocks forbear;   355
Attest the heav'ns, and call the Gods to hear:
Content, an innocent repast display,
By *Circe* giv'n, and fly the dang'rous prey.

Thus I: and while to shore the vessel flies,
With hands uplifted they attest the skies;   360
Then where a fountain's gurgling waters play,
They rush to land, and end in feasts the day:
They feed; they quaff; and now (their hunger fled)

---

obedient to the decrees of the Gods. And what still heightens the panegyric is,
that it is spoken by an enemy, who must therefore be free from all suspicion of
flattery. *Dacier.*

363.   —*And now (their hunger fled)*
          Sigh for their friends devour'd, and mourn the dead.]

Sigh for their friends devour'd, and mourn the dead.
Nor cease the tears, 'till each in slumber shares　　365
A sweet forgetfulness of human cares.
　　Now far the night advanc'd her gloomy reign,
And setting stars roll'd down the azure plain;
When, at the voice of *Jove*, wild whirlwinds rise,
And clouds and double darkness veil the skies;　　370
The moon, the stars, the bright ætherial host
Seem as extinct, and all their splendors lost;
The furious tempest roars with dreadful sound:
Air thunders, rolls the ocean, groans the ground.
All night it rag'd; when morning rose, to land　　375
We haul'd our bark, and moor'd it on the strand,
Where in a beauteous Grotto's cool recess
Dance the green *Nereids* of the neighb'ring seas.
　　There while the wild winds whistled o'er the main,
Thus careful I addrest the list'ning train.　　380
　　O friends be wise! nor dare the flocks destroy
Of these fair pastures: If ye touch, ye die.
Warn'd by the high command of heav'n, be aw'd;
Holy the flocks, and dreadful is the God!
That God who spreads the radiant beams of light,　　385
And views wide earth and heav'n's unmeasur'd height.

This conduct may seem somewhat extraordinary; the companions of *Ulysses* appear to have forgot their lost friends, they entertain themselves with a due refreshment, and then find leisure to mourn; whereas a true sorrow would more probably have taken away all appetite. But the practice of *Ulysses*'s friends is consonant to the customs of Antiquity: It was esteem'd a prophanation and a piece of ingratitude to the Gods, to mix sorrow with their entertainments: The hours of repast were allotted to joy, and thanksgiving to heaven for the bounty it gave to man by sustenance. Besides, this practice bears a secret instruction, *viz.* that the principal care is owing to the living; and when that is over, the dead are not to be neglected. *Æneas* and his friends are drawn in the same attitude by *Virgil* ⟨1 216–21⟩:

> Postquam exempta fames epulis, mensæque remotæ,
> Amissos longo socios sermone requirunt;
> Præcipue pius Æneas, nunc acris Oronti,
> Nunc Amyci casum gemit, &c.

And now the Moon had run her monthly round,
The south-east blust'ring with a dreadful sound;
Unhurt the beeves, untouch'd the woolly train
Low thro' the grove, or range the flow'ry plain: 390
Then fail'd our food; then fish we make our prey,
Or fowl that screaming haunt the wat'ry way.
'Till now from sea or flood no succour found,
Famine and meager want besieg'd us round.
Pensive and pale from grove to grove I stray'd,   395
From the loud storms to find a *Sylvan* shade;
There o'er my hands the living wave I pour;
And heav'n and heav'n's immortal thrones adore,
To calm the roarings of the stormy main,
And grant me peaceful to my realms again.   400
Then o'er my eyes the Gods soft slumber shed,
While thus *Eurylochus* arising said.

   O friends, a thousand ways frail mortals lead
To the cold tomb, and dreadful all to tread;
But dreadful most, when by a slow decay   405
Pale hunger wastes the manly strength away.
Why cease ye then t' implore the pow'rs above,
And offer hecatombs to thund'ring *Jove?*
Why seize ye not yon beeves, and fleecy prey?
Arise unanimous; arise and slay!   410

---

395. *Pensive and pale from grove to grove I stray'd.*] It was necessary (remarks *Eustathius*) for the Poet to invent some pretext to remove *Ulysses*: If he had been present, his companions dar'd not to have disobey'd him openly; of if they had, it would have shew'd a want of authority, which would have been a disparagement to that Heroe. Now what pretext could be more rational than to suppose him withdrawn to offer up his devotions to the Gods? His affairs are brought to the utmost extremity, his companions murmur, and hunger oppresses. The Poet therefore, to bring about the crime of these offenders by probable methods, represents *Ulysses* retiring to supplicate the Gods; a conduct which they ought to have imitated: Besides, there is a poetical justice observ'd in the whole relation, and by the piety of *Ulysses*, and the guilt of his companions, we acknowledge the equity when we see them perish, and *Ulysses* preserv'd from all his dangers.

And if the Gods ordain a safe return,
To *Phœbus* shrines shall rise, and altars burn.
But should the pow'rs that o'er mankind preside,
Decree to plunge us in the whelming tide,
Better to rush at once to shades below,   415
Then linger life away, and nourish woe!
    Thus he: the beeves around securely stray,
When swift to ruin they invade the prey.
They seize, they kill!—but for the rite divine,
The barley fail'd, and for libations, wine.   420
Swift from the oak they strip the shady pride;
And verdant leaves the flow'ry cake supply'd.
    With pray'r they now address th' æthereal train,
Slay the selected beeves, and flea the slain;
The thighs, with fat involv'd, divide with art,   425
Strow'd o'er with morsels cut from ev'ry part.
Water, instead of wine, is brought in urns,
And pour'd prophanely as the victim burns.
The thighs thus offer'd, and the entrails drest,
They roast the fragments, and prepare the feast.   430
    'Twas then soft slumber fled my troubled brain:
Back to the bark I speed along the main.
When lo! an odour from the feast exhales,

---

412. *To* Phœbus *shrines shall rise*—] *Eurylochus* puts on an air of piety to persuade his companions to commit sacrilege: *Let us sacrifice*, says he, *to the Gods:* as
if obedience were not better than sacrifice. *Homer* understood the nature of man,
which is studious to find excuses to justifie our crimes; and we often offend,
merely thro' hopes of a pardon. *Dacier.*
    The word in the original is ἀγάλματα, which does not signifie statues, but
ornaments, ἀναθήματα, hung up, or reposited in the temples; such as
        —Ἀγλαΐης ἕνεκα κομόωσιν ἄνακτες. ⟨xvii 310⟩
or as it is expressed in the *Iliad* ⟨iv 144⟩,
        —βασιλῆι δὲ κεῖται ἄγαλμα.
Hesychius ⟨*Lexicon s.v.*⟩ interprets ἄγαλμα to be, πᾶν ἐφ' ᾧ τις ἀγάλλεται, οὐχ
ὡς ἡ συνήθεια, τὸ ξόανον; that is, ἄγαλμα signifies every ornament with which
a person is delighted or adorn'd; not a statue, as it is understood by the generality.
Dacier, Eustathius.

Spreads o'er the coast, and scents the tainted gales;
A chilly fear congeal'd my vital blood,   435
And thus, obtesting Heav'n I mourn'd aloud.
    O Sire of men and Gods, immortal *Jove!*
Oh all ye blissful pow'rs that reign above!
Why were my cares beguil'd in short repose?
O fatal slumber, paid with lasting woes!   440
A deed so dreadful all the Gods alarms,
Vengeance is on the wing, and heav'n in arms!
    Mean-time *Lampetiè* mounts th' aereal way,
And kindles into rage the God of day:
    Vengeance, ye Pow'rs, (he cries) and thou whose hand
Aims the red bolt, and hurls the writhen brand!   446
Slain are those herds which I with pride survey, ⎫
When thro' the ports of heav'n I pour the day, ⎬
Or deep in Ocean plunge the burning ray.   ⎭
Vengeance, ye Gods! or I the skies forego,   450
And bear the lamp of heav'n to shades below.

---

451. *And bear the lamp of heav'n to shades below.*] This is a very bold fiction, for how can the Sun be imagin'd to illuminate the regions of the dead; that is, to shine within the earth, for there the realm of *Pluto* is plac'd by *Homer*? I am persuaded the meaning is only that he would no more rise, but leave the earth and heavens in perpetual darkness. *Erebus* is placed in the west, where the Sun sets, and consequently when he disappears he may be said to be sunk into the realms of darkness or *Erebus*.

Perhaps the whole fiction might be founded really upon the observation of some unusual darkness of the Sun, either from a total eclipse or other causes, which happen'd at the time when some remarkable crime was committed, and gave the Poets liberty to feign that the Sun withdrew his light from the view of it. Thus at the death of *Cæsar* the globe of the Sun was obscured, or gave but a weak light, (says *Plutarch* ⟨Life of Caesar lxix⟩) a whole year; and *Plin. lib.* 2. 80 ⟨II xxx 98⟩, *fiunt prodigiosi & longiores solis defectus,* ⟨ . . . ⟩ *totius pæne anni pallore continuo.* This *Virgil* directly applies to the horror the Sun conceiv'd at the death of *Cæsar, Georg.* 1 ⟨466–8⟩.

> *Ille etiam exstincto miseratus Cæsare Romam,*
> *Cum caput obscura nitidum ferrugine texit,*
> *Impiaque æternam timuerunt sæcula noctem.*

And if *Virgil* might say that the Sun withdrew his beams at the impiety of the *Romans,* why may not *Homer* say the same, concerning the crime of the compan-

To whom the thund'ring Pow'r: O source of day!
Whose radiant lamp adorns the azure way,
Still may thy beams thro' heav'n's bright portals rise,
The joy of earth, and glory of the skies;   455
Lo! my red arm I bare, my thunders guide,
To dash th' offenders in the whelming tyde.

   To fair *Calypso*, from the bright abodes,
Hermes convey'd these counsels of the Gods.

   Mean-time from man to man my tongue exclaims,   460
My wrath is kindled, and my soul in flames.
In vain! I view perform'd the direful deed,
Beeves, slain by heaps, along the ocean bleed.

   Now heav'n gave signs of wrath; along the ground ⎫
Crept the raw hides, and with a bellowing sound   ⎬
Roar'd the dead limbs; the burning entrails groan'd. ⎭

---

ions of *Ulysses? Dacier* imagines that *Homer* had heard of the Sun's standing still
at the voice of *Joshua*; for if (says she) he could stand still in the upper region, why
might he not do the same in the contrary Hemisphere, that is, in the language of
Homer, bear his lamp to shades below? But this seems to be spoken without any
foundation, there being no occasion to have recourse to that miraculous event
for a solution.

    458.   *To fair* Calypso, *from the bright abodes,*
                Hermes *convey'd these counsels of the Gods.*]
These lines are inserted (as *Eustathius* observes) solely to reconcile the story to
credibility: For how was it possible for *Ulysses* to arrive at the knowledge of
what was done in heaven, without a discovery made by some of the Deities? The
persons by whom these discourses of the Gods are discover'd are happily chosen;
Mercury was the messenger of heaven, and it is this God who descends to *Calypso*
in the fifth of the *Odyssey*; so that there was a correspondence between *Calypso* and
Mercury; and therefore he is a proper person to make this discovery to that
Goddess, and she, out of affection, to *Ulysses*.

    464.   *Now heav'n gave signs of wrath; along the ground*
                Crept the raw hides—]
This passage (says *Eustathius*) gave an occasion of laughter, to men dispos'd to be
merry. Λαβὰς γελοιασμοῦ δέδωκε τοῖς παίζειν ἐθέλουσι. He adds, that the
terrors of a guilty conscience drove the companions of *Ulysses* into these imagina-
tions: Guilt is able to create a phantom in a moment, so that these appearances
were nothing but the illusions of a disturb'd imagination. He cites a passage from
the *Calliope* of *Herodotus* ⟨IX 116–20⟩ to vindicate *Homer*: *Artayctes* a *Persian*

Six guilty days my wretched mates employ   467
In impious feasting, and unhallow'd joy;
The sev'nth arose, and now the Sire of Gods
Rein'd the rough storms, and calm'd the tossing floods:
With speed the bark we climb: the spacious sails   471
Loos'd from the yards invite th' impelling gales.
Past sight of shore, along the surge we bound,
And all above is sky, and ocean all around!
When lo! a murky cloud the Thund'rer forms   475

General had plunder'd a temple in which was the tomb of *Protesilaus*, where great riches were deposited; afterwards he was besieg'd in *Sestus*, and taken prisoner: One day, one of his guards was boiling salted fishes (τάριχοι) and they leap'd, and moved as if they had been alive, and newly taken out of the water: Divers persons crouded about the place, and wonder'd at the miracle; when *Artayctes* said, *Friends, you are not at all concern'd in this miracle:* Protesilaus, *tho' dead, admonishes me by this sign, that the Gods have given him power to revenge the injury I offer'd to his monument in* Eleus. But this is justifying one fable by another; and this looks also like the effects of a guilty conscience.

This is not among the passages condemn'd by *Longinus*; and indeed it is no way blameable, if we consider the times when it was spoken, and the persons to whom it is related: I mean *Phæacians*, who were delighted with such wonders. What was said injudiciously by a great Writer, may very properly be apply'd to these people, *Credo, quia impossible est* ⟨Tertullian, *De Carne Christi*, c. 5, ll. 28–9 (*Corpus Scriptorum Eccles. Lat.*, LXX): "certum est, quia impossibile."⟩. But we need not have recourse to their credulity for a vindication of this story: *Homer* has given us an account of all the abstruse arts, such as Necromancy, Witchcraft, and natural portents; here he relates a prodigy, the belief of which universally prevailed among the Ancients: Let any one read *Livy*, and he will find innumerable instances of prodigies, equally incredible as this, which were related by the wise, and believed at least by the vulgar. Thus we read of speaking Oxen, the sweating of the statues of the Gods, in the best *Roman* Histories. If such wonders might have a place in History, they may certainly be allow'd room in Poetry, whose province is fable: it signifies nothing whether a story be true or false, provided it be establish'd by common belief, or common fame; this is a sufficient foundation for Poetry. *Virgil, Georg.* I. 478 ⟨478–9⟩.

> —*Pecudesque locutæ*
> *Infandum! sistunt amnes, &c.*

These days of wonder are now over, and therefore a Poet would be blameable to make use of such impossibilities in these ages: They are now almost universally disbeliev'd, and therefore would not be approv'd as bold fictions, but exploded as wild extravagancies.

Full o'er our heads, and blackens heav'n with storms.
Night dwells o'er all the deep: and now out flies
The gloomy West, and whistles in the skies.
The mounting billows roar: the furious blast
Howls o'er the shroud, and rends it from the mast: 480
The mast gives way, and crackling as it bends,
Tears up the deck; then all at once descends:
The pilot by the tumbling ruin slain,

477.   *—And now out flies*
                    The gloomy West, &c.]
Longinus ⟨ɪx 14⟩, while he condemns the *Odyssey* as wanting fire, thro' the decay
of *Homer's* fancy, excepts the descriptions of the Tempests, which he allows to be
painted with the boldest and strongest strokes of Poetry. Let any person read that
passage in the 5th Book ⟨291–4⟩, and he will be convinc'd of the fire of *Homer's*
fancy.

὿Ως εἰπὼν σύναγεν νεφέλας ἐτάραξε δὲ πόντον,
Χερσὶ τρίαιναν ἑλών, πάσας δ᾽ ὀρόθυνεν ἀέλλας
Παντοίων ἀνέμων, σὺν δὲ νεφέεσσι κάλυψε
Γαῖαν ὁμοῦ καὶ πόντον. ὀρώρει δ᾽ οὐρανόθεν νύξ.

The two last lines are here repeated; and *Scaliger,* a second *Zoilus* of *Homer,* allows
them to be *omnia pulchra, plena, gravia.* p. 469 ⟨*Poet.* v ii, p. 215 D2⟩. There is a
storm in the very words, and the horrours of it are visible in the verses.

Virgil was master of too much judgment, not to embellish his *Æneid* with this
description ⟨ɪ 84–9, omitting 87⟩.

                    Incubuere mari, totumque a sedibus imis
                    Unà Eurusque Notusque ruunt, creberque procellis
                    Africus, & vastos volvunt ad litora fluctus.
                    Eripiunt subito nubes caelumque diemque
                    Teucrorum ex oculis: ponto nox incubat atra.

These are almost literally translated from the above-mention'd verses of
Homer, and these following ⟨295–6⟩.

Σὺν δ᾽ Εὖρός τε Νότος τ᾽ ἔπεσον, Ζέφυρός τε δυσαὴς
Καὶ Βορέης αἰθρηγενέτης, μέγα κῦμα κυλίνδων.

Scaliger ⟨*Poet.* v iii, p. 217 B2⟩ calls the Verses of *Homer, divina oratio,* but prefers
those of *Virgil. Totumque a sedibus imis,* is stronger than ἐτάραξε πόντον, &*c.* and
Αἰθρηγενέτης is an ill-chosen Epithet, to be used to describe a storm, for it carries
an image of serenity. But that is to be understood of the general nature of that
wind: As a river may be said to be gentle, tho' capable to be swell'd into a flood.
But I leave the preference to the Reader's judgment.

483. *The pilot by the tumbling ruin slain.*] There is a great similitude between this
passage and some verses in *Virgil* ⟨ɪ 114–18⟩, in which, as *Scaliger* judges ⟨*Poet.*
v iii, p. 218 cɪ⟩ and perhaps with reason, the preference is to be given to the

Dash'd from the helm falls headlong in the main.
Then *Jove* in anger bids his thunders roll, 485
And forky lightnings flash from pole to pole;
Fierce at our heads his deadly bolt he aims,
Red with uncommon wrath, and wrapt in flames:
Full on the bark it fell; now high, now low,
Tost and retost, it reel'd beneath the blow; 490
At once into the main the crew it shook:
Sulphureous odors rose, and smould'ring smoke.
Like fowl that haunt the floods, they sink, they rise, ⎫
Now lost, now seen, with shrieks and dreadful cries; ⎬
And strive to gain the bark; but *Jove* denies. ⎭ 495
Firm at the helm I stand, when fierce the main
Rush'd with dire noise, and dash'd the sides in twain;
Again impetuous drove the furious blast,
Snapt the strong helm, and bore to sea the mast.
Firm to the mast with cords the helm I bind, ⎫ 500
And ride aloft, to Providence resign'd, ⎬
Thro' tumbling billows, and a war of wind. ⎭

Roman Poet. *Tenuissima,* says that Critic, *& levissima utitur narratione Homerus.*
Πλῆξε κυβερνήτεω κεφαλήν, σὺν δ᾽ ὀστέ ἄραξε
Πάντ᾽ ἄμυδις κεφαλῆς, ὁ δ᾽ ἄρ᾽ νευτῆρι ἐοικὼς
Κάππεσ᾽.

And again   —πέσον δ᾽ ἐκ νηὸς ἑταῖροι
Οἱ δὲ κορώνῃσιν ἴκελοι περὶ νῆα μέλαιναν
Κύμασιν ἐμφορέοντο.
   —*Ingens a vertice Pontus*
In puppim ferit. excutitur, pronusque magister
Volvitur in caput.
    Ast illam ter fluctus ibidem
Torquet agens circum, & rapidus vorat æquore vortex,
Apparent rari nantes in gurgite vasto.

There is certainly better versification in these lines of *Virgil,* than in those of
Homer: There is better colouring, and they set the thing they describe full before
our Eyes. *Virgil* has omitted the two short similitudes of the Diver, and Sea-mews,
despairing perhaps to make them shine in the *Roman* language. There is a third
simile in *Homer* of the Bat or Bird of night Νυκτερίς, which is introduc'd to represent *Ulysses* clinging round the Fig-tree. 'Tis true the whole three are taken from
low subjects, but they very well paint the thing they were intended to illustrate.

Now sunk the West, and now a southern breeze
More dreadful than the tempest, lash'd the seas;
For on the rocks it bore where *Scylla* raves, 505
And dire *Charybdis* rolls her thund'ring waves.
All night I drove; and at the dawn of day
Fast by the rocks beheld the desp'rate way:
Just when the sea within her gulphs subsides,
And in the roaring whirlpools rush the tides. 510
Swift from the float I vaulted with a bound,
The lofty figtree seiz'd, and clung around.
So to the beam the Bat tenacious clings,
And pendent round it clasps his leathern wings.
High in the air the tree its boughs display'd, 515
And o'er the dungeon cast a dreadful shade.
All unsustain'd between the wave and sky,
Beneath my feet the whirling billows fly.
What-time the Judge forsakes the noisy bar
To take repast, and stills the wordy war; 520

519. *What-time the Judge forsakes the noisy bar*
    To take repast.—]
This passage has been egregiously misunderstood by Mons. *Perrault* ⟨II 60⟩.
Ulysses being carried (says that author) on his mast toward *Charybdis*, leaps from
it, and clings like a Bat round a Fig-tree, waiting till the return of the mast from
the gulphs of it; and adds, that when he saw it, he was as glad as a Judge when
he rises from his seat to go to dinner, after having try'd several causes. But *Boileau*
fully vindicates *Homer* in his reflexions on *Longinus* ⟨*Réflexions Critiques* vi, *Œuvres
Complètes*, Paris, 1942, v 91⟩: Before the use of dials or clocks the Ancients distinguish'd the day by some remarkable offices, or stated employments: as from
the dining of the labourer,
  —*What-time in some sequester'd vale*
  The weary Woodman spreads his sparing meal.
Iliad XI. ver. 119. See the Annotation; so here from the rising of the Judges, and
both denote the Mid-day, or Noontide hour. Thus it is used by *Hippocrates*, who
speaking of a person wounded with a Javelin in the Liver, says he dy'd πρὶν
ἀγορὴν λυθῆναι ⟨cited by Mme Dacier in *L'Odyssée* (Paris, 1716), II 412⟩, a little
before the breaking up of the Assembly, or before the Judge rises from his tribunal; or as some understand it, a little before the finishing of the market:
There is a parallel expression in *Xenophon*, καὶ ἤδη τε ἀμφὶ ἀγορὰν πλήθουσαν
⟨*Anab.* I viii 1⟩. This rising of the Judge *Perrault* mistakes for a comparison, to

Charybdis rumbling from her inmost caves,
The mast refunded on her refluent waves.
Swift from the tree, the floating mast to gain,
Sudden I drop'd amidst the flashing main;
Once more undaunted on the ruin rode,   525
And oar'd with lab'ring arms along the flood.
Unseen I pass'd by *Scylla*'s dire abodes:
So *Jove* decreed, (dread Sire of men and Gods.)
Then nine long days I plow'd the calmer seas,
Heav'd by the surge and wafted by the breeze.   530
Weary and wet th' *Ogygian* shores I gain,
When the tenth sun descended to the main.

---

express the joy which *Ulysses* conceived at the sight of the return of his mast; than which nothing can be more distant from *Homer*'s sentiment.

From this description we may precisely learn the time that pass'd while *Ulysses* clung round the Fig-tree.

> —*At the dawn of Day*
> *Fast by the Rocks I plow'd the desp'rate way.*
>   ⟨507–8; *I plowed* reads *beheld*⟩

So that at Morning he leap'd from his float, and about Noon recover'd it: Now *Eustathius* affirms, that in the space of twenty four hours there are three Tydes, and dividing that time into three parts, *Ulysses* will appear to have remained upon the Rock eight hours. The exact time when the Judge rose from his tribunal is not apparent: *Boileau* supposes it to be about three a Clock in the Afternoon, *Dacier* about two; but the time was certain among the Ancients, and is only dubious to us, as we are ignorant of the hour of the day when the Judge enter'd his Tribunal, and when he left it.

532. *When the tenth Sun descended to the main.*] This account is very extraordinary. *Ulysses* continued upon the Mast ten days, and consequently ten days without any nourishment. *Longinus* ⟨IX 14⟩ brings this passage as an instance of the decay of *Homer*'s Genius, and his launching out into extravagant Fables. I wonder *Eustathius* should be silent about this Objection; but *Dacier* endeavours to vindicate *Homer*, from a similar place in the *Acts of the Apostles, Cap.* 27. ver. 33. where Saint *Paul* says to the Sailors, *this is the fourteenth day that ye have tarried, and continued fasting, having taken nothing.* Now if the Sailors in the *Acts* could fast fourteen days, why might not *Ulysses* fast ten? But this place by no means comes up to the point. The words are τεσσαρεσκαιδεκάτην σήμερον ἡμέραν προσδοκοῦντες, that is, expecting the fourteenth day, (which is to-day) you continue without eating; so the meaning is, they had taken no food all that day; the danger was so great that they had no leisure to think upon hunger: This is the literal construction of the Words, and implies that out of expectation of the fourteenth Day, (which they

There in *Calypso*'s ever-fragrant bow'rs
Refresh'd I lay, and Joy beguil'd the hours.
My following fates to thee oh King, are known, 535
And the bright partner of thy royal throne.
Enough: In misery, can words avail?
And what so tedious as a twice-told tale?

---

look'd upon as a critical time when their danger would be at the highest) they had
forgot to take their usual repast; and not, that they had fasted fourteen Days. But
if any Person thinks that the fasting is to be apply'd to the whole fourteen Days,
it must be in that latitude wherein Interpreters expound *Hesiod* ⟨ *Works and Days*
147–6⟩,

—οὐδέ τε σῖτον
Ἤσθιον—

which signifies not that they eat no Meat at all, but that they had not leisure
thro' their danger to observe the usual and stated hours of repast: They eat in
their Arms, with their Hands foul'd with Blood. But I take the former sense to be
the better. Besides, it is impossible to make this place of any service to *Homer*; for
if these Men continued so long fasting, it was a miraculous fast; and how can this
be apply'd to *Ulysses*, who is not imagin'd to owe his power of fasting to any supernatural assistance? But it is almost a demonstration that the sailors in the *Acts* eat
during the tempest: Why should they abstain? It was not for want of food; for at
St. *Paul's* injunction they take some sustenance: Now it is absurd to imagine a
miracle to be perform'd, when common and easy means were at hand to make
such a supernatural act unnecessary. If they had been without food, then indeed
a miracle might have been suppos'd to supply it. If they had dy'd thro' fasting,
when meat was at hand, they would have been guilty of starving themselves. If
therefore we suppose a miracle, we must suppose it to be wrought, to prevent men
from being guilty of wilful self-murder, which is an absurdity.

Besides, the word ἄσιτος is used to denote a person who takes no food for the
space of one day only, as μονόσιτος signifies a person who eats but one meal in
the compass of one day; this therefore is an evidence, that the sailors in the *Acts*
had not been without sustenance fourteen days.

In short, I am not in the number of those who think *Homer* has no faults; and
unless we imagine *Ulysses* to have fasted ten days by the assistance of the Gods, this
passage must be allow'd to be extravagant: 'Tis true, *Homer* says, the Gods
guided him to the *Ogygian* shores; but he says not a word to soften the incredibility
of the fasting of *Ulysses*, thro' any assistance of the Gods. I am therefore inclin'd to
subscribe to the opinion of *Longinus*, that this relation is faulty; but say with
Horace ⟨ *Ars Poet.* 351–3⟩,

—*Non ego paucis*
Offendar maculis, quas aut incuria fudit,
Aut humana parum cavit natura.

ADDENDUM

p. 100. *Pope's note on* III 289 *reads as follows:*

Happier his lot, who &c.] Nothing can be better imagin'd to encourage *Tele-machus,* than what the Poet here delivers: She sets *Agamemnon* in opposition to *Ulysses*: *Agamemnon* made a speedy voyage to his country, and there fell by treachery; *Ulysses* has long been absent, but yet is happier than *Agamemnon*: the Gods perhaps reserve him for better fortunes, at least nothing can be concluded from his long absence, and this is sufficient to teach *Telemachus* not to despair. *Eustathius.*